The Jazz Singers

Also by Scott Yanow

Swing
Bebop
Classic Jazz
Trumpet Kings
Afro-Cuban Jazz
Jazz On Film
Jazz On Record: The First Sixty Years
Duke Ellington
Jazz: A Regional Exploration

The Jazz Singers

The Ultimate Guide

Scott Yanow

An Imprint of Hal Leonard Corporation
New York

Published in 2008 by Backbeat Books
An Imprint of Hal Leonard Corporation
7777 West Bluemound Road
Milwaukee, WI 53213

Trade Book Division Editorial Offices
19 West 21st Street, New York, NY 10010

Printed in the United States of America

Book design by Snow Creative Services

Library of Congress Cataloging-in-Publication Data

Yanow, Scott.
  The jazz singers : the ultimate guide / Scott Yanow.
      p. cm.
  ISBN 978-0-87930-825-4
  1. Jazz singers--United States--Biography. 2. Jazz--History and criticism. I. Title.

  ML400.Y35 2008
  782.42165092'2--dc22
  [B]
                          2008039171

www.backbeatbooks.com

CONTENTS

ACKNOWLEDGMENTS

In addition to the contributions of all of the singers who took the time to answer my questionnaire, quite a few people assisted me along the way in helping to track down the addresses and e-mails of vocalists, some of whom were quite elusive. I wish to thank (in alphabetical order) the late David L. Abell, Nich Anderson, Alan Bates (of Candid Records), Dr. Karl Berger, Ann Braithwaite, Monifa Brown (of Shanachie Entertainment), Mike Campbell, Mark Cantor, Lynn Coles, Roger Crane (the Song Scout), Bob Dorough, Jo Foster (formerly of Concord Records), Janna Gadden, Richard Ginell, Sandy Graham, Anita Gravine, Dory Green, Laura Hart, Terri Hinte, Tamm E. Hunt, Dick Hyman, Munyungo Jackson, Dan Jacobson, Amandah Jantzen, Niranjan Jhaveri, Leslie Johnson (of the *Mississippi Rag*), Regina Joskow (of Verve Music Group), Marla Kleman, Janet Lawson, Carol Leigh, Sara Leib, the late Floyd Levin, David Martin, Chris McNulty, Mike Metheny, Cassie Miller (of the Society of Singers), Antoinette Montague, Wayne Nowland, Ted Ono, Tryggve Palmquist, Chantal Phaire, Margaret Moos Pick (of Riverwalk Jazz), Ken Poston, Tina Quist, Bob Ringwald, Daryl Sherman, Carol Sloane, Lavay Smith, Brooke Vigoda, Roseanna Vitro, Lynn Wiggins, Mike Wilpizeski (of Telarc Records) and Anthony Wilson.

I wish to thank the four copy editors who did their best to give this book consistency and additional logic as well as to eliminate my misspellings. They worked awfully hard, so Colleen Coyne, Loren Kleinman, Claudine Krystyniak and Laura Sassano deserve my heartfelt appreciation. I also want to thank the staff at Hal Leonard for their patience and their belief in a project that took much longer to complete than I had originally expected.

INTRODUCTION

Although it would seem that picking out 521 jazz singers for this book would not be that difficult a task, it was more complex than expected. When I wrote *Trumpet Kings*, I was able to come up with 479 trumpeters in a relatively brief period of time and apparently did not leave out anyone all that significant, although new giants have naturally emerged since then. It may seem that there were more trumpeters to choose from than singers, particularly since big bands have three to five trumpeters. But by restricting myself to soloists rather than including section players and lead trumpeters, I was able to put together a pretty comprehensive trumpet book. I had little internal debate over who was a jazz trumpeter and who was not. Herb Albert? No. Hugh Masekela? Based on his earliest work, yes. Chris Botti and Rick Braun? Oh okay, but with reservations about the commercial nature of their careers. Otherwise, all of the other choices were easy.

That was not the case when it came to singers. The borderline between jazz singers and middle-of-the-road pop singing is vague, not to mention the overlapping fields of cabaret, R&B, blues and world music. Every week seems to bring the debut of another promising female jazz singer, and if I included every single jazz-inspired vocalist of today, this book would never be completed.

So why these 521, and what were the criteria? First, each singer has to have an interesting if not necessarily virtuosic voice. The singer's overall career or at least an important part of his or her musical life had to be of some significance to the jazz world. And among the current singers, they have to at least have the potential to be influential in the future.

Picking the historic singers was fairly easy in most cases, though there were borderline cases. One could argue that some of the classic blues singers of the 1920s, the big band vocalists of the 1930s and the later crooners do not belong in this book because they tended to present a song in a certain way and probably did not vary their interpretations much from night to night.

I decided to err on the side of inclusiveness. There are several singers in this book whom I do not think of as jazz singers, such as Frank Sinatra or Tony Bennett; one can add five or six more. Certainly their improvising was very minor and they would not stand a chance trading fours with Mel Tormé or Ella. But on the other hand, Sinatra and Bennett have had a strong influence on many jazz singers, they can swing and they frequently recorded in jazz settings. Their importance to the jazz world ultimately outweighed the fact that technically they did not sing jazz.

I wanted to make sure that the current jazz scene was well covered. Too many jazz history books cut off at 1980 or 1990, acting as if jazz is in its declining days because there are not one or two dominant innovators who are leading the way as it was when Charlie Parker, Miles Davis and John Coltrane were alive. Truth is, jazz entered its golden age around 1920 and it is still in it. The lazier jazz commentators who bemoan the passing of the earlier jazz greats without recognizing the richness of the current scene are to be given sympathy and largely ignored.

Two-thirds of the singers in this book are alive and most are still performing. In addition to the veterans, I have included many jazz vocalists who are in the first decade of their careers. To a certain extent I am taking a chance, stating that, as of late 2007, these are the singers who I think will contribute the most to creative music during the next 30 years. In some cases I will be proven wrong as a few inevitably drop out of the jazz scene and possibly out of music altogether, but I will stand by my guesses.

In addition to feeling that these current young vocalists are quite talented and destined to grow in their significance in the future, I also note that most of these singers are marketing themselves well, an important consideration. Jazz musicians and singers need to be as inventive in planning their careers as they are in creating music. This is a self-help industry with performers creating their own jobs. While some of these singers are at present quite obscure, only known in their home towns, there are strong hints that their deep commitment will result in them becoming household names (at least in the jazz world) in the future. This book is a way of encouraging them and of making it a little easier for today's jazz fans to discover lots of talents.

Those of you who are jazz singers and did not make the top 521, do not despair. A few hundred of you are in the Other Jazz Singers section and most of those came close to making the 521. If you did not make either section, just know that if this book featured another 100 singers, chances are you would have made the cut. And feel free to prove me wrong in the future.

So how did I arrive at the number 521? That's just how it turned out! 500 would not have been quite enough.

The Story Behind *The Jazz Singers*

Because there has been an explosion in the number of female jazz singers on the current scene, while ironically there has been a shortage of male jazz singers, I thought it was time to write about it all in a new book. I always envisioned *The Jazz Singers* having entries on the 500 top jazz singers of all time, with a liberal amount of space being allocated to the many talented vocalists who are around today. There was never any question of ranking all of the singers in some kind of order, because how would one compare, say, Ida Cox to Jane Monheit, or Maxine Sullivan to Dianne Reeves? Coming up with the top ten jazz singers of all time would be easier than deciding who is #297. Saying that someone is in the top 500 seems more logical than debating about the individual merits of singers who are separated by decades and from completely different time periods. Jazz is a continuum and, while the new "replaces" the old due to death and the rise of younger voices, it does not necessarily mean that the new is superior to the old, or vice versa.

Also, dividing the book into decades or styles would lead to some contradictions due to some singers being active for 40 or 50 years, so alphabetical order makes the most sense. At least one can find Ella Fitzgerald quickly rather than trying to decide whether she has been placed in the 1930s or the 1970s.

In putting together *The Jazz Singers*, I wanted, in as many cases as possible, to include new comments from the vocalists themselves about their lives and careers. After drawing up an initial list of singers to include in the book and dividing it into those who have passed away and those who are around, it was a matter of tracking down as many of the latter as possible and e-mailing them a copy of the questionnaire. Over a period of a year, and with the help of others, I was able to locate and gain responses from approximately 300 out of the 360 living singers. Some sent so much information that it could have served as a first draft for a memoir. In contrast, there were a few who only sent in a few fragmented sentences that were of little use. In a few cases (which I cite in the individual entries), I utilized past interviews with the singers. Some vocalists preferred to be interviewed over the phone rather than write their responses down, although I kept those to a minimum. Cleo Laine, rather than filling out the questionnaire, sent me two books, including one on how to sing! If she had ever heard me sing, she would have realized that that was a lost cause.

Of the singers who did not send in anything, some claimed to be too busy, including one whose manager said that she did not have time because she had to work on her wardrobe! A manager of a teenaged singer said that she was also too busy, even though I told her that, since she was so young, it would take only ten minutes to tell her complete life story. Both the one with the wardrobe problem and the teenager were minor anyway and were quickly demoted to the Other Jazz Singers section. I figured that if a singer did not recognize the value of gaining free publicity in a book, he or she would probably make other unwise career decisions and not go as far as he or she should.

Some of the other singers were too obscure to be found despite my best efforts, while a few were really way too busy and famous, having successfully surrounded themselves with an excess of "protectors" who actually limit their opportunities to stretch beyond their sheltered worlds. A few (Ray Charles and Jackie Paris among them) passed away just as I was near to getting in touch with them. While many vocalists wrote back quickly and with enthusiasm (Lorraine Feather and Jim Ferguson were the first to respond, with Lorraine's questionnaire winning that race by ten minutes), with some of the others I had to keep on setting final deadlines (all of which ended up being artificial) and *final* final deadlines. Some singers stalled me forever, and a few sent me their completed questionnaires a year after the alleged deadline which, because this book took longer to complete than expected, was still early enough. I will not be surprised if I receive some finished questionnaires in 2010.

Writing *The Jazz Singers* was an adventure, one that kept on being extended due to the need to make a living in the meantime. That this book got completed at all is a minor miracle, for the longer it took, the more new vocalists arrived on the scene. While I believe that it includes every significant jazz singer up until the end of 2007, I have no doubt that I will someday regret leaving out a few vocalists who drastically improve in the future or of whom I am not currently aware.

What Is a Jazz Singer?

This is one of the most difficult questions asked in jazz, and one that has yet to be agreed upon because the music keeps on evolving and changing.

Here is what I have come up with: A jazz singer is a vocalist who improvises at least in subtle ways through notes, words, sounds and/or phrasing. In order to be a jazz singer it is not necessary to scat (witness Billie Holiday), or to swing, or even to be any good. But it is important that a singer not put on the exact same performance night after night, year after year. Some vocalists, such as Betty Carter and Mark Murphy, proved to be radically different from night to night while others, including Lady Day and Oscar Brown Jr., changed their shows gradually

over time. Cabaret singers and middle-of-the-road crooners tend to keep things the same once they are worked out and often prefer that their sidemen also play set solos.

Of course there are many singers who are borderline or cross over the artificial boundary lines altogether. Practically every jazz singer has sung music that would be considered outside of jazz at one time or another, including Ella Fitzgerald, Sarah Vaughan and Mel Tormé. And an awful lot of vocalists from other fields have occasionally sung (or tried to sing) jazz. I have not included all of them in this book, preferring to concentrate on the ones who took jazz most seriously and worked at it. For one does not simply wake up one day and decide to sing jazz. As with playing an instrument, it takes dedication, research and a real feeling for the music. Any singers from any field can sing the words of a blues song, but can they make the audience believe in the words they are interpreting?

A Brief History of Jazz Singing

Jazz singing prior to the first jazz recordings in 1917, as with the history of jazz itself, is largely lost to history, shrouded in legend without much documentation. Jazz singing can be traced to the field hollers and work songs of African-American slaves and the singing of spirituals in churches (many jazz singers, even today, recall that their first important singing was in church), minstrel shows and vaudeville. Ma Rainey sang blues in tent shows as early as 1902, and many of the classic blues singers, including Bessie Smith, gained much of their early experience and livelihood performing in traveling revues. While singers were not part of New Orleans brass bands and were not all that major in New Orleans jazz groups prior to 1920, they were part of the music scene, particularly such singing jazz pianists as Jelly Roll Morton and Tony Jackson.

Vaudeville and live musical productions were two of the key ways that new songs were introduced. When a performer on the level of an Al Jolson or a Sophie Tucker adopted a song, there was a good chance that it would catch on.

In the pre-microphone days, it was important for singers to be able to both sing clearly and at a loud volume in live performances. However, singing at a loud volume was not as necessary in making records. Two of the most listenable pre-1917 male singers, Billy Murray and Gene Greene, were not belters. Murray was very popular due to his enthusiasm and accessible voice. Gene Greene, who was billed as "The Ragtime King," was the first singer to ever scat on records, recording "King Of The Bungaloos" several times and as early as 1911. He was one of several singers who sought to emulate ragtime rhythms in some of his hotter vocals, taking worked-out double-time breaks that were full of syncopation and sometimes imitating military drums.

The first singer to record jazz was Marian Harris. She recorded "I Ain't Got Nobody Much" (which soon became better known as "I Ain't Got Nobody") and "I'm Gonna Make Hay While The Sun Shines In Virginia" in 1916, before the Original Dixieland Jazz Band made the first official jazz records. Whether or not her first two performances are technically jazz, they were certainly ahead of their time, with Harris displaying a relaxed phrasing that would not catch on until over a decade later. Her recordings of the next few years swung, and although she never became a huge name, she set the stage for what was to come.

The next vocal milestone was Mamie Smith's recording of "Crazy Blues" in 1920, the first time a black female singer was documented singing a blues song. The surprise success of this record woke up many in the record industry toward the potential of marketing records to black audiences. The "blues craze" of 1921 to 1924 found many singers, mostly black and female, being taken to the studios and recorded in hopes of duplicating the hit. During this period Alberta Hunter, Ethel Waters, Ma Rainey and Bessie Smith were among those making their recording debuts.

With the exception of the classic blues singers and the major stars, such as Al Jolson, who were usually accompanied by unidentified studio orchestras, most singers up until the late 1920s were treated by musicians as necessary evils, tools of the record companies who were used to help sell songs. White bands in particular were often saddled with unsuitable vocalists, but there were exceptions. Cliff Edwards, best known as "Ukulele Ike," was among the first male jazz singers on records, scatting, singing rhythmically and often holding his own with top jazz musicians. Carleton Coon and Joe Sanders, co-leaders of the Coon-Sanders Nighthawks, were also both skilled jazz singers.

However, it was up to Louis Armstrong to show the jazz and pop worlds how jazz phrasing and improvising could be used in singing, making every note and pause count while no longer treating sheet music as if each note and word was sacred and unchangeable. He was not the first jazz singer, nor the first scat singer, but he popularized both and moved the art of singing jazz a decade ahead. Bing Crosby listened closely, and with his rise to prominence, both with the Rhythm Boys and as a soloist, he brought the feeling of jazz into pop singing.

On the female side, Ethel Waters proved to be the most flexible of the classic blues singers, moving into classic jazz, pop and swing by the late 1920s. She influenced Mildred Bailey, who was herself an influence on Lee Wiley. The Boswell Sisters became one of the best jazz vocal groups ever, featuring exciting arrangements full of tempo and mood changes along with heated scatting. Annette Hanshaw had a real feeling for jazz, while Ruth Etting became a female equivalent for Bing Crosby, bridging the gap between jazz and pop.

In the 1930s with the rise of swinging big bands, many orchestras featured both male and female singers. The most significant graduates from the big bands were Ella Fitzgerald (who was with Chick Webb), Frank Sinatra (Tommy Dorsey), Jimmy Rushing (Count Basie), Helen Humes (Count Basie), Billy Eckstine (Earl Hines), Anita O'Day (Gene Krupa), Peggy Lee (Benny Goodman), Doris Day (Les Brown) and Sarah Vaughan (Billy Eckstine), not to mention Cab Calloway, who led his own orchestra. Billie Holiday's laid-back phrasing and dramatic life made her an unclassifiable icon, Fats Waller evoked pure joy in his small-group recordings, and Nat King Cole evolved from being a swing pianist to an influential crooner.

By the beginning years of the bebop era, female jazz singing was dominated by Ella Fitzgerald, Sarah Vaughan and Billie Holiday, with the newcomer Dinah Washington being the top up-and-comer. No longer connected with big bands, all four and many others were involved in busy solo careers. The rise of the jive singing of Slim Gaillard and Leo Watson was an outgrowth of Cab Calloway and helped lead to the bebop-oriented singing of Babs Gonzalez. Vocalese, the writing of lyrics set to the notes of recorded solos, had been pioneered by Bee Palmer (1929) and Marian Harris (1934) but was really birthed in the late 1940s by Eddie Jefferson, who was soon followed by King Pleasure, Dave Lambert, Jon Hendricks and Annie Ross. Lambert, Hendricks and Ross in the late 1950s became the greatest of all vocalese groups, and their legacy is partly kept alive today by Manhattan Transfer, a very eclectic vocal ensemble.

The 1950s featured a variety of cool-toned female singers (Peggy Lee, June Christy, Chris Connor, Helen Merrill and Julie London), the improbable rise of Chet Baker, major new names in Carmen McRae, Joe Williams and Ray Charles (who brought the passion of gospel music into the new soul music), a continuation of the blues/jazz tradition with Big Joe Turner and Jimmy Witherspoon and the dominance of Ella Fitzgerald and Sarah Vaughan.

By the 1960s, jazz singers were grappling with the rise of rock, and many were either recording commercial albums or spending years being absent from records altogether. Among the exceptions were the country blues/bebop philosopher Mose Allison, the passionate and political Abbey Lincoln, the first bossa nova queen Astrud Gilberto and a few brave avant-garde pioneers, including Patty Waters. Fusion of the late 1960s/ early 1970s mostly left little room for singers, although Flora Purim's brand of Brazilian fusion made her a star.

But with the renewed popularity of acoustic jazz from the mid-1970s on and the realization that there was nothing wrong with exploring older styles creatively, jazz singing (just as is true of jazz in general) has headed in many directions at once. Susannah McCorkle became one of the first major young singers of the generation born after World War II to be exploring older standards, starting a movement that has since included such individualists as Banu Gibson, Rebecca Kilgore, Diana Krall (the most famous living jazz singer today) and Jane Monheit. Sheila Jordan and Shirley Horn were two of the many slightly older singers who returned to records and carved out productive careers. The jazz singer/songwriter tradition founded by Hoagy Carmichael was revitalized by the work of Dave Frishberg, Bob Dorough and Blossom Dearie. Betty Carter and Mark Murphy, while often singing standards, stretched the bebop tradition way beyond the breaking point in their always-fascinating improvisations. While Al Jarreau and Bobby McFerrin displayed remarkable voices but contributed less to jazz than one would have expected given their unlimited potential, Kurt Elling has become the leading male jazz singer of the past decade (along with Mark Murphy).

While the shortage of male jazz singers has been worrisome, there are a remarkable number of talented female jazz singers on the scene today. In addition to the ones mentioned, no list would be complete without including Dianne Reeves, Cassandra Wilson, Dee Dee Bridgewater, Diane Schuur, Nnenna Freelon, Roseanna Vitro, Karrin Allyson, Kendra Shank, Adi Braun and Roberta Gambarini, with many more sure to become prominent during the next few years.

Difficulties for Today's Jazz Singers

While there is little debate that Freddie Hubbard was a great jazz trumpeter or that John Coltrane played remarkable solos, when it comes to jazz singers, opinions vary widely. Perhaps it is because nearly everyone can sing a little as opposed to play trumpet. Even the obvious immortals like Ella Fitzgerald ("she sounds too happy all the time") and Sarah Vaughan ("she sings too many notes") have been criticized through the years and accused of not singing jazz, remarkable as that seems now. Virtually every singer in this book has been criticized somewhere along the way for their tone, appearance, dedication to jazz (Mel Tormé, on an episode of Ralph Gleason's *Jazz Casual* television series from the 1960s, stated with a straight face that Mark Murphy was not a jazz singer), improvising skills and repertoire.

Perhaps it stems from a scene that most of us have witnessed. An excellent jazz group plays a few instrumentals to indifferent applause. Out comes an attractive female singer of limited talent. The audience wakes up, loves her appearance and gives her much more applause for her mediocre performance than they had for a virtuoso saxophone solo. Add to that the excessive publicity that pop singers receive whenever they "discover" jazz and put out a standards album, and many musicians and jazz fans end up resenting vocalists in general.

Not that all of the resentment is unfair. Too many beginning singers show up at sessions not knowing what key is best for them, how to set a tempo, where to come in, how to end a song, how to treat instrumentalists, etc. Some appear at jam sessions and expect to be the star of the show with the music built around them, violating the democracy of jazz, while others seem completely lost and helpless without their accompanist, unable to ad-lib without an arrangement. None of this helps the image of jazz singers.

The great jazz singers are constantly faced with this resentment through no fault of their own and constantly have to prove themselves until they have built up a strong reputation in the jazz world.

Another major problem for jazz singers, especially today, is the matter of repertoire. While jazz instrumentalists can write new originals since they are only dealing with the music, vocalists, unless they are singer/songwriters, are often faced with singing the same lyrics as their predecessors, with lyrics that are increasingly dated. Is there any purpose left to singing the words of "I Can't Get Started" with its references to 1930s personalities? Are there any Gershwin songs worth rediscovering for the umpteenth time?

During the golden age of the American popular song (roughly 1920–60), there was a constant flow of new material written for Broadway shows, radio, movies, record dates and big bands, most of which could be interpreted by singers in dozens of different ways. But with the rise of rock and singer/songwriters, a large percentage of the most popular songs only sound right when performed by the originators. Ella never sounded comfortable singing Beatles songs no matter how much she swung them, and one cannot imagine most jazz singers today interpreting rap pieces.

So jazz vocalists of the 21st century not only have to overcome the missteps of the amateurs but also need to build a fresh repertoire. Some singers become archivists who revive obscure songs from the past. A few manage to reinvent standards in new ways, while others sift through pop music of the past 40 years, bringing back songs that meant a lot to them in their early years, transforming them (with varying success) into creative jazz. The latter can be a difficult task, for the hits of the Monkees would not exactly have been worthy of Cole Porter, and there is not as much to be found in the repertoire of Radiohead as in the songs of Irving Berlin. Jazz definitely needs many more songwriters who have the ability to write timeless lyrics and melodies that are open to scores of different interpretations (many more Dave Frishbergs).

A third serious problem is that for the past 15 years, there has been a serious shortage of creative male jazz singers under the age of 60. Eliminate Kurt Elling and a handful of others, and the field is nearly empty. It seems a bit surprising that there are not more male vocalists who see this gap and decide to sing jazz, along with songwriters from other areas of the music business who decide to fill the repertoire needs of today's singers.

Instead of resentment for the amount of unearned applause that some jazz singers receive, they are deserving of sympathy and (in the cases of the great ones) affection and admiration. They have a difficult job, for they have to develop their own voice, skills, reputation and repertoire. And we should treasure the really talented singers, for they could undoubtedly make a lot more money singing in another field!

Ten Songs That Should Be Avoided

Building on the idea of dated repertoire and tunes that have been done to death (just as instrumentalists should avoid "On Green Dolphin Street" and "Stella By Starlight," blues singers should forget about "Stormy Monday," and Dixieland groups should drop "Sweet Georgia Brown"), here is a helpful list of the top ten songs that should be banished from the repertoire of virtually all singers and a suggested number of years that should pass before they are attempted again:

"Over The Rainbow"—It's been done! Skip it except as an instrumental for 5 years.
"'Round Midnight"—5 years
"Love For Sale"—10 years
"Lover Man"—15 years
"Summertime"—20 years
"All Blues"—The world is truly sick of this song. 25 years
"Send In The Clowns"—30 years
"God Bless The Child"—40 years
"Stolen Moments"—Why does anyone sing a theme which repeats the same three notes 11 straight times? 50 years
"My Funny Valentine"—Forever

Close But Not Quite

In picking out the 521 singers who form the bulk of this book, I considered nearly twice as many vocalists. Some of the more promising current ones have ended up briefly mentioned in the "198 Other Jazz Singers of Today" section, while some of the instrumentalists who occasionally take vocals are listed in "55 Others Who Have Also Sung Jazz." Many of the others are in this chapter.

Throughout the history of jazz, there have been many vocalists who, to one extent or another, were grouped with jazz, although they were not jazz singers themselves. Some came closer than others, and a few occasionally sung jazz, but it was not the main direction of their careers. So included in this section are some of the key singers who fall into this gray area, in loosely chronological rather than alphabetical order. In addition, this chapter mentions some of the historic singers and a few of today's veterans who have been left out either because they have not worked all that much in jazz or because their discography is so small. However, do yourself a favor and check out the work of most of the singers who are in this section, for the great majority have made important contributions along the way to one style of music or another if not necessarily jazz.

First, the male singers. Prior to the first recordings of jazz in 1917, and not counting Gene "The Ragtime King" Greene (who does have an entry in this book), two of the vocalists who came closest to singing jazz were Billy Murray and Bert Williams. Murray, one of the most popular singers of the pre-1920 era, is quite listenable today, and at his best still has his period charm. One of the top interpreters of George M. Cohan songs, he can be heard at his peak throughout much of *The Denver Nightingale* (Archeophone 5501).

Bert Williams, a pioneering African-American vaudeville and Broadway performer, was best-known for his philosophical comedy dialogues. His occasional vocals show a feeling for jazz, although his death in 1922 kept him from becoming involved in the jazz world. "You Can't Get Away From It" swung in its own way while paying tribute to ragtime musicians. All of Williams' recordings are available on *The*

Early Years 1901–1909 (Archeophone 5004), *The Middle Years 1910–1918* (Archeophone 5003) and *His Final Releases 1919–1922* (Archeophone 5002).

With the exception of Bing Crosby, Al Rinker and Harry Barris from the Rhythm Boys and a very few others, the only male jazz singers worth hearing in the 1920s were musicians themselves. Record labels, under pressure from song pluggers and publishers, often insisted on the inclusion of a vocal chorus from a stable of busy if often unsuitable singers who were hired more for their volume and ability to articulate clearly than any jazz or swinging qualities. A countless number of recordings by white bands from 1925 to 1933 feature a vocal by the likes of Irving Kaufman, Scrappy Lambert, Smith Ballew, Dick Robertson, Chick Bullock, the nasally Seger Ellis or worse. The results range from tolerable to insipid, often wasting a chorus that could have been played by a soloist.

Other singers from the era include the likable if high-pitched Gene Austin (whose "My Blue Heaven" was a huge hit), bandleader Ben Bernie (his half-spoken half-sung version of "Crazy Rhythm" is a classic), the vaudevillian John W. Bubbles (who teamed up with pianist Buck Washington as Buck and Bubbles) and the enthusiastic but not particularly swinging Noble Sissle. The early country singer Jimmie Rodgers sometimes sang blues (he used Louis Armstrong as a sideman on "Blue Yodel No. 9"), while Emmett Miller, whose yodeling is intriguing, was a throwback to minstrel shows but was often backed by jazz greats on his recordings. As for Al Jolson, the star of 1927's *The Jazz Singer* and one of the world's top entertainers, he could be jazzy at times, particularly during the second choruses of his performances. But once he had a routine set, it stayed that way for decades.

In the early 1930s, two of the most popular singers were Rudy Vallee, who liked jazz but never seriously attempted to sing or play it (he was an occasional saxophonist), and the short-lived Russ Colombo, who mostly stuck to ballads while at times sounding eerily like Bing Crosby. Many of the swing era orchestras had both a male and a female singer, with the male often being confined to pop music and ballads; Jimmy Rushing with Count Basie was a major exception. Among the ballad singers who almost always fall outside of jazz are Al Bowlly (long associated with Ray Noble), Bob Eberly (Jimmy Dorsey), Ray Eberle (Glenn Miller), Skinny Ennis (Hal Kemp), Dan Grissom (Jimmie Lunceford), Dick Haymes (Harry James), Harlan Lattimore (Don Redman), Jack Leonard (famous for singing "Marie" with Tommy Dorsey) and Pha Terrell (taking high-pitched vocals with Andy Kirk). Buddy Clark first gained some notice with Benny Goodman but never really crossed over into jazz. Art Lund made a memorable vocal on "Blue Skies" with Goodman but mostly worked as an actor. The actor Dick Powell showed that he could sing jazz in some of his movies, particularly when he was teamed with the Mills Brothers ("Lulu's Back In Town"), but he never pursued jazz as his career. Ozzie Nelson led a swinging big band for over a decade but did not really excel as a singer before becoming a full-time actor. Tony Pastor, who could have been a jazz singer, mostly confined himself to happy novelties in his many years as a bandleader. The Ink Spots originally started out patterned as a hot vocal group in the mold of the 1930s Mills Brothers, but they soon switched to their highly successful if very predictable brand of pop presentations. And Bob Crosby, Bing's younger brother, proved to be a cheerful but mediocre singer who mostly stuck to ballads while wisely laying out of most of his all-star orchestra's hits.

With the rise of the bebop era and the separation of jazz from the pop music world, there has been much more of a division between most jazz and pop singers, with the debate centering on whether Frank Sinatra or Tony Bennett sang jazz.

Some singers who gained fame in the middle-of-the-road pop world occasionally hinted at jazz during the six decades since the end of the swing era or briefly popped into the jazz world. Johnny Mathis started out singing standards. Harry Belafonte recorded an intriguing jazz-oriented album in 1958 (*Harry Belafonte Sings The Blues*—RCA 27095) in which he is joined by top West Coast jazz players plus Roy Eldridge. Sammy Davis Jr., who probably could have succeeded at anything in show business that he attempted, recorded a fine album with Count Basie's orchestra. Frankie Laine started out in jazz and cut a decent album with Buck Clayton. Brooke Benton recorded a few popular duets with Dinah Washington. Bobby Darin swung the heck out of "Mack The Knife" and "Beyond The Sea." Bobby Short loved swing and the music of Duke Ellington, but his singing (unlike his jazz-oriented piano playing) was strictly cabaret. Arthur Prysock, who was often heard with big bands, including Buddy Johnson's, mostly stuck to fairly straight renditions of ballads.

A few singers from other fields who were briefly considered for this book include the jump blues pianist-singer Floyd Dixon, poet and visionary Gil Scott-Heron, the great composer Antonio Carlos Jobim (who was never really just a vocalist), Michael Franks (a so-so pop singer but a fine lyricist), Van Morrison and the unique Tom Waits. Not seriously considered were Barry Manilow, Boz Scaggs or Rod Stewart. Stewart, whose very popular renditions of vintage songs could accurately be re-titled *Murdering The Standards*, should have taken lessons in hipness from Jon Hendricks.

Among the females, a long debate took place over whether to include Sophie Tucker among the jazz singers. She certainly had the feeling of jazz in some of her recordings, including her many versions of "Some Of These Days" which she first recorded in 1911, but most of her performances fall into the areas of vaudeville, early pop music and (after 1930) nostalgia.

The major classic blues singers of the 1920s are included in this book. A couple who just missed the cut are Lavinia Turner and Elzadie Robinson. Lillie Delk Christian was one of the worst of the classic blues singers, but she had Louis Armstrong on a few titles; his vocal duet with her on "Too Busy" is unintentionally funny. Helen Morgan, one of the top torch singers of the 1920s and '30s, and the boop-boop-a-doop girl Helen Kane, are associated more with the jazz age than with jazz itself, while Esther Walker, Margaret Young and the immortal Nora Bayes (famous for "Shine On Harvest Moon") were just not jazz-oriented enough.

In 1929 when she was three years old, Rose Marie Mazetta, as "Baby Rose Marie," sang "What Can I Say, Dear, After I Say I'm Sorry" on stage, growling like a mature blues singer. She was considered a sensation for a few years, making film appearances and recording with Fletcher Henderson; in the 1960s she re-emerged as one of the stars of *The Dick Van Dyke Show*. It is a pity that as a child she did not record more extensively.

Among those female singers from the swing era who were considered for this book are Ginny Simms (Kay Kyser), Marion Hutton (Glenn Miller), Edythe Wright (Tommy Dorsey), Connie Haynes (Tommy Dorsey), Liza Morrow (Harry James and Benny Goodman), Jane Harvey (Benny Goodman), Nan Wynn, Ella Logan, Martha Raye (an early influence on Anita O'Day) and Jo Stafford (Tommy Dorsey). Jo Stafford came the closest due to the universal admiration that jazz musicians of the 1940s and '50s felt toward her beautiful voice, but she never improvised, even when teamed with Ella Fitzgerald.

Pearl Bailey, a major personality in show business, only sang jazz on a very occasional basis. The same can be said for the talented, humorous and apparently ageless Eartha Kitt. Mabel

Mercer was the queen of cabaret, and other cabaret singers who were briefly considered include Margaret Whiting, Joyce Breach, Anita Ellis, Dardanelle, Toni Lee Scott, Morgana King, Maureen McGovern and Monica Mancini. Barbara Carroll, a superior jazz pianist who would certainly belong in any book on jazz piano, is much more of a cabaret artist when she sings. Mary Ford was a country singer who teamed perfectly with Les Paul on a long series of enjoyable recordings. Marilyn Moore, the first wife of Al Cohn and mother of guitarist Joe Cohn, on her lone album (*Moody Marilyn Moore*) sounded remarkably like Billie Holiday, but her career was brief.

Doris Day always had a beautiful voice, and she could have sung jazz, coming close on the rare occasions when she recorded with just a rhythm section. Teresa Brewer had some of the greatest backup musicians in the world (from the Duke Ellington Orchestra and Count Basie to Ruby Braff, Stephane Grappelli and Earl Hines) on some of her records but always sounded like a novelty act. Aretha Franklin, who was packaged as a type of jazz singer in her early days for Columbia, has always had a tremendous voice that needed to go over-the-top and infuse R&B with the power of gospel; singing jazz would simply have been too much of a restraint on her. Etta James always lacked the subtlety to sing jazz, although she made a few good attempts in her career. Diana Ross was the only good thing about the movie *Lady Sings The Blues*, and during that period her Billie Holiday–influenced vocals were a revelation, but she did not stick to that course for long. Anita Baker and K. D. Lang have hinted at having an interest in jazz, but neither have made much of a commitment; Lang's duets with Tony Bennett do not count. One famous singer, who I wish would record a full-fledged set of swing standards, is Bette Midler. Her *Sings The Rosemary Clooney Songbook* (Columbia 90350) was good but not the classic that she is capable of. Check her out in the movie *For The Boys* for proof of her untapped potential as a jazz singer.

Other singers who almost made it to the top 521 include Savannah Churchill (a versatile performer who had some hits in the 1940s), the jump/R&B singer-pianist Camille Howard, Audrey Morris (her potential in the 1950s was never quite realized, though she is still active), Doris Drew and Laurie Allyn (both of whom recorded just a single if very good jazz record in the mid-1950s), Jo Ann Greer (who was excellent with Les Brown), Lurlean Hunter (her five albums in the 1950s combine jazz, R&B and pop), Lucy Reed (a Chicago-based cool-toned singer in the 1950s who largely faded from the scene by 1960), Ann Marie Moss (long associated with her husband, the late Jackie Paris, and a fine singer who has recorded far too little) and Gayle Moran (who sang with her husband Chick Corea in the 1970s and with the second version of the Mahavishnu Orchestra). Marilyn Scott, although sometimes grouped with jazz, is more on the crossover pop side of the music, but she did a good job on *Every Time We Say Goodbye* (Venus 35419). Ricky Lee Jones, who like her associate Tom Waits has a jazz sensibility, has mostly performed in the rock area, although her *Pop Pop* (Geffen 19293) is jazz-oriented and features Joe Henderson and Charlie Haden in the supporting cast. June Tyson, long with Sun Ra's Arkestra, was a talented avant-garde singer but did not have much of a career apart from her association with Ra.

Linda Ronstadt, although never really a jazz singer, recorded three influential standards sets in the 1980s with an orchestra arranged and conducted by Nelson Riddle. This was a surprise move considering Ronstadt's great commercial success in light pop and country/folk music, leading to many other singers from pop (and some up-and-coming jazz vocalists) exploring standards from the swing era. While one wishes that her interpretations of the tunes on *What's New*

(Asylum 60260), *Lush Life* (Asylum 60387) and *For Sentimental Reasons* (Asylum 60474) were less straight and took some chances, her interest was heartfelt and could be said to have foreshadowed the great success of Diana Krall. In 2004 her lesser-known *Hummin' To Myself* (Verve 88702) was a brief return to standards with a big band arranged by Alan Broadbent.

While I have included some singers in this book who are really not jazz singers but have had a strong influence on other jazz vocalists, missing is Norah Jones. I personally like Norah Jones' voice, but she has yet to record anything that could be remotely considered jazz, even on the rare occasions when she has interpreted a standard. The fact that she has recorded for Blue Note (one of the most famous of all jazz labels) seemed to blind many in the jazz industry, desperate to have higher sales figures for jazz recordings, to the fact that her singing is in the country/pop field. Perhaps she will explore jazz someday, but that time has not arrived yet.

Probably the most difficult decision was deciding to leave Joni Mitchell out of the top 521. Although she has been involved in occasional jazz projects through the years, Mitchell is essentially a folk/light rock singer. She has been very influential on many of today's jazz singers, such as Cassandra Wilson, in her very open repertoire and her willingness to regularly reinvent and stretch herself à la Miles Davis. Some of her recordings, particularly 1976's *Hejira* (Asylum 1087) which features Jaco Pastorius, *Don Juan's Reckless Daughter* (Elektra 81227 46642), *Mingus* (Asylum 505) which was Charles Mingus' final project and 2000's *Both Sides Now* (Reprise 47620), border and even cross over into jazz, but her vocals are usually the least jazz-oriented aspect of these projects.

So Who Are the Jazz Singing Giants?

I am regularly asked who I think the best jazz singers of all time are, so here is a list of the top 30, in loosely chronological order. I am leaving out Frank Sinatra, a huge influence who I do not feel is a jazz singer. Of the 30, I think that each one is irreplaceable, quite influential and innovative in his or her own way. And who is #1? How does one decide between Ella Fitzgerald and Sarah Vaughan, not to mention Louis Armstrong?

Feel free to argue among yourselves.

Bessie Smith
Louis Armstrong
Ethel Waters
Bing Crosby
Annette Hanshaw
Cab Calloway
Mildred Bailey
Billie Holiday
Ella Fitzgerald
Jimmy Rushing
Helen Humes
Nat King Cole
Anita O'Day
Peggy Lee
Sarah Vaughan
Eddie Jefferson
Dinah Washington
Carmen McRae
Joe Williams
Mel Tormé

Jon Hendricks
Abbey Lincoln
Shirley Horn
Mark Murphy
Betty Carter
Sheila Jordan
Dianne Reeves
Karrin Allyson
Diana Krall
Kurt Elling

Best bet to enter the top 30 in the future:

Roberta Gambarini

A Quick Introduction to the Entries

A few words should be said about the 521 entries. They comprise 397 females (286 are alive, 111 deceased) and 124 males (59 alive, 65 deceased). With the exception of the bebop era and the vocalese singers in general, females have always greatly outnumbered males among the full-time jazz vocalists in every era, not counting many of the instrumentalists who also occasionally sing.

While most of the singers have birthdates included, a few chose to leave that section blank on their questionnaires. I know better than to pressure female singers to tell me how old they are. That research can be left for braver authors in the future. I, however, do include clues in those entries when possible as to their probable ages.

I put a singer's birth name in parentheses if it differs drastically from the name by which he or she is best known. The length of each entry does not necessarily convey the importance of the singer but often has much more to do with how interesting his or her answers were in the questionnaire or how colorful a life he or she has led. Their quotes are, unless stated otherwise, taken from the questionnaire and often just an excerpt of their full responses. The list and brief reviews included in each singer's Recommended CDs part are not meant to form a complete discography, although that is true in the cases of current singers who only have a few releases out thus far. The listings are mostly in chronological order.

All of the singers who have entries in the main portion of this book plus the ones listed in other sections deserve to be heard. I truly hope that *The Jazz Singers* does justice to the art of vocal jazz.

THE 521 GREAT JAZZ SINGERS

Susanne Abbuehl

b. July 30, 1970, Bern, Switzerland

One of the very few singers to record as a leader for the ECM label, Susanne Abbuehl (who is Swiss and Dutch) made a strong impression with her 2001 recording, *April*.

"My father listened to a lot of jazz and, although he chose to become a mathematician rather than a trumpet player, music meant a lot to him. My mother was more into classical music. Both my parents went to concerts very often and took me with them to hear live music. As a child, I used to make up little melodies, songs, in a kind of syllable-language. It was in between speaking and singing, combining words with pitch and melody and rhythm." When Abbuehl was seven, she began studying baroque music on the harpsichord, and at 17 switched to taking jazz piano lessons. By that time, she was singing for the fun of it. "I was in a high school exchange program in Los Angeles in 1987 where I was part of the jazz ensemble. I returned to Europe after graduating from high school and I knew that I wanted to be a singer."

Abbuehl earned a master's degree in jazz voice from the Royal Conservatory of The Hague in the Netherlands and has studied North Indian classical singing in India with Dr. Prabha Atre. She met pianist Wolfert Brederode in 1992, and they have worked together ever since. Another longtime associate is clarinetist Christof May, and Abbuehl is proud that she had an opportunity to work briefly in a group with Jeanne Lee. She names Lee as one of her main inspirations, along with Shirley Horn, Helen Merrill and Cassandra Wilson. Susanne Abbuehl has been active throughout Europe, performing at jazz festivals, in jazz productions and lecturing as a professor.

"I love composing music for poems. I seek to create musical environments for language in which the unspoken and unspeakable parts of language can live and linger."

Recommended CDs: *April* (ECM 1766) features Susanne Abbuehl singing both wordlessly and performing five poems of E.E. Cummings in addition to introducing her lyrics to Carla Bley's "Ida Lupino." Her attractive voice is haunting (particularly on "'Round Midnight") and stretches beyond the jazz tradition to classical and Indian music in an intimate setting with piano, clarinet/bass clarinet and occasional percussion. From 2006 her second release, *Compass* (ECM 1906), utilizes a similar band and displays her growth over the past few years, during which she has continued to chart a very individual path. Few other singers would tackle such material as "A Call For All Demons," "Where Flamingos Fly" and "Black Is The Color."

Website: www.susanneabbuehl.com

Claudia Acuña

(Claudia Lorena Acuña Barrales)
b. July 3, 1971, Santiago, Chile

It has long been Claudia Acuña's dream to sing jazz in her native Spanish tongue, but she originally did not think that there would be a place for her in jazz. Born and raised in Chile, she remembers, "I sang around my house and the neighborhood, beginning when I was five. I was a member of the choir and did solo performances. I made sure I was involved in any activity which allowed me to sing."

She originally sang folk songs and pop music, but at the age of 15 discovered jazz, hearing it on the radio and seeing American jazz stars on film. She remembers the turning point in her career. "It was when Dizzy Gillespie came to Chile to perform with the United Nations Orchestra. It made me realize that I could perform jazz in Spanish. Dizzy's gift of embracing Latin music and its musicians made me confident that I could do it."

Acuña performed in Santiago, learned about the music and occasionally sat in with visiting American jazz musicians. In 1995, although knowing very little English, she took a chance and moved to New York. At first she worked at odd jobs before gradually getting gigs singing in clubs. By 1996 she was collaborating with pianist Jason Linder, and her career was seriously underway. She appeared at Birdland and met one of her idols, Abbey Lincoln. With the help of bassist Avishai Cohen, she put together a demo that in 1999 landed her a contract with the Verve label. After her CD *The Wind From The South* was released in 2000, Claudia Acuña began touring, appearing at jazz festivals and gaining recognition for her powerful singing. A highlight for her was returning to Chile in 2002 to perform as a leader at a music festival.

Although her occasional vocals in English are charming (her rendition of "Bewitched, Bothered And Bewildered" is particularly memorable), Claudia Acuña has achieved her goal of mostly singing in Spanish while accompanied by a modern jazz rhythm section. In the future she says that she wants to "continue walking on the path of truth and confidence in my musical journey, to never be afraid, and to remain open to see where the music takes me."

Recommended CDs: The year 2000's *Wind From The South* (Verve 543521) has Claudia Acuña mostly singing in English (including "Bewitched, Bothered And Bewildered") and was a very impressive debut. *Rhythm Of Life* (Verve 589547) from two years later includes haunting versions of "More Than You Know" and "Nature Boy," and shows the singer's growth and increasing desire to take chances. *Luna* (Maxjazz 117) has her singing in Spanish on all but one of the 11 songs.

Website: www.claudiaacuna.com

Kris Adams

b. November 25, 1956, Brunswick, GA

An excellent singer who brings her own fresh interpretations to standards and modern jazz originals, Kris Adams is based in the New England area.

She gained her earliest experience singing in musical theater, being part of a touring children's theater that performed on weekends. Adams played French horn in sixth grade and organ in high school and also had guitar and piano lessons. She attended the Berklee College of Music in 1982 and the New England Conservatory of Music in 1993.

"In the '80s I met and married jazz pianist/composer/educator Steve Prosser. He produced my first two CDs, arranged music and played piano on them. Besides being involved in those two projects together, we taught at the same college and I learned a great deal about teaching from him. Also, I was fortunate to study at NEC at the same time that Luciana Souza was there. Through her I developed more of my interest in Brazilian music. Along with Lisa Thorson, who was also there at the same time, we three would practice and jam together all the time. Other high points for me in my career include recording with the great pianist Paul Bley while at NEC, being asked to the stage by Michele Hendricks to sing with her on 'Air Mail Special' in Spoleto, Italy in 2003, and meeting and singing with Sheila Jordan and Jay Clayton."

Whether singing standards, scatting or interpreting her own lyrics, Kris Adams has developed a fresh and stimulating style.

Recommended CDs: *This Thing Called Love* (KA 2289) is Kris Adams' excellent debut from 1999, and *Weaver Of Dreams* (Jazzbird 002) from 2002 has such songs as "The Peacocks," "It Could Happen To You," Norma Winstone's "Ladies In Mercedes" and even "The 'In' Crowd."

Website: www.krisadams.com

Lorez Alexandria

(Dolorez Alexandria Turner)
b. August 14, 1929, Chicago, IL; d. May 22, 2001, Gardena, CA

A vocalist with a soulful sound who loved telling stories in her music but was also a fine scat singer, Lorez Alexandria never became famous beyond the jazz world despite her talents. She was always in the shadow of Ella Fitzgerald and Sarah Vaughan but had a lot to contribute of her own.

Alexandria started out performing religious music in church choirs and gospel groups in the Chicago area, often with her family, including 11 years with an a cappella singing group. In the early 1950s she switched to secular music and began singing in local nightclubs. Four albums made for the King label during 1957–59 (including *This Is Lorez Alexandria* and the Lester Young tribute *Lorez Alexandria Sings Pres*) gave her some initial fame.

Alexandria, who worked with pianist King Fleming in that period and (during 1958) with the Ramsey Lewis Trio, made four albums for the Argo label. By 1964 she had moved to Los Angeles, where she recorded two of her finest records for Impulse: *Alexandria The Great* and *More Of The Great Lorez Alexandria*, which have been combined on one CD). Although she worked often in Los Angeles, becoming a fixture at both the Parisian Room and Marla's Memory Lane, Alexandria fell victim to the changes in the music world of the mid-1960s. Her only recordings of the 1965–76 period were two commercial albums cut for the tiny Pzazz label in 1971.

However, Alexandria showed that she was still in prime form on six albums made for Discovery during 1978–87, including two sets on which shve interpreted the lyrics of Johnny Mercer. A trio of albums for Muse (including 1993's *Star Eyes*, her last recording) find the singer showing her age a bit but still retaining her distinctive phrasing and her joy at performing standards. Lorez Alexandria retired from performing in 1996 when she was 67, suffered a stroke soon afterwards and her health declined until she passed away in 2001.

Recommended CDs: *Lorez Alexandria Sings Pres* (Deluxe/King 565) is a concept that works very well as she performs swing standards from the repertoire of tenor-saxophonist Lester Young. *Alexandria The Great/More Of The Great Lorez Alexandria* (MCA/Impulse 33116) features the singer at the peak of her powers, while *I'll Never Stop Loving You* (Muse 5457) is one of her best recordings from her later years.

LPs to Search For: *This Is Lorez Alexandria* (King 542) is her debut from 1957. *Deep Roots* (Argo 694) from 1962 teams Alexandria with trumpeter Howard McGhee and the John Young Quartet. *The Songs Of Johnny Mercer* (Discovery 826) and *Harlem Butterfly* (Discovery 905) are two albums in which she expertly interprets and swings Johnny Mercer's timeless lyrics.

Jackie Allen

b. February 19, 1959, Milwaukee, WI

A jazz singer who often interprets pop songs, Jackie Allen has long been a major performer in Chicago.

"My dad is a Dixieland tuba player. Now in his 70s, he still plays part time. We attended many early jazz and polka festivals as kids growing up in Wisconsin. He also has a large album collection that we had access to. I remember in fifth grade the entire class took a music aptitude test. I was in most respects a pretty average student, but I finished at the top of my class on that test. I think my music teachers from then on treated me a little differently." Her father taught each of his five children how to play a brass instrument, so Jackie played the French horn throughout school along with some basic piano.

While attending the University of Wisconsin–Madison, she decided to make a career as a jazz singer. "Even though Madison didn't have a jazz vocal major, I could take the classes that the instrumental jazz majors did. I soon learned that if I put together a book of standards in my keys with a few nice arrangements, I could perform with any jazz musician anywhere in the world and have a solo career, longer than most classical singers."

During 1987–90, Allen performed four or five nights a week in the Wyndham Hotel lobby lounge in Milwaukee with organist Melvin Rhyne. "Musicians who were performing in town would often stay at the hotel where we performed. I got comments from Branford Marsalis, the Modern Jazz Quartet, and others asking me where I was from. They assumed I was from New York. Those comments made me start to think that perhaps I should set my sights higher so I moved to Chicago. My first real gig in Chicago was at the Moosehead Bar and Grill where the owner, Roger Wolf, just adored me and my voice. I convinced him to put up $10,000 for my first CD." The year 1994's *Never Let Me Go*, recorded for the Lake Shore Jazz label, features Allen as a singer straddling the boundary between jazz and cabaret while also being open to folk/pop influences.

Gradually during the past decade, Jackie Allen has been becoming better known outside Chicago. Although she sings her share of standards, she is not shy to include material from other sources in her repertoire, including songs by Joni Mitchell, James Taylor, Sting and herself. Still, she sings primarily from a jazz base and with the spirit of improvised music. She says this about jazz: "One has no time to reflect. It's like a sport. You must prepare but then live totally in the moment on game day. When you're doing this with top-level musicians, it's thrilling. When the audience is with you for the ride, it's life at its best."

Recommended CDs: *Never Let Me Go* (Lake Shore Jazz 005) was an impressive debut. *Which* (Naxos 86042), recorded in Los Angeles in 1999 with such players as pianist Bill Cunliffe, tenor-saxophonist Red Holloway and altoist Gary Foster, is the most overtly jazz-oriented of Allen's recordings, emphasizing swinging standards. *Of The Men In My Life* (A440 4005), *Love Is Blue* (A440 4041) and *Tangled* (Blue Note 300080) each alternate a few jazz cuts with pop and folk material.

Website: www.jackieallen.com

Mose Allison
b. November 11, 1927, Tippo, MS

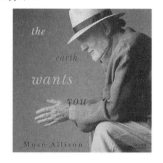

Mose Allison has always been a unique performer. His voice makes him sound like a country blues performer, his lyrics are full of his sly wit and wisdom, and his sophisticated piano playing, which has become increasingly eccentric through the years, conjures up the image of someone in a pickup truck driving on a country road, stopping here and there before continuing the journey.

He was born on a farm just outside of Tippo, Mississippi, which had a population of 200. His father played piano for the fun of it, a cousin introduced him to her jazz records and he heard blues on a local jukebox. Allison was self-taught on piano and trumpet (only recording on the latter once) and in 1945 entered the University of Mississippi, majoring in chemical engineering. After a semester, he started an 18-month period in the Army, which gave him the opportunity to play with the 179th Army Ground Forces Band and to learn to

write arrangements. After his discharge, he returned briefly to the University of Mississippi before earning an English degree at Louisiana State University, graduating in 1953. By then he had been working in clubs for a few years with a trio. In 1955, Allison moved to New York, met Al Cohn (with whom he made his recording debut) and began working with Cohn and Zoot Sims. He also worked with Stan Getz and Gerry Mulligan during 1957–58.

Signed to a record contract with Prestige in 1957, partly due to his "Back Country Suite," Allison recorded six albums in two years. Only 13 pieces have vocals, though these include "One Room Country Shack," "Young Man Blues," "Parchman Farm," "Lost Mind," "If You Live" and "The Seventh Son." Allison then spent a transitional period on Columbia and Epic during 1959–61, singing on half of the pieces, including "Fools' Paradise" and "I Love The Life I Live." The Atlantic years (1962–76) are when Mose Allison was finally recognized as a philosophizing singer/songwriter, gaining many fans among rock musicians, including the Rolling Stones (for whom he opened in 1964), the Who (they recorded his "Young Man Blues"), Leon Russell, Tom Waits and Van Morrison.

Among Mose Allison's other famous originals are "Your Mind Is On Vacation," "If You're Goin' To The City," "One Of These Days," "Everybody's Cryin' Mercy," "Your Molecular Structure," "I Don't Worry About A Thing," "Ever Since The World Ended," "You Call It Joggin,'" "Who's In, Who's Out" and "Certified Senior Citizen." Also, his sloweddown minor-toned version of "You Are My Sunshine" (which has been adopted by a few other singers) and his humorous renditions of "Meet Me At No Special Place" are always memorable.

Mose Allison has stayed active up to the present time, usually appearing with a duo or trio and dispensing his wisdom around the world.

Recommended CDs: *Mose Allison Sings* (Prestige 207279) has Allison's vocals from his Prestige period. *High Jinks!* (Columbia/Epic Legacy 64275) is a three-CD set reissuing his Columbia recordings. Of Allison's work for Atlantic, *I Don't Worry About A Thing* (Rhino 71417), *The Sage Of Tippo* (32 Jazz 32068), which is a two-CD set reissuing four albums (*Swingin' Machine*, *The Word From Mose*, *Wild Man On The Loose* and *I've Been Doin' Some Thinkin'*) and *Your Mind Is On Vacation* (Koch 8537) do an excellent job of summing up this fertile period. *Middle Class White Boy* (Collectables 6535) and *Lessons In Living* (Collectables 6536) bring back Allison's two projects for Elektra/Musician from the early 1980s. From more recent times, *Ever Since The World Ended* (Blue Note 48015), *My Backyard* (Blue Note 38402), *The Earth Wants You* (Blue Note 27640), *Gimcracks And Gewgaws* (Blue Note 23211) and 2001's *Mose Chronicles—Live In London Vols. 1 And 2* (Blue Note 29747 and 29748) show that his message remains both topical and timeless.

Website: www.moseallison.com

David Allyn
(Albert DiLello)
b. July 19, 1923, Hartford, CT

A superior ballad singer with a warm baritone voice, David Allyn was not an improviser, but he appeared in many jazz settings throughout the years.

"I remember hearing late night/early morning radio broadcasts of the big bands in the middle '30s, including Jimmy Lunceford, Erskine Hawkins and Duke Ellington." The son of a father who played French horn and a mother who sang, David Allyn was a professional by the time he was a teenager. "My dad taught me some harmony and ear exercises while my mom taught me voice lessons to obtain tone and quality. I was lucky to have a huge walk-in closet where I could spend all day singing exercises. When I was 16 years old, I called radio stations, asking for auditions." Allyn performed and recorded with the Jack Teagarden Big Band during 1940–42. "In the beginning, all singers liked Bing Crosby, but after being with Jack Teagarden, I heard the cry in his voice and his trombone, which influenced my future work."

Allyn served in the Army during World War II, earning a Purple Heart when he was wounded in Africa. After his discharge, he had short stints with the orchestras of Van Alexander and Henry Jerome. While with Boyd Raeburn during 1945–46, Allyn displayed his ability to sing melodies perfectly in tune despite some rather adventurous accompaniment written by arranger George Handy on such songs as "I Only Have Eyes For You" and "Forgetful."

The association with Raeburn should have made Allyn a star, but his addiction to heroin (which began with pain killers prescribed after he had suffered the combat injuries in World War II.) led to a directionless period and lost opportunities. He recorded six titles for Atomic as a leader in 1946 and seven selections for Discovery in 1949; some of the latter have been reissued by Savoy. A two-year jail sentence for drug possession put him out of action, although it did lead to him kicking his bad habits. Allyn made a comeback for a time, recording four excellent albums for World Pacific and Warner Bros. during 1957–61 that were reissued by Discovery and one for Everest during the same era. In each situation, he was backed by a large orchestra (Johnny Mandel and Bill Holman were among the arrangers) and permitted the opportunity to stretch out on the ballads he loved. "A high point of my career was releasing the Kern album I did with Johnny Mandel on the *Steve Allen Show* in 1960."

But the music world soon changed, and Allyn's lyrical style was considered out of vogue. He found work as an addiction counselor at a Veterans Administration hospital and gradually dropped out of music, other than recording a duet album with pianist Barry Harris for Xanadu in 1975 and a set with pianist Loonis McGloohan in 1976. While living in Minneapolis in the early 1980s, working as a night manager in a hardware store, Allyn heard one of his earlier recordings being played on the radio. He called the disc jockey to thank him, an interview soon took place, and Allyn began to perform locally. After a few years, he moved to New York, sang regularly at a club called Gregory's and recorded a new album for Discovery, one with pianist Clare Fischer that unfortunately has never been released. He led a big band briefly in the early 1990s and has been sporadically active ever since, including performing in Spain in 2002. In 2005, David Allyn's autobiography, *There Ain't No Such Word As Can't*, was published by Author House.

"I have relished the incredible beauty of life through my music, and also the stench of hell in WWII in North Africa along with pain through nine years of addiction to heroin. I realize how lucky I am to have pulled through all of that wasted time. If you really listen to my voice, you can hear my heart."

Recommended CDs: *Jewells* (Savoy 081757027328) includes David Allyn's relatively few recorded vocals with Boyd Raeburn, including "Forgetful" and "I Only Have Eyes For You." The 1975 Xanadu date *Don't Look Back* (Xanadu 101) is only available as a Japanese import, but *Soft As Spring* (Audiophile 155) from 1976 features Allyn in prime form.

LPs to Search For: David Allyn's late 1950s albums, *Sure Thing* (Discovery 900), *Yours Sincerely* (Discovery 916), *I Only Have Eyes For You* (Discovery 803) and *In The Blue Evening* (Discovery 794), are scarce and long overdue to be reissued.

Karrin Allyson
b. July 27, Great Bend, KS

When she emerged on the national scene fully formed in 1992, Karrin Allyson ranked immediately as one of the top singers in bebop. She has since stretched herself, sometimes singing in French, Portuguese and Italian and recently exploring 1970s pop tunes, while still being one of the very best in straight-ahead jazz.

Karrin Allyson was born in Great Bend, Kansas, but only lived there one year before spending five years in Kansas City and growing up in Omaha and Oakland. "I started on classical piano with my mother before she moved me to another teacher. While studying classical piano (with a French minor) at the University of Nebraska at Omaha, I started singing in different kinds of groups; variety/wedding bands and an 'all-girls' rock band plus also having solo piano/vocal gigs in restaurants and clubs. I discovered jazz through classmates and became hooked. Someone gave me the Nancy Wilson/ Cannonball Adderley recording, along with some Bill Evans, Monk, Ella, Sarah, Dinah Washington and Carmen McRae records."

Allyson was in a jazz ensemble with classmates in the Omaha area. After graduating from college in 1987, she sang in Minneapolis for three and a half years. "Then my uncle, who owned a jazz club in Kansas City called The Phoenix, hired me to sub for someone. I ended up loving Kansas City and moved there, singing regularly in the club. While in Kansas City, I met the players whom I would work with for years: guitarists Danny Embrey and Rod Fleeman, bassist Bob Bowman, drummer Todd Strait and pianist Paul Smith."

In 1992, she produced her debut recording, *I Didn't Know About You*. Carl Jefferson signed her to Concord where he reissued that album. She has since recorded nine other records for the label. Over the past 13 years, Allyson has become quite well known in the jazz world, performing regularly at clubs and jazz festivals. She moved to New York in 2000.

"My career has not been a catapulting type. It has been a long, steady climb. It is a lot of hard work and takes much self-determination. I booked and managed myself and the group until a few years ago, but it's been worth it. I love to perform and travel the world, learning about different cultures. For me, jazz encompasses all the great things in art and life: humor, soul, intellect, individualism, creative freedom and interaction between band members. I look forward to the future."

Recommended CDs: Each of Karrin Allyson's recordings has moments to recommend them. Bop lovers are particularly advised to pick up her earliest dates: *I Didn't Know About You* (Concord Jazz 4543), *Sweet Home Cookin'* (Concord Jazz 4593), *Azure-Té* (Concord Jazz 4641), *Collage* (Concord Jazz 4709) and *Daydream* (Concord Jazz 4773), with *Collage* having some of her hottest performances, while *Daydream* concentrates more on ballads (including a touching version of "Everything Must Change"). *From Paris To Rio* (Concord Jazz 4865) has Allyson mostly singing in French and Italian on many of the tunes, *Ballads* (Concord Jazz 4950) is her memorable tribute to John Coltrane's album of the same name, *In Blue* (Concord Jazz 2106) primarily features blues, and the pop-oriented *Wild For You* (Concord Jazz 2220) is her tribute to the 1970s singer-songwriters who originally got her interested in singing music. *Footprints* (Concord 2243) features Allyson singing new lyrics (mostly by Chris Caswell) to classic jazz instrumentals while occasionally being joined by Nancy King and Jon Hendricks.

Website: www.karrin.com

April Aloisio

b. April 20, 1951, Chicago, IL

Throughout her musical career, April Aloisio has had a strong love for Brazilian music, but has also developed into a top-notch bop singer. Her voice is soft, and she can be quite sensitive, but her subtlety should never be mistaken for weakness; Aloisio is never shy about taking chances.

"My mother was a professional big band singer in the 1940s and '50s and my father had a beautiful singing voice, too. My childhood was surrounded by music. There was a radio in every room in the house. My mother says I could sing before I could talk, and she always knew where I was because she could hear me singing."

Born in Chicago, young April took jazz dancing lessons and spent many hours listening to recordings of Broadway musicals. As a teenager, she sang and played guitar and harmonica, performing pop and folk music. While in high school, her family relocated to Cincinnati where she attended Ohio State University and the Cincinnati Public School of Nursing (1974–75). "I knew that I would be a professional singer when I was fired from a nursing job for bringing my guitar to work and singing for the patients. It was the fuel that I needed to go out and audition for my first professional gig, a job that lasted one and a half years. I formed my own trio, which played everything from the Lovin' Spoonful and Dan Hicks and the Hot Licks to Thelonious Monk and Miles Davis." She learned to sing jazz and scat by performing with such local Cincinnati jazz players as Jimmy McGary, Kenny Poole and Dee Felice while at the same time becoming very interested in Brazilian music. She recorded a self-titled LP, and in the late 1980s moved to Chicago.

In the 1990s April Aloisio recorded three well-received albums for Southport and made appearances on CDs by King Fleming, Paulinho Garcia, Marshall Vente, Bradley Parker-Sparrow and Joannie Pallatto. By 2001 she had returned to Cleveland where she works as a nurse by day and a singer at night. Most recently she recorded *Close Your Eyes* for her own label.

"In the future, I want to stay in Brazil for an extended period of time to absorb as much of the culture and Brazilian music as is humanly possible. To me, jazz is freedom. It allows you to open up, closing your eyes and drifting into a dreamstate, leaving reality behind, just letting go and expressing how you feel at that moment. There's nothing better than singing jazz."

Recommended CDs: "My CDs are all my 'children' and I love them for what they are, an extension of myself, the many levels of April, layer by layer." Her formerly rare debut, *April Aloisio* (Aloisio Music 915), has been reissued on her own label and shows her strong potential from 20 years ago. *Brazilian Heart*

(Southport 23) is half bossa nova, half straight-ahead jazz. Dating from 1985 to 1994, the set ranges from a bossa nova version of "The Man I Love" and five Jobim pieces (including "One Note Samba") to a cooking rendition of Bud Powell's "Duid Deed." Joannie Pallatto's voice guests on four numbers. *Footprints* (Southport 40) also has Brazilian ("Desafinado" and "Besame Mucho") and bop ("In Walked Bud" and "Yardbird Suite") numbers but also a bit of free jazz (the three-part "Sparrow Suite" and "Light Fear"). *Easy To Love* (Southport 55) is highlighted by "Song For My Father," "Invitation" and "Night And Day." While the Southport sets have the singer joined by Chicago musicians (including tenor-saxophonist Von Freeman), her recent *Close Your Eyes* (Aloisio Music 561) finds her back in Cincinnati, interacting with local players on a Brazilian-oriented program.

Website: www.aprilaloisio.com

Ernestine Anderson

b. November 11, 1928, Houston, TX

Ernestine Anderson's soulful singing style blurs the lines between swinging jazz, blues and R&B, appealing to several audiences. She has had a long career, and her style has become more influential as time passes.

Anderson remembers, "My parents used to tell me that when I was three years old, I would sit on the front porch, singing to whatever was playing on the Victrola such as Bessie Smith. When I was a little older, I used to listen to the radio station late at night. They would play music from such big bands as Jimmie Lunceford, Count Basie, Buddy Johnson, Andy Kirk, Billy Eckstine and Cab Calloway. I sang in the church with my grandmother on Sundays from the time I was three, sometimes taking solos. My father used to sing in the church in a quartet. The quartet went to different churches and sang, and he would take me. My parents bought me a piano. I taught myself to play by ear. I could hear a song two times and then pick it out. Later on when I heard Sarah Vaughan, I said 'I'm going to learn to sing like that'. I learned to sing her songs verbatim, everybody said I sounded just like her, and I thought I had reached the pinnacle. Then someone told me that I had to gain my own identity, so I stopped listening to singers and listened to instrumentalists. That's how I learned to be myself."

Ernestine Anderson's career began early. She sang with Russell Jacquet's group in 1943 when she was 15, picking up important experience singing with Johnny Otis (1947–49) and Lionel Hampton (1952–53) and making her recording debut with a few titles in 1947. She recorded with Gigi Gryce in 1955 (including the definitive version of "Social Call"), and after trumpeter Rolf Ericson heard the record, he booked her on a three-month Scandinavian tour. "I toured with them for three-and-a-half months and stayed three more months. The reason I came home was that my mom got sick. Otherwise, I was thinking of living there. They gave everybody the star treatment who was jazz and who was from America. It was the first time I knew what it felt like to be free, to feel free. And by that, I mean not to be judged by your skin, or anything except your heart and your music. The whole Swedish experience was a turning point in my career."

While in Sweden, she recorded her first full album, *Hot Cargo*, which became a bit of a hit when it was released in the United States in 1958. Anderson recorded regularly for Mercury into the early 1960s, giving swing standards and more recent songs her soulful treatment. Her star faded a bit as the music world changed in the 1960s, and in 1965 she moved to England. A bit forgotten by the mid-1970s, she made a full comeback after bassist Ray Brown heard her sing at the Turnwater Festival in Canada. He became her manager and got her booked at the 1976 Concord Jazz Festival, and soon she was signed to the Concord label and recording regularly again.

Ernestine Anderson was at the height of her powers during her 15 years with the Concord label, and she recorded two versions of her famous "Never Make Your Move Too Soon." Since the early 1990s, she has continued recording and performing regularly, and even though her voice has naturally aged through the years, she has lost none of her expressive powers or joy of performing. "I just want to keep on doing what I love...singing."

Recommended CDs: *The Toast Of The Nation's Critics* (Mercury 314 514 076) is an excellent session with a big band from 1958 to 1959. *Live From Concord To London* (Concord Jazz 4054) has her comeback set from the 1976 Concord Jazz Festival. Other worthy Concord releases include *Hello Like Before* (Concord Jazz 4031) with Hank Jones and Ray Brown in a trio, *Sunshine* (Concord Jazz 4109) with the Monty Alexander Trio, *Never Make Your Move Too Soon* (Concord Jazz 4147), *Big City* (Concord Jazz 4214), *When The Sun Goes Down* (Concord Jazz 4263) with tenor-saxophonist Red Holloway and Gene Harris, and meetings with Benny Carter on *Be Mine Tonight* (Concord Jazz 4319) and George Shearing on *A Perfect Match* (Concord 4357). Other more recent recordings include *Now And Then* (Qwest 45249), *Blues, Dues And Love News* (Qwest 45900), and *Love Makes The Changes* (High Note 7118). "Two of my favorite recordings are *Live At The Concord Jazz Festival Third Set*, which has been reissued as *I Love Being Here With You* (Concord Jazz 2126) since it has 'Skylark' and my signature song 'Never Make Your Move Too Soon,' and *Isn't It Romantic* (Koch 6906), on which I sing some of my favorite ballads with the Metropole Orchestra."

LPs to Search For: *Hot Cargo* (Mercury 20354) has long been a scarce album despite its original popularity.

Ivie Anderson

b. July 10, 1905, Gilroy, CA; d. December 28, 1949, Los Angeles, CA

Although the song "Sophisticated Lady" was not written with her in mind, the term certainly fit Ivie Anderson, whose classy delivery was greatly appreciated by Duke Ellington, his sidemen and their audience.

Anderson had her first vocal lessons at a convent and also studied privately. She worked regularly in Los Angeles starting in early 1925, and among her more notable early activities were performing at the Los Angeles version of the Cotton Club, touring with the show *Shuffle Along* and singing with Curtis Mosby's Blue Blowers, Paul Howard's Quality Serenaders and Sonny Clay (including on a tour of Australia). Unfortunately she did not record with any of these groups nor with Earl Hines, with whom she worked briefly in Chicago.

Anderson became Duke Ellington's first full-time vocalist in February 1931, and she remained with the band for 11 years.

Her first recording took place the following year and was the hit "It Don't Mean A Thing If It Ain't Got That Swing." In the 1930s, many of her recordings with Ellington found her singing material less significant than the band's instrumentals, including such songs as "Isn't Love The Strangest Thing," "Love Is Like A Cigarette," "Oh Babe, Maybe Someday," "It's Swell Of You" and "Alabamy Home." Much more rewarding are her renditions of "Happy As The Day Is Long," "Raising The Rent," "Truckin'" and "I'm Checkin' Out, Goo'm Bye." Anderson sounds equally at home on up-tempo material as on ballads, and although her improvising tends to be very subtle, she always swings. She rarely performed away from the world of Duke Ellington during her prime years. A rare exception was her only major film appearance: during a scene in the Marx Brothers' *A Day At The Races* where Anderson is featured as a soloist, leading a musical parade while singing "All God's Children Got Rhythm."

On the record date of February 14, 1940, Anderson can be heard in prime form singing "Stormy Weather," "Solitude" and "Mood Indigo," but ironically not "Sophisticated Lady," which was taken by the band as an instrumental. A year later she had her greatest hit with Ellington, introducing "I Got It Bad And That Ain't Good" both on record and in the short-lived stage show *Jump For Joy*.

Chronic asthma was plaguing her by then and led to Anderson leaving Duke Ellington in August 1942, staying off the road and opening up a Chicken Shack restaurant in Los Angeles. She continued singing locally, but mostly maintained a low profile. Anderson recorded a dozen songs on three record dates as a leader during 1945–46 for the Excellent and Black & White labels (including a remake of "I Got It Bad," but these have rarely been reissued).

Asthma cut short Ivie Anderson's life in 1949 when the much-beloved singer passed away at the age of 44.

Recommended CDs: Most of Ivie Anderson's best recordings are on *It Don't Mean A Thing If It Ain't Got That Swing* (ASV 5420).

Leny Andrade

b. January 25, 1943, Rio de Janeiro, Brazil

One of the world's top interpreters of bossa nova, Leny Andrade is still a powerful performer 40 years after the bossa nova first caught on.

She started piano lessons at the age of six, and three years later was singing on the radio. Andrade studied at the Brazilian Conservatory of Music, and at 15 sang with Perminio Goncalves' Orchestra. She worked steadily and was popular early on, for a time using Sergio Mendes' trio as her backup group. Her first album, *A Sensação*, was recorded in 1961. By 1965 she had become well known in Brazil with the stage show *Gemini V*. She lived in Mexico during 1966–70. In the 1970s Andrade sought to stretch the boundaries of bossa nova, using elements of avant-garde music. By the 1980s, however, she was back to performing more conventional, but powerful versions of the bossa nova.

Leny Andrade started visiting the United States in the 1980s, and she moved to New York in 1993, dividing her time in the years since between the United States and Brazil where she is a nationally known figure. She differs from most bossa nova singers in her ability to improvise, and her high-energy approach to what is usually a gentle music. She is often thought of as the Ella Fitzgerald of Brazil.

Recommended CDs: In general Leny Andrade's early recordings are difficult to find, although her debut, *A Sensação* (BMG 664130), has been reissued on CD. Of her more recent sets, *Interpreta Cartola* (Sony 270184), *Luz Neon* (Timeless 11014) and *Canta Altay Verlosa* (Obi 26305) are all worth acquiring. *Maiden Voyage* (Chesky 9113) from 1993 with pianist Fred Hersch is a rare American release, while *Embraceable You* (Timeless 365) has her singing jazz standards, giving the songs the flavor of bossa nova.

Ernie Andrews

b. December 25, 1927, Philadelphia, PA

Ernie Andrews is, at this writing, one of the last survivors of a tradition of swinging and bluesy big band vocalists, a genre that included Jimmy Rushing, Billy Eckstine (though he became best known for his ballads) and Joe Williams. Andrews grew up in Los Angeles where he has spent most of his life and career. He started off singing in a church choir and was discovered while still in high school, recording a dozen numbers (including the regional hit "Soothe Me") for the G&G label. He caught the tail end of the Central Avenue era in Los Angeles and decades later was featured prominently in the documentary *Blues For Central Avenue*.

Andrews recorded for the Aladdin, Columbia and London labels in the late 1940s but faded in popularity during the first half of the 1950s despite maturing as a blues, ballads and standards singer. He cut two big band albums for GNP/Crescendo in 1956 and 1959, sang with the Harry James Orchestra during 1959–67 and 1968–69, and recorded with Cannonball Adderley but remained a minor name and was barely documented at all in the 1970s, being very much in Joe Williams' shadow.

As time passed, Ernie Andrews' artistry has gradually been recognized, which was particularly helped by the shortage of major male jazz singers. In the 1980s he recorded with the Capp/Pierce Juggernaut, Gene Harris' Superband, Jay McShann and the Harper Brothers, and he has since led albums for the Muse and High Note labels. Influenced by Joe Williams and the phrasing of Al Hibbler, Ernie Andrews has long been an original whose singing is well worth celebrating and savoring.

Recommended CDs: Few of Ernie Andrews' earlier records have been reissued on CD, and even his excellent Muse CDs from the 1990s, *No Regrets* (Muse 5484) and *The Great City* (Muse 5543), are out of print since that label is defunct. An exception is *Ernie Andrews* (GNP/Crescendo 2274), which reissues some of the selections from his two GNP LPs of the 1950s, *In The Dark* and *Travelin' Light*. Although sounding older, Andrews is still in excellent form on *The Many Faces Of Ernie Andrews* (High Note 7018), *Girl Talk* (High Note 7073), *Jump For Joy* (High Note 7103) and *How About Me* (High Note 7151) from 1997 to 2005.

LPs to Search For: *From The Heart* (Discovery 825) from 1980 is pretty definitive, featuring Edwards with support from trumpeter Harry "Sweets" Edison and tenor-saxophonist Red Holloway performing such tunes as "On Broadway,"

"Don't Let The Sun Catch You Crying" and "I Cover The Waterfront."

Website: www.ernieandrews.com

Susie Arioli

b. December 19, 1963, Toronto, Ontario, Canada

Since her first album was released in March 2000, Susie Arioli has been one of Canada's top swing singers. Her soft and subtle voice is consistently delightful, and she swings well in her collaborations with guitarist Jordan Officer.

"We had a lovely collection of Billie Holiday records with Teddy Wilson from the 1930s when I was growing up. The songs were known to my mom, so she'd sing them with me and my sibs. Singing became a normal thing to do. In high school, I hung around the guys in the stage band and I went out to jazz clubs with them. When I was a young adult, I regularly attended a local blues jam where the musicians learned to play the jazzy tunes and we had fun. I got into a hotel pop cover band, but there are limits to how often one can sing Gloria Estefan in a small jazz ensemble."

After a few false starts and gaining some experience playing snare drum with pianist-singer Big Moose Walker, Arioli mostly worked outside of music. "Years later, I began playing with a singer and guitar player, Dean Cotrill. We shared singing duties and I accompanied with the snare drum. Then I met Jordan Officer in 1996, and everything just fell into place for me. When we started the Susie Arioli Band, we had a drummer with a full kit, but as we developed and our style became personal, I picked up the snare drum again."

The turning point for the group occurred in 1998 when they were asked to open at the Montreal International Jazz Festival for Ray Charles, filling in for an ailing Charles Brown. "Suddenly we were thrust into a concert hall situation, in front of a couple of thousand people, and it went really well. We were so fortunate that we received a lot of press coverage from that gig." That performance led to the band recording their debut CD, *It's Wonderful*, in 2000, and they have played their brand of swing music at festivals and in clubs ever since.

Susie Arioli names as her main inspirations Billie Holiday, Ray Charles, Nina Simone and Frank Sinatra. "I think what these folks have in common is a wonderful way of filling space with a strong tenderness, firm but gentle. That's what I aspire to do as a singer, and with the band. One of the more horrifying yet educational moments came soon after one of my first forays onto the stage, when my mother asked me, 'What the hell are you singing like Billie Holiday for?' It's true that I would have preferred unconditional adoration, but I certainly started thinking about having my own voice, and I believe that I have been using it ever since."

Recommended CDs: Susie Arioli's Swing Band, which consists of her singing and playing snare drum, two guitars (including Jordan Officer) and bass, has thus far recorded three excellent swing-based CDs: *It's Wonderful* (Justin Time 8493), *Pennies From Heaven* (Justin Time 181), which has guest appearances from stride pianist Ralph Sutton, and *That's For Me*

(Justin Time 195). *Learn To Smile Again* (Justin Time 214) is a change of pace, for it includes six Roger Miller songs (though not "King Of The Road"). *Live At The Montreal International Jazz Festival* (Justin Time 5102) is a delightful DVD of the band, with all of the music also available on an accompanying CD.

Website: www.susiearioli.com

Lil Armstrong
(Lillian Hardin)
b. February 3, 1898, Memphis, TN; d. August 27, 1971, Chicago, IL

Lil Hardin Armstrong is best remembered for her important role as Louis Armstrong's second wife and for her piano playing with King Oliver's Creole Jazz Band and her husband's Hot Five and Hot Seven in the 1920s. However, her own lesser-known recordings of 1936 to 1938 show that she was also a fine singer.

Originally Lil Hardin studied music at Fisk University with hopes of becoming a concert pianist. That plan was unrealistic during that era for a black woman, so instead she moved to Chicago in 1917, working as a song demonstrator. Her strong classical background and a feeling for jazz resulted in her securing work with Sugar Johnny's Creole Orchestra and Freddie Keppard's Original Creole Jazz Band. Hardin led her own band at the Dreamland before becoming King Oliver's pianist in 1921. The following year she met Louis Armstrong when Oliver sent to New Orleans for the young cornetist. Although they were opposites, with Lil being much more sophisticated (and three years older) than Louis, they became close and were married on February 5, 1924. The previous year they had both made their recording debuts with Oliver. Lil did not solo with the Creole Jazz Band, but her on-the-beat chordings helped make the rhythm section solid.

One can certainly argue that Lil Armstrong's main importance to jazz history is her insistence that her husband leave Oliver's band (where he played second cornet) and join Fletcher Henderson's orchestra in New York. The result was that Louis became a solo star and revolutionized jazz. Lil, in the meantime, led a band in Chicago and spent most of a year away from her husband. When Louis returned to Chicago near the end of 1925, at first he was a featured soloist with her group. But after being ribbed constantly by other musicians about being a sideman in his wife's band, Armstrong left to play with Carroll Dickerson's orchestra. However, in his Hot Five and Hot Seven recordings of 1925 to 1927, he used Lil as his pianist. She not only solidified the rhythm (the only other player in the rhythm section of the Hot Five was banjoist Johnny St. Cyr) but contributed notable originals ("Struttin' With Some Barbecue," "Jazz Lips" and "Skid-Dat-De-Dat" among them) and took vocals on "Georgia Grind" and the comedy song "That's When I'll Come Back To You."

The Armstrong marriage was doomed to failure as Louis rose to fame and Lil was pushed into the background. They separated in 1931 and were officially divorced in 1938. Lil never remarried and always proudly kept the Armstrong name. She toured with Freddie Keppard (1928) and Johnny Dodds (1928–29) and earned a teacher's degree at the Chicago College of Music and a post-graduate diploma from the New York College of Music, freelancing as a pianist during the 1930s.

In 1932 Lil recorded "Virginia" as a vocalist while backed by pianist Clarence Williams, and she also cut two vocal duets with Eva Taylor. But it was after she became a house pianist at Decca (where she backed some of the top urban blues artists) that she recorded her most important vocals. On 22 selections recorded during five sessions from 1936 to 1938, Armstrong is well featured as a singer, only playing piano on the final four numbers. She is quite effective on her "Just For A Thrill" (which became a standard), "Brown Gal," "Doin' The Suzie-Q," "Harlem On Saturday Night" and the more obscure material while joined by hot swing combos. But surprisingly she did not continue in that direction, and her last Decca date (1940) featured her strictly as a pianist.

In the 1940s Armstrong studied tailoring and planned to retire from music, but instead found plenty of work in Chicago clubs due to the popularity of New Orleans jazz. She sang on only a very infrequent basis from then on, preferring to play and teach piano. In 1961 she appeared in the *Chicago And All That Jazz* television special and made her final recordings. When Lil died in 1971, it was while playing "St. Louis Blues" at a Louis Armstrong memorial concert, less than two months after his death.

Recommended CDs: *1936–1940* (Classics 564) has all of Lil Armstrong's Decca sessions as a leader and includes her most important vocals.

Louis Armstrong
b. August 4, 1901, New Orleans, LA; d. July 6, 1971, New York, NY

Although it is not accurate to say that jazz singing began with Louis Armstrong, it would not be an exaggeration to say that he was the most important jazz singer of all time. A master at "telling a story" in his trumpet solos, Armstrong did the same thing as a vocalist, altering melody lines and lyrics to give them a catchier rhythm, using space dramatically and often emulating his own trumpet playing. On "Ding Dong Daddy" from 1930, Armstrong takes a superb vocal: after getting the words and the melody out of the way during a chorus, he claims, "I dun forgot the words" and then scats a horn-like solo. The trumpet solo that follows, which borrows phrases from his vocal as it builds and builds, can be thought of as a horn emulating a vocal emulating a horn.

Louis "Satchmo" Armstrong was extremely significant to jazz history in three areas. His trumpet playing was so outstanding and irresistible that it was partly responsible for jazz changing from an ensemble-oriented music to one emphasizing solos. With his beautiful, highly expressive tone, impressive range and ability to build up solos, it would have been a waste for him to be confined to ensembles. It was not until the bebop era that jazz trumpeters moved far ahead of Armstrong while still being indirectly influenced by him. As an entertainer, Satch was impossible to top, always stealing the show with his comedic abilities, his good-humored personality and his lovable nature. And as a singer, his gravelly voice was imitated by a countless number of performers, amateurs and fans. He influenced Bing Crosby, Billie Holiday, Jack Teagarden, Cab Calloway, the Boswell Sisters, Ella Fitzgerald, Louis Prima and virtually every jazz singer that followed. He was the most accessible of all jazz performers, the most significant and is still the most famous name in jazz.

Louis Armstrong was such a beloved performer that it seemed only right that he was thought to have been born in New Orleans on July 4, 1900. Only after his death was it found that he was actually born on August 4, 1901. No matter, he was an American hero, and the more one digs into his history, the more remarkable he looks.

Born in a very poor environment, Louis and his family were abandoned by his father early on, and he was raised as best as possible by his mother, although he was frequently left unsupervised. As a child, Armstrong sang on the streets in a vocal group for pennies. Since he loved the many brass bands that played at parades in New Orleans, he managed to get his first cornet when he was 11. On New Year's Eve of 1912, Armstrong shot off a pistol in the air in celebration and was quickly arrested. He was sent to live in a waif's home as punishment since it was decided that his mother could not take care of him properly. It ended up being the biggest break of his life.

Thriving under the discipline of the home, young Louis seriously practiced the cornet and eventually earned a featured position with the school's band. Released after two years, he was considered a promising young musician. He worked at odd jobs during the day while spending nights playing with local bands. Often called "Little Louis" during this era, he idolized the older cornetist Joe "King" Oliver. Oliver's departure from New Orleans in 1918 left a position open with trombonist Kid Ory's popular band, and he recommended Armstrong. He also gained important experience playing with Fate Marable's band on riverboats. In 1922 when King Oliver sent for Armstrong to join his Creole Jazz Band at the Lincoln Gardens in Chicago, he was ready.

Playing second cornet with Oliver was important experience for Armstrong. He made his recording debut with the Creole Jazz Band in 1923, and married the band's pianist Lil Hardin (his second of four wives). But he was too strong a talent to be confined to a subsidiary role, a situation that was recognized by his wife, who successfully persuaded him in 1924 to leave Oliver and accept an offer to be in Fletcher Henderson's orchestra in New York. Armstrong's arrival in New York to join the band had a major impact on jazz, for his legato phrasing, tone and solo style moved jazz in New York ahead five years, setting the stage for the swing era a decade before it officially started. He became the band's solo star but was unsuccessful in persuading Henderson to let him sing. Other than a few brief breaks on "Everybody Loves My Baby," there are no existing Armstrong vocals from this period. Instead, he played on records behind a variety of blues singers, many of whom he could have outsung.

After leaving Henderson in November 1925, he returned to Chicago. Satch began a series of rather remarkable recordings under the title of Louis Armstrong's Hot Five, plus in 1927 some dates as the Hot Seven. No longer stuck in an ensemble-oriented New Orleans group or a tightly arranged big band, Armstrong was free to take solos, lead ensembles and sing. His voice is heard for the first time with the Hot Five on "Gutbucket Blues" (where he humorously introduces the musicians), and on "Heebies Jeebies" he scats masterfully. The legendary story was that while recording his vocal on "Heebies Jeebies," he dropped the music in the studio and desperately

made up nonsense syllables to cover up not knowing the words, thereby inventing scat-singing. However, Armstrong sounds so confident on the recording that that oft-told story is clearly not the truth. It is possible that that near-disaster occurred on an earlier unreleased version and the producer thought that he should repeat it for the real record. In any case, there are quite a few examples of scatting on record by others during 1923–24, and Gene "The Ragtime King" Greene predated everyone in that area.

More accurately, Armstrong's vocal on "Heebies Jeebies" and other recordings popularized scatting, from novelty "boop-boop-a-doop" 1920s flappers to much more adventurous vocals and eventually vocalese. His scatting, which developed through the years, was inventive not only in his choice of notes but in his variety of nonsense syllables and his inventive humor. Among the more significant Hot Five and Hot Seven recordings that include Armstrong vocals are "Georgia Grind," "Don't Forget To Mess Around," the atmospheric "Skid-Dat-De-Dat," "S.O.L. Blues," "The Last Time" and a dazzling trade-off with guitarist Lonnie Johnson on "Hotter Than That."

The Hot Five (which also included Lil Armstrong, Kid Ory, clarinetist Johnny Dodds and guitarist Johnny St. Cyr) was strictly a recording group, only appearing in public once. Armstrong appeared on a nightly basis during this era with Erskine Tate's Vendome Orchestra or Carroll Dickerson's big band. Very popular in Chicago, Satch played stirring solos, sang and clowned to the delight of audiences.

During 1928, Armstrong appeared on records with an entirely different group, the Savoy Ballroom Five, which co-starred pianist Earl Hines. His trumpet playing was rarely more modern than it sounded that year (check out his duet with Hines on "Weatherbird"), and his vocals included "A Monday Date," "Sugar Foot Strut," "Basin Street Blues," "St. James Infirmary" and his wordless singing on arguably his finest recording, "West End Blues."

In 1929 Louis Armstrong began to become nationally famous, on his way to being an international star. This came about because he moved to New York (which had become the center of the music world), he was accompanied by various orchestras (rather than sharing space with other major soloists), and he was recording new popular numbers rather than New Orleans favorites and originals. During 1929–32 Armstrong's recordings and vocals helped make these songs into standards: "I Can't Give You Anything But Love," "Ain't Misbehavin'," "Black and Blue" (possibly the first anti-racism song), "When You're Smiling," "Rockin' Chair," "I Can't Believe That You're In Love With Me," "Exactly Like You," "I'm Confessin' That I Love You," "If I Could Be With You One Hour Tonight," "Body And Soul," "Sweethearts On Parade," "You're Driving Me Crazy," "Them There Eyes," "When Your Lover Has Gone," "Lazy River," "Star Dust," "Georgia On My Mind," "Between The Devil And The Deep Blue Sea," "All Of Me" and his theme song, "Sleepy Time Down South." In many cases, Armstrong's version became the definitive one, particularly during that era.

Armstrong fronted Luis Russell's band for six months in 1930, spent nine months in California and visited Europe for the first time in July 1932. While his recordings of 1932 to 1933 were not at the same level as his earlier gems (often due to the bands not being rehearsed sufficiently), they still had their bright moments. He spent much of 1933 in Europe, escaping his problems with managers and organized crime. When he returned to the United States in 1935, the swing era was underway, but he was still a major star. Of his big bands recordings of 1935 to 1944, some of the high points were "I'm In The Mood For Love," "Thanks A Million," "Swing

That Music," "Once In A While," "I Double Dare You" and "Jeepers Creepers." As the swing era advanced, Armstrong was thought of more as a tie to the past and a bit of a nostalgia act rather than a pacesetter, even though most trumpeters and singers named him as an important influence. Armstrong appeared in films, was always touring and remained a popular attraction, even if there were no major hits.

During 1944–47, many of his most rewarding performances were with small groups (including in the movie *New Orleans*) while he continued to lead his orchestra. Finally in 1947, Satch broke up his big band and put together the Louis Armstrong All-Stars. The sextet, originally comprising Jack Teagarden, clarinetist Barney Bigard, pianist Dick Cary, bassist Arvell Shaw and drummer Sid Catlett, played New Orleans jazz, swing and novelty numbers with equal skill and joy. The group, with personnel changes through the years, would be Armstrong's main touring and recording band for the remainder of his life. Velma Middleton was part of the band until her death in 1961, joining Satch in comedy numbers. Teagarden had his chances to be featured, and his version of "Rockin' Chair" with Armstrong became a classic. When he departed, his eventual replacement was Trummy Young, who was succeeded in 1964 by Tyree Glenn. Each of the trombonists sang occasional numbers with the master. Satch was heard in top form singing such songs as "Back O'Town Blues," "Pennies From Heaven" and his own "Someday I'll Be Sorry."

In addition Armstrong, whose gravelly voice became deeper through the years, had occasional recording dates with studio orchestras. His 1949 version of "Blueberry Hill" introduced that standard, and other popular numbers were "C'est Si Bon," "La Vie En Rose," "Gone Fishin'" (a duet with Bing Crosby), "A Kiss To Build A Dream On," and a giant hit in 1955 with "Mack The Knife." His three projects with Ella Fitzgerald were delightful, Armstrong appeared in many films, and he was a fixture on television in addition to constantly touring the world, which earned him the nickname "Ambassador Satch."

While a 1959 heart attack slowed him down temporarily, he was soon back on the road. As his range on the trumpet steadily declined during the 1960s, he emphasized his singing, and 1964's "Hello Dolly" became a #1 hit. Rarely able to play the trumpet after 1968, he spent his last years appearing as a singer with the All-Stars, always eager to entertain and having a posthumous hit with "What A Wonderful World." Even though his 70th birthday was celebrated worldwide on July 4, 1970, he actually passed away the following year at the age of 69. Decades later, Louis Armstrong still symbolizes the best in jazz.

Recommended CDs: Nearly all of Louis Armstrong's recordings are easily available. He took vocals on virtually every project that he recorded after 1925. Every record collection has to have the four-CD box *The Complete Hot Five And Hot Seven Recordings* (Columbia/Legacy 63527). His influential 1929 to 1932 recordings are on *Vol. 5: Louis In New York* (Columbia/Legacy 46148), *Vol. 6: St. Louis Blues* (Columbia/Legacy 46996) and *Vol. 7: You're Driving Me Crazy* (Columbia/Legacy 48828). Armstrong's swing era recordings are reissued on *1934–1936* (Classics 509), *1936–1937* (Classics 512), *1937–1938* (Classics 515), *1938–1939* (Classics 523), *1939–1940* (Classics 615) and *1940–1942* (Classics 685). The four-CD *Complete RCA Victor Recordings* (RCA 68682) has his 1932 to 1933 and 1946 to 1947 recordings. Of his All-Star sets, *Satchmo At Symphony Hall* (GRP/Decca 661*), Louis Armstrong Plays W.C. Handy* (Columbia/Legacy 64925), *Louis Armstrong Plays Fats Waller* (Columbia/Legacy 64927) and *The California Concerts* (four CDs—GRP/Decca

4-613) are four of the best, while the three-CD *American Icon* (Hip-O 40138) has his later hits and some of his most memorable vocals of his final 25 years. His collaborations with Ella Fitzgerald are listed in her entry.

Frank Assunto

b. January 29, 1932, New Orleans, LA;
d. February 25, 1974, New Orleans, LA

Dixieland and New Orleans jazz bands, starting in the revival era of the 1940s and continuing up to the present day, often feature a musician or two singing, whether or not they have a worthwhile voice. Unlike the swing era orchestras, most of these bands cannot afford full-time singers, so usually the trumpeter or a horn player is pressed into service. While this satisfies well-lubricated customers in clubs and at festivals, few of these performances are worth preserving. Obvious exceptions are the vocal greats such as Louis Armstrong, Jack Teagarden, Clancy Hayes and the somewhat forgotten Frank Assunto.

Assunto was the long-time trumpeter and leader of the Dukes of Dixieland, a group that included his older brother, Fred Assunto, on trombone and their father, Papa Jac Assunto, on banjo and second trombone. In high school he led the Basin Street Four, Five or Six (depending on the need for musicians), and in January 1949 formed the Dukes of Dixieland to play at a Horace Heidt talent show. Their group won and toured with Heidt (under the temporary name of the Junior Dixie Band) for a few weeks. The Dukes of Dixieland became very popular during a 44-month run at the Famous Door in New Orleans. They recorded for Band Wagon, Imperial, Okeh, Vik (a 1955 album with Pete Fountain on clarinet) and 14 albums for the Audio Fidelity label during 1956–59, including two that featured Louis Armstrong, who loved the band. The Dukes reached the height of their success during six albums for Columbia (1961–64) and finished off with five final sets for Decca (1965–66).

The Dukes in their early days featured Betty Owen (Mrs. Fred Assunto) as their singer. Frank Assunto took his first vocal on "St. James Infirmary" in 1951, but rarely sang until the Dukes signed with Columbia. He displays a warm and very musical voice on "How Are Things In Glocca Morra" (from *Breakin' It Up On Broadway*), "Blue Turning Grey Over You" (*Now Hear This*) and "Sweethearts On Parade" (*Struttin' At The World's Fair*). "Do You Know What It Means To Miss New Orleans?" (from *Live At Bourbon Street*) has his most intriguing singing since he is way behind the beat and phrasing with a lot of originality. Other vocals include "My Kind Of Town" and "Someday You'll Be Sorry" from *Come On And Hear* in 1965, "Mame" (*Sunrise, Sunset*), "Baby Face" and "Jazz Baby" (*Thoroughly Modern Millie*), an excellent version of "Ace In The Hole" (*Dixieland's Greatest Hits*) and "Rosie" and "I Wonder Who's Kissing Her Now" from the Dukes' final album, 1966's *Come To The Cabaret*.

Unfortunately Assunto always confined himself to (at most) one or two vocals per album, probably never taking himself too seriously as a singer despite his talent. In fact, the one Dukes set that has been reissued on CD, *The Dukes Of Dixieland At Disneyland*, is purely instrumental. The Dukes of Dixieland suffered a major blow when Fred Assunto passed away in 1966 from cancer at the age of 36 and a fatal one when Frank Assunto was also stricken by cancer, dying in 1974 when he was 42. The current version of the Dukes has no real connection with the original group other than its name.

If there were justice, there would be a Frank Assunto collection comprising all of his recorded vocals; it might fill up a single CD. His vocalizing is a perfect example of the level that one wishes most of the other Dixieland musicians could reach when they sing.

Fred Astaire
(Frederick Austerlitz)
b. May 10, 1899, Omaha, NE; d. June 22, 1987, Los Angeles, CA

Fred Astaire never made his living strictly as a vocalist nor appeared on a regular basis with jazz bands, but he was certainly a jazz singer. Although he tended to stick close to melodies, he improvised in his own way. He used his small range expertly, his phrasing always swung (even on ballads), and he introduced dozens of songs that became standards. It is no wonder that Irving Berlin and the Gershwins loved to write for him.

Astaire grew up in New York, where he took dancing lessons, as did his older sister Adele. They both developed so quickly that they began playing vaudeville together in 1905 when Fred was six. The Astaires worked steadily with gradually increasing success on both the New York and London stages, hitting their peak with the Gershwin shows *Lady Be Good* and *Funny Face*. After Adele got married in 1932 and retired, Fred Astaire worked solo in the hit play *The Gay Divorce* (introducing "Night And Day") before moving to Los Angeles to work in the movies. He appeared as a guest in the Joan Crawford film *Dancing Lady*, teamed up with Ginger Rogers for the first time in *Flying Down To Rio* and starred with Rogers in the renamed *The Gay Divorcee*, the beginning of a long string of beloved Astaire and Rogers movies.

In addition to his remarkable dancing, Astaire sang in all of his classic films. Among the songs that he helped introduce were "I Won't Dance," "Isn't This A Lovely Day," "Top Hat, White Tie And Tails," "Cheek To Cheek," "Let Yourself Go," "I'm Putting All My Eggs In One Basket," "Let's Face The Music And Dance," "Pick Yourself Up," "The Way You Look Tonight," "A Fine Romance," "They All Laughed," "Let's Call The Whole Thing Off," "They Can't Take That Away From Me" "One For The Road" and "A Foggy Day." In addition, he wrote "I'm Building Up To An Awful Let Down" and is featured in the film *Follow The Fleet* playing very credible stride piano on that piece, live. Astaire also played drums for the fun of it.

Astaire followed up his string of 1930s movies with other worthy projects in the next decade, even interacting with Artie Shaw in *Second Chorus*. Although he recorded on a sporadic basis in the 1930s and '40s, and there have been collections of his singing from movies, his most rewarding jazz vocal project is the three-CD set *The Astaire Story* from 1952. At the age of 53, he sang 34 of the songs that he had performed (and often introduced) in the movies with a Jazz at the Philharmonic group organized by Norman Granz that includes trumpeter Charlie Shavers, Flip Phillips on tenor and pianist Oscar Peterson. If proof were ever needed that Astaire was a fine jazz singer, this set is perfect evidence.

Fred Astaire continued appearing in movies (although only one musical after 1957) into the 1970s, never losing his popularity or tarnishing his image as pure class.

Recommended CDs: *The Essential Fred Astaire* (Sony 87141) and *The Cream Of Fred Astaire* (Pearl Flapper 7013) have the best of his recordings from the 1930s, while *The Astaire Story* (Verve 835 649) reissues in full his 1952 JATP set.

Eden Atwood
b. January 11, 1969, Memphis, TN

Eden Atwood has had several careers. She gained her greatest recognition in jazz early on with four well-received Concord recordings.

The daughter of composer-arranger Hub Atwood (who wrote for Frank Sinatra, Harry James, Stan Kenton and Nat King Cole) and the granddaughter of Pulitzer Prize–winning author A.B. Guthrie, Jr., she first sang in public when she was three. "My father would accompany me while I sang 'I Can't Give You Anything But Love.' My folks also took me down to Shakey's Pizza Parlor in Memphis and I would sit in with the Dixie trio and sing 'Doodily Doo.' I remember the guys asking me what key I wanted to sing it in and I said, 'Doesn't matter.'"

After her parents were divorced when she was five, Atwood lived with her mother in Montana. She took eight years of classical piano lessons, and later privately studied jazz piano. At 15, Atwood began singing with her own band locally. She attended the University of Montana's drama department, and in 1989 was enrolled in the American Conservatory of Music in Chicago but only stayed a year because she had too much work. "At first I thought I would be an actress. But one night after the singer at the restaurant I worked in took ill and the band let me sit in, I knew that that was what I really wanted to do most."

Atwood sang at the Gold Star Sardine Bar in Chicago for eight years in addition to working as an actress and model. She learned an important lesson during this period. "I used to dress in a very provocative style for performing. I also chose material designed to titillate the crowd. One night during a ballad, I heard my pianist say 'yeah' under his breath and from then on I only wanted to sing in a true and genuine way." In 1992 she gained a role on ABC's *The Commish* and starred for nine months on the ABC soap opera *Loving*. She also had a role in the movie *The Untouchables*, but singing jazz was her true love. In 1993 she recorded her first CD, *Today*. It was heard by Marian McPartland and forwarded it to Carl Jefferson, the president of the Concord label. He was so impressed that he signed her to a contract. *Today* was re-released as *No One Ever Tells You* (the title cut was one of her father's songs), and it was followed by *Cat On A Hot Tin Roof*, *There Again* and *A Night In The Life*.

"At first I was very inspired by Sarah Vaughan and Ella Fitzgerald. Later, I knew that my voice was not like those women and I started looking to singers who were able to express the most emotionally, whatever their vocal range might be. I found Shirley Horn and Jimmy Scott and, ever since, they have been my touchstones for what jazz singing is all about for me." On her Concord recordings, Atwood's singing falls into both jazz and cabaret, and she is particularly effective on ballads.

Since her Concord period ended, Eden Atwood has toured Hong Kong and Thailand, headlined at the first Bangkok Jazz Festival and performed at the Ritz Carlton in Shanghai, China for two months. "I got a chance to go to Singapore for a four-month gig in 2000. It was the most singing, night after night, I had ever done. I sang four sets a night six nights a week. I lowered all my keys by a fourth and developed my lower register to save my voice. As a result, I began to sound more like a woman and less like a little girl." Since signing with Groove Note, she has recorded two of her best albums: *Waves—The Bossa Nova Session* and *This Is Always—The Ballad Session.*

Now living in Montana, Eden Atwood is happily married, has adopted a boy, teaches, works with children and sings with the Last Best Band and the soul/funk band Blue Talk and Love. "Jazz, in its highest form, is about telling the truth without artifice. It can be swinging and fun and greasy, but it still has to be true. It is a noble calling. It is also a never-ending learning process. It challenges you musically and personally to know who you are and find a way to say that through music."

Recommended CDs: Of Eden Atwood's Concord recordings, *No One Ever Tells You* (Concord Jazz 4560), *Cat On A Hot Tin Roof* (Concord Jazz 4599), *There Again* (Concord Jazz 4645) and *A Night In The Life* (Concord Jazz 4730), the first and the fourth ones are the most rewarding, though each of them have their moments. Her personal favorites are her most recent sets, *Waves:The Bossa Nova Session* (Groove Note 1012) and *This Is Always:The Ballad Session* (Groove Note 1022). Those two CDs show that she has grown and matured into a potentially significant jazz singer.

Website: www.edenatwood.com

Claire Austin
(Augusta Marie)
b. November 21, 1918, Yakima, WA; d. June 17, 1994, Willits, CA

Claire Austin spent much of her life as a housewife, but she had a gift for singing 1920s blues, vintage jazz and swing.

Austin sang as a child, studied piano and often attended vaudeville shows with her father. After graduating from high school, she worked at a nightclub in Seattle and seemed poised to start her career. However, a short-lived first marriage, becoming a mother, surviving a serious illness and having a second marriage to drummer Chuck Austin, who was in the Army during World War II, made music very secondary for years, although Austin performed whenever the opportunity arose.

On Mother's Day in 1947, she was given a Bessie Smith album by a family friend, pianist Bob Moseley, and that rekindled her interest in singing. Claire Austin began to perform more regularly, having her highest profile during the first half of the 1950s. She worked and recorded with Turk Murphy, and for her own blues-oriented ten-inch album she used trombonist Kid Ory and his rhythm section. While Austin hinted at Bessie Smith (always a strong influence) and the classic blues singers on the latter project, a year later she recorded an album for the Contemporary label of tunes from the 1930s, coming across as a sophisticated if bluesy swing singer. That set, which has trumpeter Bob Scobey and guitarist Barney Kessel in the quintet, displays Austin's versatility.

After working with Scobey's band during 1955–56, Claire Austin faded from the scene, going back to being a housewife.

She returned for an obscure 1965 album with the Great Excelsior Jazz Band and re-emerged one last time in 1975 when she was living in Cincinnati, recording a sextet with cornetist Ernie Carson and Gene Mayl's Dixieland Rhythm Kings and a particularly rewarding album of duets with pianist Don Ewell. At 56, Claire Austin still retained 90 percent of her singing abilities despite her long period off the scene, but the Ewell set went unreleased for decades, and she once again slipped away.

Apparently Claire Austin, who ended up back in Northern California, felt forgotten by the jazz world in her later years, and she did not attempt another comeback. She never seemed to realize how much she was loved by the trad jazz world.

Recommended CDs: The essential *When Your Lover Has Gone* (Original Jazz Classics 1711) has all of the music from Claire Austin's blues set with Kid Ory and her swing session with Bob Scobey. *Turk Murphy At The Italian Village 1952–53* (San Francisco Trad Jazz Foundation 318) has some selections on which Austin sings with Murphy's band. *Memories Of You* (Audiophile 143) is her excellent 1975 duet project with Don Ewell.

LPs to Search For: Not yet reissued on CD are *Claire Austin And The Great Excelsior Jazz Band* (GHB 22) from 1965 and 1975's *Goin' Crazy With The Blues* (Jazzology 52).

Patti Austin
b. August 10, 1948, New York, NY

A major R&B singer whose music only on rare occasions came close to bordering on jazz, Patti Austin surprised and impressed everyone in 2001 when she recorded a brilliant tribute to Ella Fitzgerald. She has been singing jazz standards regularly ever since.

Patti Austin made her debut at the age of four when she appeared at the Apollo Theater. She was the goddaughter of Dinah Washington and Quincy Jones, and one of her early boosters was Sammy Davis Jr. Austin began recording as a teenager, was very busy initially in the jingle and session scene (singing on hundreds of commercials) and mostly stuck to the soul/R&B field, having hits with 1969's "Family Tree," 1981's "Baby Come To Me," "The Heat Of Heat" and "How Do You Keep The Music Playing."

Although she was on George Benson's 1980 recording of "Moody's Mood For Love," and her 1988 album *The Real Me* contains standards, nothing in Austin's early career showed that she would be switching eventually to swinging jazz.

In 2000, Austin performed with the WDR Big Band. When she was asked to have a return engagement the following year, she decided to make it a tribute to Ella Fitzgerald. After two months of listening to Ella's records and three weeks of learning some of the singer's most virtuosic performances note-for-note (while improvising in her own style on some of the other songs), she recorded *For Ella*. Of all the Ella tribute albums of the period (including a fine one by Dee Dee Bridgewater), this was the most successful one, with Austin bringing back Fitzgerald's style and her joyful sound.

The success of *For Ella* has launched a new jazz-oriented period for Patti Austin, who has performed that material and other jazz standards with big bands on numerous occasions ever since.

Recommended CDs: *For Ella* (Playboy Jazz 7503) is the Patti Austin jazz CD to get, a remarkable effort that contains such highlights as "Mr. Paganini," "A-Tisket, A-Tasket" and "How High The Moon." Also worth picking up because of her interpretations of standards are *The Real Me* (Qwest 25696) and *Street Of Dreams* (Intersound 9576).

Alice Babs
(Hildur Alice Nilson)
b. January 26, 1924, Kalmar, Sweden

One of Europe's top jazz singers since she was a teenager, Alice Babs is a celebrity in her native Sweden and a legend in Europe, while in the United States (where she has rarely visited) she is chiefly known for her occasional association with Duke Ellington.

Since Babs was an early nickname, she adopted Alice Babs as her stage name at the beginning of her career. She began making records when she was only 15, having a hit with "Swing It Magistern" ("Swing It, Teacher"). Babs' cheerful style, youthful enthusiasm and ability to incorporate occasional yodeling into her singing made her the symbol of swing in Sweden, while her versatility and impressive musicianship allowed her to have a long career.

Alice Babs worked as an actress in the 1940s, appearing in more than a dozen films in Swedish, although most of her recordings were of swing standards in English. While open to aspects of bebop, she was not really a bop singer, although her tone and sense of swing fit into the 1950s Swedish cool jazz movement quite comfortably. She recorded steadily, sometimes with violinist Svend Asmussen, the Harry Arnold Orchestra or altoist Arne Domnerus, and occasionally ventured outside the world of jazz into pop and classical music.

In 1963 Babs recorded a notable album with Duke Ellington that unfortunately remains out of print. She later worked with Ellington on his second and third Sacred Concerts, sounding particularly beautiful on "Heaven." She also performed with Ellington during part of his last European tour in 1973. While less active since the early 1990s, Alice Babs still makes occasional public appearances.

Recommended CDs: *Swing It* (Phontastic 9302) has most of Alice Babs' recorded high points from 1939 to 1953, showing why she was such a sensation in Sweden. *Music With A Jazz Flavour* (Celeste 549936) from 1973 and *Serenading Duke Ellington* (Prophone 21) from 1974 to 1975 are excellent examples of her middle-period work, while *Don't Be Blue* (Prophone 62) finds her in 2001 at the age of 77 still sounding youthful and very musical with the same sweet and innocent voice that made her famous 62 years earlier.

LP to Search For: Duke Ellington's *Serenade To Sweden* (Reprise 5024) from 1963 has thus far unfortunately been bypassed by all reissue programs.

Judy Bady
b. September 3, Grand Rapids, MI

A fine vocalist with a large soulful voice and the willingness to take chances, Judy Bady has made a strong impression with her long overdue debut as a leader, *Blackbird*.

Gospel music was an important early influence on her development, and she sang in several choirs and in a gospel group called the Sounds Unlimited. She studied piano, played violin briefly, took drum lessons and owns a wooden marimba.

Bady considers Aretha Franklin to be her main vocal influence. "I've always had a deep voice and used to give myself headaches when I was young, walking around the house screeching and screaming, trying to sing like her. Another great vocal influence is Vivian Lord, who sounds very much like Carmen McRae and was my vocal professor at William Paterson University." She also mentions altoist Oliver Lake, tenor-saxophonist Billy Harper, baritonist Hamiet Bluiett and pianist Barry Harris as being very significant in helping her musical development.

Bady decided to become a professional singer in the late 1980s when "Bobby McFerrin told me twice to leave Kalamazoo, Michigan, and pursue a singing career. Before that, I sang in church, and did community theater." Since becoming a full-time singer, Judy Bady has won three Down Beat Music Awards while gaining her music degree at William Paterson University in the 1990s; she appeared in the documentary *Jazz Women: The Female Side of Jazz*; and she recorded with Oliver Lake and pianist Francesca Tanksley. The biggest step forward in her career for both visibility and in documenting her singing has been recording her 2003 CD, *Blackbird*.

Judy Bady's goal for the future is simple and universal among jazz singers: "To work with as many of the masters of the genre of jazz as possible and to be able to make a comfortable living doing nothing but singing."

Recommended CD: *Blackbird* (Original Woman Productions 687877) has Judy Bady and pianist Misha Piatigorsky's trio performing fresh versions of standards (including an up-tempo "The Nearness Of You" and a soulful "Battle Hymn Of The Republic") plus her own "Je Me Souvien'." She can also be heard on four songs on Oliver Lake's *Have Yourself A Merry...* (Passin' Thru 564355), five numbers on *Gospel-Jazz Mass: Live At Ascension Lutheran Church* (Spirit 730 025) with Hamiet Bluiett and John Hicks and featured on one selection on Francesca Tanksley's *Journey* (Dream Caller 617 617).

Website: www.judybady.com

Mildred Bailey
(Mildred Rinker)
b. February 27, 1907, Toledo, WA;
d. December 12, 1951, Poughkeepsie, NY

Mildred Bailey, one of the finest jazz singers of the 1930s and '40s, had a little girl's voice that contrasted with her large body. She could sing low-down blues and was particularly effective on ballads, which she delivered with great sincerity and feeling. Her life was not as happy as it should have been (she always felt self-conscious about her looks), but she had several major accomplishments along the way and was an influential force.

In the mid-1920s, she moved from her native Washington, working in Los Angeles first as a song demonstrator and then as a radio singer. Influenced initially by Louis Armstrong and

Ethel Waters, Bailey's voice was always distinctive. When her brother Al Rinker and his friend Bing Crosby showed up on her doorstep one day in 1926, she gave them shelter, secured some work for the duo, and helped them land jobs with Paul Whiteman's orchestra as two-thirds of the Rhythm Boys. In 1929 they returned the favor, arranging for Whiteman to hear her at a party. When Whiteman hired her, Mildred Bailey became the first female band singer.

Her initial recordings were "What Kind Of Man Is You" with an Eddie Lang pickup group in 1929 and one title ("I Like To Do Things For You") with Frank Trumbauer in 1930. However, she was underutilized by Whiteman. In 1931 Bailey began seriously appearing on records, including the first two sessions under her own name. She made both "Georgia On My Mind" and "Rockin' Chair" famous and was billed as "The Rockin' Chair Lady."

By 1933 Bailey was married to xylophonist Red Norvo and starting her own successful solo career. Of her recordings during 1933–35, highlights include "There's A Cabin In The Pines," "Someday Sweetheart" and four songs (including "Squeeze Me" and "Honeysuckle Rose") on which she holds her own with the quartet of trumpeter Bunny Berigan, altoist Johnny Hodges, pianist Teddy Wilson and bassist Grachan Moncur. During 1936–39, she was regularly featured with the Red Norvo Orchestra, an ensemble featuring the advanced arrangements of Eddie Sauter. Norvo and Bailey were known to the public as "Mr. and Mrs. Swing."

Bailey, who recorded during that period with and without Norvo's band (including "For Sentimental Reasons," "More Than You Know," "There's A Lull In My Life," "Just A Stone's Throw From Heaven" and "The Lamp Is Low"), worked for a short while with Benny Goodman in 1939 after the Norvo big band broke up. She remained in prime voice during 1940–47, even while her personal life was in turmoil.

She and Norvo were divorced (though they still worked together occasionally), and Bailey's health started to become shaky due to her weight and excessive drinking. However, she remained popular and during 1944–45 hosted a regular radio show on CBS featuring jazz all-stars (that will hopefully be made available on CD in full someday). Some of the performances have come out through the years, but most remain unreleased.

After 1947, Mildred Bailey was less active, making her final record date in 1950. She died in 1951 when she was just 44, and considering her lifelong inferiority complex, she would have been amazed to know that four decades later her picture would appear on a postage stamp.

Recommended CDs: The limited-edition ten-CD box, *The Complete Columbia Recordings* (Mosaic 10-204), has 214 Mildred Bailey recordings and is a must for her fans, but it has already gone out of print. Her earliest recordings (predating the Columbias) were last out on *Volume One* (The Old Masters 103) and *Volume Two* (The Old Masters 104). *The Rockin' Chair Lady* (GRP/Decca 644) has most of Bailey's non-Columbia recordings, including the date with the Berigan quartet. *The Blue Angel Years 1945–1947* (Baldwin St. Music 306) includes Bailey's 1946 sessions and some obscurities, while *Me And The Blues* (Savoy 17089) has the majority of her 1946 to 1947 recordings for Majestic and Savoy. Difficult to find but worth the search is the *Legendary V-Disc Sessions* (Vintage Jazz Classics 1006), which not only has V-Discs and appearances by Norvo, Benny Goodman's orchestra, Teddy Wilson and the Delta Rhythm Boys but radio appearances, including two numbers from the spring of 1951 that are the last documentation of Mildred Bailey.

Chet Baker

(Chesney Baker)
b. December 23, 1929, Yale, OK;
d. May 13, 1988, Amsterdam, The Netherlands

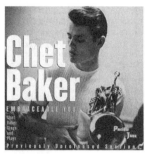

There was always something special and unexplainable about Chet Baker, an odd charisma that resulted in him being rated higher than his abilities might have deserved. Was he really a much better trumpeter than, say, Art Farmer? He was certainly much more famous. Baker expressed vulnerability in his quiet middle-register playing that reached beyond the jazz world, and the same could be said about his singing, even if it was often unintentional.

Chet Baker is one of the most controversial singers included in this book because he did not have much of a voice. His singing was more often than not flat, his high voice sometimes sounded similar to Chris Connor (though Connor sings in tune), and there were times when one got the impression that Baker did not know what he was singing about. And yet, he was one of the most popular singers in jazz during the second half of the 1950s, at least until his move to Europe and jail sentences took him off the scene.

The son of a country music guitarist, Baker was born in Oklahoma and moved to Los Angeles with his family when he was ten. He sang in church choirs and, at his father's urging, was going to start playing trombone, except that his arms were too short. At 13 he instead took up the trumpet, playing in school bands. Baker dropped out of school in 1946 when he was 16 to enlist in the Army, claiming to be 17. He served for two years, played in an Army band while in Germany and spent 1948 to 1950 in Los Angeles where he sometimes sat in at jam sessions. Since his life was aimless, he re-enlisted in the Army in 1950, but after a year was transferred to Arizona. Bored, Baker deserted. After much discussion and intense negotiations, he was able to get a general discharge and return to Los Angeles.

In 1952 Charlie Parker was in Los Angeles, trying out trumpeters to play with his quintet while in town. Baker won the audition and gained some attention due to his performances with Bird. Shortly after, baritonist Gerry Mulligan heard Baker play, enjoyed his soft sound and lyrical style and hired him for his new quartet. The Mulligan pianoless quartet caught on big, playing at the Haig in Los Angeles and recording for the new Pacific Jazz label, symbolizing West Coast Jazz for much of the jazz world. Among the group's recordings was "My Funny Valentine," which became an unofficial theme song for Baker throughout his career.

When Mulligan was busted for heroin possession in June 1953, the quartet broke up. As it turned out, Baker and Mulligan did not care for each other much anyway (despite the musical telepathy that resulted whenever they played together), and when the baritonist was released from prison a few months later and Baker asked him for a raise, he turned him down. They would only have two recorded reunions in the future.

By then, Baker did not need Mulligan. He had formed his own successful quartet with pianist Russ Freeman and was becoming quite famous. In fact, he would soon be a bit embarrassed when he began winning polls for *Downbeat* and *Metronome* over such trumpeters as Dizzy Gillespie, Clifford Brown and Miles Davis.

On his record date of October 27, 1953, Baker took his initial vocals on "I Fall In Love Too Easily" and "The Thrill Is Gone." Baker also took vocals on the sessions of February 15, 1954 (including "My Funny Valentine") and February 28, 1955. He occasionally sang a song or two in clubs, but otherwise concentrated primarily on the trumpet during the next few years. However, his vocal records sold well and added to his popularity, especially among women.

If Baker had self-discipline and better judgment, he could have been a movie star by the late 1950s and gained a fortune to go with his fame. But despite the examples of Gerry Mulligan, pianist Dick Twardzik (who had a fatal overdose during a European tour with Chet's quartet) and Charlie Parker (who died in 1955), Baker became a heroin addict in 1956. Throughout his life, drugs would be very important to him even as they continually destroyed his potential. After he was busted in the United States. and spent two months in jail, his chance for a career in movies was over. He recorded a few albums for Riverside during 1958–59 (including the vocal set *It Could Happen To You*), moved to Italy in the fall of 1959 and spent five years in Europe, including time in an Italian prison during 1961–62. Baker recorded some vocals on the album *Chet Baker With Fifty Italian Strings* (including "When I Fall In Love" and "Deep In A Dream"), but his best sets were instrumentals.

Back in the United States in 1964, Baker started making a comeback, recording seven fine albums during 1964–65, including a partly vocalized tribute to Billie Holiday called *Baker's Holiday*. But a string of dismal commercial records for World Pacific during 1965–66 gave one the impression that he no longer cared much about his career. Baker was beaten up and had some of his teeth knocked out after a botched drug deal in 1966. He came back briefly to record two additional terrible albums and then retired.

Amazingly enough, Baker made a complete comeback in the 1970s. He was fitted for dentures, practiced for three years and in 1973 with Dizzy Gillespie's help was playing in New York clubs. His trumpet chops came back, and during his final decade, Baker on good days played even better than he had in the 1950s.

In 1975 Chet Baker moved back to Europe, where he had a nomadic lifestyle, playing and recording regularly while living the life of a homeless drug addict. While his trumpet playing was back in its prime, his singing remained an acquired taste. Baker was fine for occasional scatting since his choice of notes was excellent, but the sound of his declining voice on ballads made him sound washed up and sometimes completely lost.

Fifteen days after performing at a well-received and re-corded concert with the NDR Big Band and a radio orchestra on April 28, 1988 (singing "My Funny Valentine" and "I Fall In Love Too Easily"), Chet Baker either slipped or was pushed out of a second-story window in Amsterdam, falling to his death. He was 58.

Recommended CDs: *Grey December* (Pacific Jazz 97160) has the four vocals from Chet Baker's February 28, 1955 date. *Embraceable You* (Pacific Jazz 31676, recorded in 1957 but not released until the 1990s), *It Could Happen To You* (Original Jazz Classics 303), *Baby Breeze* (Verve 314 538 328) and *Baker's Holiday* (Emarcy 838 204) include most of the best examples of his singing.

Jeff Baker
b. 1979, Boise, ID

Jeff Baker, who thus far has three CDs out on the Origin label, has a warm voice and a sophisticated style based in the jazz mainstream.

Born and raised in the Boise, Idaho area, he discovered jazz early in life. "I learned to improvise by constantly listening to records and singing along with Dizzy Gillespie's recordings. I also listened to Joe Williams, Chet Baker and Ella Fitzgerald, then later to Mark Murphy. When I was a teenager and people were listening to grunge music, I really got into jazz."

Baker, who was inspired by seeing Gene Harris play often, went to the Lionel Hampton Jazz Festival with his high school group when he was 16, winning the solo vocal competition. He earned a degree in music education from Willamette University and sang at gigs with his group One Way to Where.

After graduation, Jeff Baker took a chance. "I had saved up a lot of money to go to grad school but decided to instead put the money into making a really good CD." He recorded songs associated with Chet Baker for his *Baker Sings Chet* album in 2003.

The gamble paid off. Baker gained a longtime position working at a church music ministry job, and he has since successfully recorded two more CDs while gradually gaining recognition for his singing abilities.

Recommended CDs: *Baker Sings Chet* (Origin 22010) from 2003 has Jeff Baker singing 13 songs associated with Chet Baker but in his own voice, which is much stronger than Chet's. *Monologue* (Origin 22019) and *Shopping For Your Heart* (Origin 22031) are excellent follow-ups.

Website: www.jeffbakerjazz.com

Josephine Baker
(Freda Carson)
b. June 3, 1906, St. Louis, MO; d. April 12, 1975, Paris, France

A living legend by the late 1920s, Josephine Baker was best known as a personality, dancer and comic and for appearing onstage with a bare minimum of clothes (and sometimes less). However, she was also an underrated singer and in her early days often sang jazz, even if her voice was semi-operatic at times.

An uninhibited character when appearing in productions and giving the impression of being a primitive without a care in the world, the future Josephine Baker (who was born as Freda Carson) grew up in poverty and had a difficult childhood. When she was 13, she auditioned at a vaudeville theater and spontaneously ran away from home to join a traveling road show. At 15 she auditioned for the touring company of the innovative Eubie Blake/Noble Sissle show *Shuffle Along*, but was turned down because her skin was considered too dark for her to be a showgirl. She was hired instead to be a dresser, but one night, when one of the dancers had to leave the show because she was expecting a baby, Baker was given the spot. Her mugging and outlandish dancing made her a surprise hit.

By then, her name was Josephine Baker; her second husband's name was Willie Baker. Sissle and Blake wrote special material for her to perform in their 1924 revue, *Chocolate Dandies*, and Baker became a star on Broadway due to her comedic talents. The turning point of her career occurred when she was hired for *La Revue Nègre*, an American show that played in Paris. Her entrance, which found her entirely nude except for a large pink flamingo feather while she did a split on the shoulder of a tall black man, made the 19-year old a sensation overseas. By 1926, she was the star of the Folies Bergère, dancing the Charleston while only wearing bananas tied to her waist.

Internationally famous and a major part of French society, Baker had her own club (Chez Josephine), starred in the 1927 film *La Sirène Des Tropiques* and (starting in 1926) began to make records. Although jazz was only part of what she sang, her records during the 1926–39 period include such numbers as "Dinah," "Sleepy Time Gal," "I Found A New Baby," "Bye Bye Blackbird," "Breezing Along With The Breeze," "Blue Skies," "He's The Last Word" and "You're Driving Me Crazy." Baker was a symbol of "Le Jazz Hot" and the exotic side of America in France during the second half of the 1920s.

In the 1930s, Josephine Baker starred in the French films *Zou Zou*, *Princess Tam-Tam* and *Fausse Alerte*. She was back in the United States briefly in 1936 as one of the stars of the *Ziegfeld Follies* and, after becoming a naturalized French citizen, joined the French Resistance against the Nazis, becoming a war hero behind the scenes. Baker worked on and off during the postwar years, adopted many children from diverse backgrounds (which she called her "rainbow family") and tried unsuccessfully in the 1950s to fight for civil rights in the United States. A decade later she had better luck when she starred in a one-woman show on Broadway in 1964.

Josephine Baker was still world famous when she passed away in 1975 at the age of 68.

Recommended CDs: The two-CD set *Elysee* (DCC Compact Classics 2-614) has most of Josephine Baker's early jazz-oriented recordings.

LaVern Baker

(Delores Baker)
b. November 11, 1929, Chicago, IL;
d. March 10, 1997, New York, NY

LaVern Baker, like Ruth Brown, spent most of her career singing R&B, helping to lead the way toward rock and roll. But also like Brown, she could sing jazz quite credibly whenever she wanted to, as she proved on her Bessie Smith tribute album.

Baker, who was distantly related to blues singer-guitarist Memphis Minnie and whose aunt Merline Johnson recorded as "The Yas Yas Girl" in the 1930s, began her career singing in Chicago clubs when she was 17. She was billed as "Little Miss Sharecropper," dressing to fit the part. Baker recorded under

that name with Eddie "Sugarman" Penigar's band in 1949 and on her own debut set as a leader for the National label in 1950. She reinvented herself as Bea Baker when she recorded in 1951 with Maurice King's Wolverines and switched permanently to LaVern the following year. After singing with Todd Rhodes' group (with whom she recorded for King), Baker signed with Atlantic in 1953.

During 1954–63, LaVern Baker had quite a few hits, including "Tweedle Dee," "Bop-Ting-A-Ling," "Play It Fair," "Still," "Tra La La," "Jim Dandy," its follow-up "Jim Dandy Got Married," "I Cried A Tear," "I Waited Too Long," "So High, So Low" and "See See Rider." "Tweedle Dee" was such a big seller that white pop singer Georgia Gibbs recorded an exact note-for-note copy for Mercury. Baker petitioned Congress to make it illegal to copy an arrangement without permission. The bill failed, but it did gain a lot of publicity. When she went on a tour of Australia in 1957, Baker took out an insurance policy, naming Georgia Gibbs as her beneficiary. She sent it to Gibbs with a letter saying that she was concerned that if something happened to her, she didn't want Gibbs to suffer a hardship from not being able to copy her records.

The 1958 album *LaVern Baker Sings Bessie Smith* was a change of pace, and a complete surprise. While Baker does not imitate Smith, her shouting passionate style is reminiscent of the Empress. She is backed by an all-star swing group that includes trumpeter Buck Clayton, trombonist Vic Dickenson and Paul Quinichette on tenor, and she fares quite well in this rare jazz setting, an underrated gem.

LaVern Baker continued to be a popular attraction during the 1960s. In 1969 during a trip to Vietnam to entertain the troops, she became seriously ill, recovered in the Philippines, and decided to stay, performing locally and running a club for 19 years. In 1988 Baker was invited to Carnegie Hall to participate in the Atlantic label's 40th anniversary celebration. She sounded so strong that she settled back in the United States and launched a comeback, which reached its peak when she replaced Ruth Brown in the Broadway musical *Black And Blue*, recording an album for DRG. Despite health problems, LaVern Baker continued performing up until shortly before her death at the age of 67 in 1997.

Recommended CDs: *Precious Memories/LaVern Baker Sings Bessie Smith* (Collectables 6415) includes Baker's memorable Bessie Smith tribute album. *Woke Up This Mornin'* (DRG 8433) is a good example of her singing in her later years.

Toni Ballard

b. July 12, 1946, Chicago, IL

Best known to those in the jazz industry for her work as a publicist for the Berklee College of Music during 1998–2004, Toni Ballard is a very good jazz singer, as can be heard on her one CD as a leader, *I'm Your Pal*.

"When I was growing up, my mother, who played piano and organ by ear and also sang (but only at home), played records by the likes of André Previn and Erroll Garner. I was always singing and dancing as a child. I took dancing lessons from about age three into my early teens, and the dance recitals invariably involved singing. And then there were the various variety shows I produced in our garage."

Ballard played brass instruments during her school years, including mellophone, cornet and especially French horn. She also studied piano and played guitar a bit. "After singing with my second rock band, in 1974, I heard a Billie Holliday record, and started to get serious. I began studying with a series of voice teachers over the next ten years that included Dee Kohanna, Janet Lawson, and Sidra Cohn Rausch. I've been singing jazz in New England since the early '80s, mostly with big bands, including the Nelson Riddle Orchestra (1992), the Boston Big Band (1989–94), the White Heat Swing Orchestra (1997), and the Ryles Jazz Orchestra (2000–03). From 1989 to 2002, I was the vocalist with the Boston-based, 17-piece Silver Bullet Swing Orchestra, led by drummer Don Pentleton. I'm honored to have had the opportunity (in my former role as publicist at Berklee College of Music) to lend support to some of today's new jazz singers—Christine Fawson, Sara Leib, Daniela Schächter, Christy Bluhm, Alisa Miles, and Jeremy Ragsdale."

In addition to singing in Boston-area jazz clubs, Toni Ballard created, produced and hosted the jazz show *Studio 3* on WGMC-TV in Worcester, which resulted in 100 half-hour music and interview programs. She has also been seen as a host on BET *Jazz's Jazz Scene* and *Impressions*. Although a 1984–85 album of children's songs, *Songs For The Young At Heart*, remains unreleased, 1997's *I'm Your Pal* is a good example of Toni Ballard's jazz singing.

Recommended CDs: *I'm Your Pal* (Dolphin Recordings 6008) features Toni Ballard's warm and inviting voice in a variety of settings, including a trio with pianist Bevan Manson, a duo with guitarist Larry Coryell and larger groups.

Nancie Banks

(Nancy Manzuk)

b. July 29, 1951, Morgantown, WV;
d. November 13, 2002, New York, NY

Late in her life, Nancie Banks said "I will consider myself a success if I can be a vehicle for positive energy, have the respect of musicians that I respect, and continue to survive playing music I feel good about." Judged by that criteria, she was a definite success.

Born in West Virginia, she grew up in Pittsburgh. Both of her parents were musicians. Her father sang in the church choir, while her mother was a pianist who gave Nancie lessons starting at the age of four. Well trained in music, Nancie Banks moved to New York when she was 17, taking lessons from pianist Barry Harris, Latin jazz flutist and pioneer Alberto Socarras and at workshops put on by Billy Taylor's Jazzmobile.

Banks debuted as a singer at a Barry Harris Strings and Voice concert and led a quartet/quintet in New York for a decade. She first sang with a big band that was headed by guitarist Charlie Byrd. He introduced her to her future husband, trombonist Clarence Banks. She sang with the Lionel Hampton Orchestra and Jon Hendricks' Vocalstra plus with such all-stars as Dexter Gordon, Woody Shaw, Walter Bishop Jr. and Charli Persip.

In 1989, Banks was given a scholarship to study in the jazz department at the New School University. While working with the school's student big band led by Cecil Bridgewater, she decided to form her own orchestra, resulting in the 19-piece Nancie Banks Orchestra. The big band played fairly regularly in the New York area and at festivals, featuring the writing and the singing of its leader, who proved to be a skilled arranger, composer, lyricist and producer. The orchestra recorded four albums during 1992–2002, two apiece for Consolidated Artists (*Waves Of Peace* and *Bert's Blues*) and GFI (*Ear Candy* and *Out Of It*).

Nancie Banks, who taught music both privately and at clinics, also worked as a music copyist for Broadway shows and as a music preparation supervisor for films. Her passing at the age of 51 was unexpected; her body was discovered in her apartment.

Recommended CDs: The Nancie Banks Orchestra's Consolidated Artists recordings, *Waves Of Peace* (Consolidated Artists 902) and *Bert's Blues* (Consolidated Artists 904), are easier to locate than her sets for GFI, *Ear Candy* and *Out Of It*.

Patricia Barber

b. November 8, 1955, Lisle, IL

A unique jazz singer/ songwriter who is also a fine pianist, Patricia Barber stands apart from musical trends to create her own unusual and fresh music.

"My father, Floyd Barber, was a jazz musician. He played alto saxophone with lots of Chicago legends, Bud Freeman, Barrett Deems, and also with Glenn Miller. I started singing when I decided I wanted the lead in the high school musical. I had been a pianist and saxophonist up until that point. I found that singing was a way to get gigs at first." She was a piano major at the University of Iowa during 1973–77, and decided in her senior year that she going to work toward being both a professional jazz musician and a singer.

Years of playing in Chicago clubs, bars and dives followed, including working regularly at the Gold Star Sardine Bar during 1984–95. Barber built up her own repertoire of intelligent and continually surprising lyrics, her low voice gained attention, and her piano playing became so skilled that she also worked instrumental dates. But it is as a singer-composer-pianist that she became well known, really starting with her 1995 recording, *Café Blue*, which along with originals has her unusual versions of "A Taste Of Honey," "The Thrill Is Gone" and "Ode To Billy Joe." Since then her audience has grown, although she still remains a bit of a cult figure in jazz due to her highly personal music. She plays at the now-legendary Green Mill in Chicago when she is home, has recorded intriguing sets for Premonition and Blue Note and in 2003 received the Guggenheim Fellowship for composition/songwriting, using the grant to create a song cycle based on Ovid's *Metamorphoses*, resulting in the CD *Mythologies*.

"For the future I just want to do exactly what I'm doing: writing music, arranging it and performing it."

Recommended CDs: Patricia Barber's first recording was *Split* (Koch 5742), a 1989 release that she originally put out on her own Floyd label. *A Distortion Of Love* (Antilles 512235), *Café Blue* (Premonition 90760), *Modern Cool* (Premonition 90761), *Companion* (Premonition 90762), *Night Club* (Premonition 90763), *Verse* (Blue Note 39856), *Live: A Fortnight In Paris*

(Blue Note 78213) and *Mythologies* (Blue Note 59564) document her unique (if sometimes downbeat) originals and her transformations of pop tunes.

Blue Lu Barker

(Louisa Dupont)
b. November 13, 1913, New Orleans, LA;
d. May 7, 1998, New Orleans, LA

Blue Lu Barker was one of the most unlikely of all jazz and blues singers. She was so shy that she preferred not to perform in public at all if it could be avoided.

Her father ran a grocery store and pool hall but made a more lucrative living selling bootleg liquor during the Prohibition era. Young Louisa Dupont left school at the age of 13 to marry banjoist-guitarist Danny Barker. Despite the odds against it, their marriage worked, lasting until Danny's death in 1994, 67 years later. Louisa moved to New York with her husband in 1930 as he freelanced during the Depression years. In 1938 Ms. Barker, who had mostly just sung around the house and had a rather limited voice, was featured on a record date organized by Danny, who supplied the songs. One tune, "Don't You Make Me High," became best known as "Don't You Feel My Leg." Louisa, who was dubbed "Blue Lu" at the session by the producer, became famous due to that saucy song, and she recorded five additional sessions with all-star musicians during 1938–39.

Blue Lu only performed on rare occasions during 1939–46 as her husband played and toured regularly as a member of Cab Calloway's big band. During 1946–49 Blue Lu recorded for Apollo and Capitol, performing such songs as "I Feel Like Laying In Another Woman's Husband's Arms," "Buy Me Some Juice," "Leave My Man Alone," "Loan Me Your Husband" and "Bow-Legged Daddy." Danny Barker's witty and double-entendre lyrics that she sang were a major contrast to her soft-spoken personality. Blue Lu preferred to have a quieter lifestyle and only performed sporadically during her final 40 years, including five final songs that were recorded at the 1989 New Orleans Jazz and Heritage Festival.

Recommended CDs: All of the recordings from Blue Lu Barker's prime years have been reissued on *1938–1939* (Classics 704) and *1946–1949* (Classics 1130).

Danny Barker

b. January 13, 1909, New Orleans, LA;
d. March 13, 1994, New Orleans, LA

A storyteller who was a New Orleans historian and teacher, Danny Barker was also a banjoist, a guitarist, a skilled lyricist and a singer. Barker grew up around music, taking up the banjo quite young. He played music on the streets of New Orleans with the Boozan Kings (a kids' band) and toured Mississippi with blues pianist Little Brother Montgomery. Barker married Louisa Dupont (who later became Blue Lu Barker) in 1927 when he was 18 and she was 13. Three years later they moved to New York where he switched to guitar and played with such groups as those led by Jelly Roll Morton, Sidney Bechet, Fess Williams, Albert Nicholas and James P. Johnson and the big bands of Lucky Millinder (1937–38) and Benny Carter. Barker gained a record date for his wife in 1938 and wrote the lyrics to four songs, including the big hit "Don't You Feel My Leg" (originally called "Don't You Make Me High"). He appeared on Blue Lu's other five sessions of 1938 to 1939

and then had a seven-year stint as the rhythm guitarist with Cab Calloway's orchestra. Though he never cared for bebop, he was part of a fairly modern rhythm section (with pianist Bennie Payne, bassist Milt Hinton and drummer Cozy Cole) in Calloway's big band that for two years featured the young Dizzy Gillespie as its trumpet soloist.

After leaving Calloway, Barker recorded on his wife's sessions for Apollo and Capitol during 1946–49, contributing witty double-entendre lyrics. He also wrote "Save The Bones For Henry Jones" (which was recorded by Nat King Cole and Johnny Mercer), was part of the Dixieland revival, began playing banjo again, appeared on Rudi Blesh's *This Is Jazz* radio series in 1947 and recorded with Bunk Johnson. Barker spent the 1950s playing Dixieland in New York, usually at Ryan's. He moved back to New Orleans with Blue Lu in 1965, working as the assistant curator of the New Orleans Jazz Museum, writing his memoirs (*A Life In Jazz*), leading the Onward Brass Band and encouraging younger players.

Barker took occasional vocals during his post-Calloway years and was best captured on the 1988 solo album *Save The Bones*, on which he is heard accompanying his singing with his guitar. His rendition of "St. James Infirmary" (which, as with most of the songs on this definitive set, contains some of his own lyrics) is a classic. Danny Barker, whose lyrics and vocabulary were both dated and eternally hip, was active until shortly before his death in 1994, singing and playing guitar with bassist Milt Hinton at the 1993 Monterey Jazz Festival.

Recommended CDs: To hear Danny Barker's singing at its most spirited, get *Live At The New Orleans Jazz Festival* (Orleans 2111), which teams him with Blue Lu in 1989, and especially the memorable *Save The Bones* (Orleans 1018).

Emilie-Claire Barlow

b. June 6, 1976, Toronto, Ontario, Canada

One of the more promising singers based in Canada, Emilie-Claire Barlow has been part of the music world for a long time.

The daughter of jazz drummer Brian Barlow, she worked at voice-overs from the time she was seven, often singing on jingles. She studied piano, violin, cello and clarinet and attended the Etobicoke School of the Arts for five years. While a student at Hunter College, she led a quartet that played in Toronto.

The year 1998 brought her recording debut in *Emilie-Claire Barlow Sings*, featuring arrangements from her father. While continuing to work on commercials and voice-overs, Barlow has performed jazz regularly in the years since and grown steadily as an improviser, excelling at scat singing, vocalese and interpreting lyrics. Her young and sweet voice has matured in recent years, and her improvisations have become increasingly sophisticated.

Recommended CDs: Emilie-Claire Barlow, who is so far best known in Canada, has thus far recorded five excellent CDs. *Sings* (Rhythm Tracks 0001) from 1998 was a strong start to her recording career, even if some of the lyrics seem more mature than the innocent voice that was interpreting them.

While *Winter Wonderland* (Empress Music Group 442) is a pleasant and swinging if a little lightweight set of Christmas tunes, both *Tribute* (Rhythm Tracks 0003) and *Happy Feet* (Rhythm Tracks 0004) find the singer growing rapidly into an increasingly individual vocalist. The most rewarding of all of her recordings thus far, and an underrated classic, is *Like A Lover* (Empress Music Group 441), a set on which everything works well.

Website: www.emilieclairebarlow.com

Mae Barnes
(Edith May Stith)
b. Jan 7, 1907, New York, NY; d. December 13, 1996, Boston, MA

Mae Barnes was a fine vocalist whose versatile singing ranged from cabaret to middle-of-the-road pop music. She also fared quite well on her two jazz albums.

At the age of 12, Barnes dropped out of school to work as a singer and a tap-dancer. She was a chorus girl at Harlem's Plantation Club, toured the South in vaudeville and in 1924 was on Broadway in *Runnin' Wild*, the show that introduced the Charleston. She also appeared in *Shuffle Along* and the *Ziegfeld Follies*. During that era, Bill "Bojangles" Robinson called her "the greatest living female tap dancer." However, a serious car accident in 1938 ended her dancing days, and she became a full-time singer. Barnes sang for seven years at the Greenwich Village club Boite, graduated to the Blue Angel and by the early 1950s was performing regularly at the Bon Soir in New York.

A ten-inch album cut for Atlantic in 1953 features Barnes singing swing standards. She is heard at her best on her self-titled Vanguard set from 1958, which has been reissued by DRG.

In the 1960s Mae Barnes retired, and she passed away in 1996 from cancer at the age of 89.

Recommended CDs: *Mae Barnes* (DRG 8434) has the singer joined by a quartet that includes trumpeter Buck Clayton and either Ray Bryant or Ray Tunia on piano. Throughout this fine set, which includes "Blues In My Heart," "'S Wonderful" and "A Foggy Day," she shows that she could have been a strong jazz singer if she had chosen to make that her career.

LPs to Search For: *Fun With Mae Barnes* (Atlantic 404) is the singer's only other jazz-oriented set; it is a pity that there were not many more.

Christy Baron
b. November 1, 1963, Pittsburgh, PA

A fine jazz singer who also loves the pop music of the past 30 years, Christy Baron incorporates recent standards in her repertoire along with some vintage songs.

"My mother, a wonderful pianist, had a music room filled with what, to-day, many recognize as the 'jazz standards' but were the pop songs of her generation. They were the first pieces I played on piano. By the time I was 10 or 11, I would spend hours on end in our music room playing piano and singing. At one point, my parents asked my brother to set up a small microphone by the piano. He also set up a pair of speakers in the living room and ran the speaker cable all the way from the music room into the living room so they could sit out there and listen. I remember, one of the first tunes I sang on mic is one that I chose to do on my third recording with Chesky: 'A House Is Not A Home.' With my mother's consent and wholehearted support, at the age of 14, I started playing solo piano gigs and singing at various clubs around town." At 16, Baron was performing most nights in a nightclub. At Carnegie Mellon University she studied music, dance and drama and, since moving to New York in 1984, has had a dual career as an actress (in film, television, commercials and onstage) and as a singer.

Christy Baron signed with the Chesky label in 1996 and has since recorded three CDs that display her versatility and wide musical interests. "When you surround yourself with great musicians with great ideas and really listen, it makes you a better singer. Each song is unique and fresh each time we perform it."

Recommended CDs: Christy Baron's debut, *I Thought About You* (Chesky 152), ranges from Cole Porter to the Beatles and is highlighted by three Stevie Wonder songs. She proves equally adept at interpreting all of the diverse material in her own distinctive manner. *Steppin'* (Chesky 201) leans heavily toward pop songs, while *Take This Journey* (Chesky 239) balances "Old Devil Moon" with the Turtles' "Happy Together" and three Carole King songs.

Website: www.christybaron.com

Sweet Emma Barrett
b. March 25, 1897, New Orleans, LA;
d. January 28, 1983, New Orleans, LA

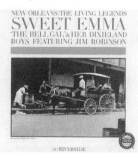

As was somewhat common with many of the New Orleans players associated with Preservation Hall in the 1960s and '70s, pianist-singer Sweet Emma Barrett ironically became better known the more she declined. Fortunately she recorded one very good album before the vestiges of age began to affect her singing and playing.

Barrett spent her entire life living in New Orleans. She played with most of the local musicians at one time or another, including Bebe Ridgley's Original Tuxedo Orchestra (which was originally co-led by Oscar Celestin) during 1923–36, John Robichaux, A.J. Piron and Sidney Desvigne. She was known as "The Bell Gal" because she wore red garters with bells that made ringing sounds while she played.

Sweet Emma Barrett did not record until she was already 63 in 1961. Her first album, made with the future frontline of the Preservation Hall Jazz Band, is her best and has been reissued in the Original Jazz Classics series. She also recorded a couple albums for Southland during 1963–64, taking vocals on half of the material, which comprised mostly Dixieland warhorses. A serious stroke in 1967 left her with a paralyzed left hand. However, she continued playing one-handed piano and singing, touring the world with the Preservation Hall Jazz Band. Sweet Emma Barrett remained a popular figure and a symbol of revival New Orleans jazz up until the time of her death in 1983 at the age of 85.

Recommended CDs: *New Orleans: The Living Legends* (Original Jazz Classics 1832) is Sweet Emma Barrett's best recording and one of the finest from the Preservation Hall-associated revivalists. In addition to her piano playing (which was rhythmic and particularly strong in ensembles), she takes spirited vocals on "St. Louis Blues," "I Ain't Gonna Give Anybody None Of My Jelly Roll" and "The Saints." Also worthwhile is the slightly later *Sweet Emma Barrett And Her New Orleans Music* (GHB 141).

April Barrows
b. April 28, 1954, Milford, CT

A fine jazz singer with a sweet voice who writes original pieces that sound like they could be vintage swing standards, April Barrows is one of those very talented but little-publicized vocalists who deserve to be discovered. Although she does not copy her musical heroes, she considers her main influences to be Ella Fitzgerald, the Boswell Sisters, Mildred Bailey, Louis Armstrong, Ivie Anderson, Bing Crosby, Ruth Etting, Annette Hanshaw and Cliff Edwards.

"I remember early on hearing my mother's prized collection of boogie-woogie 78s, including records by Meade Lux Lewis, Albert Ammons and Pinetop Smith. I'd imitate all the sounds on those records and sing the songs, intros, solos, etc. I started collecting old records in my teen years and would dig around musty record shops and flea markets discovering interesting music." Moving to the San Francisco Bay area with her family when she was five, she heard early jazz in her mother's record collection along with Bob Dylan, country music and rock of the 1960s. April Barrows played violin from third to sixth grade (which she hated), began performing professionally in high school (singing and playing rhythm guitar) and learned a lot of country roots music while she performed duets with a country singer. She also played steel guitar and electric bass.

Due to family obligations, Barrows had a day job for a time, but her real love was music. "I really wanted to become a professional musician so I finally quit my job as a chemist and ran away to Nashville in the middle of the night with my gear and 13 boxes of records." She played electric bass in Nashville for six years and had opportunities to perform with the Judds' first band, the Memphis Horns, Vassar Clements and Woody Herman. In 1985 she switched courses again and became a songwriter, at first writing country, bluegrass and blues songs. In time Barrows realized that she felt most at home singing and writing new swing tunes. Her talents can best be heard on her two CDs, *My Dream Is You* and *All You Need Is The Girl*.

"I've been lucky enough to spend my entire life doing something I love. I tried to be commercial in the music business in Nashville but it was a waste of time. Only when I quit trying to please everybody and started only playing music I cared about did I actually start getting somewhere artistically and really having fun."

Recommended CDs: It is surprising that April Barrows only has two recordings out thus far, for both are gems. *My Dream Is You* (Kokopelli 1313) has ten of her songs (including three co-written with guitarist-trombonist David Hungate) plus two standards. *All You Need Is The Girl* (Mellotone 2000) has nine more originals along with concise and hot solos. A CD with trumpeter Duke Heitger and clarinetist Evan Christopher is upcoming. Swing singers of today who have tired of reviving the same old warhorses are well advised to cover some of April Barrows' rewarding songs.

Website: www.aprilbarrows.com

Joanne Barry
b. September 5, Brooklyn, NY

A warm singer with a sincere and swinging delivery, Joanne Barry has mostly performed with her husband, guitarist Carl Barry.

"By the time I was eight, I had no desire to ever be anything but a singer," she remembers. She began her career singing cabaret music at Dangerfield's and the Playboy Club and says that she became introduced to jazz after meeting her future husband. "I also learned tremendously from some rhythm section players I worked with, including Steve LaSpina and Eliot Zigmund. My main influence was Nancy Wilson, but all the greats have had an effect on me, with Dianne Reeves being my current living favorite."

During the past 25 years, Joanne Barry has sung in the New York area with her husband, written music and given voice lessons. "I wish to sing only in settings that allow me to be as creative and versatile as I wish to be. I prefer to consider myself a stylist rather than a 'jazz singer,' because I don't wish to limit myself to certain material. My tastes in music are too varied for me not to include songs from other genres. I just believe that anything that speaks to me emotionally can be interpreted in a jazz format."

Recommended CDs: Joanne Barry has been documented surprisingly little through the years. Most recently, Joanne Barry recorded *Embraceable You* (Fat Note 102), which features Carl Barry's guitar and trumpeter Michael Morreale.

LPs to Search For: Joanne Barry's little-known debut, *This Is Me*, is a long out-of-print set for the Echo label. Her 1984 LP *Holding On* (Stash 236) gained her some visibility, not only featuring her powerful singing but her lyrics on six of the eight songs.

Website: www.carlandjoannebarry.com

Corina Bartra
b. July 8, 1963, Lima, Peru

One of the first singers to explore a mixture of Peruvian music with jazz, Corina Bartra has always blazed her own path. "My grandfather used to play me records of Charlie Parker when I was young. I started improvising with the sounds of nature, such as birds, ocean waves and what I heard in the woods." She had piano lessons from the age of five and has studied percussion since 1990. Along the way she earned degrees from the Mannes College of Music, Long Island University and Queens College (a Master's in vocal performance).

Inspired by Sarah Vaughan, Elis Regina and Flora Purim, Bartra has created her own multicultural blend of world music and jazz while being open to other avant-garde and experimental styles. Sometimes singing wordlessly and other times interpreting politically-charged lyrics, her wide range, passionate sound and expertise at utilizing unusual rhythms are consistently memorable.

"I love improvisation, exploration and interaction with other human and divine beings through the means of sound and rhythm." When Corina Bartra sings, it does not sound like a mixture of idioms but a very natural style, one that few others are currently exploring.

Recommended CDs: *Corina Bartra Quartet* (Blue Spiral 002) introduced her unique singing to American audiences. *Son Zumbon* (Orchard 3324) features the singer with a top-notch quintet, performing mostly originals that benefit from the short solos of tenor-saxophonist Peter Brainin. *Travelog* (Orchard 803 155) has plenty of variety, including a pro-democracy political message on "American People Are On The Rise," some remarkable high notes on "Kacharpari" and an inventive reworking of "How High The Moon." She is joined by pianist Eddie Martinez and the late altoist-flutist Thomas Chapin. Most recent is *Bambu Sun* (Blue Spiral 006), which includes originals "Afro Peruvian Folk Song" "Blackbird" and Wayne Shorter's "Footprints." In addition, Corina Bartra has recorded CDs more in the vein of meditation music.

Website: www.bluespiralmusic.com

David Basse

b. November 14, 1954, San Jose, CA

An entertaining jazz singer in the style of Les McCann, Ben Sidran and, to a lesser extent, Dr. John, David Basse has long been based in Kansas City.

He began on drums at age 11 and remembers, "I started playing drums at bars at 14 and somehow made it through high school. I learned to sing at 17 with the help of a bandleader who told me he would pay me more if I could sing. He didn't follow through but I did."

Basse really became involved in jazz in 1974 when he visited the Mutual Musicians Foundation in Kansas City, the same year that *The Last Of The Blue Devils* was filmed. "I played with my new heroes, including Jay McShann, LaVern Baker, Baby Lovett, Claude Williams and Ben Kynard."

Basse has gained the most attention for his singing with his City Light Orchestra starting in 1982. Other important associations included saxophonist Ahmad Alaadeen, trumpeter Pat Morrissey, pianist Mike Melvoin, drummer Bill Goodwin and, in more recent times, altoist Phil Woods. He has also hosted a regular program on Kansas Public Radio.

"I want my music to be fun. Les McCann, Red Holloway

and Jack Sheldon all have that quality. Jazz musicians have started to take themselves way too seriously. I take it in the other direction so the audience can have a good time, too."

Recommended CDs: Highlights of 1999's *Kansas City Live* (City Lights Music 1) include David Basse's renditions of "St. James Infirmary," "Caldonia" and a medley of Kansas City blues themes. On *Strike When Your Iron Is Hot* (City Lights Music 2), he performs five Mike Melvoin originals, the standards "I'm Just A Lucky So-And-So" and "Sugar" and a few offbeat choices such as Tom Waits' "Invitation To The Blues" and "New York State Of Mind." *Like Jazz* (City Lights Music 6) has the Mark Winkler title cut, more Melvoin originals and fresh versions of "Slow Boat To China" and "I've Got The World On A String."

Website: www.davidbasse.com

Winnie Beatty

b. May 22, 1925, Fayetteville, AR

An important figure in the Los Angeles jazz scene of the late 1940s and still active today, singer-pianist Winnie Beatty deserves to be better known. Though born in Arkansas, she moved with her parents to Fullerton in California when she was five, relocating to Hollywood in 1940. Early on she had the opportunity to hear many big bands, including those of Jimmie Lunceford and Stan Kenton.

"I've been playing and singing since I was seven, anytime I could find an audience. I started playing professionally at 16, accompanying myself on piano, usually adding guitar and bass. Billie Holiday and the King Cole Trio were my favorites, but I listened to Duke Ellington and Count Basie a lot and tried to emulate Basie's subtle swing. I'm basically self-taught. I'd go to the piano and try to assimilate what I'd heard after listening to good piano players."

During 1944–49, Winnie Beatty worked with Slim Gaillard, the Vivien Garry Trio (with bassist Garry and guitarist Arv Garrison) and regularly on the Make Believe Ballroom Tour in addition to appearing as a leader. "I remember playing the breaks for the Four Blazes at the Club Circle on La Cienega during that period when Frankie Laine came in and sang with them. He was working in a defense plant and trying to find work singing. He stayed to listen to me and I asked him if he'd like to close my set. We did 'West End Blues' and 'River St. Marie' and brought the house down. I think he was surprised that I knew the tunes. We became friends and I worked with him later at the Swing Club on Hollywood Boulevard and on the *Al Jarvis Show*." In addition to making records with Gaillard and Vivien Garry, she recorded 15 songs as a leader during 1944–50 for the Keynote, Lamplighter, Bel-Tone, Majestic, Coast and Crystallette labels, using such sidemen as clarinetist Barney Bigard, bassist Red Callender, drummer Zutty Singleton, Slim Gaillard and trombonist Vic Dickenson. Her vocals, influenced by Billie Holiday, are very much in her own style.

Winnie Beatty has stayed active ever since. She performed on a cruise to China in 1983, played for three months in Sweden in 1989 and has also been busy as a vocal coach. "I'm working on some material for a CD, redoing a few of my early blues that I wrote and some obscure ballads that haven't been played so much. I still do vocal coaching in my studio at home and I enjoy helping young singers with intonation, time and breathing problems. There is no greater natural high than to get caught up in the wonderful world of improvising, performing with excellent players, doing songs you love, exchanging ideas and carrying the audience along with you." Unfortunately her recordings, which include the 1966 LP *Folk Songs For Taxpayers*, are scarce.

Leslie Bee
(Leslie Michele Burris)
b. June 5, Torrance, CA

An excellent jazz singer with a witty and soulful style, Leslie Bee has also had careers as an actress, a comedian and a caterer.

"Being from a very large family, my father would wake us up to Jazz music turned up very loud. He owned a very large record collection and loved Jimmy Smith and Wes Montgomery. We would have to do house work to jazz, and even got punished (spanked) to jazz." She sang in church and school choirs, graduated from California State University at Northridge in the 1970s (majoring in Theater Arts and Pan African Studies) and worked as an actress, including in musicals. "I never thought I sang well enough to be a singer. But one day in the late '70s, a jazz musician named John Lemon asked me to sing with his group. I told him I wasn't a jazz singer but he said he would help me. That was the start. However, it did not pay much so I went back to acting and my human rights work with the Martin Luther King organization. In 1986 I went to New York to act and do stand-up comedy. Sitting at a bar with friends, I was singing along with the band when the bartender asked me to go sit in. After much urging, I did and the owner hired me to sing two days a week."

"Moving back to Los Angeles, I stopped singing again and went back to acting and catering to earn a living. In 1992 for the third time in my life, some local musicians asked me to sing with them in local clubs and parties. This time I stuck with it."

Since that time, Leslie Bee has worked in many jazz clubs, performed in Japan during a three-month tour in 1994 with bassist Henry Franklin, worked with gospel singer Kathy Audrey on her CD *My Story*, performed at European jazz festivals and spent time living in Barcelona, Spain.

Recommended CDs: Leslie Bee's debut jazz recording, *The Way I Feel* (EAC 37351) from 1999, is primarily standards, while her upcoming *What My Heart Sings* puts an emphasis on the singer's writing abilities with most of the colorful songs being co-composed with pianist Michele Faber.

Opie Bellas
(Kalliope Bellas)
b. September 8, 1958, Wheeling, WV

Named after Kalliope (the muse of music and poetry in Greek mythology), "I couldn't pronounce my whole name as a kid, so I came up with 'Opie.'" Based in the San Francisco Bay area, Opie Bellas is a top singer who often gets more recognition for her work overseas.

She began singing as a child. "I was a really shy kid, but I remember jumping on-stage to sing at a town fair, which shocked everyone. My mother gave us organ lessons when we were kids. As a young adult, I learned the piano and then the guitar. My life was altered by the loss of my father when I was six. My paternal grandparents took my two brothers and me traveling to other countries each year after that, for ten years. Those early introductions to music, art, food and customs of other cultures has influenced me personally and professionally."

Opie Bellas attended Duquesne University in Pittsburgh (graduating in 1980) as a classical vocalist, but jazz was her true love, the best vehicle for her emotional style. It took time for her career (which included a six-year break) to get going, and she is still not yet as well-known as her talent deserves.

Highlights of her career include singing with the Pittsburgh Symphony Orchestra, recording jingles and voice-overs ("I love being in the studio") and performing abroad, most notably in Capetown, South Africa in 2004 and 2006, Australia, Switzerland and Japan. "There's a deep kinship among musicians. We're family. No matter where you go, we speak the same language."

Recommended CDs: *How Do You Keep The Music Playing* (Bella Blue 302), an intimate album with piano and bass, includes "Hey John," "My Romance" and "The Late Late Show." *Live For Life* (Bella Blue 301) teams Opie Bellas with a quartet and a chamber orchestra, emphasizing ballads, including "Once Upon A Summertime," "Not While I'm Around" and her tribute to her late sibling, "My Brother John." *Faces* (Bella Blue 324), with a rhythm section and trombonist Jay Ashby, includes "Lazy Afternoon" and "Invitation."

Joy Bellis
b. August 3, Riegelsville, PA

Joy Bellis gave up a lucrative career in the finance world to pursue singing. On evidence of her first CD, *Coming Alive*, the jazz world should celebrate that move.

She took dance lessons from the age of three and started on piano when she was eight. "When I got to high school, I wanted to try out for the school musical, mostly for the dancing aspect of it, but realized you had to sing to try out too. I chose the song 'Sentimental Journey' since we had sung it for fun around my house and I loved its bluesy feel. I made the musical that year and decided to take some voice lessons during my summer breaks."

Bellis earned a degree in Finance/Financial Engineering from James Madison University in 1991 and then moved to New York. "Throughout high school and college, I thought of singing as more of a hobby, but always had the love for performing in the back of my mind. When I was job hunting after college, I wanted to try to find something in New York because I thought I could have opportunities to sing there as well. When I started doing some singing showcases at night, I knew that I wanted to give it my all and try to make it professionally." She studied jazz standards with Carol Fredette (starting in 1999) and Latin rhythms with Maura Ellyn, taking the plunge and leaving the finance world to pursue singing and work in television, film and modeling. She has also provided backup vocals in live performances for the Latin rock group Batista, and has been involved in a wide variety of studio work.

"I love music but I am really in love with the lyric, and that's one of the main reasons why I enjoy performing jazz. As a jazz performer, you really have the license to make a song your own and phrase how the song makes sense to you—how it will reach listeners the most. My favorite dream would be to have a night singing all ballads and have people truly listening and connecting with everything."

Recommended CDs: Joy Bellis' debut recording, *Coming Alive* (White Butterfly 90010), finds her displaying a clear tone that sometimes hints at Susannah McCorkle, a subtle improvising style, and phrasing that swings without wandering far from the melody. Highlights include the emotional "To Say Goodbye" and a memorable revival of the 1920s standard "Sugar."

Website: www.joybellis.com

Joan Bender
b. July 25, Iowa City, IA

A young singer with strong potential, Joan Bender has been gradually making a name for herself playing in New York-area clubs.

JOAN BENDER
Soho Jazz

"As a kid, I loved jazz, I just didn't know that was what I was listening to. I loved Vince Guaraldi's jazz piano tracks for the Charlie Brown Christmas specials on TV. Most of the enjoyable music I heard was when my mother and I went to the grocery store. I'd listen to muzak versions of 'Windmills Of My Mind' and 'I Will Wait For You' by Michel Legrand. I played clarinet from 5th through 12th grade. In my senior year of high school, I paid for my own voice lessons and entered a singing contest where we were evaluated for our renditions of Italian arias. It wasn't until college when I started singing in public that a fellow choir member turned me on to Ella, Sarah, Carmen McRae, Astrud Gilberto, Chet Baker and Blossom Dearie."

Originally she had hoped to go to Harvard University on an athletic scholarship, but a hip injury ended Joan Bender's potential career in track. Instead, she attended the University of Iowa as a theater major while also singing in the choir. After moving to New York with the intention of working in musical theater, she decided instead to become a jazz singer, particularly after seeing Blossom Dearie perform and having a chance to sing with the late pianist Frank Hewitt at Small's.

Joan Bender gained some headlines when she led a protest march against the hiring policies of the Lincoln Center Jazz Orchestra, which has rarely hired female musicians. Her 2001 debut recording, *Star Eyes*, features a strong young talent who, with the right exposure, may very well be a major name in the future.

"I think there is more of a market today for jazz vocalists than ever before. When I used to teach music in the public school system, the only time I could get the kids to behave was when I sang to them. They really loved jazz, even though

they had never heard it before. These kids worshipped Jennifer Lopez and Eminem, but I had them fascinated by this 'new' style of singing."

Recommended CDs: *Star Eyes* (Original Cast Records 2322) is an impressive start to Joan Bender's career, with fine versions of "My Heart Belongs To Daddy," "O Barquinho," "Cherokee," "Lullaby Of Birdland" and Abbey Lincoln's "Bird Alone." *Soho Jazz* (Original Cast Records 6164) is a solid follow-up.

Website: www.joanbender.com

Sathima Bea Benjamin
b. October 17, 1936, Cape Town, South Africa

A major jazz singer from South Africa and the longtime wife of pianist Abdullah Ibrahim, Sathima Bea Benjamin has carved out her own musical legacy, sometimes singing purposely between the conventional tones in order to achieve a haunting effect. That skill can be heard on *Musical Echoes* from 2002.

"I first heard jazz on the radio, especially Nat King Cole and Ella Fitzgerald." Trained to be an elementary school teacher in Cape Town, she met Abdullah Ibrahim (who was then known as Dollar Brand) in 1958. He inspired her to switch careers and become a jazz singer. After performing locally, in 1962 the married couple left the apartheid of South Africa for Europe. Duke Ellington, who was visiting Europe at the time, heard them in Switzerland and recorded them both for the Reprise label. The tape of Benjamin's 1963 recording was not issued at the time and was believed lost until it finally was released in 1997.

Benjamin and Abdullah settled in the United States, and she had an opportunity to sing with Ellington's band at the 1965 Newport Jazz Festival. She did not record again as a leader until 1976, although since then she has released a series of excellent sets for her Ekapa label. Benjamin performs ballads (including many of Duke Ellington's compositions), originals influenced by her South African heritage and jazz standards.

"Freedom plus improvising and passion is the rule that I live by. I try to be creative and expansive in all areas of my life, but feel it is best expressed when I'm singing. This is when I feel most free and unafraid to take risks and big leaps of faith. It is a safe place for me to go 'within' and express ever so truthfully who I am."

Recommended CDs: The long-awaited *Morning In Paris* (Enja 9309), Sathima Bea Benjamin's 1963 debut, has her accompanied by her husband's trio and, on two numbers apiece, Duke Ellington or Billy Strayhorn. The year 1988's *Love Light* (Enja 79605) is highlighted by "You Are My Heart's Delight." Other worthy recordings by the singer include *Southern Touch* (Ekapa 7015), 1999's *Cape Town Love* (Ekapa 001) and *Musical Echoes* (Ekapa 002).

LPs to Search For: *Sathima Sings Ellington* (Ekapa EK-001) from 1979 was the singer's first full album after the 1963 set and is an underrated gem.

Betty Bennett
(Betty Bennett Lowe)
b. October 23, 1921, Lincoln, NE

A veteran singer with a warm voice and a straightforward delivery, Betty Bennett made a strong impression in the 1950s and then in 1990 returned to recordings to show that she still had "it."

"My mother was a jazz pianist and introduced me to Fats Waller, Duke Ellington and Count Basie, the latter of whom she used to hear in Kansas City. I loved Billie, Sarah, Carmen and Ella. I did a lot of vocal swooping around as in Sarah in the beginning, before I figured out who I was."

Betty Bennett had 10 years of piano lessons but gave it up when she became a professional singer. She was originally an opera singer but soon changed her mind. "In 1940 I went to Des Moines, Iowa to college. My teacher suggested I sing in an assembly. It seemed to me that if I sang in my soprano voice I'd never get a date, so I sang a current pop tune with a piano player. The band leader offered me a job and there went my plans to be an opera singer. I never looked back."

For the next decade, she sang with a variety of important bands, including Georgie Auld (1943), Claude Thornhill (1946), Alvino Rey (1947), Charlie Ventura, an all-star Stan Kenton group, Woody Herman (1950), Benny Goodman and Charlie Barnet (1952). "I was sadly disillusioned when I sang with Claude Thornhill. The band had a very strong clique and they had some other singer in mind for my job. They made it so uncomfortable that I quit. I was a substitute on Alvino Rey's band when his singer fell ill. At the end of the gig, Alvino fired the girl and kept me. I honed my skills, learned what to leave out and generally found my style in that band, thanks to Alvino's giving me the latitude to experiment. Singing with Charlie Ventura was great fun because I got to sing lines with the band instead of the usual girl-singer gig, which consisted of bouncing around a lot and grinning. I thought that singing with Benny Goodman would be a highlight but he was very cruel to me when I was with the band. Charlie Barnet was great to work for. He let me do my 'thing,' and when I left the band he said if I ever wanted to come back, just call him."

After going out on her own, Bennett recorded albums for Trend, Atlantic and United Artists during 1953–59. Married to Andre Previn, she was largely retired by the early 1960s. After they were divorced, she had a much longer marriage to guitarist Mundell Lowe; they were married at the 1975 Monterey Jazz Festival. In 1990, 31 years after her last recording as a leader, she emerged to record *The Song Is You*.

"I do very little singing these days. However, when I'm asked, I have a great time doing it. I feel if you can't improve the melody or sing something comparable to it, stay with the melody. Some songs lend themselves to improvisation and I enjoy improvising tremendously. I, however, do not like scat singing. Musicians who scat are exceptions. It seems to me that most singers just put together phrases they've heard musicians sing or play and they never flow the way they should."

Recommended CDs: Betty Bennett's Atlantic album, *Nobody Else But Me*, has been paired with Lurlean Hunter's *Blue And Sentimental* on a single CD (Collectables 6623). Her 1990 CD *The Song Is You* (Fresh Sound 186) finds her in excellent form for a set with Mundell Lowe and tenor-saxophonist Bob Cooper, singing some of her favorite songs.

Cynthia Kaay Bennett
b. June 21, 1963, Mansfield, OH

A fine jazz singer based in Nashville who has a blues influence and a slight amount of country in her singing, Cynthia Kaay Bennett is one of the many local singers who deserves to be much better known.

"My parents played nothing but jazz and Johnny Mathis as I was growing up. I listened to Duke Ellington, Count Basie, Stan Kenton, and Charlie Parker from as early as I can remember. My mother said I began singing in the high chair—nonstop. Singing nonsensical syllables and lovely melodies came before speech." She studied piano from age five, played alto sax for 11 years and began on guitar in 1996. "While all the other kids my age were attending Journey, Kiss and Madonna concerts, I was going to as many Maynard Ferguson concerts as I could afford." She attended Ohio State University during 1981–86 and went back for a Master's in 1991.

"I didn't actually start singing for an audience made up of more than friends or family until 1987 when I sang in *Carousel* at a small little theater in town. I sang in clubs for several years while holding down a full-time teaching job, but moved to Nashville in 1997 to pursue music full-time and since then I have performed for a living." A high point of her career was touring with the 26-piece U.S. Continental Army Jazz Band in 2001. "There's no doubt in my mind that I'm doing exactly what I want to do with my life."

Recommended CDs: Cynthia Kaay Bennett has thus far recorded two albums. *I Wish I Knew* (Orchard 803 135) from 2001 starts off with a beautiful version of "Bewitched, Bothered And Bewildered" and then mostly features obscure recent songs (other than "Mood Indigo"), including two of her originals, all sung cheerfully and with enthusiasm. *That's The Spirit* (Orchard 803 136) is a Christmas jazz set with her creative versions of 14 Yuletide-oriented songs, both older favorites and some newer material.

Website: www.cynthiakaay.com

Tony Bennett
(Anthony Dominick Benedetto)
b. August 3, 1926, Queens, NY

Several things are indisputable about Tony Bennett. He is one of the nicest people in show business, he loves jazz and the gems of the Great American Songbook, and he wears superb suits. Bennett would be the first to admit that he is not a jazz singer. When he performs in concert, his second choruses to songs tend to be the same as his first, except that they might be a bit louder, and his renditions of standards do not change much from night to night, or even from year to year. However, he does justice to the lyrics that he performs, he has consistently fought against the odds to perform good music, and his enthusiasm and joy in performing is infectious.

Bennett loved swinging jazz and popular music from an early age. At ten he was already singing in public. Bennett attended New York's High School of Industrial Art where he studied music and painting. He dropped out when he was 16 to support his family, working as a singing waiter in Italian restaurants.

After serving in the Army during 1944–46, he returned to studying music and working in restaurants, singing in a variety of locations and often using the name Joe Bari. His big break occurred in 1949 when Pearl Bailey discovered him and hired him to open for her at a club. She invited Bob Hope, who was so impressed by Bennett that he took him on the road with his show. Hope advised him to use a simplified version of his name, Tony Bennett.

In 1950 Bennett was signed to Columbia, and he soon had his first hit, "Because Of You." "Cold Cold Heart," "Blue Velvet," "Rags To Riches" and "Stranger In Paradise" followed. While the rise of rock and roll was competition, Bennett continued having hit records throughout the 1950s. However, he was more interested in recording in jazz settings, and some of his albums, most notably *Cloud 7* (which featured guitarist Chuck Wayne), *The Beat Of My Heart* and two records with Count Basie's big band, gave him a chance to swing with some of the best jazz players. Throughout his career, he would enjoy adding jazz soloists to his recordings. With pianist Ralph Sharon as Bennett's musical director starting in 1957, the singer had a solid jazz-oriented trio in back of his vocals. A household name by then, Tony Bennett had his biggest hit in 1962 with "I Left My Heart In San Francisco" and also recorded "I Wanna Be Around" and "The Good Life."

By 1965, the music world was changing, and Bennett was being pressured by Columbia to record current pop tunes. While he gave in on a few occasions, he mostly resisted, and in 1972 he left the company. After a brief period on MGM, he formed his own record label, Improv Records, which allowed him to interact with jazz musicians and to perform the music he loved. Bennett recorded two classic albums with pianist Bill Evans (one apiece for Fantasy and Improv), but his own label only lasted until 1977.

By 1980, Tony Bennett's career was at a low point, and he was considered hopelessly old-fashioned by the younger generation. However, his son Danny Bennett proved to be an expert businessman and an inventive promoter. He booked his father in colleges and smaller venues where he could interact more with younger audiences, and his MTV special *Tony Bennett Unplugged* made him hip again, without changing his singing style or repertoire. Ever since then, he has continued recording regularly, performing as often as he wants to and symbolizing class in music.

Recommended CDs: Tony Bennett's most jazz-oriented projects include *Cloud 7* (Columbia 85806), *The Beat Of My Heart* (Columbia 66502), *In Person! Tony Bennett, Count Basie And His Orchestra* (Columbia/Legacy 64276), *Basie Swings, Bennett Sings* (Roulette 25072), *At Carnegie Hall, June 9, 1962* (Sony 64609), *The Tony Bennett/Bill Evans Album* (Original Jazz Classics 439), the four-CD *Complete Improv Recordings* (Concord 42255), *Bennett/Berlin* (Columbia 44029), *Perfectly Frank* (Sony 472222), *Steppin' Out* (Sony 57424), *MTV Unplugged* (Sony 66214), *On Holiday* (Sony 67774), *Bennett Sings Ellington: Hot And Cool* (Sony 63668) and the compilation *Jazz* (Sony 40424). In addition, the five-CD set *Fifty Years: The Artistry Of Tony Bennett* (Columbia/Legacy 92784) sums up his entire career quite well.

Website: www.benedettoarts.com

George Benson
b. March 22, 1943, Pittsburgh, PA

George Benson's original reputation was as one of the top jazz guitarists to emerge during the 1960s, but it was when he had a surprise #1 hit with his vocal version of Leon Russell's "This Masquerade" that he became a household name far beyond the jazz world. As with Nat King Cole two decades earlier, Benson was seen by some as a "sellout" who chose pop stardom over being a jazz innovator, but his singing is generally enjoyable.

Ironically George Benson's first recordings, four numbers in 1954 when he was just 11, were as a singer. Benson was taught the guitar by his stepfather and began playing in nightclubs when he was only eight. He led a rock band when he was 17 but soon became influenced by Charlie Christian and Wes Montgomery. Benson gained important experience playing with organist Jack McDuff's band during 1962–64, appearing on McDuff's records and matching wits with saxophonist Red Holloway. He cut his first album as a leader in 1964 (utilizing McDuff's group), and in 1965 went out on his own. Producer John Hammond "discovered" Benson and signed him to Columbia for two albums that also feature baritonist Ronnie Cuber and organist Lonnie Smith. Although his songs mostly comprise instrumentals, Benson takes vocals on "A Foggy Day," "Summertime," "Stormy Weather" and "All Of Me" during these 1965–66 albums.

Benson would not sing again on record for years, recording albums for Verve, A&M and CTI. While some of the sets are commercial, Benson's guitar playing won him many fans, and his work for CTI ranks with the best of his career.

In 1976 for his first project for Warner Bros, Benson recorded five instrumentals (including the title track to *Breezin'*) and, almost as an afterthought, cut "This Masquerade." After singing the lyrics, Benson sang along in unison with his guitar, which became his trademark. The song became such a giant hit that Benson's career was permanently changed. His next few albums, including *In Flight*, *Weekend In L.A.*, *Livin' Inside Your Love* and *Give Me The Night*, were dominated by his increasingly R&Bish vocals, with his guitar being used mostly as a prop.

Since that time, George Benson has recorded some worthwhile jazz dates, including *Big Band Basie* and *Tenderly*, but has generally coasted. His live shows, which always include his hits and a couple of examples of his guitar playing (which act as a tease), are entertaining if predictable. But Benson remains capable of greatness, both as a guitarist and as a singer, if he decided to stretch himself.

Recommended CDs: George Benson's earliest vocals (other than the four singles from his childhood which have never been reissued) are on *It's Uptown* (Columbia/Legacy 66052) and *The George Benson Cookbook* (Columbia/Legacy 66054), two high-quality hard bop sets. "This Masquerade" is on *Breezin'* (Warner Archives 76713), while *In Flight* (Warner Bros. 2983) includes "Nature Boy" and "Everything Must

Change." *Weekend In L.A.* (Warner Bros. 3139) is highlighted by "On Broadway." *Tenderly* (Warner Bros. 25907) teams Benson with pianist McCoy Tyner, while *Big Boss Band* (Warner Bros. 26295) matches him with the Count Basie Orchestra. *Live* (Verve 84353) has a typical George Benson concert from 2000.

Website: www.georgebenson.com

Cheryl Bentyne
b. January 17, 1954, Mount Vernon, WA

A member of the Manhattan Transfer since May 1979, Cheryl Bentyne will always be best known for her association with that classic vocal group. However, in recent times she has also been gradually developing a solo career that shows off her wide range and very versatile style.

"As a child I was force-fed Dixieland jazz via my father. He had a dance band and was known as the Benny Goodman of the Northwest. Of course at the time I thought it was so unhip. Little did I know it was surging through my veins like a fine, fine wine, aging and developing without my permission!"

"I often practiced singing in the rumpus room of our house and lip-synched to Barbra Streisand records. As a freshman in high school I auditioned for a musical review, belting out 'I'm The Greatest Star' from *Funny Girl* a cappella. My parents had no idea I could sing so when my mother came backstage, she was speechless. She proceeded to 'book' me as the girl singer in my dad's band at the Elks club. I got paid $20 per week for singing Friday and Saturday nights. I knew I'd hit the big time!"

Bentyne had piano lessons for seven years, and after graduating high school she performed in Seattle with the New Deal Rhythm Band. "This was eight guys in zoot suits carrying on like maniacs in the style of Cab Calloway. I was the girl singer."

After moving to Los Angeles and spending a few months developing a solo career, the turning point in Cheryl Bentyne's life was when she replaced Laurel Massé in the Manhattan Transfer, an association that has so far lasted over 26 years. "Joining the Manhattan Transfer allowed me carte blanche to meet all my musical heroes and even sing with some of them, everyone from Ella to Tony to Phil Collins to Bette to Sammy to Dizzy to Peggy Lee to the Pope to three different presidents. As a member of the Transfer, I feel our best efforts have been our recording of Joe Zawinul's 'Birdland' and our entire *Vocalese* album. My solo on the Transfer's swing of 'Nuages' is a personal best for me."

During her part-time solo career, Bentyne made an appearance on Rob Wasserman's 1988 set *Duets*, recorded a tribute to June Christy in 1992 (*Something Cool*), has made four solo albums for the Japanese King label, one of which (*Talk Of The Town*) was released in the United States by Telarc, and most recently cut an Anita O'Day tribute called *Let Me Off Uptown*.

"For me in jazz, the element of danger is the thrill along with the challenge of getting to the end of the song safely."

Recommended CDs: *Something Cool* (Columbia 48506) is out of print but worth trying to find. *Talk Of The Town* (Telarc

83583) teams Cheryl Bentyne on standards with pianist Kenny Barron and guests flugelhornist Chuck Mangione and tenor-saxophonist David "Fathead" Newman. *Let Me Off Uptown* (Telarc 83606) is a successful tribute to Anita O'Day, even though Cheryl Bentyne has a stronger voice and actually sounds nothing like O'Day. The Japanese King releases are *Moonlight Serenade* (King 453), *The Lights Still Burn* (King 462) and *Sings Waltz For Debby* (King 2100). There was also a limited-edition self-released Cole Porter set titled *Dreaming Of Mister Porter*.

Andy Bey
b. October 28, 1939, Newark, NJ

An unusual singer with a deep voice and a wide range, Andy Bey took a long time before he gained fame in the jazz world.

Bey first sang in front of audiences when he was eight. At 13 he recorded his first solo album (*Mama's Little Boy's Got The Blues*) and was on *The Star Time Kids* on television. When he was 18, he started singing with his sisters Salome and Geraldine as Andy and the Bey Sisters. The jazz-oriented ensemble, which had the passion of a gospel group, toured Europe and recorded three albums, lasting until 1967. While Andy Bey recorded a solo album in the 1970s and worked with Max Roach, Duke Pearson and Gary Bartz, he became best known for his association with pianist-composer Horace Silver. Unfortunately, Silver's lyrics during that era tended to be awkward and full of metaphysical self-help themes. Bey did not sound that comfortable singing many of his songs, but he did work with Silver on and off for 20 years, including recording the more straight-ahead *It's Got To Be Funky* in 1993.

After having a low profile, recording for tiny labels and spending two years as a vocal instructor in Austria, Andy Bey recorded *Ballads, Blues And Bey* for Evidence in 1996, gaining a bit of attention. Since that time he has recorded regularly, sometimes only accompanied by his own sparse piano, and he has risen in the jazz popularity polls. Andy Bey's use of dynamics can be jarring, and he has an eccentric style, but he is an acquired taste worth developing.

Recommended CDs: *Andy Bey And The Bey Sisters* (Prestige 24245) reissues two of the three albums recorded by this intriguing group, which blended together R&B and gospel with jazz. Andy Bey's more recent work is well represented by *Ballads, Blues And Bey* (Evidence 22162), *Shades Of Bey* (Evidence 22215), *Tuesdays In Chinatown* (N2K 4223), *American Song* (Savoy 17330) and *Ain't Necessarily So* (12th Street 292982).

Jane Blackstone
b. June 5 1955, Concord, NH

As of this writing it is surprising that Jane Blackstone has only led one commercially available CD, *Natural Habitat/NYC*. Her warm voice and flexible improvising style, which at times is a little reminiscent of Sheila Jordan, should make her a natural to be showcased in many settings.

She remembers that as a child "I was consumed with listening to records, radio, everything musical. One day when I was 12, my mom came back from the grocery store and held up an LP saying, 'Janie, I just thought you would like this record—the cover reminded me of you.' It was *Miles In The Sky*, a treasure to my ears." Blackstone began singing as a little girl, emulating what she heard on records. She played guitar and sang for the

Unitarian Church Coffee House, improvising on folk songs. As a teenager she sang with a local blues band at resorts. "On several gigs, I can remember the sensation of being so in sync with the music, the audience and with my own inner feeling that I knew I was where I wanted to be.

"All during my pre-teens and teenage years, I was totally thinking of music. I truly wanted to skip high school and simply attend the Berklee College of Music in Boston." She did not make it to Berklee until attending its summer program in 1988, mostly studying music privately, including with Joanne Brackeen in 1984 after receiving the NEA Grant for Jazz Studies. However, Blackstone has worked in New York since she turned 18, being inspired by trombonist Sam Burtis, Latin musicians in general and by constantly listening to other musicians and singers. "In the future I hope to be able to write music for a large vocal ensemble. I would like to study the harmonies of rain forest peoples, to study arranging from a Gil Evans perspective, to master singing in Spanish, and to teach kids to really appreciate music that is not the norm."

When asked to name some of the high points of her career thus far, she mentions working with Carla Bley, writing her own songs, performing in Argentina and Japan and recording *Natural Habitat/NYC.* "I think we all have to create our career from 'thin air' these days. The high points can be very subtle things that are not necessarily connected to glamour and fame. For instance, I was so turned on to be singing at the Deer Head Inn recently with Bill Goodwin's trio. We had a super audience that listened. That was a high point!"

Recommended CD: *Natural Habitat/NYC* (Motief 2002) matches Jane Blackstone with several different pianists (including Sir Roland Hanna), Bob Mover on saxophones, trombonist Sam Burtis (on the singer's original "Once") and a few rhythm sections. "Where You At," "We Kiss In A Shadow," a tribute to Nina Simone on "The Human Touch" and a few of her originals are among the highlights.

Website: www.janeblackstone.com

Terry Blaine
b. October 6, 1952, New York, NY

A very talented swing and classic jazz singer who often works with pianist Mark Shane, Terry Blaine helps keep the music of the 1920s, '30s and '40s alive not by merely recreating the past but by giving new life to the older songs through her enthusiasm and musicianship.

"I think I sang before I talked. I sang at summer camp in musicals like *The King And I* and *Destry Rides Again,* singing 'See What The Boys In The Back Room Will Have' when I was 11." She played clarinet briefly at age ten before she got braces then switched to flute, which she still plays today. Blaine graduated summa cum laude from the University of Buffalo with a Bachelor of Arts in Music in 1973. "I was torn all through high school and college because I always wanted to sing but had commitments to band and orchestra. It wasn't until after college, when I went to an audition with a sax player friend, who convinced me to

try both singing and playing the flute, that I realized I wanted to sing professionally."

"The song has always been as important to me as who performs it. Lennon/McCartney, Joni Mitchell, James Taylor, Paul Simon, Ray Davies and Elvis Costello on the pop side were early inspirations. After college, I worked in New York City for composer Charles Morrow, who gave me the complete boxed set of Billie Holiday's recordings, saying that if I was serious about being a singer, I should listen to her phrasing. She and Ethel Waters became very important to me. Through Charlie, I had the opportunity to sing lead and in a group, and also to work in New York (1974–85) as a contractor, copyist and vocal arranger." During her first decade in New York, Blaine worked with such orchestra leaders as Mark Stevens, Peter Duchin, Marty Ames, Michael Mark, Bobby Rosengarden, Leo Ursini, Denny LeRoux and Joey Mills and did a lot of studio work along with appearances on television and radio shows.

However, the turning point in her career was in 1986 when she met Mark Shane. "Mark has worked with me all these years in partnership. His artistry is unmatched and he is such a scholar of this music. He introduced me to many of the finest players in classic jazz, including Allan Vaché, Ed Polcer, Russell George, Danny D'Imperio, Frank Vignola, Ken Peplowski, Vince Giordano, Phil Flanigan, Joe Ascione, Tom Artin and many others whom I've worked with over the years. In addition my husband, Tom Desisto, has been a great producer and collaborator with Mark and me on our various CD projects and the world's most supportive spouse."

Terry Blaine and Mark Shane worked as a duo at Café Society during 1988–92, recorded *Whose Honey Are You* and have performed and recorded regularly ever since, helping keep swing music alive.

Recommended CDs: Each of Terry Blaine's recordings have their magical moments. *Whose Honey Are You* (Original Cast Records 9237) has a few selections on which she overdubs her voice to form a vocal group. *In Concert With The Mark Shane Quintet* (Jukebox Jazz 483 501) documents an enthusiastic 1994 set performed before 7,000 fans, while *With Thee I Swing* (Nagel Heyer 9004) is a 1997 performance that also features cornetist Ed Polcer and Ken Peplowski. *Too Hot For Words* (Jukebox Jazz 9904) is a tribute to Bessie Smith, Billie Holiday, Ella Fitzgerald and especially the Boswell Sisters (with more colorful overdubbing). The year 2002's *Lonesome Swallow* (Jukebox Jazz 206) is a duo CD with Mark Shane that pays particular homage to Ethel Waters and James P. Johnson. The most recent *Swingin' The Benny Goodman Songbook* (Jukebox Jazz 0407), which has Allan Vaché fitting comfortably in the role of Benny Goodman, finds Terry Blaine hinting at Helen Ward, Martha Tilton and Mildred Bailey while still sounding like herself.

Website: www.terryblaine.com

Bon Bon
(George Tunnell)
b. 1903, Reading, PA; d. May 20, 1975, Philadelphia, PA

While with Jan Savitt's orchestra, George "Bon Bon" Tunnell has the distinction of being the first African-American male singer to be featured regularly with a white big band. More importantly, he was a skilled and versatile vocalist who was equally effective on medium-tempo material and ballads and impressive at both interpreting lyrics and scatting.

Nicknamed Bon Bon early in life, he began his career in the 1920s singing and playing competent piano with a vocal group called "Bon Bon And His Buddies." That particular group broke up in 1931, but Bon Bon had better luck with the Three Keys, a hot trio similar to (if not as crazy as) the Spirits Of Rhythm. It featured guitarist Slim Furness and bassist Bob Pease with all three musicians singing together. The Three Keys recorded 16 songs during 1932–33, worked in New York City clubs, appeared on the radio and played a concert at the Palladium in London in September 1933.

The Three Keys eventually broke up, but Bon Bon found his greatest fame as the main singer with the Jan Savitt Orchestra (1937–42). He was with Savitt during the band's greatest years, and among the vocals that he recorded were "Hi-Yo Silver," "Vol Vistu Gaily Star," "It's A Wonderful World" and "Rose Of The Rio Grande." He also made two sessions under the name of Bon Bon and His Buddies during 1941–42 with small swing groups.

During 1946–50 Bon Bon recorded at least 36 titles for the Davis and Beacon labels as a solo singer, although these have never been reissued and apparently did not sell that well. In the 1950s Bon Bon moved back to Pennsylvania and only sang on a part-time basis during his last 25 years. He deserves to be remembered.

Recommended CDs: *The Three Keys/Bon Bon And His Buddies* (Classics 1141) has all of the recordings by those two groups. Jan Savitt's It's *Time To Jump And Shout* (Vintage Music Productions 0071) has some of Bon Bon's best vocals with the Savitt band plus many instrumentals.

Janice Borla
b. September 29, 1949, Chicago, IL

An adventurous jazz singer who has become as famous for her educational jazz camps as for her vocalizing, Janice Borla never coasts nor is predictable.

"I played the accordion (gasp!) from age 7 to 18, playing adaptations of classical music literature, and switched to piano thereafter. I began private vocal study at age 12 upon entering high school, and there I was afforded numerous opportunities to perform as a vocal soloist. I participated in my high school choir and often sang in vocal duo, trio and quartet settings. My college vocal training was classical in style and repertoire, but I was more interested at the time in all the vocal styles— Motown, folk, rock, soul—that emerged in popular music throughout the 1960s. As a graduate student I became involved in and interested in 'new music' as a member of a chamber vocal ensemble that performed avant-garde works."

Borla earned a degree in voice and musicology at Barat College and had graduate studies in musicology at the University of Illinois School of Music. During 1970–73 she was a member of the Ineluctable Modality, a chamber vocal group that performed modern avant-garde classical music. Borla performed regularly at various Playboy Clubs during 1979–84 with jazz trios and big bands. She put together her own quintet in 1985 and recorded her debut album, *Whatever We Imagine* (Sea Breeze). The singer began teaching in 1986 when she joined the jazz faculty at Illinois Benedictine College and the following year worked as the vocal jazz director at the Saskatchewan

School of the Arts Summer Camp in Canada. In 1989 she established the Janice Borla Vocal Jazz Camp, which each summer to the present time has provided a very valuable educational environment for up-and-coming singers. "Its mission is to encourage vocalists to regard themselves as musicians who must prepare, train, study and listen as any other musician if they wish to participate with parity in this art form." She also currently teaches at North Central College.

Based in Chicago, Janice Borla has to date recorded four albums and gigged regularly in addition to her teaching. "I approach music as a jazz instrumentalist would, participating in the interactive, collaborative process as an equal member of the ensemble rather than merely as a solo voice with accompaniment."

Recommended CDs: The 1995 CD *Lunar Octave* (DMP 3004), which includes Bill Evans' "Five," and "Very Early" plus Abbey Lincoln's "Bird Alone," is somewhat scarce. But the singer's 2003 release, *Agents Of Change* (Blujazz 3311), is very much available and is her definitive release so far. Joined by a variety of top Chicago players, Borla sings adventurous versions of such songs as "Black Narcissus," "Israel," "The Peacocks" and Joe Lovano's "Blackwell's Message." *From Every Angle* (Blujazz 3350) has her lending her imagination and giving fresh life to such jazz originals as Charlie Parker's "Segment," Thelonious Monk's "Ask Me Now," Horace Silver's "Peace" and tunes by Jeff Beal, Kenny Wheeler, John Scofield and Frank Foster.

LPs to Search For: The 1986 album *Whatever We Imagine* (Sea Breeze 2029) features Janice Borla in excellent form with a quartet that includes her husband, drummer Jack Mouse.

Website: www.janiceborla.com

Connee Boswell
(Connie Boswell)
b. December 3, 1907, New Orleans, LA;
d. October 11, 1976, New York, NY

One of the great singers to mature during the 1930s, Connee Boswell never became the major commercial success that she was expected to be, but she made a strong impact nevertheless. She was one year older than sister Martha and two years older than Helvetia. Connee (who switched her name

from Connie halfway through her career) contracted polio when she was four and was never able to walk again, a fact that was very well hidden during her performances. Early on she played cello, piano, alto sax and trombone, but it was her singing in conjunction with her sisters that gave her fame.

The Boswell Sisters first recorded as teenagers in 1925: one song as a group and a feature ("I'm Gonna Cry") for Connee. After several years of singing in New Orleans and Los Angeles, the Boswell Sisters began to catch on in 1930 when they were already one of the greatest jazz vocal groups ever. Connee was the only one of the Boswells to take solo choruses, and she was also largely responsible for the group's vocal arrangements. She recorded some sessions under her own name as early as 1931 but did not begin her solo career until 1936 when the Boswell

Sisters broke up due to both Martha and Helvetia getting married and deciding to retire. By then, Connee had already been the inspiration for Ella Fitzgerald (who always cited her as her main early influence) and had recorded definitive versions of "Time On My Hands," "Lullaby Of The Leaves," "Humming To Myself" and "Me Minus You."

For the next 20 years, Boswell worked steadily, appearing constantly on radio (particularly as a regular guest on Bing Crosby's show) and briefly in a few films, performing at concerts and recording often. Some of her more popular recordings include "Sand In My Shoes," "I Let A Song Go Out Of My Heart," "On The Isle Of May" and some of her duets with Crosby (particularly "Basin Street Blues" and "Bob White"). While too many of her sessions emphasized fairly straight readings of ballads, she was at her most exciting on her November 13, 1937 date with Bob Crosby's orchestra that resulted in very memorable versions of "Martha" and "Home On The Range."

In the 1950s Boswell acted on the short-lived television series *Pete Kelly's Blues* and recorded a jazz album long overdue to be reissued, *Connee Boswell And The Original Memphis Five*. By the early 1960s she was largely retired, although she made occasional appearances, last singing in public in 1975 with Benny Goodman's orchestra at Carnegie Hall. Connee Boswell never had a major hit record, and her solo career was less jazz-oriented than expected, but her interpretations of lyrics, solid swing and subtle improvising made her one of the greats.

Recommended CDs: The trio of *Heart And Soul* (ASV/Living Era 5221), *Deep In A Dream* (Harlequin 80) and *Moonlight And Roses* (Flare 223) do an excellent job of summing up Connee Boswell's most rewarding solo recordings of the 1930s and '40s.

LPs to Search For: *Connee Boswell And The Original Memphis Five* (Victor 1426) is well worth bidding on.

Lillian Boutté

b. August 6, 1949, New Orleans, LA

In Lillian Boutté's singing, New Orleans jazz meets gospel, soul, blues and swing. It is all part of her musical personality, and she gives each selection she interprets the sincerity and passion that it deserves.

Growing up in New Orleans, Boutté was always surrounded by music. She began singing early on, winning her first vocal contest when she was 11. She studied music and music therapy at Xavier University, sang in the gospel choir and was discovered by Allen Toussaint in 1973. "Getting to work with Allen Toussaint in his studio was the beginning of a great musical life for me." Boutté worked as a background singer for Toussaint on many recordings, including those featuring James Booker, the Neville Brothers and Dr. John. Boutté appeared in the musical *One Mo' Time* during 1979–84, recorded a gospel album with the Olympia Brass Band in 1980 and in 1982 cut her first jazz record.

Since then, Lillian Boutté has alternated between living in New Orleans and Germany. Usually joined by a New Orleans–style jazz band led by her husband, reed player Thomas L'Etienne, she has been a regular at European jazz festivals and also appeared at large gospel shows held abroad. In 1986 she was named a "Musical Ambassador" of New Orleans, an honor previously given to Louis Armstrong and one that suits her well. "My goal is to share my music!"

Recommended CDs: *Lipstick Traces* (Enja/Blues Beacon 1011) falls between jazz, blues and R&B, displaying Lillian Boutté's

versatility in 1991. *Jazz Book* (Enja/Blues Beacon 1020) from 1993 is Boutté at her most jazz-oriented, swinging soulfully through a quintet date with L'Etienne and trumpeter Leroy Jones. *But…Beautiful* (Dinosaur 84500), cited by the singer as her personal favorite, was produced by Dr. John in 1994 but has less improvising and chance-taking than the more satisfying *Jazz Book*. *I Sing Because I'm Happy* (Timeless 11003) is a strong gospel record, while *Music Is My Life* (Timeless 11002) is a particularly well-rounded and diverse set that features Lillian Boutté at her best. In addition, the singer has recorded for many other European labels, including Herman, Feel The Jazz, High Society, Turning Point, Storyville and with Humphrey Lyttelton for Calligraph.

Carmen Bradford

b. July 19, 1960, Austin, TX

When one considers Carmen Bradford's career thus far, it is surprising that she is not more famous. She was certainly born to sing music, being the daughter of vocalist Melba Joyce and trumpeter Bobby Bradford. "My mother is one of the greatest singers I've ever heard. She is a major influence on my style to this day. I knew at the age of seven that I was going to be a singer. I grew up in Altadena, California, went back to Austin, Texas when I attended Huston-Tillotson College, but left before finishing because Count Basie said, 'Come on little girl.'"

During 1982–90, Bradford was the regular singer with the Count Basie Orchestra. Basie passed away in 1984, and she never had the opportunity to record with him but she does take a few vocals on records with the Frank Foster version of the posthumous band. "Standing in front of that band was a huge responsibility. You really have to know how to sing. I'm very proud of the fact that I was the last singer that Basie hired."

After leaving the Basie band, she recorded a CD apiece for the Amazing and Evidence labels and most recently for Azica, also guesting on recordings by Dori Caymmi, George Benson (dueting with Benson on "How Do You Keep The Music Playing") and the Lincoln Center Jazz Orchestra.

In 2000, Bradford toured Europe with David Murray's 3D Family Big Band and performed obscure works by Duke Ellington and Billy Strayhorn with flutist James Newton. She has sung in recent times with the Doc Severinsen Orchestra, teaches at jazz camps and is a vocal jazz professor at the University of Southern California.

"My goal when I'm singing is to tell the story of whatever I'm singing about, to the point where you can't wait to hear what happens next."

Recommended CDs: *Finally Yours* (Amazing 1030) from 1992 is particularly rewarding for Carmen Bradford's renditions of ballads, while 1995's *With Respect* (Evidence 22115) mostly has obscure but superior material (including songs by Cedar Walton, Chick Corea and Red Mitchell) and fine solos from pianists Walton and Donald Brown. Best of all is the recent *Home With You* (Azica 72227), a set of duets with pianist Shelly Berg that shows off the singer in prime form.

Website: www.carmenbradford.com

Adi Braun
(Adreana Braun)
b. November 23, 1962, Toronto, Ontario, Canada

The release of Adi Braun's debut jazz recording, *Delishious*, displays the work of a very talented Canadian singer, one of the very few from the world of opera to successfully make the transition to jazz.

"I come from a very musical family, most of whom are classical singers. I was classically trained and worked for many years as a classical singer. Only in the last decade have I found the courage to break with family tradition and follow my dream to become a jazz vocalist."

Braun started studying piano at the age of eight. Although born in Canada, she lived in Germany most of the time until moving back to Canada in 1982. She performed musical theater a bit while in high school, although she admits, "I secretly sang pop music in the basement of my family home. As a teenager my pop senses were influenced by Stevie Wonder, ABBA and Queen." She attended the Royal Conservatory of Music and the University of Toronto, graduating in 1991. Braun worked in productions with the Canadian Opera Company and the Opera Atelier during 1990–95 and appeared in numerous cabaret and theater concerts during 1995–2001.

"The turning point in my career occurred in the summer of 2001 when, after many years of singing in the classical field, I entered a local Variety Show Competition. This was my first public jazz performance and I won a spot in the finals. This experience gave me the push I needed to embark upon this path that had always been my secret dream. I love the wonderful interplay and dialogue between the musicians in jazz, the musical spontaneity and improvisational freedom."

Adi Braun has since worked regularly in jazz, often with the Doug Riley Trio. Her debut jazz CD, *Delishious*, is such an impressive effort that it shows that she belongs in this book despite only singing jazz for a few years.

Recommended CDs: *Delishious* (Blue Rider 001) shows off Adi Braun's versatility, strong and flexible voice and her creative wit. She never sounds like a classical singer who is moonlighting, and she displays a real feel for swinging jazz. Whether the retro swing of "Crazy From The Heat," the title cut (an obscure Gershwin piece) or a sensual "Miss Celie's Blues," this is a memorable effort, one of the best jazz vocal albums released during 2003. *The Rules Of The Game* (Blue Rider 002) from 2005 builds on the success of the earlier set, featuring Adi Braun's colorful renditions of five standards, three new songs and five lesser-known tunes. Highlights include "Honeysuckle Rose," "I Got It Bad," Ann Hampton Callaway's "You Can't Rush Spring," "Lonely House," "About Last Night" and "If We Had Never Met." Adi Baun's most recent recording, *Live At The Metropolitan Room* (Blue Rider 003), is an enjoyable outing filled with more of her favorite standards plus two new originals.

Website: www.adibraun.com

Dee Dee Bridgewater
(Denise Eileen Garrett)
b. May 27, 1950, Memphis, TN

An extroverted and very entertaining singer, Dee Dee Bridgewater did not find her own individual voice in jazz until she lived in France.

"My father was a music teacher, trumpeter and band director at one of the two black high schools in Memphis. He taught many well known jazz musicians who came out of Memphis and played in a quintet headed by saxophonist Sherman Mitchell. I sang with them when I was 16. My mother loved singers and while pregnant with me and during my first year, she listened to a lot of Ella Fitzgerald." The family moved to Flint, Michigan when Dee Dee was three.

At 16, Dee Dee became a professional singer, performing with a female vocal trio modeled after the Supremes along with other soul/R&B groups. She also won talent contests and as a prize had the chance to sing in local jazz clubs. While attending Michigan State University during 1968–69, she was in the Andy Goodrich Quintet + 1. In 1970 she married trumpeter Cecil Bridgewater, moved to New York and became the singer with the Thad Jones/Mel Lewis Orchestra for four years. She also had opportunities to work with Dizzy Gillespie, Clark Terry, Max Roach, Sonny Rollins, Dexter Gordon, Rahsaan Roland Kirk, Pharoah Sanders and Frank Foster's Loud Majority Big Band.

In 1974 she moved away from jazz, playing the role of Glinda the Good Witch in *The Wiz* and winning a Tony award. She had success recording R&B and commercial music for Atlantic and Elektra, and she acted in other shows. After moving to Paris in the 1980s and appearing in the show *Lady Day*, she began returning to jazz. The 1986 album *Live In Paris* signaled her jazz "comeback," and since then she has become one of creative music's top singers.

Dee Dee Bridgewater's accomplishments of the past 20 years include tours with her quartet, Lionel Hampton (1989) and the Count Basie Orchestra under the direction of Frank Foster (1993), classic albums paying tribute to Horace Silver, Ella Fitzgerald and Kurt Weill, a recording with Ray Charles, singing for Pope John Paul II twice before huge audiences, a recent African music project, becoming the regular host of NPR's *Jazz Set* and a countless number of performances at clubs and festivals.

"The ability to communicate with other musicians through the use of my vocal chords is quite amazing to me. I love the wonderful moments when all the stars align within my bands and we make magical music on stage."

Recommended CDs: Skipping over Dee Dee Bridgewater's four R&B sets for Atlantic and Elektra, her jazz legacy really begins with 1986's *Live In Paris* (Emarcy 0143172), *In Montreux* (Verve 314 511 895) and *Keeping Tradition* (Verve 314 519 607). Her trio of tribute projects, *Love and Peace: A Tribute To Horace Silver* (Verve 527470), *Dear Ella* (Verve 537896) and the rather stunning *This Is New* (Verve 16884), represent high points in her career. Also quite worthwhile are *Live At Yoshi's* (Verve 543354), *J'ai Deux Amours* (DDB Music 9869777), which is an album sung mostly in French in thanks for her 17 years living in France, and a tribute to her African heritage and Mali called *Red Earth* (Universal/DDB Records 1722829).

Website: www.deedeebridgewater.com

Hadda Brooks
(Hadda Hopgood)
b. October 29, 1916, Los Angeles, CA;
d. November 21, 2002, Los Angeles, CA

An exciting pianist whose initial fame came due to her boo-gie-woogie records, Hadda Brooks began singing almost as an afterthought. But by her later years, she thought of herself as a sentimental ballad singer first and a pianist second.

Brooks started piano lessons at the age of four, playing classical at first before switching to popular music. In the early 1940s she gained a job playing piano for the Willie Covan dance studio, often working with Hollywood actors and dancers, including playing behind Fred Astaire and Gene Kelly. One day in 1945, while trying out different rhythms in a music store, she turned "The Poet And The Peasant" into a boogie-woogie stomp. Jules Bihari, an aspiring record producer, heard her and offered to record Brooks if she could write a new boogie-woogie within a week.

The result was "Swingin' The Boogie," a piece that Bihari used to launch his Modern label. Soon Brooks was being called the "Queen of the Boogie" and becoming a popular attraction, particularly on the West Coast and in the South. While her first records were all instrumentals, at the end of one club performance when she was called back to do an encore, she was persuaded to sing. The audience enjoyed her warm voice, and in time her recordings were split between piano features and vocals. She had hits with "That's My Desire, "Out Of The Blue" (which she sang in the film of the same name) and "I Hadn't Anyone Till You" (from another film appearance, in the Humphrey Bogart movie *In A Lonely Place*). She also was the first African-American woman to host her own television show, a 15-minute daily program on KLAC: in 1957 she hosted the nationally televised *Hadda Brooks Show* for 26 half-hour programs.

As a commercial recording artist, she peaked by 1950. Brooks recorded for London in 1950 and Okeh during 1952–53 before returning to Bihari, cutting albums for his Crown label. She continued working mostly in West Coast clubs with occasional visits to Europe. In the 1960s Brooks moved to Australia, where she again hosted her own television show. She drifted away into obscurity until she turned up in the early 1990s back in Los Angeles, playing and singing as well as ever. Hadda Brooks, considered a legend, made a couple new recordings and was once again a popular attraction in the Los Angeles area until ill health forced her retirement.

Recommended CDs: *That's My Desire* (Virgin 39687) and *Jump Back Honey: The Complete Okeh Sessions* (Columbia 65081) have many of the recorded high points of Hadda Brooks' early career, while *Anytime, Anyplace, Anywhere* (DRG 91423) and *Time Was When* (Virgin 41364) show that she was still a rewarding performer late in her life.

Charles Brown
b. September 13, 1922, Texas City, TX;
d. January 24, 1999, Oakland, CA

A smooth relaxed singer who was an underrated pianist, Charles Brown performed music that included swing-oriented jazz, blues and blues ballads. An orphan at an early age, Brown had classical training on piano and earned a degree in chemistry. After working as a teacher, he moved to the Los Angeles area in 1943.

Brown worked in pit bands and freelanced in clubs before joining guitarist Johnny Moore's Three Blazers in 1944. The group, originally based in the guitar-piano-bass music of the King Cole Trio, played swing and blues, recording for several labels, including Aladdin. In 1946 when Brown's "Driftin' Blues" became a hit, the trio began to specialize in slow blues ballads with Brown's singing and piano playing making him the star of the group. The following year his "Merry Christmas Baby" also became a standard. The only problem was that audiences often thought that Brown was Johnny Moore!

Being underpaid and feeling underpublicized, Brown went out on his own in 1948, repeating his successes with his own groups. Among his ten R&B hits of 1949 to 1952 are "Get Yourself Another Fool," "Trouble Blues" and "Hard Times." Brown's urbanized variations of the blues and his laid-back singing were major influences on Amos Milburn, Floyd Dixon (who sometimes sounded like a near-duplicate of Brown) and the young Ray Charles.

With the rise of rock and roll, Brown was overshadowed, but he rarely stopped working. While he made fewer recordings after the mid-1950s, he worked steadily in the South, Midwest and in California, each year getting some recognition around Christmas time due to "Merry Christmas Baby."

The decades of obscurity ended in 1986 when Brown recorded the well-received album *One More For The Road*. Bonnie Raitt used him as an opening act on a few tours, follow-up records revealed that Brown was a skilled jazz and blues pianist, and his regular quintet with saxophonist Clifford Solomon and guitarist Danny Caron proved to be a perfect vehicle for his music. Charles Brown had high visibility during his final decade, singing and playing piano in his timeless style for large crowds.

Recommended CDs: *1944–1945* (Classics 894), *1946* (Classics 971), *1946–1947* (Classics 1088) and *1947–1948* (Classics 1147) include all of Brown's recordings with Moore's Three Blazers, while *1948–1949* (Classics 1210) and *1949–1951* (Classics 1272) have the first 47 recordings with his own trio. From his later period (starting in 1986), *One More For The Road* (Alligator 4771), *All My Life* (Bullseye Blues 9501), *Someone In Love* (Bullseye Blues 9514), *Just A Lucky So And So* (Bullseye Blues 9521) and *These Blues* (Verve 314 523 022) all feature Charles Brown still in top form, showing that he had grown as a performer and singer through the years and was still a class act.

Cleo Brown
b. December 8, 1909, Meridian, MS; d. April 15, 1995, Denver, CO

Because her time in the spotlight was relatively brief, Cleo Brown is largely forgotten today except when Dave Brubeck mentions her as an important early inspiration. A powerful pianist, Brown was also an effective singer.

Brown sang in her father's church as a youth, moved with her family to Chicago in 1919 and took piano lessons. She developed quickly and was working in clubs and on radio by 1923. It is possible that she may have been born a few years before the listed date of 1909. She did not record until 1935, but Brown cut 18 memorable selections with rhythm sections (Gene Krupa is on one date) during 1935–36, playing and singing such good time music as "Lookie, Lookie, Lookie, Here Comes Cookie," "The Stuff Is Here And It's Mellow," "Mama Don't Want No Peas An' Rice An' Coconut Oil," "Breakin' In A Pair Of Shoes" and "Love In The First Degree." "When Hollywood Goes Black And Tan" is particularly intriguing, optimistically celebrating the black entertainment stars of the period.

An illness knocked her out of action during 1940–42, and although working steadily throughout the remainder of the 1940s, Cleo Brown never really became a major star. She recorded eight selections during 1949–51 and then dropped out of the music world, becoming a nurse. Brown became very religious, moved to Denver in 1973 and played piano on a weekly basis for the Seventh-Day Adventist Church as C. Patra Brown. In 1987 Marian McPartland discovered Brown and had her guest on her *Piano Jazz* radio show on which she sang and played piano on hymns and spiritual pieces, still sounding in excellent form. An album was recorded later that week for Audiophile. However, that moment in the spotlight was brief, and Cleo Brown soon returned to Denver, passing away eight years later.

Recommended CDs: Other than a radio transcript, some alternate takes and a date with the Hollywood Hotshots, all of Cleo Brown's recordings are available on *1935–1951* (Classics 1252) and 1987's *Living In The Afterglow* (Audiophile 216).

Deborah Brown

b. March 22, 1953, Kansas City, MO

A widely respected singer who has found her greatest recognition overseas, Deborah Brown considers her main influences to be Charlie Parker ("for his incredible timings at fast speeds and his lyrical playing") and Betty Carter, "who showed that freedom comes, not only singing with scat, but using the words to express what one feels about the lyrics in an improvisational way."

"I started on violin as a child. My mother, who was a classical pianist, decided to teach accordion lessons around the neighborhood. I loved playing that instrument and took piano lessons from my grandmother so I could accompany myself. I took a few semesters at the local university in Kansas City, Missouri (1971–72), but more importantly I learned about music through all the wonderful musicians who were happy to share their information openly." A professional singer by the time she was 20, Deborah Brown sang all over the United States. "I think the first major highlight was working opposite George Carlin in Las Vegas in 1980. I played with the big band and it was jazz; a very unusual show for Vegas at the time."

She has since toured the Far East, Japan and Indonesia, spent 1985 to 1995 living in Europe and performed in more

than 50 countries. Among her favorite experiences were playing ten duet concerts with Roger Kellaway, performing with pianists Cedar Walton and Dorothy Donegan, touring with her quartet Jazz 4 Jazz, which included pianist Horace Parlan, playing concerts with Johnny Griffin, Benny Bailey, Toots Thielemans and Harry "Sweets" Edison, being the featured vocalist with Russia's Oleg Lundstrem Orchestra, Sweden's Sandviken Big Band and Kluver's Big Band from Denmark and touring Siberia with Russian saxophonist Nicolai Panov's quintet.

Deborah Brown says that her goals for the future include singing classical music, making a tutorial CD for jazz singers, writing a book on vocal technique and recording a CD with Pat Metheny. "The jazz field today can be frustrating at best, but I learned when living in Europe that this is a profession like any other field. You have to work hard to gain respect in this line of work. Many times it's not about the money. It is a privilege to work at something that can be so fulfilling and fun."

Recommended CDs: Deborah Brown cites *International Incident* (33 Jazz 078) as a favorite because "I was only concerned with the music I loved at the time. I wasn't concerned about it having to fit into a category." Other rewarding sets include *Euroboppin'* (Alfa 32-R2-25), *Jazz 4 Jazz* (Timeless 409), *Double Trouble* (Koch 3810), *Kluvers Big Band—Live In Tivoli* (Intermusic 058), *Live At The Blue Note* (VH 1603) and *Songbird* (Jazz 'N Pulz 397). Her most recent CD, *I Found My Thrill* (Jazz Voix), is a set of duets with guitarist Joe Beck. She has led 11 CDs in all and also recorded as a guest with pianist Jon Lundgren, the Doky Brothers and the Sandviken Big Band.

Website: www.deborahbrownjazz.com

Jeri Brown

b. March 20, 1952, St. Louis, MO

Although she is an American, Jeri Brown is thought of as one of Canada's top jazz singers since she lives in Montreal and records regularly for the Canadian Justin Time label. Her dramatic interpretations, four-octave range, versatility and ability to uplift a wide variety of material have made her a significant singer for the past two decades.

"I was originally introduced to jazz through my talented and respected uncle, Virgil Carter, who was a jazz trumpeter in St. Louis at the time. He would sneak me into the jazz jam sessions at the musician's union in St. Louis to see jazz in action. Also, Miles Davis and Clark Terry would practice in our basement on a regular basis. I sat at the top of the stairs and listened to them."

Jeri Brown began singing from an early age, entertaining her family when she was just three. "As a child, I developed a sense of the dramatic when vocalizing in public. It was also during this time that I learned the importance of musically adding something unique every time in the delivery of a song, as if to add my trademark, my personal signature to a piece." She studied several instruments, including piano, violin and percussion at a conservatory and was consistently inspired and cheered on by her family.

Brown graduated from Soldan High School in St. Louis, Missouri, in 1970 with honors, earned degrees in English and Education from Westmar College in Iowa and gained a double Master's degree in Educational Administration and Counseling from Kent State University. Brown's wide-ranging career early on included performances with the Cleveland

Chamber Orchestra and the St. Louis Symphony Orchestra, work in theater and with drummer Bob McKee, whose jazz group she performed with alongside Billy Taylor and Dizzy Gillespie. After becoming one of the top jazz singers based in Cleveland, she worked extensively in Europe, moved to Canada and has been very busy ever since as a lyricist (including collaborations with Kenny Wheeler, Cyrus Chestnut and Henry Butler), arranger, playwright, side person and leader of her own groups. Brown cites Sarah Vaughan and Betty Carter as being among her favorite all-time singers, and her collaborations with Jimmy Rowles and Leon Thomas are two of her most cherished memories.

Among her other accomplishments are singing regularly in musicals (including the one-woman musical *Image In The Mirror: The Triptych*), occasionally performing classical concerts, holding several teaching positions (including ones at Corcordia University, McGill University and St. Francis Xavier University), being a regular on Canadian radio and television and traveling all around the world with her jazz group.

"Canada has provided me with a wealth of opportunities to develop as a full artist and educator. Now I would like to take all of my performance strengths to the states—of improvising and singing jazz to opera; also of acting, producing and directing. It seems a little difficult as so much typecasting goes on there, but that is my big goal for the future."

Recommended CDs: Of her recordings, Jeri Brown says, "I think *April In Paris* (Justin Time 92) provides the best example of who I am as a classic jazz artist. *A Timeless Place* (Justin Time 70) captures a haunting and intensive emotional exploration for me in a project almost overwhelmed with ballads by composer and pianist Jimmy Rowles. *Fresh Start* (Justin Time 78) is my crossover CD, which involved more of my originals and set out to make a new statement about me as an improviser and stylist. *Firm Roots* (Justin Time 184) is my laid-back crossover theme CD, which had a lot of fun moments in it." Other easily recommended Jeri Brown sets include *Unfolding—The Peacocks* (Justin Time 45), which is a CD that gained Brown a great deal of recognition, a collaboration with pianist Fred Hersch called *Mirage* (Justin Time 38), *Zaius* (Justin Time 117) with Leon Thomas, *I've Got Your Number* (Justin Time 122), *The Image In The Mirror: The Triptych* (Justin Time 151) and her intriguing tribute to Nina Simone, *Sempre Nina* (Jongleur 300).

Website: www.jeribrown.com

Oscar Brown Jr.
b. October 10, 1926, Chicago, IL; d. May 29, 2005, Chicago, IL

A remarkable multi-talented individual, Oscar Brown Jr. was a jazz singer, a lyricist, an actor, a playwright, a poet, a political activist and a humanitarian. He also put on shows that were entertaining and touching. He lived several lifetimes during his 78 years and always seemed much younger than he was.

Born and raised in Chicago, Brown at 15 acted in Studs Terkel's radio series, *Secret City*. The son of a prominent lawyer, Brown was just 16 when he entered the University of Wisconsin in 1943. It was hoped that he would become a lawyer too, but his main skill was in creative writing, and he was in and out of several universities. During 1944–48 he was on the radio on *Negro Newsfront*, the United States' first black news radio broadcast. He ran for the Illinois legislature in 1948 on the Progressive Party ticket and for Congress as a Republican in 1952 (although he was actually a member of the Communist Party during that period), losing both times. During 1948–50 Brown was back on the radio in a series called *Destination Freedom*. He served two years in the Army, began to compose songs for the fun of it and worked in real estate, advertising, public relations and the civil rights movement.

In 1960 when he was 33, Oscar Brown Jr. signed with Columbia and recorded the classic *Sin And Soul*, immediately becoming famous both in and out of the jazz world. His lyrics to such former instrumentals as Nat Adderley's "Work Song," Mongo Santamaria's "Afro Blue" and Bobby Timmons' "Dat Dere" were introduced as were his originals "Brown Baby," "Bid 'Em In" (which depicts an auctioneer selling a female slave and is quite chilling and realistic), "Signifying Monkey," "But I Was Cool," "Rags And Old Iron" and "Hum Drum Blues." A little later in his career he also wrote the lyrics to "All Blues" and "Jeannine," and much later in life he penned humorous lyrics to "Things Ain't What They Used To Be" that dealt with getting old.

Brown collaborated with Max Roach on "The Freedom Now Suite," which featured Abbey Lincoln, wrote the short-lived play *Kicks And Company* (which should be revived) and performed at major jazz clubs. Other recordings followed, his one-man show "Oscar Brown Jr. Entertains" was a hit in London, and he hosted the legendary jazz series *Jazz Scene USA*. With his warm voice, dramatic yet swinging style, brilliant writing and thoughtful interpretations, he consistently put on memorable performances.

Moving beyond jazz, Oscar Brown Jr. wrote and produced such shows as *Joy '66*, *Summer In The City*, *Lyrics Of Sunshine And Shadow*, *Joy '69*, *Big-Time Buck White*, *Slave Song* and a play that featured gang members, *Opportunity Please Knock*. In the 1970s he taught musical theater and put on works at colleges, starred in Jon Hendricks' *Evolution Of The Blues* and in 1980 hosted the PBS series *From Jump Street: The Story Of Black Music*. He also acted on television. Strangely enough, Brown was absent from records for 20 years, although 1995's *Then And Now* found him still in prime form.

During his later years, Oscar Brown Jr. stayed quite active, sometimes performing with his daughter, Maggie Brown. His life is covered quite well in a documentary by Donnie Betts: *Music Is My Life, Politics My Mistress*.

Recommended CDs: *Sin And Soul…And Then Some* (Columbia/Legacy 64994) is a classic. Also quite worthy are *Tells It Like It Is/In A New Mood* (Collectables 7436), which combines two albums from 1963 to 1964, *Mr. Oscar Brown Jr. Goes To Washington* (Verve 557452), *Finding A New Friend* (Fontana 27549), *Movin' On* (32 Jazz 32129), which includes "One Dime Away From A Hot Dog" and "Ladies' Man," *Fresh* (Warner Bros. 8122736772), the "comeback" album *Then And Now* (Weasel 3334) and *Live Every Minute* (Minor Music 801071).

LPs to Search For: Oscar Brown Jr.'s second recording, *Between Heaven And Hell* (Columbia 1774), is long overdue to be reissued.

Ruth Brown
(Ruth Alston Weston)
b. January 12, 1928, Portsmouth, VA;
d. November 17, 2006, Las Vegas, NV

Many of the singers who were fixtures on the R&B charts of 1947 to 1955 were quite capable of also singing jazz, and some of the best spent the latter part of their lives singing swing tunes, blues and ballads. Ruth Brown started her career at the end of the swing era, and like Dinah Washington (one of her early inspirations), she could sing just about anything.

Brown sang at nightclubs and USO shows while a teenager. In 1948 she was with Lucky Millinder's orchestra for a month and then was discovered by Blanche Calloway, who became her manager. She auditioned successfully for Ahmet Ertegun and Herb Abramson, who immediately signed her to the new Atlantic label. Her recording debut was stalled for a year after she suffered injuries in a car accident, but she made a full recovery. Brown quickly became a hit maker, recording "So Long" with backing by Eddie Condon's Dixieland band, and during the next six years she had big sellers in "Teardrops From My Eyes," "I'll Wait For You," "I Know," "5-10-15 Hours," "Mama, He Treats Your Daughter Mean," "Wild, Wild Young Men," "Oh What A Dream" and "Mambo Baby." Because her hits helped keep Atlantic Records alive in its early days, it became known as "The House That Ruth Built." She was called "Miss Rhythm" by Frankie Laine, and her hits kept on coming into 1960, about five years later than most of her contemporaries.

After leaving Atlantic in 1961, Brown recorded isolated dates for Philips, Mainstream, Solid State (a 1968 set with the Thad Jones/Mel Lewis Orchestra) and Skye, but this was a period of struggle. In order to raise her family, she took many jobs, including working as a maid, driving a school bus and being a teacher. Atlantic, as with the other labels of the 1950s who made millions off of artists, rarely paid royalties, leading to many of the former stars having to scuffle.

In the early 1980s, Ruth Brown started her comeback. She worked as an actress (the television series *Hello Larry* and the film *Hairspray*) and was one of the stars of the Broadway show *Black And Blue* (along with Linda Hopkins and Carrie Smith), which featured her singing vintage blues and standards. Audiences were happy to hear her in prime form. She made several jazz albums for Fantasy, and her career had a renaissance. Brown did not forget her fellow R&B artists, and she founded the Rhythm and Blues Foundation, whose purpose was to right past wrongs and have singers and instrumentalists finally receive the royalties that they were owed. It took nine years for her to recoup the money she should have been paid 30 years earlier. After years of gradually declining health, Ruth Brown passed away in 2006.

Recommended CDs: *Miss Rhythm (Greatest Hits And More)* (Rhino/Atlantic 82061) is an excellent two-CD set covering Ruth Brown's Atlantic years. *Fine Brown Frame* (Koch 51414) teams her with the Thad Jones/Mel Lewis Orchestra. *Black And Blue* (DRG 19001) is the original cast album for the Broadway show. *Have A Good Time* (Fantasy 9661), *Blues On Broadway* (Fantasy 9662), *Fine And Mellow* (Fantasy 9663), *Songs Of My Life* (Fantasy 9665), *R&B = Ruth Brown* (Bullseye Blues 9583) and *Good Day For The Blues* (Bullseye Blues 9613) show how superior and colorful a blues and jazz singer Ruth Brown could be.

Walter Brown
b. August 1916, Dallas, TX; d. June 1956, Lawton, OK

In jazz history, Walter Brown is a mystery figure of whom relatively little is known. He was discovered in his native Dallas by Jay McShann just days before the first recordings by McShann's big band. Since McShann was being pressured by the Decca label to record blues, and Brown had an expressive and likable blues style, it was a perfect match. Their initial April 30, 1941 session yielded hits in "Hootie Blues" and especially "Confessin' The Blues." Brown stayed with McShann for three years. The orchestra's next two sessions feature his vocals on all but two of the dozen selections, including "New Confessin' The Blues," "Hootie's Ignorant Oil" and "The Jumpin' Blues." Charlie Parker was the alto soloist with the band, but Brown was McShann's biggest attraction.

Drug problems and his own popularity resulted in Brown going solo in 1945. He recorded 36 songs as a leader during 1945–49 for the King, Signature, Mercury and Capitol labels and three more songs for Peacock in 1951; all of the music has been reissued on two Classics CDs. Although no hits resulted, Brown's jump blues are generally excellent, and among his sidemen are guitarist Tiny Grimes, tenor-saxophonist Ben Webster and his old boss Jay McShann.

Walter Brown opened up a nightclub in Lawton, Oklahoma, in the early 1950s, but had a low profile during the five years that preceded his death in 1956 at age 39 from drugs. If he had had his life together, he could have had a much longer career in the tradition of Jimmy Witherspoon and Big Joe Turner.

Recommended CDs: All of Walter Brown's solo recordings are on *1945–1947* (Classics 5010) and *1947–1951* (Classics 5038). His main recordings with Jay McShann are on the pianist's *Blues From Kansas City* (GRP/Decca 614).

Beryl Bryden
b. May 11, 1920, Norwich, England;
d. July 14, 1998, London, England

A beloved figure in the British trad jazz scene, Beryl Bryden seemed to sing with every major artist in that genre during the 1950s and '60s. As a jazz fan, she organized the Norwich Rhythm Club in 1939. After moving to Cambridge in 1942, she worked days as a typist and at nights sang and played washboard with local groups. Bryden continued in that vein after settling in London, even as she guested regularly with George Webb's Dixielanders starting in 1945, John Haim's Jelly Roll Kings (1948), Freddy Randall and Alex Welsh, in addition to leading her own Washboard Wonders and Backroom Boys.

In 1953 Bryden finally took the plunge and became a full-time jazz singer. She went on many tours of the European continent and appeared with the who's who of trad jazz, including Fatty George, Monty Sunshine, Lonnie Donegan (playing washboard on his hit recording of "Rock Island Line"), Humphrey Lyttelton, Chris Barber, Cy Laurie, the Dutch

Swing College Band, the Dixieland Pipers, the Downtown Jazz Band, Diz Disley, Kenny Ball, Rod Mason, Digby Fairweather and Keith Nichols, plus her own groups. A cheerful and very musical force, Bryden recorded relatively little as a leader, not making her debut until 1962.

Bryden, who was also a skillful photographer, did not perform in the United States until the 1970s, although she ended up making several successful overseas trips. Audiences loved her mixture of classic jazz, blues and vaudeville numbers, and Ella Fitzgerald called her "Britain's Queen of the Blues." Although she announced that she was retiring in the early 1980s, Beryl Bryden continued performing on a part-time basis until just weeks before her death from cancer in 1998 at the age of 78.

Recommended CDs: *Two Moods Of Beryl Bryden* (Audiophile 113) from 1975, which co-features Bud Freeman on tenor, gives listeners an excellent sampling of her singing talents and infectious spirit.

Jeanie Bryson
b. March 10, 1958, New York, NY

A cool-toned and re-strained singer with a small but very effective voice, Jeanie Bryson's style is at times a little reminiscent of Peggy Lee and Nancy Wilson. The daughter of song-writer Connie Bryson and Dizzy Gillespie, she was raised by her mother. "I grew up around people who were great apprecia-tors of music, as well as being musicians. In my mom's family, we had a songwriter, a drummer and vibist, a singer, a pianist, a classical guitarist, and an organ player. During holidays when we were all together, my family would play music. It was as natural as breathing. I remember assuming for a long time that this was what everybody's family did at Christmas.

"I often had the chance to see my father's band play when-ever he was in town, which was always a thrill as a small child, and eventually became one of the inspirations for me to focus on music and make it what I chose to do as my life's work. In college, I sang quite a bit at coffee houses and open mic nights. I also often recorded demos for my mom of the tunes she was composing."

Bryson played piano from age five and flute and piccolo starting in junior high school. She studied anthropology and ethnomusicology at Livingston College, a division of Rutgers University. One of her teachers was pianist Kenny Barron, who influenced her to explore jazz. "My very first gigs were with my mom (playing piano) and my husband (playing drums)—right after college. We had a little band, playing mostly the pop mu-sic of the day and standards, and gigged quite a bit locally for about a year. It was a great way to start in the business; I felt safe with my family right beside me, and I learned loads of great tunes. After a while my mother told me I'd better find a better piano player if I really wanted to do this for a living. I started working with some of the young musicians I went to Livingston College with and began to sing with more of a jazz sensibility."

Although she picked up plenty of experience performing, Jeanie Bryson did not make her first recording until January 1993, a couple weeks after Dizzy Gillespie's death. Since that time she has recorded several rewarding sets for the Telarc label, was part of Terence Blanchard's *Billie Holiday Songbook* project (touring with the trumpeter) and has worked frequently in the New York area. "I have so much fun when I sing—it's a joy to be making music that you love. The creative flow that I feel from everyone on stage, having that close connection with each other, is a high."

Recommended CDs: The year 1993's *I Love Being Here With You* (Telarc 83336) was a fine debut for Bryson, mostly fea-turing the singer on standards along with an all-star group that included Kenny Barron. *Tonight I Need You So* (Telarc 83348) ranges from some so-so pop to memorable renditions of "Simple Song," "Honeysuckle Rose" and "Skydive." *Some Cats Know* (Telarc 83381) is a very effective interpretation of songs either written by or associated with Peggy Lee. *Deja Blue* (Koch 7881) from 2000 features Jeanie Bryson on bluesy material, including the title cut (written by her mother), some pop and rock tunes and a couple of jazz standards, including a medley of Gillespie's "Con Alma" and "Am I Blue."

Website: www.jeaniebryson.com

Michael Bublé
b. September 9, 1975, Burnaby, BC, Canada

When Michael Bublé burst upon the scene in 2003, for many it seemed to signify the return of "good music," similar to Harry Connick Jr.'s emergence two de-cades earlier. More of a crooner than a jazz singer, Bublé loves to swing both older stan-dards and new songs in a manner not that dissimilar from Tony Bennett. However, his success was not exactly overnight.

Growing up in Canada, he remembers, "Jazz was every-where. I found it on *Sesame Street*, in restaurants, TV com-mercials and Bing Crosby's 'White Christmas' record. My earliest experiences were lip-synching to Louis Prima and trying to sing Tony Bennett songs like 'I Left My Heart In San Francisco' and 'I Wanna Be Around.' Bublé was introduced to jazz and swing through his grandfather, who had a large record collection and suggested that he learn to sing standards. "I knew I was going to be an entertainer from the time I was conscious enough to be entertained. Some of my inspirations were Tony Bennett, Dean Martin, Harry Connick, Jr., Frank Sinatra, Count Basie, Louis Prima, Bobby Darin, Ella Fitzger-ald and Sarah Vaughan."

For a time, Bublé sang in a variety of settings without gaining much attention, including appearing as Elvis in a road show and singing in the musical revue *Forever Swing*. He recorded a pair of independent albums but was still largely an unknown in 2000 when he was introduced to producer David Foster, who signed him to his company 143 Records. His al-bum *Michael Bublé* was released in 2003 and was a major hit, featuring the type of standards that Bobby Darin (whom Bublé resembled musically at the time) and Frank Sinatra would have loved to record. Since then Michael Bublé has become a household name and symbolized the modern crooner on such albums as *Come Fly With Me* and *It's Time*.

"My future musical goal is to continue to introduce jazz and standards to young people everywhere and keep the greatest style of music in the world alive. It's not even completely about jazz; it's about the songs, the melodies and the lyrics."

Recommended CDs: *Michael Bublé* (143/Reprise 48376) was the breakthrough recording for Bublé, and it is easy to see why. His versions of such songs as "Moon Dance," "Fever," "The Way You Look Tonight" and particularly "Sway" are enthusiastic, musical, slyly sensual and swinging. Also highly recommended is *It's Time* (143/Reprise 48946), his second studio CD. Bublé sounds comfortable with a wide variety of standards, including "A Foggy Day," "You Don't Love Me," "The More I See You" and even the Beatles' "Can't Buy Me Love." *Come Fly With Me* (Warner Bros. 48683) is available in both CD and DVD versions, with the former being preferable since the editing of the latter is extremely jarring. The performances are taken from concerts during Bublé's 2003 tours, highlighted by "Nice And Easy" and "Mack The Knife" but not all that significant since it repeats some of the songs (though in different versions) from *Come Fly With Me. Caught In The Act* (Reprise 49444) is a more worthwhile CD/DVD combination of live remakes of many of Bublé's recordings. Michael Bublé also recorded a five-song EP of straightforward Christmas songs, *Let It Snow* (Reprise 48599), that was later repackaged with his debut disc and reissued as a two-CD set, *Christmas* (Warner/Elektra 91529). Of interest only for completists is *Totally Bublé* (DRG 91418), which is taken from the soundtrack of *Legally Blonde*, was not sanctioned by the singer and is a lesser effort, though Bublé sounds fine on the material that was written for the movie.

Website: www.michaelbuble.com

Katie Bull
b. New York, NY

A consistently intriguing singer, Katie Bull can give listeners a false security by singing quite conventionally before suddenly improvising much more freely, pushing both herself and the other musicians.

The daughter of a jazz pianist-dancer, she grew up in the jazz scene, accompanying her father to gigs and jam sessions. During a period when they lived in upstate New York, she met drummer Lou Grassi and was affected by seeing Keith Jarrett improvising during a solo piano concert. Back in Manhattan, she sang standards at a club on a weekly basis when she was 15. She met Jay Clayton and Sheila Jordan, both of whom became friends and inspirations.

Since college Kate Bull has worked as a voice teacher, co-artistic director of the Improvisational Arts Ensembles, Inc. (where she writes, directs and performs with the Bull Family Orchestra) and has performed regularly in clubs. Thus far she has recorded four stimulating albums that are utterly unpredictable.

Recommended CDs: *Conversations With The Jokers* (Corn Hill Indie) was Kate Bull's debut in 2001, but it never finds her playing it safe, even when singing standards. *Love Spook* (Corn Hill Indie) is full of wit and eccentric moments along with impressive singing, while *Cup Of Joe, No Bull* (Corn Hill Indie) finds her taking wild chances on standards and originals in duets with bassist Joe Fonda, and *The Story So Far* (Corn Hill Indie) finds the singer stretching herself even more; the release includes a short and eccentric DVD.

Website: www.katiebull.com

Lynn Bush
(Mary Lynn Pickett)
b. October 22, 1952, Wichita, KS

"I think of myself as a storyteller," says Lynn Bush. "It is the telling of the story that counts and music is the method. Jazz is the perfect vehicle for the journey." Working in radio and other areas of the music business, Lynn Bush took a long time before she recorded her debut album, *Still Life*.

"I literally began singing on my grandfather's knee. He loved to sing his favorite Tin Pan Alley tunes to me in the evenings when I was very young. I have been singing ever since for the sheer pleasure of singing." Lynn Bush first performed professionally as a backup singer with an R&B band in Oklahoma City in 1971 and began seriously performing jazz a few years later at cocktail lounges, piano bars and small clubs. She studied piano, classical vocal techniques and audio production at the University of Central Oklahoma (1980–84) but says that she has gained most of her jazz training by working with jazz musicians. Before moving to Seattle, a couple of the high points of her career included sitting in with Max Roach's quartet in 1983 and guesting with pianist Michael Wolff. She was a longtime radio producer on KCSC-FM in addition to performing whenever she could.

"Being a professional singer was an occupational hazard of wanting to play the music. I never really thought about it as a career; it has always been my passion. It is a very emotional experience for me and not until recently did I feel that being successful on a business level was a serious possibility. As a single parent in Oklahoma, it didn't seem realistic. However, my relocation to the West in 1998 changed my perspective on this. My relocation to Seattle had a profound impact on my career. My access to musicians, the vitality of the jazz community and the support of jazz as art and my music in particular is a daily inspiration."

Since moving to Seattle, Lynn Bush has often teamed up with the New Stories Trio, including for her recording *Still Life*, was nominated by Earshot Jazz in 2004 as jazz vocalist of the year and has maintained an increasingly higher profile. "My one firm goal is to sing for the rest of my life." One hopes that she will also record much more often in the future.

Recommended CD: *Still Life* (Origin 82394) shows off Lynn Bush's warm voice and storytelling skills at their best.

Donna Byrne
(Donna Marie Wood)
b. March 2, 1950, Everett, MA

Donna Byrne is a fine swing-oriented singer based in Massachusetts. "I love the interactive nature of this music, the communication between myself and instrumentalists that takes place on a bandstand." She remembers being introduced to jazz "by attending dancing school for many years, watching the *Ed Sullivan Show* and by sitting in with Dave McKenna and gaining his approval and support. That sent me in the direction of jazz."

Byrne attended the Massachusetts College of Art as a fine arts major and raised three children. It was not until she was 26 that she decided to definitely become a jazz singer. After being hired by a pianist in Cape Cod, she was introduced to Dave McKenna and Dick Johnson who helped her ultimately become an important part of the New England jazz scene. "Dave and all the guys were great to me and offered me a tremendous amount of encouragement and support." Most influenced by Carmen McRae and Irene Kral, she considers her most important musical associations to be with Dave McKenna, guitarist Gray Sargent, trumpeter-educator Herb Pomeroy, clarinetists Dick Johnson and John LaPorta, and her husband, bassist Marshall Wood. In addition to working locally with combos and occasionally touring, she visited Hawaii a few times as the singer with the Benny Goodman Tribute Orchestra.

Recommended CDs: Donna Byrne considers her personal favorites to be *Don't Dream Of Anybody But Me* (Ol' Socks 8753) and *Licensed To Thrill* (Challenge 73230). She can also be heard in good form on her out-of-print debut, *Sweet And Lovely* (Ol' Socks 001) from 1989, *It Was Me* (Daring 3022), *Byrnin'* (Ol' Socks 3250), *All The Lonely People* (Ol' Socks 01988) and on Herb Pomeroy's *Walking On Air* (Arbors 19176).

Website: www.aahome.com/donna

Ann Hampton Callaway
b. May 30, 1958, Chicago, IL

Ann Hampton Callaway gained her original fame as a cabaret singer, but jazz has always been a strong interest of hers. Her career during the past decade has become much more jazz-oriented. An exciting and multi-faceted entertainer, Callaway puts on colorful shows that display her wide range, wit (she can do a perfect imitation of Sarah Vaughan tearing apart "Misty") and versatility.

She is the daughter of journalist John Callaway and vocal coach Shirley Callaway and the sister of cabaret singer Liz Callaway. "My father had a great record collection. He always scraped money together to bring home records by Miles, Ella, Sarah, Dizzy, Billie, you name it. I heard these artists as my late night lullaby when I was a baby and they were the soundtracks of my entire childhood. For my sixth grade graduation present I received Bill Evans' *Alone*. I was a lucky kid.

"My earliest experiences singing were with my mother on our upright piano, harmonizing on Gershwin, Rodgers, Porter and Berlin. I didn't know that we were an unusual family. I thought everyone sang and jammed and made up songs." She studied piano and was given classical voice lessons but was attracted much more to popular music. "I did lots of music at my high school, majored in acting, quit college after serving two years at University of Illinois (1976–78), moved to New York, and three days later got my first singing job at a piano bar on the east side called Sharma's. A year later I was headlining at the Algonquin."

Callaway has not looked back ever since. As a lyricist and songwriter, she had great success writing "The Nanny Named Fran" for the CBS sitcom *The Nanny*. Three of her songs have been recorded by Barbra Streisand (she has thus far written over 250 originals), she won a Tony nomination for starring in the Broadway hit musical *Swing*, and she has worked constantly in the worlds of both jazz and cabaret. Callaway is equally proud of performing live in shows with Liza Minnelli, Michael Feinstein, Margaret Whiting, Amanda McBroom and her sister Liz Callaway (in *Sibling Revelry*) as she is appearing with Wynton Marsalis, Kenny Barron, Cyrus Chestnut, Christian McBride, Bill Charlap, Randy Brecker and Benny Green. In addition to regularly working with a trio and switching to the piano during an improv song that uses words shouted out by the audience, she appears occasionally with orchestras and performs all over the world. In recent times Callaway appeared in the Matt Damon film *The Good Shepherd*, singing "Come Rain Or Come Shine." She is also busy as an educator, inspiring younger singers.

For the future, Ann Hampton Callaway says, "I want to create a body of work as a songwriter that maintains the high standards I hold from loving the great songwriters before me. I want to do more Broadway (both performance and writing) and also write and sing for film and television. I want to host my own talk-variety show called *The Ann Hampton Callaway Show* where I would interview great artists from jazz, theater and pop. And I want to continue being one of the 'keepers of the flame' for jazz, standards and quality music."

Recommended CDs: Although she was impressive from the start of her career, recording cabaret songbooks for the Painted Smiles label, in exploring Ann Hampton Callaway's recordings, it is advisable to start with her most recent sets first since they display her growth and her jazz skills the best. Taken in chronological order, *Ann Hampton Callaway* (DRG 91411), *Bring Back Romance* (DRG 91417), the cabaret-oriented *Sibling Revelry* (DRG 91443) with sister Liz, *To Ella With Love* (After 9 306), *After Ours* (Denon 18042), *Easy Living* (After 9 8934), *Signature* (After 9 4227), *Slow* (Shanachie 5118) and especially *Blues In The Night* (Telarc 83641), which includes "Hip To Be Happy" and "The 'I'm Too White To Sing The Blues' Blues," are all easily recommended.

Website: www.annhamptoncallaway.com

Blanche Calloway
b. February 9, 1902, Baltimore, MD;
d. December 16, 1978, Baltimore, MD

Due to being overshadowed by her younger brother Cab and having a relatively brief career, Blanche Calloway has been largely forgotten. However, she was an exciting performer, an excellent singer and probably the first female to lead a full-time big band.

Growing up in Baltimore, Calloway's childhood idols were Gertrude Saunders and Florence Mills. Seeing them perform inspired her to go into show business. For a little while Calloway studied music at Morgan State College, but she soon dropped out to perform in local revues, nightclubs and stage shows as a singer and a dancer. In 1923 she joined the touring company of the Eubie Blake/Noble Sissle show *Shuffle Along*. Two years later she made her recording debut, cutting two numbers ("Lazy Women's Blues" and "Lonesome Lovesick") while accompanied by cornetist Louis Armstrong and pianist Richard M. Jones. But those performances only hinted at what she could do.

Calloway toured with James P. Johnson's show *Plantation Days* and, when it closed in Chicago in 1927, she stayed in town for a few years, working in nightclubs. During this period her brother Cab (five years her junior) was studying as a pre-law student at Crane College while really wanting to be a performer. Blanche taught him all about how to be an entertainer and how to put a song over to an audience; he later thanked her several times in print.

In 1931, about the time that Cab was just becoming a hit, Blanche Calloway was at her peak. She was the headliner at Philadelphia's Pearl Theater when Andy Kirk's orchestra was also on the bill. She was so popular that Kirk asked her to join his band and go on tour across country as a special added attraction. When they returned to Philadelphia, Blanche and the Pearl's manager schemed to have her take over the band. However, Kirk got wind of the idea and soon left town, only losing trumpeters Edgar "Puddinghead" Battle (who was having a relationship with Blanche) and Clarence Smith. Battle got six members of Jap Allen's band (including the young tenor Ben Webster) to join the new big band, filling in the other spots with local players.

Blanche had an opportunity to record a session with Kirk's orchestra (under the title of Blanche Calloway and Her Joy Boys), including her trademark song "I Need Lovin'." With her own big band (which included Webster for a few months, pianist Clyde Hart and drummer Cozy Cole) she waxed such performances as "Just A Crazy Song," "Make Me Know It" and her theme song "Growlin' Dan." While the orchestra is good, it is Calloway's extroverted, flamboyant, sensual and aggressive singing that makes these selections so memorable.

The Blanche Calloway Orchestra did well for a time, touring the country and working often at the Lafayette Theater and the Harlem Opera House. However, there were only two record dates after 1931: four songs including remakes of "Growlin' Dan" and "I Need Lovin'" in 1934 and four songs (three of which were instrumentals) in 1935. There seemed to only be room for one Calloway in the music business. Blanche's band struggled for several years before she was forced to declare bankruptcy in September 1938 and break up the orchestra.

Although she never recorded again, Blanche Calloway still had several careers ahead of her. She worked as a solo act in clubs and theaters and led a short-lived all-female band in 1940. In 1944 she became semi-retired, moved to Philadelphia and soon became busy as a political leader, being involved in many social organizations. In the early 1950s, Calloway managed an after-hours club in Washington, D.C., called the Crystle Caverns, discovered Ruth Brown, and helped the young singer get started. In the 1960s she worked as a disc jockey and a programming director for a Miami radio station. And before she died of cancer in 1978, she had success founding and running a mail order company (Afram House Inc.) that specialized in cosmetics.

Recommended CDs: *1925–1935* (Classics 783) has all of Blanche Calloway's recordings (25 songs) except for three numbers (two with her vocals) from March 2, 1931 with Andy Kirk's orchestra that have been released on a Classics set under Kirk's name.

Cab Calloway
(Cabell Calloway)
b. December 25, 1907, Rochester, NY;
d. November 18, 1994, Hockessin, DE

Cab Calloway, one of the truly great entertainers, was such a colorful showman, conductor and bandleader that his singing was often underrated. His shows at the Cotton Club, which are hinted at in some of his film appearances of the 1930s, featured the constantly moving Calloway conducting wildly and singing crazy call and response refrains with his musicians.

The younger brother of singer Blanche Calloway, Cab grew up in Baltimore and for a time attended law school. He became so impressed with his sister's lifestyle that he quit school to try to make it as a singer and dancer. He learned about show business from Blanche while living in Chicago, appeared in the revue *Plantation Days*, and in 1928 worked at the Sunset Café as the emcee and substitute drummer although he was never really a musician. In 1929 Calloway took over leadership of a group called the Alabamians, and brought them to New York to appear at the Savoy Ballroom. However, the band was not strong enough to make it in the Big Apple and soon broke up. Calloway appeared in the show *Hot Chocolates*, a production that featured Louis Armstrong and had a score by Fats Waller and lyricist Andy Razaf.

Calloway had much better luck with his next group, the Missourians, a hot jazz combo that recorded three exciting record dates during 1929–30, and was on the brink of breaking up due to the Depression. Calloway took over the ten-piece band, renamed it the Cab Calloway Orchestra and added a third trumpeter. Cab made his first recordings on July 24, 1930, a session that included a spectacular version of "St. Louis Blues." Four record sessions in 1930 resulted in nine titles, highlighted by "Some Of These Days," "St. James Infirmary" and a version of "Nobody's Sweetheart" on which he makes up his own melody as he goes along. Calloway was already quite recognizable, extroverted and taking wild chances in his singing while backed by an excellent band.

1931 was the year that Cab Calloway became famous. In February, his orchestra became the house band at the Cotton Club, succeeding Duke Ellington. The regular radio broadcasts led to Calloway becoming nationally famous within a short time. On March 3 he recorded the original version of "Minnie The Moocher," his most famous song. Few listeners knew that he was singing about opium use or had much of an idea what the lyrics were about. The "hi-de-ho" call and response with the band became his trademark and made him into a sensation. Other songs in a similar fashion, some of which deal with the further adventures of Minnie and Smoky Joe, followed including "Kickin' The Gong Around," "Minnie The Moocher's Wedding Day," "You Gotta Hi-De-Ho To Get Along With Me," "Zaz Zuh Zaz," "Keep That Hi-De-Hi In Your Soul," "The Hi-De-Ho Miracle Man," "Hi-De-Ho Romeo" and "The Ghost Of Smoky Joe."

Calloway combined together the influence of Louis Armstrong (particularly his scatting), Al Jolson, opera singers,

Bing Crosby and minstrel shows in creating an eternally hip character. Sometimes his singing went over-the-top in joyous fashion and at other times it was just plain silly. Jazz critics never really knew where to place him and tended to overlook him altogether even though in reality he was one of the top jazz singers of the 1930s and '40s, and was the only jazz vocalist (beyond Bob Crosby who really was not much of a jazz singer) to lead a successful swing big band during the period. Calloway could be touching on ballads while his often-bizarre jive talk led the way to Slim Gaillard.

Calloway also headed a major jazz orchestra even though the musicians' contributions were secondary to that of the leader. None of the alumni of the Missourians became household names although they were all effective players. Turnover resulted in such musicians as pianist Bennie Payne (who was with Cab for many years), Doc Cheatham (who had the role of a non-soloing lead trumpeter), trumpeter Shad Collins and tenor-saxophonist Ben Webster spending time with the band. In 1939 Calloway's orchestra included the young trumpeter Dizzy Gillespie, Chu Berry as the tenor soloist and musical director, and an impressive rhythm section comprised of Payne, rhythm guitarist Danny Barker, bassist Milt Hinton and drummer Cozy Cole. Later stars included trumpeter Jonah Jones, trombonist Tyree Glenn and Ike Quebec on tenor.

For black musicians in the 1930s who did not mind Calloway's gyrations and showboating, playing in the Calloway Orchestra was one of the best jobs in the profession. The musicians were well paid, had fringe benefits and enjoyed regular vacations. All they had to do was show up on time, play flawlessly and look like they were enjoying themselves onstage.

Calloway kept up a busy schedule of nightclub appearances, regular radio broadcasts and occasional film work (including 1943's *Stormy Weather*) through the mid-1940s. The end of the big band era and the rise of bebop (which he brilliantly satirized in his hilarious "I Beeped When I Should Have Bopped" in 1949) resulted in him reluctantly breaking up his big band in April 1948. For a time Calloway toured with a sextet which by 1950 was down to a quartet that included Jonah Jones and Milt Hinton. In 1952 he gave up the band altogether and played the role of "Sportin' Life" in George Gershwin's *Porgy And Bess* for two years. Getting the role was quite fitting since Gershwin had originally based the part on Calloway's personality. From the mid-1950s until his death in 1994, Cab Calloway remained a famous celebrity who performed in public whenever the mood struck him. An inspiration for the Retro Swing movement of the 1990s, Cab was always happy to perform "Minnie The Moocher" for his fans.

Recommended CDs: All of Calloway's recordings during his main years have been made available by the French Classics series on *1930–1931* (Classics 516), *1931–1932* (Classics 526), *1932* (Classics 537), *1932–1934* (Classics 544), *1934–1937* (Classics 554), *1937–1938* (Classics 568), *1938–1939* (Classics 576), *1939–1940* (Classics 595), *1940* (Classics 614), *1940–1941* (Classics 629), *1941–1942* (Classics 682), *1942–1947* (Classics 996) and *1949–1955* (Classics 1287). It may seem excessive to recommend all 13 CDs, but each set has plenty of enjoyable gems. Start with *1930–1931*.

Mike Campbell

b. February 21, 1944, Hollywood, CA

Known primarily as a well-respected vocal instructor in the Los Angeles area, Mike Campbell is also an underrated singer whose warm voice is at its best on ballads. The son of a drummer,

dancer and actor who introduced him to jazz, "I started singing when I graduated high school. My first 'gig' was my brother's five-year high school reunion. My brother also got me an audition at Capitol Records for Dave Cavanaugh. He didn't sign me, but I caught the disease." A more successful audition resulted in Campbell joining the Doodletown Pipers, a middle-of-the-road pop group that recorded three albums for Epic, appeared on the *Ed Sullivan Show* six times, had their own television summer show titled *Our Place* and were featured on a series of TV specials called *Here Come The Doodletown Pipers*. The group also guested on many television shows, played 20–25 weeks a year in Las Vegas and toured the United States and Canada.

After going out on his own, Campbell worked as a single, often utilizing pianist Tom Garvin. Since that time, Campbell has been the department head of the Vocal Institute of Technology (following ten years as the chairman of the vocal department of the Grove School of Music), conducted a countless number of vocal clinics, and taught in the Los Angeles area. He also plays guitar (one of his teachers was Ted Greene) and has worked on jingles and movie soundtracks, taking bit parts in films and on television.

"Some of the high points of my career have been performing with Nancy Wilson at the Greek Theater, Count Basie and his band with Quincy Jones conducting on the NBC TV special *Rodgers And Hart Today*, with Ella Fitzgerald on the *Ed Sullivan Show*, opening for Sarah Vaughan and performing with Frank Sinatra. Just being able to make a living making music is the real high point of my life."

Recommended CDs: *One On One* (Audiophile 259) has Campbell in a trio with pianist Tom Garvin and bassist John Heard from 1982 to 1985, while *Loving Friends* (Audiophile 279) from 1994 teams Campbell with pianist Loonis McGloohan in a quartet/quintet that sometimes includes guitarist Gene Bertoncini. Those two are the ones to acquire first although *Easy Chair Jazz* (Audiophile 272), *My Romance* (Audiophile 287) and *Let's Get Away From It All* (Audiophile 303) are also enjoyable, featuring Campbell's subtle improvising and swinging.

LPs to Search For: Mike Campbell's first two solo recordings, *Secret Fantasy* (Palo Alto 8020) and *Blackberry Winter* (I.T.I. 72959), are scarce but worthy.

Website: www.members.aol.com/mcampbell4

Ana Caram
(Ana Lucia Ribeiro Caram)
b. October 1, 1958, Presidente Prudente, São Paulo, Brazil

A top jazz and samba singer from Brazil, Ana Caram has been impressing American audiences ever since she began recording for Chesky.

Born in São Paulo, she remembers, "Since I was a little child, I used to listen to my uncle and his friends playing jazz at home on the weekends. I started to sing at school parties and festivals very early. I

recorded my first jingle when I was thirteen." She studied flute and guitar in addition to earning a degree in composition and conducting from São Paulo University.

Moving to Rio, she met Antonio Carlos Jobim who was impressed by her and became an important mentor. After gaining a strong reputation in Brazil, Caram appeared at the Sea Jazz Festival in Finland, met Paquito D'Rivera and was invited to sing with his band at Carnegie Hall at the 1989 JVC Jazz Festival. A representative from the Chesky audience was in the audience and she was immediately signed to the label. She has recorded and toured regularly ever since, being one of the most significant Brazilian jazz singers on the scene during the past 20 years.

Recommended CDs: *Rio After Dark* (Chesky 28), *Amazonia* (Chesky 45), *The Other Side Of Jobim* (Chesky 73), *Maracana* (Chesky 104), *Bossa Nova* (Chesky 129), *Postcards From Rio* (Chesky 182), *Blue Bossa* (Chesky 219) and *Hollywood Rio* (Chesky 276) are all quite consistent, featuring Ana Caram's voice and acoustic guitar with musicians who are sympathetic to Brazilian music. *Sunflower Time* (Mercury 5322342) from 1996 is a departure, being more pop-oriented although it still has its pleasing moments.

Website: www.anacaram.com.br

Hoagy Carmichael
(Howard Hoagland Carmichael)
b. November 11, 1899, Bloomington, IN;
d. December 27, 1981, Palm Springs, CA

While several of the great American songwriters of the 1930s recorded as vocalists (including Harold Arlen and Cole Porter), Hoagy Carmichael had a much more extensive performance career. Carmichael, who played piano reasonably well, tended to sing flat but his likable personality and delivery (not to mention brilliance as a writer) overcame his technical faults. He paved the way for other piano-playing jazz-inspired singer/songwriters such as Dave Frishberg, Bob Dorough, Blossom Dearie and Mose Allison.

It is doubtful if Hoagy Carmichael ever thought of himself as a great singer, though he loved to perform. In his early days he was more interested in playing hot jazz on piano, trying to be a cornetist and writing songs. He reluctantly studied to be a lawyer and attended Indiana University but found time to play piano in Indianapolis at dances while still in school, sometimes heading a group called Carmichael's Collegians. Bix Beiderbecke became a good friend by 1924 and Bix with the Wolverines was the first to record a Carmichael composition, the Dixieland standard "Riverboat Shuffle."

Even though he earned a law degree in 1926, Carmichael found the pull of music to be irresistible. He recorded with Hitch's Happy Harmonists in 1925, worked a bit with Jean Goldkette in 1927, led his first two record dates that year (including an uptempo instrumental version of his new song "Star Dust") and recorded "Washboard Blues" with Paul

Whiteman, both singing and playing piano on the latter. Other record dates of 1927–30 found him leading bands mostly filled with regional musicians but on a couple occasions utilizing musicians the caliber of Bubber Miley, Tommy Dorsey, Benny Goodman, Bud Freeman, Joe Venuti, Eddie Lang, Gene Krupa, Jack Teagarden, Jimmy Dorsey and Bix. Among the compositions that he debuted during this period were "Rockin' Chair," "Georgia On My Mind" and "Up The Lazy River."

Carmichael, who moved to New York from Indiana in 1929, at first worked for a brokerage house during the day while he wrote songs at night. But by the time he and lyricist Johnny Mercer collaborated on "Lazy Bones" in 1933, there was no longer a need for a day job. "Star Dust" had been given lyrics by Mitchell Parrish and its tempo slowed down. The success of that song alone would have made him famous.

In 1936 Carmichael moved to Hollywood where he wrote music for films and, after a successful appearance in the 1937 film *Topper*, was constantly offered work as an actor. Carmichael invariably played a wisecracking pianist who sang and offered homespun advice, usually being the best friend of the lead. He appeared in 14 films during 1937–54 with some of his best appearances being in *To Have And Have Not* (1942), *The Best Years Of Our Lives* (1946) and *Young Man With A Horn* (1950), with the latter being the most musical of his films. Along the way he wrote such songs as "Two Sleepy People," "Small Fry," "Heart And Soul," "Ole Buttermilk Sky," "Skylark," "The Nearness Of You," "New Orleans," "Baltimore Oriole" and "In The Cool, Cool, Cool Of The Evening."

In addition to his film work, Carmichael had a regular series on the radio for years and he recorded as a singer-pianist including six songs in 1942 as the leader of a trio and a few isolated items during 1946–49. In 1956 he recorded one of his finest sessions, *Hoagy Sings Carmichael*. Backed by an 11-piece West Coast jazz group arranged by Johnny Mandel and including altoist Art Pepper and trumpeter Harry "Sweets" Edison, Carmichael sounds in prime form singing ten of his songs. It is a pity that there were no further projects like that one. With the change in popular music, by the mid-1950s Carmichael was in less demand than he had been in 25 years.

The 1960s and '70s were a slow and frustrating final period for Carmichael, whose music and talents were considered out-of-date. Though he was never forgotten, "Georgia On My Mind" became Ray Charles' signature song and "Star Dust" remained famous, Hoagy Carmichael was only heard from on an occasional basis during the final two decades before his death in 1981.

Recommended CDs: The ten-CD imported set *Hoagy Carmichael In Person 1925–1955* (Avid 150) has virtually everything that Carmichael recorded before his lone Pacific Jazz album, including his studio recordings as a leader and sideman, radio broadcasts, radio transcriptions and quite a bit of previously unissued material. The four-CD set, *The First Of The Singer Songwriters* (JSP 918), which was compiled by Richard Sudhalter, covers the high points of Hoagy Carmichael's career from 1924 to 1946. Although he is not on every one of the 101 selections, virtually all of his most significant recordings from that 23-year period are included along with other definitive versions of his compositions. *Stardust, And Much More* (Bluebird 8333) includes some of the same numbers along with a few additional tunes, *Mr. Music Master* (Naxos 25742) contains some rarities from the 1940s and *Hoagy Sings Carmichael* (Pacific Jazz 46862) is his classic 1956 album.

Thelma Carpenter

b. January 15, 1922, Brooklyn, NY; d. May 14, 1997, New York, NY

Thelma Carpenter is best remembered in jazz for her stint with the Count Basie Orchestra, but that was only one short period in a 70-year career in show business. When she was five, she debuted on the *Kiddies' Hour* radio show. Six years later she had her own radio show and was performing with her childhood friend pianist Hazel Scott around New York City. At 16 Carpenter won an amateur night at the Apollo, and succeeded Maxine Sullivan at the Onyx Club on 52nd Street. John Hammond liked what he heard and got her a job singing with Teddy Wilson's short-lived big band; she recorded three songs with Wilson. In 1940 she was in Coleman Hawkins' equally brief orchestra, recording "He's Funny That Way." After that band broke up, she worked in various clubs on 52nd Street, further developing her style, which was influenced by Ethel Waters and Mabel Mercer but already quite original, full of her own sauciness and soul.

After appearing on Broadway in the Bill Robinson show *Memphis Bound*, Carpenter replaced Helen Humes with the Count Basie Orchestra. During her two years with Basie (1943–45), which unfortunately was mostly dominated by a musicians' recording strike, she only recorded one commercial side ("I Didn't Know About You") but can be heard on several radio broadcasts. Leaving Basie, she was a regular on the Eddie Cantor radio show and had a successful solo career. Carpenter recorded for the Majestic label during 1945–46 (including "Hurry Home," "Can't Help Lovin' That Man" and "American Lullaby") and a few selections for Musicraft and Columbia, was in the 1952 revival of *Shuffle Along* and was popular in Paris and Rome in the 1950s. After Elvis Presley hit it big with "Are You Lonesome Tonight," she recorded "Yes, I'm Lonesome Tonight," which became a minor hit.

Despite her successes (including a 1963 album for Coral that gained good reviews if low sales), Carpenter was always in and out of the music world, having such day jobs as running a coat-check concession in a restaurant, working as a file clerk and selling cigarettes at a newsstand. She kept her spirits high and worked when she could in New York clubs, was Pearl Bailey's understudy in *Hello, Dolly!* (a role which she eventually took over), was on the short-lived television series *Barefoot In The Park*, appeared in the filmed version of *The Wiz* and was cast as the mother of Gregory and Maurice Hines in *The Cotton Club*. While her recordings are mostly unavailable, an Audiophile CD has her appearance on Alec Wilder's radio show *American Popular Songs* in 1975 (she was Wilder's first guest) plus an unreleased duo date with pianist Ellis Larkins from 1970. Thelma Carpenter packed a lot of life into her 75 years.

Recommended CDs: *A Souvenir* (Audiophile 111) features Thelma Carpenter at the ages of 48 and 53 still sounding youthful and full of enthusiasm.

LPs to Search For: Thelma Carpenter did not record all that often despite her talents. 1963's *Thinking Of You Tonight* (Coral 57433) is well worth acquiring if it can be found.

Helen Carr

b. 1922 or 1924, Salt Lake City, UT; d. 1960

Helen Carr had a short life, only recorded on a few occasions, and many of the details of her existence are quite sketchy. However, she made a strong impression upon those lucky enough to hear her.

She wanted to be a singer from the time she was a child and she succeeded, if only for a relatively brief number of years. In 1946 she made her recording debut in Los Angeles, singing "Say It Isn't So" with a group led by Charles Mingus. Carr married pianist-arranger Donn Trenner and they had a group called the Donn Trio and Helen. She had short stints with the big bands of Charlie Barnet (appearing in a Snader Telescription singing "My Old Flame"), Chuck Foster, Skinnay Ennis, Buddy Morrow and Georgie Auld without recording with any of these orchestras. A month with Stan Kenton's band in 1952 resulted in a lone recording, "Everything Happens To Me." On at least two occasions she had opportunities to sit in with Charlie Parker. She also appeared on an album led by violinist Paul Nero (on Nero's label Rhythm Records) singing "Sittin' 'Neath The Willow Tree."

Carr recorded two albums as a leader for Bethlehem, both of which have been reissued on the single CD *The Complete Bethlehem Collection*. These are probably from 1953 and 1954 although one discography lists them both as taking place in 1955. The supporting cast includes trumpeter Don Fagerquist, altoist Charlie Mariano and Carr's husband Donn Trenner on one date, and trumpeter Cappy Lewis and guitarist Howard Roberts on the other. The singer displays a basic delivery, a lightly swinging style and honesty in her interpretations of lyrics. Her soft sound and quiet tone sounds eerily like Norah Jones in spots although she is more jazz-oriented, and her phrasing is influenced by Billie Holiday.

Helen Carr recorded two songs for a Max Bennett Bethlehem album in 1955 and had a very minor role on two selections for a King Curtis single for Atco in 1958. Otherwise she maintained a low profile during her final years. Three sources apiece report that she died in a car accident or from breast cancer in 1960, at the age of 36 or 38. In any case, she is a talent well worth rediscovering.

Recommended CDs: *The Complete Bethlehem Collection* (Bethlehem 4002) has both of Helen Carr's two albums as a leader.

Joe "Bebop" Carroll

(Joseph Paul Taylor)
b. November 25, 1919, Philadelphia, PA;
d. February 1, 1981, Brooklyn, NY

Like Babs Gonzalez, Joe "Bebop" Carroll was a very enthusiastic bop singer. Carroll was an expert scatter and sounded almost deliriously happy on uptempo tunes although ballads were never one of his strong points.

Carroll sang with Paul Bascomb's orchestra early on but became most famous for his association with Dizzy Gillespie. He joined Gillespie's big band in 1949 (replacing Poncho Hagood) and was featured on "Jump Did-Le-Ba," "Hey Pete, Let's Eat Mo' Meat," the bebop fable "In The Land Of Oo-Bla-Dee" and "Honeysuckle Rose." Gillespie broke up the orchestra in early 1950 but the following year Carroll rejoined him, being an extra added attraction with Dizzy's combo. His versions of "School Days," "Oo-Shoo-Be-Doo-Bee," "Lady Be Good," "The Champ" and "The Bluest Blues" are bop singing at its most exuberant and his recording of "Pop's Confessin'" had him expertly imitating Louis Armstrong. After touring Europe in 1953, Carroll left Gillespie and worked most of the rest of his career as a single other than occasional reunions with Dizzy (including a 1961 Carnegie Hall concert) and a tour with Woody Herman during 1964–65.

As a leader, Carroll (who considered Leo Watson to be his main inspiration) led a four-song session in 1952 (reissued on Prestige's *The Bop Singers*), a date in France the following year and three albums (for Epic in 1956, the Charlie Parker label in 1962 and a final set for Jazzmania in 1978). The 1962 record has been reissued on CD by Collectables and is pretty definitive.

Joe Carroll never really grew as a singer or performer beyond where he was during his Gillespie years and he faded from the jazz world by the mid-1960s, working in obscurity.

Recommended CDs: *Man With A Happy Sound* (Collectables 5797) and the double-CD *Dizzy Digs Paris* (Giant Steps 016), which features him at a 1953 concert with Dizzy Gillespie, sums up Joe Carroll's style and career quite well.

Betty Carter
(Lillie Mae Jones)
b. May 16, 1930, Flint, MI; d. September 26, 1998, Brooklyn, NY

Arguably the most innovative jazz singer since 1970 and certainly a major influence on the generations that followed, Betty Carter constantly took chances. She often interpreted ballads at remarkably slow tempos and then would follow up by racing her way through a standard that she would ruth-

lessly de-construct. She loved sliding between notes, and changing tempos, songs and moods on a moment's notice, never playing it safe. Sometimes she sounded sarcastic but on other numbers she would be unexpectedly sweet. The name of one of her albums, *It's Not About The Melody*, seemed to express her musical philosophy. As a singer, she was a true jazz musician.

Born Lillie Mae Jones, she studied piano and began working as a vocalist in Detroit in 1946. Early on she was attracted to bebop and had an opportunity to sit in with Charlie Parker. A potential big break was being the singer with the Lionel Hampton Orchestra during 1948–51. She was known at the time as Lorraine Carter. However, Hampton nicknamed her "Bebop Betty" due to her love for bop and she eventually adopted Betty as her first name.

While Betty Carter made a few appearances on Lionel Hampton recordings, the association did not lead her

anywhere. She freelanced in New York during most of the 1950s, making an appearance on King Pleasure's recording of "Red Top" and recording her first album as a leader in 1956. Her recordings between 1956 and 1965 are fascinating because during this period Carter was basically a forward-looking bebop singer. On such numbers as "Social Call," "Tell Him I Said Hello," "I Can't Help It" (in which she seems to predict her future in music), "You're Driving Me Crazy," "What A Little Moonlight Can Do," "Jazz (Ain't Nothin' But Soul)," "This Is Always" and "You're A Sweetheart," she sounds quite distinctive although tied to the bebop tradition. An album of vocal duets with Ray Charles in 1961 gave her some recognition, but by the mid-1960s she was struggling and she was off records altogether during 1966–68.

During that period of time, Carter freed up her style, became a very adventurous improviser and her connections to bebop and standard singing became much more abstract. She also started her own Betcar record label so she could record whatever she wanted. Carter became an underground legend and her reputation gradually grew. By the time she recorded a duet album with Carmen McRae in 1987, she was considered McRae's equal. The following year she signed with Verve, and finally Carter's recordings (including her earlier ones) became more widely available. She refused to ever compromise, won jazz polls and worked as often as she wanted. Carter was also a skillful talent scout, constantly pushing her sidemen, which included pianists John Hicks, Mulgrew Miller, Benny Green, Stephen Scott, Jacky Terrasson and Cyrus Chestnut.

She could be abrasive and erratic and could slip out of tune at times, but it was from her constant desire to stretch herself rather than any musical deficiency. During her final decade, Betty Carter was considered by many to be jazz's top singer. She always sounded like herself.

Recommended CDs: *I Can't Help It* (GRP/Impulse 114), which has sessions from 1958 and 1960, is the most rewarding of Carter's early reissues. Also of interest are *Meet Betty Carter And Ray Bryant* (Columbia/Legacy 64936), *'Round Midnight* (Atco 80453) and *Inside Betty Carter* (Capitol 89702). Six sets, *Finally* (Roulette 795332), *'Round Midnight* (Roulette 95999), *Live At The Village Vanguard* (Verve 835 681), *The Betty Carter Album* (Verve 835682), *The Audience With Betty Carter* (Verve 835 684) and *Whatever Happened To Love* (Verve 835 683), cover the 1969–82 period with the Verves being reissues of most of her Betcar recordings. The mature Betty Carter of 1988–1996 can be definitively experienced by acquiring *Look What I Got* (Verve 835 661), *Droppin' Things* (Verve 843 991), *It's Not About The Melody* (Verve 314 513 870), *Feed The Fire* (Verve 314 523 600) and *I'm Yours, You're Mine* (Verve 314 533 182).

Katharine "Katchie" Cartwright
b. July 17, 1952, New York, NY

An intriguing singer whose adventurous wordless improvisations are always stirring (she also interprets lyrics well), Katharine "Katchie" Cartwright has been part of the New York jazz scene since the 1980s.

She remembers hearing a wide variety of recordings while growing up including Miles Davis' *Walkin'*, Ornette Coleman's *Free Jazz*, the Swingle Singers' *Going Baroque*, Nina Simone, Julius Baker's recording of Bach's flute sonatas, *West Side Story*, Miriam Makeba, Yma Sumac and Mickey Katz. "As a child, I sang all the time. At home, our extended family sang folk songs around a big bonfire all summer long. As a teenager, I became friends with jazz musicians in the local community of Delaware Water Gap, Pennsylvania. My most important mentors and role models in jazz were Flo and Al Cohn, Phil Woods, Bob Dorough, John Coates, Jay Cameron (owner of a music store), Bob and Fay Lehr (owners of the Deer Head Inn), and Jerry Harris (an incredible singer). Among my local peers were singers Kim Parker, Michele Bautier, Nancy Reed, Janet Lawson, and Stephanie Nakasian."

Cartwright primarily studied flute, not becoming a professional singer until she was in her twenties when she spent a couple of years working as a solo singer-pianist. An ethnomusicologist, she studied extensively at the City University of New York, earning a Ph.D. in 1998. "I come from a family of artists and artisans, and they inspired me. My eclecticism and interest in ethnomusicology are perhaps most influenced by my father and maternal grandfather. My father was a pilot and world traveler who constantly brought back interesting music from all over the world, including early bossa nova and African music. My grandparents traveled the world also, bringing back art and music from South America, Spain, and other places."

Although she appeared on records as a side person on congas, flute and as a vocalist as early as 1981, her first album as a leader was 1994's *Katchie Cartwright Quintet Live At The Deer Head Inn*. In more recent times she recorded a set of improvisations with saxophonist Richard Oppenheim and several Indian musicians and jazz interpretations of John Cage pieces. Cartwright teaches music and movement at the Third Street Music Settlement School and at Hunter College/City University of New York in addition to conducting workshops internationally.

"Jazz has so much of what I love about music: heart, eloquence, freedom, integrity, humor. My main goal is to continue to grow, learn, and create. I am definitely a traveler; it's simply in my blood. There are so many musical ideas to explore, people to meet, conversations to become involved in."

Recommended CDs: In the 1980s Katchie Cartwright recorded on congas with Mark Holen and the Flint Brothers, flute with Gregory Alper and her voice in the film project *Alexa*. But it is her projects as a singer with her quartet of saxophonist Richard Oppenheim, pianist James Weidman, Cameron Brown or Belden Bullock on bass and drummer Bill Goodwin that are most significant: *Katchie Cartwright Quintet Live At The Deer Head Inn* (Harriton Carved Wax 941), *Soulmates* (Pacific Street Records 015) and the very ambitious *La Faute De La Musique: Songs Of John Cage* (Harriton Carved Wax 031). Also important is her collaboration with Oppenheim and three Indian musicians, *A Mumbai Of The Mind: Ferlinghetti Improvisations* (Harriton Carved Wax 032), which utilizes the poems of Lawrence Ferlinghetti. These four CDs are Katchie Cartwright's most important contributions to jazz and improvised music so far.

Website: www.katchie.com

Eva Cassidy

b. February 2, 1963, Washington, D.C.;
d. November 2, 1996, Bowie, MD

Eva Cassidy died much too young. She was on the brink of becoming well known, she had not yet set a direction in her music and her future looked limitless. Her recordings are few and she has become an underground legend since her death.

Cassidy grew up in Bowie, Maryland, learned guitar from her father, and particularly loved jazz and folk music. As a teenager she sang with a rock group in high school but

did not like the experience because it forced her to always sing at top volume. After graduating high school, she studied art, got bored and worked at a plant nursery. Cassidy sang background vocals for rock groups, funk bands and even a gangsta rapper.

In the late 1980s, she formed a group and performed at local clubs even though she was very shy and not always that comfortable singing before audiences. In 1992 Eva Cassidy recorded an album (*The Other Side*) with Chuck Brown, a funk vocalist who had long been wanting to record a set of jazz and blues standards. There was interest from record labels in signing Cassidy, who had a wide range, a beautiful tone and the ability to put emotion into everything she sang. But because her music was so eclectic, ranging from jazz and blues to folk, gospel and R&B, they thought she would be impossible to classify and market so they passed her by. In 1994 she briefly teamed up with the pop jazz group Pieces of a Dream, but that association did not last.

Cassidy mostly worked locally, gradually building up a following. In 1996 her *Live At Blues Alley* was recorded but, shortly after it was released, she died from bone cancer. Eva Cassidy was 33.

Recommended CDs: *The Other Side* (Blix Street 210166) is Eva Cassidy's set of duets with Chuck Brown and it includes her famous version of "Over The Rainbow." *Live At Blues Alley* (Blix Street 10046) features her at her most powerful and haunting on jazz and folk ballads. *Eva By Heart* (Blix Street 10047) was a partially completed set that was finished after her death. *Songbird* (Blix Street 10045) is a sampler with the best selections from the three albums (although only one cut from *The Other Side*). *Songbird* reached #1 on the British charts in 2001, more than four years after Eva Cassidy's death. Adding to her slim discography is *Time After Time* (Blix Street 10073), a posthumous release. A few less significant releases of leftover material have come out in recent years, but get *Live At Blues Alley* first.

Patti Cathcart

b. October 4, 1949, San Francisco, CA

The vocal half of Tuck and Patti, Patti Cathcart has a beautiful voice that she has used to sing jazz, folk music, pop and originals, usually as duets with guitarist Tuck Andress.

"From my earliest memories there was always music in my home including jazz, blues, opera, country, rock and roll and  movie soundtracks. My mother was a music lover and passed this on to us." Cathcart sang early on in her church choir and in the chorus at school. She played violin for years and a little bit of piano and guitar. "The first day that I sang with the orchestra during a first rehearsal for *The Sound Of Music*, the wall of sound washing over me was so intoxicating that I was hooked." She attended college during 1967–68, but "I realized when I had dropped all my classes except theater that my college days were numbered." Instead she became a professional singer, performing in a wide variety of settings during the next decade.

In 1978 she met Tuck Andress at an audition for a band that they both joined. A couple of months later, they were practicing as a duo. Married in 1983, they waited until 1987 to record so they would have a unique sound and a reputation before their debut. Since then Tuck and Patti have performed together a countless number of times, performing everything from jazz standards and unique versions of pop tunes to folk, rock, soul and R&B as well as originals that are mostly written by Patti.

"I love when we take unexpected tunes and give them a new perspective. The high points happen every time we walk on a stage together."

Recommended CDs: Fans of Tuck and Patti will enjoy all of their recordings, for they have consistently stayed true to their original vision, playing the music that they love most. Their discography consists of *Tears Of Joy* (Windham Hill 0111), *Love Warriors* (Windham Hill 0116), *Dream* (Windham Hill 0130), *Learning How To Fly* (Epic 64439), *Paradise Found* (Windham Hill 11336), *Taking The Long Way Home* (Windham Hill 11507), *Chocolate Moment* (T and P/33rd Street 3310) and *A Gift Of Love* (T and P/33rd Street 3331). While Tuck Andress has recorded a couple of solo sets, surprisingly Patti Cathcart has not yet recorded without her husband.

Website: www.tuckandpatti.com

Maye Cavallaro
b. May 15, 1945, San Jose, CA

A warm singer based in the San Francisco Bay area, Maye Cavallaro has only recorded a few albums in her career, but she has been a popular attraction for many years.

"Both of my parents were music lovers. My mother was trained as a professional singer. We had tons of recordings at home, mostly the popular singers of the day like Perry Como, Rosemary Clooney, Andy Williams and such. My older brother loved the blues singers like Brownie McGhee and Sonny Terry, and Lightnin' Hopkins. When he brought home a Billie Holiday recording and I heard popular songs sung like that I was hooked."

Maye Cavallaro played violin and drums in her school orchestra, learned piano and sang in the chorus throughout school in addition to her church choir. She attended the University of California in Santa Barbara as an English major, mostly studying music privately and learning on the job. "I didn't know I was going to be a professional singer until I was in my late twenties. I had always sung at parties and with friends. One night a friend offered me a professional gig at a local delicatessen. Singing live for an audience of more than just friends was frightening, thrilling and totally engaging. I've sung professionally ever since that fateful deli gig."

Cavallaro considers her main influences to be Billie Holiday, Sarah Vaughan and Esther Phillips. She also teaches stagecraft and jazz singing at the Jazz School in Berkeley. "The musical high point of my career is that I've had the privilege to be a professional singer for 30 years. I've sung in all kinds of venues from the aforementioned deli, to Town Hall in New York, to

stages in Japan, to nightclubs all over the United States and in Europe. The high points come when it 'clicks.'"

Recommended CDs: Thus far Maye Cavallaro has four CDs out. 1995's *In The Middle Of A Kiss* (Redhead 001), *Never Let Me Go* (Redhead 002), *Hearts* (Redhead 003), which co-stars the brilliant guitarist Mimi Fox (a longtime associate) and *In The Middle Of A Kiss* (Redhead 004). While the instrumental backing changes from project to project, the singer's ability to caress ballads, her musicality and her ability to tell a story are consistent and rewarding.

Website: www.redheadmusic.com

Page Cavanaugh
(Walter Page Cavanaugh)
b. January 26, 1922, Cherokee, KS

A charming singer and a talented swing pianist, Page Cavanaugh has been making tasteful music for over 60 years at this writing, always giving one the impression that he knows every song written between 1930 and 1950.

"We were farmers and my dad, Clover Cavanaugh, played great ragtime piano. My Grandpa Page was both a coal miner and a heck of a fiddler. My Mom, Mary Page Cavanaugh, played piano as well; some hymns and standard tunes and one ragtime called 'Tickled To Death.' At age six or seven I learned to play chords on the ukulele and sang several songs such as 'Five Foot Two' and some minstrel songs which fortunately we don't hear anymore." Cavanaugh began taking piano lessons when he was nine and within three years was already playing at dances. He worked with Ernie Williamson's band during 1938–39, attended Kansas State Teachers College on scholarship for one semester, and dropped out to continue working as a musician. Cavanaugh was with Bobby Sherwood's orchestra in 1942 when he was drafted.

The following year while in the Signal Corps, he met guitarist Al Viola, who started a group called the Three Sergeants. The piano-guitar-bass trio (with bassist Lloyd Pratt) was popular from the start, originally emulating the Nat King Cole Trio while featuring some group singing along with the instrumentals. Upon their discharge in 1945, Cavanaugh, Viola and Pratt settled in the Los Angeles area and became known as the Page Cavanaugh Trio.

"Bullets Durgom signed us to a management contract and placed us in The King Cole Room at The Trocadero along with the Modernaires, while Nat and his trio were at The Copa in New York. In November 1946, we opened a new club called Le Bocage. Frank Sinatra came to hear us and took us to New York to back him in The Wedgewood Room at The Waldorf. Frank stood in the center of my trio on the floor in front of Emil Coleman's orchestra. He added strings to the orchestra and the bulk of the show was Frank and the trio with the orchestra joining in on five or six tunes."

In 1947 the Page Cavanaugh Trio appeared in Doris Day's debut film, *Romance On The High Seas*, playing with her on "It's You Or No One" and "Put 'Em In A Box, Tie 'Em

With A Ribbon." The trio also appeared with Danny Kaye in *A Song Is Born*, the Danny Thomas film *Big City* and in 1949 in *Lullaby Of Birdland* with Doris Day. They appeared regularly on the radio and recorded such hit numbers as Bobby Troup's "Three Little Bears," "All Of Me" and "Walkin' My Baby Back Home."

In 1949 Al Viola left the trio to work in the studios, becoming Frank Sinatra's guitarist in 1951. Cavanaugh continued leading trios for the next few decades, working steadily in Los Angeles. In the early 1960s he led the Page 7, a septet that augmented his trio with drums, two trombones and baritone sax. Although Cavanaugh recorded now and then, he was largely taken for granted until he was rediscovered in the 1980s when Al Viola rejoined his trio for a few years. In more recent times his trio has consisted of bassist Phil Mallory and either David Tull or Jason Lingle on drums. Even at the age of 85, Page Cavanaugh still plays in clubs a couple of times a week.

"I just hope it continues a while longer. I do want to give my deepest thanks to the people I've accompanied: Frank Sinatra, Johnny Desmond, Beryl Davis, Jo Stafford, Connie Haines, Stephanie Powers, Helen O'Connell, Kay Starr, June Christy, Dick Haynes, Helen Forrest and my dear friend, Michael Feinstein."

Recommended CDs: Page Cavanaugh's early recordings have never been coherently reissued, on LP or CD, which is a major omission. *Page One* (Star Line 9001) and *Page Two* (Star Line 9006) feature Cavanaugh, Al Viola and bassist Alvin Jackson in prime form during 1989 while the slightly earlier *Page Three* (Star Line 9012) was not released until 1996 but actually showcases Cavanaugh's 1967 trio with bassist Jerry Pulera and drummer Warren Nelson. All of these sets expertly mix together vocals with occasional instrumentals while displaying the Page Cavanaugh charm. *Return To Elegance* (Moon Over Leg 2993) has Cavanaugh, Phil Mallory and Jason Lingle in 2006 with Page singing some of his favorite vintage songs and showing that he is still an impressive pianist.

Website: www.pagecavanaugh.com

Judy Chamberlain
b. September 26, 1944, New York, NY

An important force in the Southern California jazz scene, Judy Chamberlain has a 4,000 song repertoire, a flexible style that ranges from swing to rock and roll, and a knack for picking good material, players and setting the right tempos. She has such close communication with her rhythm section that she can start a song without calling out its title, the tempo or even the key and her sidemen jump in within two beats.

"My parents had a radio show in New York in the 1930s, before I was born. He played guitar, she sang. As a little girl in post-WWII New York, I performed all the time at parties, because that was what we did in my family. I was also regularly taken to nightclubs and forced to drink Shirley Temples and listen to the most wonderful music in the world. I hung out in kitchens, talking to the chefs, stayed up all night and slept till noon. And that was before I started kindergarten. It was a lot like now."

She performed at her first big band gigs at the age of 13, had violin lessons and also played bass and acoustic guitar. After moving to Southern California in 1980, she worked not only as a performer and bandleader but as a radio and television personality, a restaurant critic, a newspaper columnist and a producer of musical events. "I'm proud to have put a lot of musicians to work in the events that I've produced over the years." During the past decade she has appeared at many different venues. She considers one of the main high points of her career to be the opportunity to have worked regularly with guitarist Al Viola. "I got to work with Al from 2001 until a month or two before he passed away in 2007. There will never be anyone like him again. He taught me Sinatra's vocal warm up intervals and encouraged my progress as a bandleader."

"Every song tells a story. Jazz is a living, breathing medium that happens 'in the moment.' It makes us transparent, and we have no choice but to be real."

Recommended CD: *Road Trip* (Jazz Baby 3412) features Judy Chamberlain in excellent form with a quartet that include pianist Bill Cunliffe and guitarist Ron Eschete. The privately issued *Live In Hollywood* is also quite worthy.

Website: www.judychamberlain.com

Phyllis Chapell
b. October 19, 1958, Philadelphia, PA

Although best known for singing Brazilian music, Phyllis Chapell has explored music from a variety of countries, singing in 11 different languages. She gives every song a jazz sensibility while remaining true to its heritage, whether it originates from Latin America, Europe or the Middle East.

"My father taught me popular songs from the '40s while my mother played recordings of music ranging from folk music from around the world, to classical, Broadway and popular. As a child I sang in choirs and school plays performing Jewish music (religious and secular Israeli). As a teenager, I sang folk music of the '60s. I studied piano as a child but switched to guitar when I was 13."

Although she attended the University of Pennsylvania, she did not take music classes, instead studying voice and guitar with private coaches. Phyllis Chapell became serious about becoming a professional singer in 1983, with a turning point in her career being meeting Dan Kleiman in 1991. "He is a gifted pianist/composer/arranger. We formed a duo (keys and vocals/guitar) and then in 1995 formed our ensemble SIORA. We have been collaborating, performing and recording ever since."

"I consider myself a ballad singer/songstress who can express herself through jazz. It's really about the song for me... that magical chemistry that goes into the creation of a great song. I search for it wherever I can find it, in whatever genre or language—and I endeavor to communicate it in my own way."

Recommended CDs: Phyllis Chapell made a duo CD with Dan Kleiman in 1994, *Infinite Lover* (Miowan Music). Otherwise she recorded a solo voice and guitar CD in 1999, *World Songs* (Orchard 2246), and two sets with Siora: *Siora* (Orchard 4401) and *Vis-A-Vis* (Miowan Music 1003). "*Vis-A-Vis* is my best recording thus far, a culminating vehicle for my multilingual jazz expression. I had sung many of the songs on this CD for years and with this CD placed these songs into a jazz context." Her upcoming CD, *Voice In Flight*, features Phyllis Chapell growing even more as an improviser.

Websites: www.siorajazz.com and www.phyllischapell.com

Topsy Chapman

b. August 9, 1947, New Orleans, LA

One of the many fine singers who was born in New Orleans, Topsy Chapman has performed with trad bands, gospel groups and in R&B settings.

She grew up in Kentwood, Louisiana, where her father was a vocal music instructor. "I started playing piano for churches at the age of seven or eight. In high school I had a group that performed at other schools." After graduating high school, she moved to New Orleans and worked with her own gospel group, the Chapmans, not only singing, but composing and arranging material for the group.

The turning point of her career was when Topsy Chapman became one of the original cast members of *One Mo' Time*, a New Orleans jazz and blues revue that became a hit on Broadway. She toured with the cast to Europe and her association with the show gave her a strong reputation. Since then she has appeared in New Orleans in the production of *Staggerlee*, worked on cruises for the Delta Steamboat Company, toured with the Magnolia Jazz Band and recorded and/or performed with many classic jazz and New Orleans greats including Willie Humphrey, Louie Nelson, Orange Kellin, the New Orleans Jazz Ladies, Jim Cullum (including on his *Live From The Landing* radio series), Lars Edegran, Nicholas Payton, Butch Thompson and Dick Hyman. She has also toured with the Chapman Singers (which was later renamed Solid Harmony), a spirited gospel-oriented group that features her two daughters.

"When I'm singing, I'm relating to every word, telling you a story with that song. I'm a sucker for ballads and I love stories with great melodies."

Recommended CDs: *My One And Only Love* (GHB 520) from 2001 is Topsy Chapman's definitive jazz recording while *Fine And Mellow* (GHB 320) is an excellent collaboration from 1994 with the Magnolia Jazz Band.

Website: www.topsychapman.com

Ray Charles

(Ray Charles Robinson)
b. September 23, 1930, Albany, GA;
d. June 10, 2004, Beverly Hills, CA

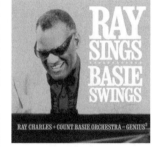

RAY CHARLES + COUNT BASIE ORCHESTRA = GENIUS²

One of the most famous American entertainers of the 20th century, Ray Charles is perhaps most significant for putting the emotional intensity and power of gospel into popular music, becoming a major force in the formation of soul music. Charles could also sing and play R&B, blues, pop, country and jazz. While never a full-time jazz singer, jazz was a major influence in Charles' music, and he sounded quite at home singing with the Count Basie Orchestra and with his own swinging big band.

Raised in a very poor family in Florida, Ray Charles went blind between the ages of six and seven, possibly from glaucoma. While attending the St. Augustine School for the Deaf and the Blind, he learned to write music and started playing piano. He also developed into a fine saxophonist. Leaving school as a teenager, he worked in several local bands including the Florida Playboys and in jazz combos.

Charles moved to Seattle in 1947 and made his first records for the Swingtime label. At the time his singing was very close to that of Charles Brown and, to a lesser extent, Nat King Cole, and his bluesy swing piano was similar. He had a minor hit in 1951 with "Baby, Let Me Hold Your Hand." Charles had opportunities to tour with Lowell Fulson and work with Guitar Slim in New Orleans.

By the time he signed with Atlantic in 1952, Ray Charles was sounding much more original. He had hits from the start with "Mess Around" and "It Should Have Been Me," and 1955's "I Got A Woman" really made him famous. No longer an emulator, Charles represented the new sound in R&B and eventually soul, yet traveled with a big band and enjoyed starting his usual program with some jazz, occasionally taking an alto solo.

Ray Charles never lost his popularity. 1959's "What'd I Say," "Hit The Road Jack" and his always-passionate version of Hoagy Carmichael's "Georgia On My Mind" became classics. No one infused "America The Beautiful" with as much emotion as Brother Ray. He had a slew of other hits through the years including "Unchain My Heart," "Hallelujah I Love Her So" and "I Can't Stop Loving You." Jazzwise, he recorded vocal duets with the young Betty Carter, was featured on organ with the Count Basie Orchestra, had such key soloists as altoist Hank Crawford and tenor-saxophonist David "Fathead" Newman in his big band for years, played alto and piano on two instrumental albums with vibraphonist Milt Jackson in the 1950s, and late in his career played very effective jazz piano on several songs included on a CD led by trombonist Steve Turre. He may have coasted after the mid-1960s, but Ray Charles was always capable of greatness, and he never lost his love of jazz.

Recommended CDs: Ray Charles has a huge discography. Those primarily interested in his singing in jazz-oriented settings will find these discs of interest. *The Very Best Of The Early Years* (Metro 580) is a two-CD set that has the better selections from Ray Charles' pre-Atlantic recordings. *The Definitive Soul Collection* (Rhino 77664) is a nice two-CD overview of Charles' Atlantic years including his biggest hits of the period. *Ray Charles And Betty Carter/Dedicated To You* (Rhino 75259) has their famous duets. *Genius + Soul = Jazz/My Kind Of Jazz* (Rhino 72814), although comprised mostly of instrumentals, does have Charles' famous vocals on "I'm Going To Move To The Outskirts Of Town" and "I've Got News For You." *Ray Sings, Basie Swings* (Concord 30026) is a successful oddity, combining Ray Charles' vocals from a 1973 concert with playing by the 2006 Count Basie Orchestra. It works and sounds lifelike.

Jeannie Cheatham

b. August 14, 1927, Akron, OH

Jeannie Cheatham is best known for being the singer-pianist with the Sweet Baby Blues Band, an exciting Kansas City swing ensemble that she has long co-led with her husband, the late bass trombonist-arranger Jimmy Cheatham.

"I played piano by ear in church from five years of age and then studied formally for ten years. My uncle Richard Smart, who was first trumpeter for many local big bands, played records for us as children." Jeannie Cheatham lists such diverse musical inspirations as the Wings Over Jordan

Gospel Choir, Jay McShann, Charlie Parker, Count Basie, Earl Hines, Jo Jones and several classical composers. She attended the University of Akron for a short time but mostly worked as a pianist from the mid-1940s on while developing into a fine singer. She enjoyed accompanying other vocalists including Al Hibbler, T-Bone Walker, Dinah Washington, Joe Williams, Big Mama Thornton, Jimmy Witherspoon, Cab Calloway and Dakota Staton. Jeannie met Jimmy Cheatham in the mid-1950s and often worked with him during the next few decades.

Jeannie Cheatham was featured with Big Mama Thornton and Sippie Wallace on the PBS special *Three Generations Of The Blues* and she taught at the University of Wisconsin. Although there were occasional recordings, including *Academy Awards In Jazz* with fellow pianist Roberta Como and an avant-garde CD with trombonist George Lewis (*Changing With The Times*), it was not until Jeannie and Jimmy Cheatham formed the Sweet Baby Blues Band in 1984 that they finally began to gain the recognition they deserved.

Their group, also known as the Cheathams, usually featured at least four horn soloists plus Jeannie's piano and vocals. They were always exciting to hear and see. The band played spirited and joyous renditions of swing, blues and romps inspired by Jay McShann, Count Basie and the feel of Kansas City jam sessions. Their string of recordings for Concord during 1984–95 was popular and they had a hit in "Meet Me With Your Black Drawers On." The Sweet Baby Blues Band became much more part-time since their association with Concord ended.

"Jazz is truly a way of life. The mechanics of it can be taught in school, but the spirit of it cannot. I live to make music with the marvelous marriage of facility and spirit by those that do it best."

Recommended CDs: All of the Sweet Baby Blues Band's Concord recordings are fun and swinging, with Jeannie taking vocals on roughly half of the selections. One cannot go wrong by acquiring *Sweet Baby Blues* (Concord Jazz 4258), *Midnight Mama* (Concord Jazz 4297), *Homeward Bound* (Concord Jazz 4321), *Back In The Neighborhood* (Concord Jazz 4373), *Luv In the Afternoon* (Concord Jazz 4429), *Basket Full Of Blues* (Concord Jazz 4501), *Blues And The Boogie Masters* (Concord Jazz 4579) and *Gud Nuz Bluz* (Concord Jazz 4690).

Website: www.jeanniecheatham.com

Ellen Christi
b. March 7, 1958, Chicago, IL

An adventurous and consistently intriguing singer with a flexible voice who is not shy to tackle art songs, avant-garde jazz or standards, Ellen Christi is always well worth hearing.

"I knew what I wanted to do when I was 11. I started performing when I was sixteen years old in

Chicago." She names Jaki Byard, John Coltrane, Red Garland and Jeanne Lee as being among her inspirations. Christi, who also plays piano and flute, studied privately with pianist Jack Hubble and studied composing, technique and arranging with Jaki Byard.

Since coming to New York in the mid-1970s, Ellen Christi has worked in a wide variety of challenging situations, from solo vocal concerts to theatrical productions. Among the artists who she has collaborated with are Ray Anderson, Mark Dresser, Andrew Cyrille, Reggie Workman, Rashied Ali, Tony Scott, Ed Blackwell, William Parker, Lisa Sokolov, Kenny Wheeler, Butch Morris, Carlo Actis Dato, the trio Illustrio, the 22-piece ensemble Joe Gallatin's Illuminati and her own group Aliens' Talk. She was one of the co-founders of the New York City Artists' Collective, an organization that conducts seminars, concerts and the N.Y.C.A.C. record label. In addition, she teachers master classes in vocal technique/ improvisation and movement.

"My life is something that I have etched out by following my heart through a creative process. I have chosen to make sacrifices in an effort to realize a dream. The creative process is exhilarating and a constant challenge. But as a female it can be lonely and unforgiving. I am only a channel for the creative spirit which comes through the music. The music is precious, universal, and a beacon of hope for many when they begin to understand the sounds."

Recommended CDs: Ellen Christi's recordings have consistently been for tiny labels but are well worth seeking out. A strong sampling to start with includes *Live At Irving Plaza* (Soul Note 121097), *Instant Reality* (Network 2001), *Vocal Desires* (CMC 1050), *Reconstruction Of Sound* (Network 1051), *Aliens' Talk* (Saragasso 20025) and *Deep Beat* (Blissco 07827).

Website: www.ellenchristi.com

June Christy
(Shirley Luster)
b. November 20, 1925, Springfield, IL;
d. June 21, 1990, Los Angeles, CA

One of the most beloved of the jazz singers to rise to prominence in the 1940s, June Christy's friendly girl-next-door musical personality was a major asset to the Stan Kenton Orchestra before she started her own successful solo career.

Growing up in Decatur, Illinois, Shirley Luster became a professional singer at the age of 13, performing in Chicago with local bands. As Sharon Leslie, she sang for four years with a band led by Bill Oetzel. She was with Boyd Raeburn's unrecorded swing orchestra for four months during 1943–44, but had to leave when she contracted scarlet fever. After singing with Benny Strong's big band and changing her name to June Christy, she auditioned for her favorite group, the Stan Kenton Orchestra. Anita O'Day had just left Kenton and the bandleader decided to take a chance on the 19-year-old Christy, who at the time was strongly influenced by O'Day. Her first record date with Kenton yielded a million seller, "Tampico."

Christy learned fast and became popular immediately. Her recordings with Kenton, which include such hits as "Across The Alley From The Alamo," "Shoo Fly Pie" and "How High The Moon," made the band money that helped finance some of Kenton's more adventurous projects. While with Kenton in 1946, she married his tenor-saxophonist Bob Cooper, a marriage that worked and lasted for 44 years. Christy did not read music and sometimes sang a little flat, but she had a definite charm and also the will power to learn and master the most difficult arrangements, many of which were provided by Pete Rugolo.

Christy made some radio transcriptions in 1946, headed her first record date the following year and in December 1948, when Kenton broke up his big band, she started her solo career. She returned to Kenton's orchestra to tour with the radical Innovations orchestra in 1950–51 and had several reunions with Kenton through the years including a memorable album, *Duet*, on which she is accompanied just by Kenton's piano.

After making some singles for Capitol during 1947–50, Christy recorded a series of notable albums for the label (many of which were arranged by Rugolo), including her trademark set *Something Cool* (the haunting title track, which has her sounding as if she is mentally on-the-edge, is a classic), *The Misty Miss Christy* and *Gone For The Day*. Christy's singing in the 1950s helped to define cool jazz for she sounded laid-back and emotionally reserved, with deep feelings being hinted at but kept just beneath the surface.

After 1965, the 40-year old June Christy retired except for special occasions, which included a reunion with Kenton at the 1972 Newport Jazz Festival, a final album in 1977 (*Impromptu*) on which she sounds a little rusty, and an appearance at a European jazz festival as late as 1985. But although she was mostly off the scene during her final 25 years, June Christy was greatly mourned in the jazz world when she passed away in 1990.

Recommended CDs: *Tampico* (Memoir 526) has most of June Christy's recordings with Kenton, while June Christy's singles from 1947 to 1950 are on *Day Dreams* (Capitol Jazz 32083). Among Christy's most rewarding CDs are *Something Cool* (Capitol Jazz 96329), *The Misty Miss Christy* (Capitol Jazz 98452), *Duet* (Capitol Jazz 89285), *Gone For The Day And Fair And Warmer* (Capitol Jazz 95448) and *The Song Is June* (Capitol Jazz 55455).

Peter Cincotti

b. July 11, 1983, New York, NY

In 2003 when Peter Cincotti's self-titled debut was released by Concord, it was easy to write him off as a Harry Connick Jr. wannabe, particularly if one did not listen to his music closely. After all, Cincotti also played piano and sang, wrote some of his own songs, enjoyed playing vintage swing standards, was being hired by fashion magazines, and was being pushed as the flavor of the month. But there were differences. Chief among them were that Cincotti does not have a New Orleans connection and he is a better pianist than Connick, enjoying ripping through Fats Waller's "Handful Of Keys" as an encore. As time has passed, his individuality has shone through even if the show biz elements of how he is being marketed have sometimes overshadowed his jazz abilities.

At the age of three, Cincotti was playing a toy piano given to him by his grandmother, leading to him taking piano lessons the following year. He developed quickly and at the age of seven he impressed Harry Connick Jr., who had him sit in at one of his shows in Atlantic City. Cincotti studied classical piano at the Manhattan School of Music as well as jazz with Ellis Marsalis. He began playing Manhattan-area clubs when he was 12 and a few years later began to also sing. At 16 he toured with Connick and the following year appeared at the Montreux Jazz Festival, winning a piano competition.

In 2002, after becoming the youngest performer to ever headline at the Algonquin Hotel, the 18-year old was signed to Concord. He has since recorded two CDs and an abbreviated Christmas set, toured the world and appeared at many jazz festivals. His personable singing, songwriting ability (with lyrics from his mother Cynthia Cincotti) and piano playing are still in their early stages and whether Peter Cincotti will become a significant jazz singer in the future is not certain. Certainly he has a great deal of potential and a love for vintage jazz.

Recommended CDs: *Peter Cincotti* (Concord 2159) mixes together pop standards from different eras (including "Spinning Wheel," "Nature Boy" and "Ain't Misbehavin'") along with a few of his originals on a trio/quartet set. *My Favorite Time Of Year* (Concord 0036) just has two songs and is a certain collector's item. *On The Moon* (Concord 2221) adds funk and touches of rock to the mix while Cincotti still plays such numbers as "St. Louis Blues" and an instrumental "Cherokee." Some of the selections match his voice with a larger group that includes strings and are closer to middle-of-the-road pop.

Website: www.petercincotti.com

Linda Ciofalo

b. August 28, 1961, Brooklyn, NY

Linda Ciofalo took a long time before deciding to become a full-time professional singer but, based on the performances that she recorded on her debut *Take The High Road*, she made the right decision.

She sang in a church choir when she was nine and also sang classical music. Her brother was a songwriter so she was his demo singer, and together they did a few radio commercials. As a teenager, Ciofalo worked as a backup singer in rock bands and sang professionally in wedding and club date groups. "However, that was not enough to convince my old-fashioned parents and so I was encouraged to do something with a secure future. I got a license in cosmetology, became a beauty advisor for Revlon and later worked in the laboratory for Avon Cosmetics in their testing center until I started a family. I sang as a hobby and it grew into a career as I began to sing to earn extra money to help support our family of six. I first realized I wanted to be a jazz singer when I heard Sarah Vaughan with a big band sing 'I'll Remember April' on television. Up until then I was singing with a band doing top-forty songs by Aretha Franklin, Whitney Houston, Donna Summers and Madonna. The next week I left my club date band and auditioned for a big band, competing against 300 auditioning vocalists, and got the gig."

In 1999, after attending Molloy College (1995) and Juilliard (1996–98), Linda Ciofalo became a bandleader and began performing regularly in the New York area. She studied with Mark Murphy and in 2000 released *Take The High Road.*

Recommended CD: *Take The High Road* (Orchard 2357) consists of two originals and a variety of standards ranging from "You Do Something To Me" to Abbey Lincoln's "Throw It Away" and, despite its brevity (38 minutes), is a particularly strong all-around set. *Sun Set* (Lucky Jazz 001), which includes support and solos from tenor-saxophonist Joel Frahm, guitarist John Hart and the John DiMartino Trio, is even better. The repertoire includes "You Took Advantage Of Me," "Comes Love" and various songs having to do with the sun.

Soesja Citroen

b. September 25, 1948, Den Haag, The Netherlands

One of the Netherlands' top jazz singers, Soesja Citroen's background in avant-garde jazz has resulted in her sounding quite original when she sings standards and interprets lyrics.

"I sang originally in church. When I was 15 I started really singing, first with an old-style jazz band some blues that I learned from Bessie Smith records, and then later in my teens with more modern jazz groups."

Citroen moved to Amsterdam and earned a master's degree in social psychology before deciding to become a full-time jazz singer. "In 1981 we were driving to a gig. At that time I was leading a sextet with trumpeter Nedly Elstak, Willem Breuker (on bass clarinet) and bass player Arjen Gorter. I remember asking Arjen how he had become a professional. He said 'When I'd played bass for half a year, Willem asked me to join his band.' 'That's the way to do it, as easy as that,' I thought. So I quit my job and started to be a professional jazz singer."

Fortunately she had the talent to successfully switch careers. Soesja Citroen recorded her debut album *To Build* in 1980 when she was 32 and has made numerous recordings since that time. Her 1983 set *Soesja Citroen Sings Thelonious Monk* gained her a great deal of attention in Europe.

When asked to name some of the highlights, Citroen mentions her early avant-garde group, recording the Monk album with pianist Cees Slinger's octet, her three albums with the Metropole Orchestra that she made between 1984 and 1989 and working with her current trio. "When I started to sing professionally, I favored avant-garde jazz. I tried to reach the highest heights with my voice, together with the trumpeter I often worked with. I enjoyed the sheer improvising but soon realized that though my voice was high and versatile enough, I lacked some of the basic knowledge. Within a few years I started to study the standards. As I studied the lyrics of songs and started to make some lyrics of my own, I got more and more interested in the interpretation of songs. I enjoyed the feeling of diving into a song and getting close to its meaning. I love singing about subjects that are part of my daily experiences."

Recommended CDs: *Soesja Citroen Sings Thelonious Monk* (Timeless 11021), which has the singer's interpretation of eight Monk songs, including five with lyrics of her own, was her breakthrough album. Some of her more recent CDs give one a particularly strong sampling of her talents, including *Shall We Dance Or Keep On Moping* (Timeless 11007), *Here And Now* (Challenge 70003), *Songs For Lovers And Losers* (Timeless 70034), *Song For Ma* (Challenge 70056), *Soesja Sings Citroen* (Challenge 70101) and *Don't Cry Baby* (Challenge 70127); the latter three sets feature her original compositions and lyrics.

Fay Claasen

b. December 2, 1969, Nijmegen, The Netherlands

A major jazz singer from the Netherlands, Fay Claasen sometimes sings in Dutch, French and Portuguese but also excels in English. She has a beautiful and subtle voice, whether interpreting lyrics or singing wordlessly. Her main influence is Ella Fitzgerald, although she has her own sound.

Although she took guitar and piano lessons when she was young, Fay Claasen did not really hear jazz until she was 18. "A friend of mine introduced me to it. The way that people played around the melody, improvising, got to me the most, especially when I heard what some of the singers could do with their voice, singing like an instrument and being so free with the music. I got deeply moved by singer Deborah Brown and I listened to a tape of her during a whole summer until I could learn every embellishment."

She studied at the Royal Conservatory, worked with several groups including the Amsterdam Jazz Quintet and in 1994 was featured on saxophonist Carolyn Breuer's *Simply Be* CD on Challenge. Fay Claasen made her first album as a leader, *With A Song In My Heart*, in 1999, and has become increasingly well known in Europe ever since. She had an opportunity with her second CD, *Rhythms And Rhymes*, to record in New York with Mike Stern and Kenny Werner, although she is primarily famous in the European jazz world where she teaches vocal improvisation.

"I am very grateful that I can sing this music which has brought me so much freedom and a way to express the most playful and serious feelings that are within me."

Recommended CDs: *With A Song In My Heart* (Challenge 70096), *Rhythms And Rhymes* (Jazz 'N Pulz 380) and the two-CD *A Night At The Music Village* (BMCD 395), which has Fay Claasen guesting with the Benelux Orchestra and pianist Ivan Paduart are impressive. But *Specially Arranged For Fay* (Jazz 'N Pulz 381), which teams her voice with the Millenium Jazz Orchestra, and the two-CD *Two Portraits Of Chet Baker* (Jazz 'N Pulz 497), which features her paying tribute to Baker the trumpeter (improvising wordlessly with a Gerry Mulligan-type group) and singer (interpreting lyrics with the support of a rhythm section), are the most essential Fay Claasen recordings so far.

Website: www.fayclaassen.nl

Clairdee

(Barbara Wright Clardy French)
b. November 19, 1951, Tucson, AZ

A soulful singer who until recently was one of the San Francisco Bay area's best-kept secrets, Clairdee is equally skilled at singing swinging jazz, R&B tunes and vintage pop.

Clairdee grew up in Denver, Colorado. One of eight children, she remembers singing three-part harmony with her sisters from the time she was six. Clairdee played the viola and later picked up piano. However, she did not really discover jazz until she attended the University of Colorado in Boulder and was particularly impressed by seeing Nancy Wilson in concert. After graduating in December 1972, she got married and taught seventh-grade English and Social Studies for a year. However, it was not long before Clairdee was concentrating on being a vocalist. "I always knew that I wanted to sing. There has never been a time in my life that I don't remember wanting to be a professional singer. During the early stages of my professional career, I had the pleasure of working with the very fine pianist/organist, William 'Big Daddy' Sailes in Omaha, Nebraska, during 1977–80 before I moved to California." Settling in the San Francisco Bay area in 1986, Clairdee sang a wide variety of music including pop, cabaret, country and soul before dedicating herself to jazz in the mid-1990s. She has worked with John Handy, Eddie Henderson, Roland Hanna, Allen Farnham and with altoist Dick Crest's big bands and ensembles, naming Billy Higgins as an important mentor. She is also the vocal instructor for the University of California, Berkeley jazz department and teaches at Diablo Valley College.

"In the future, I want to do more writing, arranging and producing, with the hope of releasing a new recording every 18 months. I want to uplift and inspire people through music. In that regard, I call myself a 'soul singer'—not in terms of the rhythmic style—but in terms of making a connection with the listener to make him/her feel good. Many times I begin my performances with the words, 'Welcome to my living room.' A good host makes their guests feel comfortable and entertained. That's what I strive to do."

Recommended CDs: Clairdee's debut CD *Destination Moon* (Declare 72301) for the first time spread her fame beyond Northern California, and it features an enthusiastic and soulful jazz-inspired storyteller mostly singing jazz standards. *This Christmas* (Declare 2701), which has her versions of Yuletide favorites, is more R&B-oriented, while *Moves* (Declare 3102) is an exciting live set that features her effectively melting the boundary lines between jazz, pop and classic R&B.

Website: www.clairdee.com

Jay Clayton
b. October 28, 1941, Youngstown, OH

Of all of the current singers, Jay Clayton, Sheila Jordan and Mark Murphy were mentioned the most times by other vocalists in the questionnaires as being among the most important in their careers. But Jay Clayton has always been more than a significant teacher and mentor, for she has been a highly versatile and adventurous singer since the beginning.

"Early on my cousin gave me three records, one apiece from Miles Davis, Dave Brubeck and Ramsey Lewis. I didn't really know what it was, but I had to hear more!" Her mother used to sing standards around the house so Jay Clayton learned songs very early. She took piano lessons and studied briefly at the St. Louis Institute for Music. Clayton graduated from Miami University in Oxford, Ohio, in 1963 with a B.S. in Music Education. While studying classical music at school (this was before there was much jazz education), she sang jazz on the weekends. "I sang a lot with a jazz group and then decided to move to New York. After I was in New York a couple of years, I knew it would take a long time, but I was compelled to sing and learn more about jazz music."

She began her career in New York singing standards but soon became one of the first vocalists performing with free jazz musicians; Clayton has utilized electronics and poetry at various times in her career. Most inspired by Sheila Jordan, her many musical associations have included Mark Whitecage, Jeanne Lee, Perry Robinson, Steve Lacy, Jane Ira Bloom, Jerry Granelli, Muhal Richard Abrams, Gary Bartz, George Cables and Julian Priester. In addition, she worked with Vocal Summit, an a cappella group with Urszula Dudziak, Bobby McFerrin, Jeanne Lee and Norma Winstone. A fearless improviser who can also sing standards when it fits her conception, she has been consistently unpredictable except in the constant high quality of her music.

As an educator, Jay Clayton was on the jazz faculty of Cornish College of the Arts for 20 years. She has also taught at Universität für Musik in Austria, the Bud Shank Jazz Workshop, City College, the New School in New York City, with Sheila Jordan at the Vermont Jazz Workshop and at the Banff Center in Canada in addition to conducting many workshops, seminars and master classes.

Jay Clayton's 65th birthday was celebrated at a performance at Sweet Rhythm, playing with a challenging quintet that included Jane Ira Bloom and Gary Thomas.

Recommended CDs: Fortunately, Jay Clayton has recorded fairly often including *All Out* (Anima 1335), *The Jazz Alley Tapes* (Hep 2046) with Don Lanphere, *With The String Trio Of New York* (West Wind 2008), *Live At Jazz Alley* (ITM 970065), *Tito's Acid Trip* (ITM 970072), *Sound Songs* (Winter and Winter 919006) and *An American Garden* (Sound Winds 1701). She names as her personal favorites her duo set of standards with pianist Fred Hersch (*Beautiful Love*, Sunnyside 1066), *Circle Dancing* (Sunnyside 1076) and *Brooklyn 2000* (Sunnyside 1096).

Website: www.jayclayton.com

Rosemary Clooney
b. May 23, 1928, Maysville, KY; d. June 29, 2002, Beverly Hills, CA

Rosemary Clooney is one of perhaps ten vocalists in this book of whom it is probably a bit of a stretch to call a jazz singer. But because of her long string of Concord recordings during the last part of her career, many of which team her with tenor-saxophonist Scott Hamilton and a swinging rhythm section, and because she headlined quite a few jazz events and was part of the jazz world, she is included.

A warm singer who stuck to the lyrics and the melody of each song, but also swung the music lightly, Clooney was always a delight to hear. The happiness in her voice hid the inner scars that a rough childhood must have caused. She came from a broken home that included an alcoholic father and a mother who remarried and abandoned Rosemary and her younger sister Betty. While struggling in poverty and trying to raise themselves, the Clooney Sisters won a singing audition at a Cincinnati radio station and appeared regularly on WLW in 1945. Shortly after, Tony

Pastor heard their singing on the radio and hired them for his big band.

During 1945–48, the Clooney Sisters were a major attraction with the Tony Pastor Orchestra, making recordings, being featured on the radio and playing concerts. In 1948 Betty returned to Cincinnati to work on the radio and the following year Rosemary left Pastor to start her solo career. Signed to Columbia, she was mostly stuck recording novelties at first and in 1951 had a major hit with the bizarre "Come On-A My House." That recording made her famous, but fortunately she had opportunities during the remainder of the decade to display her versatility and to grow musically. Clooney appeared regularly on radio, met and sang with Bing Crosby (a lifelong friend) and was one of the stars in 1954's *White Christmas*. Although she appeared in a few other films, Clooney never became a movie star. Instead she recorded a string of excellent albums (including *Blue Rose*, a memorable meeting with Duke Ellington's orchestra), married actor Jose Ferrer, and was a fixture on television, including hosting the *Rosemary Clooney Show*, which aired during 1956–57 and teamed her voice with Nelson Riddle arrangements.

After having five children in five years, Clooney's marriage fell apart, she became addicted to tranquilizers and sleeping pills, and her life was erratic. A mental breakdown in 1968 stopped her career for a time although she remained a household name. In 1976 she made her comeback, singing with Bing Crosby on his final tour. She signed with the Concord label and during the next 25 years recorded 25 albums for the label. The first 15 or so find Clooney at the peak of her singing powers, interpreting superior songs from the golden age of the American popular song while accompanied by jazz combos that usually included Scott Hamilton and sometimes cornetist Warren Vache.

Rosemary Clooney's voice began to decline in the mid-1990s as she neared the age of 70, but she kept up a busy performance and recording schedule up until the time of her death from cancer.

Recommended CDs: The two-CD set *Songs From The Girl Singer* (Concord 4870) has a disc of vintage material from 1946 to 1963 and a CD that contains some of the best numbers from Clooney's Concord years. *Blue Rose* (Columbia/Legacy 65506) with Duke Ellington in 1956 is a gem. *Jazz Singer* (Columbia/Legacy 86883) repeats four songs from *Blue Rose* and otherwise has some of her more jazz-oriented performances from the 1950s. *Rosie Solves The Swingin' Riddle* (Koch 7991) is a set from 1960 with the Nelson Riddle Orchestra. Skipping to her Concord period, Clooney is in particularly excellent form on *Everything's Coming Up Rosie* (Concord Jazz 4047), *Rosie Sings Bing* (Concord Jazz 4060), *Tribute To Billie Holiday* (Concord Jazz 4081), *Sings The Lyrics Of Ira Gershwin* (Concord Jazz 41112), *Sings The Music Of Cole Porter* (Concord Jazz 4195), *Sings The Music Of Harold Arlen* (Concord Jazz 4210), *Sings The Music Of Irving Berlin* (Concord Jazz 4255), *Sings The Music Of Jimmy Van Heusen* (Concord Jazz 4308), *Sings The Lyrics Of Johnny Mercer* (Concord Jazz 4333), *Show Tunes* (Concord Jazz 4364), *For The Duration* (Concord Jazz 4444) and *Dedicated To Nelson* (Concord Jazz 4685).

Freddy Cole
(Lionel Frederick Coles)
b. October 15, 1931, Chicago, IL

The younger brother of Nat King Cole, Freddy Cole remained in Nat's shadow as a singer and pianist until 20 years after

his death, when he finally began to emerge as an important performer himself.

In addition to Freddy and Nat, older brother bassist Eddie Coles and singer-pianist Ike Cole were musicians who had opportunities to record. Freddy Cole began playing piano when he was five and entertained thoughts of playing football professionally although a hand injury ended that dream. When he was 17, he decided to work seriously toward becoming a musician. Nat was already on the verge of becoming a major star by then.

Cole recorded a single ("The Joke's On Me") in 1952, had a little success with the following year's "Whispering Grass" and cut a full album for Dot in 1959, but he remained in obscurity for a long time. A mid-1970s album for Audiophile documented his progress but he would not really begin to be noticed until his Sunnyside, Laserlight and Muse albums of the early 1990s, with his breakthrough being his recordings for the Fantasy label. By then Freddy Cole was already 15 years older than Nat had been when he passed away. His voice, while sometimes sounding similar to his brother, was darker and deeper while his piano playing was boppish and much more modern.

Since the mid-1990s, Freddy Cole (who considers Billy Eckstine and Dick Haymes to be his main inspirations as a vocalist) has worked and recorded regularly, being recognized as one of jazz's top veteran singers while de-emphasizing his piano. It is a pity that it took him so long to become successful, but at least he is a survivor.

Recommended CDs: *Waiter, Ask The Man To Play The Blues* (GRP 268902) reissues an obscure 1964 album for Dot. *I'm Not My Brother, I'm Me* (Sunnyside 1054) from 1990 really started the discovery of Freddy Cole. Other enjoyable sets are *Live At Birdland West* (Laserlight 17 015), *This Is The Life* (Muse 5503), *A Circle Of Love* (Fantasy 9874), *Always* (Fantasy 7670), *I Want A Smile For Christmas* (Fantasy 9672), *It's Crazy But I'm In Love* (After 9 2008), *To The Ends Of The Earth* (Fantasy 9675), *Love Makes The Changes* (Fantasy 9881), *Le Grand Freddy* (Fantasy 9683), *Merry-Go-Round* (Telarc 83493), *Rio De Janeiro Blue* (Telarc 83525), *In The Name Of Love* (Telarc 83545), *This Love Of Mine* (Highnote 7140) and *Because Of You* (Highnote 7156).

Nat King Cole
(Nathaniel Coles)
b. March 17, 1917, Montgomery, AL;
d. February 15, 1965, Santa Monica, CA

In the 1940s, Nat King Cole was a brilliant jazz pianist who also sang. The following decade he was a very popular crooner who also played a little piano. Cole handled both of his roles and the transition in between with class, charm and obvious talent.

Nat Cole (who changed his name from Coles early in his career) was raised in Chicago and was influenced pianistically by Earl Hines. He led the Royal Dukes in 1934 and in 1936 made his recording debut with his older brother bassist Eddie Coles. Cole left Chicago the following year on a tour with a revival of the show *Shuffle Along*. When the band broke up in Los Angeles, he was stranded, picked up work in local nightclubs and decided to stay. Cole formed a trio with guitarist Oscar Moore and bassist Wesley Prince, which by 1940 was causing a stir, first locally and then, after they recorded for Decca, nationally. Called the King Cole Trio, they alternated instrumentals with rhythmic group vocals. Their recording of "Sweet Lorraine," a minor hit, featured Cole as a solo singer and pointed the way toward his future.

After signing with Capitol in 1943, the King Cole Trio recorded prolifically, with Nat Cole getting more and more features as a vocalist although usually in a jazz setting. Throughout the 1940s, he had hits in "Straighten Up And Fly Right," "Nature Boy," "Route 66," Mel Tormé's "The Christmas Song" and Billy Strayhorn's "Lush Life." Each of those songs became standards thanks to Cole's version.

The King Cole Trio, with guitarist Irving Ashby and bassist Johnny Miller succeeding Moore and Prince, became a quartet with the addition of Jack Costanzo on bongos. A much bigger change took place in 1950 when Nat Cole recorded "Mona Lisa" with a string orchestra. "Mona Lisa" became a #1 hit and suddenly Cole was a pop star. His trio was de-emphasized and then disbanded as he began touring and recording regularly with orchestras. Few of his new fans seemed to realize that Nat King Cole was a great pianist and, although he generally played a number or two during his concerts, he was now best known as a ballad singer who also sounded quite comfortable in front of big bands.

Cole's warm tone and likable style cast him as a black equivalent of Bing Crosby in that his vocals were attractive to women and non-threatening to men. Like Crosby, Cole's vocal style always sounded effortless and natural and there was a smile in his voice. During 1950–64, he had a continuous string of vocal hits including "Unforgettable," "Smile," "(I Love You) For Sentimental Reasons," "Too Young," "Walkin' My Baby Back Home," "Send For Me," "When I Fall In Love," "Pretend," "Answer Me, My Love" and finally "L-O-V-E." Nearly as popular as Frank Sinatra, Cole became an international star. While the jazz influence can barely be felt on his ballad albums with Gordon Jenkins, his dates with arrangers Billy May and Nelson Riddle sometimes put him in the role of a big band singer. He did record a few sets on piano, including a sort-of King Cole Trio reunion in 1956 (titled *After Midnight* and featuring guest soloists) and, on his groundbreaking 1956–57 television series, there were usually some jazz performances amongst the ballads. But in general, many in the jazz world felt abandoned, particularly when Cole recorded a few hit country albums, noticeably 1962's *Ramblin' Rose*.

Nat King Cole's career mostly went as smooth as his style until he was struck down by lung cancer in 1965 when he was only 47. On piano he was a major influence on Oscar Peterson and his piano-guitar-bass trio spawned similar trios led by Peterson, Art Tatum and Ahmad Jamal. His approach to taking vocals and his easy-going style have been influential on John Pizzarelli, Diana Krall and countless others. In both of his careers, Nat King Cole made a strong impact and was a class act.

Recommended CDs: There are a countless number of Nat King Cole CDs available, many duplicating each other. The most relevant from the vocal standpoint are listed here. Prior to signing with Decca, the King Cole Trio made an extensive number of radio transcriptions. *The Complete Early Transcriptions* (Vintage Jazz Classics 1026–29) is a difficult-to-locate four-CD set and the well-titled *Birth Of The Cole: 1938–1939* (Savoy 1205) has an additional disc. Later transcriptions from 1941 to 1945 are on the five-CD *The Trio Recordings* (Laserlight 15 915), the four-CD *The MacGregor Years* (Music and Arts

911) and the single disc *WWII Transcriptions* (Music and Arts 808). *Hit That Jive Jack: The Earliest Recordings* (MCA/Decca 42350) has the trio's Decca recordings. Collectors with huge budgets will want to bid on the out-of-print limited-edition 18-CD box *The Complete Capitol Recordings Of The Nat King Cole Trio* (Mosaic 138). Some of the same material is more readily available in *Jumpin' At Capitol* (Rhino 71009), *Jazz Encounters* (Capitol 96693), *The Best Of The Nat King Cole Trio: Vocal Classics Vol. 1 1941–46* (Capitol 33571) and *The Best Of The Nat King Cole Trio: Vocal Classics Vol. 2 1947–50* (Capitol 33572). The four-CD *Nat King Cole* (Capitol 99777) has 100 selections dating from 1943 to 1964 that include virtually all of Cole's pop hits plus a good sampling of his jazz performances. *The Capitol Collector's Series* (Capitol 93590) consists of 20 of those songs and is an excellent single-disc introduction to Cole. Nat King Cole the jazz-inspired vocalist is well featured on *Lush Life* (Capitol 80595), *Big Band Cole* (Capitol 96259), *The Billy May Sessions* (Capitol 89545), *Welcome To The Club/Tell Me All About Yourself* (Collector's Choice 823), *L-O-V-E* (Collector's Choice 876) and the *Complete After Midnight Sessions* (Capitol 48328), with the latter also including quite a few piano solos. Nat King Cole the ballad singer is in the spotlight on *Sings For Two In Love/Sings Ballads Of The Day* (Collector's Choice 827), *Love Is The Thing/Where Did Everyone Go* (Collector's Choice 825) and *The Touch Of Your Lips/I Don't Want To Be Hurt Anymore* (Collectors' Choice 821). *The Nat King Cole Story* (Capitol 95129) is a two-CD set of remakes of Cole's hits, well done in 1961. *Nat King Cole Sings, George Shearing Plays* (Capitol 48332) from 1962 has some inventive string charts by Ralph Carmichael and memorable Nat Cole versions of "September Song" and "Pick Yourself Up."

Natalie Cole
b. February 6, 1950, Los Angeles, CA

Natalie Cole has had two successful careers, the same number as her father Nat King Cole although in a different way.

Her father was already world famous at the time that Natalie was born and she was just 15 when he died from cancer. She began performing when she was 11 and appeared with her dad on a few occasions in the early 1960s. When she began her solo career in the early 1970s, although it was no secret that she was Nat King Cole's daughter, her music was purposely far removed from his. Cole was able to carve out her own very successful niche in R&B, starting with her 1975 album *Inseparable*. Although she had some difficulties with drugs in the early 1980s, she overcame her problems and continued to have a very successful career in pop music. In 1987 one of her singles was "When I Fall In Love," the first hint that she was interested in her father's music, but just viewed at the time as a brief moment of nostalgia.

In 1991 Natalie Cole began her second career, recording her versions of Nat King Cole's hits on *Unforgettable...With Love*, including everything from "It's Only A Paper Moon" and "Route 66" to "L-O-V-E." The CD was a major hit, selling over five million copies and winning many awards. Most touching was her spliced duet with her father on the title cut, which was also made into a video.

Since that time, Natalie Cole has developed into a more mature and versatile singer even though standards and jazz remain only part of her repertoire. *Ask A Woman Who Knows* from 2002 is her most jazz-oriented set and one that pleased both her father's fans and those who enjoyed *Unforgettable... With Love*. Since that time she has returned to pop, but at least now jazz and swing standards remain an option.

Recommended CDs: From the jazz standpoint, *Unforgettable... With Love* (Elektra 61049), *Take A Look* (Elektra 61496), *Stardust* (Elektra/Asylum 75596 19902) and *Ask A Woman Who Knows* (Verve 589 774) are certainly the Natalie Cole CDs to get. She shows on these four sets that she could be an appealing jazz singer if that were her main goal.

Earl Coleman

b. August 12, 1925, Port Huron, MI; d. July 12, 1995, New York, NY

Earl Coleman was strongly influenced by Billy Eckstine's voice throughout his life. Coleman had a very episodic career, one in which he was regularly being rediscovered.

Coleman grew up in Leland, Mississippi and, although he hitchhiked to Chicago when he was 13 in search of music, he eventually returned to Leland and finished high school. In addition to Eckstine, he considered his other main influence to be Roy Felton, who sang with Benny Carter's big band. Coleman first started singing professionally as a teenager, and he was with several big bands at the tail-end of the swing era, including those of Ernie Fields, Jay McShann (1943) and Earl Hines (1944), where he succeeded Eckstine and King Kolax. He made his recording debut in 1946 on a date featuring Miles Davis and Gene Ammons, but it went unreleased for decades. Coleman gained his greatest fame in 1947 when Charlie Parker, who was making his first record date after being released from Camarillo State Hospital, insisted that the reluctant Ross Russell (owner of the Dial label) let him use Coleman on his session with the Erroll Garner Trio. Coleman recorded "Dark Shadows" and "This Is Always," with the latter being the biggest seller in Dial's catalog.

Coleman recorded 11 songs in 1948; a single apiece for the Savoy, Atlantic and Jade labels plus five songs for Dial with the latter having Coleman backed by a sextet including trumpeter Fats Navarro, tenor-saxophonist Don Lanphere and pianist Linton Garner (Erroll's brother). But then Coleman fell into obscurity, only leading one album (1956's *Earl Coleman Returns*) during 1949–76. He did cut a few songs as a guest on Gene Ammons, Sonny Rollins and Elmo Hope records but otherwise went undocumented despite working with the Gerald Wilson Orchestra, Don Byas (while in Paris) and Billy Taylor.

Coleman's deep baritone voice still sounds in prime form on albums cut for Atlantic (1967), Xanadu (one apiece in 1977

and 1979) and Stash (1984), but record sales were light and he never became famous beyond a small cult following despite always being a superior ballad singer. He died a month short of his 70th birthday in 1995.

Recommended CDs: *Earl Coleman Returns* (Original Jazz Classics 187) from 1956 should have led to a major comeback. This reissue, which is highlighted by a definitive version of Gigi Gryce's "Social Call," is augmented by Coleman's recordings with Gene Ammons. Coleman's two numbers with Charlie Parker can be found on many Parker collections. *Cool Whaling* (Spotlite 235) has four of Coleman's 1948 recordings plus early performances by Joe Carroll, Babs Gonzales, Poncho Hagood, Eddie Jefferson and the obscure Frankie Passions (with Thelonious Monk).

LPs to Search For: Coleman's other main recordings, which include *Love Songs* (Atlantic 8172), *A Song For You* (Xanadu 147), *There's Something About An Old Love* (Xanadu 175) and *Stardust* (Stash 243), are unfortunately quite scarce.

Melissa Collard

b. November 6, Indiana

A fine swing singer and guitarist based in Northern California who has perfect articulation, Melissa Collard on her *Old Fashioned Love* CD shows that she is already one of the best in her field.

She grew up in Southern California and remembers: "My grandmother was a ragtime and stride pianist, so that first turned my ear when I was very young to something other than the pop music of the day. When I was in my teens I met a group of musician friends and we all explored more in the jazz arena—listening to Fats Waller, Mose Allison, Billie Holiday, Charlie Parker, Lambert, Hendricks and Ross. We would sneak in at the Lighthouse Jazz Club in Hermosa Beach and hear some great shows there."

Melissa Collard first sang professionally as a teenager when her brother's rock band needed a backup singer. She started playing guitar when she was 12, not just sticking originally to such vintage jazz heroes as Eddie Lang, Django Reinhardt and Charlie Christian, but also being inspired by Pat Metheny and Jimi Hendrix. At 14 she was singing regularly at a lounge on the Redondo Beach Pier.

After graduating high school, Collard studied English at Berkeley where she met quite a few trad jazz musicians who introduced her to early jazz. "These guys were a part of the New Orleans Revival in the 1940s in the Bay Area. They included Dick Oxtot, Bob Mielke, Richard Hadlock, Bill Bardin, Bob Helm, Bill Napier, Ray Skjelbred, Leon Oakley, Jim Goodwin, Jack Minger, Jim Rothermel and Bob Schultz. I got to play gigs on guitar and vocals with different combinations of these people, usually under the leadership of Oxtot. Simultaneously, I was in a Hot Club of France type quartet that played in North Beach which, in addition to the Django numbers, had an extensive swing repertoire."

Collard moved to Sacramento in the late 1980s and sang more modern standards with piano trios in hotels. She also worked with the ghost bands of Tommy Dorsey and Nelson Riddle, sang Western Swing with the Lost Weekend big band and traveled to Europe with the Cosumes River College jazz band. Most important to her career was recording *Old Fashioned Love* in 2004, which features trombonist Dan Barrett and banjoist-guitarist Eddie Erickson in the supporting cast. Hopefully there will be many more recordings in the future from Melissa Collard.

Recommended CD: *Old Fashioned Love* (Melismatic 101) is Melissa Collard's only CD thus far, but it is a delight. Swing standards and obscurities, outfitted with Dan Barrett arrangements, are well served by Collard's infectious singing.

Website: www.melissacollard.com

Joyce Collins

b. May 5, 1930, Battle Mountain, NV

An expressive storyteller (her "The Job Application" is a classic of its kind) and a fine bop-oriented pianist, Joyce Collins is also a well respected educator and teacher in the Los Angeles area.

She remembers being given records by Fats Waller and Teddy Wilson by an uncle and "that was it." Collins played piano from age four. Although she sang along with the radio and records as a youth, "I really didn't plan to become a singer. In the early 1950s I joined an instrumental quartet and reluctantly sang a song or two a night to secure the job. But as I grew to understand, appreciate and love lyrics, I started to really enjoy it." She attended Stockton Junior College and San Francisco State, was very impressed by seeing Peggy Lee perform and, after working in Northern California (including with the Frankie Carle band in 1954 and Oscar Pettiford), she settled in the Los Angeles area in the late 1950s.

Since that time Joyce Collins has worked with Bob Cooper at the Lighthouse, played with Benny Carter, recorded with the Gene Estes Big Band, toured with Paul Horn, worked on a variety of assignments in the studios and for films (including coaching Beau and Jeff Bridges who played pianists in *The Fabulous Baker Boys*) and has been a popular and influential piano and vocal teacher. She has also worked and recorded with Bill Henderson and Dave Mackay and led her own trio in clubs, having opportunities to tour Brazil, Europe and Japan.

"In terms of singing, I prefer to tell the story. I just want to serve the song. A great lyric wedded to a wonderful melody thrills me."

Recommended CDs: A trio set, *Sweet Madness* (Audiophile 262) from 1990, just has two vocals, but it includes "The Job Application."

LPs to Search For: Joyce Collins' second album, 1981's *Moment To Moment* (Discovery 828), has not been reissued yet.

Peggy Cone

b. 1947, New York, NY; d. February 5, 2001, New York, NY

Although she came to professional singing late in life, Peggy Cone was one of the bright new voices of Retro Swing in the 1990s.

"My stepdad, who was a painter, was very much into jazz and my mom was an actress, so I was always around the theater. I knew early on that I wanted to be a singer and a dancer although that didn't happen for quite a few years."

She sang with her mother onstage on a few occasions as a child but pursued several other careers first. Cone worked for a fashion magazine, had a costume jewelry business, started a cooking school, worked as a caterer for private parties, was an image fashion consultant worked for a children's photographer, and shot album jacket photos for Atlantic Records. While she was successful at each of those careers, she decided in 1989 to switch course and take voice lessons. "The first time that I sat on the piano with a microphone in my hand, I knew that I had found exactly what I wanted to do with my life."

Peggy Cone sang standards with a trio during 1993–98 in the New York City area. In 1998 she formed the Central Park Stompers, one of New York's top swing bands (Jon-Erik Kellso was their trumpeter) and for two years her extroverted and joyous singing, stylish period wardrobe and high-quality band gained a lot of publicity and work. "One thing that is different in our group is that we are very visual-oriented. I change outfits, two, three, and even four times during an evening; we put on a show. I'm thrilled to be involved with Swing music. I'm doing what I wanted to do since I was five years old and I'm living my dreams."

Sadly it did not last long. Peggy Cone died from liver cancer in 2001 at the age of 53.

Recommended CDs: *Peggy Cone And The Central Park Stompers* (Cone un-numbered) is a brief (20-minute) CD that has six infectious numbers. *Bad Girl Shoes* (Cone 6300) is a full-length disc that features Cone and her nine-piece group at their best. A slightly earlier CD, *Peggy Cone Sings* (Cone un-numbered), features the singer in her pre-swing days with her trio.

Mary Foster Conklin

b. December 29, 1957, New York, NY

Although she has a voice that could easily fit into the cabaret world, Mary Foster Conklin in recent times has proven to be a superior jazz singer, sounding at her best on her tribute CD to songwriter Matt Dennis.

The only musician in her family, she played the piano and clarinet in grade school and, while attending college, was a disc jockey at WRVR. She graduated from Connecticut College in 1979 with a major in theater. "I came to New York City right after college to go to theater school. My twenties were spent doing theater—I ran a non-profit theater company for six years, did a little musical theater and sang in a garage band, but didn't really get serious about my singing until 1988, when I left the theater company. I made the decision then to focus on music, as that's what made me happiest."

She has sung regularly with Art Lillard's 15-piece Heavenly Band since 1994, recorded three CDs, appeared regularly in New York clubs and occasionally on the West Coast. "Recently, I've gotten more interested in researching lesser known, out of print music and have just discovered the vast collection at the Library of Congress. Time and life experience are tremendous teachers. I don't think a singer really comes into the meat of their work till after forty. By then, there is plenty of history to draw upon."

Recommended CDs: *Crazy Eyes* (Mock Turtle 219) from 1998 was an impressive start for Mary Foster Conklin, ranging from singing lyrics for Dexter Gordon's "Fried Bananas" to swing standards, some pop and bits of cabaret while backed by a jazz trio. *You'd Be Paradise* (Mock Turtle 220) is a stronger jazz date and includes four Bob Dorough songs plus Matt Dennis' "Everything Happens To Me." The latter was a hint of what was to come, a full set of Dennis songs on *Blues For Breakfast* (Rhombus 7064), an inspired project that is her finest recording to date.

Website: www.maryfosterconklin.com

Harry Connick Jr.
b. September 11, 1967, New Orleans, LA

Harry Connick Jr. has had a multi-faceted career, as a pianist, bandleader, arranger, actor and, most of all, a good-natured singer. His rise to prominence preceded most of the current crooners by a decade, paving the way. Connick's father, Harry Connick, Sr. was the district attorney of New Orleans and a jazz lover who occasionally sang. The younger Connick started on piano when he was three and within a few years was performing in public, occasionally singing. Many years later, a CD came out of him playing (and singing "Doctor Jazz") with a Dixieland group when he was 11. Connick studied at the New Orleans Center for the Creative Arts (Ellis Marsalis and James Booker were influential teachers) and in New York at Hunter College and the Manhattan School of Music.

Signed to Columbia when he was 19, Connick first gained attention as a Thelonious Monk–inspired stride pianist. He took his initial vocals on his second CD, *20*, and became famous when he was heard throughout the soundtrack of *When Harry Met Sally* in 1989, singing standards in a charming fashion. From that point on, Connick has been a major name, crooning à la Frank Sinatra at times, leading a big band for which he writes most of the arrangements, acting effectively in films, and recording everything from pop (which usually flops) to New Orleans-flavored jazz. He concentrated on pop and funk during 1994–96, but most of his work since then is jazz-oriented. In recent times, he has alternated between vocal albums for Columbia and instrumental piano records for Marsalis Music. In addition, after Hurricane Katrina and the Federal government's incompetence at helping New Orleans, Connick has been involved in raising money for his hometown and working closely with Habitat for Humanity.

Harry Connick Jr. puts on colorful shows, singing standards from several decades, performing some original material and always leaving space for a tribute to New Orleans.

Recommended CDs: These recordings are the ones with Harry Connick Jr.'s best vocals, most of which are jazz-oriented: *20* (Columbia 44369), *When Harry Met Sally* (Columbia 45319), *We Are In Love* (Columbia 46146), *To See You* (Columbia 68787), *Come By Me* (Columbia 69618), *Songs I Heard* (Columbia 86177), *Only You* (Columbia 90551) and *Oh My NOLA* (Columbia 88851).

Chris Connor
b. November 8, 1927, Kansas City, MO

Chris Connor, along with June Christy and Peggy Lee, symbolizes cool jazz of the 1950s. Her straightforward vibratoless delivery gives one the impression that she is both vulnerable and very guarded toward expressing her deepest feelings, keeping all but a few at a distance. She makes every note and sound count. Her subtle interpretations of songs mean that her recordings need to be listened to closely in order to feel the emotions that are bubbling just beneath the surface.

Connor studied clarinet when she was young but being a singer was always her main dream. While working as a secretary, she performed on weekends at the University of Missouri with a college band influenced by Stan Kenton, and it was her goal to sing with Kenton. In 1949 she moved to New York, singing with the Claude Thornhill Orchestra during the next few years. She was briefly with Jerry Wald when June Christy heard her on the radio and recommended her to Stan Kenton. Connor was only with Kenton for ten months during 1952–53, quickly tiring of the endless traveling which she had already undergone with Thornhill, but she did record a hit: "All About Ronnie."

From then on, Chris Connor was a solo artist. She recorded three albums for Bethlehem prior to doing her most significant work, 12 records for Atlantic cut during 1956–62. Her career suffered when rock became the dominant music, but she toured Japan, recorded for a few obscure labels and made a full comeback by the early 1980s.

Although her voice has inevitably aged and she only makes infrequent appearances today, Chris Connor maintains the same cool approach as in her earlier days, with subtlety and quiet (but passionate) feelings still being felt in her interpretations.

Recommended CDs: Chris Connor's excellent Bethlehem releases are available as *Chris* (Bethlehem 75988), *This Is Chris* (Bethlehem 76684) and *Sings Lullabys Of Birdland* (Bethlehem 79851). Eight of the Atlantics have returned as four single CDs that have all of the music from two former LPs apiece: *Chris Connor/He Loves Me, He Loves Me Not* (Collectables 6239), *A Jazz Date With Chris Connor/Chris Craft* (Rhino 71747), *I Miss You So/Witchcraft* (Collectables 6814) and *Chris In Person/Sings George Gershwin* (Collectables 6887). Three of the other Atlantics are also available on CD. *Double Exposure* (Collectors Choice 319) teams Connor with the Maynard Ferguson Orchestra, *Free Spirits* (Collectables 6521) is one of her more adventurous sets and *A Portrait Of Chris* (Collectables 236) is also well worth picking up. Of Connor's later recordings, *Sweet And Swinging* (Audiophile 208), *The London Connection* (Audiophile 246), *Classic* (Contemporary 14023), *New Again* (Contemporary 14038), *As Time Goes By* (Enja 7061), *Haunted Heart* (High Note 7079) and 2002's *I Walk With Music* (High Note 7095) also have their moments of interest, but get her Bethlehems and Atlantics first.

LPs to Search For: *No Strings* (Atlantic 1383) is currently the one Chris Connor Atlantic LP not yet available on CD.

Website: www.chrisconnorjazz.com

Carla Cook

b. January 19, 1962, Detroit, MI

In the late 1990s, MaxJazz emerged as one of the top labels involved in documenting current jazz singers. One of their most important discoveries was Carla Cook, an exciting singer who was quite capable of performing both creative jazz and very expressive R&B.

"I started singing in the Angelic Choir at the age of five in the Christian Methodist Episcopal Church. I studied piano from ages seven to 16 and string bass in the junior high and high school orchestras. At the age of 12 or 13 I knew that I wanted to sing jazz for a living." She attended the highly regarded Cass Technical High School where she sang in the choir, studied voice at the Detroit Community Music School and earned a Bachelor of Science in Speech Communication at Northeastern University in 1985.

While Carla Cook brings a jazz sensibility and the willingness to improvise to each song she sings, her repertoire includes R&B songs, Motown, blues, gospel, pop and rock tunes in addition to jazz standards. In 1990 she moved to New York, appearing in nightclubs but also teaching social studies at a junior high school until the work picked up. Signing with MaxJazz in 1998 and recording three CDs has given her a well-deserved national reputation.

"I love improvising and the thrill of creating music on the spot was always fascinating to me. I remember being dumbfounded when I learned that Ella's solos were different every time! But while I am a jazz vocalist, I also love other forms of music. I've been influenced by it all on some level and I'd be musically dishonest if I omitted that influence from what I'm doing."

Recommended CDs: Thus far Carla Cook has recorded three diverse and well-conceived albums: *It's All About Love* (MaxJazz 106), which also features pianist Cyrus Chestnut, *Dem Bones* (MaxJazz 111) and 2002's *Simply Natural* (Max Jazz 115).

Website: www.carlacook.com

Carleton Coon

b. February 5, 1894, Rochester, MN; d. May 4, 1932, Chicago, IL

Prior to the rise of Louis Armstrong in 1926, very few of the male singers who made it into the recording studios had much of a feel for jazz (other than Cliff Edwards). Carleton Coon and his musical partner Joe Sanders were two of the few exceptions.

Coon, who began playing drums early on, led a band when he was a teenager. He served in World War I, becoming a captain. In December 1918, while on leave in Kansas City, he happened to go into a music store where he heard pianist Joe Sanders trying out a few new songs by singing. Coon spontaneously harmonized with him and a friendship was born.

After they were discharged from the military the following year, they formed the Coon-Sanders Novelty Orchestra. The interplay between the co-leaders along with their individual vocals made the group popular from the start. They recorded one instrumental in 1921 and on December 5, 1922, the band appeared for the first time on the radio, broadcasting from WOAF in Kansas City. Since their radio show did not start until midnight, the group was renamed the Coon-Sanders Nighthawks.

The Nighthawks were among the first bands to become famous due to radio. By 1924 they had relocated to Chicago where they were based at the Blackhawk Restaurant during 1926–30. It was also in 1924 that the band began seriously recording, signing with Victor. Most of the group's selections had vocals by either both or one of the co-leaders but, unlike the singing on most recordings of the era, the vocalizing was jazz-oriented. Instead of pompous interpretations by semi-classical baritones who displayed awkward phrasing, both Coon and Sanders had styles that swung. Among Coon's best solo numbers were "Yes, Sir! That's My Baby," "That's All There Is (There Ain't No More)" and "Too Busy," but it was his duet performances with Sanders such as "I'm Gonna Charleston Back To Charleston," "I Ain't Got Nobody" and "Sluefoot," that were generally most exciting.

The Coon-Sanders Orchestra weathered the first years of the Depression well and was reasonably successful during a six-month stay in New York (1931–32), though the group became homesick for Chicago. Settling into the Hotel Sherman in Chicago, they were poised to continue their success, but Coon was having difficulty with an abscessed tooth that he had neglected for months. When he went in for surgery, it was disastrous. He contracted blood poisoning from the operation and died on May 4, 1932, when he was 38. The Nighthawks struggled on for a year but, without Carleton Coon, the spirit was gone and they broke up within a year.

Recommended CDs: All of the recordings by Carleton Coon and Joe Sanders are on *Coon-Sanders Nighthawks, Vols. 1–4* (The Old Masters 111, 112, 113 and 114).

Eve Cornelious

(Eve Cornelious Crawford)
b. August 9, Newark, NJ

Based in North Carolina, Eve Cornelious is such a talented singer that it is surprising she only recorded two CDs under her own name.

She remembers seeing the movie *Lady Sings The Blues* early on and then being really inspired when she heard a real album by Lady Day. "I sang some in the children's choir at a Baptist church, but I sang more regularly in the high school chorus and quite a bit around school with two other young girls mostly harmonizing pop tunes of the day." She graduated from Hampton University with a business degree, and from North Carolina Central University with degrees in jazz and music.

"I had always wanted to sing, but I did not think that it would be a viable career that would make me self-supporting. After graduating from college, I took a job with one of the giant cigarette companies. I would ride around in the company car all day from job to job singing and many people told me that it sounded really good. It got to a point where I didn't like the job and I knew that the only way that I would be happy was to pursue a singing career, so I threw caution to the wind." She married pianist-arranger Chip Crawford, and has pursued music ever since.

In addition to her husband and her own groups, Eve Cornelious has worked with Ramsey Lewis, Norman Connors,

Grady Tate, Roy Hargrove's Cristol, Chucho Valdes, Russell Malone, Mulgrew Miller, Billy Taylor, John Hicks, Jon Hendricks, Mark Whitfield, Tim Warfield and Javon Jackson (with whom she recorded *Easy Does It*), touring Europe, Japan and Cuba. She is also the jazz vocal teacher at East Carolina University.

Recommended CDs: While Eve Cornelius' debut CD *Faces Of Eve* is scarce, *I Feel Like Some Jazz Today* (Pooky/Looky 9904) is a definitive outing. The repertoire is primarily standards and includes tributes to Miles Davis (new lyrics to "Flamenco Sketches"), Carmen McRae, Esther Phillips, Betty Carter and Ella Fitzgerald ("Air Mail Special").

Website: www.evecornelious.com

Roz Corral
b. June 7, 1947, Lakeport, CA

It took Roz Corral a surprisingly long period of time before she dedicated herself to becoming a jazz singer, but her one recording, *Telling Tales*, is a particularly memorable effort.

Corral took dance lessons from an early age and sang publicly for the first time when her dance teacher gave her a singing spot at one of their recitals. She sang professionally when she was 19, taking a semester off from college to tour with a variety revue. "But until the end of the 1980s, I worked as a senior publicist in a high powered, major film/entertainment P.R. firm (PMK Associates). It was all consuming." She had begun seriously singing jazz in 1985 when she started studying with Barry Harris. Torn between keeping her day job or pursuing her dream, her decision was made for her when she was laid off. "In 1989 I made a demo with Vic Juris, Ray Anderson and Jeff Hirschfield and started working rather quickly."

Since then, Roz Corrall has worked steadily in the New York area, often with pianist Bruce Barth. "I'm not sure what took me so long to put out my first CD, *Telling Tales*, for its release was certainly a turning point for me. Musically, my main inspiration is Carmen McRae. She has always been my favorite because she incorporated so much soulfulness and heart into her delivery. At this point, I certainly want to record more and make up for lost time although performing live is my first love. When singing the standards, or even a contemporary composition, it can sound stilted if you stick to the way it was written rhythmically. That freedom to put your own stamp on it allows you to give your own interpretation."

Recommended CDs: Roz Corral's one CD, *Telling Tales* (Blujazz 3335), finds her as a very capable storyteller and a singer capable of expressing a wide variety of emotions. She swings throughout, hints at Ella Fitzgerald on "Too Close For Comfort," and benefits from the inventive arrangements of Bruce Barth.

Website: www.rozcorral.com

Christine Correa
b. July 8, 1955, Bombay, India

ROUNDABOUT

An adventurous avant-garde singer, Christine Correa has a very flexible voice and is never shy to push herself into new areas of music.

"My father, Micky Correa, led a big band at the Taj Mahal Hotel in Bombay for 21 years. During his tenure he met several well-known musicians including Louis Armstrong, Duke Ellington, Jack Teagarden, Dave Brubeck and Paul Desmond, and I was thus introduced to this art form." She sang from an early age, participating in local concerts and school functions, and played the piano since she was five.

The turning point of her musical career occurred in 1979 when she moved to the United States and began studying at the New England Conservatory of Music. Correa studied with Ran Blake, Jaki Byard and Joe Maneri among others, and her open-minded approach led to performances with Blake, Jimmy Giuffre, Steve Lacy and John LaPorta. "They taught me that articulation, clarity and being true to oneself is the basis for this music. Studying and performing with pianist Ran Blake encouraged me to tap into my ethnic heritage which for so long had been suppressed in my music. And meeting my partner, pianist/composer Frank Carlberg, who wrote specific art songs tailored to my voice with regard to style and range, opened another range of possibilities and creativity, presenting an entirely new repertoire."

Christine Correa, who directs the Maine Jazz Camp so as to pass down her musical lessons to the next generations, says, "The spontaneous quality of the music can make a performance a real thrill. In the music with which I am involved, the singer is not in the foreground but is instead an integral part of the whole ensemble."

Recommended CDs: Christine Correa's duo album with Ran Blake, *Roundabout* (Music and Arts 807), put her on the jazz map as she not only holds her own with the unique pianist but inspires him on a mixture of standards and his quirky originals. Correa's other CDs have generally been recorded under Frank Carlberg's leadership but she is very much an equal partner: the duo set *Ugly Beauty* (Northeastern 5015), *The Crazy Woman* (Accurate 4401), *Variations On A Summer Day* (Fresh Sound New Talent 083) and *In The Land Of Art* (Fresh Sound New Talent 167).

Baby Cox
(Gertrude Cox)
Birth and death dates and places are not known

One of the advantages of having 521 entries in this book rather than 200 is that it allows me to include a few mystery figures; talented singers of whom very little is known beyond their recordings. In the case of Baby Cox, one wonders who this exciting early scat-singer was, and why she became lost to history.

A year after, Adelaide Hall made a very strong impression with her wordless vocal on "Creole Love Call," Duke Ellington

Ida Cox

again reached beyond his orchestra to use a voice as one of his instruments. On the session of October 1, 1928, Baby Cox scats on "The Mooche" (interacting with guest guitarist Lonnie Johnson) and trades off quite heatedly with Bubber Miley's wa-wa cornet on a classic rendition of "Hot And Bothered." On October 30 she returned to Duke's band to scat a chorus of "I Can't Give You Anything But Love" (Irving Mills took the straight part), and on November 10 she recorded a remake with Ellington that was originally rejected but released over a half-century later. That is her entire recorded legacy.

Record collectors have long speculated who Baby Cox was, and even whether she might have been a man. Some have thought that Cox could be Adelaide Hall under another name. Neither of those theories is true, since Baby Cox had a role in the Broadway musical *Hot Chocolates* in 1929 and also appeared in the obscure *Humming Sam* in 1933.

Otherwise nothing is known about her. But Baby Cox was certainly one of the most stirring jazz singers of 1928.

Recommended CDs: Three of the four Baby Cox performances (all but the originally rejected version of "I Can't Give You Anything But Love") are on *1928* (Classics 550).

Ida Cox
(Ida Prather)
b. February 25, 1896, Cedartown, GA;
d. November 10, 1967, Knoxville, TN

Ida Cox was one of the most important classic blues singers to rise to fame in the early 1920s. While some of those vocalists were vaudevillians swept up in the blues fad and others would change their style to adapt to popular music of the late 1920s, Cox stuck to the jazz-influenced blues that she knew best throughout her career.

IDA COX
Complete Recorded Works 1923–1938 In Chronological Order

VOLUME 3
1925–1927

Featuring:
TOMMY LADNIER
LOVIE AUSTIN
JIMMY O'BRYANT
PAPA CHARLIE JACKSON
BOB SHOFFNER
a. o.

document
RECORDS
DOCD-5324

She first sang in church choirs as a child in Georgia. As a teenager she ran away from home in 1910 to tour with White and Clark's Minstrels. She learned about show business, developed her talents as a singer and writer, and married Alder Cox who also worked in minstrel shows. That marriage did not last long but Ida kept her husband's name, even after she started a much more successful second marriage to pianist Jesse "Tiny" Crump who was often her accompanist.

Cox became a major draw in vaudeville and in theaters, at first in the South and eventually up in Chicago where she moved in 1922. She signed with the Paramount label the following year and recorded 86 songs during 1923–29. Billed by Paramount as "The Uncrowned Queen of the Blues," Cox was often joined on her recordings by small groups headed by pianist Lovie Austin. Among her best-known recordings are "Wild Women Don't Have The Blues," "I've Got The Blues For Rampart Street," "Graveyard Dream Blues," "'Fore Day Creep" and "Death Letter Blues." For "Chicken Monkey Man Blues," the lyrics she wrote are very similar to the ones featured years later by Jimmy Rushing and Joe Williams on "Goin' To Chicago Blues."

Ida Cox, ranked second to Bessie Smith in popularity among blues singers by the mid-1920s, toured with her own

companies including shows titled *Raisin' Cain* and *Darktown Scandals*. Her recordings stopped after two final songs in 1929, but she continued working during the Depression years even when her style was considered out of vogue. Producer John Hammond hoped to showcase Bessie Smith at his first *Spirituals To Swing* concert in December 1938, but the Empress had died by then. For his second production a year later, he featured Ida Cox, who at 43 was still very much in her prime. In fact, Cox was having a very good year, performing at Café Society in New York and starring in two record dates that included versions of "Death Letter Blues," "One Hour Mama" and "'Fore Day Creep" while backed by an all-star swing combo. There was one more record date the following year and she appeared briefly in a film, singing two blues songs while assisted by Jesse Crump.

After suffering a stroke in the mid-1940s, Cox retired from music, moving to Knoxville, Tennessee. She performed now and then in the 1950s and in 1961 made her final recordings, a full album for the Riverside label in which (at age 65) she sounded fine while backed by a quintet including Coleman Hawkins and Roy Eldridge. It was her last act, since she soon went back into retirement. Ida Cox, who died from cancer in 1967, is still considered one of the early giants of the blues and an unacknowledged influence on jazz singers.

Recommended CDs: *Vol. 1* (Document 5322), *Vol. 2* (Document 5323), *Vol. 3* (Document 5324), *Vol. 4* (Document 5325) and *Vol. 5* (Document 5651) have all of Ida Cox's recordings from 1923 to 1940. *Blues For Rampart Street* (Original Jazz Classics 1758) is a reissue of her underrated 1961 album.

Christina Crerar
b. June 12, 1972, PA

Christina Crerar's *Little Jazz Bird* is a very impressive debut not only for her singing but for the well-conceived arrangements and the inspired repertoire on the CD.

She grew up in New Jersey, singing show tunes and standards for school functions and at home. "It is a magical thing to spontaneously launch into harmony with one's siblings. At somewhere around 10 or 11, no one had taught us how; we just did it whenever we felt like it. Jazz seems to me to be the closest thing a group of people can come to creating something harmonious and meaningful out of thin air."

Crerar played piano and flute while growing up. She earned a Bachelor of Music from Catholic University of America in 1994. "A turning point for me was in 1997 when I decided to specifically sing jazz. I stopped auditioning for shows and started fronting groups. It started with big bands, then smaller combos. I feel incredibly fortunate to have been taught entirely 'on the bandstand' by some incredible musicians here in the D.C. area. My good friend Geoff Reecer (guitarist with the Airmen of Note) and I started working together with small groups and guitar duo work around 1999. His influence allowed me to freely discover my voice."

Based in the area of Washington, D.C., Christina Crerar is a regular member of the swing band Blue Sky 5, leads her vocal swing trio Swing It Sister, sometimes sings with George Gee's orchestra in New York and guests with the Boilermaker Jazz Band. In addition, she acts in plays, has sung in Amsterdam with the musical revue *In The Mood* and entertained American troops in Japan and Korea.

Recommended CDs: The privately issued *Little Jazz Bird* is a joy. Among the songs that Christina Crerar interprets are such offbeat items as "An Occasional Man," "Solid Potato Salad," "Down With Love" and "No Moon At All." Her voice is flexible, versatile and quite attractive, and she clearly has a promising future.

Website: www.littlejazzbird.com

Bing Crosby
(Harry Lillis Crosby)
b. May 3, 1903, Tacoma, WA;
d. October 14, 1977, Madrid, Spain

Because he was so famous as a middle-of-the-road pop singer, actor and a TV personality in his later years, Bing Crosby's early contributions to jazz and popular music are sometimes forgotten. Probably the first great white male jazz singer who was not a musician, Crosby brought the innovations of jazz (particularly the phrasing of Louis Armstrong) into popular music, setting the stage for swing singing.

Crosby sang in his high school band in Washington and taught himself the drums. Although he studied law at Gonzaga University in Spokane, he was much more interested in performing. He met singer Al Rinker and played drums and sang with Rinker's Musicaleaders. Crosby made so much money with the group that he dropped out of school during his final year. After forming a duo with Rinker, they worked a bit in vaudeville but were scuffling when they came down to Los Angeles to visit Rinker's sister, Mildred Bailey. Through Bailey, Crosby and Rinker met bandleader Paul Whiteman, who hired them, and soon teamed them with singer-pianist Harry Barris as the Rhythm Boys.

Crosby, Rinker and Barris not only worked as an independent group but were joined by other less jazz-oriented singers on some of Whiteman's recordings. While with Whiteman during 1926–30, Crosby also had some solo vocals, most notably "Muddy Water," "Mary," "Ol' Man River," "Make Believe" and "'Tain't So, Honey, 'Tain't So." He had opportunities to learn about jazz by observing cornetist Bix Beiderbecke and C-melody saxophonist Frank Trumbauer. The Rhythm Boys appeared with Whiteman in the 1930 film *The King Of Jazz,* though Bing missed an opportunity to have a solo number due to his excessive drinking (which he gave up in the 1930s).

The Rhythm Boys, whose act was quite humorous, caused Whiteman plenty of headaches and, when the bandleader was forced to cut back when the Depression hit, the Rhythm Boys were cut loose. They settled in Los Angeles and worked with Gus Arnheim's orchestra. However, by then Crosby was becoming such a big attraction that he broke away to start his solo career.

Most earlier male pop singers came across as frustrated opera singers, boy tenors or very pompous in their phrasing. In contrast, Crosby was one of the first vocalists to take full advantage of the development of the microphone to sing intimately in a relaxed and friendly fashion, influenced not only by Armstrong (he was a lifelong fan) but Beiderbecke and Jack Teagarden. He also had the knack to make everything look easy and his often-brilliant vocals appear so natural as to seem effortless.

A series of 15-minute radio programs for CBS helped make Crosby famous, as did his series of recordings, which included such hits as "Just One More Chance," "I Found A Million-Dollar Baby," "I Surrender Dear," "Wrap Your Troubles In Dreams," "Please," "Brother Can You Spare A Dime" and "June In January." During the first half of the 1930s, Crosby showed on numerous occasions that he was one of the top jazz singers around. His recordings of "Dinah," "Shine," "Some Of These Days" (which has some creative scatting), "St. Louis Blues" (with Duke Ellington) and "My Honey's Loving Arms" (with the Mills Brothers) rank with the best vocal performances of the classic jazz era.

By the mid-1930s, Crosby was a superstar, the most popular singer in the world. His recordings for Decca covered a wide variety of music and his jazz-oriented past was de-emphasized. He had remarkable success on records, on the radio (hosting the *Kraft Music Hall* during 1936–46), in movies (he was in 79 films in all, starring in 55 of them) and in live performances, breaking records in all four areas, and those were joined in later years by his successes on television. Crosby introduced scores of songs that became standards, everything from "I'm An Old Cowhand" to "White Christmas."

Although jazz formed only a small part of his post-1935 repertoire and career, Crosby always loved Dixieland and Louis Armstrong. He had Armstrong appear in some of his movies, most notably *Pennies From Heaven* and *High Society* (they sang together on "Now You Has Jazz"), and along the way there were occasional projects in jazz settings. To name a few, in 1932's *Big Broadcast*, Crosby sings a hot version of "Dinah" with his regular accompanist of the period, the great guitarist Eddie Lang. The 1940 film *Birth Of The Blues*, while being a fictional history of jazz, has Crosby singing quite a few jazz numbers. He welcomed trumpeter Wingy Manone and Harry Barris (playing a saxophonist) to his film *Rhythm On The River*, Armstrong and Teagarden appeared on his radio show in the late 1940s/early '50s on several occasions, Bing recorded "Gone Fishin'" with Satch, and as late as the late 1950s, he used Bob Scobey's Dixieland band as his backup group on a record.

Even with the emergence of worthy competitors such as Frank Sinatra in the 1940s, Bing Crosby never declined in popularity, staying active up until the time of his 1977 death.

Recommended CDs: *1928–1932* (Timeless 1-004) is an excellent sampler of Bing Crosby's early recordings, particularly his work from 1927 to 1929 with Paul Whiteman. *Bing—His Legendary Years: 1931 to 1957* (MCA 4-10887) is a four-CD set that is a superior overview of Crosby's most influential and successful years. *Bing Crosby In Hollywood, Vol. One: 1930–1934* (Collectables 605) and *Bing Crosby In Hollywood, Vol. Two: 1930–1934* (Collectables 606) contain songs that Crosby mostly recorded in films including many hot performances. *And Some Jazz Friends* (GRP/Decca 603) has some of Crosby's best jazz dates of the 1934–51 period, highlighted by meetings with the likes of Louis Jordan, Connie Boswell, Louis Armstrong, Jack Teagarden, Lionel Hampton, Eddie Condon, Lee Wiley, Woody Herman and Bing's younger brother Bob Crosby. The three-CD *Swingin' With Bing! Bing Crosby's Lost Radio Performances* (Shout! Factory 31507) has a variety of performances, many jazz-oriented, from his radio shows of the 1940s. *Havin' Fun* (Storyville 8405) is a two-CD set of Crosby's radio shows with guests Louis Armstrong, Jack Teagarden and violinist Joe Venuti. The mutual love and often hilarious humor is as rewarding as the music. From 1956 to 1957, two of Crosby's finest recordings of his later years are *Bing Sings Whilst Bregman Swings* (Verve 549367) and *Bing With A Beat* (RCA 60142); the latter is Crosby's outing with trumpeter Bob Scobey. And for the true completists, the British

Jonzo label has released a complete chronological reissue of Bing Crosby's recordings through 1949, on 49 CDs.

LPs to Search For: A superb single-album summary of Crosby's early hits, *Wrap Your Troubles In Dreams* (RCA 584), features Bing Crosby at his youthful best.

Joan Crowe
b. Indianapolis, IN

Originally known as an actress, cabaret singer and comedian, Joan Crowe made a strong impression in the jazz world with the release of *Bird On The Wire*, showing that she is a memorable jazz singer, too.

She grew up in Indianapolis and spent summers in Germany at her grandparents' dairy farm. Crowe picked up experience performing at shows in community theater and high school musicals. After earning a degree in theater from Indiana University, she gained a Masters from the Asolo State Theater.

Joan Crowe has since worked in films, television and on stage. She took 1992 to 1998 off to raise a family, and then in 1999 began to concentrate on her singing career, gradually shifting from cabaret to jazz. She currently leads a trio (High Society Rhythm), and her larger band (High Society Rhythm Orchestra), mostly in the New York area.

Recommended CD: 2005's *Bird On The Wire* (Evensong Music 8703) features Joan Crowe on one inspired number after another, putting plenty of surprises and her wit into jazz, cabaret and pop songs, using her acting skills and her versatile voice to cover nearly all emotions.

Website: www.joancrowe.com

Jamie Cullum
b. August 20, 1979, Essex, England

One of the most interesting new performers of the past decade, singer-pianist Jamie Cullum is a major attraction in England and an increasingly famous name in the United States. His music is based in both jazz and pop music, his shows are colorful, and he has the potential to be either an important new force in music or a forgettable pop star, depending on the decisions he makes during the next few years.

Self-taught, Cullum first gained attention in 1999 when he released his debut album, *Jamie Cullum Trio—Heard It All Before*, printing up only 500 copies. He sang and played standards dating from the 1930s and '40s with his trio yet sounded fresh and contemporary. After graduating from the University of Redding in 2001, he recorded *Pointless Nostalgic*, a CD that caught on in England and became a major seller. All but three of the 13 songs were jazz standards, yet Cullum brought a pop sensibility and wit to the music that made it seem brand new and relevant to young people. He was signed to Universal and his 2003 album *Twentysomething* sold over a million copies, making Cullum a star. Ever since then he has constantly toured, including visiting the United States several times.

Relying less on standards and more on originals during the past couple of years, Jamie Cullum can still croon a ballad with the best, or do something outlandish in his high energy concerts like end a song by putting his foot on the piano. His future adventures will certainly be worth following.

Recommended CDs: Cullum's debut, *Heard It All Before*, is a collector's item and very difficult to find. *Pointless Nostalgic* (Candid 79782) has Cullum finding something fresh to say on slyly inventive renditions of "You And The Night And The Music," "Devil May Care," "In The Wee Small Hours Of The Morning" and Thelonious Monk's "Well You Needn't" plus his own "I Want To Be A Pop Star." *Twentysomething* (Verve 227302) has fewer jazz tunes (though "I Could Have Danced All Night" is a highlight), a memorable title cut that seems to symbolize his generation, and erratic but never dull material. 2005's *Catching Tales* (Verve 80005478) includes ten Cullum originals and features him as more of a singer/songwriter but still has its jazz-oriented moments. From the jazz standpoint, *Pointless Nostalgic* is Jamie Cullum's most rewarding recording but hopefully his most significant work is in the future.

Website: www.jamiecullum.com

Adela Dalto
b. November 18, 1953, Weslaco, TX

Adela Dalto, who originally performed with her late husband pianist Jorge Dalto, has carved out an individual career for herself, performing Brazilian and Afro-Cuban jazz.

Born in Texas, she grew up in East Chicago and Gary, Indiana. "Standing on the sofa at the age of three, when my parents would have company, I was the entertainment. Years later, my first paid performance was opening for Ramsey Lewis back in 1971." She played violin as a youth and studied privately with voice teachers.

"A month after I married my husband in 1973, I didn't like the idea that I would be sitting at the table with the ladies while my husband played on stage. I was 19 and quickly decided I belonged on stage." When Jorge Dalto had groups, Adela was usually his singer, and she was featured in 1985 on his recording of "Ease My Pain." When he was involved in other projects or touring, she worked on her own music and took flute lessons from Alberto Socarras. She also recorded jingles for the studios and sang Brazilian music in restaurants.

Jorge Dalto's death in 1987, when he was just 39, forced Adela Dalto to go out on her own. She recorded *A Brazilian Affair* the following year and worked during 1989–92 five nights a week at the Rainbow Room with Mauricio Smith. She also toured Europe with Mario Bauza's band in 1991 and has since worked with Patato Valdes, Chucho Valdes, Jerry Gonzalez and Hilton Ruiz. In 2000 Dalto formed an all-women's group, Mujeres Latinas, that played several styles of Latin jazz, salsas and Latin rock. In addition, she earned a B.A. in Music from Empire State College in Jazz and Latin Jazz Vocal Performance.

A versatile singer who performs in English, Spanish and Portuguese, Adela Dalto has successfully moved out from her late husband's shadow. She has become a versatile and skilled singer in both Afro-Cuban and Brazilian music.

Recommended CDs: *Papa Boco* (Milestone 9253) ranges from sambas to salsa along with some straightforward jazz pieces. Dalto has recorded three CDs for the Japanese Venus label, *A Brazilian Affair* (Venus 9253), *Peace* (Venus 79805) and *Exotica* (Venus 35011), and guested on sets by Lee Konitz (*Brazilian Rhapsody*) and Mario Bauza (*My Time Is Now* and *944 Christopher Avenue*). However, she is proudest of *La Crème Latina*, which has been released by her own Mujeres Latinas label and features the remarkable pianist Chucho Valdes.

Website: www.adeladalto.com

Meredith D'Ambrosio
b. March 20, 1941, Boston, MA

A thoughtful, introverted, quiet, sometimes-haunting and often-melancholy singer, Meredith d'Ambrosio has had a strong underground following for years.

Her father sang with big bands while her mother was a pianist. "Perhaps the many sadnesses I've experienced through my life may be a factor in the way I feel and interpret a song. I was very fortunate to have parents who were professional musicians. My father was a bass-baritone singer who helped me to understand the importance of breathing, intonation and phrasing. Both parents allowed me to discover my own voice without the help of a vocal coach. They felt that studying classical piano, solfege and jazz theory would put me on the path they trusted me to follow. Also, my ears were glued to the radio in the mid-forties with the great singers, songs and bands. But in the end, I had to believe in my musical art enough to want to nurture and direct it."

D'Ambrosio had classical piano lessons from the time she was six, and performed on local television in Boston as a teenager. Her first professional gig took place in 1958 in a Boston jazz club with pianist Roger Kellaway. She has worked steadily ever since, often accompanying herself on piano, starting in 1963. D'Ambrosio, who is married to pianist Eddie Higgins, made her first recording in 1978, moved to New York in 1981 and began her long-time association with the Sunnyside label in 1985. She has worked and/or recorded with pianists Harold Danko, Bob Dorough, Dave Frishberg, Fred Hersch, Dick Hyman, Hank Jones, Lee Musiker, Mike Renzi, Richard Wyands and Eddie Higgins, bassist Jay Leonhart, altoists Lee Konitz and Phil Woods, guitarist Gene Bertoncini and violinist Johnny Frigo in addition to featuring many players in her rhythm section. She is also a lyricist, composer, teacher, a calligrapher, a watercolorist and a creator of eggshell mosaics.

When asked about her future goals, Meredith d'Ambrosio says, "To record all the songs I've written, to study orchestral arranging and score writing, and to help singers learn how to find their own voice."

Recommended CDs: Fans of Meredith d'Ambrosio's unique style of singing and piano playing will want all of her releases since she has been very consistent through the years. The ones given an asterisk have been cited by her as her personal favorites: *Lost In His Arms* (Sunnyside 1018—originally on Spring Inc.), *Another Time (*Sunnyside 1017—originally on Shiah*), *Little Jazz Bird* (Sunnyside 1040—originally on Palo Alto), *It's Your Dance* (Sunnyside 1011), *The Cove* (Sunnyside 1028), *South To A Warmer Place* (Sunnyside 1039), *Love Is Not A Game* (Sunnyside 1051), *Shadowland* (Sunnyside 1060), *Sleep Warm* (Sunnyside 1063), *Beware Of Spring* (Sunnyside 1069), *Silent Passion* (Sunnyside 1075), *Echo Of A Kiss* (Sunnyside 1078), *Out Of Nowhere* (Sunnyside 1085) and *Love Is For The Birds* (Sunnyside 2002).

Website: www.meredithdambrosio.com

Putney Dandridge
(Louis Dandridge)
b. January 13, 1902, Richmond, VA;
d. February 15, 1946, Wall Township, NJ

Relatively little is known about Putney Dandridge, who for two years came out of obscurity to be in the spotlight before disappearing again. A pianist-vocalist, Dandridge worked regularly as part of the *Drake And Walker Show* starting in 1918 and continuing for quite a few years. Buffalo, New York, was his home base for much of the 1920s. Dandridge worked as the piano accompanist for tap dancer Bill "Bojangles" Robinson during 1930–32, and had a small part in the Bojangles film *Harlem Is Heaven* in 1932. That year he put together a band that was based in Cleveland during 1932–34.

After the group broke up, Dandridge put together a solo act and moved to New York City where he worked on 52nd Street, including at the Hickory House. In 1935 he spent some time playing piano and occasionally singing in bass saxophonist Adrian Rollini's band, based at Rollini's Tap Room.

Because Fats Waller's recordings were selling so well for Bluebird, Putney Dandridge (whose singing style was similar to Waller's) was signed by Vocalion to lead a series of hot jazz combos. Bob Howard fulfilled the same role for the Decca label during this period. During 1935–36, Dandridge recorded 44 selections as a vocalist, only playing piano on five of the numbers. Dandridge's good-natured voice is heard at its best on such numbers as "Chasin' Shadows," "You Hit The Spot," "Dinner For One Please, James" and "When A Lady Meets A Gentleman Down South." He was usually backed by all-stars including such notables as trumpeters Roy Eldridge, Henry "Red" Allen and Doc Cheatham, clarinetists Buster Bailey and Joe Marsala, tenors Chu Berry and Ben Webster, pianists Teddy Wilson and Clyde Hart, bassist John Kirby and drummers Cozy Cole and Big Sid Catlett. Dandridge also recorded six songs with Adrian Rollini's Tap Room Gang on June 14, 1935, mostly playing piano but also singing on "Nagasaki" and sharing the vocal with Wingy Manone on "Weather Man."

Unfortunately, the Vocalion records did not sell that well (particularly compared to Waller's output), and the recordings stopped after 1936. Putney Dandridge slipped away, never recorded again and passed away in 1946.

Recommended Recordings: Putney Dandridge's 44 recordings as a leader are all available on the two-CD set *Putney Dandridge* (Timeless 23) or on the two single discs *1935–1936* (Classics 846) and *1936* (Classics 869). They contain many enjoyable moments, both from Dandridge and his illustrious sidemen.

Barbara Dane
(Barbara Jean Spillman)
b. May 12, 1927, Detroit, MI

Barbara Dane has always stood out from the crowd. She may be white and have matured in the 1950s, but her singing often reminds one of the classic blues singers of the 1920s. Blessed with a strong social conscience, she has spent her life singing classic jazz, blues, folk music and protest songs, excelling in all areas and staying true to herself.

Dane remembers growing up in Detroit, listening to the jazz-oriented singers on the jukeboxes and seeing swing bands (thanks to a fake ID) at the Eastwood Gardens, including Glenn Miller, Harry James, Tommy Dorsey, Count Basie, Artie Shaw and Benny Goodman. "I collected 78s of musicians from Dizzy Gillespie and Charlie Parker to Claude Thornhill and Louis Jordan and the great boogie pianists. I stuck my ear in the late night radio, too. There was all kinds of music there, including live local gospel, country, etc. I was a pretty alienated teenager, so I didn't go to high school many days. But at the dances sometimes I got to sing with kid bands, usually 'Embraceable You' or 'Blue Moon.' My first paid job was at age 14 when I got hired for the Fireman's Ball."

Dane attended Wayne Street College for a few weeks but then realized that there was nothing she cared to learn there and asked for her money back. In 1946, when she was 19, she was offered a job to go on the road with Alvino Rey's band. "I turned it down, having by this time become a purist who wanted nothing to do with sleazy promoters and pop music." Dane was more interested in socially conscious songs and the music of Leadbelly. "Once someone loaned me his records, I couldn't get enough and soaked up his rhythms, his passion and his eclectic repertory that proved to me you don't have to put borders on your choice of songs. It never occurred to me to see myself as anything other than a singer, whether I would be paid for it or not. There was no 'trying' about it. It felt like a calling, not a choice. Pete Seeger's coming to Detroit in 1946 and encouraging me in what I was doing with the folk and union songs was fundamental. But he also said, 'some of us ought to get deeper into jazz,' so that was a kind of license to go where most folkies dared not tread."

Since that time, Barbara Dane has had a very wide-ranging career. She was involved in the folk movement, leading the Gateway Singers for a year. However, she was also very interested in classic blues and jazz, and was inspired to perform trad jazz in the mid-1950s by Dick Oxtot. Dane sat in regularly with Bob Mielke's Bearcats, trombonist Kid Ory and clarinetist George Lewis and worked with trombonist Turk Murphy. She became known for reviving obscurities from the 1920s, and she names among her inspirations Bessie Smith, Ma Rainey, Ida Cox, Sippie Wallace, Memphis Minnie, Hociel Thomas and two veteran singers who she knew well: Mama Yancey and Lizzie Miles. Dane was careful not to copy her predecessors too closely. "On the job, I developed my own style, flying by the seat of my pants but based on my strengths learned from vocal training in my teens as well as my weaknesses. I couldn't

hit certain top notes reliably, so I invented a sort of slide up to them. Then once on the note, I could open up the power." She also taught herself the guitar. "I played guitar and sang solo for more than 30 years, as a folksinger, an agitator, as a blues singer."

Barbara Dane's jazz bands in the late 1950s and early '60s usually featured pianist Kenny Whitson (who frequently played cornet and piano at the same time) and either Pete Allen, Pops Foster or Wellman Braud on bass. Braud came out of retirement to work with the singer, turning down other work. In addition, Dane sang with Louis Armstrong on one of the Timex Jazz TV specials, worked with pianist Art Hodes, toured the Northeast with Jack Teagarden and Don Ewell, and appeared a few times on Bobby Troup's *Stars Of Jazz* telecasts in addition to recording a few notable albums. Dane was also active in the blues world, including having the Muddy Waters band with pianist Otis Spann working with her for a week, appearing opposite major blues greats (such as Rev. Gary Davis and Lightnin' Hopkins) at the Ash Grove, and opening her own blues club in San Francisco, which was called Sugar Hill. Her work in the folk music field included being heavily involved in the civil rights and antiwar movements, recording several albums for Folkways and even appearing on Cuban television for a few hours on a Saturday evening in 1964.

Barbara Dane has remained active up to the present time and is currently starting work on what should be a very colorful autobiography. "Several performances this past year proved to me that I can still do plenty of interesting things with my voice even at my age. I feel humbled by the privilege of living my life as a singer. I love never knowing exactly what I'm going to sing, how I'm going to bend a note or phrase a line. I love the freedom to never have to repeat myself. I would have died if I had to sing the exact same thing the exact same way every night."

Recommended CDs: Barbara Dane's most important early albums were out-of-print for years until, typically, she took matters in her own hand and reissued them on her Dreadnaught label. *Trouble In Mind* (Dreadnaught 1601) has Dane singing classic blues and 1920s material with a quintet comprised of trumpeter P.T. Stanton, trombonist Bob Mielke, clarinetist Darnell Howard, pianist Don Ewell and bassist Pops Foster. *Livin' With The Blues* (Dreadnaught 1603) from 1959 is in the same vein but has quite an all-star group including Benny Carter (heard exclusively on trumpet), tenor-saxophonist Plas Johnson and drummer Shelly Manne. While Dane made the mistake of signing with Capitol (they tried to pigeonhole and the association was not a happy one), the lone album that was released is one of her best, *On My Way* (Dreadnaught 1602), focusing on her working group of Kenny Whitson and Wellman Braud plus such guests as drummer Earl Palmer and the Andrews Gospel Sisters. Dane makes the vintage material, which includes "Wild Women Don't Get The Blues," "Crazy Blues" and "Mama Don't Allow," sound contemporary, topical and relevant. *Live At The Ash Grove* (Dreadnaught 1604) documents Dane, Whitson and Braud during a live engagement on New Year's Eve, December 31, 1961. One of her best blues sets is a CD that she shares with Lightnin' Hopkins, *Sometimes I Believe She Loves Me* (Arhoolie 451), that features the co-leaders on vocal duets on half of the selections. Much more recently, *What Are You Gonna Do When There Ain't No Jazz* (GHB 240) showcases Dane with hot trad bands in 1988 and 2000 singing the early jazz songs and blues that she always loved.

Website: www.barbaradane.net

Dee Daniels

b. January 11, 1947, Berkeley, CA

A fine singer influenced by Sarah Vaughan, R&B and gospel, Dee Daniels is probably better known in Europe than in the United States.

Daniels sang in church from age nine and took piano lessons, playing for the choirs of her stepfather's Baptist church. "However, art was my passion so I earned a degree in art education from the University of Montana in 1970. I sang in a couple of bands for fun and money to help pay for school. It wasn't until after I graduated and began teaching art in a Seattle high school that I found myself being seriously drawn into the world of music. I joined a rock/R&B band for weekend gigs which expanded into six nights a week. I loved it and soon realized that music was my true calling. In 1972 I resigned from teaching and haven't looked back since."

To keep from being bored performing the same songs every night, she began altering the songs. It was some time before she realized that she was improvising and really a jazz singer. A versatile and colorful performer, Dee Daniels learned her craft and has been singing steadily for the past 35 years. She lived in Europe during 1982–87 where she had opportunities to perform with John Clayton, Toots Thielemans, Monty Alexander, Johnny Griffin and others. She has returned regularly since then, also performing in Canada, Australia, Hong Kong and 11 African countries in addition to the United States. Dee Daniels has sung with jazz groups and pops orchestras, and appeared in theater productions, including the musical comedy *Wang Dang Doodle* and starring in 2001's *Calgary Stampede*.

For the future she has many goals: "To record my 'Great Ladies Of Swing' pops program, to create new symphonic pops programs, to complete and release my *Total-Self Approach To Singing* vocal instruction DVD and book, to record a gospel CD and to continue to stretch musically."

Recommended CDs: *Let's Talk Business* (Capri 74027) from 1990 teams Dee Daniels with a quartet that includes the Clayton Brothers while *Wish Me Love* (Mons 874769) is an impressive effort with the Metropole Orchestra. In recent times, she has recorded *Love Story* (Three XD Music 502), *Feels So Good* (Three XD Music 503) and the very eclectic *Jazzinit* (Origin 82483) in addition to releasing a DVD, *Live At Biblo* (Challenge 71025).

Website: www.deedaniels.com

Daria

b. August 15, San Francisco, CA

An adventurous yet accessible singer whose music ranges from swing to world music, Daria has long been a popular attraction in the San Francisco Bay area.

"My father was a classical violinist with the San Francisco Symphony. I played classical piano, and my father bought me a Scott Joplin ragtime book when he noticed my musical tastes were leaning in other directions. Then, when I was 13 years old I was listening to the radio one day and stumbled upon a station by sheer accident that played jazz of all kinds. I was hooked from then on."

Daria sang in choirs and magridal groups through high school. She earned a degree in Humanities and Early Childhood Music Education in 1993 from the New College of California. Daria studied voice privately from several teachers including Mark Murphy (1988–90) and was encouraged by Maye Cavallaro. "I always knew that I wanted to be a professional singer, but I didn't make a go of it until I was in my early twenties."

She has since recorded two CDs and, in addition to her solo projects, has been touring with Dan Hicks and the Hot Licks (along with Roberta Donnay) since 2005.

Recommended CDs: *Just The Beginning* (Jazz 'm Up 350) is a brief five-song disc that displays some of Daria's singing talents in 1997. *Feel The Rhythm* from 2005 (Jazz 'm Up 360) ranges from jazz standards to world music and colorful mixtures of different styles. Daria excels in every setting.

Website: www.dariajazz.com

Kay Davis

b. December 5, 1920, Evanston, IL

Kay Davis had a brief career in jazz, all of it spent with Duke Ellington's orchestra. She was trained as a classical vocalist, earning a degree at Northeastern University in 1943. She performed at recitals around the Chicago area for a year and came to the attention of Ellington, who was impressed by her soprano voice. He hired Davis for his orchestra primarily to sing wordless vocals, extending the legacy of Adelaide Hall. In addition to her work with the big band, Davis accompanied Ellington and Ray Nance on a visit to England in 1948.

During 1944–50, Davis was heard at her best on "Transbluency," "On A Turquoise Cloud," a remake of "Creole Love Call" and "A City Called Heaven," settings on which her voice could sound angelic. The rare times that she sang words, usually on broadcasts (including occasionally on the Treasury Shows of 1944–45) and during a ballad such as "The More I See You," her "legit" tone and unswinging style were very much out-of-place.

In 1950, Kay Davis married and dropped out of music. Although she attended the Duke Ellington Society's conference in England in 1997, very little has been heard from her since her retirement.

Recommended CDs: The three-CD Duke Ellington set *Black, Brown And Beige* (Bluebird 86641) has some of Kay Davis' best vocals, along with features for Ellington's instrumentalists and other singers.

Irene Daye

b. January 17, 1918, Lawrence, MA;
d. November 1, 1971, Greenville, SC

Irene Daye was the singer with Gene Krupa's orchestra before Anita O'Day, and was Mrs. Charlie Spivak for two decades. She had a light and pleasing voice, improvising with subtlety and sticking very much to the swing style throughout her career.

A few weeks short of graduating from high school in 1935, she joined Jan Murphy's big band, although she did fly back home to get her diploma. Daye acquired two years of experience singing with Murphy and had a short stint with Mal Hallett before joining Gene Krupa's big band in May 1938. She gained her greatest fame with Krupa, being featured on 63 recordings. While some of the material was comprised of throwaways, her better vocals include "Jeepers Creepers," "Bolero At The Savoy," "The Lady's In Love With You," "Drummin' Man," "The Rumba Jumps," "Rhumboogie," "Yes, My Darling Daughter" and, from her final record date with Krupa on January 17, 1941, her biggest hit "Drum Boogie." She also ghosted for Barbara Stanwyck's singing voice in the movie *Ball Of Fire*, singing "Drum Boogie." The Gene Krupa Orchestra was on the brink of making it big when Daye, one of the band's main assets, left to marry trumpeter Corky Cornelius. Her replacement was Anita O'Day. Would Irene Daye have been featured on "Let Me Off Uptown" (recorded by O'Day in May, 1941) if she had stayed?

Instead, Irene Daye retired when Cornelius joined the Casa Loma Orchestra. She gave birth to a daughter in 1943 and was all ready to become a housewife when Cornelius unexpectedly died the following year. Needing to support herself, Daye began to sing again although she never regained her former fame. She succeeded June Hutton with the Charlie Spivak Orchestra in 1944 and sang with the band for six years, although no real hits resulted. In 1950 she married Spivak and again retired from performing, handling her husband's business activities, living in Miami and later near the Ye Olde Fireplace restaurant in Greenville, South Carolina, which became his home base. Irene Daye Cornelius Spivak died from cancer in 1971, still best known for "Drum Boogie."

Recommended CDs: Most of Irene Daye's vocals with Krupa are on *Gene Krupa 1938* (Classics 767), *Gene Krupa 1939–1940* (Classics 834) and *Gene Krupa—Best Of Big Bands* (Columbia 53425).

Blossom Dearie

b. April 28, 1926, East Durham, NY

As unusual as her name, Blossom Dearie has always been a unique performer. Dearie's singing voice, particularly in her earlier years, made her sound like a little girl (between six and twelve), a real contrast to her bop-based piano playing and her witty and sophisticated lyrics.

Dearie began her career singing with vocal groups. She was part of the Blue Flames when they sang with Woody Herman's orchestra, and the Blue Rey's when they were part of the Alvino Rey Orchestra. Dearie was on the original recording of "Moody's Mood For Love" with King Pleasure and, while living in Paris during 1952–56, she formed the Blue Stars, a group that had a hit recording of "Lullaby Of Birdland." She married Belgium tenor-saxophonist Bobby Jaspar and sang with Annie Ross on occasion while developing her own solo career.

After moving back to the United States in 1956, Dearie (who had made one solo record in Paris in 1955) recorded six albums for Verve during 1956–60, which made her reputation. She also cut one album apiece for Japanese DIW and Capitol as well as four for the British Fontana label. In 1973 she founded her own Daffodil label, which has released at least 19 of her albums since then.

A longtime regular on the New York cabaret circuit with her trio, Blossom Dearie has long had a cult following and the admiration of other singer/songwriters.

Recommended CDs: Most of Blossom Dearie's Verve albums are available. *Blossom Dearie* (Verve 837 934) mostly sticks to swinging standards while *Give Him The Ooh-La-La* (Verve 314 517 067) has her making such offbeat material as "Bang Goes The Drum," "The Riviera" and the title cut sound like they were written for her. *Sings Comden And Green* (314 589 102) has her personal versions of "Lucky To Be Me," "Some Other Time" and "The Party's Over." *My Gentleman Friend* (Verve 314 519 905) finds her taking "ownership" of the Gershwin's "Little Jazz Bird" and Cy Coleman's "You Fascinate Me," while *Soubrette* (Verve 2687-02) has her definitive versions of "Rhode Island Is Famous For You" and "Always True To You In My Fashion." Her Capitol set, 1964's *May I Come In* (Blue Note 95449), despite some cutesy moments, is also worth acquiring. Blossom Dearie's long string of Daffodil recordings, mostly just available from her website, include *My New Celebrity Is You* (Daffodil 103), *Our Favorite Songs* (Daffodil 117) and a two-CD retrospective called *Blossom's Own Treasures*. Other songs that she helped make famous are "I'm Hip" (by Dave Frishberg and Bob Dorough) and her own "Dear John."

LPs to Search For: *Once Upon A Summertime* (Verve 2111) from 1958 is the only Blossom Dearie Verve album not reissued on CD at this writing. Also worth finding are Dearie's London sets: *Blossom Time At Ronnie's* (Fontana 5352), *Sweet Blossom Dearie* (Fontana 5399), *Soon It's Gonna Rain* (Fontana 5454) and *That's Just The Way I Want To Be* (Fontana 6309015).

Website: www.blossomdearie.com

Vaughn DeLeath
(Leonore Vonderlieth)
b. September 26, 1894, Mount Pulaski, IL;
d. March 27, 1943, Buffalo, NY

One of the very first radio crooners and a major star in the 1920s, Vaughn De-Leath is largely forgotten today despite being a pioneer in several areas. At a time when female singers were rarely heard on the radio because their high voices did not carry well, DeLeath's comparatively low, soft and warm voice paved the way. She had a wide range, very good control of dynamics, and could sing anything from jazz to novelties, dialects to sentimental love songs. Her phrasing in spots recalls the much younger Annette Hanshaw while on the more dramatic pieces she shows the influence of Al Jolson.

Born to a rich family, DeLeath spent her teenage years living in Los Angeles. She wrote songs early on (publishing two tunes in 1912), attended Mills College for two years and dropped out to become a professional singer. She learned her craft in vaudeville, and in 1919 moved to New York where she soon changed her name from Leonore Vonderlieth to Vaughn DeLeath. She made history in January, 1920, when she was invited to sing a cappella for a demonstration of radio. Her rendition of "Swanee River" is considered the earliest example of a vocalist singing over the air.

DeLeath became heavily involved in radio, working as the station manager of the radio station WDT in New York in 1923. Accompanying herself on banjo, ukulele, guitar or piano, she often performed live on the air for hours at a time. In addition to her radio work, which continued into the early 1940s and earned her the titles of "The Original Radio Girl" and the "First Lady Of The Radio," she appeared in Broadway shows (including *Laugh Clown Laugh* in 1923 and 1925's *Easy Come, Easy Go*) and was even a pioneer in television. DeLeath appeared on a very early TV production in 1930 and was featured on CBS-TV twice a week during part of 1931.

Vaughn DeLeath first recorded in 1922 and was prolific throughout the decade, often recording under various pseudonyms (most often Gloria Geer). On 1923's "Comin' Home," she scats a chorus more than two years before Louis Armstrong's "Heebies Jeebies." Her recording of "The Man I Love" with Paul Whiteman's orchestra was popular, and in 1927 she had a hit with "Are You Lonesome Tonight," 33 years before Elvis Presley. A strong sampling of her 1928 to 1929 performances for the Edison label (most of which are jazz-oriented) has been reissued by Diamond Cut Productions, although her earlier work remains quite scarce.

Vaughan DeLeath was much less prominent after the early 1930s, but she continued working in radio up until the time of her death in 1943.

Recommended CDs: *The Original Radio Girl* (Diamond Cut Productions 304) has most of Vaughn DeLeath's 1928 to 1929 recordings. More of her rare recordings deserve to be reissued.

Rick DellaRatta

b. October 23, 1961, Schenectady, NY

A Chet Baker-influenced singer and a fluent pianist who is inspired by McCoy Tyner, Rick DellaRatta has been touring with his *Jazz For Peace* program in recent years.

DellaRatta started his career singing in a teenage rock band, working at casuals and touring as a piano bar singer/entertainer in Europe. He studied extensively at the New England Conservatory during 1981–88 while playing jazz, including in trios and quartets with drummer Alan Dawson. Since then he has worked with drummer Denis Charles (off and on during 1993–98), Brazilian bassist Beto, Guillherme Franco's group Pe de Boi and led a trio that at times has included bassist Eddie Gomez and drummer Lenny White.

He formed *Jazz For Peace* for an October 4, 2001 concert and has used that format and theme ever since in performances including in Brazil, Japan and Hong Kong. "For the future, I hope to continue to perform my original compositions and interpretations of other people's music on stage all over the world. When we fill our souls up with creativity, artistry and intelligence, we have a better chance at avoiding the behavior that leads to destruction."

Recommended CDs: Rick DellaRatta has thus far led six sets. Best are *Take It Or Leave It* (Original Cast 1214), *Live In Brazil And The Blue Note* (Stella 449233) and the solo set *Alone Together* (Stella 4214)

Website: www.rickdellaratta.com

Dena DeRose

b. February 15, 1966, Binghamton, NY

Dena DeRose never set out to be a singer, and it was only through an odd twist of fate that her very expressive voice had a chance to be heard.

"I started playing piano at age three, switched to classical organ for a number of years, played percussion from grades 5 to 12, including performing with the school orchestra, youth orchestra (tri-state area), and all school bands (marching, wind ensemble, concert band), played piano in the jazz band, and accompanied the musicals throughout college." She also worked in a top-40 wedding band as a teenager for four years, playing two or three weddings most weekends. While DeRose took classes in classical piano at S.U.N.Y. Binghamton, her main goal was to become a top jazz pianist and she was well on her way, performing in upstate New York. But then disaster struck in the combination of arthritis and carpal tunnel syndrome, which mostly affected her right hand and made it impossible for her to play piano for two years in the mid-1980s. She had two operations and her career appeared over before it had begun.

On a lark, while sitting in a jazz club with some musician friends, DeRose answered a dare and sang with the group. She received good applause and enjoyed the experience. Within a couple of weeks, she was booking herself as a singer. By the time her hand had completely recovered, Dena DeRose was a singer-pianist, equally skilled at both and now paying much more attention to melodies and phrasing as an instrumentalist, learning to sing through the piano in addition to her voice.

In 1991 she moved to New York and built up her reputation. She made her first recording, *Introducing Dena DeRose*, in 1997 and since then has played with Randy Brecker, Bruce Forman, Ingrid Jensen, the Ray Brown Trio, Clark Terry, Benny Golson, Bill Henderson, Houston Person, Ken Peplowski and quite a few other musicians on the jazz party circuit. Dena DeRose, a fixture at jazz parties and festivals, has also been a very busy music educator.

Recommended CDs: *Introducing Dena DeRose* (Sharp Nine 1009), *Another World* (Sharp Nine 1016) and *I Can See Clearly Now* (Sharp Nine 1018) got her career off to a strong start, with *I Can See Clearly Now* having quite a few memorable examples of her singing. *Love's Holiday* (Sharp Nine 1024), *In The Park* (Max Jazz 502) and *Live At Jazz Standard, Vol. 1* (MaxJazz 504) are all solid examples of her artistry and her equal skills as a singer and pianist.

Website: www.denaderose.com

Tony DeSare

b. 1976, Glens Falls, NY

One of the better crooners on the scene today, Tony DeSare has two impressive releases out thus far.

The son of an amateur guitarist-singer, DeSare started on violin, switching to piano when he was 10 or 11. He began singing when he was 16, and at 18 was performing at gigs with his trio. He attended Ithaca College and worked regularly in upstate New York during that period. DeSare moved to New York City in 1999, playing at the Marquis Hotel in Times Square and starring in the off-Broadway musical *Our Sinatra*. He was picked by Sam Arlen, son of Harold Arlen, to be in the tribute show *Arlen On Arlen*. Since then, Tony DeSare has signed with Telarc, and his two releases have given him more exposure and a strong reputation.

Recommended CDs: *Want You* (Telarc 83620) has DeSare joined by a band that includes guitarist Bucky Pizzarelli, mixing together standards, older obscurities and high-quality originals generally co-written with bassist Mike Lee. *Last Kiss* (Telarc 83651) is similar except that it also includes some pop/rock songs turned into jazz, and benefits from the tenor solos of Harry Allen.

Website: www.tonydesare.com

Trudy Desmond

b. 1946, United States;
d. February 19, 1999, Toronto, Ontario, Canada

All her life, Trudy Desmond wanted to sing jazz. She had several other successful careers before she found time to sing, almost waiting too long, but ultimately achieving all of her dreams in her relatively brief life.

Desmond sang jazz in college but, instead of becoming a professional vocalist, she concentrated on working as an actress, producing cabaret shows and having a successful interior design business. As she turned 40, she finally began working as a singer, emphasizing the beauty of lyrics and only improvising slightly. What was most important to her were the messages in the songs. Her cool sensuous voice did the words justice, and she was recognized during her lifetime as one of Canada's best jazz-influenced singers.

Trudy Desmond recorded four CDs during 1988–97 before being struck down by cancer in 1999 at the age of 53.

Recommended CDs: Each of Trudy Desmond's recordings is well worth picking up by listeners who love to hear lyrics treated with sensitivity and good taste. *RSVP* (The Jazz Alliance 10024), *Tailor Made* (The Jazz Alliance 10015), *Make Me Rainbows* (Koch 7803) and *My One And Only: A Gershwin Celebration* (Justin Time 8648) comprise her musical legacy.

Denise Donatelli

b. May 26, Bethlehem, PA

Considering her talent, it seems strange that Denise Donatelli has thus far only led one CD, but it is a great one.

"My mother was a singer in New York before my parents married, and while my father was a clothing manufacturer by trade, he played the piano even though he couldn't read a note of music. But it was my sister who introduced me to jazz. She was a member of the Capital and Columbia Music Clubs and, from a very early age, I was listening to all the greats of jazz. My mother told me that when I was a baby, I used to sneak into the living room during my sister's voice lessons. Her voice teacher would have to chase me out because I was doing all the singing."

Donatelli studied classical piano for 14 years, starting when she was three, winning awards and gaining local recognition. "However, I became burned out on piano study and I thought I'd have a better chance of earning a living if I pursued a career

in fashion. That didn't work out too well as I ended up spending my earnings on clothes. I soon married and started a family." Living in Atlanta, she did not begin singing professionally until her children were almost grown up. "A friend took me to a jazz jam. I lost a bet and, after a couple of glasses of wine, I found myself sitting in with the band. Word spread among the musicians and I soon started getting calls for gigs."

In 2000, Denise Donatelli moved to Los Angeles. She met Dave Pell who introduced her to Les Brown Jr., leading to her signing with the Les Brown Orchestra. She has also led combos in the Los Angeles area, performing in clubs.

"I love to sing. If I can continue to do that and build an audience that appreciates what I'm doing, my life is complete."

Recommended CD: Denise Donatelli's one CD, *In The Company Of Friends* (Jazzed Media 1008), is a great one. Her voice sounds consistently beautiful and displays very appealing phrasing while being framed by pianist Tom Garvin's inventive arrangements for a tentet. A memorable outing.

Website: www.denisedonatelli.com

Roberta Donnay

b. August 10, 1964, Washington, D.C.

Roberta Donnay's *What's Your Story* was one of the most rewarding jazz vocal CDs released in 2006, and it was her first full-fledged jazz recording in a diverse career.

"At five years old, I sang at my uncle's wedding in NYC. I snuck up to the stage when the band took their break and sang 'Five Foot Two, Eyes Of Blue' to thunderous applause. I had already decided I was a singer and would continue on this career path. I sang solos at school, at parties, and won a talent contest at the age of 12 in front of 900 people. My prize was a plaque and a Hershey's candy bar. I remarked, 'Where's my money?' Yes, a diva was born."

She first heard jazz in her parents' records, particularly Billie Holiday, Louis Armstrong and Duke Ellington. She also hung out at a Washington, D.C., after-hours jazz club. "All of the music I learned was on the 'street' and from other jazz musicians." She worked with Dick Oxtot's Golden Age Jazz Band while a teenager during 1977–78, and primarily with San Francisco Bay area musicians in the years since.

"I was a teenage runaway. I was lucky to find music at such a young age. Music saved my life. It gave me a destination, a goal. I could use the yardstick of the great artists I studied to measure myself and see my own growth toward inner expression. It took me many years of struggle and study to produce a sound and tone I could even listen to myself. I am truly grateful for having the gift of my voice. It is a precious thing to me."

Donnay has had major success as a singer/songwriter. Her original songs have often been used on television shows, including soap operas. Her "One World" was adopted as a theme for the United Nations' 50th anniversary and is considered a world peace anthem. Donnay's first records were outside of jazz, making the inventiveness and high quality of *What's Your Story* a major surprise.

"Jazz has restored my creativity. When I am singing jazz, I feel completely free.

I love the interplay and improvisation between musicians that happens naturally when everyone listens to one another. For the future, I'd love to record a jazz album with alternative instruments (banjo, mandolin, accordion), record a jazz album in Nashville, do some film composing, and write some more alternative, modern jazz."

Recommended CDs: Roberta Donnay's first jazz CD, *What's Your Story* (Pacific Coast Jazz 1295), was produced by Orrin Keepnews and matches her with a trio/quartet that includes pianist Eric Reed and occasionally tenor-saxophonist Dave Ellis. Her version of "No Regrets" is particularly memorable with other high points, including the Crusaders' "Put It Where You Want It," "Drinkin' Again" and two Bob Dorough songs.

Bob Dorough

b. December 12, 1923, Cherry Hill, AR

Bob Dorough has always been a unique singer/pianist/songwriter. His voice has touches of both Cliff Edwards and Hoagy Carmichael along with an Arkansas drawl, his lyrics generally display a sly wit, and he is a top-notch bebop pianist. Although there were stretches of time when he did not record enough, Dorough has been a popular performer among those "in the know" for a half century.

"Aunt Florence urged me onto the stage when I was three or four during an amateur show at the local movie house. I sang a cappella 'My Blue Heaven' and 'When Polly Was A Little Girl.' The audience threw pennies, nickels and dimes onto the stage and I gathered them up without embarrassment of any degree. I remember I didn't win the contest (a fiddler beat me out), but I liked the pay."

Bob Dorough grew up in Texas. "My first piano teacher was a lady who ran a grocery store and lived in the back. My Dad delivered bread for a bakery and enrolled me for six lessons to pay off her debt to the bakery. Since I couldn't quite play what was written on the sheet music, I began to do it in my 'own style.'" Dorough also played clarinet and wrote arrangements for a high school jazz band. He attended Texas Tech for three semesters, taking music classes. When he served in the military during World War II, he had an opportunity to play in the Army band. After his discharge, he was introduced to bebop, earned a music degree from North Texas State Teachers College in 1949, served for two years as boxer Sugar Ray Robinson's musical director and began to sing.

"On piano I was inspired by Bud Powell, Al Haig and hosts of earlier cats like Teddy Wilson and Earl Hines. I sort of found my own way from there, but never became a truly trained pianist. In NYC, I found that I could get jobs by singing at the piano. While the cool and hot attitudes of my fellow beboppers made me a bit reluctant to sing in public unless it was needed (to get the gig), I secretly practiced at home with a tape recorder, trying to get my 'sound' and style. As the songwriting developed, I decided that I would be a singing piano man and entertain the folks till they were ready to listen

to me. My personal appearances brought me to Bethlehem Records where I made my first LP as a leader, recording 12 songs, eleven of them vocals. By now I'd been swayed also by King Pleasure, Annie Ross and Eddie Jefferson."

Dorough, who spent part of 1953–54 living and performing music in Paris (occasionally with Blossom Dearie), recorded a memorable debut set for Bethlehem in 1956, which is highlighted by "Baltimore Oriole," his lyrics on "Yardbird Suite" and one of his best known songs, "Devil May Care." Strangely enough there was no follow up. Dorough did record a jazz and poetry project for World Pacific in 1958 and songs from the show Oliver in 1963 but, two titles with Miles Davis from 1962 aside ("Blue Xmas" and "Nothing Like You"), his next significant recording would not take place until 1966 (the album *Just About Everything*) and then another decade passed before he recorded again. Nevertheless, Dorough kept busy performing and writing music. In the 1970s he became the musical director for *Schoolhouse Rock*, writing kids' songs for television that became influential and beloved even though many of the viewers probably never knew that he was responsible for much of the music.

Always on the verge of being discovered, Dorough and his longtime bassist Bill Takas recorded for Laissez-Faire, 52 Rue East, Philogy, Red, Bloomdido, Pinnacle and Orange Blue. At 73 Bob Dorough was signed to Blue Note in 1997 where he made two CDs that gave him some long overdue recognition. But as usual, that did not last and, after cutting a CD for Candid, he is as of this writing working on forming his own Dee Bees label and writing his autobiography.

Recommended CDs: *Devil May Care* (Bethlehem 75994) is a classic that features Bob Dorough at his early best. 1966's *Just About Everything* (Evidence 22094) has three Dorough originals, including the title cut. *Beginning To See The Light* (Laissez-Faire 002) from 1976 is a fine tribute to the Bob Dorough-Bill Takas musical partnership and features Dorough singing "I'm Hip" (a song that he co-wrote with Dave Frishberg) and "Small Day Tomorrow" (Dorough's music and Fran Landesman's words). *Right On My Way Home* (Blue Note 57729) gave Bob Dorough some attention, but *Too Much Coffee* Man (Blue Note 99239) is the better buy, for it includes such memorable performances as "Wake Up Sally, It's Saturday," "Too Much Coffee Man" and the funny "Where Is The Song?" *Sunday At Iridium* (Arbors 19305) lets one hear an entire live set by Dorough in 2004 (including many of his originals), *Who's On First* (Blue Note 23403) is a wonderful duo set with Dave Frishberg that includes songs by both of the pianists-singers, plus the classic title cut. *Small Day Tomorrow* (Candid 984 428) is a tribute to Fran Landesman. Bob Dorough, in his mid-eighties, still is full of enthusiasm and a creative spirit.

Website: www.bobdorough.com

Urszula Dudziak

b. October 22, 1943, Straconka, Poland

Sporting a five-octave range and a fearlessness that allows her to improvise freely, utilize electronics and come up with very original versions of standards, Urszula Dudziak is a major innovator even though too few of her recordings have been widely available in the United States.

She played accordion from age five and later took up piano. "As a teenager living in Poland, I discovered jazz through *Voice of America's Jazz Hour*, broadcast by Willis Conover for jazz fans in Eastern Europe. I started to sing as a 15 year old girl, mostly Polish pop songs. When I was 17, I was discovered by Polish jazz giant composer Krzysztof Komeda." She worked with Komeda, attended music school and met violinist Michael Urbaniak who she married and worked with for much of the next 20 years; they have since divorced.

Dudziak performed and lived in Scandinavia for several years, moving to New York in 1973. Her first few American records for Arista and Inner City gained her a lot of attention due to her very wide range, the variety of new sounds that she created, and her use of electronics on her voice. In addition to her work with Urbaniak, she performed with Vocal Summit (next to Jane Clayton, Norma Winstone, Jeanne Lee and Bobby McFerrin) starting in 1982, the Gil Evans Orchestra in 1987, Archie Shepp, Lester Bowie, and the Vienna Art Orchestra (1997–2000), making records along the way with Herbie Hancock, Jaco Pastorius, the Brecker Brothers, Kenny Kirkland and Adam Makowicz. Still, it is surprising that she has not had a higher profile during the past 15 years.

"My thing is expressing myself through sounds, using electronics like samples, harmonizers and octavers, creating live new grooves and sounds, always looking for something unusual, something that I've never heard before."

Recommended CDs: Urszula Dudziak's most recent recordings, *Magic Lady* (In and Out 70082), *High House* (CTI 9015), *And Life Goes On* (Dreadlines 001) and 1998's *Painted Bird* (Polonia 050), are undeservedly obscure.

LPs to Search For: *Newborn Light* (Cameo 101) is a 1972 duet album with Adam Makowicz, who matches Dudziak's electronics with his playing on electric keyboards. *Urszula* (Arista 4065), *Midnight Rain* (Arista 4132) and *Future Talk* (Inner City 1066) are the albums that made Urszula Dudziak well known in the United States, but all are still awaiting reissue on CD. Urszula Dudziak's versions of "Lover," "Misty," "A Night In Tunisia" and "Bluesette" on *Midnight Rain* are unlike any others. Dudziak is also well featured on *Ulla* (Popeye 101) and *Sorrow Is Not Forever...But Love Is* (Keytone 726).

Catherine Dupuis
b. Columbus, GA

Catherine Dupuis is a subtle yet dramatic interpreter who enjoys uplifting obscure lyrics. "I grew up in small towns in the Midwest and Pennsylvania where opportunities were pretty rare for live jazz, but my parents had a small but solid collection of jazz LPs to choose from and we listened to them nonstop: Louis Armstrong, Dave Brubeck and Charlie Byrd. I also listened to Sinatra and Ella on the radio. My grandmother had piano music and vocal selections, including Gershwin and Cole Porter. By ninth grade I knew more than 50 Cole Porter tunes. My uncle was (and is) a huge bebopper—he turned me on to Miles, Dexter Gordon and 'Trane."

By high school, Dupuis was constantly listening to jazz, learning every possible song and occasionally singing with a Dixieland band at a pizza parlor. She was also involved in competitive choral work, appearing in plays and studying

piano, which she has played since she was seven. She earned a double degree in music (voice) and theater (performance) from Indiana University in 1979, spending her summers performing in musical theater. Dupuis performed regularly with the Pittsburgh Civic Light Opera and studied for a semester with Eileen Farrell. "It was a wonderful experience. The best thing she taught me was that if you're not singing about sex, shut up."

Catherine Dupuis worked both as a singer and an actor in Pennsylvania, earning an MFA in acting from Penn State. She moved to New York in 1985, performed in a stage production about Doris Day called *Daydream* and has recorded three CDs. "My acting technique really helps in performance and song delivery. I really think my strong point is lyric interpretation; dealing with the lyric as poetry first and a song second."

Recommended CDs: 1997's *I Hear Music* (KBQ 103), *Moments* (Bearheart 001) and *The Rules Of The Road* (Bearheart 002) are all fine showcases for Catherine Dupuis' voice and interpretative skills. She always respects the lyrics while coming up with fresh variations.

Website: www.catherinedupuis.com

Ann Dyer
b. April 29, 1958, Newport Beach, CA

In the mid-1990s, Ann Dyer made a very strong impression with her debut CD *Ann Dyer And The No Good Time Fairies* and her memorable appearance at the 1994 Monterey Jazz Festival. She has not found the stardom one would expect in the years since, but the huge potential is still there.

Dyer was a fan of the Beatles as a child, played piano in her high school jazz band, performed on oboe for a period and graduated with a B.A. in Dance from Mills College. "When I left college as a dancer, I already had the bug to sing. It took me several years to segue from dancer/choreographer to vocalist, but by the time I was in my mid to late twenties, I was committed to a life in music." She was always interested in all types of art and music. "I am inspired by musicians who possess a certain intensity—pure, brilliant, focused—like looking into the sun, like hearin0g the Islamic call to prayer. I would include Astor Piazzolla, Paco de Lucia, Miles Davis, John Coltrane, Kurt Cobain, Celia Cruz and Pandit Jasraj in that category."

In the early 1990s, Ann Dyer put together her band, the No Good Time Fairies, a perfect vehicle for her singing. "Guitarist Jeff Buenz, bassist John Shifflett, and drummer Jason Lewis formed the nucleus of a band that would eventually shape and define my sound as an artist. Saxophonists Hafez Modirzadeh and Peter Apfelbaum later joined us, then Rob Burger on accordion, and Carla Kihlstedt on violin (both of whom would be in the Tin Hat Trio). The band was built on a premise of minimal structure with maximum group improvisation. The looseness, the empathy, the adventure of the individual personalities and the band's overall approach became my signature sound." Three very different CDs resulted.

In recent times, Ann Dyer has taken a hiatus from performing to work on what she calls "the yoga of sound," giving workshops on her beliefs and philosophies dealing with the power of music.

Recommended CDs: Her debut recording, *Ann Dyer And The No Good Time Fairies* (Mr. Brown 896), is her finest jazz set to date. Dyer's adventurous treatments of "I Remember April," "Social Call," "Pinocchio" and a particularly passionate rendition of Ornette Coleman's "Lonely Woman" are innovative and unique. *Revolver: A New Spin* (Mr. Brown 907) reinvents the Beatles' 1966 *Revolver* album while *When I Close My Eyes* (Sunnyside 1113) features many of Dyer's originals but is often more bizarre than compelling.

Website: www.anndyer.com

Dominique Eade
b. June 16, 1958, Ruislip, England

A stimulating singer who is able to sing between conventional tones when it fits her music, Dominique Eade is quite versatile and also significant as an educator.

Though born in England, she is an American who came to the United States when she was six months old. Eade lived in many places in the United States and Europe while growing up. "Both of my parents loved music and listened to jazz. My mother was Swiss and my father was an American Air force officer. I am the youngest of five children and everyone took piano lessons. We sang together at home, too. In the middle of the '60s, the folk wave hit us all the way out in Nebraska and everyone got guitars and learned Bob Dylan songs as well as all the rediscovered folk songs. I used to perform on guitar in high school." Keeping her mind open, she listened to everything in jazz from Bessie Smith and Billie Holiday to Jay Clayton and Jeanne Lee. While attending Vassar College (1976–78), Eade performed in New York. "With my band at the time, I had no problem singing a Fats Waller song and then a tune that Flora Purim sang with Return to Forever. It was all jazz and all good."

She went to Berklee for two semesters before transferring to the New England Conservatory of Music, becoming strongly influenced by pianist-educator Ran Blake and open not only to other jazz singers, but Indian classical music and performers from Brazil. Eade earned a Bachelors of Music from NEC in 1982 and since then her solo career has found her using such musicians as flutist Jamie Baum, guitarist Mick Goodrick, pianists Donald Brown, Stanley Cowell, Bruce Barth and Jed Wilson, drummer Alan Dawson and saxophonist Bill Pierce, in addition to working on an occasional basis with Ran Blake and with her husband, saxophonist Allan Chase. She has also been a soloist in two Anthony Braxton operas, had a duo with bassist Mark Helias, worked often with Fred Hersch and guested with Butch Morris, Orange Then Blue and the Either/Orchestra.

As a professor at the New England Conservatory of Music, Dominique Eade has been influential and her students have included Roberta Gambarini, Luciana Souza, Kris Adams, Lisa Thorson, Christine Correa, Kate McGarry and Julie Hardy. "I cannot think of many life experiences that surpass the amazing sense of connection I can feel with others when playing improvised music. The combination of trust and awareness brings me into the moment in a very powerful way."

Recommended CDs: Dominique Eade began her recording career with two impressive self-produced efforts released on Accurate: *The Ruby And The Pearl* (Accurate 3924) and *My Resistance Is Low* (Accurate CD 3925). *The Long Way Home* (RCA 63296) has the singer providing all of the arrangements.

When The Wind Was Cool (RCA 68858) is an intriguing tribute to June Christy and Chris Connor; the supporting cast includes Fred Hersch, Benny Golson and vibraphonist Steve Nelson. The singer's most intimate recording is *Open* (Jazz Project 3001), a set of often-haunting duets with pianist Jed Wilson for which Dominique Eade contributed seven of the 11 selections.

Website: www.dominiqueeade.com

Madeline Eastman
b. June 27, 1954, San Francisco, CA

A major jazz singer from the San Francisco Bay area, Madeline Eastman has the vocal chops and knowledge to succeed at everything she tries, a wit that always makes her music accessible, and a sense of adventure that keeps her music from ever being predictable.

Eastman first seriously thought of becoming a jazz singer after seeing the Diana Ross movie *Lady Sings The Blues* when she was 18. She studied at the College of San Mateo, and made her recording debut in 1983 with the big band Full Faith and Credit. In 1989 she co-founded the Mad-Kat label with Kitty Margolis and has thus far recorded five CDs for her company. A measure of the quality of her music can be ascertained by realizing that altoist Phil Woods, trumpeter Tom Harrell, pianists Cedar Walton and Kenny Barron, drummer Tony Williams and Mark Murphy have been sidemen on her CDs.

Madeline Eastman is also a very popular and respected jazz and vocal educator, giving many clinics and workshops in addition to being the department chair of Jazz Vocal Studies at Berkeley's Jazzschool and teaching at the Stanford Jazz Workshop. As a singer, she has appeared at many jazz festivals around the world, having developed her own style and approach out of bebop, and the approaches of Betty Carter and Shirley Horn while sounding unlike anyone else.

Recommended CDs: Thus far Madeline Eastman has recorded *Point Of Departure* (Mad-Kat 1002), the especially rewarding program *Mad About Madeline* (Mad-Kat 1003), *Art Attack* (Mad-Kat 1005), *Bare: A Collection Of Ballads* (Mad-Kat 1007), which is a set of duets with pianist Tom Garvin, and *The Speed Of Life* (Mad-Kat 1009).

Website: www.madelineeastman.com

Billy Eckstine
(William Clarence Eckstine)
b. July 8, 1914, Pittsburgh, PA; d. March 8, 1993, Pittsburgh, PA

A singer with a deep baritone voice, Billy Eckstine made a major impact in the 1940s that continued for the next 30 years. One could not imagine such singers as Johnny Hartman, Earl Coleman or Arthur Prysock without there having been an Eckstine first, counteracting the popular high-toned tenors (such as Pha Terrell) of the 1930s. While Eckstine spent a large portion of his life performing middle-of-the-road pop music, he was a hero to the bebop generation for having led and kept together as long as possible the second significant bop big band. A jazz influence was felt even in his later vocals, and Eckstine was an underrated if infrequent scat-singer and improviser.

Born and raised in Pittsburgh, Billy Eckstine, as early as 1930, won a talent contest by imitating Cab Calloway. He sang with Tommy Myles' group while attending college. In 1939 Eckstine immediately entered the big time by joining the Earl Hines Orchestra. He soon became Hines' biggest attraction, recording 13 selections during 1940–42, including a minor hit in the blues "Jelly, Jelly." In 1943 Eckstine, who passed the time by teaching himself trumpet and valve trombone, urged Hines to hire Charlie Parker (for the tenor chair), trumpeter Dizzy Gillespie and Sarah Vaughan. Eckstine was responsible for Hines modernizing his band and having the first bebop orchestra. Unfortunately, the recording strike of the period resulted in this Hines big band going completely unrecorded and not even a radio broadcast has yet surfaced.

In 1944 Eckstine had a big enough name to have a solo career, but he surprised many of his fans by forming his own big band. His orchestra, which initially featured Parker (on alto), Gillespie and Vaughan, during 1944–47 was an important training ground for such young modernists as tenors Gene Ammons, Dexter Gordon, Wardell Gray and Frank Wess, trumpeters Fats Navarro, Miles Davis, Freddie Webster and Kenny Dorham, altoist Sonny Stitt, baritonist Leo Parker and drummer Art Blakey. Eckstine recorded big hits with "A Cottage For Sale" and "Prisoner Of Love" and his version of "Blowing The Blues Away" has a classic tenor tradeoff by Gordon and Ammons. Eckstine alternated uptempo bop romps (some of which have him scatting while others were instrumentals) and his own ballad features. Unfortunately whenever the band left New York, it tended to be disastrous because crowds that were more accustomed to Glenn Miller or even Count Basie found Eckstine's music to be undanceable. And since the big band era was ending, the Eckstine Orchestra was doomed from the start. However, Billy Eckstine resisted the pressure to start his own lucrative career until he finally had to give up in mid-1947.

Signed to the MGM record label, Eckstine had a string of hits during 1947–52, including "Everything I Have Is Yours," "Blue Moon," "Caravan," "My Foolish Heart" and "I Apologize." Much of the time his warm voice was surrounded by large string sections and he was marketed successfully as a black pop singer, helping pave the way for Nat King Cole's later successes. Despite the commercial settings, Eckstine (who was known as "Mr. B") remained popular in the jazz world and he occasionally returned to jazz for short periods. In 1952 he recorded a fine album while accompanied by his regular accompanist pianist Bobby Tucker and a quartet. Eckstine is excellent on two hot jazz numbers with the 1953 Metronome All-Stars, and in 1959 was joined by the Count Basie Orchestra for one of his finest recordings. In addition, the 1960 live album *No Cover, No Minimum*, which is mostly jazz-oriented, even has Eckstine taking a few effective solos on trumpet, but these were exceptions. One has to pick and choose when it comes to Billy Eckstine recordings for much of his work was in the pop field including two sets from 1965 to 1966 that were made for Motown.

In a different time period, Eckstine would have become a movie star by the mid-1940s, playing leads as romantic as many of his vocals, but there was no such opening for African-Americans. Instead, he had a busy solo career as a singer and Mr. B., who was heard at his best live in concert with his rhythm section, remained popular and active up until his death in 1993 when he was 78.

Recommended CDs: *The Legendary Big Band* (Savoy 17125) is a two-CD set that has all of the Eckstine Orchestra's most important bop recordings including selections recorded for Deluxe and National in 1944 and the best of his output for Savoy. *Everything I Have Is Yours* (Verve 819 442), which is also a twofer, has Eckstine's commercial hits of 1947–57. Many of the performances are with strings, but the program also contains eight selections with the Bobby Tucker Quartet, some ballad duets with Sarah Vaughan and Eckstine's two numbers with the 1953 Metronome All Stars. *Basie And Eckstine, Inc.* (Roulette 52029) and *No Cover, No Minimum* (Roulette 98583) are a pair of the singer's finest jazz albums. *Billy Eckstine Sings With Benny Carter* (Verve 832 011), although he shows his age in his voice (he was 72 at the time of this 1986 recording), serves as an excellent swan song.

Cliff Edwards

*b. June 14, 1895, Montreal, Quebec, Canada;
d. July 18, 1971, Hollywood, CA*

Cliff Edwards, who was widely known as Ukulele Ike, was arguably the first important male jazz singer on record. However, he had such an odd career that, by the mid-1930s, few realized his importance, and he was underrated and generally overlooked throughout his career, especially by the jazz world.

Edwards left home as a teenager to work in show business and vaudeville. He sang, played ukulele and kazoo, and learned to scat in a style that he called "effin," which alternated with his falsetto. He started out working in the St. Louis area, traveled with carnivals and had menial day jobs when times got slow. In 1917 Edwards moved to Chicago, worked at local clubs, introduced the song "Jada" and gained the stage title of "Ukulele Ike" when an emcee could not remember his name. Edwards teamed up with the stuttering comedian Joe Frisco in an act that made it to the Palace in New York and the Ziegfeld Follies. After that team broke up, Edwards spent time working with singers Pierce Keegan and Lou Clayton. In 1922 he made his first records, sitting in on kazoo with Ladd's Black Aces and Bailey's Lucky Seven.

In 1924, Ukulele Ike hit the big time when he introduced "Fascinatin' Rhythm" in the show *Lady Be Good* on Broadway. The next few years were full of major successes. Edwards helped popularize the ukulele in the 1920s (it became part of popular culture during that era), was one of the stars of the *Ziegfeld Follies* in 1927 (where he was the first to sing "I'll See You In My Dreams") and in the film *Hollywood Revue Of 1929* he made "Singin' In The Rain" into a standard.

Cliff Edwards began recording as a leader in 1923. He was among the very first singers to scat on record and he recorded over 125 songs during the next ten years. Among his hits were "Singin' In The Rain," "I Can't Give You Anything But Love," "Sunday," "Somebody Loves Me," "Fascinatin' Rhythm," "Oh, Lady Be Good" and "I'll See You In My Dreams," all songs that are still performed today. He also introduced "Toot

Toot Tootsie" before it was adopted by Al Jolson, and in 1933 helped make "It Is Only A Paper Moon" into a standard. Many of his records featured him with a small jazz group called his Hot Combination, which often included such players as Red Nichols, Miff Mole, Jimmy Dorsey, Adrian Rollini, Eddie Lang and Vic Berton.

After his appearance onscreen performing "Singin' In The Rain," Cliff Edwards should have experienced greater success in the 1930s, but this is where the Ukulele Ike Story starts to become erratic. Although he appeared in over 100 films in the 1930s and '40s, it was usually as either a second banana in a B movie (including many Westerns) or as a bit player in major films. He was in *Dance Fools Dance* with Joan Crawford, *His Girl Friday* with Cary Grant and *Gone With The Wind*, but his roles were so small that they are forgettable. Although he sang occasional numbers (including "I Wonder Who's Kissing Her Now" in 1935's *Red Salute*), mostly he offered weak comedy relief. A gambler and an alcoholic, Edwards managed to lose all of the fortune he had gained in the 1920s, and he could barely afford the alimony owed to his ex-wives much less resolve his continual income tax problems. He declared bankruptcy on four separate occasions in the 1930s and '40s.

Ukulele Ike did not record much after the early 1930s and the jazz world failed to recognize his early achievements. And yet, in 1939 he received a very big break. Walt Disney loved Edwards' vocalizing so much that he cast him as the singing voice of Jiminy Cricket in the animated feature *Pinocchio* where he sang "When You Wish Upon A Star." That performance helped the tune win the Oscar for best song of 1940.

Edwards also provided the voice to one of the main crows in the animated film *Dumbo* and made some radio transcriptions in the mid-1940s. But he drank away his opportunities, continued gambling and slipped away into obscurity again.

There was one more chance for Ukulele Ike. A few years after hosting *The Cliff Edwards Show* on CBS three nights a week in 1949, he started making regular guest appearances on *The Mickey Mouse Club Show*. A 1956 album for the Disney label features him sounding fine on remakes of some of his early hits in a Dixieland setting. But the drinking continued, and he soon blew his last opportunity. Edwards ended up on welfare, living in a home for indigent actors. He died in 1971 as a charity patient at a convalescent hospital, and his body went completely unclaimed until Walt Disney found out about it and arranged for a proper burial.

In his career, the pioneering jazz singer Cliff Edwards sold 74 million records, but he ended up broke and forgotten.

Recommended CDs: *Singin' In The Rain* (ASV/Living Era 5313), *The Vintage Recordings Of Cliff Edwards* (Take Two 419) and *Singing In The Rain* (Audiophile 17) have some of the high points of Ukulele Ike's large 1920s output, but a complete chronological reissue is long overdue. *Ukulele Ike Sings Again* (Disney 60408) reissues his final album from 1956.

LPs to Search For: *Cliff Edwards And His Hot Combination 1925–26* (Retrieval 203) has some of Edwards' more jazz-oriented selections from the mid-1920s.

Karen Egert
b. August 31, Brooklyn, NY

Karen Egert may not be a household name yet in the jazz world, but her CD *That Thing Called Love* is a particularly impressive and creative effort that lets one know of her great potential.

Raised on Long Island, she heard recordings of Broadway shows along with the Beatles while growing up, and was introduced to standards in high school. "I started out my career singing pop and Broadway show tunes in cafes. In college I studied acting and after graduation I became an actress. However, I found out that every time I auditioned for a role that required singing, I got the job, but the acting part was more difficult. I decided to concentrate on singing." Egert, who always had a beautiful voice, toured the Midwest for a year with a show band that played pop and rock songs. Back in New York, she landed a role in a short-lived Broadway musical *Rock And Roll—The First 5,000 Years*, playing Cher because of her ability to imitate her voice. After being the lead vocalist with the female pop group the Flirts and working on cruise ships and other shows, in 1984 she became a solo singer-pianist at the Sheraton Center in New York. Egert spent 1986–91 performing regularly at the Peacock Alley Lounge in the Waldorf-Astoria. "Cole Porter used to stay at that hotel and he had donated his piano. It was thrilling working there night after night, playing that piano."

After taking time off to raise a family, she returned as a full-time singer in 2003 and has since performed regularly in clubs in New York and New Jersey, recorded two CDs and written songs of her own.

Recommended CDs: *Let's Get Lost* debuts two of Karen Egert's thoughtful originals, "Wait Until I'm Through With You" and "Please Go Away," plus a dozen standards that include three Cole Porter songs. *That Thing Called Love* includes her original "Could You Be Mine" and memorable versions of "All Or Nothing At All," "So Nice (Summer Samba)" and "I Remember You." She is assisted by John and Bucky Pizzarelli on guitars and tenorman Harry Allen. Both CDs are privately issued by the singer.

Website: www.karenegert.com

Kelly Eisenhour
(Kelly Conelly)
b. April 17, 1960, Tucson, AZ

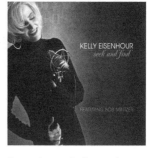

Although Kelly Eisenhour has been singing for over 25 years, her recent *Seek And Find* CD alerted the jazz world about her talents and made one wonder why she was not already famous.

"My father is an avid jazz listener and he had jazz playing in the house practically all day and night, and it was always the latest innovative music. Later, when my musician friends would come over and hang out, they couldn't get over my dad's record collection." She sang as a child and also played piano frequently in school, having had classical piano lessons from the age of six. Eisenhour attended the University of Arizona for two years and then finished at the Berklee College of Music, graduating in 1986. Ever since she began singing in clubs when she was 19, Eisenhour has made her living from music, either as a singer or as a vocal jazz educator.

She spent time working in Las Vegas, singing in production shows. During 1989–91 she toured as a backup singer for Gladys Knight. In 2002, she helped Knight organize the gospel choir Saints Unified Voices, being the assistant choir director and co-arranger of the music, appearing on their 2006 album *One Voice*.

Since moving to Utah in 1997, Eisenhour has sung as a guest soloist with the Utah Symphony during their pops concerts and also with the Boston Pops, appeared at the Salt Lake City Jazz Festival, recorded three CDs and become the Vocal Jazz Instructor at Brigham Young University.

"I'm actually at a turning point in my career right now. I have made my living as a singer all my life, but I became complacent and comfortable in the local or regional successes that I had. I didn't pursue my career to the fullest, and really regret that.

When I reached a certain age and began reflecting on all of this, I became very sad that I didn't do some of the things that I had hoped to. Not because I failed but because I just didn't pursue them. But I've decided that it isn't too late, and here I am now."

Recommended CDs: *Now You Know* (privately issued) is a strong start to Kelly Eisenhour's recording career while *Seek And Find* (Blujazz 3356) is a very impressive effort. Highlights of the latter include her vocalese lyrics to solos by Lester Young ("I'm Confessin'") and J.J. Johnson (on Benny Golson's "Reunion"), two originals that she co-wrote, and fresh versions of a variety of standards.

Website: www.kellyeisenhour.com

Kurt Elling

b. November 2, 1967, Chicago, IL

During a period when significant male jazz singers under the age of 60 can be counted on the fingers of one hand, the rise of Kurt Elling has revitalized the field. Elling's voice and approach were initially strongly influenced by Mark Murphy, but he has always had his own musical personality and it has become stronger as the years pass. Rather than merely recreate vocalese of the past, Elling has written new lyrics to solos by the likes of Dexter Gordon, Freddie Hubbard and John Coltrane ("A Love Supreme"). He has displayed the ability to improvise stories onstage (surpassing the best Beat poets of the 1950s), sometimes sets poetry to music, and constantly pushes himself like the best jazz improvisers yet can sing standards with as much affection as anyone.

"I remember when I was eight or nine, seeing Tony Bennett and the Woody Herman band on TV and thinking, 'That would be fun—coming on in a white dinner jacket and singing in front of a band like that.'" Elling sang in choirs as a youth and played, to various levels of success, violin, French horn, piano and drums. He did not seriously pursue singing jazz until college. "Cats down the hall were playing Dexter Gordon, Herbie Hancock and Dave Brubeck. Also, on exchange in Edinburgh, Scotland, a friend took me to hear Don Cherry, Bobby Watson and others at the Queen's Hall. As this happened, I had the opportunity to sit in with a vibraphone-led quartet at college—in fact, almost at exactly the time I started listening to the music consciously. Then, right after that, I got to be the singer for the school stage band and tour down to Texas and back." However, Elling never majored or minored in music. Instead he graduated cum laude with a B.A. in History from Gustavus Adolphus College in 1989, and then put in three years on a Master's in the Philosophy of Religion at the University of Chicago Divinity School. But in 1992 he dropped out and, within a year, was singing jazz in local clubs, especially at the Green Mill opposite tenor-saxophonists Von Freeman and Ed Peterson. He was never just a singer but a musician himself in his attitude and the way he sang and improvised.

Elling sent a demo to Blue Note and was quickly signed, recording his debut (*Close Your Eyes*) in 1994 and making a strong impression from the start. He has worked constantly ever since, generally accompanied by a trio with his musical director pianist Laurence Hopgood. His activities at the 2006 Monterey Jazz Festival were typical. Not only did he perform with his regular group before an overflow crowd but he guested with the Yellowjackets, played a part in Dave Brubeck's "Cannery Row Suite," performed with a college big band (which he had helped to mentor), was interviewed onstage, and starred with the Clayton/Hamilton Jazz Orchestra including debuting a new suite called "Red Man/Black Man."

For the future, Elling says that he wants to "learn to play piano better, write better music and learn to write bigger pieces—a requiem mass and more experimental stuff. I want to work with heavier and heavier cats including Wayne Shorter, Roy Haynes, Dave Liebman and Pat Metheny. I've got a pretty long wish list." Kurt Elling, a hipster for the 21st century, has endless potential.

Recommended CDs: Each of Kurt Elling's seven CDs is excellent. His debut *Close Your Eyes* (Blue Note 30645) includes his vocalese and words to Wayne Shorter's "Delores" and Herbie Hancock's "Hurricane" plus some spoken word sections, improvised lyrics and "Ballad Of The Sad Young Men." *The Messenger* (Blue Note 52727) has fresh versions of "Nature Boy," "'April In Paris" and "Prelude To A Kiss," crazy scatting on Jimmy Heath's "Gingerbread Boy," and vocalese on Dexter Gordon's solo on "Tanya." *This Time It's Love* (Blue Note 93543) emphasizes love songs and ballads including "Too Young To Go Steady" and a charming "I Feel So Smoochie," but also vocalese for a long Freddie Hubbard statement on "Freddie's Yen For Jen." *Live In Chicago* (Blue Note 22211) includes a 12-minute "My Foolish Heart," vocalese for Wayne Shorter's solo on "Night Dreamer," an overly brief but amusing blues jam with tenors Von Freeman, Eddie Johnson and Ed Peterson, and two guest appearances by Jon Hendricks. *Flirting With Twilight* (Blue Note 31113) boasts many great moments, including vocalese for an obscure Charlie Haden bass solo on "Moonlight Serenade," a tender "Lil' Darlin'," "Not While I'm Around," "Blame It On My Youth" and two originals co-written by Elling. *Man In The Air* (Blue Note 80834) has his lyrics to Grover Washington Jr.'s hit "Winelight;" "Resolution" from John Coltrane's *A Love Supreme*; and pieces by Joe Zawinul, Herbie Hancock, Courtney Pine, Bobby Watson and Bob Mintzer. Vibraphonist Stefan Harris is a major asset throughout. *Nightmoves* (Concord 7230263) finds Elling continuing to stretch himself on pop tunes, originals, ballads and, best of all, vocalese to Dexter Gordon's "Body And Soul" solo.

Website: www.kurtelling.com

Ethel Ennis
b. November 28, 1932, Baltimore, MD

A major jazz singer, Ethel Ennis has spent her life living in Baltimore, which accounts for her being somewhat underrated despite her talent.

She began piano lessons when she was seven and sometimes substituted for her mother playing piano in the local Methodist church. "When I was 15 years old, a performing group called Abe Riley's Octet needed a piano player. So with the permission of my parents and grandmother, I started playing in the Baltimore area with this older, all-male group that performed jazz, blues and pop music. At one point, someone in a local dance hall asked Abe Riley if he knew 'In the Dark,' a blues tune made popular by Lil Green. I knew the song from listening to the blues that used to boom on Saturday night from the unit below us in the projects. I sang the song all night; the group got a big tip, and I hung out my shingle as a singer/pianist."

Ennis graduated from Cortez W. Peters Business College in 1952 before choosing to become a singer. She debuted with an album for Jubilee (*Lullabies For Losers*) in 1955, which was followed by two highly rated sets for Capitol. "The Capitol associations led to an audition with Benny Goodman, who was assembling an all-star band to tour Europe and play in the U.S. Pavilion at the Brussels World's Fair in 1958. Jimmy Rushing and I became the vocalists for that tour, my first introduction to European audiences." During 1963–64 she was at the height of her fame, recording four albums for RCA, appearing at the 1964 Newport Jazz Festival, performing with Duke Ellington on the Bell Telephone Hour on television, and dueting with Joe Williams at the Monterey Jazz Festival. She also appeared opposite Cab Calloway at the Apollo Theater.

However, Ethel Ennis resettled in Baltimore and, although she has worked as often as she wanted to in the years since, fame has eluded her. She has appeared in concerts with the Count Basie Orchestra, sung the national anthem a cappella at Richard Nixon's presidential inauguration in 1973, been part of the last live band to perform regularly on Arthur Godfrey's CBS radio series, and been recognized as Baltimore's cultural ambassador. During 1985–88, she and her husband operated Ethel's Place in Baltimore, which gave her an opportunity to perform with major musicians who were booked into the club.

Ethel Ennis has appeared at concerts with the Billy Taylor Trio and been featured at jazz festivals, including annually at the Lionel Hampton Jazz Festival (starting in 1988). "When I married for the second time in 1967, I decided to remain in Baltimore and resist blandishments to settle in New York or Los Angeles. That decision slowed my career but enabled me to lead a balanced life with select engagements, mostly concerts in recent years."

Recommended CDs: Ethel Ennis' two Capitol albums have been reissued as *Change Of Scenery/Have You Forgotten* (EMI 98886). In more recent times, 1998's *If Women Ruled The World* (Savoy 8088) and the live *Ennis Anyone?* (Jazzmont 2421) give one a good sampling of Ethel Ennis at her best.

LPs to Search For: *Lullabies For Losers* (Jubilee 1021), *This Is Ethel Ennis* (RCA 2786), *Eyes To You* (RCA 2984), three of the singer's personal favorite recordings, are unfortunately all quite scarce.

Eddie Erickson
b. April 4, 1948, San Francisco, CA

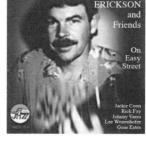

One of the funniest comedians on the jazz scene, and a frequently hilarious ad-libber, Eddie Erickson is also a fine guitarist and banjoist in addition to being an excellent jazz singer. "Easy Street" is a song he practically owns.

The son of an amateur guitarist, Erickson started playing ukulele when he was seven. He also spent a bit of time on trombone and cornet (the latter while working at Disney World) and began playing banjo when he was 13. "I started listening to Kenny Ball, Louis Armstrong, Eddie Peabody, George Van Eps—everybody I could. I learned how to play by ear. I read music, but not enough to hurt my playing."

Erickson began working professionally in music in San Jose in the mid-1960s, moved to Monterey in 1969, and spent time working at Disney World and Disneyland, also being a member of the Banjo Kings. From 1978 to 1983 he led the Riverboat Rascals on a riverboat in Disneyland. Erickson co-led *Fast Eddie And Big Mama Sue* for years with singer-washboard player Sue Kroninger, an excellent vehicle for his brand of goodtime music and humor. "I think every situation I have been in (musically) has been a learning experience, from my first job at 15 years of age singing at Me 'N Ed's Pizza Parlor, to now. I worked with a group called the Abalone Stompers, which was such a great band in its day. I met Jake Stock, the leader and mentor of the band, as well as Jackie Coon (we started the *Jack 'N Ed Show* in the late '80s), an incredible musician. I learned so much from them, especially how to swing and how to have fun doing it. The reed player/entertainer Rick Fay was also a great influence on me, and he got me started in the jazz party circuit."

In 2002, Eddie Erickson started teaming up with singer Rebecca Kilgore, trombonist Dan Barrett and eventually bassist Joel Forbes to form B.E.D. In addition to playing guitar and banjo, Erickson's vocals (both humorous and straight) and his ad-libbing have added a great deal of personality to the group.

"I love to sing, because of B.E.D., more than ever. Rebecca Kilgore has been a wonderful inspiration for me, and I have taken singing more seriously because of her."

Recommended CDs: *On Easy Street* (Arbors 19111) puts the spotlight on Erickson with assistance from Rick Fay, Jackie Coon and Johnny Varro. B.E.D.'s three recordings thus far are *Get Ready For Bed* (Blue Swing 001), *Bedlam* (Blue Swing 003) and *Watch Out* (Blue Swing 005), giving one a good idea what it is to experience B.E.D. Although the joking between songs is missing, making one hope for a live recording or a DVD in the future.

Website: www.eddieerickson.com

Dewey Erney

b. February 19, 1937, Latrobe, PA

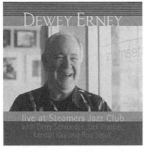

A straightforward interpreter of lyrics who swings lightly and rarely varies from the lyrics of a song, Dewey Erney has long been a popular performer in the Los Angeles area, often teaming up with guitarist Ron Eschete.

Early on he heard his brother's swing records and his father's collection of music from Broadway shows. "Much of the *Great American Songbook*, which I have sung through the years was learned by the exposure I had to these songs in my early life. In the second grade, I won some amateur contests imitating Al Jolson. I remember singing for various classrooms in elementary school, and I guess that's where and when I started enjoying performing."

Although he graduated from Indiana University of Pennsylvania with a degree in Business Education (1960), he also sang with his school jazz and dance bands. While serving in the Navy, he met pianist Jesse Tyler and began to sing more extensively in clubs. Erney moved to Long Beach in 1963, and a few years later began working with the Bill Evans-inspired pianist Dick Powell. He also had many opportunities to work with pianists Gerry Schroeder and Tom Ranier, and has been associated with Ron Eschete since 1970.

Since that time, Dewey Erney has worked at most Southern California jazz clubs, including a regular monthly engagement at Steamers in Fullerton. He has recorded extensively, mostly for the Resurgent label. "My favorite way to express myself is to work with a guitarist or pianist and a rhythm section that actually know many, many songs, so that when I call out a tune in a particular key, we can just go for it. I know over 1,500 songs by memory, so I always want to have musicians who also know a lot of material. My main focus on performing is to present the material in as honest a way as I can, with special emphasis on melody and lyrics, while making it swing and be emotionally involving at the same time."

Recommended CDs: A very consistent performer who enjoys recording standards, Dewey Erney is in fine form on *Dearly Beloved* (Resurgent 107), *You And The Night And The Music* (Resurgent 114), *Time Was* (Resurgent 118), *You'd Be So Nice To Come Home To* (Resurgent 119), *The Shades Of Love* (Resurgent 122), *Calvary's Love* (Resurgent 126), *Christmas Time Is Here* (Resurgent 125), *So In Love* (Resurgent 127) with the Tom Kubis Big Band, the two-CD *A Beautiful Friendship/Then And Now* (Resurgent 128), which reissues Erney's Discovery LP of 1982 and includes a new set from 20 years later, *What Is This Thing Called Love* (Resurgent 129), *Live At Steamers Jazz Club* (Resurgent 130), *A Tribute To Johnny Mercer* (Dewsong), *Lucky To Be Me* (Dewsong), *Live At Steamers Jazz Club 2* (Primrose Lane 004), *My Shining Hour* (Dewsong), and *I Remember You, Johnny Mercer* (Dewsong) and *Songs In Our Hearts* (Dewsong).

Website: www.deweyerney.com

Ruth Etting

b. November 23, 1897, David City, NE;
d. September 24, 1978, Colorado Springs, NE

A major pop singer of the late 1920s/early '30s, Ruth Etting had a "girl next door" persona and often had the word "Sweetheart" in her billing, whether it was "Chicago's Sweetheart," "The Radio Sweetheart" or "America's Sweetheart." She was influenced by jazz and served a similar role as Bing Crosby did at the time for male singers by bringing a relaxed and lightly swinging jazz phrasing into pop music, almost unconsciously influencing a generation of female vocalists.

Ruth Etting's mother died when she was five and she was raised by her father's parents. Her original goal was to be a costume designer and, after she moved to Chicago in 1915, she attended the Chicago Academy of Fine Arts. But after working at designing clothes for shows, her good looks and natural talent resulted in her gaining a job as a chorus girl, dancer and eventually singer. Her low voice was both sensual and non threatening, and the cry in her voice made her constantly sympathetic when she sang torch songs. She married the Chicago gangster Martin Snyder (who was known as "Moe the Gimp") in 1922, and he helped her get a job with Abe Lyman's orchestra where the regular radio broadcasts made her a star. The Gimp's strong arm tactics were at first an asset for Etting, who rose to the top of show business pretty fast, but in time his interference became a hindrance. The chances are that she would have made it as a singer eventually without his help.

During 1926–38, Ruth Etting was one of the major stars of popular music. She recorded 203 songs, was a fixture on the radio (being a regular performer on eight different network radio shows), starred in 35 film shorts and made appearances in three full-length movies. Florenz Ziegfeld, who managed her career part of the time, called her "the greatest singer of songs." She certainly was an asset to his shows, moving to New York to appear in the *Ziegfeld Follies Of 1927* where she sang the hit "Shakin' The Blues Away." In *Whoopee* she introduced "Love Me Or Leave Me" (her trademark song), 1929's *Simple Simon* had her causing a major stir with her depiction of a taxi dancer with "Ten Cents A Dance," and she successfully revived "Shine On Harvest Moon" in *The Follies Of 1931*.

Etting had over 60 hit records during this era and her sidemen included her regular pianists (Rube Bloom or Frank Signorelli) plus occasional guests such as violinist Joe Venuti, guitarist Eddie Lang, Tommy Dorsey and Jimmy Dorsey. Her successes in the early years of the Depression faded a bit with the rise of the Swing era, but she remained a household name. Etting divorced the Gimp in 1937, but the following year he followed her to Hollywood and shot her accompanist and boyfriend Myrl Alderman. The resulting trial and all the sensational publicity persuaded her that it was best to retire. She married Alderman and they lived quietly in Nebraska. Etting made a minor comeback in 1947, singing on the radio and appearing at the Copacabana in NY, but at 50 she decided to permanently retire so her fans could remember how she sounded in her prime. A semi-fictional movie on her life (*Love*

Me Or Leave Me starring Doris Day and James Cagney) was released in the mid-1950s, and Ruth Etting made rare appearances during her last few decades, passing away in 1978.

Recommended CDs: A strong sampling of Ruth Etting's best recordings can be heard on *Ten Cents A Dance* (Living Era 5008), *America's Sweetheart Of Song* (Living Era 5374), *Love Me Or Leave Me* (Pearl 7061) and *Glorifier Of American Song* (Take Two 422).

George Evans
b. January 23, 1963, Bloomington, IN

One of Canada's top ballad singers, George Evans falls between jazz and cabaret in his approach, swinging pieces lightly and improvising while paying respect to the lyricist and composer's original intent.

"With my parents in the opera field, we heard classical music at home as a rule. As a child, I was made to sing at cocktail parties for the luminaries from the opera world who would come to our home. By age three, I had learned the entire score to every musical in which Julie Andrews starred, and (much to their dismay, I imagine) sang them for all the neighbors. I was introduced to big band and theater music in films and on television at an early age and found it most accessible. In my teens, I listened to pop of the day and then, as many of us did, I became lost in the morass of disco. Finally in college I started to methodically learn the standards." He also played trombone for nine years before concentrating on singing, naming Rosemary Clooney, Mel Tormé, Carmen McRae, Nancy Wilson, Etta Jones, Johnny Hartman and Billy Eckstine as key influences.

Evans attended the College Conservatory of Music at the University of Cincinnati in the early 1980s, majoring in musical theater. "I knew at a very early age that singing was what I was going to do, but it wasn't until my late 20s that I fully realized my fate. It seems as though I'd tried to find any other suitable option first, but in the final analysis, my work as a singer has given me the greatest satisfaction and fulfillment."

George Evans performed in New York in 1990 and moved to Montreal in 1992, settling in Toronto in 1999. He has worked as a music archivist, written articles as a jazz journalist, been a regular on the radio, toured with The Three Crooners, produced compilation records and recorded six CDs of his own. "The rendering of words can be every bit as focused and intelligent in jazz as in other fields like cabaret. Jazz offers a new experience at every turn that a more rigid approach to song interpretation disqualifies."

Recommended CDs: Thus far George Evans has recorded six CDs, and his evolution toward becoming a more adventurous jazz singer is fun to follow. Each of his discs, *Moodswing* (M-Swing 23), *I'm All Smiles* (M-Swing 24), *From Moment To Moment* (M-Swing 25), *Eyes For You* (M-Swing 26), *Movie Songs* (Maximum Jazz 16532) and *Bewitched* (M-Swing 28), features fine singing and tasteful improvising.

Website: www.georgeevans.ca

Connie Evingson
b. May 7, Hibbing, MN

A highly appealing singer from Minnesota, Connie Evingson has in recent times been singing with the Hot Club of Sweden, a gypsy swing band in the tradition of Django Reinhardt and

Stephane Grappelli, but she has always been quite versatile in her tastes.

"My father had an extensive jazz record collection, so I heard the music constantly from a very early age, really from infancy." She sang in church and with school choirs, performing in musicals in high school. Evingson graduated from the University of Minnesota in 1981, starting as a music major but, since there was no jazz program, she earned a degree in Speech Communications. "I think I always knew, growing up, that singing was what I was meant to do. I tried to avoid it, knowing that it is a very difficult way to make a living, but I kept getting pulled back in. Immediately after graduating from college, I started singing in nightclubs in Minneapolis and St. Paul. It felt very natural to me, like it was what I was supposed to do. I took a break from the music business at one point and worked in advertising for a few years, but I couldn't stay away. When I came back, it was like coming home."

Connie Evingson particularly appreciates her association with Doc Severinsen. "I began working with him when he was the guest Pops conductor of the Minnesota Orchestra in 1996. I've done several orchestra programs with him; he's a real inspiration." In addition, she has worked with the vocal ensemble Moore By Four, toured Europe and Japan, performed with Bobby McFerrin and Vocalessence, has had a long-time radio show on KBEM and created and starred in the stage production *Fever: A Tribute To Peggy Lee*.

"I love the freedom of jazz, the creativity, the fact that there really aren't any boundaries. Most of all, there's nothing like the feeling of swing."

Recommended CDs: Each of Connie Evingson's recordings has its own personality. *I Have Dreamed* (Minnehaha 2001) consists of jazz versions of show tunes, *Fever—A Tribute To Peggy Lee* (Minnehaha 2002) revives songs associated with Lee, *Some Cats Know* (Minnehaha 2003) has guest appearances by Doc Severinsen and trombonist Al Grey plus local heroes, *The Secret Of Christmas* (Minnehaha 2004) is one of the better Christmas jazz CDs, and *Let It Be Jazz: Connie Evingson Sings The Beatles* (Summit 1021/Minnehaha 2005) features creative jazz versions of 13 Lennon/McCartney songs. *Gypsy In My Soul* (Minnehaha 2006) finds the singer joined by three different gypsy jazz groups (including Pearl Django) while *Stockholm Sweetnin'* (Minnehaha 2007), a collaboration with the Hot Club of Sweden, has her building upon the concept, even performing effective versions of Abbey Lincoln's "Throw It Away" and "Windmills Of Your Mind" in the 1930s swing setting. *Little Did I Dream* (Minnehaha 2008) features Connie Evingson singing Dave Frishberg compositions with a quintet that includes the composer on piano.

Website: www.connieevingson.com

Georgie Fame
(Clive Powell)
b. June 26, 1943, Leigh, Lancashire, England

Georgie Fame has had an unusually wide-ranging musical career, one based originally in rock and roll but often crossing over into jazz.

The son of an amateur musician, he had piano lessons at the age of seven but did not take music very seriously until rock and roll became the dominant popular music. At 15 he left school to work as an apprentice cotton weaver in a local mill (as many in his family had), but he also spent time playing piano with a group called the Dominoes. In the summer of 1959 the teenager

Lorraine Feather

landed a full-time job playing with Rory and the Blackjacks. When the band broke up, he struggled in London for a time until gaining a job with impresario Larry Parnes, who renamed him Georgie Fame. He gained a lot of experience playing with top British musicians and began to discover jazz, being particularly attracted to the trad jazz of Humphrey Lyttelton.

After some time spent playing piano with Billy Fury's Blue Flames, Fame became its leader in 1962, starting doubling on organ, and landed them a job as the house band at the Flamingo Club in London for three years. The music of the Blue Flames was essentially R&B with some rock and jazz. In 1963 Fame recorded a live album and during the next few years he had a series of hit records including "Yeh Yeh," "Getaway" and "The Ballad Of Bonnie And Clyde." At the same time, he recorded a jazz album, *Sound Venture*, with the Harry South Big Band and during 1967–68 had opportunities to sing with the Count Basie Orchestra when it visited Europe.

Much of the 1970s was spent performing R&B and pop, including on a television series that he shared with keyboardist Alan Price called *The Price Of Fame*, and leading a new version of the Blue Flames. In 1981, he teamed up with Annie Ross to record a tribute album to Hoagy Carmichael called *In Hoagland*. Fame also recorded tribute albums to Benny Goodman (*In Goodmanland*) and Chet Baker (*A Portrait Of Chet*).

Georgie Fame worked regularly with Van Morrison during 1988–97, including a tribute album to Mose Allison. He recorded some of his most jazz-oriented CDs during that time, particularly for Ben Sidran's Go Jazz label, including *Cool Cat Blues*, *The Blues And Me* and *Name Droppin'*. Later projects have included playing in the Rhythm Kings with bassist Bill Wyman, regrouping the Blue Flames and recording *Poet In New York* and *Relationships*.

Even at the age of 63, Georgie Fame is a difficult singer and pianist to categorize (sort of like Mose Allison meets Fats Domino), yet he is able to excel at a broad range of music without losing his musical personality.

Recommended CDs: Georgie Fame has recorded a lot of music through the years. His most rewarding jazz sets include *In Hoagland* (DRG 5197), *Cool Cat Blues* (Blue Moon 6002), *The Blues And Me* (Blue Moon 6005), *Name Droppin'* (Blue Moon 6021) and *Poet In New York* (Blue Moon 6044).

LPs to Search For: Two historic Georgie Fame albums await CD reissue: *Rhythm And Blues At The Flamingo* (Columbia 1599) and *Sound Venture* (Columbia 1676).

Website: www.georgiefame.absoluteelsewhere.net

Lorraine Feather
(Billie Jane Lee Lorraine Feather)
b. September 10, 1948, New York, NY

Although she has had a wide-ranging career as a singer, lyricist and songwriter, it seemed inevitable that Lorraine Feather would find her own niche in jazz. After all, her father was the notable jazz critic/ producer/songwriter Leonard Feather and her godmother was Billie Holiday.

Born in Manhattan, Feather grew up in Los Angeles. After being a theater arts

major for two years, she moved back to New York in hopes of becoming an actress. Although she had parts in regional theater, gained some off-Broadway work and, appeared in the Broadway version of *Jesus Christ Superstar*, work was infrequent. "I was 25 and had been singing with small groups to make a few bucks when I was out of work as an actress, which was almost all the time. I'd been to a depressing 'cattle call' for a show and said to my then-boyfriend, 'Forget this acting thing. From now on, I'm a singer.' The next day I got a call to sing backup for Petula Clark in Vegas and had a ball."

After a period of time performing with top-40 and occasional jazz bands on the East Coast, she moved back to Los Angeles, recording a jazz album for Concord. In 1980 she joined the vocal trio Full Swing, developing as a songwriter (writing 23 songs for the band's recordings) and appearing with the group regularly during the next eight years, including backing Bette Midler and recording with Barry Manilow. The vocal ensemble recorded a wide variety of music that ranged from pop to Feather's lyrics for Duke Ellington's "Rockin' In Rhythm," Fletcher Henderson's "Big John's Special" and the Yellowjackets' "Ballad Of The Whale." After the group broke up, Feather primarily worked as a songwriter. Her lyrics were recorded by a variety of R&B and pop groups plus Eric Marienthal, David Benoit, Tom Scott, Diane Schuur and Cleo Laine (who recorded several of her lyrics for Duke Ellington instrumentals). She also wrote for television shows and films (gaining seven Emmy nominations) and worked as a singer now and then.

In 1999, Lorraine Feather returned to jazz when she wrote contemporary lyrics to the piano pieces of Fats Waller. The resulting album, *New York City Drag*, is a gem full of wit, particularly the now-classic "You're Outta Here" (her lyrics to Waller's "Minor Drag"). Her follow-up recording *Café Society* has her lyrics to a variety of tunes by Duke Ellington, Johnny Mandel, Don Grusin, Russell Ferrante and others, while *Such Sweet Thunder* features her words to a full set of Duke Ellington instrumentals. The Waller and Ellington albums in particular are Lorraine Feather's most important contributions to jazz thus far and they find her voice in prime form.

Lorraine Feather names Annie Ross and Joni Mitchell as her main singing inspirations. "I relate to them because, aside from being brainy women who swing, each of them has a light upper register the way I do. I consider myself a writer more than a singer, but what's funny is that I didn't begin doing either one in earnest till I was in my 30s. It took me a long time to get good as a singer; writing comes to me more easily. Now, though, recording albums and performing have become a real thrill."

Recommended CDs: *New York City Drag* (Rhombus 7020) and *Such Sweet Thunder* (Sanctuary 8653) contain some of Feather's most witty and inventive lyrics. The nostalgic *Café Society* (Sanctuary 84597) also has its memorable moments while *Dooji Wooji* (Sanctuary 34101) contains four more Duke Ellington songs with new lyrics plus some more recent material; "Indiana Lana" ("Jubilee Stomp") is the classic of the CD.

LPs to Search For: *Sweet Lorraine* (Concord Jazz 78) gives one an opportunity to hear Lorraine Feather early in her career.

Website: www.lorrainefeather.com

Jim Ferguson
b. December 10, 1950, Jefferson City, MO

Few singers in this book are bass players who are based in Nashville, but Jim Ferguson has always stood out from the crowd.

His father, formerly a high school music teacher, was involved in church music by 1950, moving the family to South Carolina when Jim was two. He sang in a children's choir when he was four and studied voice at the University of South Carolina while still a junior in high school. Ferguson had piano lessons but they did not take. However, as a senior in high school, a bass was needed in his father's youth choir, so he played the string bass for the first time. He entered the University of South Carolina in 1969 with a major in voice and had his first bass lessons, but it would be ten years before he gained a degree.

"I began gigging around Columbia, South Carolina. My main mentors were guitarist Terry Rosen and trumpeter Johnny Helms. They wanted the sound of the string bass badly enough to put up with my inexperience. I did not begin singing jazz until my sophomore year. I found that, though I was hired to play bass on gigs, band leaders would discover that I sang and they would ask me to do a ballad or a medium swing tune. Gradually, I became more comfortable with singing while playing string bass."

During his junior year in college, Ferguson joined the New Christy Minstrels since there was an opening for a high-voiced male singer who could play bass. He toured for six months. In 1978 he played bass in a musical, *On Green Pond*, that though in production in South Carolina, was going to be performed in Brooklyn. Ferguson's time in New York included meeting Red Mitchell, befriending Chuck Israels, taking lessons from Michael Moore and soaking up the jazz scene.

Back in South Carolina, Ferguson was motivated to finish school, following it up by quickly earning a Master's in Jazz Studies. In 1981, he moved to Nashville where he has since played with such major jazz artists as Teddy Wilson, Kenny Burrell, Cal Collins, Phineas Newborn, Jimmy Raney, Martin Taylor, the Hi Los, Jay McShann, Conte Candoli, Steve Allen, Marian McPartland and Mose Allison, recording with Stephane Grappelli, Al Jarreau, Lorne Lofsky and Lenny Breau. He was also the regular bassist on the NPR series *The American Popular Singer*, and has toured regularly with pop singer Crystal Gayle since 1990.

In addition to his work as a sideman, Jim Ferguson has led two albums of his own that feature both his friendly singing and his bass playing. "I look for strong melodies and interesting lyrics. If the song is familiar, I try to do it differently; if it is obscure, so much the better. My hope is that the lyrics and vocals help make my music more accessible to a wider audience, even when it includes extended solos."

Recommended CDs: *Not Just Another Pretty Bass* (Challenge 73160) features Ferguson singing a variety of ballads and *Deep Summer Music* (Challenge 73201) is equally charming as the bassist comes across as a rural Dave Frishberg. Tenor-saxophonist Chris Potter is the solo star on both sets.

Website: www.jimfergusonmusic.com

Nina Ferro

b. September 6, 1973, Melbourne, Australia

A versatile singer from Australia, Nina Ferro is best known in the United States for her many appearances with the Jim Cullum Jazz Band on his *Live From The Landing* radio series. But although she sings classic jazz well, Ferro's musical interests are much more diverse.

"Some of my earliest experiences singing were with family members around my grandmother's house. At school I was involved in practically every music ensemble and school musical production time would allow. At 15, I was asked to sing a couple of songs at wedding for a friend of my mother's; that was my first paid job. I began doing more regular gigs around town at 16." In school she learned piano, drums and played clarinet for four years. As a singer, Ferro says that she was inspired as a youth by Stevie Wonder, Elvis Presley, Motown, Italian opera, Aretha Franklin and later on the jazz greats including Billie Holiday and Louis Armstrong.

Ferro studied at the Victorian College of the Arts for a little over a year but left to go on an overseas tour. "I was holding down part time jobs and never really having enough time and energy to put into my music career, so I decided to quit all my other jobs and focus on singing for a living. It was tough at first, but I figured if you really want to do something and you set your mind to it, you'll be fine."

Since then, Nina Ferro has performed all over the world, made at least 30 appearances with Jim Cullum's band for his radio series in San Antonio including sharing the stage with Dick Hyman and Benny Carter, performed five times at the Sacramento Jazz Festival, relocated to England and led five CDs. She has been a regular performer at Ronnie Scott's Club in London. While she has wide musical tastes and talents, her heart remains with vintage jazz. "It's a different feeling to when I'm singing contemporary pop, soul, funk or classical. It has a richness and diversity that I enjoy interpreting."

Recommended CDs: Thus far Nina Ferro has mostly stuck to swing standards on her CDs along with a few originals. Her first two releases, *Just You Just Me* and *Out Of The Blue*, are out of print. *Tender Is The Night* from 2001 and 2004's *Crazy Way Of Lovin'* are her strongest sets to date. Recollection is a sampling of music from her first four albums while *Nina Ferro And Dominic Grant* is a recent EP. All of her recordings have been released on her Ferro-cious Entertainment label.

Website: www.ninaferro.com

Ella Fitzgerald

b. April 25, 1917, Newport News, VA;
d. June 15, 1996, Beverly, Hills, CA

No one could out-swing Ella Fitzgerald. She could trade four-bar phrases with any horn player and come out on top; her scatting was second to none. But Ella also deserved the title of "The First Lady Of Song" due to her ability to sing the definitive versions of hundreds of standards. Her in-terpretations tended to be full of joy and she was criticized by some for lacking emotional depth, but Ella could also sing a lowdown ballad or blues and make one really feel the words. It is just that she loved singing so much, it was an escape from her early past, and she wanted audiences to love her. What she did not always seem to realize is that from the 1940s on, they always loved her, before she even opened her mouth to sing.

Ella Fitzgerald's early life was as grim as Billie Holiday's, but she reacted to it much differently. Growing up very poor, Ella was actually homeless for a year as a teenager. She lacked Holiday's looks, was somewhat gawky, and was very unsure about her future. She hoped to become a dancer but she was a much better singer. In 1934 she won the Apollo Theater's amateur contest, singing "Judy" in the style of her early idol Connie Boswell. Ella sang briefly with Tiny Bradshaw's orchestra, but Fletcher Henderson turned down the chance to hire her. Benny Carter, who had been in the audience at the amateur contest, told Chick Webb that he should add her to his band. Webb was not impressed by her appearance and her shabby clothes (she was virtually penniless at the time), but gave her a chance one night. The audience was enthusiastic about her spirited singing and Webb grudgingly hired her. Within a year, she was the band's main attraction.

Ella began recording with Webb in 1935, alternating juvenile novelties with ballads. Her 1938 recording of "A-Tisket, A-Tasket" was a huge hit and she helped make "Undecided" into a standard. She also began to record under her own name, using Webb's sidemen.

Chick Webb, who had been in shaky health for years, passed away in June 1939. Ella Fitzgerald at 22 was already such a big name that she was made the leader of the "ghost" band even though she actually had nothing to do with its music. She acted as the front man and took vocals on the majority of the performances, being the most significant female singer to lead a big band during the swing era. The Ella Fitzgerald Orchestra lasted into 1941 before she began her solo career.

A household name by then, Ella was a strong-selling artist from the start and never declined nor lost her popularity. She recorded regularly for Decca for the next 15 years, soon dropping the juvenile novelties in favor of swing standards, blues and ballads. She rarely scatted at all during her Chick Webb years, but by the mid-1940s she was on her way to becoming its leader as she showed on famous recordings of "Lady Be Good," "How High The Moon" and "Flying Home." Touring with the Dizzy Gillespie big band gave her an opportunity to learn bebop although she remained essentially a swing singer. Ella first toured with *Jazz At The Philharmonic* in 1946 (keeping up with its masterful horn players) and Norman Granz became her manager. She was married to bassist Ray Brown during 1948–52, but her private life was mostly uneventful; she lived through singing.

The 1950s found Ella Fitzgerald at the peak of her powers. She recorded superb duet sets with pianist Ellis Larkins in 1950 and 1954, appeared in a few movies including 1955's *Pete Kelly's Blues*, and in 1956 switched to Norman Granz's Verve label, which he had formed specifically to record her. Her series of songbooks featured her singing entire sets of the music of major composers. Lee Wiley had recorded songbooks first (starting in 1939) but Ella's was much more extensive with full-length programs devoted to the music of Cole Porter, the Gershwins, Rodgers and Hart, Duke Ellington, Harold Arlen, Jerome Kern and lyricist Johnny Mercer.

There was no slowdown during the 1960s and '70s as she constantly toured and sang. After the Verve years ended, Ella made records for Capitol and Reprise that were sometimes sub-par due to the material. But in the 1970s Norman Granz formed the Pablo label, and Ella was back in good company again, singing with everyone from Count Basie and Oscar Peterson to guitarist Joe Pass and pianist Tommy Flanagan. Her voice began to decline slightly in the mid-1970s and then gradually after that but she never lost her impeccable timing or her joy at singing. Her last recording was in 1989, and she retired a few years later, passing away in 1996 at the age of 79.

In the decade that has passed since then, no new singer has appeared who is on the level of Ella Fitzgerald, but that is not surprising. There is only one Ella.

Recommended CDs: Ella Fitzgerald recorded a very large number of recordings during 1935–96, and an awful lot are essential. The best way to acquire all of her early studio recordings is by getting the comprehensive releases of the French Classics label since the American equivalents tend to be incomplete "best of" collections. Ella's earliest years are fully covered on *1935–1937* (Classics 500), *1937–1938* (Classics 506), *1938–1939* (Classics 518), *1939* (Classics 525), *1939–1940* (Classics 566) and *1940–1941* (Classics 644), which feature her recordings with Chick Webb and with her own orchestra. *1941–1944* (Classics 840) has her first recordings after breaking up the big band. *1945–1947* (Classics 998), *1947–1948* (Classics 1049) and *1949* (Classics 1153) get her through the bebop era although, in addition to scat fests, Ella sings ballads, swing tunes and novelties, sometimes "assisted" by background vocalists. *1950* (Classics 1195) has the first eight-song collaboration with Ellis Larkins in addition to including a wide variety of material. *1951* (Classics 1261) is highlighted by four duets with Louis Armstrong. *1952* (Classics 1328) and *1953–1954* (Classics 1404) find Ella doing her best to overcome weak material, occasionally recording gems and, in *1953–1954*, sounding in prime form on her second set with Larkins. Both of her Larkins duet projects are also available on *Pure Ella* (Decca 636). All of Ella's songbook sessions are on the 16-CD box set *The Complete Ella Fitzgerald Songbooks* (Verve 314 519 832 8487) and fortunately most of them are also available individually (as *The Cole Porter Songbook*, *The Rodgers And Hart Songbook*, etc.). Among the other excellent projects recorded by Ella during her Verve years are *Ella At The Opera House* (Verve 831 2697), *Get Happy* (Verve 314 523 3217), *Like Someone In Love* (Verve 314 511 5247), *Ella Swings Brightly* (Verve 314 519 3477), *Ella Swings Gently* (Verve 314 519 548), *The Complete Ella In Berlin* (Verve 314 519 584), which includes her famous ad-lib version of "Mack The Knife" (she forgot the words), *The Intimate Ella* (Verve 839 838), *Ella Returns To Berlin* (Verve 837 758), *Clap Hands Here Comes Charlie* (Verve 835 646), *These Are The Blues* (Verve 829 536) and *Ella At Duke's Place* (314 529 700). Only *Sunshine Of Your Love* (Verve 314 533 102) from 1969 is a misfire, unless one really wants to hear Ella trying to swing "Hey Jude." *Newport Jazz Festival/Live At Carnegie Hall* (Columbia/Legacy 66809) is a two-CD set from 1973 that serves as a solid retrospective, including a reunion of the Chick Webb band. *The Concert Years* (Pablo 4414) is an excellent four-CD set that has Ella live in 1953, with Duke Ellington during 1966–67, and during her Pablo-era concerts from 1971 to 1983, including her rather hilarious version of "C Jam Blues" from 1972. Other worthy Pablo sets include *Ella À Nice* (Original Jazz Classics 442), *Take Love Easy* (Pablo 2310-702), *Fine And Mellow* (Pablo 2310-829), *Ella In London* (Original Jazz Classics 974), *Ella And Oscar* (Pablo 2310-759), *At The Montreux Jazz Festival* (Original Jazz Classics 789), *Fitzgerald And Pass...Again* (Pablo 2310-772), *Montreux '77* (Original Jazz Classics 376) and *Lady Time* (Original Jazz Classics 864) from 1978. Ella's four Pablo recordings from the 1980s are quite a bit weaker, and be sure to avoid her rather sad finale, *All That Jazz*.

LPs to Search For: There are so many Ella Fitzgerald recordings currently available on CD that it seems somewhat remarkable that one of her finest albums, *Ella In Hollywood* (Verve 4052), has not been reissued. On this very jazz-oriented set from 1961, Ella takes her longest-ever recorded scat vocal on a nine-and-a-half minute version of "Take The 'A' Train," one of the high points in her very productive career.

Fleurine
(Fleurine Varloop)
b. April 3, 1969, The Netherlands.

A major jazz singer originally from Holland, a country with more than its share of top-notch vocalists, Fleurine is unusual in that she purposely does not record standards. "I've never felt that I could possibly add to the many outstanding versions of vocal standards that all of my heroes recorded. Thus, I have always tried to create a different repertoire, either by writing lyrics to jazz instrumentals, by re-arranging more contemporary songs, or by writing my own material."

Her father had a huge jazz record collection. "From age four to about seven my favorite repertoire was either from *Ella And Louis* or the Beatles' red double-album.

Later I got into Al Jarreau, Earth Wind and Fire, and Frank Sinatra, who pretty much stuck with me all through my teens. I always fell asleep singing. With Frank, the keys were always wrong for me, so I ended up singing the different horn parts of Nelson Riddle or Count Basie instead." Although she played guitar, piano, electric bass, alto sax and percussion at various times, Fleurine's main interest was singing. She attended the Amsterdam School of High Arts Music Conservatory during 1990–94 and moved to New York in 1998. Since then she has performed extensively in Europe and parts of the United States.

Among some of the highlights of Fleurine's career that she mentioned were playing with the Metropole Orchestra and Rita Reys in 1995, touring with Roy Hargrove and his quintet in Cuba in 1996, and recording and touring the world in a duo with Brad Mehldau. "For the future I want to grow grow grow, develop my voice further, play with many more inspiring people and further develop my skills as a songwriter."

Recommended CDs: 1995's *Meant To Be* (Emarcy 159 085), in addition to some beautiful singing, has Fleurine's lyrics to songs by Kenny Dorham, Thelonious Monk, Thad Jones, Joshua Redman and Tom Harrell while joined by top American players with arrangements by Don Sickler. *Close Enough For Love* (Emarcy 157 748) is a ballad-oriented duo set with Brad Mehldau that includes songs by Pat Metheny, Michel Legrand, Jimi Hendrix, Antonio Carlos Jobim and Supertramp. *Fire* (Coast To Coast 2990447) has Fleurine exploring pop-oriented material that she turns into jazz, featuring solos from Mehldau, tenor-saxophonist Seamus Blake, guitarist Peter Bernstein and Gil Goldstein on accordion.

Website: www.fleurine.com

Pat Flowers
(Ivelee Flowers)
b. October 16, 1917, Detroit, MI; d. October 6, 2000, Detroit, MI

It was always Pat Flowers' goal to follow in Fats Waller's footsteps. A skilled stride pianist who also sang quite well (particularly on his last recordings), Flowers never became famous and spent decades playing in obscurity in his native Detroit.

Flowers was classically trained at music conservatories as a youth. In 1936 or 1937 he met Waller, who encouraged and inspired him. Flowers first came to New York in 1939 where he landed a job playing piano in the lobby of the Yacht Club during a period when Fats played in the main room. He soon returned to Detroit before making a second attempt at the Big Apple, playing on 52nd Street and recording two solo numbers in 1941.

When Waller died prematurely in 1943, his manager Ed Kirkeby decided to work with Flowers, seeing him as a possible successor and remembering that Fats once said of him, "This young man will carry on where I leave off." Flowers was cast in the role of Waller on an all-star memorial radio show that was recorded (February 11, 1945) and is available on the *1941–1945 Classics* CD. During 1946–47 he recorded 20 selections for Victor (Waller's old label), including a dozen titles that feature him leading a group that includes some of Fats' former sidemen including trumpeter Herman Autrey and tenor-saxophonist Gene Sedric. While Flowers' jivey vocals lack Waller's charm and comic genius, his piano playing is excellent and on a few of the selections he shows potential as a vocalist.

1948 brought a musicians union recording strike and Flowers' record contract was not renewed in 1949. By then, he had returned to Detroit, where he played regularly at Baker's Keyboard Lounge through 1954. Flowers remained an entertaining singing pianist for decades but played low-level jobs, often functioning as background music for partiers. Other than two singles for Dot in 1956, he did not record again until cutting five songs for Black and Blue in 1972 and nine more for the same French label in 1975, the latter in the company of guitarist Jimmy Shirley, bassist Slam Stewart and drummer Jackie Williams. Flowers sings on half of the later selections, displaying the charm missing on the earlier dates and sounding quite musical. That year Pat Flowers toured Europe for the only time as part of a Waller tribute show. But his life ended quietly for he spent his final 15 years back in the Detroit area where he was completely forgotten by the jazz world.

Recommended CDs: *1941–1945* (Classics 1060) has its moments including the Waller radio tribute, but *1945–1947* (Classics 1093) features Pat Flowers at his best, showing potential that was never quite realized.

LPs to Search For: *I Ain't Got Nobody* (Black and Blue 33.157) features Pat Flowers in the 1970s.

Helen Forrest
(Helen Fogel)
b. April 12, 1917, Atlantic City, NJ;
d. July 11, 1999, Los Angeles, CA

If one took a poll in 1942, asking which of the big band singers was destined to have the most rewarding solo career, the winner would not have been Peggy Lee, Doris Day or Anita O'Day. Helen Forrest, a very well respected vocalist who was in the process of gaining her greatest fame with Harry James, seemed to have the most promising future. And yet after 1945, her career became aimless and she spent decades trying to duplicate the magic of her earlier hits.

Forrest started her career as a teenager singing on radio station WNEW out of New York. She graduated to CBS Radio where she was billed as Bonnie Blue. Artie Shaw heard her in the fall of 1938, saw her potential, and hired her for his big band, which was rapidly rising to the top of the swing world. Among the 40 songs that she recorded during her year with Shaw are "They Say," "Deep Purple," "Moonray" and "All The Things You Are." Although quite young during this period, Helen Forrest's voice was already quite recognizable. Not really an improviser, she was a masterful interpreter of lyrics, always sang in-tune, swung lightly and was a joyful presence on the bandstand.

When Artie Shaw buckled under the pressure of having the #1 swing band and fled to Mexico in late 1939, resulting in the breakup of his orchestra, Forrest called Benny Goodman and said that she was available. She soon regretted her decision for her relations with Goodman were stormy, although the association did help her career. Among her 55 recordings with Goodman are "The Man I Love," "Taking A Chance On Love," "More Than You Know," "The Fable Of The Rose" and "Shake Down The Stars." But Forrest did not care for the very adventurous (and sometimes abrasive) Eddie Sauter arrangements that frequently were heard behind her singing (much preferring Fletcher Henderson's charts), she felt that Goodman treated her as a necessary evil, and she was almost always confined to one vocal chorus per record, as were most band singers.

A much happier association, at first, was when she quit Goodman in late 1941 to join Harry James. James featured her extensively, casting her in a starring role on many of her records, usually giving two choruses, opening and closing the records. Forrest had three major hits while with the trumpeter's band ("I Had The Craziest Dream," "I Don't Want To Walk Without You" and "I've Heard That Song Before"), each of which topped the charts during the World War II years. She also sounds wonderful on "But Not For Me," "I Remember You" and "I Cried For You." Due to the recording strike of 1942–44, Forrest only recorded 19 songs with James, but these made a strong impact and are considered the high points of her career. Forrest also appeared in several films with James, including *Private Buckeroo* in which she sang "You Made Me Love You," which James originally had a big hit with as an instrumental.

However, Forrest's love affair with James, which undoubtedly added to the passion in her recordings of the era, came to an abrupt end when he became involved with his future wife Betty Grable. Forrest left the trumpeter's band in 1943. She teamed up with Dick Haymes (another James alumnus) on the radio and they recorded a series of popular duets including "Long Ago And Far Away," "It Had To Be You," "Together," "I'll Buy That Dream," "Some Sunday Morning," "I'm Always Chasing Rainbows" and "Oh! What It Seemed To Be." However, those performances are very much outside of jazz and, after 1946, Forrest was on her way to becoming a nostalgia figure, despite still only being 29 years old.

Bad career choices and being overshadowed by the next generation of singers partly explains Forrest slipping away into obscurity in the 1950s although it is still puzzling. As her "World Transcriptions" of 1949–50 and her later recordings show, she could certainly sing. But Forrest only gained attention when she was occasionally brought back for swing recreations. She sang with the Tommy Dorsey ghost band in the early 1960s when it was led by Sam Donahue, had a recorded reunion with Harry James in the late 1960s, and in the mid-1970s toured with James, Haymes, the Pied Pipers and the Ink Spots in a touring revue called *The Big Broadcast*

Of 1944. Helen Forrest wrote an autobiography, *I Had The Craziest Dream*, which has the same name as her final album from 1983. She passed away in 1999 at the age of 82; her last 55 years were largely anti-climatic.

Recommended CDs: The three-CD set *The Complete Helen Forrest With The Benny Goodman Orchestra* (Collectors Choice Music 245) and the single disc *The Complete Helen Forrest With The Harry James Orchestra* (Collectors Choice Music 81), along with various Artie Shaw samplers, have the most significant recordings of her career. The two-CD *Complete World Transcriptions* (Soundies 4114) shows how much more Helen Forrest still had to give after the swing era ended.

Calabria Foti
b. January 23, Fredonia, NY

A studio singer and violinist based in Los Angeles, Calabria Foti emerged in 2007 to record *A Lovely Way To Spend An Evening*, a set of high-quality romantic jazz.

Born into a family of musicians (her father plays trombone and her mother is a pianist), she grew up attending both classical concerts and jazz clubs. Foti started on guitar and bass, but also studied the violin. At the age of 12 she began singing and playing bass in nightclubs and hotels.

"I attended music camps from about age 13 on. I was studying jazz and violin intensely. I went briefly to college to pursue a performance degree as a violinist. It was during my second year that I auditioned for an orchestra and got the job of Associate Concertmaster. Soon after, I quit and have been working as a musician ever since."

She moved to Los Angeles in her early twenties. Since then, Calabria Foti has become an important studio singer and violinist, developed into a songwriter, vocal arranger and educator, married trombonist Bob McChesney, and has produced two CDs of her own, to date.

"I consider myself a throwback to the 1930s and '40s. I love the popular music of that time and the artists that performed those songs, so my recordings reflect that. In addition to bringing my own songs out on CDs, I want to keep recording the old tunes. I want to keep the glamour and sensibilities of that era alive, and keep those beautiful songs around for a long, long time."

Recommended CDs: So far Calabria Foti has led two CDs: *When A Woman Loves A Man* (Faccia Bella) and *A Lovely Way To Spend An Evening* (MoCo). Both contain lush ballads and Broadway show tunes. The subtle arrangements (some of which are by Ms. Foti) perfectly show off her flexible voice.

Website: www.calabriafoti.com; www.foticd.com

Ya Ya Fournier
b. November 26, 1951, Chicago, IL

Ya Ya Fournier took a long time to become a jazz singer and finally record, but she did create a very good CD, *Bearcat*.

"Aside from school and church choirs, I remember best

the times I spent with my grandmother, who was a retired opera singer. We would sing along to opera on the radio while following the score in her old music books." She had some piano lessons as a child but soon lost interest. In 1979 she married drummer Vernel Fournier, famous for having been in the Ahmad Jamal Trio. "It was around 1983 when music started demanding my attention. I was entirely too self-conscious up until then to ever consider performing. But step-by-step, I learned how to get out of my own way and let the music out."

After her husband's death in 2000, Ya Ya Fournier began working toward recording a CD, resulting in 2003's *Bearcat*, which also features tenor-saxophonist David Murray. While visiting Haiti in 2003 to add some traditional Haitian rhythms to the *Bearcat* CD, Fournier was surprised to find that she felt very much at home, and she moved to Haiti the following year. Although she still performs locally, no further CDs have been released yet.

Recommended CDs: *Bearcat* (Random Chance 3) is a mixture of originals and songs by the likes of Duke Ellington, Clifford Jordan, Jimmy Heath and David Murray. Ya Ya Fournier sounds creative and enthusiastic, making one wish for a follow-up.

Carol Fredette
(Carol Frances White)
b. Bronx, New York

Carol Fredette's superior exploration of the songs of Dave Frishberg and Bob Dorough on *Everything I Need* made it obvious that she is an important jazz singer. It is surprising that she has not recorded more often in her career for that CD is a classic of its kind.

Everyone in Carol Fredette's family loved music. Her uncle Marty Bell was a trumpeter and singer in the cool jazz style of Chet Baker, recording an album in the 1950s with Don Elliott. "As a child my father would call me in to sing for company. He'd accompany me by ear on an old upright piano. I sang at special events and school functions, performing 'For All We Know' at my high school prom. By that time, I knew I was going to be a singer."

She attended Florida State University for a year but, after hearing the Stan Kenton Orchestra play at her college, she was determined to return to New York as a jazz vocalist. Fredette dropped out of college and never had a need to return. She spent that summer singing with her uncle on weekends, an invaluable experience during which she learned dozens of standards. She gigged around New York, sang with Sal Salvador's 17-piece band, performed with the orchestras of Larry Elgart and Neal Hefti, and spent a lot of time on the road during the next two decades. In 1978, after performing regularly on three continents, she re-established herself in New York. Among her most important musical associations were pianists Mike Abene, Mike Renzi, Hank Jones and Steve Kuhn (who she had been playing with off and on since 1963), Bucky Pizzarelli's trio, Al Cohn (1986–87) and Dave Frishberg.

Although never gaining the fame that she deserves, due to spending so much time outside of New York, Carol Fredette has had a colorful career, been an important educator

and recorded three excellent albums. "Singing this music is ultimately about swinging and telling the story, phrasing in a way that makes sense lyrically, thereby bringing the words of the song to life, from your experience, from your soul, and from your truth."

Recommended CDs: *In The Shadows* (Owl 075 830 484) is a duet CD with Steve Kuhn from 1993 and has its great moments. But the Carol Fredette set to get is 1995's *Everything I Need* (Brownstone 9903), which features her witty and fresh renditions of Frishberg and Dorough songs with a band also including Lee Konitz, Lew Soloff, Chris Potter and Ronnie Cuber.

LPs to Search For: *Love Dance* (Devil Moon 001) teams Carol Fredette in 1983 with Steve Kuhn and guitarist John Basile in a quintet.

Nnenna Freelon
(Chinyere Nnenna Freelon)
b, July 28, 1956, Boston, MA

A very attractive singer who sometimes breaks away from the safety of performing standards in order to come up with fresh ideas, Nnenna Freelon started her career later than most but quickly rose to near the top of her field.

"I began singing in church at a very young age around seven. I took piano lessons briefly and used to accompany myself on my grandmother's piano playing by ear. I would listen to recordings in the living room and run to the parlor with the notes in my head to try and figure it out on the piano."

Instead of pursuing a career in music, Freelon graduated from Simmons College in 1979 with a BA degree in Health Care Administration, had three children and worked in health services in Durham, North Carolina. It was not until the birth of her third child in 1982 that she seriously toyed with the idea of becoming a professional singer. She sang throughout North Carolina during 1987–92 and conducted many workshops. Ellis Marsalis noticed her at a 1990 jam session and, with his recommendation, she was signed to Columbia in 1992 and made her first record. While her debut found her a bit too influenced by Sarah Vaughan, her next couple of albums emphasized her individuality and she has had a busy career ever since, switching to the Concord label in 1996, touring regularly, and being active as a music educator.

Recommended CDs: After paying a bit too much homage to Sarah Vaughan on *Nnenna Freelon* (Columbia 49891), her second album, *Heritage* (Columbia 53566), shows just how strong and individual a singer Nnenna Freelon can be, particularly on such songs as "'Tis Autumn," "Heritage" and "Comes Love." *Listen* (Columbia 64323) ended her period on Columbia on a high level as she stretched herself on a variety of ballads. *Shaking Free* (Concord 4714) includes a 5/4 version of "Out of This World," "Black Is The Color Of My True Love's Hair" and "Birk's Works." *Maiden Voyage* (Concord 4794) puts the focus on songs by female composers; *Soulcall* (Concord 4896) has a remarkable amount of variety; *Tales Of Wonder* (Concord 2107) is a set of Stevie Wonder songs; and *Live* (Concord 2184) is an intriguing mixture of offbeat numbers, including "If I Only Had a Brain," "Button Up Your Overcoat" and her own "Circle Song." While one appreciates Nnenna Freelon's willingness to take chances on Billie Holiday–associated tunes during *Blueprint Of A Lady* (Concord 2289), the occasional substitution of dull funky vamps for some of the chord changes is a misfire, with the contemporary touches often taking away from the essence and joy of some of the songs such as "All Of Me." But, as usual, Nnenna Freelon herself sounds highly appealing.

Website: www.nnenna.com

Dave Frishberg
b. March 23, 1933, St. Paul, MN

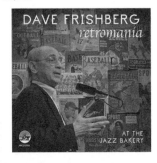

In some ways, Dave Frishberg is like a modern-day Hoagy Carmichael. He is a pianist-singer who writes and performs most of his own material, some of which has caught on among jazz musicians and singers. More of a lyricist than Carmichael, who mostly wrote music, Frishberg is a skilled jazz pianist, a personable and witty vocalist, and an important contributor to the repertoire of many of today's singers.

"I first heard jazz through the 78 rpm records collected by my older brothers. They included Benny Goodman, Artie Shaw, Cab Calloway, Mildred Bailey, Art Tatum, Count Basie with Jimmy Rushing, Lee Wiley and the Eddie Condon gang. I used to sing along with Bing Crosby records alone in the living room. At age eight, I took piano lessons and discovered that piano came easily to me. I learned the pieces very quickly and immediately began playing around with the music. I brought my Mozart assignment back to my teacher, played it accurately, then showed her how I had changed it to a conga rhythm. She explained to me that this was not to be done. I quit piano lessons shortly thereafter at the age of nine."

When he was 13, Frishberg learned to play boogie-woogie by listening to records of Pete Johnson and Albert Ammons. At 15 he took some informal lessons from a bop pianist (Jimmy Mulcrone). "After listening to Jimmy Rowles play on the Woody Herman Woodchoppers sides on Columbia, I knew that I wanted to learn professional skills as a pianist. My main goal was to play well enough to play with the best players. I never once thought that I would someday be a 'professional singer' and I still don't consider myself in that category."

Frishberg graduated from the University of Minnesota in 1955 with a major in journalism. He served in the Air Force (1955–57) during which time he began to write songs and lyrics for radio jingles. After his discharge, he briefly had a day job and then in 1958 took the plunge and began working full-time as a pianist. Frishberg was Carmen McRae's accompanist during 1959–60, was a member of Ben Webster's quartet (1962–63) and freelanced in New York throughout the 1960s, playing with Kai Winding, Gene Krupa, Wild Bill Davison, Bud Freeman, the Al Cohn–Zoot Sims Quintet, Bobby Hackett and Jimmy Rushing, among others. In 1968 he sang for the first time on records, recording a mostly commercial album for CTI (*Oklahoma Toad*) that had a surprise hit in "Van Lingle

Mungo," a song whose lyrics are comprised entirely of the names of old baseball players.

In 1971, Frishberg moved to Los Angeles to join the staff of the NBC weekly comedy show *The Funny Side*, writing some of its music. After the show flopped, he worked in the studios and played jazz in local clubs, eventually settling in Portland. In 1977 he recorded as a pianist-singer for Concord and opened a show at the Concord Pavilion for Bing Crosby, singing in public for the first time. He had already written "Peel Me A Grape" and co-written "I'm Hip" with Bob Dorough. Since his career shift, Frishberg has composed such witty and wistful songs as "Dear Bix," "The Underdog," "Saratoga Hunch," "Slappin' The Cakes On Me," "Gotta Get Me Some Z's," "My Attorney Bernie," "Blizzard Of Lies," "Another Song About Paris," "You Are There," "El Cajon," "Can't Take You Nowhere," "Let's Eat Home," "Quality Time," "You Would Rather Have The Blues," "The Hopi Way," "I Want To Be A Sideman" and "The Dear Departed Past." Many of his songs are nostalgic for the past and slightly gloomy but leavened with insightful humor. And while other singers have adopted some of his songs, his interpretations are usually the definitive versions.

Dave Frishberg has recorded for a variety of labels and worked as often as he likes ever since he began performing as a singer/songwriter, though he never neglects his piano playing. In addition to his solo work, he has recorded with Bill Berry, Jack Sheldon, Richie Kamuca, trumpeter Jim Goodwin, Susannah McCorkle, Ken Peplowski and Rebecca Kilgore.

"The jazz of the 1930s and 1940s came naturally to me, and as a young pianist I was charmed. But I don't think I'd be interested in contemporary jazz if I were growing up today, and that goes for pop music in general. If I were a young kid today, musically sensitive, I'd steer clear of the music industry. I'd learn to be a classical ensemble player (cello or viola), or maybe a librarian or English professor."

Recommended CDs: Among the many excellent Dave Frishberg CDs are 1977's *Getting Some Fun Out Of Life* (Concord Jazz 4037), *Classics* (Concord Jazz 4462), *Live At Vine Street* (Original Jazz Classics 832), *Can't Take You Nowhere* (Fantasy 9651), *Let's Eat Home* (Concord Jazz 4402), *Where You At* (Bloomdido 010), the instrumental *Double Play* (Arbors 19118) with Jim Goodwin, *Quality Time* (Sterling 1006), *By Himself* (Arbors 19185), *Do You Miss New York* (Arbors 19291) and *Retromania* (Arbors 19334).

LPs to Search For: *Trio* (Seeds 4) and *You're A Lucky Guy* (Concord Jazz 74) deserve to be reissued.

Laura Fygi
b. August 27, 1955, Amsterdam, The Netherlands

Laura Fygi followed a rather unusual and circular path to becoming a jazz singer. The daughter of a Dutch father and an Egyptian mother, she spent the early part of her life in South America. In Holland, Fygi sang whenever she had an opportunity. In 1980 she became a member of the group Terra. During 1983–91 she was a member of Centerfold, a very popular Dutch disco/rock all-female group in which the performers dressed like centerfolds. The glamorous band was very popular in Europe and Japan.

In 1991 when Centerfold broke up, the 35-year old Fygi started a band called the Backlot and, after just one concert, she was signed by Mercury to record a solo album. In what must have been a major surprise to Centerfold fans, Fygi sang jazz on *Introducing Laura Fygi*. The album sold over 120,000 copies in the Netherlands and Japan.

Ever since then, Laura Fygi has developed into a first-class jazz singer. She may have started late, but her jazz abilities proved to be quite natural.

Recommended CDs: *Introducing* (Mercury 510 700) was Laura Fygi's 1991 debut as a jazz singer. Clark Terry and Johnny Griffin guest on 1992's *Bewitched* (Verve Forecast 314 514 724) and *The Lady Wants To Know* (Verve Forecast 314 522 438) is a set of bossa novas. *Watch What Happens* (Verve Forecast 314 534 598) features Michel Legrand songs with the composer contributing the arrangements. Other worthy Laura Fygi CDs include *Turn Out The Lamplight* (Verve Forecast 528 787), *Live Your Dreams* (Polygram 112 568), *Live* (Polygram 120490), *The Latin Touch* (Polygram 424 752), *Change* (Universal 586 5072), *Live at Ronnie Scott's* (Verve 38017) and *The Very Best Time Of Year* (Universal 986859).

Website: www.laurafygi.nl

Slim Gaillard
(Bulee Gaillard)
b. January 1, 1916, Santa Clara, Cuba;
d. February 26, 1991, London, England

"Jive" is a form of singing that is a step beyond scatting, improvising words to create a party atmosphere. In the case of Slim Gaillard, he improvised an entire nonsensical language, one that was frequently both humorous and nutty.

A true eccentric, Gaillard started his show biz career in the 1930s in vaudeville, having an act in which he played guitar and tap danced at the same time, which must have been quite a trick. Gaillard could play guitar well, was a basic pianist and on rare occasions performed on vibes and various horns. However, it was his jive singing that made him famous. He formed a quartet with bassist Slam Stewart that was known as Slim and Slam. Their first recording, "Flat Foot Floogie (With The Floy Floy)," was a huge novelty hit. Influenced by Louis Armstrong, Cab Calloway and Fats Waller, Gaillard's comments between songs at the group's nightclub appearances were as notable as the music itself.

Slim and Slam recorded such tunes as "Chicken Rhythm," "Buck Dance Rhythm," "Laughin' In Rhythm" (which lived up to its billing), "Tutti Frutti," "Matzoh Balls," "Boot-Ta-La-Za," "Sploghm" and "African Jive." Their group stayed popular until it broke up in 1943 when Gaillard was drafted. By 1945, Gaillard had been discharged and was working in the Los Angeles area with bassist Bam Brown, whose singing was as demented as Slim's, being somewhat hysterical while Gaillard's was cool and laid-back. Slim performed often at Billy Berg's, liberally using such words as "o-voutie," "o-rooney" and "vout" in his singing and monologues. Most of the songs that Gaillard performed with a great flourish were based on "Flying Home" or the blues.

At the height of his fame in 1945, Gaillard used Charlie Parker and Dizzy Gillespie as sidemen on one date, and other associates included pianist Dodo Marmarosa and drummer-singers Leo Watson and Scatman Crothers. Gaillard's tunes from the era include "Cement Mixer (Puttee Puttee)," "Dunkin' Bagel," "Laguna," "Ya Ha Ha," "Ding Dong

Oreenee," "Penicillin Boogie," "Minuet In Vout," "Popity Pop," "Chicken Rhythm" (on which he imitated the clucking of a chicken), "Matzoh Balls," "Oxydol Highball," "When Banana Skins Are Falling," "Avocado Seed Soup Symphony" and the four-part "Opera In Vout."

By 1948, the novelty was wearing off. Gaillard's music was being called immoral by right-wingers who did not understand that his lyrics purposely made no sense while sounding hilarious. "Yip Roc Heresy" was banned from one radio station and called degenerate although it primarily featured Slim singing the contents of an Armenian menu. During the early 1950s, Gaillard was based in New York where he often played at Birdland and recorded some dates for Norman Granz's Clef and Norgran labels including "Babalu," "Yo Yo Yo," "Potato Chips," "Mishugana Mambo," "Serenade To A Poodle" and the remarkable "Genius." The latter (modestly titled) has Gaillard overdubbed on vocals, trumpet, trombone, tenor, vibes, piano, organ, bass, drums and tap dancing, concluding with two remarkably funny choruses.

After 1953, Gaillard was off records (other than a 1958 album) for many years. Although he appeared in the films *Go, Man, Go* (1954) and *Too Late Blues* (1961), he was in obscurity for decades, running a motel in San Diego for a few years and just working part-time in music. In the 1980s, Slim Gaillard was rediscovered, had a few gigs, and showed on "How High The Moon" from his 1982 album *Anytime, Anyplace, Anywhere* that he was still the master of jive singing.

Recommended CDs: The three-CD set *Complete Recordings 1938–1942* (Affinity 1034-3) has all of the Slim and Slam recordings. *1945* (Classics 864), *The Absolute Voutest* (Hep 28), *In Birdland 1951* (Hep 21) and *Laughing In Rhythm* (Verve 314 521 651) cover the 1945–53 period, both in the studio and in some of his more rambunctious live radio broadcasts. *Anytime, Anyplace, Anywhere* (Hep 2020) features Slim Gaillard still sounding funny late in life.

Roberta Gambarini
b. November 30, 1969, Torino, Italy

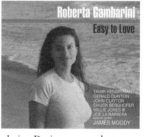

When Roberta Gambarini's CD *Easy To Love* came out in 2006, it was many years overdue. She had already impressed those lucky enough to see her in concert during the past few years with her warm voice, wide range, scatting abilities and sensitive approach to interpreting lyrics. During an era when many jazz singers and instrumentalists seem to record too often, she was almost completely absent on records, a situation that has fortunately ended.

"My parents and most of my family members are long time jazz fans. My parents met at a jazz concert. My dad played tenor saxophone as a young man in gigs and, even after he stopped playing in public, he used to practice and play for fun in our apartment. The first music I ever heard in my life was jazz and my earliest recollections are of hearing Duke, Armstrong, Basie, Billie and Ella—when I hadn't learned to speak, yet. My parents named me after the musical revue *Roberta*, which contains some of their favorite songs, such as 'Yesterdays' and 'Smoke Gets In Your Eyes.' They brought me along to hear concerts when I was still a child and I had the chance to see Basie, Eddie Lockjaw Davis, Sweets Edison, Sarah and many more at a young age. I always loved singing, since the age of two, and that remains to this day the biggest fun I can think of."

Because her parents noticed that she had a knack for picking up words from foreign languages, Roberta Gambarini studied English for nine years as a child. She also took clarinet lessons as a teenager. Gambarini sang in church and at weddings from an early age, and at 17 started performing in jazz clubs in northern Italy, moving to Milan the following year to work as a jazz singer. She taught herself to play jazz piano and spent a few years studying classical piano and composition. After coming in third place in a national jazz radio competition on television, she was hired to perform at jazz festivals throughout Italy, making her recording debut as a leader in 1991.

However, it was not until 1998 that Roberta Gambarini began to be noticed outside of Italy. After gaining a scholarship from the New England Conservatory, she moved to the United States. Two weeks later she came in third place in the Thelonious Monk International Jazz Vocal Competition and, after a few months, she dropped out of school because she was working so often in New York. Soon she was gaining a strong reputation despite being absent on records. "I had the fortune to be able to sing with many of my idols. The most important of these experiences has been meeting the great Benny Carter in 2000. He honored me with his friendship and was my mentor for the last years of his existence." She also mentioned having the honor of performing with Billy Higgins, Harold Land, Ron Carter, Johnny Griffin, Herbie Hancock, Michael Brecker, Roy Hargrove, Chucho Valdes, Cedar Walton, Jimmy Heath, Toots Thielemans, Clark Terry, Hank Jones and James Moody.

In recent times Roberta Gambarini, in addition to her *Easy To Love* CD, recorded and performed with the Dizzy Gillespie All Stars and the Pratt Brothers Big Band. "My life history is in my music and vice versa; I couldn't tell one from the other. There were and are a lot of struggles and hardships in my life as in any human being's. But ultimately, it's all about communication on a human level. I am trying to tell a story."

Recommended CDs: One of the most elusive CDs is Roberta Gambarini's little-known 1991 set with guitarist Antonio Scarana, *Apreslude* (Splasch 356). *Easy To Love* (Groovin' High 1122) is her long-overdue American debut and a classic set, one of the top vocal releases of 2006. She also steals the show on the Pratt Brothers Big Band's *16 Men And A Chick Singer* (CAP 985) from 2005. Her most recent recording to date, *You Are There* (Emarcy 10622), teams Robert Gambarini on a ballad-oriented program of duets with veteran pianist Hank Jones.

Website: www.robertagambarini.com

Paulinho Garcia
(Paulo Garcia)
b. August 16, 1948, Belo Horizonte, Brazil

A warm jazz singer from Brazil, Paulinho Garcia always has the spirit and chance taking of jazz in his performances, even when he performs folk music.

"Though Nat King Cole is my all-time favorite singer, it was Chet Baker who brought me to jazz. I started singing when I was nine years old in a Sunday program for kids at my city's main radio station at the time: *Radio Inconfidencia.*" His first instrument was the drums on which as a youth he performed Brazilian music and rock. Garcia was a self-taught bassist for

years, playing in bands from the time he was 14. He began playing guitar for the fun of it when he was 16, but did not perform on it in public until he moved to the United States. Garcia earned a degree in physics, but soon chose music as his career. He led his band Os Agitadores, recording two albums, and doing a lot of studio work in his native Brazil.

In 1979 Paulinho Garcia moved to Chicago, recording two albums with his group Made In Brazil and touring Japan for six months. In the 1990s he led Jazzmineiro, and he has toured all over the world in recent years. He started teaming up with tenor-saxophonist Greg Fishman in a duo called Two for Brazil starting in 2001, bringing to mind what a group might have sounded like if it consisted solely of João Gilberto and Stan Getz. Garcia and Fishman have a wider repertoire than the early 1960s bossa novas of Antonio Carlos Jobim and deserve to be much more widely recorded. During 2001–2002 they temporarily added Polish singer Grazyna Auguscik to the group, renaming the unit Three for Brazil.

"I sing music from South America to North America, from Europe and Asia. If it is music I probably have done it. I have sung British rock and Cuban boleros, tangos and sambas, in four languages. But in all those styles what stays constant is my own character and my Brazilian roots. I tried many different things in life but never gave up my music, even when I was told that I was going to starve to death. It hasn't happened yet and I think that it never will. I raised my son and daughter and live comfortably, and it was all done by being an honest musician."

Recommended CDs: The most readily available of Paulinho Garcia's recordings are *Jazzmineiro* (Southport 26), *Solo* (Southport 49) and Two For Brazil's superb *Take Five* (Jazzmin 3375).

Website: www.paulinhogarcia.com

Abbie Gardner
(Abigail Washburn Gardner)
b. March 3, 1975, Nyack, NY

The release of *My Craziest Dream* in 2004 was the debut for Abbie Gardner, a fine young singer who sounded quite at home performing vintage swing standards. Although she has since become more involved in folk and Americana music, she always brings a jazz sensitivity to the music.

The daughter of pianist Herb Gardner who played with Roy Eldridge, Gene Krupa and Bobby Hackett, she grew up around jazz. "As a kid I tagged along to all sorts of gigs. Everyone seemed to have so much fun and they'd laugh at the end of each song. My dad would smile and chuckle when he said he had to go to 'work' because he couldn't believe he was getting paid for having so much fun." Abbie Gardner played violin for a year, studied classical flute for 13 years, and in more recent times has taken up the guitar and the dobro. She began to sing in front of people as a senior in high school and in college was a member of the Inner Strength Boston University Gospel Choir, working with a cappella groups and becoming the musical director for the Treblemakers. She earned a degree in Occupational Therapy at Boston University but always wanted to be a singer. "I don't feel like I can be happy doing anything else, to be honest."

Gardner began singing jazz in 2000 with the Galvanized Jazz Band and has since worked with Stan Rubin's Tigertown Five, the Stan Rubin Orchestra, Vince Giordano's Nighthawks, the New Deal Orchestra and Herb Gardner's Groundhog Band. She recorded *My Craziest Dream* with her father's group, displaying her love for Billie Holiday's music while still sounding like herself. "The melodies of those old standards are something you don't see in other types of music. And the best part about it is that I get to share it with my father."

Since 2004, Abbie Gardner has also performed as part of the female trio Red Molly, performing Appalachian ballads, contemporary folk and country standards.

Recommended CD: *My Craziest Dream* (GSRM 1), which features both Gardners and clarinetist Dan Levinson, was an impressive start to Abbie Gardner's career.

Website: www.abbiegardner.com

Giacomo Gates
(Giacomo Agostini)
b. September 14, 1950, Bridgeport, CT

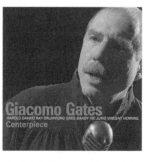

A successor to Eddie Jefferson in his hipness, ability to write clever vocalese lyrics and his bop-oriented style, Giacomo Gates is gradually getting noticed.

Gates took guitar lessons when he was eight, discovering jazz within a short time. "I started with Brubeck and Monk, then Dexter Gordon, Miles, and on and on. I discovered all the lyrics to songs beneath the notes in the old Fake Book. That got me interested in words and stories." He also took some piano lessons and studied arranging with Bill Finegan. However, Gates' life took a detour and during 1975–88 he worked as a heavy equipment operator in Alaska, building roads. A turning point occurred in 1987. "I attended a workshop at the *Fairbanks Summer Arts Festival* given by Chris Calloway. I received some very positive feedback from some of the instrumental and vocal instructors, as well as from Grover Sales, who was writing an article about the festival. I knew it was time for a change and, after a few months, I decided that I would return to the East Coast and try to make some noise." Gates recorded a self-produced cassette in 1989 (Bebop and Blues), began performing in New York

and he worked on mastering his craft. 1994's CD *Blue Skies* showed that he was worthy of further attention. He also began writing lyrics, including "Five Cooper Square," which is set to the music of Thelonious Monk's "Five Spot Blues."

Gates has had the chance to sit in with Jon Hendricks on a few occasions, he toured with Kurt Elling, Mark Murphy and Andy Bey in *Four Brothers*, and he has been working as a soloist. He has also taught classes and private students at Wesleyan University, the Hartford Conservatory of Music and the Neighborhood Music School in New Haven, keeping the bebop and vocalese message alive.

For the future, Giacomo Gates says that his goals are "to keep swinging, to tour at a comfortable pace, to teach, to continue recording, to record some of my own lyrics to classic jazz tunes, and to have fun with this great music. I have always been a fan and a student of this music, so to perform it is terrific."

Recommended CDs: *Blue Skies* (DMP 3001) and *Fly Rite* (Sharp Nine 71011) are both excellent sets, but *Centerpiece* (Origin 72428) is Giacomo Gates' finest hour on records thus far. He is also showcased on organist Eddie Landsberg's *Remembering Eddie Jefferson* (Berghem 802275).

Website: www.giacomogates.com

Rachael Gavoni
b. October 18, Los Angeles, CA

A talented singer, saxophonist, flutist, pianist, guitarist and educator, Rachael Gavoni recently recorded her long overdue debut CD as a leader. "Each instrument that I play attracted me passionately with its power, depth and beauty into a life long love affair. I need to play them all as they each have something important to say and are an extension of my music, my voice."

Her grandfather was a jazz guitarist, her grandmother was a professional singer, and her mother was a classically trained pianist with perfect pitch. She started playing piano at three, performed in the school orchestra at seven and played in all of the school music performing groups through college. She had a guitar-vocal duo in junior high school, constantly composed new music, and was a professional musician at 14, appearing on local radio. "I woke up to jazz when I was 15, and then I couldn't get enough. It dawned on me then that jazz is infinite. There is never a dull moment, as you can explore new ideas your entire lifetime and still have an endless amount of exciting music left to play and get into. I knew then that I had to be a jazz musician." At 18, she was busy in the studios, singing commercials for radio and television in addition to performing in jazz groups at night while studying guitar and voice in college.

Rachael Gavoni became a studio musician in Northern California, involved in writing and arranging for commercials, and a well respected educator. Due to her beautiful voice and four-octave range, she was noticed by record producers and sang on albums by such R&B stars as the Temptations, Michael Cooper of Confunktion, La Toya Jackson and Club Nouveau, earning a platinum album. She was offered a contract to RCA, but turned it down, and instead she decided to work on her own music and perform jazz.

During the past few years, Rachael Gavoni has worked with local musicians at jazz festivals, concert halls and live on the radio. Her debut CD, *Valentine Kisses*, is mostly comprised of colorful original songs that display her versatility and musical talents.

"My greatest love will always be singing, writing music, performing live and getting into the creative confluence while playing with other great jazz players. But in my spare time I have started writing a book called *The River Of Ideas*, inspired by the place I go to when I improvise or compose music, or do anything creative. I've learned so much while teaching my students how to open up and be inspired to write their own music. I wanted to share these ideas and help other people find their own creative space."

Recommended CD: Rachael Gavoni's debut album *Valentine Kisses* (River of Ideas, 1004) includes a few songs that are used in the plot of her upcoming novel plus some modern jazz originals and standards. Highlights include the swing of "Valentine Kisses," is a Basie-inspired swing tune, the Wes Montgomery–inspired "I Won't Do It," the Brazilian samba "Rio Bonito" and an uptempo "It Don't Mean A Thing." Her skills as a vocalist and as a saxophonist, flutist, pianist and guitarist are well displayed during this impressive effort.

Website: www.theriverofideas.com/rachael_gavoni

Carmen Getit
(Patricia Marie Smith)
b. November 13, 1963, St. Clair Shores, MI

One of the top singers to emerge from the Retro Swing movement (along with Lavay Smith), Carmen Getit is best known for her association with Steve Lucky's Rhumba Bums.

She was introduced to jazz early on by her father. "He particularly loved the early hot jazz sound and was a big fan of Sidney Bechet and Bessie Smith. He had a vast record collection which he loved to listen to, and I became the one of the eight of us who was thrilled to join him." She had piano lessons starting when she was eight and began to play acoustic guitar the following year, playing and singing in a kid's group. She attended the University of Michigan (1981–86), but was primarily self-taught in music in addition to taking some private voice and guitar lessons.

Despite some earlier musical experiences, her career as Carmen Getit really began when she met pianist-singer Steve Lucky in 1986. Lucky bought her her first electric guitar and gave her coaching and encouragement. "I got my first break in 1991 when Steve Lucky asked me to join him on some solo piano gigs he was working in Switzerland. He took me on as a vocalist/guitarist and we performed six nights a week for a month straight as a duet. That was my first paying gig. After a move to the San Francisco area in 1993, I started performing in his quartet. He asked me to join his quintet the Rhumba Bums in 1994 and a real turning point was the success of our first CD, *Come Out Swingin'*, in 1998." The Rhumba Bums have long been a major attraction in San Francisco's swing circuit and the perfect outlet for Carmen Getit's powerful singing (influenced by Ruth Brown, Dinah Washington and Etta James) and T-Bone Walker-inspired guitar playing. In addition, she has recorded with pianist Pinetop Perkins (*Ladies Man*), worked with singer-pianist Carol Fran, and performed in the show *Crazy In Love With Patsy Cline* along with Lavay Smith and Ingrid Lucia.

"In the near future I'm planning on writing and recording albums for both my Carmen Getit band and another group I'm in, the Hammond Cheese Combo."

Recommended CD: 1998's *Steve Lucky And The Rhumba Bums' Come Out Swingin'* (Rumpus 65902) features hard-swinging late 1940s jump jazz and blues.

Banu Gibson
b. October 24, 1947, Dayton, OH

When Banu Gibson first formed her Hot Jazz Band in 1981, she practically stood alone. Few other singers were interpreting music from the 1920s and '30s, and many of those were either amateurs, vocalists who chose to satirize the vintage material or just plain corny. Banu, with her trained voice, very large repertoire, witty showmanship and desire to be creative with the music while having fun, was at the top of her field and she still is.

She grew up in Hollywood, Florida. "I was first introduced to jazz by an early boyfriend, a drummer, who listened to Thelonious Monk, Sonny Rollins, Art Blakey, Ahmad Jamal and Dave Brubeck. I was 16 at the time and most of the music was very abstract to me. Ironically, I started out listening to contemporary jazz, but kept moving backwards to the beginnings of jazz."

Banu attended Broward Community College in Florida with a triple major in Music, Theater and Dance, but eventually dropped out so as to work in music. "I knew my whole life that I would end up in the business in one area or another. I just had no idea whether it would be in singing, dancing, choreography, or all of the above." After working in a pair of Las Vegas–style shows, she sang and danced with *Your Father's Mustache*, a 1920s banjo band revue at the Miami Beach Hilton. "We worked opposite Phil Napoleon and his Emperors, which was my first real exposure to live Dixieland. I moved to NYC to join the Mustache's road band and began looking around for new material to sing. I was given LPs of Paul Whiteman, Bing Crosby and Bix Beiderbecke, as well as the RCA Vintage series that featured people like Irving Aaronson and Ethel Waters. I absolutely fell in love with the original sound of the period. I had been exposed to the '50s rehash of the '20s music, but that was a caricature of the real thing. I found I had a knack for singing the entire spectrum of the '20s from Bessie Smith to Betty Boop, as well as pop singers like Ruth Etting, Annette Hanshaw, and Ethel Waters. A few years later I discovered Fats Waller, Mildred Bailey and Lee Wiley, and my repertoire began to include songs from the 1930s."

Banu worked at Disneyland in the *Class Of '27* during 1972–78. She moved to New Orleans in 1973, and regularly commuted to Los Angeles during her Disneyland years. During this period, she learned how to play rhythm banjo and guitar. Banu went on a European tour with Wild Bill Davison, formed her New Orleans Hot Jazz Band in 1981, and within a few years was a major attraction at classic jazz festivals. Her group evolved to include (at different times) Charlie Fardella, Duke Heitger and Randy Reinhardt on trumpets, trombonist David Sager and either Tom Fischer or Dan Levinson on reeds. Banu's musical director since near the beginning has been pianist David Boeddinghaus. Their repertoire (which includes fresh versions of standards, lots of obscurities and occasional instrumentals), the colorful and concise arrangements, the excellent musicians, Banu's versatile singing and her wit make this a group always well worth seeing.

It is surprising that Banu Gibson has not found much fame

in jazz beyond the trad circuit since her repertoire now includes many songs from the late '30s and 1940s and she has been one of the very best jazz singers in any style of the past 25 years.

When asked what it is like to perform with her band, she says, "There is both a freedom to be an individual and, at the same time, a responsibility to be a part of the group to make the song work. I sometimes describe it as everyone getting in the same car and all going to the same place, with no back-seat drivers and no one demanding to pull off the road for a side trip. Everyone is just focused on getting there while enjoying the trip."

Recommended CDs: An early version of Banu Gibson's "Hot Jazz" is featured on *Jazz Baby* (Stomp Off 1073), including pianist David Boeddinghaus and trumpeter Charlie Fardella, but no clarinetist, and a tuba rather than a string bassist. "Rose Of Washington Square," "Sweet Man" and "Changes" are highlights. Some of the material is repeated on the sampler *Vintage Banu* (Swing Out 109), which has the best of her earliest recordings from the first half of the 1980s. *Let Yourself Go* (Swing Out 103) with "I Got Rhythm," "Let Yourself Go" and "Put That Sun Back In The Sky"; 1989's *You Don't Know My Mind* (Swing Out 104), which has "Ol' Pappy," "I've Got My Fingers Crossed" and "Truckin,'"; and the swing-oriented *Love Is Good For Anything That Ails You* (Swing Out 107) are the three finest recordings by Banu with her band. *Livin' In A Great Big Way* (Swing Out 105) has the singer backed by one of two pianists (David Boeddinghaus or John Sheridan) as does *My Romance* (Swing Out 108). *'Zat You Santa Claus* (Swing Out 106) is a set of swinging Christmas songs. *Steppin' Out* (Swing Out 109) has Banu joined by a quartet with guitarist Bucky Pizzarelli and a few guest horns, and *Sings Johnny Mercer* (Swing Out 1111) features her in a similar setting with John Sheridan.

Website: www.banugibson.com

Harry "The Hipster" Gibson
(Harry Raab)
b. August 1914, New York, NY; d. May 9, 1991, CA

Harry "The Hipster" Gibson was a crazy rock and roll personality, vocalist and pianist who emerged in the mid-1940s, a decade too soon. Although the music he played and sang was not technically rock and roll (being essentially swing), Gibson's persona as a demented drug user who took outrageous vocals would have worked much better in the Elvis Presley era than it did during the Glenn Miller-to-bebop years.

Gibson started his career as a stride pianist who played in 52nd Street clubs. The high point from his early period was performing Bix Beiderbecke's "In A Mist" at an Eddie Condon Town Hall concert. However, he soon reinvented himself as a singer-pianist who went out of his way to be over-the-top. His prime recordings, made for Musicraft during 1944 and 1947, include "Stop That Dancin' Up There," "4F Ferdinand The Frantic Freak," "Get Your Juices At The Deuces," "I Stay Brown All Year Round" and his famous "Who Put The Benzedrine In Mrs. Murphy's Ovaltine." His music was considered so frantic and scandalous that it was banned from several Los Angeles radio stations during the period.

Excessive drug use and general unreliability resulted in the Hipster fading from the scene after 1947. He made a few obscure records for Diamond (1947), Aladdin (four spaced-out versions of children's stories in 1953) and Hip (two titles in 1957, including "Live Fast, Die Young, And Have A Good Lookin' Corpse"), but was long forgotten by the time rock and roll began. Being 42 in 1956, he was too old to be a teen idol anyway.

Harry "The Hipster" Gibson mostly scuffled and played low-level jobs during the remainder of his life, only re-emerging to record a demented Christmas jazz record in 1974, and a couple of live albums with mostly amateur players in the 1980s. By then he had wasted his huge potential.

Recommended CDs: *Boogie Woogie In Blue* (Musicraft 70063) has all of The Hipster's prime Musicraft recordings while *Who Put The Benzedrine In Mrs. Murphy's Ovaltine?* (Delmark 687) from 1976 and 1989 has some effective piano playing and hilarious storytelling from Gibson.

Astrud Gilberto
b. March 30, 1940, Salvador, Bahia, Brazil

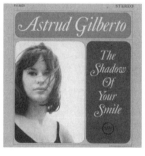

Astrud Gilberto's career began as an accident and she went remarkably far with a limited voice, a trademark hit and an understated charisma.

Born in Brazil and married at the time to João Gilberto, an increasingly famous singer, Astrud Gilberto moved with João to the United States in 1962. A housewife, she happened to be at the record date that resulted in *Getz/Gilberto*, one of the classic bossa nova albums, a set featuring Stan Getz, Antonio Carlos Jobim on piano and João Gilberto. When João was unable to sing the English lyrics to "The Girl From Ipanema," he suggested that his wife try it. Astrud had no ambitions to be a singer and no professional experience but João liked the sound of her voice. Her quiet tone and naïve interpretation perfectly fit the song (and "Quiet Nights" from the same album), which became a giant hit, launching her unexpected career.

As soon as the record was released, Astrud Gilberto was famous. She appeared on a Stan Getz live album *Getz Au Go Go*, was signed to Verve and recorded a string of popular albums. None featured a hit on the level of "The Girl From Ipanema," but they sold well throughout the 1960s. Astrud Gilberto's profile has dropped a bit since the early 1970s, but she has remained active, recording on an occasional basis (including a 1977 vocal duet on "Far Away" with Chet Baker), developing as a songwriter, and still being the most famous bossa nova singer for many in the United States.

Recommended CDs: *Getz/Gilberto* (Verve 810 048) is an essential acquisition for its beautiful mixture of cool jazz and Brazilian music, although Astrud Gilberto is only heard on two numbers. Gilberto is on half of 1964's *Getz Au Go Go* (Verve 821 725) and is heard in excellent form on *The Astrud Gilberto Album* (Verve 314 526 951), *The Shadow Of Your*

Smile (Verve 314 557 184), *Look To The Rainbow* (Verve 821 556), *A Certain Smile—A Certain Sadness* (Verve 314 557 449) and the intriguing 1972 set *Astrud Gilberto Now* (Perception 81218). 1987's *Astrud Gilberto Plus The James Last Orchestra* (Polygram 831 123) and *Jungle* (Magya 581861) from 2002 feature Gilberto in more recent times.

Website: www.astrudgilberto.com

João Gilberto
b. June 10, 1931, Salvador, Bahia, Brazil

Miles Davis once said of João Gilberto: "He could read a newspaper and sound good." Gilberto has the definitive male voice for Brazilian music and, along with composer Antonio Carlos Jobim, he was the one most responsible for the bossa nova catching on worldwide.

João Gilberto began playing guitar when he was 14 and within a year was leading a band. Even at that early stage, he was singing and playing melodic jazz over Brazilian rhythms. At 18 he began working on the radio. He spent a year in Rio de Janeiro (1950) as the lead singer in the popular band Garotos da Lua, but was fired for being unreliable, often showing up late for performances. Little was heard of Gilberto for a few years as he freelanced and drifted aimlessly, although he did make a few early recordings starting in 1951.

Gilberto reappeared in the late 1950s, teaming up with singer Luis Telles, developing his unique breathy and whispery singing, and recording his first album, *Chega De Saudade*, one of the very first bossa nova records. In 1962, he moved to the United States where he lived for the next 18 years. His work on *Getz/Gilberto* (with his wife of the time Astrud Gilberto; they were divorced in 1965) made him well known to American listeners and he worked constantly, often as a soloist. Gilberto moved back to Brazil in the early 1980s, teaming up with some of the top Brazilian performers but becoming increasingly reclusive. Nowadays he performs on only an occasional basis, but his highly influential voice can still be heard in prime form.

Recommended CDs: João Gilberto recorded ten songs during 1951–58 on 78s, but his first album, *Chega De Saudade* (Odeon 3073), was his breakthrough. The three-CD set *O Mito* (EMI 164-79115) has all of the music from *Chega de Saudade* plus his next two albums, *O Amor, O Sorriso E A Flor* and *João Gilberto*. Other significant CDs from his career include *Getz/Gilberto* (Verve 810 048), *João Gilberto En Mexico* (Polygram 848426), *Amoroso/Brazil* (Warner Archives 45165) and *Live In Montreux* (Warner Bros. 36215/76).

LPs to Search For: A pair of João Gilberto's early American albums, *Boss Of The Bossa Nova* (Atlantic 8070) and *The Warm World Of João Gilberto* (Atlantic 8076), have not been reissued on CD yet.

Website: www.joaogilberto.org

Dizzy Gillespie
(John Birks Gillespie)
b. October 21, 1917, Cheraw, SC;
d. January 6, 1993, Englewood, NJ

A true giant who ranks as one of the greatest jazz trumpeters of all time (possibly the top), Dizzy Gillespie was (with Charlie Parker) one of the main founders of bebop. He was also a very significant force in forming Afro-Cuban jazz, the leader of three major orchestras and quite a few combos, an inspired wisecracker and a very important if informal jazz educator. In addition, on an irregular basis, Gillespie sang. He never made his living as a vocalist, but he was one of the most inventive and fastest scat-singers ever.

John Birks Gillespie was nicknamed Dizzy as a teenager due to his sly wit. He started on trombone, switched to trumpet, and studied music at an agricultural school, the Laurinburg Institute in North Carolina. In 1935 he dropped out of school to pursue music, moving to Philadelphia where he played with Frankie Fairfax's orchestra.

Influenced originally by the exciting and harmonically advanced playing of Roy Eldridge, Gillespie was in Eldridge's former spot when he was with the Teddy Hill Orchestra in 1937. Even at that early stage, he was criticized by some musicians for taking chances during his solos as he sought to develop his own approach. Dizzy continued to evolve during his two years with Cab Calloway (1939–41) to the point where he was improvising over more complex chord changes than the rhythm section was playing. Calloway called some of Gillespie's solos "Chinese music" and, in hindsight, he did hit a fair number of "wrong" notes during this period. After performing with ten different big bands during 1941–42 (including Lucky Millinder, Les Hite and four weeks subbing with Duke Ellington) and meeting Charlie Parker, Gillespie joined the 1943 Earl Hines big band, an organization that is considered the first bebop orchestra (Parker, Sarah Vaughan and Billy Eckstine were among the other sidemen) but tragically never recorded. The following year, Gillespie spent much of the time with the Billy Eckstine Orchestra (which did make a few records) and participated in the first bebop record dates, led by Coleman Hawkins.

In 1945 Dizzy Gillespie became a major force in jazz, recording highly influential performances with Charlie Parker and becoming the spokesman for the new bebop music. He also took his first vocal on "Salt Peanuts" and led a short-lived big band. The following year after visiting the West Coast with Parker, Gillespie formed a more successful orchestra that lasted for over three years. Dizzy took vocals on "Oop-Bop-Sh-Bam" during a combo date in 1946, an alternate rendition of "He Beeped When He Shoulda Bopped" (the version with Alice Roberts is better known), "Oop-Pop-A-Da," "I'm Be Boppin' Too," "Hey Pete, Let's Eat Mo' Meat" and "You Stole My Wife You Horsethief" (not a classic), but gave most of the vocals with his big band to Kenny "Poncho" Hagood, Joe "Bebop" Carroll (who replaced Hagood by 1949) or Johnny Hartman. For Gillespie, singing was just a diversion, but as it turned out, he was a much better scat singer than either Hagood or Carroll. While Carroll was featured on a couple

European tours with Gillespie's quintet in 1952–53, Dizzy usually joined in on the hotter scat numbers (most notably "The Champ") and eventually realized that he did not need another vocalist. Among the other numbers on which he sang during the 1950s are "She's Gone Again," his long-time comedy number "Swing Low, Sweet Cadillac," "Cripple Crapple Crutch" (using blues lyrics "borrowed" from Pleasant Joseph), "Pretty Eyed Baby" (sharing the vocal with Roy Eldridge), "Oo-Shoo-Bee-Doo-Bee," "Ool-Ya-Koo" and "School Days." Gillespie also often sang "Lady Be Good," including on a remarkable date with Sonny Rollins and Sonny Stitt.

Dizzy evolved from being a musical revolutionary in the mid-1940s to a senior statesman in the 1960s and '70s. While his trumpet playing started to fade after the early '70s, his occasional singing, which mostly emphasized scatting, remained as heated, creative and witty as ever. He could hold his own with Jon Hendricks (although he never did vocalese) and it is a pity that no one thought of having Dizzy record a vocal album. At the time of his death in 1993 at the age of 75, Dizzy Gillespie had been one of the most beloved of all jazz musicians for nearly five decades.

Recommended CDs: Dozens of Dizzy Gillespie recordings are recommended for his trumpet playing but only a few feature much of his singing. *Dizzy Gillespie In Paris, Vol. 2* (Vogue 68361) has Dizzy singing during 1952–53 on "Afro-Paris," "Say Eh," "Cripple Crapple Crutch" and "Always," while the two-CD *Birk's Works: The Verve Big Band Sessions* (Verve 314 527 900) has vocalizing by Gillespie on "Hey Pete," "The Champ," "School Days" and "Umbrella Man." Singing may have been just an afterthought for Dizzy but the great trumpeter was one of the very best scat-singers.

Wendee Glick
(Wendy Dee Glick)
b. February 23, 1959, Brookline, MA

A fine vocalist with a warm voice and an infectious delivery, Wendee Glick took some time before finally appearing on records.

"When I was young, my mom would sing a lot of the old standards at home. I think I filed them in the back of my memory for a later time. In 1990 when I met pianist Steve Heck, his bluesy interpretations of the standards drew me in. It inspired me to start singing all of the old tunes my mom used to sing around the house." As a child, Wendee Glick sang harmony with her mother and older sister. She took voice lessons in junior high school, appeared in musicals, and grew to love singing. Glick sang in choral groups in high school, performed some light operas, and studied opera at the University of Lowell for three semesters. But she changed course, earned a degree in business and spent a few years outside of music.

In 1990 she met Steve Heck, sat in with him at the '57 in Boston, sang "The Wind Beneath My Wings," and received a standing ovation. It was the first time that she had ever used a microphone. "It was such a great feeling to know that I could bring that much joy to people, that I decided it was something I had to pursue. For the next few years I made my way from pop ballads to cabaret, and finally to jazz."

Since that time, Wendee Glick has worked regularly in the New England area, been featured with the Compaq Big Band, and performed swinging jazz and ballads at restaurants, clubs, occasional concerts and private parties.

Recommended CDs: *Baby I'm Fine* (Jazzy Plus 111) from 2002 teams Wendee Glick in a group with Ken Peplowski on clarinet and tenor and either Steve Heck or Paul Broadnax on piano.

She used a similar group (with Hack or Eddie Higgins on piano) throughout 2005's *True Colors* (Jazzy Plus 794 421). The latter has most but not all of the song titles having something to do with colors (such as "Orange Colored Sky" and "Deep Purple"). In both cases, her enthusiastic delivery and appealing voice make the CDs well worth acquiring.

Website: www.jazzyplus.com

Babs Gonzales
(Lee Brown)
b. October 27, 1919, Newark, NJ; d. January 23, 1980, Newark, NJ

In some ways, Babs Gonzales was the Jelly Roll Morton of the bebop era. Like Morton, Gonzales tended to brag a lot and was constantly working on ways to get ahead. Unlike Jelly Roll, Babs was not a genius or a major innovator. While Morton tended to obscure his own very real accomplishments with his bragging, Gonzales succeeded in getting a lot of attention, at least for a few years.

He studied piano and drums as a youth, but Gonzales ended up dropping both to concentrate exclusively on singing. He worked briefly with the big bands of Charlie Barnet and Lionel Hampton before forming the Three Bips and a Bop in 1946. Although he had a limited voice, Gonzales loved to sing bebop and developed a scatting style that emphasized vowels over consonants. He recorded "Oop-Pop-A-Da" before Dizzy Gillespie and during 1947–49 documented such bop fantasies as "Weird Lullaby," "A Lesson In Bopology," "Professor Bop" and "Prelude To A Nightmare." Gonzales was able to use a wide variety of top sidemen on those record dates including tenor-saxophonist Sonny Rollins (on his recording debut), trombonists J.J. Johnson and Bennie Green, altoist Art Pepper, James Moody on tenor, clarinetist Tony Scott, pianists Wynton Kelly, Tadd Dameron and Linton Garner, flutist Alberto Socarras, Don Redman on soprano, Julius Watkins on French horn and violinist Ray Nance.

With the end of the classic bebop era in 1950, the musically inflexible Gonzales found his services in much less demand. He worked with James Moody's group during 1951–54, and had jobs as a disc jockey and a promoter. There were some isolated record dates, including three singles for his own short-lived Crazy label in 1953, two songs with Jimmy Smith's trio in 1956, a single for Savoy, a few titles for King (including "The Bebop Santa Claus") and an album apiece for Hope, Jaro and Dauntless, some of which involved Gonzales talking as much as singing. He also made at least three albums for his own Expubidence label in the late 1960s. Babs documented his adventures in the two colorful, semi-fictional autobiographies *I Paid My Dues* and *Movin' On Down De Line*.

Perhaps if Babs Gonzales had worked more on developing his singing and less on self-promotion, he would have had a more significant career. But then again, maybe we would not have heard of him.

Recommended CDs: *Weird Lullaby* (Blue Note 84464) is easily Babs Gonzales' definitive set, including all of his 1947–49 recordings except for two sessions that were released on sampler collections by Delmark and Xanadu. All of the aforementioned tunes are on this CD plus boppish renditions of "St. Louis Blues" and "Stompin' At The Savoy," "Babs' Dream," "Real Crazy" and other entertaining performances.

LPs to Search For: *Live At Small's Paradise* (Dauntless 4311) has Gonzales in fine form in 1963 with an all-star quintet that includes flugelhornist Clark Terry and tenor-saxophonist Johnny Griffin.

Teddy Grace

(Stella Gloria Crowson)
b. June 26, 1905, Arcadia, LA; d. January 4, 1992, La Mirada, CA

One of the best jazz singers of the late 1930s, Teddy Grace is today one of the forgotten greats. Her entire performing career spanned only 13 years with her most significant period being just six years, but she left behind many fine recordings.

She gained the nickname of Teddy as a child and played piano and guitar as a youth. Married for the first time when she was 18, Grace spent several years as a housewife in Montgomery, Alabama. In 1931, while at a country club function, she was singing to herself while listening to a live band broadcasting on the radio. A friend dared her to sing onstage and she bravely performed "St. Louis Blues." Grace was immediately discovered and within two weeks had become a radio star in the South. She appeared with Blue Steele's Orchestra, Al Stanley's Arcadians, and Al Katz's Kittens. Grace went to New York with Katz, worked with Tommy Christian and toured with Mal Hallett's big band during 1934–35. She married a second time and briefly retired, but was back with Hallett by early 1937. Grace made her recording debut with Mal Hallett (cutting ten numbers) and in 1937 also recorded her first of seven sessions as a leader for Decca.

The 30 songs that she made during her 1937–40 dates usually teamed her with jazz all-stars including cornetist Bobby Hackett, trumpeters Charlie Shavers and Max Kaminsky, trombonist Jack Teagarden, clarinetists Buster Bailey and Pee Wee Russell, tenor-saxophonist Bud Freeman and pianists Frank Froeba and Billy Kyle. Teddy Grace, who was white, showed that she could sing the blues with the best black vocalists of the era, especially during the three May 1939 sessions with Shavers that were released as a 78 album titled *Blues Sung By Teddy Grace*. She also showed that she could sing swing tunes such as "Love Me Or Love Me" and "Sing (It's Good For Ya)."

In addition, Grace recorded 11 numbers with Bob Crosby's orchestra during July-December 1939 (best are "The Little Man Who Wasn't There," "I Thought About You" and "Angry") and two with Lou Holden's Disciples of Rhythm. But after making her last date as a leader on September 26, 1940, she dropped out, discouraged by having to fight with Decca to record the material she wanted and burnt out by the music business in general.

After a few years of inactivity, Grace joined the WACs in 1943, working as a recruiter for the Army, organizing revues, and singing constantly at bond rallies and shows for the military. Her schedule was so hectic that in 1944 she completely lost her voice and was unable to make a sound for six months. Over time, her speaking voice came back but she was never able to sing again. Grace was discharged in 1946, and worked as a typist and secretary for decades.

The jazz world completely lost track of Teddy Grace after 1940 and she was considered a lost legend among record collectors, who had assumed that she was long dead. In 1991, writer David McCain located her at a nursing home near Los Angeles. Although ill from cancer, she was happy to be extensively interviewed by McCain on several occasions, and his article alerted jazz fans that the legendary singer was still around. Before she passed away on January 4, 1992, Teddy Grace was aware that she had not been forgotten and that her contributions to jazz were appreciated.

Recommended CDs: Shortly after Teddy Grace's death, David McCain wrote the liner notes for the definitive release *Teddy Grace* (Timeless 1-016), which has 22 of her 30 recordings as a leader; all of her prime material. A complementary set is *Teddy Grace* (Hep 1054), which contains four more songs from her dates, all of Grace's recordings with Mal Hallett, 10 of the 11 selections made with Bob Crosby and one of the cuts with Lou Holden. Acquire these two CDs and you will have the very best of Teddy Grace.

Sandy Graham

b. November 14, 1947, Santa Barbara, CA

An excellent singer based in Los Angeles who has not recorded often enough, Sandy Graham has had a lengthy career filled with musical high points.

She grew up in a musical household and heard jazz constantly as a child. "My earliest singing experiences were in the Baptist church when I was five or six years old. The people we lived with taught us to harmonize on Christmas carols. Even then I loved singing. My music teachings came from public schools, my father and listening to the jazz greats. There are many jazz-singing giants that I appreciated and learned to imitate until I found my own voice. Sarah Vaughan first, then Billie Holiday, later Carmen McRae."

Sandy Graham began her career sitting in at jam sessions, getting her first engagement at the Sapphire Room in West Los Angeles when she was 19. She has performed at many venues and in many different situations since then. Among the situations that she fondly remembers are performing with the Jimmy Rowles Trio at Sonny's in 1973, recording with the Colorado Springs Air Force Band in 1975, her work for television, performing with the Nat Pierce/Frankie Capp Juggernaut Band starting in 1979, recording with Lalo Schifrin (although it was ruined by bad editing from its producer), performing with Bill Berry's L.A. Big Band and the Gerald Wilson Orchestra, touring Japan several times, being accompanied by pianist Gerald Wiggins, and touring Europe in the 1990s with the Duke Ellington All-Stars. She has also worked as a model and an actress.

"I've had some really tough times, but I am grateful that God blessed me with a talent that no one can take away from me. I've been so fortunate to have worked with musicians that I used to listen to as a child, never dreaming for one minute that I'd ever meet them."

Recommended CDs: Each of Sandy Graham's three CDs feature her in top form: *Sandy Graham* (Muse 5425), *Comes Love* (Jazz Link 40062) and *Sandy Graham By Request* (Jazz Link 44005).

Website: www.sandygraham.com

Anita Gravine

b. April 11, 1946, Carbondale, PA

Anita Gravine's first two albums, *Dream Dancing* and *I Never Knew* from the mid-1980s were so enjoyable that it is surprising that she has not accomplished more in jazz since that time, but other careers took precedent.

Her father had booked swing era bands in the 1930s, and her older brother Mickey Gravine was a studio musician. "As a young girl, I usually begged to go along with Mickey whenever he could possibly take me, especially to the NBC radio programs he performed on every Sunday. I just loved the aura surrounding every aspect of the creative process." In addition, her mother played piano and sang in the house, teaching her many songs.

As a young teenager, Anita Gravine sang with local bands in Jersey City, New Jersey, moving up to Hoboken, Newark, Atlantic City and New York City, using such players as Roy Eldridge, Hank Jones and Marty Napoleon. She sang with such big bands as that of Larry Elgart, the Tommy Dorsey ghost band, Les Elgart, Urbie Green, Buddy Morrow and Kai Winding. "The piano player in the Tommy Dorsey/Warren Covington band was Chick Corea."

For a few years in the 1970s, Anita Gravine lived and performed in Europe before returning to New York. She finally recorded as a leader for the first time in the mid-1980s, making very good albums for Progressive and Stash that have not been reissued yet on CD, and a set for Jazz Alliance that was not released until 1993. Gravine worked as a teacher of jazz singing and in the 1990s was active in video and film production, being off of records almost entirely until late in the decade. "Several years ago, I formed a small video company (Sargasso Productions) to produce documentaries. My first project was a half-hour pilot on the history of Italian-Americans. I would like to continue gathering stories which in turn feeds my singing ideas. After all, it's all story telling, in one way or another."

Recommended CDs: Anita Gravine's only two available CDs hint at her potential although they are not as rewarding overall as her earlier LPs. *Welcome To My Dream* (Jazz Alliance 10021) has her singing ten songs from the Bing Crosby/Bob Hope road movies, but the arrangements take themselves too seriously and, with a few exceptions, the material is weak. *Lights, Camera, Passion* (Soul Note 121 306) has Gravine interpreting 13 songs from Italian films, some of which are more rewarding than others although the jazz content is generally low.

LPs to Search For: Anita Gravine's two most rewarding albums, *Dream Dancing* (Progressive 7074) and *I Always Knew* (Stash 255), which is a real unknown classic, remain out of print. The latter is highlighted by memorable versions of "Thanks A Million," "I'm Confessin'" (taken as a duet with bassist George Mraz), "Not For All the Rice In China," "Look For The Silver Lining" and a delightful version of "The Coffee Song."

Buddy Greco
(Armando Greco)
b. August 14, 1926, Philadelphia, PA

A colorful singer and pianist whose roots are in jazz but whose career has stretched in many directions, Buddy Greco has been a household name for over a half-century.

When asked when he knew that he was going to try to be a professional singer, Greco says that "The

day I was born! My father had a record store and I grew up with music. My father started my piano lessons when I was four. I first heard jazz when I heard Art Tatum when I was a kid." Greco performed on the radio for nine years starting when he was just five, singing on a program that featured Italian operas. He attended the Curtis Institute of Music as a teenager during 1941–42. He then dropped out of school, formed a trio and worked in Philadelphia night clubs. Greco recorded a few records and had a hit in 1946 with "Ohh, Look A There, Ain't She Pretty?"

In 1949 when he was 23, Buddy Greco began a two-year stint with Benny Goodman on both piano and as a singer. He was in Goodman's brief bebop orchestra, but also felt comfortable playing with Goodman's later swing groups.

Since then, Buddy Greco has had a busy solo career, appearing at nightclubs, concert halls, with symphonies and on television. One of his high points was appearing at the same concert as the Beatles (before they came to the United States) for a command performance for Queen Elizabeth. He had big hits in his versions of "The Lady Is A Tramp" and "Around The World," has recorded over 65 albums and his music has ranged from jazz to middle-of-the-road pop and country. He has been a regular in Las Vegas, produced a nationally syndicated live radio show *Vegas Live Tonite* and has opened Buddy Greco Dinner Club, in Cathedral Springs, California.

Recommended CDs: Two 1950s albums are reissued on the single CD *My Buddy/On Stage* (Collectables 6079). *Route 66* (Celebrity 1901), *Back To Basics* (USA 1645) and *Like Young* (USA 1655) are strong examples of how Buddy Greco sounds today.

LPs to Search For: Quite worthwhile are *Buddy Greco At Mister Kelly's* (Carol 1013), *Songs For Swingin' Losers* (Epic 585), *I Like It Swinging* (Epic 602) and 1968's *Big Band And Ballads* (Reprise 6220), which Greco named as one of his favorites.

Website: www.buddygrecoproductions.com

Jane Green
(Martha Jane Green)
b. January 2, 1897, Louisville, KY;
d. August 28, 1931, San Francisco, CA

Jane Green's relatively short life has resulted in her being forgotten, but for a time in the 1920s she was a major name. Her mother was an actress who taught her the popular songs of the time. Green grew up in Los Angeles and began working in clubs when she was 14, specializing in ragtime-oriented songs and blues. She also appeared now and then in rodeos (being a champion trick horse rider) and graduated from business college. Her first husband Jimmy Blyer was her piano accompanist and musical director. The team of Green and Blyler (who died in 1924) was a hit in New York in 1918, they frequently worked with Eddie Cantor in the early 1920s, and during this period Green introduced "I Never Knew I Could Love Anybody" and "Everybody Loves My Baby," although she never recorded either.

Jane Green, who worked in many productions, made her first recordings in 1920 with the bulk of her records cut for Victor during 1923–27. She worked with Isham Jones during 1924–25, became the first female singer featured regularly with a top dance orchestra (predating Mildred Bailey, who was with Paul Whiteman in 1929) and headlined for two months in London in September 1925.

In 1927, at the height of her fame, Green was a passenger in a car accident that broke her nose and caused internal damage.

She made a comeback but soon stopped recording, a second marriage caused her problems and she lost most of her money in the Wall Street crash of 1929. During her last two years, Jane Green was active in radio, and for a time she hosted a 45-minute weekly show called *Jane Green's Manhattan*. But her health failed, and she died of a stroke at the age of 34.

Recommended CD: All of Jane Green's record dates are on *Complete Recordings 1920–1929* (Superbatone 732). Among the selections that best show off her singing are "The Blues Have Got Me," "You Went Away Too Far (And Stayed Away Too Long)," "My Castle In Spain" (which Isham Jones wrote for her) and "I'm Gonna Meet My Sweetie Now."

Lil Green
(Lillian Johnson)
b. December 22, 1919, MS; d. April 14, 1954, Chicago, IL

A top blues singer who crossed over into jazz and early R&B, Lil Green might have had a more significant career if she had not died prematurely.

She was born on the Mississippi Delta as one of ten children. Lil's parents died when she was ten and the orphan moved to Chicago, where she went to school. In 1934, she dropped out to become a singing waitress. After a few years of experience, she had become one of the top female blues/jazz singers based in Chicago, and in 1940 she began recording for Bluebird.

Green recorded 28 songs for Bluebird during 1940–42, all with Big Bill Broonzy on guitar. Her first session resulted in her most famous original, "Romance In The Dark," and on April 3, 1941 she became the first to record Joe McCoy's "Why Don't You Do Right," a year before Peggy Lee cut the hit version with Benny Goodman. Green's sensuous voice, an appealing twang and her versatility made her quite popular in the Chicago area. Some of her other early recordings include "Knockin' Myself Out," "I'm Going To Copyright Your Kisses" and "You're Just Full Of Jive."

Green worked with Broonzy in clubs, played theaters with the Tiny Bradshaw Orchestra, toured with Luis Russell's big band in 1944, and for a time she fronted the Milt Larkin big band (which was temporarily renamed the Lil Green Orchestra). After the recording strike of 1943–44 ended, she returned to records, making 22 more sides for Bluebird and Victor during 1945–47, often backed by larger groups. However, no new hits resulted. She recorded two further numbers in 1949 for Aladdin (including "My Be Bop Daddy") and in 1951 sang on three songs for Atlantic in an R&Bish setting.

Although Lil Green was being overshadowed by other singers by the early 1950s, her possible association with Atlantic and R&B looked promising. But, despite being a clean liver who did not smoke or drink, she caught bronchial pneumonia and died in 1954 when she was only 34.

Recommended CDs: *1940–1941* (Jazz Classics 5072) and *Complete Recorded Works 1946–1951* (Document 1527) have all of Lil Green's recordings (including her hits) except her 12 selections from 1942 and 1945.

Everett Greene
b. February 16, 1934, Washington, D.C.

A warm ballad singer who can swing, Everett Greene, has only been gaining recognition for his deep baritone voice in recent years.

"I was originally a doo-wop singer until I served in the Marines during the Korean War and then moved to Indianapolis, Indiana in 1955. I had the opportunity to hear many local musicians such as Wes Montgomery, David Baker, Freddie Hubbard and Larry Ridley. After hearing those musicians, I found a new love for jazz." However, it was a long time before Greene performed jazz regularly for he had a longtime day job as a laborer/machinist, singing gospel in his spare time.

When he did enter show business on a full-time basis after his retirement, it was as a stage actor in a few touring shows. But gradually he turned toward jazz, where his baritone (hinting at times at Billy Eckstine and Arthur Prysock but sounding individual) was a welcome addition. By 1994 he was being noticed, and he made his long overdue recording debut on *At Last*, at the age of 60.

Since then, Everett Greene has stayed active, working with such greats as Houston Person, Junior Mance, Lou Donaldson and David "Fathead" Newman. "My goals are to sing as long as I still enjoy it and can make people happy listening. It gives me a wonderful feeling to see people leave an engagement happy about something they heard me sing."

Recommended CDs: *At Last* (Evergreen 1), *My Foolish Heart* (Savant 2014) and *I've Got Love* (Evergreen 2) feature Everett Greene sounding quite happy to finally be performing the ballads and jazz tunes that he loves.

Website: www.everettgreene.com

Gene Greene "The Ragtime King"
(Eugene Greene)
b. June 9, 1877; IN; d. April 5, 1930, New York, NY

Legend has it that scat-singing began in 1926 when Louis Armstrong, in the midst of recording "Heebies Jeebies" with his Hot Five, dropped the music and began improvising nonsense syllables to cover himself. It is a great story, except that Satch sounds quite comfortable during the recording, and that there are quite a few examples of scat singing on record during 1923–25. In 1924, Don Redman with Fletcher Henderson's orchestra, scats a little on "My Papa Doesn't Two-Time No Time." That same year an unidentified musician scats on several records by George Olsen's Orchestra, and Cliff Edwards (Ukulele Ike) scatted on some of his performances from 1923.

However, more than a decade earlier, vaudeville performer Gene Greene recorded "King Of The Bungaloos." This 1911 recording, which mostly features some silly lyrics about Greene becoming the king of the jungle, also has Greene scatting for two choruses. According to Mark Berresford's informative liner notes to the CD that contains this track, *From Ragtime To Jazz Volume 3 1902–1923* (Timeless 1-070), scat singing is thought to have been invented by ragtime singer-pianist-composer Ben Harney (1872–1938) in the mid-1890s. Unfortunately, Harney never recorded, but he was considered the main influence on Greene.

Gene Greene worked in vaudeville during its prime years, and since he often sang in a ragged fashion, and because it rhymed with his last name, he gained the title of "The Ragtime King." "King Of The Bungaloos" was his most popular recording and he recorded it five times during 1911–17. Greene often had Charley Straight (a bandleader in the 1920s) as his pianist and co-composer and sometimes worked with his wife Blanche Werner as Greene and Werner. They sailed to London in 1912 on an extensive tour. She died while in Germany. Gene Greene returned to the United States in 1914, after recording 64 selections in London during the previous two years.

In his American and British recordings, Gene Greene performed all types of material considered humorous at the time. Quite a few have "Rag" in their titles and, although not technically ragtime, the rhythms are influenced by that music. In 1916 he recorded "The Chinese Blues" (four years before Mamie Smith's "Crazy Blues"), and in 1917 he recorded an answer to "Alexander's Ragtime Band" called "Alexander's Got A Jazz Band Now." Unfortunately, that was his last recording. Greene's rare and historic recordings deserve to be coherently reissued.

Greene continued performing during the 1920s before retiring to manage a restaurant in Grand Rapids, Michigan, that was eventually closed due to violating Prohibition. During a comeback in New York, Greene strained himself physically during his performance and, after accepting curtain calls, he died of a heart attack backstage. He was just 52. What Gene Greene "The Ragtime King" thought of the scat singers of the late 1920s is unknown.

Marty Grosz

b. February 28, 1930, Berlin, Germany

Marty Grosz has long been a triple threat as a chordal acoustic guitarist (in the tradition of Carl Kress and Dick McDonough), a Fats Waller-inspired vocalist and a frequently hilarious wit. He has been involved in some of the hottest small-group swing sessions of the past 30 years, some of which have been recorded.

Born in Germany and the son of artist George Grosz, he moved to New York with his family when he was three. Marty Grosz first heard jazz on the radio, began playing ukulele when he was eight and switched to acoustic guitar at 13. He attended Columbia University for a year, got drafted and, after his discharge, he attended the University of Chicago before leaving after six months to play jazz. In 1950, he made his first record in a group with pianist Dick Wellstood and bassist Pops Foster. Grosz moved to Chicago in 1954, staying 20 years and working with a variety of Dixieland bands on guitar and banjo. "I sang backstage or in the band room; never on stage. Finally a leader said 'Hey, we need all the help we can get. Do that on stage.' I did, reluctantly. Gradually it dawned on me that that was what the audience wanted. I've never thought of myself as anything but a rhythm guitarist. Singing is a sideline, but it's become what the fans enjoy, so I 'lay it on 'em' (pardon the old hipster talk)."

Although quite active in Chicago, playing with Art Hodes, Albert Nicholas, Dave Remington, clarinetist Frank Chace and the visiting greats of trad jazz, Marty Grosz went largely unnoticed until he joined Soprano Summit in 1975, the year that he returned to New York. "One of the highlights was moving back to New York and two weeks later performing at Carnegie Hall with Soprano Summit, singing 'Milenburg Joys' to riotous applause. I haven't sung it since. Another highlight of the period was playing my first entirely solo concert in England; I didn't know I was to be alone until 20 minutes before."

Grosz took occasional vocals with Soprano Summit during 1975–79, and was a member of the Classic Jazz Quartet with Dick Wellstood. Starting in the 1980s, his ability to quickly organize small groups to play obscurities from the 1930s, along with his musicianship, joyful vocals and unique ad-libs, made him a great favorite at jazz parties and trad festivals.

When asked about future goals, Marty Grosz says, "To play in a dump with a combo. Of course there are no more dumps that hire old tooters, so I'll have to say to explore the guitar and try some of the forgotten songs that I like. What I'm after is swing and perhaps some theater of the absurd or Dada if you like. The stuff they produce at Juilliard, the Berklee School, etc. bores me. Jazzmen used to be part of the underground, anti-establishment. Now they're on their way to becoming teachers, jingle writers and movie score technicians. There's a world of difference between what the academics produce and the sort of music that my heroes laid down."

Recommended CDs: Marty Grosz has recorded frequently as a leader since 1988, performing the type of good-humored hot swing that he loves. Among his many rewarding and fun CDs are *Swing It* (Jazzology 180), *Extra* (Jazzology 190), *Unsaturated Fats* (Stomp Off 1214), *Songs I Learned At My Mother's Knee And Other Low Joints* (Jazzology 220), *Thanks* (Jazzology 310), *Rhythm For Sale* (Jazzology 280), *Keep A Song In Your Soul* (Jazzology 250), *Left To His Own Devices* (Jazzology 330), *Ring Dem Bells* (Nagel-Heyer 022), *Just For Fun* (Nagel Heyer 039), *Rhythm Is Our Business* (Sackville 2060), *Chasin' The Spots* (Jump 1228) and *Marty Grosz And His Hot Combination* (Arbors 19319). He is featured interacting with and inspiring other current swing greats, leading groups going under the names of the Orphan Newsboys, Destiny's Tots, Paswonky Serenaders, the Sugar Daddies and the Hot Puppies.

Maria Guida

b. May 1, 1953, New York, NY

Maria Guida's long overdue debut CD *Soul Eyes*, features her very attractive voice, skill at scatting, some original vocalese and her warm renditions of ballads. Although she has been doing it for some time, she is one of the top "new" voices in New York jazz.

"As a child, I always sang while my grandfather, who made stringed instruments, played the mandolin or guitar. I studied violin for 12 years, the piano for two and I also played mandolin and guitar." However, Maria Guida's early direction was toward a career as an actor. She worked for 15 years on Broadway, in regional theater and on television. But a turning point came when she saw Bill Evans play in a local club in the late 1970s and realized that she loved jazz. "I had been working as an actor and had done a number of roles in Shakespeare, Chekhov, Tennessee Williams and other plays from the classical repertoire. In 1980, Joseph Papp hired me to a musical at the New York Shakespeare Festival, his original production of the *Pirates Of Penzance* with Linda Ronstadt and Kevin Kline. I performed on stage each night for its entire Broadway run and, while it was a valuable experience, I decided that I absolutely had to sing the music that I was passionate about. That's when I started singing jazz and began studying with Jay Clayton." She also studied with Sheila Jordan at City

College, in addition to private instruction with Mark Murphy and Janet Lawson.

Since dedicating herself to jazz, Maria Guida has often performed in New York area clubs including with pianists Kenny Werner, Pete Malinverni, Bruce Barth and James Weidman. "The spirit of improvisation and spontaneity in jazz provide enormous room for personal expression so, for me, there's a feeling of liberation in performing this music. That makes it joyful for me, even when I'm singing 'sad' lyrics."

Recommended CDs: *Soul Eyes* (Larknote 1001) is a particularly impressive effort, particularly when one realizes that all 12 standards were recorded in a single day. Highlights include a touching version of "How Little We Know," her recreation of John Coltrane's solo on "Bessie's Blues," "Soul Eyes" and Maria Guida's vocalese lyrics to "The Way You Look Tonight."

Website: www.mariaguida.com

Kirsten Gustafson

b. March 25, 1953, Lansing, MI

One of the better jazz singers based in Chicago, Kirsten Gustafson has thus far recorded far too little for one with her singing talents.

"My mother, who had studied voice, piano and harp, taught me how to sing when I was little. She told me that when I was a baby, I pulled myself up in front of the TV and sang along with the commercial jingles. In the fifth grade, the teacher asked us to walk up to the blackboard and write what we wanted to be when we grew up. I wrote SINGER and sat down, beaming."

She played French horn while in school and graduated from Northern Michigan University, majoring in German language and culture, but did not have any formal music lessons. Kirsten Gustafson has worked in a wide variety of settings including rock bands and many types of jazz groups. In 1992 she recorded her first CD, *You Taught My Heart To Sing*, and gained some attention. That year she performed at the Montreux Jazz Festival. In 1994, she joined the Latin group Samba Bamba. She has since worked on voiceovers and jingles, recorded a little-known second CD, *Live At Montreux* that was released in 2000, performed with pianist-arranger Frank Mantooth and violinist Johnny Frigo, toured with the Nelson Riddle Orchestra and appeared regularly in Paris clubs.

Recommended CD: *You Taught My Heart To Sing* (Atlantic 82387), which should have been a breakthrough album, is still Kirsten Gustafson's best recording. Her versions of standards sound fresh and lively, helped out by Frank Mantooth's arrangements.

Angela Hagenbach

b. March 7, Kansas City, MO

Angela Hagenbach is a major singer based in Kansas City who specializes in jazz standards and Brazilian music.

She did not start out to be a singer and did not even care for jazz all that much in her early days although she studied piano and played trombone, her father was a saxophonist and her mother a pianist. "I would sing harmony parts around my house with my sisters while our mom played the piano. I played trombone in the high school marching and stage bands and was a member of the One Way Band, a garage band with nine members. We were a funk-oriented group focusing

mainly on Earth, Wind and Fire, The Ohio Players, etc., with vocals and horns."

Hagenbach attended the University of Kansas City, majored in Child Psychology, and pursued a successful career as a model. She did not neglect music, singing in a gospel choir starting in 1985, but it was in December, 1989 that she reached the turning point. "I truly 'heard' Sarah Vaughan singing, 'Black Coffee,' and it changed my life forever. After that it took me six rigorous months of religiously attending jam sessions, hearing live jazz as often as possible and private study with three musicians in Kansas City before I felt ready to sit in and pursue jazz as a professional singer. On June 13, 1990 I sat in at a jam session, singing 'Black Coffee,' and that was the beginning of my career." She worked regularly at Kansas City's Ritz-Carlton Hotel for four years, started becoming a regular at jazz festivals in the Midwest, and developed the ability to sing quite comfortably in both English and Portuguese. In 1994 she recorded her debut CD, *Come Fly With Me*, starting her own Amazon record label.

In 1998 and 2000, Hagenbach and her group served as Jazz Ambassadors for the United States Information Agency and the Kennedy Center for the Performing Arts, touring Africa and the world. Although it has taken time, Angela Hagenbach has been gradually gaining recognition in the United States. "The multiple options available to keeping the music fresh and new, and the synergy I feel when my band and I come together to present great music to an audience who truly gets it is, for me, the most enjoyable aspect of performing jazz."

Recommended CDs: Angela Hagenbach's debut CD, *Come Fly With Me* (Amazon 7592), set the stage for the ones to follow, featuring unusual treatments of standards including a double time "Tenderly," a funky "Lazy Afternoon" and lots of chance taking.

Her other recordings, *Hot Latin Jazz* (Amazon 3940), *Weaver Of Dreams* (Amazon 8664), *Feel The Magic* (Amazon 3756) and *Poetry Of Love* (Amazon 2822), find her growing in strength, power and daring.

Website: www.amazonrecords.com

Adelaide Hall

b. October 20, 1901, Brooklyn, NY;
d. November 7, 1993, London, England

Adelaide Hall is chiefly remembered for a three-minute recording that she made on October 26, 1927. Her haunting wordless vocal on "Creole Love Call" with Duke Ellington is her main claim to fame although she had a lengthy and productive career.

Hall grew up in Harlem, was an acrobatic roller skater as a child and in 1921 was in the chorus line of *Shuffle Along*. She worked in theaters and shows, went to Europe in May 1925 with the *Chocolate Kiddies* revue and, back in New York, was in the show *Desires Of 1927*. Hall made her recording debut with Ellington, although she was never a member of his orchestra. In addition to "Creole Love Call," she was featured on "The Blues I Love To Sing" and "Chicago Stomp Down," showing that she was a fine early scat singer.

As a performer in *Blackbirds Of 1928* on Broadway, Adelaide Hall helped to introduce "I Can't Give You Anything But Love." That year Hall recorded two numbers from the show with Lew Leslie's Blackbirds Orchestra: "I Must Have That Man" and "Baby." In 1931 she visited England, recording some songs with the backing of a two piano duet comprised of Francis J. Carter and Bennie Paine. Back in the United States, she often utilized two pianists, which in 1932 included Carter and Art Tatum. Tatum, who she brought to New York, made his recording debut with the singer. Hall appeared in the shows *Brown Bodies* and the *Cotton Club Revue*, recorded with Ellington in 1932 (again performing "I Must Have That Man" and "Baby") and visited Europe in 1936.

Adelaide Hall had a strong reputation as a musical comedy star overseas and she decided to stay, settling in England and becoming a British citizen in 1938. That year she finally recorded "I Can't Give You Anything But Love" (along with "That Old Feeling") while accompanied by the visiting Fats Waller. She was a popular attraction in England for decades, uplifting British spirits when she entertained during World War II in underground shelters during air raids. Although she visited the United States in 1957 to appear in the show Jamaica, Hall soon returned to England where she continued to work in a variety of theaters and clubs, more as a cabaret than a jazz singer. In 1988, Adelaide Hall summed up her long career during her one-woman show at Carnegie Hall. She lived to be 92, outliving everyone else associated with Duke Ellington in the 1920s.

Recommended CDs: *Hall Of Memories* (Conifer 169) has the most significant of Adelaide Hall's early recordings.

LPs to Search For: *That Wonderful Adelaide Hall* (Monmouth Evergreen 7080) and *Hall Of Ellington* (Columbia 6586) feature the vocalist in her later years, revisiting past glories and still singing quite well.

Kate Hammett-Vaughan

b. May 1, 1957, Halifax, NS, Canada

Kate Hammett-Vaughan convincingly sings standards yet also holds her own with the most avant-garde improvisers.

"I used to sit at the piano when I was young and sing along with the songs in my beginner piano books. Around the age of ten, I took up folk guitar and played in our church and local coffee houses. Through my teens I sang back-ups for my brother's rock bands and eventually started forming my own groups in my late teens when I went to the university." She names Joni Mitchell, Sheila Jordan and Betty Carter as three of her main inspirations. Hammett-Vaughan attended music school for one year (1975–76) at Acadia University but otherwise just had occasional private lessons. "I started singing 'professionally' (getting some money for gigs) in my middle teens. I got more serious about it in my early twenties when I moved to Vancouver, and really felt quite settled about it by my early thirties."

While she worked regularly in Vancouver during 1979–85, 1986 was a breakthrough year. "I attended the month-long Banff Jazz Workshop and had the opportunity to take classes with Jay Clayton, George Lewis, Muhal Richard Abrams, Dave Holland, Dave Liebman, Richie Beirach and others. This was my first encounter with modern harmonic concepts, open-form music and new ideas for personal expression." Vaughan began seriously exploring avant-garde music and

she has since worked with the NOW Orchestra (starting in 1988) and Garbo's Hat. "My work with the trio Garbo's Hat (with bassist Paul Blaney and saxophonist Graham Ord) during 1988–94 helped to establish a lot of stylistic ideas for me. Since then, my quintet (pianist Chris Gestrin, bassist André Lachance, saxophonist Jim Pinchin and drummer Tom Foster) has been my main musical project. I also have played in a voice/bass duo with André Lachance since 1992."

Few singers are as comfortable as Kate Hammett-Vaughan in exploring both free improvisations and standards. "I love the fact that the complete jazz tradition embraces both structured form and open improvisation, and that it offers a place where I can explore technical work and personal expression at the same time."

Recommended CDs: On *How My Heart Sings* (Maximum 063), *Devil May Care* (Maximum 201) and *Eclipse* (Maximum 14782), Kate Hammett-Vaughan stretches standards, being both respectful and constantly creative. *Face The Music* (Word Of Mouth 1006) from Garbo's Hat in 1994 features the singer really excelling in a freer setting.

Website: www.katehv.com

Annette Hanshaw

b. October 18, 1910, New York, NY;
d. March 13, 1985, New York, NY

One of the finest female jazz singers of the late 1920s/early '30s, Annette Hanshaw would be much better known today if she had had the desire to perform instead of choosing to retire so early from music.

Although she wanted to be a painter, in 1926 when she was just 15 she found that she could make money by singing. Hanshaw was discovered by her future husband Herman Rose who was the A&R man for the Pathe label, and she made her recording debut that year. Even at her very young age, she could be considered one of the first great female jazz singers. Annette spontaneously said "That's all!" when she finished one of her recordings and that became her trademark line, which was repeated at the end of numerous records. Billed as "The Personality Girl," she showed from the start that she knew how to swing lyrics. She was a superior interpreter of words, sometimes wrote additional verses to songs and she could improvise.

Considered a competitor of Ruth Etting (who was more of a pop singer), Hanshaw was Etting's equivalent in jazz. Her recordings of 1926 to 1934 are quite jazz-oriented, and include such sidemen as cornetists/trumpeters Red Nichols, Manny Klein, Phil Napoleon and Muggsy Spanier, trombonists Miff Mole, Tommy Dorsey and Jack Teagarden, clarinetists Jimmy Lytell, Benny Goodman and Jimmy Dorsey, bass saxophonist Adrian Rollini, violinist Joe Venuti, guitarist Eddie Lang and drummer Vic Berton. Among the songs that became closely identified with Hanshaw are "I'm Gonna Meet My Sweetie Now," "It All Depends On You," "Get Out And Get Under The Moon," "Daddy, Won't You Please Come Home," "Lovable And Sweet," "My Future Just Passed" and "We Just

Couldn't Say Goodbye." Her one film appearance, from a 1933 short (*Captain Henry's Showboat*), features her performing the latter song. In addition to singing in her own voice, Hanshaw also recorded some records under different names in which she expertly imitated the boop-boop-a-doop girl Helen Kane (a stereotyped flapper), using such pseudonyms as Gay Ellis, Patsy Young and Dot Dere.

Being an introvert, Annette Hanshaw much preferred recording and appearing on radio then singing in public or having a career in movies. In 1937, three years after her last recordings, the 26-year old retired from singing and slipped away into history. She was happily married for many years and worked at normal office jobs, being very surprised on the rare occasions when record collectors found her and raved about how much they loved her singing.

Recommended CDs: A comprehensive reissue of all of Annette Hanshaw's recordings was started by the Canadian Sensation label although the death of label head Jeff Healy may have ended it. So far they have released *Volume 5, 1928–29* (Sensation 769 748 022), *Volume 6, 1929* (Sensation 769 748 023) and *Volume 7, 1929–30* (Sensation 769 748 028). For more general collectors, *Lovable But Sweet* (Living Era 5220) is an excellent sampler that spans her entire career while *It Was So Beautiful* (Old Bean 614) has her final recordings from 1932 to 1934.

Julie Hardy
b. February 4, 1977, Danvers, MA

A promising singer who made her recording debut with 2005's *A Moment's Glance*, Julie Hardy is influenced in her improvising by Wayne Shorter and her teacher Dominique Eade.

"I have always been a singer. As a child I would make up songs that sounded like scat; I think it drove my parents crazy. When I was a little older I tried to sing like Whitney Houston and Mariah Carey and performed in my middle school variety show. Many of my early experiences singing jazz were with pianist Rob Martin. I started on piano at nine and was pretty serious about it in high school. I started as a piano major at the University of New Hampshire during my freshman year, but then switched to voice half way through."

Julie Hardy earned a Bachelor's degree in music theory and composition in 1999 from the University of New Hampshire and a Master's in Jazz Performance in 2001 from New England Conservatory, where she studied with Dominique Eade. She has since moved to New York, become associated musically and personally with pianist Randy Ingram and been inspired by her friend Fred Hersch. She became the first American singer ever signed to the Fresh Sound New Talent label in 2004, an early step in what promises to be a significant career.

Recommended CD: *A Moment's Glance* (Fresh Sound New Talent 215) features four of Julie Hardy's adventurous originals and a few reinvented versions of standards. Equally skilled at creating wordless sounds and expressing herself through lyrics, Hardy is an impressive force throughout her debut and on its follow-up, *The Wish* (World Culture 0003).

Website: www.juliehardy.com

Allen Harris
(John Allan Harris, III)
b. April 4, 1957, Brooklyn, NY

Allen Harris has an appealing baritone voice that is a mix between Nat King Cole and Tony Bennett. "In Catholic school

in the third grade, I sang 'Blue Velvet' for a talent contest. That's when the singing bug hit me." He played guitar from an early age and always knew that he'd be a singer and a guitarist. "What others call a profession I call my life. I don't know that I ever had a choice."

Allen Harris spent a long period learning his craft, but he really began to get noticed in the 1990s. Tony Bennett called him one of his favorite singers and Harris's recordings gained him attention. He had opportunities to be accompanied by such pianists as Tommy Flanagan, Cyrus Chestnut, Bill Charlap, Eric Reed and Benny Green. Harris performed and recorded with the Metropole Orchestra, revived the music of Billy Strayhorn, and recorded Duke Ellington's Sacred Mass. He also paid tribute to Nat King Cole at special concerts and, most recently in his project *Cross That River*, he paid homage to African-American cowboys, writing the material and singing in a vintage country style.

"Through my talent, I have been able to travel the world and be befriended by people of all cultures and walks of life. I hope in the future to keep touching people with my voice and my art, and to write the perfect song."

Recommended CDs: Thus far Allen Harris has recorded six albums: *Setting The Standard* (Love Productions 0001), *It's A Wonderful World* (Mons 874-765), *Here Comes Allan Harris* (Mons 874-771), which was recorded with the Metropole Orchestra, *Love Came—The Songs Of Strayhorn* (Love Productions 0002), *Cross That River* (Love Productions 0003) and a tribute to Nat King Cole called *Long Live The King* (Love Productions 0005).

Website: www.allanharris.com

Asa Harris
b. August 11, 1946, New York, NY

Although she has mostly been a part-time singer, Asa Harris sounds very impressive on her MaxJazz CD *All In Good Time*.

The daughter of pianist Ace Harris and the niece of Erskine Hawkins, Asa Harris grew up surrounded by music. "My earliest singing experiences were in choirs and plays in Catholic grade school. The sisters appreciated my family background and they made sure I developed my gifts for music and theater." She was a speech and drama major at Catholic University of America (later earning a degree elsewhere in Applied Behavioral Science and a Master's in Theology), was active as an actress in theater for years (appearing in the 1996 Robert Duvall movie *A Family Thing*), and has worked as a home hospice chaplain. In addition, she sang with Erskine Hawkins' band in the Catskills, taught jazz vocal performance at Webster University and has been active in bringing jazz into elementary and junior high schools.

"A major turning point for me was the deaths of my family members in the early nineties, ending with Erskine's in November 1993. I performed his music for a couple of years after, but understandably it wasn't the same. His music, because it was written for dancers, has been virtually overlooked by the academicians who dominate much of the recent resurgence in jazz repertory."

In 1999 Asa Harris finally had an opportunity to lead her own record date, and *All In Good Time*, which has her winning interpretations of standards (including Erskine Hawkins' theme song "Tuxedo Junction"), is a definitive outing. "My husband, son and other family members continue to express how much they miss my singing. I hope that eventually I'll find the time and energy to venture back into performance on a more full-time level."

Recommended CD: *All In Good Time* (Max Jazz 108) gives one a rare chance to experience the singing of Asa Harris.

Marion Harris
(Mary Ellen Harrison)
b. 1896, IN; d. April 23, 1944, New York, NY

MARION HARRIS
The Complete Victor Releases

Five months before the Original Dixieland Jazz Band became the first group to record jazz, Marion Harris was documented singing "I Ain't Got Nobody Much" (the "Much" would soon be dropped from its title) and "I'm Gonna Make Hay While The Sun Shines In Virginia." While those performances may not technically be jazz, they are awful close and show that Harris certainly had a feel for the new music. One of the top singers on records during 1916–20, Harris was one of the pioneering jazz vocalists, displaying a subtle laid-back delivery (a contrast to the "in-your-face" aggressiveness of an Al Jolson) that often hints at Ruth Etting and Annette Hanshaw from a decade later. She also made jazz history during her very last record date in 1934.

Marion Harris' early life is shrouded in mystery, including the exact date of her birth. Some accounts state that she ran away from a convent when she was 14 to sing on the stage. In any case, it was not long before she had prominent roles in such productions as Irving Berlin's *Stop, Look And Listen*, *Midnight Frolic* and *Yours Truly*. She was 20 when she first started recording for Victor in 1916 and among the other excellent (and surprisingly modern) recordings that she made during the following three years are "Paradise Blues," "My Syncopated Melody Man," "They Go Wild, Simply Wild, Over Me," "When I Hear That Jazz Band Play," "When Alexander Takes His Ragtime Band To France" and important early versions of such future standards as "After You've Gone," "A Good Man Is Hard To Find" and "Take Me To The Land Of Jazz."

Harris recorded in the 1920s for Columbia and Brunswick plus an additional date for Victor. Among the songs she helped popularize were "Look For The Silver Lining," "I'm Nobody's Baby," "Carolina In The Morning," "It Had To Be You," "Tea For Two," "I'll See You In My Dreams," "The Man I Love" and "More Than You Know." She worked steadily on the stage and starred in the hit *A Night In Spain* in 1927. Harris moved to London in 1931 where she continued her career as a cabaret performer.

For what would be her very last recording date, on August 2, 1934, Marion Harris recorded the second-ever example of vocalese. Bee Palmer, a dancer and vaudevillian, in 1929 had recorded a rendition of "Singin' The Blues" that had words written to parts of the recorded solo of Frank Trumbauer; she scatted the Bix chorus. However, Palmer's voice was not good, and the performance was not released until the 1990s. In 1934 Harris had her own crack at "Singin' The Blues," a coincidence since it is rather doubtful that she ever heard the unreleased Bee Palmer recording. Harris' version is far superior. After

taking the verse fairly straight, Harris sings words to both the Bix and Trumbauer solos (reversing the order of the original record) and sounds a bit like Eddie Jefferson from 20 years later. However, this record would have no real impact and vocalese would have to be "invented" again.

Marion Harris continued working in London until her home was destroyed during the Blitz in the early 1940s. She returned to New York, her health began to fail and she died one night when she fell asleep with a lit cigarette in her hand.

Recommended CD: *The Complete Victor Releases* (Archeophone 5001) has the very valuable early Marion Harris recordings. *Look For The Silver Lining* (Living Era 5330) is a good overview of her recordings although it leaves off "Singin' The Blues." Unfortunately most of her work in the 1920s has not yet been reissued, which is one reason she tends to be overlooked in discussions of early jazz singers. Few seem to realize that Marion Harris was the first jazz singer to record.

Wynonie Harris
b. August 24, 1915, Omaha, NE;
d. June 14, 1969, Los Angeles, CA

WYNONIE HARRIS
with ILLINOIS JACQUET · JACK McVEA · OSCAR PETTIFORD
Everybody Boogie!

Wynonie Harris sang swing, blues and R&B with passion and power, gaining the nickname of "Mr. Blues." But despite his versatility and the accessible subjects that he sang about (which quite often dealt with good times, parties and booze), he had a relatively brief career.

Harris began in show business as a dancer and drummer in addition to his singing, performing in shows in his native Omaha. Big Joe Turner was his idol. After moving to Los Angeles in 1940 and working as a singing emcee, Harris caught on while with the Lucky Millinder Orchestra in 1944. His hits, "Who Threw The Whiskey In The Well" and "Hurry, Hurry," resulted in him successfully beginning his solo career in 1945. Harris toured with Illinois Jacquet and Lionel Hampton, recording as a leader for Apollo, Aladdin and King. Among his biggest sellers were "Playful Baby," "Good Rockin' Tonight" (a major influence on early rock and roll), "All She Wants To Do Is Rock," "Good Morning Judge," "Lovin' Machine" and "Grandma Plays The Numbers." A constant on the R&B charts during 1946–52, he also had an opportunity to record a pair of duets with Big Joe Turner in 1947.

Harris was at the peak of his popularity in the early 1950s when he recorded for King. However, when his contract with the label ended in 1954, he slipped away into obscurity, one of the many victims of the rise of rock and roll that he ironically had helped inspire. Harris only recorded a total of 11 songs during 1956–64, none of which sold well. Although he lived until 1969 (passing away from cancer), Wynonie Harris spent his last decade running bars in Brooklyn and Los Angeles, being completely out of the spotlight and only singing on an occasional basis.

Recommended CDs: *Everybody Boogie* (Delmark 683) has Wynonie Harris' first selections as a leader other than his initial session and features such sidemen as tenors Illinois Jacquet, Jack McVea and Johnny Alston. *1945–1947* (Classics 1013) has the Harris-Turner duets (including the two-sided "Battle Of The Blues") and such songs as "In The Evening Blues," "Drinkin' By Myself," "Mr. Blues Jumped The Rabbit," "Big City Blues" and "Dig This Boogie"; the latter has the future avant-garde pianist Sun Ra featured during his recording debut. *1947–1949* (Classics 1139) and *1950–1952* (Classics 1289) have most of Harris' other hits and feature him and his brand of jump blues during the prime of his career.

Nancy Harrow
b. October 3, 1930, New York, NY

Nancy Harrow is a superior singer of standards who in recent times has developed into a fine songwriter herself. She took classical piano lessons from the age of seven from her aunt and continued through her college years. Harrow studied literature and dance, and planned originally to become a dancer. She toured with the Bennington Dance Group and choreographed dances to jazz scores. But instead she worked as an editor at William Morrow and Company for five years before deciding to become a singer.

Harrow worked briefly with the Tommy Dorsey Orchestra under the direction of Warren Covington and appeared in New York City clubs. "About a year before my first album, I sat in at Minton's with Kenny Burrell's group, and I was astonished to hear the audience talking back to me about the story I was telling. It made the song come alive for me, and I never forgot that experience."

Inspired by Billie Holiday, Lester Young, Ben Webster and Thelonious Monk, Harrow was heard singing in a club one night in 1960 by writer Nat Hentoff who at the time was running the Candid label. He soon produced her first album, *Wild Women Don't Have The Blues.* "The first album was a high point for me, because of the exhilaration of working with Buck Clayton, Dick Wellstood, and those great horn players from the Basie band. Another high point was when John Lewis heard me singing in a Paris club in 1961 (the Mars Club) and asked me to record with him for Atlantic Records. Working closely with John and then recording with that great quartet (John, Connie Kay, Jim Hall, and Richard Davis) was the best part of that experience." The latter album, *You Never Know,* should have really launched Nancy Harrow's career, but it would be 16 years before she recorded again. She raised a family and, although she had opportunities to perform in New York and Paris, her brand of jazz was overshadowed by rock. Harrow instead worked as the editor of *American Journal.*

In 1975 when she was 45, Nancy Harrow returned to singing, performing at the Cookery in New York. In 1978, she recorded *Anything Goes* with guitarist Jack Wilkins in a trio and has since recorded fairly regularly. In 1981, she wrote some lyrics to John Lewis' songs and by 1990 was writing both the words and music for her own originals. Harrow composed all of the music for her *The Lost Lady* CD and has written extensively for a children's jazz puppet show (*The Adventures Of Maya The Bee*), *The Cat Who Came To Heaven,* Nathaniel Hawthorne's *The Marble Faun* and *Winter Dreams: The Life And Passions Of F. Scott Fitzgerald,* often utilizing Roland Hanna's arrangements and the singing of Grady Tate.

"The albums I did with Dick Katz for Soul Note were a milestone (*Secrets* and *Lost Lady*) because they were the first recordings of tunes I had written myself and the first time I wrote songs based on a literary work. My 16-year association with Roland Hanna was the most significant to me in every way—first as an accompanist, he was the most empathic and perceptive accompanist I ever worked with—almost a mind

reader. And then to work with him as a collaborator on my tunes was extraordinary—he was so supportive and encouraging and involved, and patient. We did two albums together of standards (*You're Nearer* and the Beatles album) and three CDs of my songs—(*Maya, Marble Faun* and *Winter Dreams*) as well as club dates and concerts."

As far as future musical goals go, Nancy Harrow says that she wants "to continue to write songs based on literary works that I admire and to see where this leads me. So far it has led me to a theatrical presentation, to the world of puppetry, perhaps to animated film, even to doll manufacturing. I look forward to whatever adventure awaits me."

Recommended CDs: *Wild Women Don't Have The Blues* (Candid 79006) from late 1960 features the young Nancy Harrow in a swing setting. *Anything Goes* (Audiophile 142) from 1978 signaled the beginning of her second career and among the many recordings that have followed are *You're Nearer* (Baldwin Street Music 203), *Street Of Dreams* (Gazell 2005), *Secrets* (Soul Note 121133), *Lost Lady* (Soul Note 121263), *The Marble Faun* (Harbringer 1707) and *Winter Dreams* (Artist's House 0001).

LPs to Search For: Harrow's second album, *You Never Know* (Atlantic 8075), and a set of duets with guitarist Jack Wilkins titled *Two's Company* (Inner City 1159), are long overdue to be reissued.

Website: www.nancyharrow.com

Johnny Hartman
b. July 13 (also listed as July 3 and 23), 1923, Chicago, IL; d. September 15, 1983, New York, NY

Johnny Hartman would be famous in jazz if only for his 1963 classic ballad album *John Coltrane And Johnny Hartman,* which includes the definitive versions of "Lush Life" and "My One And Only Love." His warm baritone voice made him a perfect singer of ballads and romantic material.

Hartman actually took a long time to get his career going and he never did prosper. He studied voice at the Chicago Musical College, served in the military, sang with the last Earl Hines big band (recording four numbers in 1947) and was a member of the Dizzy Gillespie Orchestra (1948–49). His ballad recordings with Gillespie were sincere, but not very memorable (particularly compared to the band's instrumentals) with Hartman sounding like a substitute for his main influence, Billy Eckstine. The same can be said for his early solo sides, which include ten titles for Savoy (1947) and eight for Mercury (1948–49), including four with the Erroll Garner Trio with whom he worked regularly for two months.

By the mid-1950s, Hartman was in his prime. He recorded two excellent albums for Bethlehem (1955–56) and one for Roost (1958) that mostly focus on ballads although there are a few medium-tempo selections, too. Despite the albums' excellence, he remained fairly obscure in jazz, working in clubs but not getting much recognition.

The 1963 collaboration with Coltrane made Hartman immortal. He followed that set up with two other excellent Impulse albums (*I Just Dropped By To Say Hello* and *The Voice That Is*). But although his voice remained strong, and there were a few more worthy recordings (for Perception, Japanese Capitol, Bee Hive and Audiophile), Hartman never really caught on commercially. Perhaps Hartman was just too limited or inflexible to carve out a major career for himself. Although not completely forgotten, at the time of his death at the age of 60, Johnny Hartman had had a fairly low profile for years. Ironically in 1995, 12 years after his death, Hartman came the closest he ever did to becoming a household name when Clint Eastwood used some of his recordings in the soundtrack of his romantic movie *Bridges Of Madison County*.

Recommended CDs: No vocal jazz collection is complete without *John Coltrane And Johnny Hartman* (Impulse 157). *The Johnny Hartman Collection 1947–1972* (Hip-O 40137), a two-CD set, has most of the high points from Hartman's career, including the best of his early titles and only missing his last five albums, three of which are less significant. *Song From The Heart* (Bethlehem 79773), *All Of Me* (Bethlehem 79849) and *And I Thought About You* (Roost 57456) show how mature a singer Hartman was by the mid-1950s. The follow-up to the Coltrane/Hartman classic was *I Just Dropped By To Say Hello* (Impulse 176), which teams Hartman with tenor great Illinois Jacquet quite successfully. *The Voice That Is* (Impulse 144) is also quite worthwhile. *For Trane* (Blue Note 35346) reissues all but four titles from a pair of Japanese Capitol albums from 1972. *Thank You For Everything* (Audiophile 165) has all of the music from a pair of radio shows that Hartman made with Alec Wilder in which he focused on the music of Cole Porter and Billy Strayhorn (including a remake of "Lush Life") while *This One's For Tedi* (Audiophile 181) from 1980 shows that Hartman never did decline musically.

LPs to Search For: 1980's *Once In Every Life* (Bee Hive 7012), recorded 12 days before *This One's For Tedi*, has not been reissued, yet although many of the numbers were used by Clint Eastwood in *Bridges Of Madison County*.

Clancy Hayes
(Clarence Leonard Hayes)
b. November 14, 1908, Caney, KS;
d. March 3, 1972, San Francisco, CA

Most Dixieland bands feature one or two of their musicians taking occasional vocals for variety, allowing the horn players to rest. While often effective when heard live, these vocals are rarely worth documenting for the musicians generally do not have great voices. Clancy Hayes was a major exception.

Hayes had a long career, but did not really come into his own on records until the 1950s. As a banjoist and singer, Hayes led the Harmony Aces when he was a teenager. He came West in 1923, playing in his brother's band in Oakland and touring the Midwest with a vaudeville show. Hayes worked in San Francisco from 1927 on, appearing regularly on the radio as a member of the NBC staff and in clubs. He met trumpeter Lu Watters in 1938, helped put together an orchestra for Watters that lasted two years, and then spent the 1940s off and on with Watters' Yerba Buena Jazz Band, a very important group in the New Orleans revival movement. Ironically Hayes played banjo, rhythm guitar and occasionally drums with Watters, but did not record any vocals. Instead he made his vocal debut on records in 1946 when he cut a few titles with the Frisco Jazz Band including his most famous composition, "A-Huggin' And A-Chalkin'." While Hayes' version (cut for the tiny Pacific label) is obscure, the song became a hit for Hoagy Carmichael. Hayes also recorded a handful of titles for Mercury and Down Home as a leader during 1949–50.

Clancy Hayes gained his greatest fame during 1949–59 when he was a member of Bob Scobey's band. He was well featured on vocals with Scobey, particularly on their records for Good Time Jazz and Verve, singing such numbers as "Coney Island Washboard," "Sailin' Down Chesapeake Bay," "Ace In The Hole," "Silver Dollar," "St. James Infirmary," a remake of "A-Huggin' And A-Chalkin'" and a variety of good time standards. After Scobey relocated to Chicago, Hayes became homesick for San Francisco and departed in 1959.

In the 1960s, Hayes recorded five albums as a leader (including one with the perfectly fitting title of *Swingin' Minstrel*), he worked with Turk Murphy, the Firehouse Five Plus Two and an early version of the World's Greatest Jazz Band, and toured as a single. He remained a popular figure in San Francisco up until the time of his death. As a good-humored interpreter of vintage standards with a Dixieland backing, Clancy Hayes has never been topped.

Recommended CDs: *Swingin' Minstrel* (Good Time Jazz 10050) and *Oh! By Jingo* (Delmark 210) from 1963 to 1964 are Hayes' definitive sets as leader. His singing is also well featured with Bob Scobey on *Vol. 1, The Scobey Story* (Good Time Jazz 12032), *The Scobey Story, Vol. 2* (Good Time Jazz 12033), *Bob Scobey's Frisco Band* (Good Time Jazz 12006), *Direct From San Francisco* (Good Time Jazz 12023) and the best of the lot, *Scobey And Clancy* (Good Time Jazz 12009).

LPs to Search For: Hayes' other albums as a leader, *Dixieland* (Audio Fidelity 1937), *Happy Melodies* (ABC-Paramount 519) with the Lawson-Haggart Band and *Live At Earthquake McGoon's* (ABC-Paramount 591) with Turk Murphy, are all quite scarce. Also quite enjoyable are a pair of long out-of-print Scobey albums: *Bob Scobey's Frisco Band With Clancy Hayes* (Verve 1001) and *The San Francisco Jazz Of Bob Scobey* (Verve 1011).

Stephanie Haynes
b. July 31, 1945, Glendale, CA

Stephanie Haynes has long had one of the best voices in Los Angeles, although she has not recorded half as often as one wishes.

"My earliest experience singing was in a kids' choir in a Lutheran Church circa 1950. I started taking piano lessons when I was about five or six. I had a lot of trouble with the concept of reading music, but would occasionally get over just by having a good ear. I began flute lessons at age eight, and continued on until after I had married and dropped out of college, when I was about 22. I first imagined being a singer in the middle of my second year at UCSB. I remember telling one of the faculty that I wanted to be a jazz singer and his response being 'You've chosen a rough row to hoe.' It wasn't until many years later, after moving around a lot and being

Lucille Hegamin

divorced, that I actually began what you could call a career as a singer." In 1974, while living in Albuquerque, Stephanie Haynes began to sing professionally, at first with top-40 groups and at lounge and funk/dance clubs. By 1980 she had moved to Orange County and was singing jazz in Laguna Beach clubs with the late pianist Kent Glenn, her mentor. "He taught me good from bad, musically speaking. I am indebted to him for my repertoire of almost 600 songs."

In the 1990s, Haynes often performed duets with the adventurous pianist Dave Mackay, staying perfectly in-tune and close to the melody while Mackay played wildly behind her; it was a perfect matchup. She also sang with vocalist-bassist Jack Prather in Bopsicle and appeared in a variety of settings in Los Angeles. "I enjoy the challenge of reworking material, listening for twist and turns in the music that I didn't hear the last time. I respect the composer's intent and at the same time I attempt to add something of my own."

Recommended CDs: Stephanie Haynes made her recording debut with 1988's *Here's That Rainy Day* (Discovery 70556) and teamed up with pianist Pete Jolly and tenor-saxophonist Jack Montrose on *Dawn At Dana Point* (Holt 3305). She is also on *Bopsicle* (Why Not 1002), but her best recording is *Two On A Swing* (Why Not 1001), a set of challenging and sometimes hair-raising duets with pianist Dave Mackay.

Lucille Hegamin
(Lucille Nelson)
b. November 29, 1894, Macon, GA;
d. March 1, 1970, New York, NY

The surprise success of Mamie Smith's "Crazy Blues" recording in 1920 led to scores of female African-American singers getting a chance to make records during 1920–23 before most were dropped by the labels as the blues fad passed. Lucille Hegamin was the first to be signed up after Mamie Smith, making her initial record in November 1920, just three months after "Crazy Blues."

She first sang in a church choir in her native Georgia. At 15 in 1910, young Lucille Nelson toured with the Leonard Harper Minstrel Stock Company, working in the South before moving to Chicago. She hooked up with pianist Bill Hegamin in 1914. Their marriage lasted until 1923. The singer also worked with pianists Jelly Roll Morton and Tony Jackson (introducing the latter's "Pretty Baby"), and she spent time living in Los Angeles.

Near the end of 1919, Hegamin moved to New York where she immediately made a strong impression. A vaudevillian rather than a lowdown blues singer, Hegamin was versatile and able to sound quite credible on both blues and current pop tunes. Her early recordings, although primitively recorded, still sound good today. Hegamin's renditions of "I'll Be Good But I'll Be Lonesome" and "Arkansas Blues" were hits in 1921 and she introduced "He May Be Your Man But He Comes To See Me Sometimes." She toured with her Blue Flame Syncopators (a couple years later her group was renamed the Dixie Daisies) and was billed as "The Chicago Cyclone—Blues Singer Supreme." Hegamin recorded 94 songs during 1920–26 and worked in several Broadway shows, including Sissle and Blake's famous *Shuffle Along*. But by the late 1920s, Hegamin was a minor figure, particularly compared to Bessie Smith and Ethel Waters, and her style was considered out-of-date. She recorded two final selections in 1932, worked at Atlantic City during 1933–34 and then left music altogether, becoming a nurse in 1938.

Over 20 years later, Lucille Hegamin re-emerged, recording four songs for a Bluesville LP that featured survivors of the 1920s and singing three numbers on a 1962 album on the Spivey label. But she did not make a serious comeback and, other than appearing at a few charity benefits, she went back into retirement, living to the age of 75.

Recommended CDs: All of Lucille Hegamin's recordings from 1920 to 1932 are on *Vol. 1–3* (Document 5419, 5420 and 5421).

Lenora Zenzalai Helm
b. August 15, 1961, Chicago, IL

A versatile singer and educator, Lenora Zenzalai Helm keeps so busy that she tends to be a bit underrated, except by those who are familiar with her talents.

"My father, who was a painter, always played jazz music at home. He would sing all the jazz standards to me. When I was in high school, I sang in an R&B band and after band practice the musicians would play albums of many different types of music. It was then that I first heard John Coltrane and Billie Holiday." Sarah Vaughan became her favorite singer and, while retaining a love for R&B, she began to move toward jazz. Helm attended the Berklee College of Music during 1979–82, graduating with a BA in Film Music Compositions and Voice. While at Berklee she met Donald Brown (originally her piano teacher), with whom she collaborated on many projects since that time. She also became good friends with Branford Marsalis who gave her ideas on how to focus her goals. "From the time I arrived in NY in 1987 there have been countless musicians who have taught me various things, including Geri Allen, Ron Carter, Stanley Cowell, Andrew Hill, Dr. Billy Taylor, Nasheet Waits (my significant other) and Antonio Hart."

Since moving to New York, she has worked with Andrew Hill, Michael Franks, Freddie Jackson, Kenny Garrett, Illinois Jacquet, Javon Jackson, Dave Liebman, Greg Osby, Antonio Hart, Branford Marsalis, Mark Whitfield, Geri Allen, Stanley Cowell, Junior Mance, James Williams and Donald Brown. Helm led her jazz trio the Zenzalai Project, was involved with an R&B/jazz vocal group Sepia and recorded with Andrew Hill during his 2003 Jazzpar tour. Her compositions and lyrics have been recorded by others and she wrote for the off-Broadway musical play *The Sun And The Moon Live In The Sky*. Leonora Helm was a U.S. Jazz Ambassador during 1998–99, touring abroad and representing the United States.

"A huge turning point for me was the decision to start teaching and to develop my skills and resume as a teaching artist. Teaching has developed my performance and creativity in ways I never imagined. Teaching is like learning twice." She has worked steadily as a music teacher and clinician, lobbied to get jazz into schools and is the artistic director and co-founder of HARMONY, which has college music students teaching youngsters living in public housing. Helm also heads the vocal jazz department at Cultural Arts Performing Arts High School in Syosset, New York.

"In the future I hope to record a CD of all original compositions, write music, arrange composers' works for Langston Hughes text, score for film and grow HARMONY until it is available in every large city across the country. I am also writing a book profiling about 25 teaching artists and demystifying the field for aspiring teaching artists."

Recommended CDs: Since independently releasing *Awakenings* in 1995, Lenora Zenzalai Helm's three releases are *Spirit Child* (Jcurve 1005), which is a mixture of jazz and R&B; *Precipice* (Baoule 604998) on which she performs challenging material with a quartet that includes pianist Stanley Cowell and trumpeter Duane Eubanks; and *Voice Paintings* (Midlantic 207). The latter is her strongest set to date, featuring her singing, some of her composing and lyrics, and consistently superior material.

Website: www.lenorahelm.com

Carla Helmbrecht
b. November 11, 1967, Nennah, WI

A very good singer who reshapes standards in subtle ways, Carla Helmbrecht is based in the San Francisco Bay area.

"I have a large, music-loving family. When I was five years old, I recall my best friend asking me on the playground, 'What are you going to be when you grow up?' I confidently replied, 'A professional singer.' I'm not sure how long I had the idea brewing before that moment, but I was so glad that someone finally asked me." She began playing piano when she was eight, started singing professionally at weddings when she was 12, played oboe for six years in junior and high school concert bands, and discovered jazz as a teenager. At 18 her father and uncle took her to Nashville where she recorded four songs on 45s.

Helmbrecht attended Texas Tech University where she earned bachelor's and master's degrees in Speech-Language Pathology, graduating Summa Cum Laude both times. She also played and sang with the TTU big band (they recorded the Sea Breeze album *Seein' The Light…Hearin' The Hub-tones*) and supported herself by singing in nightclubs and jazz bars. In 1994 Helmbrecht recorded her debut solo recording, *One For My Baby*, and she soon relocated to the San Francisco Bay area. Since that time Carla Helmbrecht has performed with the Black Market Jazz Orchestra (and is on their 1998 CD *Season's Greetings*), worked regularly in Northern California and made two further solo recordings.

Recommended CDs: *One For My Baby* (Heart 10) features Carla Helmbrecht at her best on such ballads as "It Never Entered My Mind," "Song To A Seagull" and "Dream A Little Dream Of Me," assisted in the octet by pianist Frank Mantooth who contributed the arrangements. 2001's *Be Cool, Be Kind* (Heart 24) features tenor-saxophonist Ernie Watts with "Easy Love" (which she co-wrote with pianist Peter Horvath), "The Party's Over" and "Windmills Of Your Mind" being

most impressive. *Here's To Love* (Pony Canyon) from 2004 has thus far only been released in Japan.

Website: www.carlahelmbrecht.com

Bill Henderson
b. March 19, 1926, Chicago, IL

Bill Henderson has always had a deep voice and a likable style. He can be compared to Joe Williams and Ernie Andrews, but also has his own melodic approach to interpreting lyrics.

"My father had the first voice I wanted to sound like and he was not in show business. My brother Finis was a great tap dancer. He knew everybody and first introduced me to Joe Williams; I admired him so." Henderson began singing professionally in 1952 after being discharged from the military. Other than a few singles, he first recorded with Vee Jay in Chicago in 1958. Henderson worked with Ramsey Lewis, moved to New York, and had a hit with Horace Silver's "Senor Blues." Although he made a variety of strong sessions for Vee Jay during 1959–61, recorded with the Oscar Peterson Trio in 1963 and worked with the Count Basie Orchestra during 1965–66, he never really made it big in a commercial fashion.

Henderson settled in Los Angeles, worked as an actor, and in the 1970s performed and recorded with a group that also featured pianist Dave Mackay and pianist-singer Joyce Collins. Today his voice is still in prime form. Bill Henderson is long overdue to be recorded again and to be celebrated for his fine singing.

Recommended CDs: *His Complete Vee Jay Recordings, Vol. 1* (Koch 8548) teams Henderson up with the Ramsey Lewis Trio, Booker Little, Yusef Lateef, Frank Wess and others throughout a superlative program. His *Complete Vee Jay Recordings, Vol. 2* (Koch 8572) continues the complete reissue of all of his 1959–61 recordings as Henderson is heard with the Count Basie Orchestra, string ensembles and combos with Eddie Harris and Tommy Flanagan. *Bill Henderson With The Oscar Peterson Trio* (Verve 283 793 729) features the singer in 1963 at his peak while inspired by the accompaniment of Oscar Peterson, Ray Brown and Ed Thigpen. Of his 1970s work on Discovery, *Land At The Times* (Discovery 779) and *Something's Gotta Give* (Discovery 932) have returned on CD.

LPs to Search For: *Street Of Dreams* (Discovery 882) and *Tribute To Johnny Mercer* (Discovery 846) feature Bill Henderson during his middle period.

Rosa Henderson
(Rosa Deschamps)
b. November 24, 1896, Henderson, KY;
d. April 6, 1968, New York, NY

A fine classic blues singer whose career peaked in the 1920s, Rosa Henderson was not related to Fletcher Henderson, although he appeared on some of her records. She started her career in 1913, singing with her uncle's carnival troupe. She worked in vaudeville, married comedian Douglas "Slim" Henderson in 1918, and in the 1920s performed in such musical comedies and shows as *The Priceless Funny Revue*, *Quintard Miller's Revue*, *Seventh Avenue Affairs*, *The Harlem Rounders Revue* and *Brunettes Preferred*.

Henderson recorded 88 selections during 1923–27, including "Good Woman's Blues," "I Ain't No Man's Slave," the classic "So Long To You And The Blues," "He May Be Your Dog But He's Wearing My Collar," "Don't Advertise Your Man" and "Somebody's Doin' What You Wouldn't Do." In addition to using her own name, Henderson recorded under such pseudonyms as Flora Dale, Rosa Green, Mae Harris, Mamie Harris, Sara Johnson, Sally Ritz (her sister's name), Josephine Thomas, Gladys White and Bessie Williams.

In 1928 Henderson's husband died, and she began to lose interest in performing. She did visit London that year to perform in *Showboat*. Her final record date, two songs cut in 1931 with backing by James P. Johnson, show that Henderson had continued to evolve and mature as a singer. But she chose to retire altogether the following year, working in a department store. Unlike other classic blues singers who survived into the 1960s, Rosa Henderson never attempted to make a comeback or record again. Other than appearing at a few charity benefits, her career was completely over by the time she made it into her late thirties, although she lived to be 71.

Recommended CDs: All of Bertha Henderson's recordings are available on *Vols. 1–4* (Document 5401, 5402, 5403 and 5404).

Jon Hendricks

b. September 16, 1921, Newark, OH

The "genius of vocalese," Jon Hendricks is at the top of the field in writing lyrics to recorded solos. He is also a brilliant lyricist in general, one of the best of the bop singers and the epitome of hip.

Growing up in Toledo as one of 17 children, Hendricks sang as a kid with a local pianist named Art Tatum. He had opportunities to work on the radio, but it would be some time before his career took off. Hendricks served in the military during 1942–46 and, after his discharge, he studied law but music interested him much more. He played drums for two years and was inspired when Charlie Parker, passing through Ohio, heard him sing and urged him to move to New York and be a jazz singer.

In 1952 Hendricks took Bird's advice, and he had a little luck as a songwriter when Louis Jordan recorded his "I Want You To Be My Baby." In 1955, he recorded his vocalese versions of "Four Brothers" and "Cloudburst" on a Decca single with backing by the Dave Lambert Singers, but it failed to create a stir. In 1957, he was urged by Dave Lambert to write vocalese lyrics to the music of Count Basie. At first they recorded with a group of other singers but, other than Annie Ross, the other vocalists did not have the right feel for the music. After much discussion, Lambert, Hendricks and Ross overdubbed their voices several times to emulate a big band and the resulting recording, *Sing A Song Of Basie*, was a hit in the jazz world. Lambert, Hendricks and Ross performed and recorded frequently during the next five years. When Ross

dropped out in 1962, Yolande Bevan took her place until the group broke up in 1964.

During his period with Lambert, Hendricks and Ross (or Bevan), Hendricks led five albums of his own, including a tribute to João Gilberto and songs from his 1960 show *Evolution Of The Blues*, which had played at the Monterey Jazz Festival. After he resumed his solo career, Hendricks lived in Europe during 1968–72, not recording again until 1972. He moved to San Francisco, taught, wrote about jazz for a period for the *San Francisco Chronicle*, revived *Evolution Of The Blues* (which ran for years) and resumed recording. He was able to build upon the legacy of Lambert, Hendricks and Ross when he formed Hendricks and Company, enlisting his wife Judith, his daughter Michelle and a fourth singer, which for a time was Bobby McFerrin. Among his other projects during the years since have been writing and recording with the Manhattan Transfer for their *Vocalese* project, playing one of the lead roles in Wynton Marsalis' *Blood In The Fields*, having a few reunions with Annie Ross, performing in clubs and at festivals, making guest appearances on recordings by Kurt Elling and Karrin Allyson, being the Professor of Jazz Studies at the University of Toledo since 2000, touring in 2003 with Kurt Elling, Mark Murphy and Kevin Mahogany as "Four Brothers," and always writing new lyrics. Although his voice at 86 has naturally faded, his brilliance and storytelling abilities remain undiminished and he is still the hippest cat around.

Recommended CDs: *A Good Git Together* (EMI 69812), Jon Hendricks' first album as a leader, is an underrated gem from 1959 that teams him with Wes Montgomery, the Adderley Brothers and altoist Pony Poindexter, singing bebop rather than vocalese (as a contrast to his work with Lambert, Hendricks and Ross). *Evolution Of The Blues Song* (Columbia Special Products 8383) goes through the history of the blues from spirituals to swing and bebop with Hendricks joined by Big Miller and Jimmy Witherspoon. *Recorded In Person At The Trident* (Smash 314 510 601) has Hendricks summing up his musical career up to 1965, highlighted by "Watermelon Man," "Old Folks," "Cloudburst," "Shiny Stockings" and the always-funny "Gimme That Wine." *Cloudburst* (Enja 4032) from 1972 ended Hendricks' long period off of records with a solid quartet date. *Tell Me The Truth* (BMG 37392) from 1975 is notable for Hendricks' versions of "Naima," "On The Trail" and "Old Folks," with the Pointer Sisters helping out on "Flat Foot Floogie." *Love* (Muse 5258) features Hendricks and Company performing his lyrics to such numbers as "Groove Merchant," "Bright Moments" and "Harlem Airshaft"; there are also spots for trumpeter Harry "Sweets" Edison and Jerome Richardson on tenor.

Freddie Freeloader (Denon 81757 6302) is a classic outing from 1989 to 1990. The title cut has Hendricks (John Coltrane), Bobby McFerrin (Wynton Kelly), George Benson (Cannonball Adderley) and Al Jarreau (Miles Davis) bringing back the 1959 recording in memorable fashion. Other selections feature the Manhattan Transfer, the Count Basie Orchestra, Wynton Marsalis, Al Grey and Stanley Turrentine plus Judith Hendricks, who sings Louis Armstrong's solos on "Star Dust" and "Swing That Music." *Boppin' At The Blue Note* (Telarc 83320) from 1993 has Hendricks scatting, sounding jubilant on "Get Me To The Church On Time," persuading Wynton Marsalis to make his vocal debut (scatting on "Everybody's Boppin'"), featuring Michelle Hendricks on some numbers, and performing three Count Basie vocalese charts with Kevin Burke and Judith, Michele and Aria Hendricks.

LPs to Search For: *Fast Livin' Blues* (Columbia 1805) and *Salud! João Gilberto* (Reprise (20167), which includes some of

Hendricks' lyrics to Antonio Carlos Jobim songs, are both from 1963 and remain scarce.

Website: www.jonhendricks.com

Michele Hendricks

Michele Hendricks, a fine singer in her own right, is the daughter of Jon Hendricks. She grew up around jazz, started singing when she was eight and sometimes accompanied her father on road trips, occasionally singing with him on stage. She was a dance and drama student at Gradison College in London, in the 1970s; joined Jon Hendricks and Company; and in the 1980s performed in the *Evolution Of The Blues* show.

Unlike her mother, who has not had a solo career, Michele Hendricks has performed outside of her father's groups. She recorded three albums of her own for Muse during 1987–90. Although still appearing with her father on an occasional basis, Michele Hendricks lives in Paris, teaches in schools, directs workshops and occasionally performs at concerts. A talented vocalist, she deserves to record more frequently.

Recommended CDs: All three of Michele Hendricks' CDs, *Carryin' On* (Muse 5336), *Keepin' Me Satisfied* (Muse 5363) and *Me And My Shadow* (Muse 5404), are out-of-print due to the sale of Muse. *Carryin' On* features Stan Getz, Ralph Moore and pianist David Leonhart on a boppish set. *Keepin' Me Satisfied* teams Hendricks with Leonhart, Claudio Roditi, David "Fathead" Newman and Slide Hampton (Jon Hendricks sits in on "Everybody's Boppin'"), and *Me And My Shadow* is the most individual of the programs, with her joined by just a trio. In each case, Michele Hendricks contributes a few originals. She has since recorded *A Little Bit Of Ella* with the late pianist Tommy Flanagan but that set has only thus far been available in Europe.

Nicole Henry
b. March 17, Philadelphia, PA

Nicole Henry made a strong impression in 2005 with the release of her CD *The Nearness Of You*. She sang in school and church choirs as a youth and studied cello for six years. "I will always remember the 'charge' my fifth grade teacher, Susan Boyle, gave me. She empowered me to continue sharing whatever good I felt, and she told me that it would make a difference in people's lives." In college she received a scholarship to study architecture but graduated with a degree in advertising and theater.

Nicole Henry knew that she wanted to be a singer in 2000. "I knew it after the first few days of a six week tour as a background singer for Robert Bradley's *Blackwater Surprise* in 2000. I had traveled to gigs that lasted one or two days when I was singing dance music right out of college, but once I was able to do it day after day, city after city, I knew there was nothing else for me to do."

Nicole Henry has worked as an actress, a spokesperson and as an R&B singer. She was introduced to jazz when she sang in Miami Beach. "I was opening for a few jazz and R&B bands. One night a bass player named Paul Shewchuk invited me to learn some jazz tunes and do a gig with his trio. I had never truly, consciously, listened to jazz before, particularly, not straight-ahead jazz but I soon found that I loved it." Since then the Florida-based singer has performed throughout the United States, Korea, Japan, Mexico and England.

Recommended CDs: *The Nearness Of You* (Banister 2798) features Nicole Henry performing ten standards and two of

her originals ("Get Here" is memorable), singing in a passionate style that falls between jazz and R&B. Her second release, *Teach Me Tonight* (Venus 35346) with the Eddie Higgins Trio is thus far only available in Japan.

Website: www.nicolehenry.com

Woody Herman
b. May 16, 1913, Milwaukee, WI;
d. October 19, 1987, Los Angeles, CA

Woody Herman was very significant as a leader of big bands, he was a masterful talent scout and he was an underrated clarinetist and alto-saxophonist. However, few of his fans probably realize that in his first band, the majority of the recordings feature Herman's effective ballad singing.

Herman had a lengthy and very productive career. He began performing as a singer and dancer in vaudeville while still a child. He was 11 when he started playing alto and 14 when he began doubling on clarinet. Herman was just 15 when he worked with the bands of Myron Stewart and Joe Lichter in 1928. A five-year stint with Tom Gerun's orchestra (1929–34) was followed by brief stays with the big bands of Harry Sosnick and Gus Arnheim. As a member of Isham Jones' dance band during 1934–36, Herman had occasional solos and also recorded a few vocals including "There Is No Greater Love," "I've Had The Blues So Long" and "Fan It."

In the summer of 1936, Jones broke up his group and Herman took over the nucleus to form his first big band. Of the Woody Herman Orchestra's initial 33 recordings from its first two years, 28 have vocals by the leader. While some of the tunes are dated ballads and throwaways, Herman sounds best on "Doctor Jazz," "Dupree Blues," "Trouble In Mind" and "Lullaby In Rhythm." After struggling for a long time without a musical personality, on April 12, 1939, the Woody Herman Orchestra's recording of "Woodchopper's Ball" became a hit and the group started being billed as "the band that plays the blues." While its jazz content rose a bit and there were more instrumentals, Herman remained the orchestra's main attraction, having vocals on 30 of its 45 recordings from 1940. Herman's most convincing vocals from 1939 to 1942 are on "Jumpin' Blues," "Fine And Dandy," "Blue Prelude," "Mister Meadowlark," a remake of "Fan It," "Amen" and "Four Or Five Times."

During 1943–44, Herman's orchestra gradually evolved from being a second-level swing dance band into the rollicking and witty First Herd. Although he was occasionally featured on a ballad vocal (most notably "Laura," which he was the first to sing), Herman's vocalizing became more jazz-oriented starting with 1943's "Do Nothin' Till You Hear From Me." The songs "Milkman, Keep Those Bottles Quiet," "It Must Be Jelly," "Caldonia," "I've Got The World On A String," "Put That Ring On My Finger," "Your Father's Mustache," "Let It Snow, Let It Snow, Let It Snow," and yet another version of "Fan It," show the range of his singing during 1943–46.

The First Herd (with tenor-saxophonist Flip Phillips, trombonist Bill Harris and frequently riotous ensembles) was

Al Hibbler

Herman's most popular band. He broke it up near the end of 1946 so as to spend more time with his family, but after a year out of the band business (during which he recorded quite a few vocals with both small groups and large orchestras), he came back with his Second Herd (nicknamed "The Four Brothers" band) in the fall of 1947. Herman's vocals (best on "I Told Ya I Love Ya, Now Get Out" and "I've Got News For You") were an accessible element in the repertoire of the cool bop orchestra, best known for its sax section (tenors Stan Getz, Zoot Sims and Herbie Steward plus baritonist Serge Chaloff) and such songs as "Four Brothers" and "Early Autumn."

The Second Herd failed to make money and disbanded at the end of 1949. Herman put together the Third Herd (a slightly more danceable variation of the first two Herds) in 1950, and led big bands on and off during the decade. In addition to singing on every fourth or fifth song with the big band ("Laura" and "Caldonia" remained in the band's book), Herman recorded a pair of fine vocal albums: *Music For Tired Lovers* and *Songs For Hip Lovers.*

After being a hit at the 1959 Monterey Jazz Festival with a specially assembled orchestra, Herman had success in the early 1960s with his Young Thundering Herd featuring tenor-saxophonist Sal Nistico, trombonist Phil Wilson and high-note trumpeter Bill Chase. Herman rarely sang with that particular outfit with one unfortunate exception. For unexplainable reasons, in 1966 Herman recorded a full album of vocals (*The Jazz Swinger*) of tunes associated with Al Jolson. It was a flop on all levels.

While many instrumentalists sing more often in their later years, Woody Herman went in the opposite direction. After 1966, other than "Caldonia" (which he recorded again as late as 1983) and, less often, "I've Got News For You," Woody Herman rarely sang. He continued leading his big band up until the time of his death in 1987, 51 years after forming his first orchestra.

Recommended CDs: Woody Herman's early vocals are reissued on *1936–1937* (Classics 1042), *1937–1938* (Classics 1090), *1939* (Classics 1128), *1939–1940* (Classics 1163), *1940* (Classics 1243) and *1940–1941* (Classics 1304). *Songs For Hip Lovers* (Verve 314 559 872) from 1956 has Herman sticking exclusively to singing while joined by an all-star cast, which includes trumpeters Harry "Sweets" Edison and Charlie Shavers and tenor-saxophonist Ben Webster. *The Jazz Swinger/Music For Tired Lovers* (Collectables 6679) combines together the odd Jolson tribute with *Music For Tired Lovers*, a fine 1954 album that teams Herman with the Erroll Garner Trio.

Al Hibbler
b. August 16, 1915, Tyro, MS; d. April 24, 2001, Chicago, IL

Al Hibbler had an eccentric style that Duke Ellington called "tonal pantomime." His unusual accents of syllables and his fast vibrato were odd enough but his occasional use of a British accent often seemed bizarre. Hibbler could sing conventionally, but he relished in being unpredictable.

Born blind, Al Hibbler first sang in a school choir, graduating to singing the blues in Texas and Arkansas. His early influences were Pha Terrell (who was with Andy Kirk's orchestra), Bing Crosby and Russ Columbo. Hibbler toured with Dub Jenkins and Boots And His Buddies. He came to the attention of Duke Ellington in 1942 and, after singing with Ellington one night, he thought that he had been offered a job and he celebrated excessively. The next day Ellington turned him down, saying that although he was prepared to hire a blind man, he was not so sure about a blind drunk!

Instead, Hibbler worked with Jay McShann's orchestra for 18 months, making his recording debut on "Get Me On Your Mind" in 1942. The following year he finally joined Ellington, becoming a special feature with the band for eight years. Among the songs that he helped introduce are "Do Nothin' Till You Hear From Me," "I'm Just A Lucky So And So," "I Ain't Got Nothin' But The Blues" and "I Like The Sunrise." Hibbler left Ellington in 1951 when Duke refused to give him a $50 raise.

By then, Al Hibbler had been recording his own record dates (often with Ellington sidemen) since 1946. He signed with Norman Granz and recorded a few albums in the 1950s, having hits with "Unchained Melody," "After The Lights Go Down Low" and "He." Just to show that there were no hard feelings, a 1954 album was titled *Al Hibbler Sings Duke Ellington.* Hibbler had a weakness for sentimental songs that often delivered in slightly over-the-top interpretations, but he also performed blues and swing standards.

After he became involved in the civil rights movement, work became harder to find for Hibbler. His 1961 Reprise album, *Monday Every Day* (with backing from the Gerald Wilson Orchestra), was one of his few for a major label. An unusual later recording, 1972's *A Meeting Of The Times*, teamed him successfully with multi-instrumentalist Rahsaan Roland Kirk.

Al Hibbler continued working on an occasional basis into the 1990s but was out of the spotlight except for special occasions during most of his final 25 years before his death in 2001 at age 85.

Recommended CDs: *1946–1949* (Classics 1234) has Hibbler's earliest recordings as a leader, seven sessions that often use sidemen drawn from the Ellington band. Highlights include "I Got It Bad," the blues "Fat And Forty," "Solitude," "Trees," "Tonight I Shall Sleep" and "Poor Butterfly." *1950–1952* (Classics 1300) has his last recordings under his own name before leaving Ellington and the first selections that launched his solo career. Included are his own special interpretations of "Star Dust," "Honeysuckle Rose," "Summertime," "Old Man River" and "On A Slow Boat To China." Most of Hibbler's best-known recordings with Ellington are included on the three-CD set *Black, Brown And Beige* (Bluebird 6641).

LPs to Search For: Hibbler's later albums are scarce, including *Al Hibbler Sings Love Songs* (Verve 4000), *Monday Every Day* (Reprise 2005) and Rahsaan Roland Kirk's *A Meeting Of The Times* (Atlantic 1630).

Bertha "Chippie" Hill
b. March 15, 1905, Charleston, SC; d. May 7, 1950, New York, NY

One of the last of the classic blues singers discovered during the blues craze of the 1920s, Bertha "Chippie" Hill was a limited but powerful singer who put plenty of feeling into her performances. She was one of 16 children, and she left home at the age of 13 to work as a singer and dancer, including at LeRoy's, a club in Harlem. Hill was soon being called "Chippie" because of her youth. She toured as a singer and dancer with Ma Rainey's troupe and appeared in theaters and black vaudeville. In 1925 Hill settled in Chicago, where she worked for seven months at the Palladium dance hall with King Oliver.

During 1925–29, Hill recorded 24 selections, all of which are available on a single CD. Ten of the songs have her joined by Louis Armstrong, including the original version of "Trouble In Mind." Other notable recordings include "Lonesome, All Alone And Blue," "Georgia Man," "Some Cold Rainy Day" and "Hangman Blues."

In 1930 Hill became semi-retired in music because the blues was considered out of style, and she needed a steadier income in order to raise her seven children. In 1946 when she was 41 and working in a bakery, she was discovered by writer Rudi Blesh. He recorded her on eight songs for his Circle label that year (including "Trouble In Mind," "Careless Love" and "How Long Blues") and used her as regular guest on his *This Is Jazz* radio series the following year. Hill made a complete comeback, sang regularly at New York clubs, performed at Carnegie Hall with Kid Ory, appeared at the 1948 Paris Jazz Festival and worked with Art Hodes in Chicago. During a period when very few of the classic blues singers were active (the handful that had made comebacks in the late 1930s had already been forgotten), Bertha "Chippie" Hill was a major link to 1920s blues/jazz. But her renaissance came to a sudden end when she was hit by a car in 1950, dying at the age of 45.

Recommended CDs: *Complete Recorded Works* (Document 5330) has all of Chippie Hill's 1920s recordings. Her eight songs for Circle from 1946 with a group including trumpeter Lee Collins are available on *Mutt Carey And Lee Collins* (American Music 72).

Hinda Hoffman

b. March 25, 1953, Chicago, IL

Although she did not start not singing professionally until she was nearly 40, Hinda Hoffman has since become a popular fixture in the Chicago area.

"In 1963, when I was 10 years old, I was at a the home of a friend whose father listened to jazz radio. I heard Nancy Wilson and Cannonball Adderley, and I was hooked. But when I was 12, the music teacher at my grammar school asked me to sing at the next PTA meeting for all of the parents and teachers. I was a nervous wreck. I got about four bars out and threw up. I didn't sing again in public until I was in my late thirties."

Years later in 1988, Hinda Hoffman took a jazz vocal class at the Blooms School of Jazz. The following year, she began sitting in on jam sessions and open mikes a few nights a week. She was bitten by the bug and soon was performing at clubs. Two of her early supporters were Sheila Jordan (whom she met at a jazz camp) and Steve Allen. Since that time, she has appeared at several festivals throughout the United States (including the Amherst Jazz Festival and the Chicago Jazz Festival) and worked regularly in the Chicago area.

"In the future I hope to tour Europe, singing jazz with great musicians wherever I can. I love popular standards and jazz standards by jazz musicians. To me, it's sacred, spiritual music. I feel so lucky to be able to sing it."

Recommended CDs: Hinda Hoffman's two recordings *You Are There* (HH 508033) and *Moon And Sand* (HH 506122), were both self-produced but are quite professional. She shows on the standards that she can swing lyrics while making them sound fresh and new with her attractive voice.

Billie Holiday
(Eleanora Harris)
b. April 7, 1915, Baltimore, MD; d. July 17, 1959, New York, NY

One of the most famous of all jazz singers and a living legend by the 1940s, Billie Holiday broke many musical rules. She had a small voice that was subtle yet very expressive and could be heartbreaking in her interpretations. She sang behind the beat and, like her good friend tenor-saxophonist Lester Young, was "cool" when "hot" was the fashion. She never scatted and her improvisation involved the placement of notes and her phrasing rather than altering lyrics. And, unlike many singers who are a bit like actresses, Billie Holiday meant every word she sang, particularly during the second half of her career.

She was born Eleanora Harris and was the daughter of rhythm guitarist Clarence Holiday, who for a few years played with Fletcher Henderson's orchestra. Her parents never married and she had a terrible and at times dangerous childhood, never really feeling loved or wanted. She named herself Billie and took the last name of her father since she wanted to somehow get close to him and be part of the music world.

In 1933, her life changed. Billie Holiday was heard by jazz fan and record producer John Hammond in a Harlem club. He made it possible for her to record two numbers with pickup bands led by Benny Goodman. While the two songs, "Your Mother's Son-In-Law" and "Riffin' The Scotch," were doomed for obscurity and the records did not sell, it was the start. Holiday sang with several groups during the next couple of years and appeared in *Symphony In Black*, a short film with Duke Ellington (singing a single blues chorus). In 1935 her career really got going when Hammond teamed her with pianist Teddy Wilson. Joined by all-stars taken from the top swing bands, Holiday and Wilson recorded a classic series of performances during the next four years. In 1937, Holiday started leading her own similar sessions with other pianists; those recordings lasted into 1942. Generally on the Wilson-led dates, Billie Holiday took her turn with the other horns, frequently taking a chorus in the middle of the song. On her own recordings, she usually opened and closed each song but there was almost always room for major soloists to make their mark. Starting in 1937, Lester Young (who named her "Lady Day," she named him "Pres," short for "president of the saxophone") appeared on many of her records and the interplay between his horn and her voice (both had similar tones) was remarkable, particularly when he played behind her. Trumpeter Buck Clayton was frequently on those recordings too and added perfectly complementary solos.

Scores of recordings from this early period are classic with just a few of the high points including "What A Little Moonlight Can Do," "I Cried For You," "This Year's Kisses," "I Must Have That Man," "I'll Get By," "Mean To Me," "Foolin' Myself," "Easy Living," "My Man," "When You're Smiling," "I Can't Believe That You're In Love With Me," "If Dreams Come True," "Sugar," "Billie's Blues," "A Fine Romance," "A Sailboat In The Moonlight," "Without Your Love," "When A Woman Loves A Man," "Them There Eyes,"

"Swing, Brother Swing," "Falling In Love Again," "All Of Me," "Let's Do It," "I Cover The Waterfront," "Gloomy Sunday" and her own "God Bless The Child." On "I Can't Give You Anything But Love," Holiday's phrasing sounds exactly like Louis Armstrong's.

Billie Holiday spent much of 1937 singing with the Count Basie Orchestra and part of 1938 with Artie Shaw but, because she was signed to a different record label, all that exists of these two associations are three songs from a radio broadcast with Basie and a lone selection ("Any Old Time") with Shaw. In 1939 when her record company did not want to take a chance with her recording the somewhat scary anti-racism song "Strange Fruit," she worked out a deal where that poem and three other songs (including "Fine And Mellow") could be recorded for the much smaller Commodore label.

Lady Day's voice was at its peak throughout the 1940s. After recording further titles for Commodore, she signed with Decca where she immediately had her biggest seller in 1944 with the original version of "Lover Man." While with Decca, she recorded in settings ranging from a trio to a string orchestra and studio big bands, sometimes even using background vocalists. While some of the settings were a little commercial, she sounded particularly strong during her Decca years and added such numbers to her repertoire as "Don't Explain," "Good Morning Heartache," "Ain't Nobody's Business If I Do" and "Crazy He Calls Me."

While her recordings of 1944–50 feature her at her peak, Holiday's personal life was constantly in turmoil. She always made bad decisions with boyfriends and husbands, preferring those who were physically strong over others who were mentally wise and caring. She also became a heroin addict, which did not affect her voice as much as smoking and drinking later would, but it did make her life rather difficult. She appeared in her only movie, *New Orleans*, in 1946 opposite Louis Armstrong, overcoming the stereotypical role of a maid with her singing and beauty. But she was busted for heroin possession soon afterward and served a year in prison. When she was released, she was considered rather notorious due to all of the publicity.

The 1950s should have been Billie Holiday's golden age. After recording four titles for Aladdin in 1951 (including "Detour Ahead" and "Now Or Never") she signed with Norman Granz. Her recordings of 1952–57, which would later be reissued by Verve, match her with jazz greats (often Charlie Shavers or Harry "Sweets" Edison ontrumpet and Flip Phillips or Ben Webster on tenor) on superior tunes from the Great American Songbook. While the settings were very sympathetic, Lady Day's voice steadily declined during the decade. Sometimes she would sound better than expected but on other occasions her voice was very rough. There are some great moments (such as "Comes Love"), but this is a very different Billie Holiday than she had been in the 1930s, sounding beaten down by life. Her emotional intensity had grown but her voice was slipping.

She visited Europe a few times, made excellent money, and should have been prospering but her messy private life was affecting her health and her frame of mind. Lady Day rallied regularly, including for the 1957 telecast of *The Sound Of Jazz* where she sang "Fine And Mellow" with a group of talented friends that included an ill but determined Lester Young. But 1958's *Lady In Satin*, which has her backed by the commercial string arrangements of Ray Ellis, was her most controversial recording. Some listeners love the feeling that she put into the songs, particularly on "You've Changed" and "You Don't Know What Love Is." But at 42, Holiday could have passed for a singer in her seventies. It was her next-to-last recording.

Billie Holiday died the following year. Nearly a half-century after her death, she is still a household name.

Recommended CDs: It is fairly easy to acquire every studio recording of Billie Holiday. There are also a countless number of "best of" samplers from each of her periods. The 10-CD box set *The Complete Billie Holiday On Columbia 1933–1944* (Columbia/Legacy 85470) cannot be improved upon since it has everything that Lady Day recorded during that period (except the one title with Artie Shaw and the Commodore dates) including all of the existing alternate takes. Listeners who just prefer to listen to Holiday without the alternates and radio broadcasts will find *The Quintessential Billie Holiday Volumes 1–9* (Columbia 40646, 40790, 44048, 44252, 44423, 45449, 46180, 47030 and 47031) to be quite satisfying. A pair of two-CD sets, *The Complete Commodore Recordings* (GRP/Commodore 2-401) and *The Complete Decca Recordings* (GRP/Decca 2-601), has all of her work for those two labels; the Decca box is particularly essential. *Billie's Blues* (Blue Note 48786) has a 1954 concert, her session for Aladdin and a version of "Trav'lin' Light" from 1942 with Paul Whiteman's orchestra. *The Complete Billie Holiday On Verve* (Verve 314 513 860-869) is a 10-CD box set that has every note that Holiday recorded for Norman Granz's labels (warts and all) including Jazz At The Philharmonic performances of 1945–46, the 1952–57 studio sessions, a couple of lengthy rehearsals that are full of talking, and her final album from 1959. General collectors will be more satisfied with some of the many single-disc reissues from this period. Finally, there is *Lady In Satin* (Columbia/Legacy 65144), which is mostly of interest to her greatest (and most tolerant) fans.

Linda Hopkins
(Melinda Helen Mathews)
b. December 14, 1924, New Orleans, LA

Throughout her career, Linda Hopkins has performed a wide variety of music, all of which she gives bluesy interpretations, whether it be gospel, R&B, blues or jazz.

Her father was a Baptist preacher and she began singing in church. When she was 11, she phoned the great gospel singer  Mahalia Jackson and convinced her to perform at a benefit concert at her father's church. During the benefit, the youth sang "God Shall Wipe Your Tears Away," so impressing Jackson that she arranged for her to become a member of the Southern Harp Spiritual Singers. Linda Hopkins (who was performing at the time as Helen Mathews) sang with the group for 11 years, making her recording debut with the ensemble in 1947. Not long after the benefit, she saw Bessie Smith perform in 1936, an encounter that convinced her that she should sing blues and secular music too.

In 1951 she met Little Esther Phillips, who took Johnny Otis to see her, resulting not only in her singing with Otis and recording for Savoy but her being convinced to change her name to Linda Hopkins. She made a handful of recordings for various labels, spent two years living in Japan and adapted well to the changes in music, touring with the Rock N' Roll Cavalcade. In 1959 she portrayed Bessie Smith in the Broadway show *Jazz Train*, touring Europe with the production (which was renamed *Broadway Express*) the following year. In 1963 Hopkins recorded a gospel-oriented album with Jackie Wilson and one of their singles, "Shake A Hand," became a hit. Later in the decade she began working as an actress, landing a role in the Broadway musical *Purlie* in 1970 and acting in movies and television, including playing a singer in *Roots: The Next Generations* and having a part in 1982's *Honky Tonk Man*. During 1974–75 Hopkins conceived, wrote and starred in the one-woman show *Me And Bessie*, starring in 453 performances on Broadway. In 1985 she started appearing in the musical revue *Black And Blue*, having 829 Broadway performances and working with the show on and off through 1997. During 1997–99 she appeared as part of *Wild Woman Blues*, mostly in Europe.

Linda Hopkins has always been quite active, performing in clubs and festivals in addition to her stage work. At 82, her voice remains in its prime.

Recommended CDs: Linda Hopkins recorded a total of 40 selections during 1951–62 for a variety of labels, most of which are pretty scarce although her four selections for Savoy sometimes appear on samplers. *How Blue Can You Get* (Quicksilver 4002) from 1982 is a strong blues-oriented set in which Hopkins is assisted by trumpeter Clora Bryant and saxophonist Red Holloway. *The Living Legend Live* (Free Ham 3747) features Linda Hopkins in recent times in excellent voice even if the oft-recorded material offers no real surprises.

LPs to Search For: *Me And Bessie* (Columbia 34032) from 1976 documents the songs that Linda Hopkins sang in her tribute show to Bessie Smith although her R&Bish interpretations are just as close to Aretha Franklin in style as to the Empress of the Blues.

Website: www.global-mojo.com/specialsite/hopkins

Shirley Horn

b. May 2, 1934, Washington, DC;
d. October 20, 2005, Washington, DC

When it came to relaxed and laid-back singing, few were in Shirley Horn's league. Her ability to express the most intense emotions at a low volume and a slow tempo became very influential after she finally became famous in the 1980s, when she was in her fifties.

Shirley Horn began taking piano lessons when she was four, played throughout her childhood, and attended Howard University. She organized her first trio in 1954, and made her recording debut with Stuff Smith in 1959, although her identity was largely hidden for years; the record mistakenly listed John Eaton as the pianist on all of the selections. In 1960 she cut her first album as a leader, an obscure effort for Stereo-O-Craft. Championed by Miles Davis (who had her open for him at the Village Vanguard) and Quincy Jones, Horn recorded three albums for Mercury and ABC/Paramount during 1963–65, but then she decided decided to only play locally in Washington, DC, for years while raising her daughter. Other than a few songs made for a soundtrack

and a 1972 Perception album, she did not record again until making the first of three Steeplechase albums in 1978. But her breakthrough did not take place until 1987, when she began recording for Verve.

During her final 18 years, Shirley Horn was a major name in the jazz world, leading a trio that included bassist Charles Ables and drummer Steve Williams. She made "Here's To Life" into a standard, displayed the ability to quickly quiet audiences at any venue (including at noisy festivals) by simply singing softly, had guest appearances on several records (including playing piano on Carmen McRae's last CD) and became an influential force including on Diana Krall. Near the end she suffered from diabetes, resulting in the loss of her left leg, and she reluctantly decided to let others play piano behind her singing; George Mesterhazy was her pianist during her last few years.

Shirley Horn's final recordings were a few titles in January 2005 that were included in a "Best Of" collection. She passed away nine months later at the age of 71.

Recommended CDs: *Loads Of Love/Shirley Horn With Horns* (Mercury 843 454) reissues Horn's two Mercury albums on a single CD. *Travelin' Light* (ABC 538) features Horn in 1965 before her long hiatus from recordings. *Where Are You Going/ The Real Thing* (Perception 5618) is from 1972, while *A Lazy Afternoon* (Steeplechase 31111), *At Northsea* (Steeplechase 37015) and *Garden Of The Blues* (Steeplechase 31203) feature Horn and her trio during 1978–84. 1987's *I Thought About You* (Verve 833 235) made Shirley Horn into a jazz star and it was followed by such popular discs as *Softly* (Audiophile 224), *Close Enough For Love* (Verve 837 933), *You Won't Forget Me* (Verve 847 482), *Here's To Life* (Verve 314 511 879), *I Love You Paris* (Verve 314 523 486), *Light Out Of Darkness* (Verve 314 519 703), *The Main Ingredient* (Verve 314 529 555), *Loving You* (Verve 314 537 022), *I Remember Miles* (Verve 314 557 199) and *May The Music Never End* (Verve 440 076 028). For many Shirley Horn fans, the *Here's To Life* CD is essential, featuring her backed by an orchestra arranged by Johnny Mandel.

LPs to Search For: *Embers And Ashes* (Stereo-O-Craft 16) has Shirley Horn already sounding quite recognizable with a trio in 1960 while *Live At The Village Vanguard* (Can-Am 6106) features her in her early prime in 1961.

Lena Horne

b. June 30, 1917, Brooklyn, NY

Lena Horne is almost as well known for being a timeless beauty as she is for her singing. Though she spent much of her career performing in a style closer to cabaret and middle-of-the-road pop than jazz, in the 1940s she often proved to be a satisfying swing singer.

She first performed in public when she was six, and by 1934 was working at the Cotton Club. Horne sang with Noble Sissle's orchestra during 1935–36 when she was still a teenager and starred in the B picture *The Duke Is Tops*. Her jazz career included working with Teddy Wilson in the late 1930s, performing with Charlie Barnet during 1940–41, recording with Artie Shaw, appearing in the jazz short *Boogie Woogie Dream* and being one of the stars of two big-budget all-black films: *Cabin In The Sky* (with Ethel Waters) and *Stormy Weather* (next to Bill "Bojangles" Robinson). But signed to MGM, she was primarily used by the company in specialty numbers that could easily be cut out of versions of the films sent to Southern audiences. Eventually, she became fed up with the situation and stuck to music full-time. In 1946, Horne recorded a set of jazz songs with Phil Moore's orchestra, but otherwise her career was going in a different direction, toward cabaret and middle-of-the-road pop music. Lena Horne teamed up with her husband, arranger-pianist Lennie Hayton, and became quite successful in a lengthy singing career that after the mid-1940s barely touched on jazz.

Recommended CDs: *Stormy Weather* (Bluebird 9985) has Horne's best swing era work including her recordings with Barnet, Shaw and Horace Henderson. *Lena Horne At MGM* (Rhino 72246) has most of the music from her film appearances (other than her performances in *Stormy Weather*) and is jazz-oriented. Definitely worth searching for are *The Original Black And White Recordings* (Simitar 56782), which shows the direction Lena Horne could have gone toward if she had wanted to remain dedicated to jazz. Solos are taken by trumpeter Gerald Wilson, altoist Willie Smith, trombonist Tyree Glenn and Lucky Thompson on tenor. Most of her many later recordings are of lesser interest to jazz listeners.

Bob Howard
(Bob Joyner)
b. June 20, 1906, West Newton, MA;
d. December 3, 1986, Mount Kisco, NY

After Fats Waller began his series of popular recordings for Victor in 1934, some of the other record labels jumped on the bandwagon and signed up similar sounding singer-pianists. Bob Howard was a decent pianist (though never on Waller's level) who was also a jivey singer a bit reminiscent of Fats. He made practically all of his recordings for Decca during 1935–38 but actually had a fairly extensive career in show business.

Born Bob Joyner, he attended the Howard University Medical School for a time before enrolling in the New England Conservatory of Music. He worked in vaudeville as half of Joyner and Hopkins (backing dancer Morris Hopkins), moved to New York in 1926, and worked in local clubs. He also recorded five obscure numbers during 1931–32 as a singing pianist.

After being signed with Decca in 1935 (by which time he had changed his name), Howard recorded 84 songs (not counting alternate takes) during the next three years, strictly as a singer except for four good-time medleys on which he is showcased on piano. Among his sidemen on these all-star dates are Benny Carter (on trumpet and alto), clarinetists Buster Bailey and Artie Shaw, Ben Webster on tenor, cornetist Rex Stewart, trumpeter Bunny Berigan, pianists Teddy Wilson, Zinky Cohn, Frank Froeba and Billy Kyle, guitarist Teddy Bunn and drummer Cozy Cole. Although Howard's singing was limited and his yelling over people's solos (which Waller and Cab Calloway did with more charm) sometimes gets repetitive, he displays an appealing voice and the performances contain some underrated gems.

Howard only recorded two more numbers after his Decca association ended in 1938, but he remained very active. He worked regularly on 52nd Street, accompanied singer Billy Daniels at Mamie's Chicken Shack in the late 1930s, appeared in the films *Howard's House Party*, *Junction 88* and *Stars on Parade*, and was on Broadway in 1943's *Early To Bed* (for which Fats Waller contributed the score). He was on the radio often and was possibly the first black performer to appear regularly on television, having his own 15-minute show on CBS from July 1948 to December 1951.

Even with the lack of recordings (which is perplexing), Bob Howard sang and played piano at nightclubs and restaurants until shortly before his death in 1986.

Recommended CDs: All of Bob Howard's recordings are contained on *1932–1935* (Classics 1152), *1935–1936* (Classics 1121), *1936–1937* (Classics 1076) and *1937–1947* (Classics 1055). *1935–1936* is the most satisfying of the quartet.

Rosetta Howard
b. ca. 1914, Chicago, IL; d. 1974, Chicago, IL

Rosetta Howard could have been one of the major classic blues singers were she not born so late. Her style would have fit well in the 1920s: she could sing the blues, was flexible enough to sing some less bluesy material, and worked well with jazz sidemen.

Very little is known about Rosetta Howard's life. She started her career in the early 1930s as a dancer before switching to singing in 1932. She often worked in the mid-1930s with the Harlem Hamfats, an intriguing group consisting of trumpeter Herb Morand, the primitive clarinetist Odell Rand, piano, guitar, mandolin, bass and drums. At three record dates during 1937–38 that were released under her name, she fronted the Hamfats for 18 selections. Among the titles are "If You're A Viper," "Rosetta Blues" and "Delta Bound."

Howard worked with clarinetist Jimmie Noone in 1938, and with Eddie Smith's band. In New York she led two record dates in 1939 that feature such sidemen as Charlie Shavers or Henry "Red" Allen on trumpet, clarinetist Buster Bailey and sometimes pianist Lil Armstrong. Her straightforward singing bridges the gap between classic blues, swing and jive music of the 1940s.

Rosetta Howard worked in Chicago during most of the 1940s and in 1947 cut eight numbers with the Big Three (which has Willie Dixon on bass) and four others on a session with a three-horn septet that includes guitarist Big Bill Broonzy. Despite her talents, Howard never recorded again. She worked on Chicago television in the late 1940s, left show business to work in religion, sang with Thomas A. Dorsey at Pilgrim Baptist Church and slipped away into obscurity.

Recommended CDs: *Complete Recorded Works 1939–47* (RST 1514), *The Harlem Hamfats Vol. 3* (Document 5273) and *Vol. 4* (Document 5274) contain virtually all of Rosetta Howard's recordings.

Diane Hubka
b. March 18, 1957, Pleasantville, NY

A quiet and subtle singer with a pleasing voice, Diane Hubka puts a lot of care into each recording project, and the attention to detail shows in each of her rewarding CDs.

"I always sang—whether with my family, in church choirs or the school Glee Club. I took violin lessons for two years starting when I was six, and in fourth grade I took trombone. After a year of carrying the heavy trombone to and from school, I was relieved to switch to the much lighter guitar. That was 1968, when I was 11 years old. Folk guitar was popular and, since I enjoyed singing, it became a natural choice. While

I was in college in Frostburg, Maryland, majoring in business and accounting, I started taking jazz and blues guitar lessons from Bill Bittner, who in the 1950s had backed top artists including Anita O'Day. He asked if I wanted to sing in his band and he recorded a tape for me of standards. As soon as I heard Carmen McRae's rendition of 'Our Love Is Here To Stay,' I knew that I wanted to be a professional jazz singer."

She performed with Bittner's group for several years, gaining important experience. Along the way, Hubka studied with guitarist Paul Wingo, Connie Crothers, Harold Danko, Sheila Jordan, Barry Harris, Gene Bertoncini and Howard Alden. She won a grant from the National Endowment for the Arts to study with Anne Marie Moss in 1982 and three years later, moved to New York.

Diane Hubka had opportunities to perform with Bob Dorough, Lee Konitz and Bucky Pizzarelli, and in 1997 made her first CD. By then she often accompanied herself on guitar, and in 2002 she began playing seven-string guitar. Since moving to Los Angeles, she has continued recording, performs locally, teaches and conducts workshops on jazz improvisation.

"I've always felt that singing jazz was not something I chose to do, but rather, discovered I was born to do. I'm equally drawn to the rhythm and harmonies of jazz. I love to harmonize and I love the freedom of improvising, both with and without words."

Recommended CDs: *Haven't We Met* (Challenge 73128) has Diane Hubka holding her own with Lee Konitz and guitarist John Hart. *Look No Further* (Challenge 73182) continues her welcome practice of performing little-known songs (Herbie Hancock's "Dolphin Dance" is rarely sung) and fresh versions of standards. *You Inspire Me* (VSOJazz 5173) matches her with seven top guitarists while *Diane Hubka Goes To The Movies* (18th and Vine 1054) features her performing songs that debuted in films during the past 75 years.

Website: www.dianehubka.com

Ilse Huizinga

b. October 15, 1967, Beverwijk, The Netherlands

One of several very talented jazz singers from the Netherlands, Isle Huizinga has thus far recorded seven albums.

"As a child of six, I used to sing in front of my class. Later I was extremely shy as a teenager, but in my last year of high school I debuted on stage before an audience of 700 and I sang 'Songbird.'" She took piano lessons from the age of six and at 17 took lessons in classical singing. However, at that time she became much more attracted to jazz singing. "I had tapes of Ella Fitzgerald, Sarah Vaughan, Abbey Lincoln and Billie Holiday when I was 18 and I took my tapes everywhere." After spending a year living in Australia and earning a degree in Public Administration at the University of Amsterdam, she switched to music. "I was attending a vocal jam session at Café Casablanca in the heart of Amsterdam's Red Light district. I sang two songs with the band and suddenly I felt

convinced that I had to change my future completely." Huizinga attended the Conservatory of Amsterdam during 1993–96. Since that time she has performed all over Europe, usually with her husband, pianist-arranger Erik Van Der Luijt.

"I chose to produce my first record myself after I had been through the mill of several record companies. I was promised a lot, but I never got a copy of the contract I was supposed to sign before the production would take place, so I decided to run my own show." After her first two CDs were well received, she recorded for Daybreak. Today, Ilse Huizinga mostly performs standards.

"I sing many songs from the American Songbook and I particularly enjoy the melody and lyrics of the older songs. It's a challenge for me to create my own rendition of a song; and often I find that it's all about 'less is more.'"

Recommended CDs: *Out Of A Dream* and *Voices Within* (the latter has Ilse Huizinga's voice overdubbed five times) were privately released and are available through her website. *The Sweetest Sounds* (Daybreak 75093) features her winning interpretations of Richard Rodgers songs. *Easy To Idolize* (Daybreak 727478) and *Beyond Broadway* (Maxanter 611148) are in a similar vein, *The Club Sessions* is thus far only available in Japan and the recent two-CD set *Intimate Jazz Sessions* (Foreign Media 8329) features her dueting with her husband pianist Erik Van Der Luijt.

Website: www.ilsehuizinga.com

Helen Humes

b. June 23, 1913, Louisville, KY;
d. September 9, 1981, Santa Monica, CA

One of the great singers to emerge from the swing era, Helen Humes was equally skilled on blues, standards and ballads, always having a smile in her voice even on sadder songs. She had a long career that can be divided into four parts.

Humes grew up in New York and sang as a child. In 1927 she became the youngest classic blues singer to record during the decade, performing 10 songs including two before she turned 14. Years later she would claim that she did not understand the words of these double-entendre blues, which include "Do What You Did Last Night," "If Papa Has Outside Lovin'" and "Race Horse Blues."

Humes picked up experience in the early 1930s, performing in theaters and working with Stuff Smith, Al Sears and Vernon Andrade's orchestra. In 1938 Helen Humes replaced Billie Holiday with the Count Basie Orchestra, gaining some fame during her three years with Basie despite being underutilized. While most male band singers of the era stuck to ballads, Jimmy Rushing was Basie's main singer and got most of the blues and the best material. Humes tended to be assigned the novelties and the ballads, sounding best on "Blame It On My Last Affair," "If I Could Be With You One Hour Tonight" and "Don't Worry 'Bout Me."

Helen Humes' third period (1942–63) was her most rewarding. Although never quite becoming a household name, her versatility came in handy during her busy solo career. She had a hit in 1945 with "Be Baba Leba," appeared in both bop (the Dizzy Gillespie big band) and R&B settings, and wrote the humorous "Million Dollar Secret," which explains why it makes logical sense for young women to go after elderly men, and older women to date youngsters. Humes was on records frequently during 1944–52 and cut three classic albums for Contemporary during 1959–61, particularly *Songs I Like To Sing*. In her late forties, she was at the peak of her powers.

Humes spent 1964–67 living in Australia. She returned to the U.S. and, after her mother died, she was completely retired from music for six years, working day jobs including one with a munitions factory. In 1973 she was persuaded by writer Stanley Dance to sing at a Basie reunion at the Newport Jazz Festival and it led in a full-fledged comeback. During the next seven years she recorded for Black & Blue (the memorable album *Let The Good Times Roll*), Audiophile, Black Lion, Jazzology, Columbia and Muse. Helen Humes' final appearance was at the 1981 Playboy Jazz Festival less than three months before her death, sharing a vocal duet with Joe Williams on "If I Could Be With You."

Recommended CDs: The three-CD set *Complete 1927–50 Studio Recordings* (Jazz Factory 22844) perfectly covers Helen Humes' early years since it has everything except for her Basie recordings. *Tain't Nobody's Biz-Ness If I Do* (Original Jazz Classics 453), *Songs I Like To Sing* (Original Jazz Classics 171) and *Swinging With Humes* (Original Jazz Classics 608) feature the singer at her very best during 1959–61. From her last period, *Let The Good Times Roll* (Black & Blue 871) is highlighted by "That Old Feeling," "They Raided The Joint," "Million Dollar Secret" and "He May Be Your Man" while the scarce *Helen Humes And The Muse All Stars* (Muse 5473) is well worth a search.

Tamm E. Hunt

b. June 19, 1954, New York, NY

An important force in the Baltimore jazz scene, Tamm E. Hunt deserves to be much better known.

"My aunt, Hannah Sylvester, was a jazz and blues singer who performed at the Celebrity Club in Harlem. Her husband, Uncle Benny Clark, owned a record company and my father, K.D. Searcy, was a tap dancer who danced at the Apollo Theater with Tip, Tap and Toe." Growing up around music, she remembers hearing Dakota Staton's "The Late Late Show" and knowing that she wanted to sing jazz.

Tamm E. Hunt sang throughout her childhood including R&B with girl groups. She had commercial success singing disco in the early 1980s, but she was more impressed by Billie Holiday and Shirley Horn and eventually switched to jazz. "I have been mentored and encouraged by Betty Carter, Sarah Vaughan and Dorothy Donegan. I made singing a goal early in life and pursued it with great persistence." Among her key associations through the years are Gary Bartz, T.S. Monk, Clifford Jordan, Ronnie Matthews, Buster Williams, Bill Saxton and Larry Willis. She has performed in Europe, Canada and Japan in addition to throughout the U.S.

In addition, Hunt founded the Harlem Jazz Foundation and has written jazz education programs, including Adopt A Kid 4 Jazz and Jazz 4 The Beginner. She produced and starred in the off-Broadway show *Billie Holiday: The Legend* and appeared in a dramatic film with Gary Bartz called *A Jazz Story*. In recent times, she has lived and worked in Baltimore and been the executive/artistic director of the Maryland Center

for the Preservation of Jazz & Blues, working behind the scenes to help jazz.

Recommended CD: *Live At Birdland* (New Jazz Audience 111) from 2004 features Tamm E. Hunt in excellent form with fine playing from Gary Bartz.

Alberta Hunter

b. April 1, 1895, Memphis, TN; d. October 18, 1984, New York, NY

Alberta Hunter had a unique and very long career, making a major comeback when she was 82, after having been one of the pioneering classic blues singers of the 1920s.

She ran away from home when she was 11 and was soon working as a singer, performing in Chicago area clubs by 1907. Hunter worked in vaudeville and in shows before jazz had even been heard up North. She moved to New York and started recording in 1921, less than a year after Mamie Smith had opened the door for black female blues singers. Hunter always had a wider repertoire than blues although she was responsible for writing "Downhearted Blues," which in 1923 became Bessie Smith's first hit. Hunter usually used the best possible musicians on her records including Louis Armstrong, Sidney Bechet, Fats Waller, King Oliver, Fletcher Henderson, the Original Memphis Five, Duke Ellington and Eubie Blake.

During 1928–29, Hunter was in London starring opposite Paul Robeson in *Showboat*. She greatly modified her style to work in Paris as a cabaret and ballad singer, recording in England with John Jackson's orchestra. She stayed in Europe throughout the 1930s until it was obvious that a war was coming. Hunter returned to New York in 1939, showed on records that she was an excellent swing singer (other than Ethel Waters, few classic blues singers of the 1920s were able to make the transition), and she did extensive touring with the U.S.O. during both World War II. and the Korean War.

After her mother died in 1954, Alberta Hunter decided to switch careers. In 1956 she retired from singing to become a nurse, lying about her age (she was 61 but said that she was 44) and claiming that she had graduated from high school. Her nursing career was quite successful, lasting 21 years. Although she was persuaded to record again in 1961, she was otherwise out of music until 1977, when it was decided that she should be retired because it was thought that she had reached the age of 65. She was actually 82.

So Alberta Hunter went back to singing again, appearing regularly at the Cookery in New York. Despite being in her eighties, she sounded quite spirited and ageless while singing double-entendre blues (a favorite was "My Handy Man") and material that she had recorded 50 years earlier. She recorded four albums for Columbia, was considered a unique sensation and was (along with Sippie Wallace who outlived her) the last survivor of the 1920s classic blues singers. Better known in her eighties than she had been in her original heyday, Alberta Hunter toured Europe and South America, appeared on television, and seemed to thoroughly enjoy the seven years of her comeback before her death at age 89.

Recommended CDs: All of Alberta Hunter's recordings during a 25-year period (other than her dull cabaret dates with John Jackson) are on *1921–1923* (Document 5422), *1923–1924* (Document 5423), *1924–1927* (Document 5424) and *1927–1946* (Document 5425) plus the less essential *Alternate Takes* (Document 1006). She also recorded eight selections in 1950, and in 1961 made appearances on *Chicago: The Living Legends* (Original Blues Classics 510), which she co-led with pianist Lovie Austin, and on four numbers on *Songs We Taught Your Mother* (Original Blues Classics 520), a historic set that she shared with singers Lucille Hegamin and Victoria Spivey. *Amtrak Blues* (Columbia 36430) is from her comeback years.

LPs to Search For: Three of Alberta Hunter's four recordings from her last period, *Remember My Name* (Columbia 35553), *The Glory Of Alberta Hunter* (Columbia 35606) and *Look For The Silver Lining* (Columbia 38970), have surprisingly not been reissued on CD yet.

Ina Ray Hutton
(Odessa Cowan)
b. March 13, 1916, Chicago, IL; d. February 19, 1984, Ventura, CA

Ina Ray Hutton found fame by leading one of the first major all-female big bands. Although her good looks, colorful conducting and dancing helped to sell the orchestra, she was also an effective, if underrated, vocalist.

Hutton first appeared on stage as a child in 1924 as a tap dancer. After gaining experience in various areas of show business, including appearing in several Broadway shows and the *Ziegfeld Follies*, her career went in another direction in 1934. With the assistance of manager-producer Irving Mills, she put together Ina Ray Hutton and Her Melodears.

During its five years, Hutton's Melodears gained a lot of attention, appearing in several film shorts and also the feature-length *Big Broadcast Of 1936*. Surprisingly, the band only recorded six songs (all in 1934), with Hutton singing spirited versions of "How's About Tomorrow Night" and "Twenty-Four Hours In Georgia" although she was more extensively featured in the film shorts, including a memorable rendition of "Truckin'."

After breaking up the Melodears in 1939, Hutton formed an all-male orchestra that featured tenor-saxophonist George Paxton (the band's musical director) and pianist Hal Schaefer. The Ina Ray Hutton Orchestra recorded a dozen numbers during 1940–41 with the leader taking four vocals including "Five O'Clock Whistle" and "Nobody's Sweetheart." This orchestra performed often on the radio and several of the broadcasts have since been released on LPs and CDs.

After giving up the band in 1946, Hutton briefly led a new male orchestra in 1948. She married trumpeter Randy Brooks, and in the early 1950s headed an all-female big band that appeared on television regularly. After hosting her own nationally televised *Ina Ray Hutton Show* in the summer of 1956, Ina Ray Hutton went into semi-retirement in California. Although it seems like she should have done much more with her career, Ina Ray Hutton is still remembered for the Melodears.

Recommended CD: *Ina Ray Hutton And Her Melodears 1934–1944* (Vintage Music Productions 0081) has all of Hutton's most important studio recordings along with soundtracks from film and radio appearances.

Jacintha
(Jacintha Abisheganaden)
b. October 3, 1957, Singapore

An actress from Singapore, Jacintha has developed into an effective jazz singer, as can be heard on her series of Groove Note releases. Although she has a powerful voice, she prefers to sing quietly at slow tempos and with subtlety, which at times is reminiscent of Julie London with a touch of Ella Fitzgerald.

When she was 12, Jacintha sang on a radio program called *Voice And Guitar*, accompanied by her father on guitar. Jacintha joined the Singapore Youth Choir at 14. "We covered everything from atonal 'post modern' stuff, a lot of Latin hymns with beautiful arrangements and madrigals to pop. We actually won the first prize for Best Choir in the Llangollen Eisteddfod in Wales in 1974—I'm not sure anyone taking part even knew where Singapore was." Influenced by her father, who took her to record stores each Saturday, she grew to love jazz standards and won a nationwide contest by singing jazz when she was 18. Jacintha sang on TV regularly with a group called the Accidentals, did Christmas specials and recorded five pop and Latin albums in Singapore. She earned an Honor's degree in English Literature from the National University of Singapore, studied at Trinity College of London, and lived in the United States for a period in the mid-1980s. In addition to her work as an actress, she has worked as a journalist and started a booking company.

The turning point for Jacintha was in 1999 when Groove Note Records was started. She was signed and began to receive international attention as a singer. "Groove Note's production values are very high and I love recording live. It has also been a chance for collaboration with very talented musicians. What I most love about jazz and the standards are that there are stories to be told. There is irony and humor, the inner groove and, if you're good, you can tell your own story. I don't really believe in 'the voice beautiful.' Stories resonate much more to me."

Recommended CDs: *Here's To Ben* (Groove Note 1001) is an unusual tribute to tenor-saxophonist Ben Webster. Jacintha sings some of Webster's favorite songs while being assisted by tenor man Teddy Edwards. *Autumn Leaves* (Groove Note 1006) consists of ballad versions of songs with Johnny Mercer lyrics, *Lush Life* (Groove Note 1011) teams Jacintha's voice with a string section, *Jacintha Is Her Name* (Groove Note 1014) is a tribute to Julie London, *The Girl From Bossa Nova* (Groove Note 1026) has Brazilian music that fits her voice very well and *Jacintha Goes To Hollywood* (Groove Note 1040) mostly features ballads associated with movies.

Janiece Jaffe
b. June 9, 1958, Akron, OH

A creative jazz singer and an educator based in Indiana, Janiece Jaffe is never shy to take chances while improvising.

"My dad was a classical musician, so it wasn't until I was in high school and heard some of my friends in the jazz band that I even knew that jazz existed. The first vocalist's record I bought was at a garage sale for 25 cents, Sarah Vaughan. I was immediately intrigued by her voice and phrasing. My mother sang opera and was a preschool teacher. I remember my whole family singing together. We even had a Family Opera Night around the dinner table where everyone was required to sing rather than talk!" However, despite an early start, including appearing in musicals from the time she was eight, Janiece Jaffe took some time before she became a professional singer. "In 1991 when I was 33, I was running a preschool and went through a crisis about my mission in life. I just knew that I was supposed to sing, so I decided to jump in with both feet. I started taking voice lessons with David Baker, and he told me that if I was really serious about singing professionally, I should enroll in the jazz program at Indiana University." At the time, she had four children under the age of eight but managed to earn a degree in vocal jazz performance six years later.

Since then, Janiece Jaffe has worked with the big bands of David Baker, Dominic Spera, Al Cobine and Clem DeRosa, the Midcoast Jazz Project, the Simon Rowe Trio, Brazilian jazz guitarist Marcos Cavalcante, Roy Geesa's Cool City Swing Band and with her own combos.

"What I love most about jazz is being in the moment, joyful and fearless. The excitement of co-creating sounds with partners on stage and experiencing the energies of a group of people is profoundly unique."

Recommended CDs: Jacintha's recording debut was 1995's *Keep The Flame Alive* (JLJ Productions). *It Takes Two* (Catalyst 20) is a set of stimulating duets with either guitarist Marcos Cavalcante or bassist Tom Hildreth. *Heart's Desire* (JLJ Productions) has Janiece Jaffe assisted by the Simon Rowe Trio. *The Lotus And The Rose* (JLJ Productions), a live radio performance with guitarist Tyron Cooper on *Saturday's Child* (JLJ Productions), and a collaboration with Marcos Cavalcante called *Standing On The Edge* (JLJ 0060) are her most recent recordings.

Website: www.janiecejaffe.com

Denise Jannah
(Denise Johnanna Zeefuik)
b. November 5, 1956, Paramaribo, Suriname

lthough Denise Jannah has had a few CDs released by Blue Note, she has been based in Holland throughout her career. Fluent in five languages, she sings in English without any accent.

Born in Suriname, South America, she remembers singing extensively with her family at home. Jannah relocated with her family to Holland in the 1970s where for four- and-a-half years she studied law at the University of Utrecht. "I was singing on the side, and had joined my first band in my second year. It must have been somewhere in 1976 that I was on stage performing when all of a sudden it hit me: 'I'm on the wrong track with my law studies. I have to be a full-time singer.' I lacked the courage to make the switch right away so it took a few years, but since then I knew that I wanted to be a professional singer."

During 1984–92 she studied at the vocal department of the Conservatory in Hilversum, Holland, taking two years

off to tour Holland, Belgium and Germany in the musical *A Night At The Cotton Club.* Jannah recorded her first album in 1991. Ever since then, she has been quite active, touring the world, appearing at the North Sea Jazz Festival seven times and performing everywhere from the United States to South Africa and back in her native Suriname. Along the way she has worked with Cyrus Chestnut, Bob Belden's orchestra, Paquito D'Rivera, the Carnegie Hall Jazz Band, Jon Hendricks, the Willem Breuker Kollektief, the Rosenberg Trio, pianist Amina Figarova and the Metropole Orchestra. Jannah has also performed with the shows *Ain't Misbehavin', Joe: The Musical* and a tribute to soul singers, *R.E.S.P.E.C.T.* She has worked as a vocal director for several theater productions and also teaches and conducts workshops and master classes.

"We all know that music has loving and healing powers. I've had times that I had to go on that stage being very sad about something in my private life, or downright sick, very much doubting whether I could make it. But I always did, because of the music. After the gig there is no pain, sadness, fatigue or stress, just great loving energy."

Recommended CDs: 1991's *Take It From The Top* (Timeless SJP 308) and *A Heart Full Of Music* (Timeless SJP 414), the latter teaming her with Cyrus Chestnut, made Denise Jannah well known far beyond Holland. Signing with Blue Note in 1995 and releasing three CDs, *I Was Born In Love With You* (Blue Note 333902), *Different Colours* (Blue Note 54729) and *The Madness Of Our Love* (Blue Note 22642), gave her a name in the United States. Four of her first five CDs are bop and standards-oriented although colorful and never predictable. *Different Colours* was an attempt at crossover that is a lesser effort. *Gedicht Gezongen* (Plattèl Music 402) is quite a bit different, a self-produced vocal poetry album in which she wrote the music to 22 poems from poets from the Netherlands, Suriname, Aruba, South Africa and Indonesia, singing in their languages. In addition, she is featured on five songs on *Thirst! Willem Breuker Kollektief and Denise Jannah* (BV Haast 0300).

Website: www.denisejannah.com

Amandah Jantzen
b. July 11, 1960, San Francisco, CA

A subtle interpreter of standards who has her own charm and charisma, Amandah Jantzen has in recent times primarily been performing in Asia.

"I got my first radio in 1970 and played it constantly, so I know a lot of '70s tunes. When I first played guitar and eventually tried to do shows, it was 'folk' and light rock. I remember hearing Al Jarreau's version of 'Since I Fell For You.' It changed my life, my voice, the style of music I was doing, my range, and the direction I thought I was headed in. I picked that song to sing at a jam session–type show in Marin County called *Sing With A Band*. The director told me to sing it in a lower key in the alto range, I had been a soprano, and the result was a totally different range and sound for my voice." Soon she discovered Linda

Ronstadt's three albums with the Nelson Riddle Orchestra and, since she had a similar range, she was inspired to learn all of the songs. Next, she heard Sarah Vaughan for the first time and was very impressed when she saw Nancy Wilson in concert. She knew that jazz was going to be her future direction.

Unfortunately, when she was 20 and hired for a gig to sing and play guitar, she became so terrified that she did not perform in public again until 1986. Coaxed into sitting in with a guitar duo, this time she fought the feeling of fear, gained energy from it, and became determined to become a singer. "Instead of running away, I wanted to try it again and again. I was bitten by the bug and I have never recovered since. In the years that followed, I sang anywhere and everywhere I possibly could. Since I was in business and traveled all over the country, I performed in many different cities."

Amandah Jantzen eventually dropped out of the lucrative business world, moved to Portland, worked locally in clubs and at concerts, and was inspired by bassist Leroy Vinnegar and guitarist Charlie Byrd. She had played piano by ear as a child and began to accompany herself in 1997, at the suggestion of Charlie Byrd. She recorded her first CD in 1998 and picked up valuable experience performing not only in Portland and Vancouver, British Columbia but at important engagements in Dutch Harbor (Alaska), Sturgeon Bay (Wisconsin), Las Vegas, Spokane and in Florida with Ira Sullivan. In recent times, she has had lengthy engagements in Singapore, Seoul and Bali.

"Someone asked me once if I ever wanted to 'make it big' someday. My answer was, 'I get to do what I love for a living. I never have to work. I can't wait for my next gig. I get paid to have fun, to express myself through music and do the one thing I would be doing for free anyway. If that's not making it, then I can't imagine what is.'"

Recommended CDs: *Some Other Time* (Starfire 100), *Devil May Care* (Starfire 254) and *My Secret Love* (Starfire 739) each contain Amandah Jantzen's enthusiastic and heartfelt interpretations of standards. *Northern Star: The Singapore Sessions* (self-produced) is a high-quality set of standards performed by duos and trios recorded in Singapore with one of four pianists.

Website: www.amandahjantzen.com

Al Jarreau
b. March 12, 1940, Milwaukee, WI

Al Jarreau has been so successful from the standpoint of commercial success and achieving fame that it seems odd to say that he could have accomplished much more in his career. But if he had not made a conscious effort starting in the mid-1970s to steer away from jazz and toward pop/R&B, he could have been the leading jazz singer of the past 30 years.

Jarreau began singing when he was four and he performed locally in Milwaukee on several occasions while growing up. While attending Ripon College, where he earned a Bachelor of Science degree in Psychology, Jarreau sang for the fun of it with a group called the Indigos. He earned a Master's degree in

Vocational Rehabilitation at the University of Iowa and moved to San Francisco to work in rehabilitation counseling.

However, he was soon drawn toward music. In 1965 Jarreau recorded his first album, a straight-ahead jazz set cut in Illinois that finds him at the age of 25 sounding quite recognizable both in his tone and in his style, swinging such numbers as 'My Favorite Things,' "A Sleepin' Bee" and "The Masquerade Is Over." This small-label release is still one of his finest jazz sets, preceding his second recording by a decade.

In San Francisco, Jarreau worked in small clubs, often with the George Duke Trio. He also spent time singing in Los Angeles and New York before signing with Reprise in 1975. At the time, he displayed the ability to imitate instruments with remarkable expertise (even a conga), sounding to an extent like Bobby McFerrin a decade before McFerrin fully emerged. Jarreau's two-LP set *Look To The Rainbow* hints at enormous potential in the jazz world that he never realized or probably ever wanted. Instead, Jarreau tailored his albums so they would hint at jazz, sometimes including one out-and-out jazz selection, but otherwise emphasizing a likable but bland combination of light R&B and pop. Jarreau's flexible voice and winning personality, along with his unstoppable musicality, resulted in him becoming world famous within a short period of time. He has rarely looked back since, winning awards in the pop music world, filling stadiums and selling millions of CDs.

Along the way, Jarreau did record memorable versions of "Blue Rondo A La Turk," "Take Five," "Since I Fell For You," Chick Corea's "Spain" (which is on his otherwise forgettable *This Time* set) and occasionally some other jazz songs. He has starred at a countless number of jazz festivals but inevitably, despite a few nostalgic moments that look back at his roots in jazz, he has stuck to the music that has made him famous. While the greater music world knows his name well, for the jazz world the name Al Jarreau evokes the response, "If only."

Recommended CDs: From the jazz standpoint, Al Jarreau's most worthwhile recordings are the remarkable *1965* (Bainbridge 6237), *Look to The Rainbow* (Warner Bros. 3052), which includes "Take Five" and "Better Than Anything," and 2004's *Accentuate The Positive* (GRP 163402). A sampler of Jarreau's greatest jazz recordings from the rest of his otherwise R&Bish output is long overdue.

Website: www.aljarreau.com

Half Pint Jaxon
(Frankie Jaxon)
b. February 3, 1895, Montgomery, AL; d. 1944, Los Angeles, CA

Frankie "Half Pint" Jaxon was an eccentric jazz, blues and jive singer who often sang bawdy lyrics and worked as a female impersonator. He gained the title of "Half Pint" due to being 5'2".

Orphaned at an early age, Jaxon grew up in Kansas City and at 15 was singing in variety shows. He formed a song and dance team with Miss Gallie De Gaston that worked regularly in vaudeville for a couple of years before he developed his own solo act. Jaxon, who frequently worked in Atlantic City in the summer and Chicago in the winter (appearing on the same bill for a time with King Oliver and Freddie Keppard), gained a reputation for his ability to stage elaborate shows. In the 1920s he helped Bessie Smith and Ethel Waters put on their productions and also worked as a female impersonator, a pianist-singer and an occasional saxophonist.

Jaxon, who spent most of the 1926–41 period based in Chicago, recorded his first two numbers in 1926 (including "Hannah Fell In Love With My Piano"), was on records extensively during 1927–30, led two sessions in 1933, and made his final sides during 1937–40. Among the titles that he recorded were "Fifteen Cents," "I'm Gonna Dance Wit De Guy Wot Brung Me," "Can't You Wait Till You Get Home," "You Got To Wet It," "Chocolate To The Bone," "Spank It," "You Know Jam Don't Shake" and a song later recorded by Woody Herman, "Fan It." Among his sidemen on records were trumpeters Punch Miller and Henry "Red" Allen, clarinetist Barney Bigard and pianist Lil Armstrong. Jaxon also made guest appearances on records by Tampa Red and Georgia Tom Dorsey (billed as "The Black Hillbillies"), Cow Cow Davenport and the Harlem Hamfats. Jaxon often sang in a purposely-high feminine voice for comedy effect and some of his songs left little to the imagination.

In 1930 Half Pint formed the Quarts of Joy, a group that he featured while appearing regularly on the radio. By the end of the decade, his brand of double-entendre hokum music was going out of style and in 1941 he retired from music. Half Pint Jaxon worked for the Pentagon in Washington, DC, for a few years before moving to Los Angeles in 1944 before he passed away at the age of 49.

Recommended CDs: Although a little of Half Pint Jaxon goes a long way, these three CDs are valuable in reissuing all of his recordings as a leader: *1926–1929* (Document 5258), *1929–1937* (Document 5259) and *1937–1940* (Document 5260).

Eddie Jefferson

b. August 3, 1918, Pittsburgh, PA; d. May 9, 1979, Detroit, MI

Eddie Jefferson was the founder of vocalese and one of the most skilled at the art of writing lyrics to fit recorded solos. However, he was not the first to use vocalese. In 1929 Bee Palmer sang her words on "Singin' The Blues" to part of the recorded solos of Bix Beiderbecke and Frank Trumbauer, and

Marion Harris did a different variation based on the same recording in 1935. But Palmer's recording (due to her inferior voice) was not released until over six decades later and Harris' "Singin' The Blues" only came out in England and was obscure. Neither recording was known to Jefferson, who had his own special way of reinventing and improving the wheel.

As a youth, Jefferson played tuba, guitar and drums. When he became a professional, he worked as a singer and dancer, including with Coleman Hawkins in 1939. Jefferson began writing vocalese lyrics in the early 1940s, a decade before they were noticed. The earliest example of his singing is on a 1949 broadcast where he performs his lyrics to Charlie Parker's solo on "Parker's Mood" and Lester Young's on "I Cover The Waterfront." However, the first vocalese singer to make a strong impression was King Pleasure, who in 1952 made his recording of Eddie Jefferson's lyrics to James Moody's solo on "I'm In The Mood For Love," which was renamed "Moody's Mood For Love," and the following year recorded his own

lyrics to "Parker's Mood," both of which became timeless classics in the jazz world.

Jefferson never had that great of a voice, and listening to him sing his vocalese lyrics is similar to hearing Cole Porter perform his own songs. Others can do it better, but there is something special about hearing the composer interpret his own material. Jefferson, who recorded relatively little as a leader until 1959 (just 10 selections during 1952–56 including "The Birdland Story," a tribute to Coleman Hawkins on "Body And Soul" and "Strictly Instrumental") worked with James Moody's octet during 1953–57. He freelanced mostly as a single during the remainder of his career, though he worked again with Moody during 1968–73, co-led the group The Artistic Truth with drummer Roy Brooks during 1974–75 and during his last few years often teamed up with altoist Richie Cole. Jefferson recorded sets that were made available by Evidence (1959–60), Riverside/Original Jazz Classics (1961–62), Prestige (a pair during 1968–69), three for Muse (1974–76) and a final effort for Inner City in 1977.

Among Jefferson's other well-known lyrics were "Lady Be Good" (the Charlie Parker solo), "Now's The Time," "I've Got The Blues" (based on "Lester Leaps In"), "So What," "Freedom Jazz Dance," the humorous "Benny's From Heaven" and even Miles Davis' "Bitches Brew." Tragically, Eddie Jefferson was shot to death outside a Detroit club after a performance in 1979 for reasons that are still unknown.

Recommended CDs: Six of Eddie Jefferson's 10 early recordings are available on *The Bebop Singers* (Prestige 24216) along with important early titles from Annie Ross, King Pleasure, Joe Carroll and Jon Hendricks. Jefferson's post-1958 recordings are almost entirely available. *The Jazz Singer* (Evidence 22062), *Letter From Home* (Original Jazz Classics 307), *Body And Soul* (Original Jazz Classics 396) and *Come Along With Me* (Original Jazz Classics 613) completely cover the 1959–69 period. *Vocalese* (32 Jazz 32123) is a sampler drawn from Jefferson's three Muse albums, consisting of seven of the nine numbers on *Things Are Getting Better*, five of the eight tracks on *Godfather Of Vocalese* and just one number from *The Liveliest*. *Things Are Getting Better* (Muse 5043) and *Godfather Of Vocalese* (Muse 6013) were reissued on CD but, with the demise of Muse, have been out-of-print for quite a few years. His final recording as a leader, *The Main Man* (Inner City 1033) from 1977, shows that there was no sign of decline in Eddie Jefferson's creativity.

LPs to Search For: *The Live-liest* (Muse 5027) has not yet reappeared on CD.

Herb Jeffries

b. September 24, 1911, Detroit, MI

Primarily a ballad singer, Herb Jeffries is remarkable. It is not an exaggeration to say that no other 90-year old singer in the history of music has ever sounded so youthful.

Herb Jeffries' family was involved in show business and he began singing as a teenager on the radio. He sang in Chicago with Erskine Tate's orchestra and during 1931–34 was a member of the Earl Hines big band with whom he made his recording debut. He also sang briefly with Blanche Calloway. Jeffries, disturbed that there were no black cowboys depicted in films, raised the money and produced the first African-American cowboy films, starring as the "Bronze Buckaroo," the first black cowboy actor. He was in five Westerns during the second half of the 1930s, serving as a role model for young African-Americans.

Herb Jeffries found his greatest fame while with Duke Ellington's orchestra during 1940–42, ironically having a giant hit on a non-Ellington song called "Flamingo," which over time sold over 14 million copies. He has performed "Flamingo" at virtually every performance he has had during the 65 years since.

Jeffries, who recorded with Sidney Bechet in 1940, has had a successful solo career since leaving Ellington in 1942. He spent a decade living in France, where he ran a nightclub called The Flamingo. Back in the U.S., he has occasionally appeared in films and on television while always continuing to sing.

At the age of 96, Herb Jeffries appeared at the Sweet and Hot Music Festival in Los Angeles in 2007, singing "Flamingo" and other Ellington-associated songs. The last surviving member of the 1940 Duke Ellington Orchestra, his still-powerful voice can pass for 60.

Recommended CDs: *A Brief History Of Herb Jeffries/The Bronze Buckaroo* (Warner Western 7621), while celebrating Jeffries' role as a cowboy actor, contains many of his most significant jazz-oriented recordings including numbers with Hines, Bechet ("Blues For You, Johnny"), Joe Liggins' Honeydrippers and Ellington (four songs including "Flamingo" and "Jump For Joy"). *Say It Isn't So* (Bethlehem 20-3006) showcases Jeffries' warm voice in 1957 on a set of ballads with backing by the Russ Garcia Orchestra. *If I Were King/Remember The Bing* (Audiophile 317) reissues on one CD, two separate sets from 1978 in which Jeffries sings songs associated with Nat King Cole and Bing Crosby. *The Duke And I* (Flaming-o 327) was recorded in 1999 when Jeffries was 88. He should be recorded again to show just how young this 96-year-old wonder still sounds.

Pucci Amanda Jhones
(Pucci Amanda Wooten Jhones)
b. August 11, Newark, NJ

A fine modern mainstream jazz singer, it is surprising that Pucci Jhones thus far has only recorded two CDs.

Although Diana Ross was her original inspiration, seeing Betty Carter perform at the Cadillac Club in Newark convinced her that she should be a jazz singer. "That was the start of my wanting to create my own sound." Jhones earned a Bachelor of Fine Arts in Contemporary Music and Jazz from the New School but had other careers going on simultaneously with her singing, including being a model in Europe and an actress. Jhones' has mostly performed in New York clubs, where for a time Jacky Terrasson was her pianist. She impressed producer Bob Rusch and, although not an avant-garde singer, she has recorded one CD apiece for Rusch's Cadence and CIMP labels.

"The rush I get when I hit the stage and the music is oh so sweet. There's no repetition in the art form of jazz. I'm free to move about the music as I feel it. The freedom is what I crave. I have always been a bird in flight."

Recommended CDs: *Sweet Dreams* (Cadence 1088) from 1997 has Jhones effortlessly taking chances on standards and

sounding mature with a group that is anchored by pianist Kenny Barron. *Wild Is The Wind* (CIMP 170) features her joined by a pianoless quartet with guitarist Rory Stuart, sounding quite confident and soulful.

Website: www.puccijhones.com

Ella Johnson
b. June 22, 1917, Darlington, SC;
d. February 16, 2004, New York, NY

A smooth singer who could also get lowdown on the blues, Ella Johnson will always be best known for having introduced the standard "Since I Fell For You."

The younger sister of pianist-singer Buddy Johnson, Ella moved to New York in 1939 to join her brother's combo at the Savoy Ballroom. She spent virtually her entire career singing in his groups. Ella made her debut recording with Buddy on October 25, 1940, having a hit with "Please Mr. Johnson." That was followed seven months later by "Now Please Mr. Johnson."

Buddy Johnson's ensemble evolved from a swing combo to a big band, and by the late 1940s, he had a top R&B outfit. Ella Johnson grew with the group and showed quite a bit of flexibility, generally having hits on uptempo tunes but also excelling on blues and slow ballads. She was compared to Billie Holiday and Ella Fitzgerald early in her career but had her own sound. In addition to Buddy's "Since I Fell For You" (which she introduced in 1945), Ella had hits with "When My Man Comes Home," "Hittin' On Me," "Did You See Jackie Robinson Hit The Ball" and "I Don't Want Nobody."

The Buddy Johnson Orchestra had a strong following among black audiences in the 1950s, with Ella Johnson as its main attraction. It recorded for Decca (1940–52), Mercury (1953–57 and 1961) and an album for Roulette (1958–59) with Ella taking vocals on 47 selections. As a leader, Ella headed a few sessions of her own for Mercury during 1955–57 and a final date in 1964 but, even in the majority of those cases, she was accompanied by her brother's sidemen.

Buddy Johnson kept his music open to the influence of rock and roll by the late 1950s (Ella recorded "They Don't Want Me To Rock No More" in 1957) and his Roulette album was titled *Go Ahead And Rock*. But by the early 1960s, there was no longer a demand for a rock and roll big band. Ella Johnson retired after 1964, restricting her singing to the church for her final 40 years.

Recommended CDs: Ella Johnson's recordings with Buddy Johnson, along with the contributions of other singers and occasional instrumentals, are on *1939–1942* (Classics 884), *1942–1947* (Classics 1079), *1947–1949* (Classics 1115) and *Rockin' And Rollin'* (Collectables 5664). *Swing Me* (Verve 838 218) is an overview of Ella Johnson's solo dates from 1956–57 while *Say Ella* (Jukebox Lil 604) has 16 songs that she recorded with her brother's band during 1942–57 although unfortunately not "Since I Fell For You" (which is on *1942–1947*).

Ellen Johnson
b. December 18, 1954, Chicago, IL

A fine singer based in Los Angeles, Ellen Johnson's *These Days* is her most significant recording to date, a set that emphasizes voice-bass duets with bassist Darek Oles.

"My mother played piano and sang all kinds of music, so I must have heard the great standards growing up. There was a class taught by pianist Willie Pickens that was just for instrumentalists. I was allowed to attend and I sat in the horn section and learned everything from a horn player's point of view. After that, I started singing in clubs whenever and wherever I could. I sang in coffee houses, with folk music groups, pop bands, in musical theater, and classical recitals. I also sang jazz with some great local musicians." She worked extensively in Chicago, earned a Bachelor's of Music in Vocal Performance from the American Conservatory of Music in 1979, and received a Master's of Music from San Diego State University in 1990. Along the way, Johnson studied guitar and piano, gave master classes in vocal jazz, was president and founder of the Jazz Vocal Coalition, wrote lyrics, developed her own label of artists in the Vocal Visions Media Group, and currently is an adjunct professor at California Polytechnic University. But singing has always been her main focus.

Ellen Johnson, who has a four-octave range, names as her main inspirations among singers: Sheila Jordan, Joni Mitchell, Betty Carter and Urszula Dudziak. In addition to recording three CDs and working locally, she has been a featured soloist at performances of Duke Ellington's Sacred Concerts, excelling in the role originally filled by Alice Babs.

"Poetry plays an important role in my music. I write and choose material that has a sense of poetry in the lyrics and the music because I like the subtleties of sound and words, like a painter with colors."

Recommended CDs: *Too Good To Title* (Vocal Visions 02) includes such numbers as "Peggy's Blue Skylight" (with guest altoist Charles McPherson), Duke Ellington's "Heaven," "Waltz For Debby" and the singer's own "TV News Blues." *Chinchilla Serenade* (Vocal Visions 03) has among its highlights "Freedom," "Yesterdays" and "A Child Is Born." Pianist Rick Helzer is an asset on both CDs. Ellen Johnson's recent *These Days* (Vocal Visions 04) is her most intimate set, mostly duets with bassist Darek Oles, plus two special appearances by Sheila Jordan.

Website: www.ellenjohnson.net

Kelley Johnson
b. July 1, 1961, Richmond, IN

Kelley Johnson has been compared to Carmen McRae, Irene Kral and Anita O'Day. One can hear similarities in the way she makes lyrics sound personal through her phrasing while swinging the words and constantly improvising.

Growing up in Milwaukee, she remembers going to a record store and purchasing Miles Davis' *Kind Of Blue*, Billie Holiday's *Billie's Blues* and Keith Jarrett's *My Song*. "I started sneaking into The Jazz Gallery while I was still a minor (17) and I heard the locals several times a week, like Hattush Alexander, Ray Appleton, Manty Ellis and Jessie Hauck, and such young guys as Carl Allen, Brian Lynch and David Hazeltine. Many of these people became my teachers and mentors, and the musical values that they expressed gave me my foundation." Johnson sang in a rock band in high school and earned

a music degree from the Wisconsin Conservatory of Music in 1984. She worked steadily in Wisconsin starting when she was 22. "In 1988 I realized I was a jazz singer and not supposed to be anything else, and that was that."

The year 1988 was the turning point of her life. While in Seattle on vacation, she was hired to sing with the Roadside Attraction Big Band and decided to make Seattle her home. She met Mark Murphy, who became a mentor, friend and influence, and she teamed up with pianist John Hansen, who in 1997 became her husband.

Since then, she has recorded three CDs, using such notable sidemen as Brian Lynch, Fred Hersch, Geoff Keezer and Ingrid Jensen. In 2002 she won first prize in the Jazzconnect Jazz Vocal competition, which gained her a live recording date at Birdland. In 2004 the Kelley Johnson Quartet was chosen by the Kennedy Center and State Department as U.S. Jazz Ambassadors. They toured seven countries in Eastern Europe and Asia, including Russia. In addition to her singing, Kelley Johnson teaches at the Cornish College of the Arts and Musicworks Northwest, and is a skilled lyricist, with her words to Joe Henderson's "Recorda Me" being covered by other singers.

"I love the immediacy of jazz. I love flying by the seat of my pants and finding a new way to say the things I think are most important through music."

Recommended CDs: *Make Someone Happy* (Chartmaker 1100) from 1998 is a particularly impressive debut, ranging from "Stompin' At The Savoy" to Abbey Lincoln's "Throw It Away" and introducing Kelley Johnson's words to "Recorda Me."

Live At Birdland (Jazz Connect 002), which was recorded in one night, also has plenty of variety (from "Tulip Or Turnip" to Ornette Coleman's "Turnaround") and consistently top-notch singing. *Music Is The Magic* (Sapphire 7612) includes memorable versions of "Lucky To Be Me," "Tea For Two" and "Music Is The Magic," the latter a celebration of singing jazz. Kelley Johnson wrote most of the arrangements.

Lil Johnson
(birth and death dates and locations are not known)

It is odd that virtually nothing is known about three of the four most popular female blues singers of the 1930s (Lil Johnson, Merline Johnson and Georgia White), the three that are most jazz-oriented (all but Memphis Minnie). In the case of Lil Johnson, not even a photo has surfaced to show what she looked like, much less her birth and death dates or where she grew up.

What is known is that Lil Johnson was a talented singer whose music crossed over from blues to hokum and swing-oriented jazz. She recorded five titles (one of which was originally unissued) in 1929, most of which are double-entendre risqué songs such as "You'll Never Miss Your Jelly Till Your Jelly Roller's Gone." Charles Avery or Montana Taylor is on piano with guitarist Tampa Red added on "House Rent Scuffle."

All of Johnson's other 68 recordings were cut during 1935–37. Her biggest hit was "Get 'Em From The Peanut Man (Hot Nuts)," which has three different versions. Many of her other recordings are in a similar vein including "Anybody Want To Buy My Cabbage," "If You Can Dish It (I Can Take It)," "Press My Button (Ring My Bell)," "Sam The Hot Dog Man," "My Stove's In Good Condition," "Let's Get Drunk And Truck," "New Shave 'Em Dry," "Take Your Hand Off It," "Snake In The Grass" and even "Buck Naked Blues." Most of these songs are not pornographic, although "My Baby

(Squeeze Me Again)" is very close, and they generally hint at more than they actually say. Johnson sings the tunes with such exuberance and musicality that she uplifts the potentially dubious material. Other strong assets are the sidemen, which at times include the equally mysterious pianist Black Bob, guitarist Big Bill Broonzy and trumpeter Lee Collins.

Despite her productivity and the relative popularity of her recordings, Lil Johnson does not seem to have appeared in any Chicago clubs during the period, and she completely disappeared into history after 1937.

Recommended CDs: All of Lil Johnson's recordings are available on *Vol. 1* (Document 5307), *Vol. 2* (Document 5308) and *Vol. 3/Barrel House Annie* (Document 5309).

Merline Johnson
b. ca. 1912, MS; d. unknown date and location

A strong blues singer who was able to interact effectively with jazz musicians in Chicago (most notably trumpeter Lee Collins), Merline Johnson was known as "The Yas Yas Girl." As with her competitors Lil Johnson and Georgia White, virtually nothing is known about Johnson beyond her recordings and the fact that her brother's daughter was singer LaVern Baker.

Merline Johnson recorded 77 selections during 1937–41 in Chicago. While most of the earlier titles fall more into blues than jazz, her music became more jazz-oriented by mid-1938. Among her sidemen on these consistently enjoyable performances are pianists Black Bob and Blind John Davis, guitarists Big Bill Broonzy and George Barnes, and trumpeters Lee Collins and Punch Miller. In addition to blues songs and quite a few having to do with alcohol, she recorded Jelly Roll Morton's "Don't You Leave Me Here," "Old Man Mose," "Don't You Make Me High," and Billie Holiday's "Fine And Mellow."

After a five-year absence from the recording studios, Merline Johnson returned in 1947 to cut four titles, but only one was issued ("Bad Whiskey Blues") and that was decades later. That was the last that was heard musically from the mysterious Yas Yas Girl.

Recommended CDs: All of Merline Johnson's recordings are available on *The Yas Yas Girl: Vols. 1–3* (Document 5292, 5293 and 5294) and *Female Chicago Blues* (Document 5295); the latter has her final seven selections along with music from three equally obscure singers from the era.

Etta Jones
b. November 25, 1928, Aiken, SC;
d. October 16, 2001, Mount Vernon, NY

A bluesy singer who gave heartfelt interpretations of standards, ballads and blues, Etta Jones never became a household name, but was a beloved figure in jazz.

At the age of three she moved with her family to New York City. She started in the music business pretty early, faring well in a local talent contest when she was 15, which led to her discovery by bandleader Buddy Johnson who hired her for his orchestra. After a year, she began her solo career, making her first session as a leader in 1944. Jones sang four Leonard Feather songs, but since three were already hits for Dinah Washington, they did not create a stir. Jones recorded other sessions for RCA during 1946–47 and had stints with drummer J.C. Heard and Earl Hines (1949–52). In the 1950s she freelanced, working in New York clubs but also having occasional day jobs including working as a seamstress, an elevator operator, and as a stuffer of LP jackets for the London label.

In 1960 Etta Jones began recording a string of albums for Prestige and her first record generated a hit in "Don't Go To Strangers." She recorded regularly for the next five years and, although she was mostly off records during 1966–75, an important event occurred during that period. In 1968 in Washington, DC, she worked for the first time with tenor-saxophonist Houston Person. Their musical partnership lasted for the next 33 years, and they seemed so close that many mistakenly thought that they were married. Jones was married, but not to Person.

Etta Jones toured Japan with Art Blakey's Jazz Messengers in 1970, but maintained a low profile until 1976, when she began recording regularly for Muse, often with Person in her group. Her recordings during the last 25 years of her life for Muse and its successor High Note are some of the most rewarding of her career. She stayed active singing her brand of soulful jazz until she was struck down by cancer at the age of 72.

Recommended CDs: *1944–1947* (Classics 1065) has Etta Jones' first 21 recordings and finds her sounding fairly mature (particularly for her age), bluesy and versatile. *Don't Go To Strangers* (Original Jazz Classics 298), *Hollar!* (Original Jazz Classics 1061), *So Warm* (Original Jazz Classics 874), *From The Heart* (Original Jazz Classics 1016), *Lonely And Blue* (Original Jazz Classics 702) and *Love Shout* (Original Jazz Classics 941) contain all of Jones' Prestige recordings of 1960–63 and each set has its memorable moments although the one to start with is *Don't Go To Strangers*. During 1976–2000, Etta Jones recorded more than a dozen albums for Muse (those will be difficult to locate) and High Note. Some of the most rewarding are *My Mother's Eyes* (32 Jazz 32027), *I'll Be Seeing You* (Muse 5531), *Reverse The Charges* (Muse 5474), *My Gentleman Friend* (Muse 5534), which is a set of duets with pianist Benny Green, *The Melody Lingers On* (High Note 7005), *My Buddy: Songs Of Buddy Johnson* (High Note 7026), *All The Way* (High Note 7047), *Easy Living* (High Note 7059) and her final album, *Etta Jones Sings Lady Day* (High Note 7078).

LPs to Search For: *Etta Jones Sings* (King 707) from 1957 is her only recording as a leader during 1948–59. Another scarce album with the same name, *Etta Jones Sings* (Roulette 25329), is from 1965.

Maggie Jones
(Faye Barnes)
b. 1900, Hillsboro, TX; d. Probably 1940s, TX

Very little is known about the classic blues singer Maggie Jones, whose recording career stopped prematurely and whose death date is unknown. Born in Texas, she moved to New York City in 1922, working in theaters for the next five years, billed as "The Texas Nightingale." Jones recorded 38 songs during 1923–26

Louis Jordan

including six songs in 1924 in which she is accompanied by Louis Armstrong and pianist Fletcher Henderson. Of these, "Anybody Here Want To Try My Cabbage" was a minor hit while "Good Time Flat Blues" would resurface as "Farewell To Storyville" in the 1946 Armstrong movie, *New Orleans*. Some of Jones' other recordings include such notable sidemen as trombonist Charlie Green, guitarist Roy Smeck, cornetists Joe Smith and Louis Metcalf, and pianists Cliff Jackson and Clarence Williams. Jones, who rarely gets mentioned as one of the top blues singers of the 1920s, actually fares quite well, had an attractive voice and was able to hold long notes quite effectively. Her other recordings include "Don't Never Tell Nobody What Your Good Man Can Do," "Four Flushing Papa," "You May Go, But You'll Come Back Someday," "You Ain't Gonna Feed In My Pasture Now" and "Mama Stayed Out The Whole Night Long."

On evidence of her recordings, Maggie Jones was still improving as a singer in 1926 but her recordings stop there. She worked with the Clarence Muse Vaudeville Company in 1927, co-owned a dress shop and during 1928–29 had a small part in Lew Leslie's *Blackbirds Of 1928*. Jones returned to Texas in the early 1930s and was last reported performing in 1934. Unfortunately, nothing is known of Maggie Jones' life from that point on.

Recommended CDs: All of her recordings are on *Maggie Jones, Vol. 1* (Document 5348) and *Maggie Jones, Vol. 2/Gladys Bentley* (Document 5349).

Louis Jordan

b. July 8, 1908, Brinkley, AR; d. February 4, 1975, Los Angeles, CA

Louis Jordan always had the ability to sing the most complicated and humorous lyrics effortlessly while displaying a lovable personality. An excellent altoist, Jordan's string of hits during 1941–51 bridged the gap between swing and rhythm and blues, setting the stage for rock and roll. His witty and swinging jump music formed a world of its own, one that has been emulated often but never duplicated all that successfully.

Jordan began playing clarinet when he was seven, gigging as a teenager with his father's group, the Rabbit Foot Minstrels. In 1929 he played alto with Jimmy Pryor's Imperial Serenaders, and he toured with a variety of bands in the South before moving to Philadelphia in 1932. Jordan worked with trumpeter Charlie Gaines, recorded with Clarence Williams in New York in 1934, played with Leroy Smith's big band in 1935 and was a section player with the Chick Webb Orchestra during 1936–38, featured on three rather dull ballad vocals.

When Jordan formed his own band in 1938, he was 30 and completely unknown. He began to record as a leader in December 1938, and the following year named his group (which was usually a septet) the Tympani Five since his drummer occasionally added tympani to the ensembles for color. The name would stick even after the tympani was permanently discarded. Combining together catchy melodies, riff-filled ensembles, brief

but heated solos, Jordan's very accessible and hip vocals, and the ability to perform a lot of music within three minutes was a winning formula. One hit followed another in what seemed to be an endless flow, and of the 57 songs released as singles during 1944–51, 55 made the R&B top 10.

Among the numbers made famous by Louis Jordan and his Tympani Five were "Choo Choo Ch'Boogie," "Ain't Nobody Home But Us Chickens," "Is You Is Or Is You Ain't Ma Baby," "Five Guys Named Moe," "Saturday Night Fish Fry," "G.I. Jive," "Caldonia," "Let The Good Times Roll" and "What's The Use Of Getting Sober (When You Gonna Get Drunk Again)." Jordan became such a big name that he starred in several black films while making brief appearances in white ones. His group worked constantly, and he recorded duets with Bing Crosby, Louis Armstrong and Ella Fitzgerald.

And then in 1952, the success stopped. The music world was changing and Jordan made the mistake of putting together a big band, which quickly flopped. While the songs he continued recording were appealing, none were hits and, by the time rock and roll exploded in 1956, Jordan, at 48, was considered old and passé in the pop music world. He continued performing but was unable to recapture the magic except when he played his older hits. Perhaps if he had switched to jazz, Louis Jordan would have been more significant in the 1960s, but instead he essentially became a nostalgia act despite still singing and playing quite well in his classic style, as shown on 1973's *I Believe In Music*, his final recording.

Recommended CDs: *The Best Of Louis Jordan* (MCA 4079) is an excellent sampler filled with Jordan hits. Completists will prefer *1934–1940* (Classics 636), *1940–1941* (Classics 663), *1941–1943* (Classics 741), *1943–1945* (Classics 866), *1945–1946* (Classics 921) and *1946–1947* (Classics 1010). *One Guy Named Louis* (Capitol 96804) from 1954 and *Rock 'N Roll Call* (Bluebird 66145) from 1955–56 have no hits, but the performances are infectious. *I Believe In Music* (Evidence 26006) serves as his excellent last act.

Sheila Jordan

(Jeanette Dawson)
b. November 18, 1928, Detroit, MI

One of the truly great jazz singers, Sheila Jordan is always both highly expressive and very intelligent in her improvisations, whether scatting or interpreting lyrics. One of the few who can effortlessly improvise words, often making up a blues onstage to sum up her day, she is very accessible and easy to approach (loving to help out younger singers), yet creates jazz on a level few other jazz vocalists can touch.

She grew up in poverty in Pennsylvania, living near the coal mines, but loved to sing from an early age. "At 14, I moved to Detroit to live with my mother. A couple years later I heard Bird on the jukebox outside my school, and it blew my mind." A quiet rebel from the start, she mostly worked with black musicians in Detroit, being encouraged by Tommy Flanagan, Kenny Burrell, Barry Harris and the local players. Jordan was a member of the vocal trio Skeeter, Mitch and Jean, a group that sang Charlie Parker solos and predated Lambert, Hendricks and Ross by a decade.

She moved to New York in the early 1950s where she married pianist Duke Jordan (who was most famous for being with Charlie Parker during 1947–48), took a few lessons from Lennie Tristano, and gigged whenever she could. Her first voice and bass duet performance was with Charles Mingus at the Five Spot in the early 1950s. But she was unrecorded and little known until George Russell, who was very impressed by her adventurous nature and improvising skills, enlisted her to record "You Are My Sunshine" over a very advanced arrangement in his *The Outer View record*. He also helped get her signed to Blue Note where, as one of the label's very few vocalists, she recorded the classic, *Portrait Of Sheila* in 1962.

Despite the artistic successes, it was difficult for Sheila Jordan to make a living out of singing her brand of jazz, so she had a conventional day job for many years. Her second album under her own name followed her first by 13 years and was made for a Japanese label. *Sheila*, recorded in 1977, was her first duet album with a bassist (Arild Andersen), which became a specialty and a joy of hers. She co-led a group with pianist Steve Kuhn in the late 1970s and in 1982 recorded the first of several duet albums with bassist Harvey Swartz. From that point on, she has worked in jazz full-time and been recognized as a legendary singer, recording frequently, teaming in more recent times with bassist Cameron Brown, and being one of the major inspirations for scores of younger vocalists.

Referring to herself as "a frustrated bass player," she says, "The music is so much a part of me. The spirit is fulfilled when I can express what I hear and feel. I never expected to come this far in music. I'm shocked at my acceptance, so I'll keep doing the little thing I do for as much time as I have left."

Recommended CDs: *Portrait Of Sheila* (Blue Note 89002) has the singer backed by a quiet guitar-bass-drums rhythm section in 1962, with "Dat Dere" being a duet with bassist Steve Swallow. *Confirmation*, recorded in 1975, (Test Of Time 4) is highlighted by "Inch Worm," "My Favorite Things" and "Confirmation." *Sheila* (Steeplechase 31081) is her classic collaboration with Arild Anderson, *Playground* (ECM 1159) teams her with Steve Kuhn, and *Lazy Afternoon* (Muse 5366) is her initial duet album with Harvie Swartz. Other worthy recordings include *The Very Thought Of Two* (MA 5), *Songs From Within* (MA 014), *Lost And Found* (Muse 5390), *One For Junior* (Muse 5493), which has her taking delightful vocal duets with Mark Murphy in 1991, *Heart Strings* (Muse 5468), *Jazz Child* (High Note 7029), *I've Grown Accustomed To The Bass* (High Note 7042) with Cameron Brown, *Little Song* (High Note 7096) and the recent *Celebration* (High Note 7136), which is also a set of duets with Brown.

Website: www.sheilajordanjazz.com

Judi K.
(Judi K. Erickson)
b. October 15, 1942, Arcadia, WI

A fine swing singer who has also been heard in Dixieland settings, Judi K. leads the Hot Swing Revue.

"I remember when movies and television had performers that played and sang jazz and big band music; it mesmerized me. One could see Louis Armstrong, Bing Crosby, Anita O'Day, Lena Horne, Ella Fitzgerald, Rosemary Clooney, Patti Page, Judy Garland, Doris Day and others. Those people

never lost the gist of the song or the meaning of the words, yet they played with the time in ways I can only dream of." Judi K. picked up experience performing in plays in high school and in community theater. For many years, she was a guitar teacher who also sang and played. "I had my own trio called the Swing Set. That's about all we had at first was one set of swing, but it blossomed, and we added pieces and did a lot of weddings."

The turning point for Judi K. occurred in 1982, when she met country mandolinist Jethro Burns. "I was performing with my student guitar class and he was our school's guest artist. He watched my class perform, and then invited me to sing with him. The other teachers just about fell off their chairs and, after that, he told me he was going to put me to work. He had me guest in some of his concerts. I assumed this was the way it was supposed to be. It was coming too easy: airplanes, limos, dressing rooms, personal guards, well, I sure know better now. Jethro did make me realize that the music I always loved was still around, and it made me hunger for more of it. I was led to the classic jazz bands that were still playing for a living, and I was so thrilled to hear, in person, the music of my 'past' and to find out that it was still alive."

In 1987 Judi K. started singing with Gary Miller's Celebration Dixieland Band and Connie Jones' Crescent City Jazz Band. Her most important association also began that year. "Jim Beebe and Barrett Deems were guest starring at Gary Miller's anniversary show, and Jim asked me to try singing with his Chicago Jazz. Within two months, I was a regular member of that band, and the rest is 'history.' Jim had a hot, swinging, popular band that was working five and six nights a week, plus daytime corporate events. Many times, we were performing with each other two and three times a day at different gigs." She worked with Jim Beebe until he retired in 2002, two years before his death.

"At my first night club dates in Kenosha Wisconsin, the owner told me, 'Judi, always look your best, even if the room is empty. You never know who is going to come in the door.' I took him seriously then and that's the way I have tried to keep it. My style is one that evokes nostalgia and memories of the classy songbirds of the '40s."

Recommended CDs: *It's Been A Long Long Time* (Jazzology 215) features Judi K. on 15 standards, mostly from the swing era and before. Jim Beebe, Jethro Burns, cornetist Connie Jones and Franz Jackson on tenor all get their spots although Judi K's ballad singing takes honors. *I'm Nobody's Baby* (Jazzology 319) is its equal, with the highlights including "I've Got The World On A String," "Dream A Little Dream Of Me," "As Long As I Live" and "I'll See You In My Dreams."

Website: www.judikjazz.com

Kitty Kallen
b. May 25, 1922, Philadelphia, PA

Kitty Kallen was part of the later part of the swing era and she made a strong impression with her classy style.

She won an amateur contest as a child, imitating other famous singers of the period. Kallen sang on the radio on *The Children's Hour* and had her own radio show on WCAU while still just a young teenager. She sang with Jan Savitt in 1936 when she was only 14, and had stints with the orchestras of Artie Shaw (1938), Jack Teagarden (1939-40) and Bobby Sherwood. Kallen made her recording debut with Shaw and sounded mature for her age. She gained her first real

Bev Kelly

recognition in the jazz world in 1943 when she replaced Helen O'Connell with Jimmy Dorsey, having a hit with "Besame Mucho," and introducing "Star Eyes," one of several vocal duets that she had with Bob Eberly.

In late 1944, Kallen joined Harry James' band where she had major hits with Duke Ellington's "I'm Beginning To See The Light" and the perfect song with which to end World War II, "It's Been A Long Long Time." She also had good sellers in "I Guess I'll Hang My Tears Out To Dry" and "I'll Buy That Dream."

After leaving James, Kitty Kallen had a solo career, appearing regularly on the radio and recording middle-of-the-road pop records for Musicraft, Signature and Mercury. Due to having temporarily lost her voice, she was inactive during part of 1951–53. In 1954 she made an unexpected comeback, having big hits in "Little Things Mean A Lot," "In The Chapel In The Moonlight" and "I Want You All To Myself." With the rise of rock and roll, the success soon faded and she retired in 1957, but came back during 1959–62, having further strong sellers in "If I Give My Heart to You" and "My Coloring Book." Since that time, having made her mark, Kitty Kallen gradually retired.

Recommended CDs: The two-CD set *The Kitty Kallen Story* (CBS 48978) has the high points of her recording career, from "Star Eyes" to "My Coloring Book."

Bev Kelly

b. June 18, 1934, Rittman, OH

A fine singer who was a cool jazz vocalist in the 1950s, Bev Kelly has "disappeared" from the music scene on a few occasions while enjoying success in other fields.

"I was introduced to blues and jazz at a very early age. I began studying classical piano at the age of five and continued my studies through high school. I did most of my charts when I was actively singing, studied classical voice when I was 14 and performed in recitals, concerts, light opera, etc. When I was 18, I was awarded a vocal scholarship to the Conservatory of Music in Cincinnati, Ohio."

In 1954 she began teaming up with pianist Pat Moran, appearing on Steve Allen's *Tonight Show* as a duo and then, with the addition of bass and drums, they became the Pat Moran Trio featuring Bev Kelly. Most unusual was that the group sang four-part harmony. The band was signed to Bethlehem, recorded two albums, and was part of a notable recording of the music from *Porgy And Bess*. In December 1957, Kelly recorded her first album as a leader, soon leaving the group. She worked as a solo artist for a couple of years, made two albums for Riverside, and was based in San Francisco, working with pianist Flip Nunez and altoist Pony Poindexter.

"I had a young son when I began my singing career and it was difficult to be a mom and travel at the same time. In 1961, with no regrets, I opted to be with my son and his father." She retired from active performing, wrote music and poetry, worked as a vocal coach, did some session work, and was a professional photographer. Kelly resumed performing on an occasional basis in the Los Angeles area in 1966, including with pianist Hampton Hawes and trombonist Frank Rosolino. In 1972, she recorded three albums for *Reader's Digest* in London, she worked with Al Williams' quintet in Long Beach in 1976, and sang the opening and closing themes for the film *The Late Show* in 1977.

"From 1978 to 1980, I was an investor in a club in Long Beach, California, called the Jazz Safari that was owned by Al Williams. I worked there through 1979 with a number of excellent musicians." A live set from the Jazz Safari was recently released for the first time.. Her most current recording, a CD of autobiographical tone poems co-written and arranged by Jimmy Felber in 2002, is *Portrait Of Nine Dreams.*

Bev Kelly returned to school and earned a doctorate in Psychology in 1984, becoming a psychotherapist and again dropping out of music. "I approach my work with people with the same creativity I did as a singer. I encourage people to follow their passions and their dreams. They can be all that they want to be if they believe in themselves."

Recommended CDs: *Love Locked Out* (Original Jazz Classics 1798) and *Bev Kelly In Person* (Original Jazz Classics 1019) are reissues of Bev Kelly's rewarding Riverside albums. *Live At The Jazz Safari* (3D 1017) from 1979, shows what a loss it was to the jazz world when Kelly decided to become semi-retired. *Portrait Of Nine Dreams* (Jimeni 61834) is a much more recent and thoughtful release, showing how Bev Kelly sounds today.

LPs to Search For: *Beverly Kelly Sings* (Audio Fidelity 1874) and her two albums with Pat Moran, *The Pat Moran Quartet* (Bethlehem 6007) and *While At Birdland* (Bethlehem 6018) are very scarce.

Website: www.bevkellyphd.com

Beverly Kenny

b. January 29, 1932, Harrison, NJ; d. April 13, 1960, New York, NY

One of the most promising singers of the late 1950s, Beverly Kenny's tragically brief life has resulted in her being almost completely forgotten.

Inspired and slightly influenced by Billie Holiday, Ella Fitzgerald and Mel Tormé, Kenny began her career singing in Miami. She spent part of 1955 singing with the Dorsey Brothers Orchestra and made her first official album. From the start, she had her own sound, based in the jazz tradition while displaying a distinctive tone. During a five-year period she recorded six albums, three apiece for Roost and Decca. Kenny was attractive, original and always swung while putting plenty of feeling into ballads, and she fit well into the era, interacting well with both Count Basie sidemen and cool jazz players.

But she was also prone to depression, and a broken love affair plus some unseen inner demons led her to take her own life in the spring of 1960, overdosing on a combination of alcohol and sleeping pills. Beverly Kenny was 28.

Recommended CDs: Beverly Kenny's recordings, after having been scarce for decades, have reappeared on CDs. *Lonely And Blue* (Cellar Door 1022) from around 1952 has 10 selections originally recorded as radio transcriptions. The very youthful singer is heard on obscure but worthy material including "It's A Mean Old World," "Long, Lean And Lanky" and the somewhat bizarre "That Pyramid Jazz." *Snuggled On Your Shoulder* (Cellar Door 1003), a previously unreleased set from 1954 that teams the singer with pianist Tony Tamburello, was originally a demo tape and is quite listenable. *Sings for Johnny Smith* (Fresh Sound 79) released in 1955, is a gem, particularly her delightful versions of "Destination Moon," "Almost Like Being In Love" and "There Will Never Be Another You" (even if "Ball And Chain," a renamed "Sweet Lorraine," sounds dumb). *Come Swing With Me* (just available in Japan on Toshiba/EMI 679) has Kenney joined by a big band arranged by Ralph Burns while *Sings With Jimmy Jones And The Basie-ites* (Fresh Sound 33), which has spots for trumpeter Joe Newman and Frank Wess on tenor and flute, features superior versions of "Nobody Else But Me," "Isn't This A Lovely Day" and "Can't Get Out Of This Mood." *Songs For Playboys* (Universal/Decca 3044) is performed with an intimate duo consisting of pianist Ellis Larkins and bassist Joe Benjamin, *Born To Be Blue* (Universal 9327) has orchestral backing and *Like Yesterday* (Universal 9328) features contributions from Jerome Richardson on reeds and guitarist Chuck Wayne. Taken as a whole, this body of work is impressive, but leaves one wanting more.

Stacey Kent
b. March 27, 1968, South Orange, NJ

A cool-toned and laid-back singer, Stacey Kent has been building a strong audience for the past decade.

She originally had no plans to be a jazz singer, earning a degree in Comparative Literature from Sarah Lawrence College. Kent moved to England to work on a Master's, met saxophonist Jim Tomlinson (who she married in 1991) at Oxford, and decided to pursue music instead. She studied for a year at the Guidhall School Of Music. When her demo tape was sent out, she was signed to Candid in addition to appearing in the film version of *Richard III*.

Stacey Kent has since been featured on seven CDs of her own and on Jim Tomlinson's recordings including, most notably, *The Lyric*. On her most recent CD, *Breakfast On The Morning Tram*, Kent mostly foregoes singing the usual songs from the Great American Songbook in favor of performing worthy originals by Tomlinson and novelist Kazuo Ishiguro.

Recommended CDs: Each of Stacey Kent's CDs are logical steps forward in the evolution of the subtle jazz vocalist: *Close Your Eyes* (Candid 79737), *The Tender Trap* (Candid 79751), *Let Yourself Go* (Candid 79764), *Dreamsville* (Candid 79775), *In Love Again* (Candid 79786), *The Boy Next Door* (Candid 79797), Jim Tomlinson's *The Lyric* (King 507) and *Breakfast On The Morning Tram* (Blue Note 01611)

Website: www.staceykent.com

Rebecca Kilgore
b. September 24, 1949, Waltham, MA

One of the finest singers to emerge in the swing field during the 1990s, Rebecca Kilgore has an infectious and winning style. Her voice, which is influenced a bit by both Doris Day and Maxine Sullivan, is always in tune. She has the ability to place notes perfectly, and she uplifts every song she sings while swinging lightly. She is a constant joy to hear and has become a major attraction at classic jazz festivals, jazz parties and cruises.

Kilgore sang early on in her church choir and enjoyed singing along with the soundtracks of musicals. After discovering jazz she remembers, "When I became of driving age, I sang along with Ella in my car at the top of my lungs." She was an art major for two-and-a-half years at the University of Massachusetts in Amherst, studied jazz guitar for a year while in her twenties, and later in Portland took some college courses in theory, keyboard harmony and ear training, but her singing was very natural and largely self-taught.

Rebecca Kilgore did not begin singing professionally until 1981 when she joined Wholly Cats. "That association was an awakening for me, and the band was quite successful. I learned a tremendous amount about music and the music business. Next, my association with pianist Dave Frishberg, which started in 1992, was extremely gratifying." She was gradually discovered by the trad and swing jazz worlds, has appeared on over 30 recordings including many for the Arbors label, and became a key member of BED, a quartet that also includes guitarist-banjoist-singer Eddie Erickson, trombonist Dan Barrett and bassist Joel Forbes. BED gives Kilgore an opportunity to show off her humorous side, interact with the often-hilarious Erickson, and to play rhythm guitar. "My current band, BED, is the best ever: musically high-level and challenging, yet fun at the same time."

When asked about her future goals, Rebecca Kilgore responded, "To record and perform more with BED, and to learn every song written during 1930 to 1950."

Recommended CDs: Rebecca Kilgore is remarkably consistent, both in performance and on records. Her earliest recordings include *It's Easy To Remember* (Orb 1002), *Cactus Setup* (PHD 1009) and duets with Dave Frishberg on *Looking At You* (PHD 1004). 1994's *I Saw Stars* (Arbors 19136) was her breakthrough recording and it has been followed by *Not A Care In The World* (Arbors 19169), *The Starlit Hour* (Arbors 19255), *With Barrett, Ingham, Reitmeier* (Jump 12-22), *With The Keith Ingham Sextet* (Jump 12-24), *Moments Like This* (Heavywood 78871), *Harlem Butterfly* (Audiophile 308), *The Music Of Jimmy Van Heusen* (Jump 12-27) and *Make Someone Happy* (Audiophile 319). BED has thus far recorded *Get Ready For Bed* (Blue Swing 001), *Bedlam* (Blue Swing 003) and *Watch Out* (Blue Swing 005). In addition, Rebecca Kilgore has participated on dates led by pianist John Sheridan, Dan Barrett, trumpeter Duke Heitger, Lyle Ritz on ukulele and several very memorable outings by drummer Hal Smith's Roadrunners.

Website: www.rebeccakilgore.com

Marilyn King
b. May 11, 1931, Glendale, CA

Because the King Sisters gained their initial fame during the swing era, it surprises many people that Marilyn King is still performing as of this writing in the 21st century. However, she was the youngest of the King Sisters and was not a member of the group in its earliest days. Since Marilyn King can pass for being quite a few years younger than her mid-seventies, that adds more to the confusion.

"My sisters, the King Sisters, were the first four-part harmony girl vocal group in the late '30s and '40s. They had many hit records with RCA Victor and Bluebird, got their start with the Horace Heidt Orchestra and later formed their own band with Alvino Rey who my sister Luise married. They appeared in ballrooms, theaters, nightclubs, hotels, and on radio shows all over the USA and also made movies. I was

Nancy King

a little girl at the time. Mom and Dad used to take me East every summer, where I would hang out backstage and in the dressing rooms. I can even remember some of the musicians babysitting me."

Her father was a music professor who taught each of his children (six girls and two boys) how to sing and play instruments, forming a family vaudeville act before Marilyn King was born. "As my sisters became famous and started singing jazz and swing, Daddy was determined to make me a classical singer and pianist, but jazz won out. At age nine, I began substituting for each sister when she would get pregnant (which was a lot) or ill. I eventually became Alvino Rey's girl singer, replacing Blossom Dearie and Betty Bennett." She was the featured vocalist on Rey's weekly television show in 1951, and has spent the many decades since performing in a countless number of situations.

In addition to singing with the King Sisters off and on through 2004, as well as with Alvino Rey, Marilyn King has worked with Billy May, Frank DeVol, Freddy Martin, Les Brown, Harry James and Ray Anthony, and appeared on virtually all of the key variety television shows. She starred on various King Family and King Sisters television specials, performed in lead roles in 1970s productions of *Hello Dolly* and *Guys And Dolls*, had her own nightclub act for many years, and sung for five presidents. King mostly performs swing standards but also does an expert imitation of Louis Armstrong and puts on an entertaining show.

"I have been backstage and on stage all of my life. Music and love were the main theme(s) in my family's life. I loved the sound of my father giving music lessons, and listening to him compose. I loved to hear my sisters on the radio and on recordings. I had no other choice than to follow in their footsteps. To this day, I still love to hear musicians warming up their instruments before a concert, and the smell of dressing rooms."

Recommended CDs: *Solo Flight* (Alamody Prods.) features Marilyn King in recent times. She can also be heard with the King Sisters on *Spotlight On The King Sisters* (Capitol 31203) and *Imagination/Warm And Wonderful* (EMI 866904).

Website: www.marilynking.com

Nancy King
b. June 15, 1940, Eugene, OR

Until recently, when she began to emerge much more on the national scene, Nancy King had a small following that included virtually every creative singer in jazz. Her ability to improvise in any setting, along with her wit and her seemingly effortless originality, has long made her a great favorite among her fellow jazz singers.

The daughter of pianists said, "I specifically remember that Slim Gaillard and Slam Stewart (Slim and Slam) were my idols when I was four years old. I could sing 'Flat Foot Floogie' with all the 'Vouties' and 'O-Rooneys.' My first actual gig (at age

13) was with my Dad's little band at the Moose Lodge dance in Corvallis, Oregon." Nancy King played drums from the time she was eight until she was 21. "The most inspirational moment in my life was when Ella Fitzgerald and Louis Armstrong came to Eugene when I was 14. They played at the University of Oregon and it was general admission. I was the first person in the door and got the best seat—front row center. I was in heaven watching Louis, who started scat singing, and Ella, who was the best scatter on the planet. At that concert, I knew that that was what I wanted to do."

Nancy King attended the University of Oregon for one year, and then joined a band in 1959 with guitarist Ralph Towner and bassist Glen Moore, playing drums. She sang in San Francisco with Pony Poindexter in 1961, and gigged with Vince Guaraldi, Flip Nunez, Wes Montgomery, Manny Duran and many other local players. "I met Uncle Marky (Mark Murphy) in 1961 and he has been my friend ever since, along with being one of my major influences." She also studied with Jon Hendricks and Bill Henderson.

After performing at various Playboy clubs for two years, in 1970 Nancy King settled back in Eugene, raising a family and singing locally. She has since worked with pianist Steve Christofferson, bassist Glen Moore (co-leading King & Moore), Dave Frishberg, Leroy Vinnegar, John Stowell and Ray Brown, and has been very active as both a singer and an educator. Her Max Jazz recording and her guest appearances with Karrin Allyson (including a few appearances on Allyson's *Footprints* CD) have finally given her some of her recognition that she deserves.

"Jazz is something I have to do. It's life itself to me. I am my music. I get so much from performing, listening, and teaching it, passing it along to my students. If I didn't have the music, I'd have been dead long ago."

Recommended CDs: *Impending Bloom* (Justice 801), *Potato Radio* (Justice 802) and *Cliff Dance* (Justice 803) features King & Moore. *Straight Into Your Heart* (Mons 874 778) is a magnificent collaboration with the Metropole Orchestra while *Dream Lands 1* (Stellar 1008) and *Dream Lands 2* (Stellar 1014) are duet sessions with Steve Christofferson. But the best place to start in exploring Nancy King's music is *Live At Jazz Standard* (Max Jazz 122), a brilliant duet set with pianist Fred Hersch.

Website: www.nancykingjazz.com

Teddi King
b. September 18, 1929, Boston, MA;
d. November 18, 1977, New York, NY

Teddi King was a relaxed jazz/swing singer who also crossed over at times into cabaret. She put plenty of feeling into the lyrics that she interpreted (being at her best on ballads) and always swung even when heard in more commercial settings.

King first gained some attention while performing and recording with Nat Pierce in 1949. She toured with the George Shearing Quintet during 1952–54, recorded with pianist Beryl Booker in 1953 and made several records in jazz settings for Storyville. During the second half of the 1950s, Teddi King was on a verge of a breakthrough, having hit recordings of "Mr. Wonderful," "Married I Can Always Get" and "Say It Isn't So," but she chose to return to more jazz-oriented settings where she was happiest. While not quite becoming a household name, Teddi King worked steadily in the 1960s (including eight years at Playboy clubs), returned to record after a 14-year absence for a Marian McPartland date in 1973, and sang with Dave McKenna in the 1970s.

Unfortunately, she developed lupus in 1970 and, after a long battle, she passed away in 1977, when she was just 48.

Recommended CDs: *In The Beginning: 1949–1954* (Baldwin Street Music 307) features Teddi King with Pierce, Shearing and in other settings, mostly as a guest artist. *Bidin' My Time* (Cloud 9 14465) from 1955 teams the singer with an 11-piece group influenced by Count Basie and arranged by Al Cohn. *A Girl And Her Songs* (BMG 35023) is a fine all-round showcase for King from 1957 in both orchestra and combo settings. *All The King's Songs* (Audiophile 177) has her singing standards made famous earlier by male singers. From later in her life, Teddi King is teamed with the Loonis McGloohan Trio in 1976 on both *Lovers & Losers* (Audiophile 117) and *Someone To Light Up My Life* (Audiophile 150).

LPs to Search For: Teddi King's final album, *This Is New* (Inner City 1044), matches the singer with Dave McKenna and was recorded shortly before her death.

King Pleasure
(Clarence Beeks)
b. March 24, 1922, Oakdale, TN;
d. March 21, 1981, Los Angeles, CA

A somewhat mysterious personality, King Pleasure had the best voice of all the male vocalese singers. While he could have been successful singing pop music in the 1950s, his main interest was vocalese and bebop.

Born Clarence Beeks, he grew up in Cincinnati and mostly worked outside of music until he was 29. In 1951 he won a talent contest at the Apollo Theater by singing Eddie Jefferson's lyrics to "Moody's Mood For Love." When Beeks, under the name of King Pleasure, recorded that piece in 1952 (before Jefferson had an opportunity), it became a hit, featuring Blossom Dearie on the brief female vocal. In 1953 King Pleasure had a follow-up with his words to "Parker's Mood" (which differed from Jefferson's), eerie stanzas that predict Charlie Parker's death and owe a bit to "St. James Infirmary." "Parker's Mood" also caught on big.

Despite those successes, King Pleasure was not all that active as a performer during his prime years. He only recorded three album's worth of material in his career, which included memorable versions of "Red Top" (with Betty Carter), "Jumpin' With Symphony Sid," "Sometimes I'm Happy," "Don't Get Scared" (with Jon Hendricks and Eddie Jefferson) and "D.B. Blues."

King Pleasure moved to Los Angeles in 1956, made his final record in 1962 and then disappeared from the music world. The mystery of his life has not yet been figured out but his three albums are easy to enjoy and contain more than their share of gems.

Recommended CDs: *King Pleasure Sings/Annie Ross Sings* (Original Jazz Classics 217) has the dozen Pleasure numbers from 1952 to 1954, including the original version of "Moody's Mood For Love" and the first vocal rendition of "Parker's Mood." The eight Annie Ross tracks are not exactly throwaways either, highlighted by her hit recordings of "Twisted" and "Farmer's Market." *Golden Days* (Original Jazz Classics 1772) has a 1960 session originally cut for Hi Fi by King Pleasure that includes remakes of the two hits. *Moody's Mood For Love* (Blue Note 84463) consists of six songs from 1955 to 1956 that were originally put out as singles and along with all of the music from Pleasure's final album in 1962. Get all of these CDs, and one has the complete King Pleasure.

Lisa Kirchner
b. June 10, 1953, Los Angeles, CA

A subtle and inventive singer, Lisa Kirchner is the daughter of classical composer Leon Kirchner. Early on she was interested in singing and playing guitar in folk music, performing in theater and playing classical piano. "I was introduced to jazz by musician friends in high school. I was turned on to Stan Getz, Stanley Turrentine, Ornette Coleman and John Coltrane. I choreographed a dance to 'Lonely Woman,' and a jazz drummer friend started me improvising on piano, doing impressionistic imitations of Cecil Taylor."

Kirchner started singing jazz and cabaret in New York nightclubs while attending Sarah Lawrence College, but that was only a small part of her life. Her early career was quite diverse as she understudied on Broadway, sang folk songs on television, appeared as a soloist with Judy Collins, and acted in shows (both on- and off-Broadway) and on television. But in the early 1990s, she was inspired to focus more on jazz. "I heard guitarist Ron Jackson in a club in the '90s and sat in with him; that immediately flicked the switch. His harmonization, alacrity of mind and musical intelligence, along with his groove, I found extraordinary. I felt as if a swan had flown under me and lifted me into the sky. I had never experienced that kind of musical freedom and simpatico listening from an accompanist. The sense of freedom was exhilarating, that the sky was the limit and that the music of the minute, how it is heard by the musicians in the moment, is the drive and the power. That was the beginning of jazz for me."

Since then, Lisa Kirchner has performed in many clubs in the New York City area and in the Northeast, in addition to recording two jazz CDs. "My theatrical background and the journey I have taken from other mediums to jazz has created a rich field where everything I sing is jazz, and is informed by other experiences, both artistic and day to day."

Recommended CDs: *One More Rhyme* (Albany 409) includes French and Brazilian tunes while 2002's *When Lights Are Low* (Albany 551) concentrates more on jazz standards. Both feature Lisa Kirchner creating her brand of intelligent jazz with subtlety and feeling.

Website: www.lisakirchner.com

Jean Kittrell
b. June 27, 1927, Birmingham, AL

A fine stride and swing pianist who contributes vocals inspired by Bessie Smith, Jean Kittrell has been an important part of the trad jazz and festival scene for decades.

Kittrell played piano early on for her Baptist Church and used to sing hymns solo. She majored in music theory at Blue Mountain College in Mississippi although her jazz career did not really begin until 1957, when she was already 30. "My then-husband, Ed Kittrell, announced that he wanted to start playing jazz on the trumpet. Surprised, I agreed to try to accompany him on piano until he found someone who could play jazz." She and her husband organized the Chesapeake Bay Jass Band in Norfolk, Virginia and began to sing, usually two songs a night. The following year they moved to Chicago, joining the Chicago Stompers with whom they toured Germany in 1959. "I never planned to be a professional singer. As I continued to play jazz piano, I began to sing more just to broaden the band's repertoire."

Kittrell spent 1967–69 performing as a solo singer-pianist on the St. Louis waterfront at the Old Levee House on Laclede's Landing. She earned a PhD in 20th Century British Literature at Southern Illinois University-Carbondale in 1973, joining the English faculty at SIU-Edwardsville where she taught for 10 years. She followed that up by teaching at Southern Illinois University-Edwardsville for 25 years (chairing the English department for four) while playing weekends aboard the Lt. Robert E. Lee Restaurant and Saloon in St. Louis.

Jean Kittrell worked and recorded with the Mississippi Mudcats Jazz Band (1972–74) and the Boll Weevil Jass Band. Since the mid-1970s she has led three bands, the Jazz Incredibles, the St. Louis Rivermen and the OSLLB (Old St. Louis Levee Band), mostly performing in the Midwest at concerts, festivals and on cruises. Along the way, she has also performed in concerts with Tony Parenti (with whom she recorded), Johnny Wiggs, Danny Barker, Doc Evans, George Brunies and the Preservation Hall Jazz Band.

Recommended CDs: *Jean Kittrell Sings The Blues* (Jazzology 051) features Kittrell on Bessie Smith-type material in 1967 with clarinetist Tony Parenti's Blue Blowers. *You Gotta See Your Mama* (GHB 26) is a reissue of a 1970 album, showcasing Jean Kittrell performing with her Boll Weevils.

LPs to Search For: *Jean Kittrell Alone* (Fat Cat's Jazz 169) from 1970 features Kittrell in top form as a solo singer-pianist.

Website: www.jeankittrell.com

Leah Kline
b. June 29, Tachikawa, Japan

An excellent American jazz singer who has been based in the Netherlands, Leah Kline performs and records an eclectic variety of music ranging from straight-ahead to original groove-oriented singer/songwriter material.

Born in Japan due to her father being in the military, but raised in the United States, she remembers, "My mother is fully responsible for my cultural upbringing. At nine years old in Annapolis, Maryland, we all went to an underground club to listen to jazz. Later in art school I was introduced to Gershwin, Ellington repertoire and Dave Brubeck's 'Take Five,' the latter with live musicians. It made me realize what improvisation was. I used to sit in at a jazz brunch. The first time I really improvised was when the pianist played 'Route 66' four keys higher than I sing it, so I had to sing around it."

She played piano, hand bells and congas as a child, and attended North Carolina School of the Arts in Winston-Salem, graduating in 1991 with a degree in modern dance. Kline worked around the Washington, DC, area as a choreographer, dancer, actress and singer. After gaining a small role in the film *Patriot Games*, she moved to Los Angeles in 1995, where she gigged locally. A fall off of a balcony put her out of commission for a time. A USO tour of Europe convinced her that she should take singing jazz much more seriously. "I gained a contract on a cruise ship as a singer/dancer. For six months, I memorized every song on a three-CD Verve collection of the Lady of Song—Ella Fitzgerald. Every evening, I sat in and sang at the midnight jam sessions with the musicians, trying out my new songs and getting lead sheets written for me, learning my keys. I committed 150 standards to memory at sea."

Back in Los Angeles, she was part of the local jazz scene, often using Tamir Hendelman or John Rangel as her pianist. Leah Kline worked on Seabourn cruise lines, performed shows in the Far East, and in 2000 moved to Amsterdam.

"I have always had a straight clear sound with very little vibrato (probably from all of my choir training), which is good for making harmonies. In ways I am like a parrot. If I like the way someone says something then I repeat it, fascinated with how one makes that sound. This applies to singing and to speaking other languages, which is how I became quickly fluent in Dutch."

Leah Kline performed in a musical production based on the life of Irving Berlin (*There's No Business Like Show Business*), was selected to be part of *The Ann Burton Tribute*, performed in productions of *42nd Street* and *Musicals in Ahoy*, and presented her Jazz Cabaret shows in theaters in Holland, Germany and France. She has also developed as a song writer (most of the lyrics on her recent *JuzzFlirtin* CD is hers, while pianist Dirk Balthaus wrote the music), and teaches performance skills, dance and yoga in addition to co-hosting a radio show and writing articles.

"I am now expanding my repertoire looking for the *New American Songbook*; people from my generation who write. I love songs from the 1950s and earlier, but there are so many new and good writers sprouting up and the only way to introduce them to the world is to start including them in my repertoire."

Recommended CDs: Leah Kline's debut CD, *Playground* (Stemra 8240) is mostly comprised of her fresh and inventive versions of standards. *JuzzFlirtin* (Theatrics Productions 256) has her diverse and intriguing lyrics set to pianist Dirk Blathaus' music and features her increasingly original voice.

Website: www.leahkline.com

Barbara Knight
b. August 5, 1958, Cleveland, OH

One of the best jazz singers in the Cleveland area, Barbara Knight released a CD in 2007 (*Angel Eyes*) that is a continuous surprise.

Barbara Knight is a self-described late bloomer who did not concentrate on jazz until she had a chance to sing with the jazz ensemble while attending Kent State. She graduated with a degree in Voice/Music Education and started singing professionally in 1980 with the Harry Hershey Orchestra, staying with the band for 13 years. "I sang with those musicians in a show called *Stompin' At The State* that was so successful that it ran for two years at Cleveland's Playhouse Square. That show solidly established me as a big band jazz singer in northeast Ohio."

In 1993 Knight became the singer with the Cleveland Jazz Orchestra. She has also worked in the Midwest with the Nelson Riddle Orchestra, the Tommy Dorsey Orchestra, the Famous Jazz Orchestra (since 1997), and as a frequent guest artist with the Cleveland Pops Orchestra. She has recorded two CDs as a leader and currently leads a quintet that plays throughout northeastern Ohio.

"I have always been a vocalist who believes in the integrity of the melody. My interpretations of the jazz classics are not difficult to decipher nor filled with vocal pyrotechnics. Although I strive to present fresh, innovative arrangements, the melody remains the focus of my singing."

Recommended CDs: *Night And Day* from 2001, matches Barbara Knight with the Cleveland Jazz Orchestra plus strings. *Angel Eyes* features her working quintet. On the latter, the singer takes a duet apiece with each of her sidemen (including flugelhornist Jack Schantz on "Skylark") and wrote the arrangements along with bassist Dave Morgan, so the standards are full of subtle surprises. Both releases were issued by Barbara Knight through her website.

Website: www.barbaraknight.net

Ilona Knopfler
b. May 15, 1976, Paris, France

The release of *Live My Life* in 2005 alerted the jazz world to the presence of a new and potentially significant voice, Ilona Knopfler.

"My mother was a singer and my father a pianist, so I grew up listening to all the artists and composers that would later become my sources of inspiration. When I was six, I sang for the opening of the Regal Meridien Hotel in Hong Kong. I performed a medley of songs by Mistinguette, a French singer famous in the early 1900s, with apparently 'risqué' lyrics that outraged the French community. Of course at that age, I had no idea what I was making reference to when talking about how, that day on the grass, I finally experienced the great jolt and the famous little chill. I was just happy to be on stage, watching people smile."

Ilona Knopfler always knew that she would be a singer. She traveled all over the world with her parents and at 15 was working as a backup singer for a rock band in Hong Kong when she discovered jazz. During the next three years, she sang with a trio at the Jazz Club in Hong Kong and also with two big bands. "Those three years confirmed that I had made the right choice. There really was nothing else like this

feeling I had on stage." When she was 18 in 1994, Ilona moved to New York City for five years, studying at the Lee Strasberg Theater Institute. Since then, she has recorded two CDs for Mack Avenue, gigged regularly and developed into a very promising singer. She currently lives in both Atlanta and Paris.

"Jazz is very personal to me. I usually sing lyrics that I wish I'd written, expressing an emotion I would not have dared express."

Recommended CDs: Ilona Knopfler's debut recording, *Some Kind Of Wonderful* (Mack Avenue 1010), has the singer mostly interpreting rock and pop songs (including numbers by Grand Funk and the Zombies) in jazz settings. *Live The Life* (Mack Avenue 1021) is definitive as she explores more suitable material including Thomas A. Dorsey's "I'm Going To Live The Life I Sing About In My Song," Bob Dorough's "But For Now," Thelonious Monk's "Ask Me Now," Abbey Lincoln's "Throw It Away" and "This Is Always," with the assistance of Antonio Hart, Sean Jones and Paquito D'Rivera.

Website: www.ilonaknopfler.com

Ithamara Koorax
(Ita Mara Jarlicht)
b. April 28, 1965, Niteroi, Rio de Janeiro, Brazil

A versatile singer from Brazil, Ithamara Koorax has sung straight-ahead jazz, conventional bossa novas and interesting mixtures of style, all with enthusiasm and strong musicianship.

The daughter of Polish Jews who fled Europe during World War II recalls, "I started to study singing and classical piano when I was very young, just five years old. My concentration was on operatic singing, classical music, and mostly European music. But I also used to listen a lot to albums by Ella Fitzgerald (her Decca LPs), Frank Sinatra and Tony Bennett, as well as to jazz pianists like Dave Brubeck, George Shearing and Teddy Wilson, all from my parents' record collection. The most important influences on my early years, in my teens, were Elizeth Cardoso (the uncredited singer in the original Black Orpheus movie soundtrack), Carmen McRae, Elis Regina, Betty Carter, and Flora Purim. I remember that Flora's *Stories To Tell* had a huge impact on me. It was the first time I listened to a Brazilian singer phrasing in a jazz style on Brazilian songs. So I said to myself, 'That's how I want to sing.'"

She studied classical piano for nine years and attended the Niteroi Educational Center, in Rio de Janeiro. When she was 18, Koorax did backup vocals for Brazilian pop stars and recorded jingles. She had success with her first solo recording, *Iluminada*, in 1990, when the title song was included in a very popular soap opera. Soon she was touring Japan regularly, where her records became best sellers including *Ithamara Koorax Sings The Luiz Bonfa Songbook* in 1996. She worked with Hermeto Pascoal, Edu Lobo, Azymuth, Dom Um Romão and Martinho da Vila, and took part in an all-star session for CTI with Art Farmer, Eddie Gomez and Jack DeJohnette although it was never released in the U.S. In addition, her acid jazz version of "The Frog" became a dance hit in Europe in 1994 and she recorded the groundbreaking album *Bossa Nova Meets Drum 'N' Bass*. But it was her Milestone CDs, *Serenade In Blue* and *Love Dance: The Ballad Album*, that helped establish her name in the United States.

"I want to constantly expand my musical horizons. I never wanted to be known only as a Brazilian singer, never wanted to be labeled as a singer of Brazilian music exclusively. I am very proud that I was born in Brazil but my goal is to be recognized as a singer of music, good music."

Recommended CDs: Ithamara Koorax's most important early Brazilian albums include *Rio Vermelho* (Imagem 2012), *Wave 2001* (Paddle Wheel 301), *Bossa Nova Meets Drum 'N' Bass* (Paddle Wheel 665) and *Ithamara Koorax Sings The Luiz Bonfa Songbook* (Imagem 333). *Serenade In Blue* (Milestone 9301), *Love Dance: The Ballad Album* (Milestone 9327) and her first acoustic straight-ahead jazz trio album *Autumn In New York* (EMI 0473) have given her an excellent reputation in the United States. Her most recent release is the world music-oriented *Brazilian Butterfly* (JSR 60509).

Website: www.koorax.com

Simone Kopmajer
b. September 23, 1981, Schladming, Austria

A talented cool-toned jazz vocalist from Austria who sings in flawless English, Simone Kopmajer has a great deal of potential.

"I grew up in a musical family and I always sang along with my father's records (including Frank Sinatra, Louis Prima and Elvis Presley). I played classical piano from age 8 and at 12 I started taking saxophone lessons. That year I got introduced to jazz when I started playing in a teenage big band. When I was 17, I was asking my teacher Sheila Jordan if there would be any chance for me to sing professionally and she said 'There is no doubt, you are a singer.' That meant a great deal to me." She also had opportunities to study with Mark Murphy, Jay Clayton and Michele Hendricks in addition to singing in her father's band from the age of 12.

Since growing up, Simone Kopmajer has earned a master's from the University of Music and Dramatic Arts in Graz, Austria, toured the Netherlands twice with the Euro Big Band, appeared at a variety of jazz festivals in Europe and recorded three CDs, including *Romance*, which gained her a bit of attention in the United States.

"I'm from a small village in Austria and all of my dreams have already come true. I would like to sing as long as possible, write my own music and create music that touches people."

Recommended CDs: All three of Simone Kopmajer's recordings, *Moonlight Serenade* (Venus 758832), *Romance* (Zoho 200505) and *Taking A Chance On Love* (which has been privately released), feature her take on standards and are worth exploring.

Kristin Korb
b. October 29, 1969, Billings, MT

Kristin Korb is primarily known as a bassist, but she also sings quite well.

"I grew up singing at home and at church and originally listened to country music. When I was in third grade, I wanted to be Barbara Mandrell because she played guitar, sang, danced and had her own TV show. I had my guitar teacher transcribe her songs and I used to sing them while I played guitar. My mom is a school teacher and she wanted us to be well-rounded individuals. Before I reached seventh grade, I had studied guitar, piano, and violin." After attending the Soundsation Jazz Camp one summer, Korb knew that she wanted to be a jazz musician, and after being told that a seventh grade vocal jazz group did not need a guitar, she switched to electric bass, eventually focusing on the acoustic bass, starting in 11th grade.

After earning a degree in music education at Eastern Montana College in 1992, she spent the next two years working on her Master's in Classical Bass Performance at the University of California-San Diego. While in grad school, Korb took lessons from Bertram Turetzky, who encouraged her to sing and play bass at the same time. In April of 1994 she met Ray Brown. "I had the opportunity to study with him and make a recording with him at a time when I doubted my ability to really be a jazz musician. Ray gave me the confidence to dig in, study more, and grow in the music. He taught me that it wasn't about trying to be a professional jazz musician; it was about loving what you do. Everything else works out if you love what you do."

She recorded her first CD in 1995 (*Introducing Kristin Korb With The Ray Brown Trio*), taught jazz history, bass and the vocal jazz ensemble at Grossmont Community College (1996–2000), and was the Director of Jazz Studies at Central Washington University (2000–2002), before finally moving to Los Angeles in 2002. Since then she has freelanced in the L.A. area, occasionally toured, played at jazz parties, led her own trio and recorded three additional CDs as a leader.

"Every day is a new adventure. I get excited hearing what everyone else is playing. I feel like I get the best seat in the house."

Recommended CDs: *Introducing Kristin Korb With The Ray Brown Trio* (Telarc 83386) features Korb exclusively as a singer, a quiet vocalist with a small voice but with enough knowledge to create the most with what she has. *Get Happy* (Grace Bass 9775) has her singing and playing bass with seven-string electric bassist Todd Johnson and drummer Kendall Kay while *Where You'll Find Me* (Double K 1096074) and *Why Can't You Behave* (Double K 1096075) feature her in fine form with trios and quartets.

Website: www.kristinkorb.com

Irene Kral
b. January 18, 1932, Chicago, IL; d. August 15, 1978, Encino, CA

Irene Kral, who died at the age of 46 from cancer, saved her best singing for the last four years of her life, recording three classics that rank with the very best ballad albums ever.

Like Johnny Hartman before he recorded with John Coltrane, Irene Kral was a pleasing if not overly substantial singer in her early days. Ten years younger than her brother Roy Kral (of Jackie and Roy), she was performing by the time she was 16, accompanying her vocals on piano. Two years later, she joined the big band of Jay Burkhardt and sang briefly with Woody Herman and Chubby Jackson. She spent much of 1954 as a member of a jazz vocal group, the Tattle Tales, for whom she not only sang but played drums. A year later, she resumed her solo career, gaining some attention during 1957–59 when she sang regularly with Maynard Ferguson with whom she recorded.

In 1959 Irene Kral was the regular singer on *The Steve Allen Show* and the following year she sang with Shelly Manne and His Men. She then was semi-retired for years as she took time off to raise a family, just singing occasionally and guesting on Laurindo Almeida's 1964 album *Guitar From Ipanema* and appearing next to Jack Sheldon for Shelly Manne's *My Fair Lady Swings*. She made four albums as a leader during 1958–65, with Herb Pomeroy's orchestra, a set of Steve Allen tunes with a tentet arranged by Al Cohn, a strong program from 1963 with the Junior Mance trio and a half jazz/half commercial effort for Mainstream.

But nothing that she recorded previously was on the level of 1974's *Where Is Love*, a set of often-heartbreaking ballads recorded with the sparse accompaniment of pianist Alan Broadbent. Such songs as "Spring Can Really Hang You Up The Most," "A Time For Love" and "Never Let Me Go" are taken at very slow tempos and every note counts in these haunting interpretations. Irene Kral's ability to show remarkable self-restraint (using space brilliantly) while also singing with strong emotions remains unparalleled. It is impossible to listen to this music and not be moved, even if one is not aware that she was in her second year in an ultimately losing six-year battle against breast cancer.

The year 1977 brought two more classics. *Kral Space* has the singer joined by Broadbent in a quartet. In addition to the ballads such as "Small Day Tomorrow" and "Everytime We Say Goodbye," her versions of Dave Frishberg's "Wheelers And Dealers," "It Isn't So Good, It Couldn't Get Better" and the witty "It's Nice Weather For Ducks" sticks in one's mind. *Gentle Rain*, a final set of duets with Broadbent, almost reaches the heights of *Kral Space* with "You Are There," "If You Could See Me Now" and "What's New" being among the highlights.

Irene Kral performed until three weeks before her death.

Recommended CDs: *Better Than Anything* (Fresh Sound 69) has a very good session in 1963 with the Junior Mance Trio that finds Irene Kral hinting at the greatness to come. *Where Is Love* (Candid 71012) is essential for all jazz vocal collections and close behind are *Kral Space* (Collectables 7160) and *Gentle Rain* (Choice 71020). *You Are There* (Audiophile 299), which has the singer with the Loonis McGloohan Trio on a radio show in 1977, *Lady Of Lavender* (Jazzwest 2003), *Live* (Just Jazz 1002), *Just For Now* (Jazzed Media 1003) and *Angel Eyes* (TDK 5143) all add to the legacy of Irene Kral's final and very special musical period.

LPs to Search For: Irene Kral's earliest records as a leader from 1958–59, *Steveireno* (United Artists 3052) and *The Band And I* (United Artists 5016), remain out of print as does her interesting but erratic (due to the material) effort from 1965, *Wonderful Life* (Mainstream 6058)

Diana Krall
b. November 16, 1964, Nanaimo, British Columbia, Canada

The most famous living jazz singer, Diana Krall has helped to popularize swing standards during her 15 years in the limelight. An excellent pianist whose vocals are expressive and personable, Krall is both shy on stage and charismatic.

She took classical piano lessons starting when she was four. Her father's record collection contained many jazz records, which introduced her to the earlier greats. Krall played with her high school jazz band, attended the Berklee College of Music in the early 1980s, and was convinced by Ray Brown to spend time in Los Angeles and study with Jimmy Rowles. In 1990, when she moved to New York at the age of 25, Krall was an unknown, but that would change soon.

In 1993, Diana Krall recorded her first CD, *Stepping Out*, and it gained her some attention. Signing with GRP, her *Only Trust Your Heart* in 1994 was impressive but it was 1995's All For You that caused the major breakthrough. A tribute to the Nat King Cole Trio, *All For You* was a giant hit and suddenly Krall was a superstar. It was ironic that she was marketed as a sex symbol because onstage, Diana Krall was awkward whenever she was away from the piano or had to talk to the audience. It took quite a few years before she started looking much more comfortable before large crowds even though she quickly became a constant headliner at jazz festivals.

By 1997, Diana Krall's regular trio featured guitarist Russell Malone and Christian McBride. In more recent times, the group has become a quartet, often including guitarist Anthony Wilson, bassist John Clayton and drummer Jeff Hamilton. While Krall's style has not changed much in the past decade, there have been occasional departures, with string orchestras being utilized on some of her recordings and in special concerts. After marrying pop/rock star Elvis Costello in late 2003, she recorded the rather unfortunate *The Girl In The Other Room*, a set which contains quite a few forgettable originals by Krall and/or Costello. *From This Moment On*, released in 2006, finds her returning to high-quality standards.

One can sympathize with Diana Krall wanting to move ahead into new material rather than just playing older songs, but her first real attempt in that area was a misfire. For now, it is easier to enjoy her memorable versions of such songs as "East Of The Sun," "Peel Me A Grape," "All Or Nothing At All," "Devil May Care," "Let's Fall In Love" and "I've Got You Under My Skin."

Recommended CDs: *Steppin' Out* (originally on Justin Time and reissued as GRP 9825) and *Only Trust Your Heart* (GRP 9810) set the stage for a trio of gems: *All For You* (GRP/Impulse 82), *Love Scenes* (GRP/Impulse 233), and a set with the Johnny Mandel Orchestra, *When I Look In Your Eyes* (Verve/Impulse 304). *The Look Of Love* (Verve 549846) teams her with Claus Ogerman arrangements and *Live In Paris* (Verve 440065) has some of Krall's best piano solos and jazz singing, while *The Girl In The Other Room* (Verve 9862246) is sunk by its weak material. *Christmas Songs* (Verve 4717) with the Clayton-Hamilton Jazz Orchestra works well as does *From This Moment On* (Verve 7323). A historic oddity,

Heartdrops: Vince Benedetti Meets Diana Krall (TCB 2218) is from 1989 (five years before Steppin' Out) and has Krall mostly singing and playing obscure originals by trombonist Vince Benedetti.

Laurie Krauz

b. August 18, 1955, Bronx, NY

A warm singer who is comfortable in both the jazz and cabaret worlds, Laurie Krauz works regularly in the New York area.

She had piano lessons for a few years from the age of five, although those stopped a few years later when her piano teacher was killed in an accident. "Singing with my mother at the piano at home were some of my happiest childhood memories." Krauz graduated from Pennsylvania State University in 1976 and at first worked in other fields. "In 1980 I was studying toward an MBA in Finance, working in Health Care Management. The day before starting an important new job as a management trainee at a major Wall Street Bank, I took a course called 'The Gotta Sing Workshop' as a lark on the suggestion of a friend. The workshop was geared toward those who liked to 'sing in the shower.' When I got up to sing I truly had an epiphany. It was an incredibly comfortable feeling—as though I had come home. I can remember sitting on the subway on my way to my apartment, knowing that I was going to be a singer." Three years later, she made a complete break with her developing banking career to work in musical theater.

After three years on the road in the United States and Canada, she returned to New York and sang with a four-voice swing ensemble called Asque for two years. During that period, Krauz started to really love jazz and she decided to become a solo jazz singer. Among the teachers she credits with helping her are: Mark Murphy, Carla White, Daryl Kojak, Woody Mann, Stephen Tarshis and Jay Bianchi.

"My work bridges the gap between more theatrical musical genres and jazz." In 2001, Laurie Krauz released her first CD, *Catch Me If You Can*, a set that shows she is both an expert scat singer and a sensitive interpreter of lyrics. As of this writing, she is involved in *Tapestry Rewoven*, a jazz interpretation of Carole King's *Tapestry* album.

Recommended CD: *Catch Me If You Can* (LML 159) features Laurie Krauz in top form with tenor-saxophonist George Coleman and the Daryl Kojak Trio.

Website: www.lauriekrauz.com

Karin Krog

(Karin Krog Bergh)
b. May 15, 1937, Oslo, Norway

One of Norway's top jazz singers, Karin Krog has had a versatile style in a wide-ranging career that has ranged from interpreting standards to appearing in avant-garde settings. She was introduced to jazz through her father's record collection, took piano lessons, and first sang in school bands. Originally inspired by Billie Holiday, Ella Fitzgerald and Sarah Vaughan, Krog performed with local musicians while a teenager including with pianist Kjell Karlsen's sextet (1955–56) and regularly at the Humlen Restaurant in Oslo starting in 1957. She won a poll put on by the Norwegian paper Verdensrevyen in 1959 as the top female jazz singer.

Despite all of this, Krog says that she did not seriously pursue music until she was 25 in 1962, when she started taking private vocal lessons with Anne Brown, the first singer to be cast in the part of Bess in George Gershwin's *Porgy And Bess*. That year, Krog began leading her own groups, and in 1963 she made her recording debut. Since that time, she has appeared at a countless number of European festivals and recorded over 30 albums as a leader, including 10 for Meantime Records, a label she founded in 1987. When asked what her most important musical associations have been, she replied "Saxophonist and composer John Surman for 20 years, pianist Bengt Hallberg for five, Don Ellis, Dexter Gordon and Steve Kuhn."

In addition to her performances, Krog helped form the Norwegian Jazz Forum in 1965 (serving as its first chairman), an organization that worked to get jazz out of nightclubs and into concert settings. Although based primarily in Europe, in 1967 she performed in the United States with Don Ellis and Clare Fischer, and is proud that she won in the "Artist Deserving Of Wider Recognition" category in that year's Down Beat critics poll. However, it is surprising that she has visited the U.S. so rarely through the years; she has performed all over Europe, Japan, Hong Kong, India and Australia. In addition to working with Norwegian musicians, Krog had collaborations with Dexter Gordon, Red Mitchell, Archie Shepp and Warne Marsh in the 1970s, and has participated in many projects (including some that were electronic explorations) with John Surman.

"As I look back on my career, I am pleased that I have been fortunate to make music with so many excellent musicians. I think being a European and working in Europe, I have been able to work with many different kinds of styles and to explore new things without having to be commercial."

Recommended CDs: *By Myself* (Mercury 3084), which is from 1964, *Jazz Moments* (Century 0460), *Some Other Spring* (Meantime 10) with Dexter Gordon, *Gershwin With Krog* (Meantime 4), *Hi-Fly* (Meantime 3) with Archie Shepp, *I Remember You* (Meantime 8) with Warne Marsh and Red Mitchell, *Dave Frishberg & Karin Krog* (Baybridge 20404), *Bluesand* (Meantime 9) with John Surman and, *Where You At* (Enja 9144) with Steve Kuhn in 2003 are just a few of Karin Krog's more rewarding recordings. A two-CD anthology, *Jubilee* (Verve 523 716), sums up her career well, drawing its material from 1963–91.

Website: www.karinkrog.no

John Labelle

b. May 4, 1967, Greenfield Park, Quebec, Canada

A top crooner from Canada, John Labelle considers Frank Sinatra to be his main inspiration. "Frank Sinatra is not, by most people's definition, a jazz singer, but he is the true giant. His influence is too big to fathom. Ella, Sarah, Mel, and Nat are all up there, but I'd rather listen to Frank if I could have only one choice."

As a child, Labelle heard his parents' records, particularly one with hit vocal recordings from the 1940s through the '70s. He was also attracted to big band swing albums, which led him to explore other vocalists and jazz. "I sang at family gatherings, played flute in my high school orchestra, bought my first saxophone in my mid-teens, and have played tenor ever since; poorly, I might add." As a record collector, Labelle learned hundreds of lyrics and constantly practiced singing standards.

"At 21, I was working as a bartender at a well-known jazz club in Montreal called Biddle's. I became friendly with some of the musicians. One night, one of the band members didn't show up. The pianist and leader, Norman Zubis, made a joke on stage that he would call up the bartender and have him sing since I knew all the words. It started as a joke but in the end, I did go up in the next set. I sang 'A Foggy Day,' and 'Just In Time.' I was hooked." He soon landed a three-month contract at a small hotel.

In 1995 John Labelle made his recording debut and also had an important and successful appearance at the Montreal Jazz Festival. Since then he has worked regularly at Modavie Jazz Bar and Kaizen's Blue Note Lounge, performed for eight years with the Montreal Jazz Big Band, sung with two other vocalists in the Three Crooners, and worked in Shanghai, Hong Kong, Beijing, Washington, DC, and throughout Canada, frequently with guitarist Greg Clayton. "I hope to write more original music in the future and to continue earning my living doing the thing I love most, singing."

Recommended CDs: Each of John Labelle's recordings are rewarding, as he shows steady progress in gaining maturity and originality, and he has grown as an improviser. Thus far, he has recorded four CDs: *If You See Her* (Jazz Inspiration 9311), *Don't Say No* (Jazz Inspiration 9318), *Too Close For Comfort* (JLP) and *Last Time I Was Here* (JLP).

Cleo Laine
(Clementina Dinah Campbell)
b. October 28, 1927, Southall, Middlesex, England

A much-beloved singer in England and throughout the world, Cleo Laine has a beautiful voice and perfect control over her singing. Although generally grouped with jazz and married to saxophonist John Dankworth, who acts as her musical director, Laine is actually not much of an improviser.

She is at her best when singing arranged unisons with her husband that show off her very wide range.

Although she took singing lessons while a child, Cleo Laine did not really begin singing until she was already 25, having worked as a hairdresser, a librarian and for a pawnbroker. She auditioned for the Johnny Dankworth Seven in 1952, got the job, and they were married six years later. Most of her performances have been with the group that she co-leads with her husband.

Throughout her career, Laine has been both a singer and an actress, acting in several shows, including *Show Boat* in 1971. As a singer, she stretches beyond the usual standards, performing art music, special projects, and even recording one album called *Shakespeare And All That Jazz*. Since 1972, Cleo Laine has traveled the world, worked with classical musicians, recorded duet albums with Ray Charles and Mel Tormé (she was greatly outclassed by the latter), made three recordings during 1973–83 at Carnegie Hall, continued working in musical theater, and performed concerts in many prestigious venues.

Recommended CDs: *Ridin' High: The British Sessions 1960–71* (Koch 7940) is a good sampler of Cleo Laine before she became an international star. Some of her most jazz-oriented recordings have been *Shakespeare And All That Jazz* (Phillips 5504), *Cleo's Choice* (GNP/Crescendo 9024), *I Am A Song* (RCA

61670), *Born On A Friday* (RCA 61662), *Cleo Laine Live!!! At Carnegie Hall* (RCA 60960), *Cleo At Carnegie: The 10th Anniversary Concert* (RCA 61665), *That Old Feeling* (RCA 39736), *Jazz* (RCA 60548) and *Blue And Sentimental* (RCA 61469).

Natalie Lamb
(Natalie Elston)
b. November 10, 1940, New York, NY

A powerful singer whose vocalizing crosses over between classic blues and trad jazz, Natalie Lamb made her greatest impact during the late 1960s and '70s.

She studied classical singing, earned a degree from Hunter College, and worked as a folk singer early on. After hearing the album *Odetta Sings The Blues*, she became interested in early blues and her Town Hall concert in 1965 with pianist Sammy Price launched her jazz career. Lamb recorded with Price that year for Columbia but the album was never released. In 1979 she finally had the opportunity to record a similar set with Price. She started working with the Red Onion Jazz Band in 1969, marrying its leader Bob Thompson in 1972. Natalie Lamb has since primarily worked at classic jazz festivals, visiting Europe on a few occasions including recording with the Peruna Jazz Band.

Recommended CDs: *Natalie Lamb And The Blues* (GHB 84) is the long-postponed collaboration with Sammy Price, which also features Doc Cheatham. The project from 1979 is augmented by six additional selections recorded in 1999 that find the singer still in fine voice. *I'm A Woman* (GHB 329) teams Lamb with the Peruna Jazz Band in Copenhagen on classic jazz material, while *Blues Around The Clock* (GHB 419) is a bit more recent.

LPs to Search For: *Natalie Lamb Wails The Blues* (Fat Cat's Jazz 152) from 1973–74 features the singer in a jam session setting with Wild Bill Davison and Dick Wellstood.

Dave Lambert
b. June 19, 1917, Boston, MA; d. October 3, 1966, Westport, CT

Although he will always be best-known for being one of the three stars of Lambert, Hendricks and Ross, Dave Lambert had an extensive, if not too lucrative, career during the 15 years before L, H & Ross was formed.

Lambert originally worked as a drummer with the Hugh

McGuinness Trio during the summers of 1937–40. After serving in the Army (1940–43), he sang with Johnny Long's big band. By the time he was with Gene Krupa's orchestra (1944–45), Lambert was very interested in bebop, often teaming up with fellow singer Buddy Stewart. Lambert and Stewart recorded what is considered the first bebop vocal while with Krupa in 1945, "What's This."

Influenced most by Leo Watson, Lambert was a superior bop singer but he performed infrequently. He and Stewart worked together on an occasional basis up until Stewart's death in a car accident in 1950, most notably on a few recordings for the Keynote and Sittin' In With labels and on a Royal Roost broadcast in early 1949 with Charlie Parker. Lambert led a date of his own for Capitol in 1949 and he organized the Dave Lambert Singers to accompany Charlie Parker on a 1953 session that resulted in poorly balanced and bizarre versions of "Old Folks" and "In The Still Of The Night." In 1955 the Dave Lambert Singers had better luck backing Jon Hendricks on "Four Brothers" and "Cloudburst."

If it had not been for the formation of Lambert, Hendricks and Ross, chances are that Dave Lambert would have only rated a footnote in jazz history. The album *Sing A Song Of Basie* in 1957 made Lambert (who was usually the group's arranger) and the other singers immortal. Lambert, Hendricks and Ross had five busy years as one of the top jazz vocal groups of all time. When Ross dropped out in 1962, Yolande Bavan was her replacement. Lambert, Hendricks and Bavan worked until its breakup in 1964.

Dave Lambert, who had recorded an obscure solo album in 1959, freelanced during 1964–66 and made his last recording in 1965, scatting on "Donna Lee" at a Charlie Parker memorial concert. Ironically, like Buddy Stewart, he died in a car accident, being killed in 1966 when he was hit by a car while changing a tire. He was just 49.

LPs to Search For: The Lambert, Hendricks and Ross recordings are covered under their entry. Dave Lambert's one solo album, 1959's *Sing Along And Swing Along* (United Artists 3084), will be a tough one to locate and has yet to be reissued on CD.

Jeannette Lambert
(Jeannette Mukidah Schwager)
b. June 15, 1965, Leiden, Netherlands

An industrious singer with a warm voice and an eclectic style, Jeannette Lambert can sing anything from very adventurous improvisations to standards and ballads.

The daughter of Dutch and Indonesian parents who were avid jazz fans, and the sister of guitarist Reg Schwager, she remembers, "In fourth grade I presented a class project called the history of bebop. My father was the ghost writer. Reg and I were more intellectual than athletic as kids, and for fun we'd learn songs together. By the time I was 12, we were doing gigs here and there, playing parties, coffee houses and music festivals. I knew very early on that I loved to sing and I never really thought of it as a profession. I just have to sing or else I am unhappy."

As a teenager, she often listened to and eventually participated in jam sessions held at her house. "Our house became a focal point for a trio of older jazz musicians who came by often to jam and to teach Reg and I about the music in more depth. Those musicians were Herbie Spanier, Freddie McHugh and Keith (Spike) McKendry. Herbie was instrumental in teaching me how to improvise freely. I started singing my own poems around that time."

Lambert studied film production at York University in Toronto during 1984–86 while also taking some jazz classes. An early high point was attending the Banff Summer Jazz Workshop in 1985, where she participated in the Cecil Taylor Workshop Big Band and took lessons from Jay Clayton, Dave Liebman and Julian Priester. Since then she has spent time living in Paris, New York and Amsterdam, married drummer Michel Lambert (who she met in 1986), and settled in Montreal.

Jeannette Lambert has performed in Europe, Indonesia and throughout Canada, being inspired not only by jazz singers but by the traditions of flamenco, fado and jaipong. She co-founded the record label Jazz From Rant with Reg Schwager and Michel Lambert in 1991. In addition, she often writes music to her own poetry, and she was an early Internet filmmaker, combining together her loves of music, poetry and cinema. "Many of my fans are happiest when I sing lots of torch songs and ballads, but singing my own poems is vital to me. It is the end result of the creative process, finding my own voice."

Recommended CDs: *Lone Jack Pine* (Jazz From Rant 2027) is an adventurous trio set with bassist Barre Phillips and Michel Lambert. "It is an album that was completely improvised around my poems. The poems expressed many thoughts I'd gathered over the years and it really was a very personal exploration." *Bebop For Babies* (Jazz From Rant 329) and *Bebop For Babies 2* (Jazz From Rant 632) are jazz versions of children's melodies. *Sand Underfoot* (Jazz From Rant 631) is a superior all-round effort with both Lamberts, Paul Bley and Barre Phillips in different combinations, creating fresh new music.

Website: www.nette.ca

Lou Lanza
(Louis Vincent Lanza III)
b. July 20, 1970, Philadelphia, PA

A fine Philadelphia-based singer who is not shy to take chances, Lou Lanza is both a talented scat-singer and a crooner.

"I was originally introduced to jazz through my uncle, Vincent Trombetta Jr., an excellent saxophonist who taught some of the best musicians in the Philadelphia area, including Michael Brecker. I have been told that I sang before I could actually talk. Allegedly, I imitated my mother singing the Schubert 'Ave Maria' phonetically." Part of a family filled with classical musicians, Lanza began singing in public when he was a young teenager. He also played violin from the age of five and taught himself piano and guitar.

Lanza was a theater major in college and worked as a professional actor in Philadelphia and New York City for a few years. However, he really wanted to be a singer, studying improvisation with guitarist Jimmy Bruno (starting in 1994) and recording his first album in 1995. Since that time he has been a fixture in the Philadelphia and East Coast jazz scene, recording often and playing in local clubs.

Lou Lanza, who cites Frank Sinatra, Chet Baker, Ella Fitzgerald and Mark Murphy as his main influences, says, "When I sing a love song, it truly is to a real person in my past or present that I loved. The saloon songs are sung from the experience of real events and feelings that live within my emotional memory and even the comic, quirky, offbeat, and cool songs come from a desire to rail against my own personal darkness and sadness that is carried within me. I feel tremendously blessed to be able to make my greatest love my life's work."

Recommended CDs: Lou Lanza's recording debut, *The Road Not Taken* (C.A.R. 0295), is most notable for his sensitive interpretations of ballads. *Corner Pocket* (J Bird 80185) mixes together ballads and scat/vocalese pieces. *Shadows and Echoes* (Challenge 73131) is mostly laid-back and conventional but creative in subtle ways, while *Opening Doors* (Cexton 0904) is an unusual tribute to the Doors, reflecting Lanza's wide musical interests and desire to stretch himself. In contrast, *Portrait In Blue* (LL 1097039) is a very intimate set of duets with pianist Jason Long that effectively shows off Lanza's voice and wide emotional range.

Website: www.loulanza.com

Mary LaRose

b. January 16, 1956, Brooklyn, NY

In her career, Mary LaRose has sought to greatly increase the jazz repertoire available to singers, not only performing standards but the music of Ornette Coleman, Eric Dolphy, Anthony Braxton, and Charles Mingus.

"My father was a railroad man who loved to play his blue guitar and sing a repertoire of songs ranging from standards like 'Autumn Leaves' to Woody Guthrie tunes in his own rootsy fashion. My oldest brother Joe was a piano player and he loved to play jazz. He also had lots of records and was very into singers. He had several Nancy Wilson LPs, which I stole from him and still have not returned to this day."

Mary LaRose grew up singing at family gatherings, in her church choir and to rock records of the period. She had piano lessons from the age of five although, when she attended Brooklyn College, it was as a fine arts major who was mostly involved in visual arts. "As I became more involved in music, the two worlds of music and painting began to compete with each other for my focus. I picked music because I wanted to communicate with other people and art felt like a more solitary activity." She worked with another brother, Pete LaRose, who had a wedding band in New York, gradually becoming part of the jazz world.

"My biggest influence to date has been my husband Jeff Lederer, who introduced me to a new world of music. When we first got together, I remember Jeff playing an Albert Ayler record for me and me thinking to myself, 'This is noise, this isn't music!' But I had already gotten to a point where singing standards was not fulfilling me any longer and maybe I was ready for something new. I was already interested in the music of Eric Dolphy via his solo on Oliver Nelson's recording of 'Teenie's Blues' and that might have been my entry into the 'new thing.' I also think that my association with the wonderful trombonist Steve Swell has been important in opening up my ears."

Each of Mary LaRose's recordings reflects her open-minded approach and willingness to break new ground. "Stylistically,

my biggest step has been letting go of traditional jazz ideas of harmonic progression and preconceptions of the role of a singer in a jazz setting. I have always considered myself to be a musician rather than a singer. I don't think I have a polished sound or a pretty vibrato but that's not my style. I like to be an equal partner in the creative act and I hope the listener will always find something new and interesting in what they hear."

Recommended CDs: Each of Mary LaRose's recordings feature her inventive interpretations of fresh and unusual pieces, often drawn from avant-garde jazz and rock. *Cutting The Chord* (Ledhead 101), *Walking Woman* (GM 3041), *Obbligato* (CIMP 256) and *The Blue Guitar* (Little I Music), the latter drawing upon songs associated with Woody Guthrie, Johnny Cash and other veteran country/folk performers, are each intriguing, full of surprises and filled with brilliant jazz singing.

Janet Lawson

(Janet Ann Polun)
b. November 13, 1940, Baltimore, MD

A brilliant improviser and an important educator who, after recording two significant albums, has had her career plagued by illness, Janet Lawson is still an inspiration to today's jazz singers.

Her parents were professional musicians, her father a drummer and her mother a singer-lyricist. When she was three, she sang on a radio show, *Uncle Jack's Kiddy Klub* and performed in musicals at summer camp from the age of five. Lawson took classical piano lessons from age five but, by the time she was a teenager, she was much more interested in improvising. She listened to jazz records and to the radio constantly, always learning new songs along with jazz phrasing. "After going to many dances and spotting a group I liked, Bill Maisel's band, I asked if I could sit in and he said yes. At 15, he hired me for $20.00 a gig and I sang with that 15-piece band for four years right up until I left for New York at 19. It was great training and inspirational for what later became my instrumental scat style, influenced by being immersed in all those saxes, bones and brass."

In New York, one of her first gigs was singing at the Village Vanguard with Art Farmer's group. She studied with Hall Overton, toured extensively as a nightclub singer, appeared in South America, the Caribbean and the Far East, and landed a spot on Steve Allen's television show during 1968–69. Lawson began to dig seriously into more advanced jazz in the early 1970s. She studied with Warne Marsh, had an avant-garde group called Pipe Dreams with Judy Niemack, clarinetist Perry Robinson and guitarist Scott Hardy, worked with Bob Dorough, and became active as a teacher, heading the Vocal Jazz program at William Paterson College during 1981–88.

In the late 70s, she noticed that Beefsteak Charlie's had opened the club up to horn players. "I called them up and told the manager I wanted to sing there. He said, 'We don't hire singers – we hire horn players.' I said, 'I sing like a horn.' After hearing my tape he admitted, 'You do sing like a horn, you're hired.' That was the beginning of the Janet Lawson Quintet—seven years of the most supportive, adventurous, closest musical conversations I've ever had." Two highly rated recording resulted during 1980–83 that perfectly showcase her adventurous singing.

After having a lower profile in the 1990s, Janet Lawson was diagnosed with both Lyme disease and Bell's palsy in 2001, which forced her into semi-retirement as a singer, although she has continued as an educator (teaching at the New School

Barbara Lea

and at an annual jazz camp in Latvia) and is working toward making a comeback.

Recommended CDs: Janet Lawson's two albums, *The Janet Lawson Quintet* and *Dreams Can Be*, are available on the Japanese two-CD set *Janet Lawson* (Celeste Sound), which also includes selections that she recorded with Eddie Jefferson and David Lahm.

Website: www.janetlawson.hypermart.net

Barbara Lea
(Barbara Ann Le Cocq)
b. April 10, 1929, Detroit, MI

A superior swing singer from the 1950s, Barbara Lea is a survivor who had also spent periods as an actress and a cabaret singer before returning to jazz.

She grew up in a musical family and as a child learned hundreds of popular songs. "My first instrument was the ukulele; it ended when I broke it over my brother's head. Later, I took classical piano lessons, but when we moved into Detroit from Melvindale, I had a new teacher and didn't like her, so I quit, to my everlasting regret. My brother knew a woman who reviewed records for one of the Detroit newspapers. She used to give him records after she had reviewed them. That's how I got introduced to Louis Armstrong's Hot 5 and Hot 7, and Fats Waller on V-discs."

Barbara Lea first sang with a band in 1945, making $5 a night, and worked with a lot of local groups in the Detroit area. She majored in music theory at Wellesley College, graduating in 1951. During that period of time she sang with the Crimson Stompers, and in the Boston area had the opportunity to sing with such major trad musicians as Vic Dickenson, Edmond Hall, Frankie Newton, Johnny Windhurst and George Wein. A single in 1954 that included "Any Place I Hang My Hat Is Home" gained her some attention, as did her first album for Riverside in 1955, which teamed her voice with trumpeter Windhurst. She sang for nine weeks at the Village Vanguard, toured extensively and recorded two excellent albums for Prestige. But then she did not record as a leader during 1958–75.

"The bottom dropped out of jazz. Only those who had really substantial careers/names could keep going. I went into acting and thought I would never sing again." She worked in summer stock and in off-Broadway productions for years, earned an MA in Drama, and taught acting, modern drama and speech. In the jazz world, she had become a forgotten legend. "This changed in the mid-1970s when I had a little gig at a place at Third Avenue and 37th Street and my friend Charlie Bourgeois came in with Marian McPartland (whom I had known in Boston) and Alec Wilder. Alec asked me to do a couple of segments of his forthcoming radio series on NPR, *American Popular Song*. This led to a resurgence in my singing career."

Barbara Lea has been busy in jazz ever since, recording on a regular basis, performing in settings ranging from trad jazz and swing to cabaret, and appearing at jazz parties and festivals in addition to being the regular singer with Loren Schoenberg's big band for over 20 years.

"I don't like to mess with either the melody or the words when I'm singing a ballad. I do take a more relaxed view with up-tempo songs. Alec Wilder said of one that it 'has an air of permissiveness about it' and I think that's the case."

Recommended CDs: While her initial album has not been reissued yet, *Barbara Lea* (Original Jazz Classics 1713) and *Lea In Love* (Original Jazz Classics 1742) bring back her two wonderful early Prestige records. Since her "comeback," her best recordings have been released on CD, including *The Devil Is Afraid Of Music* (Audiophile 119), *Do It Again* (Audiophile 175) *Remembering Lee Wiley* (Audiophile 125), *You're The Cats* (Audiophile 252), *Sweet And Low* (Audiophile 260), *Celebrate Vincent Youmans* (A Records 73238) and a set of Hoagy Carmichael songs performed with Bob Dorough, *Hoagy's Children* (Audiophile 165).

Website: www.barbaralea.com

Jeanne Lee
b. January 29, 1939, New York, NY;
d. October 24, 2000, Tijuana, Mexico

One of the very first avant-garde jazz singers, Jeanne Lee had an adventurous spirit, a warm voice, and a great deal of versatility.

Originally, she studied modern dance and piano. While attending Bard College, she met pianist Ran Blake and their 1961 duet recording, *The Newest Sound Around*, is considered a classic. After a few years living in California, she moved to Europe in 1967, where she performed with and eventually married Gunter Hampel, who played vibes and bass clarinet. They worked together regularly, recording for Hampel's Birth label and combining advanced jazz with poetry and multimedia projects.

In addition to her work with Hampel, Lee performed with the who's who of advanced jazz, recording duet albums with cellist David Eyges and pianist Mal Waldron and appearing on records by Carla Bley, Archie Shepp, Marion Brown, Anthony Braxton, Reggie Workman and Vocal Summit. An innovator at creating wordless sounds, Lee also sounded quite natural performing lyrics, displaying a slightly heavy and husky voice. She was also a well-respected educator.

Jeanne Lee, before her death from cancer in 2000, was considered an innovator and a leader in her field.

Recommended CDs: *The Newest Sound Around* (Bluebird 6461) is her groundbreaking album with Ran Blake. *Natural Affinities* (Owl 070) features Smith in various settings in 1992, while *Here And Now* (World Of Mouth 1007) and *After Hours* (Owl 077) are her duet sets with David Eyges and Mal Waldron. *You Stepped Out Of A Cloud* (Owl 79238) is a 1989 reunion with Ran Blake that holds its own with their earlier collaboration.

Julia Lee
b. October 31, 1902, Booneville, MO;
d. December 8, 1958, Kansas City, MO

A fixture in Kansas City for over three decades, Julia Lee was well known for her singing of double-entendre lyrics (which was more cute than menacing) and her rocking piano playing. Her father was a violinist who had a string trio. Lee made her debut singing with her father's band when she was four. When she was 10, she started playing piano and at 16 she was performing intermission piano at Kansas City's Love Theater. Her brother George E. Lee led one of the top groups in Kansas City and she was featured as pianist and vocalist with his band during 1920–33. In 1927, when George E. Lee's Novelty Singing Orchestra recorded two numbers, Julia was featured on "Down Home Syncopated Blues." On November 6, 1929, the band recorded four more numbers with Julia taking the vocal on "If I Could Be With You One Hour Tonight." That same day, a contingent from the band backed Julia Lee on two numbers released under her name: "He's Tall Dark And Handsome" and "Won't You Come Over To My House."

Surprisingly, Julia Lee did not record again for 15 years, despite working steadily as a solo act at Milton's in Kansas City during 1934–48. After missing being documented at all during the swing era, Lee recorded two titles for Capitol in 1944 ("Trouble In Mind" and a hit remake of "Won't You Come Over To My House," which was renamed "Come On Over To My House") and then recorded regularly for Capitol during 1946–52. Among the suggestive songs that she made popular were "Lotus Blossom," "Gotta Gimme What'cha Got," "Snatch It And Grab It," "King Size Papa," "Do You Want It," "It Comes In Like A Lion," "Don't Save It Too Long," "You Ain't Got It No More" and "All This Beef And Big Ripe Tomatoes." Many of the songs, which were delivered innocently, closed with a punch line that showed that the subject matter was different than one initially thought. Lee also recorded standards and her recording bands mixed together top local musicians with occasional all-stars, including Benny Carter, Red Nichols, Vic Dickenson and Red Norvo.

Julia Lee, who performed at the White House for Harry Truman in 1949, made her final record session in 1956 and was active until she was struck down by a heart attack in 1958 at the age of 56.

Recommended CDs: The two-CD set *Julia Lee And Her Boyfriends* (JSP 3405) has all of Lee's 1944–47 recordings other than alternate takes. Collectors desiring the complete Julia Lee and not worried about keeping their acquisition inexpensive will want the four-CD *Kansas City Star* (Bear Family 15770).

Peggy Lee

(Norma Deloris Egstrom)
b. May 26, 1920, Jamestown, ND;
d. January 21, 2002, Bel Air, CA

Peggy Lee helped to define "the cool sound" by using understatement, singing softly, and making the most out of her small voice.

She had a rough childhood but survived and first sang professionally on local radio, gaining her own radio series while in high school. A disc jockey convinced her to change her name from Norma Egstrom to Peggy Lee. She spent some time in Los Angeles (appearing with Will Osborne's orchestra) and was singing in Chicago in 1941 when she was seen by Benny Goodman, who hired her as

Helen Forrest's replacement. Although she sounded very nervous on her first recording with Goodman ("Elmer's Tune"), she matured steadily during her two years with the King of Swing. "Somebody Else Is Taking My Place" was a hit and she really became well known after recording Lil Green's "Why Don't You Do Right," which became one of her trademark songs. In addition to the recording, she can be seen singing that number in the film *Stage Door Canteen*.

Lee married Goodman's guitarist Dave Barbour in 1943, and they both left the band. She had planned to retire and raise a family, but within a year was writing songs and recording for the Capitol label. After she had hits with "I Don't Know Enough About You," "It's A Good Day" and "Mañana" (each of which have her lyrics), she was back to singing full-time.

In the 1950s, Lee continued recording for Capitol except for a period with Decca (1952–56). Among her best-known recordings are "Fever" and "Black Coffee." She wrote the music for the classic animated film *Lady And The Tramp* (also supplying the voice for four of the characters) and was in three films during 1950–55: *Mr. Music*, which starred Bing Crosby, the remake of *The Jazz Singer*, and *Pete Kelly's Blues*, gaining an Academy Award nomination for the latter. It is surprising that she was not in more films, but she kept busy with a steady string of recordings, club appearances and work on television. She also wrote the lyrics to such songs as "I'm Gonna Go Fishin'," "The Shining Sea," "He's A Tramp" and "I Love Being Here With You."

Not all of Peggy Lee's recordings would be considered jazz, and her work from the mid-1960s on is generally less interesting, often being pop tunes. She had her last hit in 1969 with the somewhat bizarre "Is That All There Is." Lee continued performing into her last decade, but by the 1990s her voice was gone and she was in a wheelchair. But she never lost her phrasing or her ability to make a ballad such as "The Folks Who Live On The Hill" sound touching.

Recommended CDs: *Peggy Lee And Benny Goodman—The Complete Recordings* (Columbia/Legacy 65686) is a two-CD set that covers 1941–42 plus three numbers from a 1947 reunion date. Lee is on half of the limited-edition five-CD box set *The Complete Peggy Lee And June Christy Capitol Transcription Sessions* (Mosaic 5-184) and is heard on other transcriptions from 1947 on the single CD *With the Dave Barbour Band* (Laserlight 15 742). *Capitol Collectors Series* (Capitol 93195) has her most important recordings of 1945–50. The two-CD set *The Lost '40s & '50s Capitol Masters* (Collectors' Classics 9/7) has jazz-oriented rarites from 1944–52. *Black Coffee And Other Delights* (MCA/Decca 11122) is a two-CD set that covers her Decca years quite well, ranging from jazz to pop and a duet with Bing Crosby on "Winter Weather." Of her later Capitol LPs, *Beauty And The Beat* (Capitol 98454) with the George Shearing Quintet and *Mink Jazz* (Capitol 95450) are rewarding, while *Basin Street East Proudly Presents Peggy Lee* (Capitol 32744) is overarranged and a bit disappointing. Peggy Lee's final recordings for Angel and Chesky in the 1980s and early 1990s are of only historic interest, for her voice was pretty well gone.

Ranee Lee

b. October 26, 1942, Brooklyn, NY

Ranee Lee was a late bloomer in her singing career, not recording her first CD until she was 42. However, she has since emerged as one of the top jazz singers in her adopted homeland, Canada.

Sara Leib

"My mother was a big fan of the big band style and loved vocalists like Lena Horne, Billie Holiday, Pearl Bailey, Billy Eckstine and Cab Calloway. Music played in our home all the time when I was growing up. So when I chose the style of music that I would perform in my early career, I sang the songs that I was most familiar with; they just seem to live in me."

Ms. Lee gained early experience singing in doo-wop groups, her church choir and talent shows. She performed on the road with a variety of ensembles in the 1960s, joining "The Play Girls," an all-female group for which she learned how to play drums. She also taught herself the tenor sax, gaining work with several groups, and played bass in a country band. "Having to play those instruments gave me a better perspective, and respect for musicians as a vocalist. I learned how to incorporate with rhythms, phrase the voice as an instrument, and to sing with the band, not out in front of it."

After settling in Montreal, Ranee Lee recorded her first album, *Live At Le Bijou*, in 1984, starting a long association with the Justin Time label and quickly gaining recognition as an important vocalist. Along the way she has recorded with Milt Hinton, Red Mitchell, David Murray, Ray Brown, Ed Thigpen, Clark Terry and many top Canadian players. In addition to being a warm and flexible singer, Ranee Lee won an award for her portrayal of Billie Holiday in the play *Lady Day At Emerson's Bar And Grill*, starred in the film *Giant Steps* next to Billy Dee Williams, has been the jazz vocal instructor at McGill University and Laval University, toured Europe frequently, wrote and starred in her musical theatrical production *Dark Divas*, authored the children's book *Nana What Do You Say*, and hosted the television series *The Performers*.

Ranee Lee, who considers her early influences to be Dinah Washington and Nancy Wilson, has been an original for at least the past 20 years and has certainly made up for lost time.

Recommended CDs: From the start of her career, Ranee Lee was a creative force in invigorating standards and shining light on lesser-known songs. All of her Justin Time releases are rewarding: *Live At Le Bijou* (Justin Time 6), *Deep Song* (Justin Time 33), *The Musicals: Jazz on Broadway* (Justin Time 42), *I Thought About You* (Justin Time 68), *You Must Believe In Swing* (Justin Time 88), *Seasons of Love* (Justin Time 103), *Dark Divas—The Musical* (Justin Time 132/133), *Dark Divas—Highlights* (Justin Time 144), *Maple Groove* (Justin Time 194) and *Just You, Just Me* with Oliver Jones (Justin Time 213). Start off with *Deep Song*, *Dark Divas—Highlights*, and *Just You, Just Me* to get a strong overview of Ranee Lee's music and career.

Sara Leib
b. December 21, 1981, Los Angeles, CA

A fine young singer who is particularly adept at creating long scat-filled improvisations, Sara Leib made a strong start to her career with her debut recording, *It's Not The Moon*.

"I always sang. Growing up in my house, music was not an extracurricular activity but an educated discipline, just like history or math. I began studying piano, taught myself various instruments, and eventually moved on to voice. I sang in a jazz choir in high school and began listening to the recordings of Miles Davis; Lambert, Hendricks, and Ross; John Coltrane; Ella Fitzgerald; Benny Goodman; and Louis Armstrong, learning to improvise from hearing them."

Sara Leib was accepted into the Grammy High School's National Jazz Ensemble and attended Berklee (1999–2001) and the New England Conservatory (2001–2003) where she earned a Bachelor's degree in music. She studied with Dominique Eade, Steve Lacy and Jerry Bergonzi, toured Japan after college, played with pianist Art Lande, and resettled in the Los Angeles area. She has since toured, worked in the studios, taught music and recorded her first CD. "I am also writing and licensing pop music, and hope to popularize jazz with young America by fusing it with some of my singer/songwriter music."

Recommended CD: *It's Not The Moon* (Panfer 8932) from 2003 features Sara Leib as an expert scat singer despite only being 21 at the time. The title cut has her words to Gerry Mulligan's "Night Lights" and the repertoire ranges from "More Than You Know" to Tom Waits' "San Diego Serenade," alternating haunting ballads with heated straight-ahead romps, sometimes over tricky time signatures.

Website: www.saraleib.com

Carol Leigh
(Carol Ann Karney)
b. December 25, 1933, Redwood City, CA

Carol Leigh caught the tail-end of the Dixieland revival movement and has helped keep classic jazz alive ever since. She is a delightful and versatile singer who ranges from Bessie Smith to Ethel Waters and young Billie Holiday.

She grew up hearing her two older brothers' jazz records, black big bands and New Orleans jazz on the radio and, at the age of 16, the San Francisco jazz bands of Turk Murphy and Bob Scobey in person. In 1953 she married trombonist Jim Leigh. "After I finished high school at age 17, I worked in offices, as a keypunch operator, and at other office jobs. When Jim Leigh began teaching at San Francisco State College in 1958, I didn't have to have a steady day job. That year, Alan Hall (piano/trombone) asked me to come to his gig in San Mateo and sing with his band. I sang a few 1920s blues & hot jazz and was hired for $5 a night. I got occasional gigs during the next few years. In May, 1961, I began my first six-night-a-week job at a 'Roaring '20s' nightclub in San Francisco named the Hotsy Totsy. I sang old and newer blues and hot jazz tunes with just a piano player and danced the Charleston on a big specially built table. I never worked in offices after that."

During her period in San Francisco, which lasted until 1971, she had opportunities to sing with bassists Wellman Braud and Pops Foster, Slim Gaillard and Wingy Manone, not only performing classic blues and trad standards but more contemporary material. Divorced from Jim Leigh, in 1973 she met saxophonist Russ Whitman; they were married four years later. Also in 1973, she met the members of the Original Salty Dogs Jazz Band. "I sat in with them and began working with them in 1974. They regularly worked a lot of festivals in the East and Midwest. The Salty Dogs and I have worked about six times a year since I joined them. Because most of the band lives in the Chicago area and Lew Green (cornet & leader) lives in Connecticut, as do I, we don't have a steady local gig."

While most associated with the Salty Dogs (with whom she has recorded on several occasions), she has also worked with Turk Murphy (1979–81), Wild Bill Davison, Dick Wellstood, James Dapogny (1985–88), Neville Dickie, the Hall Brothers Jazz Band, the Climax Jazz Band, the Black Eagles, and in Japan with the New Orleans Rascals, touring Japan, Europe and Australia.

Carol Leigh still sings on an occasional basis. "I feel lucky to have lived at a time when there were many great players still around, when there were a lot of very good players, and when there were a lot of big and little gigs for us all. The music is bigger than anyone playing it; treat it well."

Recommended CDs: *If You Don't, I Know You Will* (Stomp Off 1064) is a great duet set with pianist Jim Dapogny. In addition to her appearances on records by the Salty Dogs, Carol Leigh is well featured on *I'm Busy And You Can't Come In* (Stomp Off 1087), which teams her with Jim Dapogny's band, *You've Got To Give Me Some* (GHB 136), *Go Back Where You Stayed Last Night* (GHB 167), *Long, Deep And Wide* (GHB 237) with the Salty Dogs, *Carol Leigh And The Dumoustier Stompers* (GHB 341), and *A Tribute To Louis And The 1920s Singers* (GHB 388).

Tom Lellis
b. April 8, 1946, Cleveland, OH

Often overlooked when one discusses the top male jazz vocalists of the past 30 years, Tom Lellis ranks pretty high in that admittedly small field.

He remembers, "My first grade teacher would put up a broomstick with a painted black tin can mic on Fridays for the kids. I sang every week and she repeatedly called me her 'little Perry Como.' At a talent show in tenth grade at Euclid High School, I sang 'What'd I Say' and 'Kansas City' and was a hit. I began working in bars professionally at 15 years old." Although Lellis had brief stints playing ukulele, electric bass, guitar and piano (which he still plays), and at 51 he started to play the nylon string guitar, he has been primarily a singer throughout his career.

By the time he was 21, he was opening for Ray Charles and Gregory Hines. In addition to his singing, Lellis has put words to the music of McCoy Tyner, Keith Jarrett, Wayne Shorter, Chick Corea and Dave Brubeck, among others. His recording debut, 1981's *And In This Corner*, gained him some recognition but it would be a decade before the follow-up, *Double Entendre*, was released. Lellis, who has stretched from bop and standards to Latin music (collaborating with Toninho Horta on his third recording, *Taken To Heart*), is proudest of *Skylark*. On that ambitious project from 2002, he performs with the Metropole Orchestra.

"Since my musical influences are both singers and musicians, I will continue to try to integrate the two. I think jazz has been divided for 60 years (since bebop) and believe that unless the best of both singers and musicians record and perform together regularly, jazz will remain a dwindling art form."

Recommended CDs: *And In This Corner* (Inner City 1090), *Double Entendre* (Beamtime 1012), *Taken To Heart* (Concord 4574), *Skylark* (Total Music Design 001), *Southern Exposure* (Adventure Music 1006) and *Avenue Of The Americas* (Beamtide 1013) all have their strong moments. *Avenue Of The Americas* is an excellent all-round overview of Tom Lellis' musical interests, while he is justifiably happy with *Skylark*.

Website: www.tomlellis.com

Jay Leonhart
(James Chancellor Leonhart)
b. Dec 6, 1940, Baltimore, MD

Jay Leonhart has had overlapping careers as a fine bassist and a witty vocalist and lyricist who has been influenced and inspired by Dave Frishberg and Tom Lehrer.

Growing up in a very musical family, by the time he was seven Jay and his older brother Bill were playing banjo, guitar, mandolin and bass. A few years later they were appearing on Baltimore television and touring, mostly on banjos where they sang and played both country music and jazz.

"I sang in church choirs but stopped when the choirmaster had the audacity to accuse me of singing flat. I knew who was singing flat and it wasn't me. I loved Dixieland when I was growing up, but my first real jazz awakenings happened when I listened to Oscar Peterson and Duke Ellington. Then I knew where I had to go." At 14, he became the bassist with the Pier Five Dixieland Jazz Band. He studied at the Peabody Institute (1946–49), the Berklee School Of Music (1960–61) and with Oscar Peterson and Ray Brown at the Advanced School Of Contemporary Music in Toronto (1961–62).

Leonhart toured with various big bands starting in the late 1950s, moving to New York in 1961. He worked with Buddy Morrow (1961) and Mike Longo (1962–63) before becoming a very busy freelance and studio musician. Among his countless number of associations have been Ethel Ennis, Urbie Green, Marian McPartland, Jim Hall, Tony Bennett, Mel Tormé, Thad Jones/Mel Lewis, Phil Woods, Gerry Mulligan, Lee Konitz, Don Sebesky, Louie Bellson, Bill Charlap and Wycliffe Gordon.

In 1968 he married singer Donna Zier and since then they have had two children: trumpeter Michael Leonhart and singer Carolyn Leonhart. "I started singing again when I had kids and began writing songs about them. It slowly dawned on me as I kept writing my songs that I was going to be the only one singing them for a while. My songs would wither and die on the vine if I didn't sing them. Besides, I really have fun singing them. I still sing mostly my own compositions."

In 2005, Jay Leonhart put together a one-man show, singing and playing bass on *The Bass Lesson*. He is currently writing a second show, *Nukular Tulips*.

Recommended CDs: Of Jay Leonhart's 15 solo albums, the ones that most feature his vocals and lyrics are *Salamander Pie* (DMP 442), *There's Gonna Be Trouble* (Sunnyside 1006), *The Double Cross* (Sunnyside 1032), *Life Out On The Road* (Nesak 19801), *Live At Fat Tuesday's* (DRG 8439), *Two Lane Highways* (Nesak 19806), *Galaxies And Planets* (Sons Of Sound 20008) and *The Bass Lesson* (Chancellor Music).

Website: www.jayleonhart.com

Dori Levine
b. November 13, 1953, Newark, NJ

A singer with a style of her own, Dori Levine has often been associated with the students of Lennie Tristano, many of whom have been her teachers.

"I can remember getting together with my girlfriends and singing along to girl group recordings that were popular at the time and trying to match the harmonies. I also remember an early performance at an open mic in my college cafeteria at the School of Visual Arts in the 1970s. I was playing slide guitar at the time and doing my Bonnie Raitt imitation. But I got introduced to jazz when I was an art student living on 114th St. around the corner from the West End Bar. Phil Schaap was emceeing and booking ex-Ellington and Basieites into the room along with a young jazz prodigy, a pianist named Brooks Kerr. Brooks had a girlfriend named Annie Hurwitz who used to get up and sing 'Pennies From Heaven' in a Billie Holiday-esque style. I thought that looked like the most fun in the world. It was around this time that I bought my first Ella Fitzgerald record and I had already worn out the Billie Holiday record I had been given. I was sold."

After discovering Betty Carter, Dori Levine knew that she had to be a jazz singer. She graduated from the School of Visual Arts in 1976, took singing lessons from Anne Marie Moss and Ann Ruckert, and put together her first band. After being impressed by a Liz Gorrill record, she found out that Gorrill studied with Lennie Tristano, so she sought out the pianist and studied with him until his death, often singing along with solos by Lester Young, Lee Konitz and Charlie Parker.

After meeting singers Bob Casanova and Sally Swisher at a free improvisation workshop taught by Jay Clayton, Ms. Levine formed a vocal trio with them called Over Easy that performed in the New York area during 1981–91. She studied jazz improvisation on piano with Connie Crothers, had a group called "Voices from the Other Side" that often performed freely improvised pieces, recorded two CDs for the New Artists label, began teaching jazz and vocal improvisation, and today often works with pianist Michael Levy, guitarist Ed Littman or pianist Giacomo Franci (her husband).

"I see myself as part of the 'voice as an instrument' lineage originating with Billie Holiday, Louis Armstrong and Ella Fitzgerald. In my opinion, this tradition has continued with other great improvising singers like Jeanne Lee, Betty Carter, Sheila Jordan, Jay Clayton and Bobby McFerrin. I always seek to find a balance between singing jazz standards and being a free improviser."

Recommended CDs: Dori Levine's two CDs are *Koo Koo* (New Artists 1031), which is a set of mostly freely-improvised music with Michael Levy, and *Click* (New Artists 1042), which is comprised of duets with Ed Littman that include standards, scatting and blues.

Website: www.dorilevine.com

Abbey Lincoln
(Anna Marie Wooldridge)
b. August 6, 1930, Chicago, IL

Abbey Lincoln symbolized the first half of the 1960s in jazz, being based in bop and standards but also very involved in the civil rights movement and looking toward the avant-garde in her adventurous and sometimes angry improvisations. She has since evolved into an important songwriter, in addition to being a vital interpreter of lyrics who, like Billie Holiday, always believes in the words she sings.

The tenth of twelve children, young Anna Marie Wooldridge sang as a teenager and then carved out a career as a glamorous supper club singer, using several names along the way including Anna Marie, Gaby Lee and Gaby Wooldridge. By the time she made her debut in 1956, she had settled on Abbey Lincoln. She sang a song in the lightweight film *The Girl Can't Help It* and then met drummer Max Roach, who was very influential on her approach and music. She began to take her singing much more seriously and was signed to Riverside where she made three very good records, using such sidemen as Sonny Rollins, Kenny Dorham, Benny Golson, Curtis Fuller, Wynton Kelly and Roach.

All of that was a warmup. She starred on Roach's intense *Freedom Now Suite* (one of the movements has her screaming), is superb on her own *Straight Ahead* (sidemen include Coleman Hawkins, Booker Little and Eric Dolphy), and her singing on "Mendacity" on Roach's *Percussion Bitter Suite* steals the show.

Lincoln and Roach were married in 1962; their marriage lasted eight years. The singer's involvement in civil rights and politics made it difficult for her to get work at time, and she did not record as a leader during 1962–72. However, she did co-star in two important movies: *Nothing But A Man* (1964) and *For Love Of Ivy* (1968). The latter also starred Sidney Poitier.

Since returning to records in 1973, Abbey Lincoln has developed into a major songwriter (her "Throw It Away" has gradually become a standard), and since 1990 she has recorded regularly for Verve, including a set of her originals on 2007's *Abbey Sings Abbey*. Now entering her late seventies, she is still relevant, contemporary and a stirring performer.

Recommended CDs: Although her voice has naturally aged through the years, there is not an unworthy Abbey Lincoln recording. All have their merit, and these definitely include *Abbey Lincoln's Affair: A Story of A Girl In Love* (Blue Note 81199), *That's Him* (Original Jazz Classics 85), *It's Magic* (Original Jazz Classics 205), *Abbey Is Blue* (Original Jazz Classics 69), *Straight Ahead* (Candid 79015), *People In Me* (ITM 1439), *Talking To The Sun* (Enja 79635), *Abbey Sings Billie, Vol. 1* (Enja 79633), *Abbey Sings Billie, Vol. 2* (Enja 7037), *The World Is Falling Down* (Verve 843476), *You Gotta Pay The Band* (Verve 511110), which also features Stan Getz, *Devil's Got Your Tongue* (Verve 513574), a set of duets with pianist Hank Jones that is called *When There Is Love* (Verve 519697), *A Turtle's Dream* (Verve 527382), *Painted Lady* (ITM 1422), which co-stars Archie Shepp, *Who Used to Dance*

(Verve 533559), *Wholly Earth* (Verve 591982), *Over the Years* (Verve 549101), *It's Me* (Verve 126802) and *Abbey Sings Abbey* (Verve 847030). Also be sure to pick up Max Roach's *We Insist: Freedom Now Suite* (Candid 79002).

LPs to Search For: So far Abbey Lincoln's *Golden Lady* (Inner City 1117) has eluded all reissue programs.

Jeanette Lindstrom
(Maria Jeanette Lindström)
b. May 29, 1971, Stockholm, Sweden

A very versatile singer from Sweden who can create vocal music without words and can improvise freely, Jeanette Lindstrom is also adept at wrapping her voice around a strong set of lyrics.

"My parents had a lot of jazz records and my father played the drums, so I guess I can say I grew up with jazz. I lived in the north of Sweden, with the forests and mountains, by a big lake. There was a lot of space. In addition to jazz, I grew up with soul, and some Brazilian music. And also, even if I haven´t been singing very much Swedish folk music, that tradition might have left some traces in me, too." She took classical piano lessons from the age of two and did some gigging in high school as an organist and a pianist but, by the time she was 18, she knew that her career would be in singing. She took music programs in school and graduated from Stockholm's Royal College of Music in 1995. While in college, Lindstrom was in a quartet called Pictures, which featured her using her voice primarily as a wordless instrument. She formed her own quintet in 1994 and recorded her first CD, *Another Country*, the following year.

When asked to name some of the high points to her career since then, she mentions her collaborations with pianist Steve Dobrogosz, an occasional quartet that she had during 1996–98. "The concept was more 'free'; we decided on some tunes to play, but then anything could happen in or between them. She also cites a project with pianist Kenny Werner, trumpeter Tim Hagans and the Norrbotten Big Band in 1998, being a guest with the Jacky Terrasson Trio, and working during 2002–03 with the Swedish singer-composers Lina Nyberg and Rigmor Gustafsson.

In addition, she has been active in other genres, performing contemporary art music, appearing with chamber orchestras, and having a repertoire ranging from Satie to Burt Bacharach. Jeanette Lindstrom's jazz recordings have ranged from nearly free improvisations to standards, and she is today considered one of Sweden's finest jazz singers. "I can think of some concerts as high points, where the audience has not been 'typical' jazz listeners, but where we still have managed to catch their attention. I love it when people come up to me and say 'Oh, that was jazz?' I've never heard that before. It was really good, I liked it!'"

Recommended CDs: Jeanette Lindstrom's versatility and consistent creativity are well displayed on her recordings. *Another Country* (Caprice 214 80), released in 1995, was a very impressive debut, while 1997's *I Saw You* (Caprice 215 49) and *Feathers* (Prophone 053), the latter a set of duets with pianist Steve Dobrogosz, feature her quite at home whether performing standards or improvised numbers. *Sinatra/Weill* (Caprice 216 24) features Ms. Lindstrom with an orchestra, Tim Hagans and Kenny Werner, singing selections associated with Frank Sinatra and Kurt Weill. *Walk* (Amigo 895) and *In The Middle Of This Riddle* (Amigo 909) are two of her most adventurous dates, utilizing medium-sized groups (there are occasional strings on *In The Middle Of This Riddle*) during originals and free pieces. In contrast, *Whistling Away The Dark* (Amigo 916) has Jeanette Lindstrom with a trio (with either Bobo Stenson or Jonas Ostholm are on piano) singing her fresh interpretations of standards.

Website: www.jeanettelindstrom.com

Virginia Liston
b. 1890; d. June 1932, St. Louis, MO

Virginia Liston was a fine classic blues singer who retired prematurely. She began performing blues in Philadelphia around 1912 and worked in theaters and vaudeville. During 1920–25 she was married to pianist Sam Gray and they toured as Liston and Liston, an unusual situation where, because she was much better known than him, he took her last name. Liston recorded 36 songs during 1923–26, 19 of which have her backed by just Clarence Williams' workman-like piano or (on three songs) reed organ. Best known are two songs ("Early In The Morning" and "You've Got The Right Key, But The Wrong Keyhole") that feature Liston with Clarence Williams' Blue Five in 1924, which at the time included Louis Armstrong and Sidney Bechet.

The recordings ended after mid-1926, and three years later Liston remarried, moved to St. Louis and spent her last years working in a church.

Recommended CDs: *Vol. 1* (Document 5446) and *Vol. 2/ Lavinia Turner* (Document 5447) have all of Virginia Liston's recordings.

Julie London
(Gayle Peck)
b. September 26, 1926, Santa Rosa, CA;
d. October 18, 2000, Los Angeles, CA

Julie London had one of the most unlikely singing careers. By the mid-1950s she was a well-regarded actress, had never even sung in films, was involved with songwriter Bobby Troup, had a small voice, and was shy to sing before audiences. And yet, after scoring a major hit with "Cry Me A River," she was reluctantly cast as a jazz singer, although she always thought of herself as an actress first.

The daughter of a song and dance vaudeville team, Julie London's beauty was recognized early on and she began appearing in movies as a teenager in 1944. A pin-up girl during World War II, she was married to actor/jazz fan Jack Webb from 1947 to 1953. After their divorce, she met Bobby Troup in 1954, six years before they married.

Annette Lowman

In 1955, she recorded four selections with a sextet headed by Bobby Troup and also made a duet album with guitarist Al Viola, *Lonely Girl*. However, a few months later, she recorded *Julie Is Her Name* (which was released before *Lonely Girl*). Her sensual renditions of standards in which her smoky voice sounded remarkably intimate while accompanied by guitarist Barney Kessel and bassist Ray Leatherwood caused a bit of a sensation. "Cry Me A River" was one of the songs and it became her biggest hit. She repeated her success by singing "Cry Me A River" in the Jayne Mansfield film *The Girl Can't Help It*, in 1956.

There would be a total of 32 albums during the next 14 years, with Julie London sometimes heard with orchestras but usually sounding at her best with small groups that accentuated her use of space. Her LPs became collectors' items due to the sexy photos of her that graced the album jackets. But after recording *Yummy, Yummy, Yummy* in 1969 (which featured her versions of current pop hits including "Light My Fire"), she retired from recording other than cutting a version of "My Funny Valentine" for the 1981 film *Sharky's Machine*.

Julie London was happy to be a full-time actress again and gained some additional fame for her role as a nurse on NBC's *Emergency* (1972–79), appearing next to Bobby Troup on a series produced by her ex-husband Jack Webb. She suffered a stroke in 1995. Troup died in 1999, and she passed away the following year.

Recommended CDs: Although the original LPs are fun to find, many are only available at high prices due to the covers. *Julie Is Her Name/Julie Is Her Name Vol. 2* (EMI 99804) has the "Cry Me A River" album plus a similar 1958 date in which she is accompanied by guitarist Howard Roberts and bassist Red Mitchell. *Lonely Girl* (The Entertainers 3841) is scarce. Two of the best EMI couplings are *Calendar Girl/Your Number Please* (EMI 59959) and *About The Blues/London By Night* (EMI 535208). Her recordings from 1959–69 include *Swing Me An Old Song* (Marginal 040), *Julie…At Home/Around Midnight* (EMI 54542), *Sophisticated Lady/For The Night People* (EMI 94992), *End Of The World/Nice Girls Don't Stay* (EMI 70238) and *All Through The Night* (Jasmine 308).

Annette Lowman
b. March 27, 1949, Denver, CO

A soulful American singer, Annette Lowman spent an important 15-year period living and performing in Europe.

While growing up in Denver, she listened to the R&B and pop music of the era, but did not discover jazz until the 1970s. "The door was kicked wide open when I started working at Charlie's Georgetown in Washington, DC in 1980. This was a classy venue which housed a clientele that nourished me musically and personally. Charlie's had two rooms: the piano bar, where I worked six nights a week with pianist Bob Diener, and the supper club room which housed great names like Sarah Vaughan, Sonny Stitt, Marian McPartland, Teddy Wilson and Mel Tormé. I would go in to listen to them on my breaks and they would come out from time to time to check

me out and offer comments on how I could improve. It was a wonderful gig and it changed my entire life."

On a bit of a lark, after hearing how Paris was a haven for jazz musicians, she moved to France in 1983. "I moved there with $1,500, no credit cards, could not speak a word of French and there was nobody to meet me at the airport. I was shocked and terrified, being all alone in Paris, France, but I was entirely too proud to return to the United States without achieving some type of a success." Somehow she managed to struggle successfully and was soon carving out a career for herself. "That was the best musical education I could have received. Every day of my life for 12 years depended on daily improvisations. There was enough good energy to keep me moving straight ahead from the expat community and the serious jazz lovers."

During her European years, Annette Lowman made her recording debut, hooked up with the Minor Music label, worked with Horace Parlan, Steve Lacy and Archie Shepp, and was treated as an artist. She moved to Portland in 1998, and has had a lower profile in recent years. "I've never been privileged enough to work consistently with the same people so every performance is completely different. Jazz gives me the freedom to move wherever I want to go and to express myself in the moment."

Recommended CDs: Annette Lowman's main recordings have been *Movies Memories* (Le Chant Du Monde 274941), which features her performing standards that were written for films, *Brown Baby* (Minor Music 84182), which is a tribute to Oscar Brown Jr., and *Annette Lowman* (Minor Music 801050). The latter has her in 1995 being joined by the group Three Of A Kind with guests Stanley Turrentine and Maceo Parker for a set of standards mostly taken at a relaxed pace along with a cooking "Surrey With The Fringe On Top" and a duet with guitarist Rodney Jones on "Lush Life."

Website: www.annettelowman.com

Nick Lucas
(Domenic Antonio Nicola Lucalese)
b. August 22, 1897, Newark, NJ; d. July 28, 1982, Newark, NJ

Nick Lucas' high-pitched voice and the fact that he introduced "Tip Toe Through The Tulips" made him an influence on Tiny Tim in the late 1960s, but he was on a higher level. A fine guitarist whose features "Pickin' The Guitar" and "Teasing The Frets" in 1922 were the very first recordings of unaccompanied jazz guitar solos (he remade both songs in 1923 and 1932), Lucas also had a charming and easy-going singing style.

Nick Lucas sang and played guitar as a youth, in time adding banjo, mandolin and ukulele. When he was 10, he and his brother played on trains for money. He picked up experience as a teenager performing in cafes and restaurants, and at 20 put together the Kentucky Five with pianist Ted Fio Rito to play in vaudeville. Lucas popped up on jazz records during the first half of the 1920s with Bailey's Lucky Seven and Sam Lanin, and his two guitar features find him predating Eddie Lang by several years. In 1924, while with Ted Fio Rito's band, Lucas was featured on the radio, which gave him fame and did wonders for his record sales. Billed as "The Singing Troubadour," it is estimated that during 1925–32 his records sold over 84 million copies. Among his hits were "My Best Girl," "I'm Looking Over A Four Leaf Clover," "I'll Get By" and "Brown Eyes, Why Are You Blue?" Lucas also starred on Broadway in *Sweetheart Time* and *Show Girl*, and appeared in the early talkies *The Show Of Shows* and *Gold*

Diggers Of Broadway. In the latter film he introduced "Tip Toe Through The Tulips" and "Painting The Clouds With Sunshine."

In 1928, the Gibson Company established their Nick Lucas model, the first guitar named after a specific artist. It is also a little-known fact that the first stylized flat guitar pick was developed by Lucas in 1932.

Although no longer a major star after the Depression hit and swing caught on, Nick Lucas continued working for decades. He was a fixture in Hollywood clubs during the 1930s, appearing in some shorts and on radio. His excellent radio transcriptions of the 1940s have been reissued on the Soundies CD *Painting The Clouds*. Lucas worked in Las Vegas in the 1950s, made many appearances on the *Ed Sullivan Show*, and in 1974 sang some of the vintage songs used on the soundtrack of the remake of *The Great Gatsby*.

Nick Lucas, whose smooth singing style is nostalgic, melodic and straightforward while lightly swinging, remained active until shortly before his death in 1982 at the age of 84.

Recommended CDs: *The Crooning Troubadour* (ASV/Living Era 5329) has some of Nick Lucas' most significant early recordings, while *Painting The Clouds* (Soundies 4134) features him at his best in the 1940s.

Carmen Lundy

b. November 1, 1954, Miami, FL

While it gets to be a cliché to call a particular jazz singer underrated (isn't everyone in jazz underrated by the general public?), Carmen Lundy is near the top of the list. Her voice is deep, versatile and very appealing, she is a masterful yet subtle improviser, writes high-quality music (some of which could be future standards), arranges for her band, and puts on intriguing performances.

Carmen Lundy had piano lessons from the age of six and she sang in her church's junior choir. She sang at local high schools in the vocal duo "Steph and Tret" and made a recording, *The Price Of Silence*, while a teenager. "I knew that I wanted to be a singer by the time I was 12. I entered college in the fall of 1972–73 as an opera major and later switched to the jazz program. I was the first Jazz Vocal major at the University Of Miami School of Music."

After gaining experience singing with the University of Miami Big Band (traveling to Europe and North Africa) and working in Miami jazz clubs, she moved to New York in 1978. "I immediately began working with some of the great jazz veterans including Walter Bishop Jr., Jaki Byard, Don Pullen, Cedar Walton, Sonny Fortune, Ronnie Matthews, John Hicks, Victor Lewis, Kenny Barron and Buster Williams plus my brother, bassist Curtis Lundy." She recorded her debut album *Good Morning Kiss* in 1986 and already had a mature and original style, even when interpreting standards.

In the years since, she has moved to Los Angeles, been active as a teacher and clinician, recorded six other albums, been an actress onstage (including playing Billie Holiday in *They Were All Gardenias* and appearing in Duke Ellington's *Sophisticated*

Ladies), and presented her original music in concert and on the CD and DVD *Jazz And The New Songbook—Live At The Madrid*. In addition, she is the composer of over 40 songs and a painter whose artwork has been exhibited in New York and Los Angeles.

"I ask the jazz community (the listeners, critics and record companies) to continue to support, embrace and reward originality."

Recommended CDs: Each of Carmen Lundy's recordings have their great moments, starting with her debut *Good Morning Kiss* (Justin Time 8495) and continuing through the Japanese release *Night And Day* (Sony 28AP-3320), *Moment To Moment* (Arabesque 102), *Self Portrait* (JVC 2047), which teams her with a large string orchestra, *Old Devil Moon* (JVC 2065), *This Is Carmen Lundy* (Justin Time 174), *Something To Believe In* (Justin Time 198) and the ambitious *The New Songbook – Live At The Madrid* (Afrasia Productions 61374).

Website: www.carmenlundy.com

Nellie Lutcher
(Nellie Lutcher Lewis)
b. October 15, 1912, Lake Charles, LA;
d. June 8, 2007, Los Angeles, CA

A very popular singer-pianist in the late 1940s, Nellie Lutcher often seemed to be singing lyrics that were more risqué than they actually were. She had a rhythmic sing-song vocal style that was immediately distinctive and she became famous for "He's A Real Gone Guy," "Fine Brown Frame" and "Hurry On Down."

One of 15 children, Nellie Lutcher had a father who worked in a packing plant and also played bass with Clarence Hart's Imperial Orchestra. Her family was very musical, whether dancing, singing or playing jazz. "I studied piano under Eugene Reynaud when I was eight years old. I was taught to play the violin, guitar, mandolin and ukulele by my Dad." When Ma Rainey came to town and needed a pianist in 1923, Nellie was recruited. She was 11. The following year, she joined Clarence Hart's band, staying with the group for five years.

After touring with the Southern Rhythm Boys and freelancing, in 1935 she moved to Los Angeles. "When I came to Los Angeles, I was not singing. My first job was at the Dunbar Hotel on Central Avenue. The customers requested me to sing by putting money in a glass. They liked what they heard, so I decided to add singing to my piano playing." She worked in a variety of settings without gaining much more than regional fame. But in 1947, Nellie Lutcher was heard playing and singing for the March of Dimes Cancer Drive on a radio broadcast by producer Dave Dexter. He immediately rushed into a studio and signed her to Capitol. Among the four songs recorded at the first session was "Hurry On Down," and three weeks later "He's A Real Gone Guy" was waxed. She recorded 40 songs for Capitol during the last nine months of 1947 and 22 more during 1949–52, not to mention a pair of vocal duets with Nat King Cole. Thirty-five years old in 1947, she was considered an overnight success despite having performed regularly for two decades, and for a five-year period was considered a regular on the R&B charts. She toured Great Britain twice during 1950–51.

But by 1952, the music world was changing and Nellie Lutcher's combination of vocal novelties, double-entendre songs and hard-driving swing piano was becoming out of style. She was dropped by Capitol and, although there were record dates for Epic, Decca, Liberty and Imperial, the hits had stopped. She performed less in public, but fortunately she had been wise enough to retain control of the publishing rights for her songs, a rarity for musicians of her generation. She invested in apartment houses, worked as a board director of the local Musicians Union, and occasionally emerged to play a high-profile engagement, including at the Cookery in New York in 1973 and on an hour-long television special in 1982. Nellie Lutcher continued performing now and then into the early 1990s and lived to be 94.

Recommended CDs: *The Best Of Nellie Lutcher* (Capitol/Blue Note 35039) has approximately one-third of her Capitol recordings including her three hits and is a definitive overview of her prime years. The four-CD set *Nellie Lutcher And Her Rhythm* (Bear Family 15910) has her complete output of 1947–57.

Gloria Lynne
b. November 23, 1931, New York, NY

Gloria Lynne, who recorded prolifically for Everest during 1958–63, seemed to disappear altogether in the 1970s and '80s, only to reappear in more recent times still in good voice.

She started out singing in church, which was natural because her mother was a gospel singer. Gloria Lynne had five years of concert training and in 1951 won the amateur competition at the Apollo Theater. In the 1950s, she sang R&B as part of both the Enchanters and the Dell-Tones, recording with both vocal groups. She also recorded a few singles, but it was her late-1958 Everest album, *Miss Gloria Lynne*, that gained her attention as a soloist.

Ms. Lynne recorded nine albums for Everest in settings ranging from hot swing groups and string orchestras to just a rhythm section (*At The Las Vegas Thunderbird*). While her recordings of "June Night," "Love I Found You" and "I'm Glad There Is You" were popular, her big hit, "I Wish You Love," was not recorded until her final Everest date in 1963 (the album *Gloria, Marty & Strings*). Her style during this period straddled the boundaries between swing, bop, middle-of-the-road pop and early soul music.

She toured as an opening or supporting act for Ray Charles, Billy Eckstine and Ella Fitzgerald and recorded frequently for Fontana during 1964—69, but the music world was changing. With the rise of rock, Gloria Lynne was never able to duplicate the commercial success of "I Wish You Love." She only recorded two commercial albums in the 1970s and was in danger of becoming a forgotten name.

But starting with 1989's *A Time For Love*, she began to record again in jazz settings for Muse and High Note, working more often and making a comeback, impressing audiences with her still-strong voice and sassy spirit.

Recommended CDs: Gloria Lynne's first full-length album, *Miss Gloria Lynne* (Evidence 22009), still sounds fresh and lively. Her other Everests have been reissued by Collectables, with two LPs worth of material on a single CD: *Gloria Lynne At Basin Street East/At The Las Vegas Thunderbird* (Collectables

5855), *Try A Little Tenderness/I'm Glad There Is You* (Collectables 5852), *He Needs Me/This Little Boy Of Mine* (Collectables 5856) and *Gloria, Marty & Strings/After Hours* (Collectables 5853). Her Fontana recordings are quite scarce. Gloria Lynne's music from her later comeback years can be heard on the out-of-print *A Time For Love* (Muse 5381), *This One's On Me* (High Note 7015) and 2007's *From My Heart To Yours* (High Note 7162), which finds her sounding ageless.

Christina Machado
b. August 19, 1970, Gainesville, FL

The release of Christina Machado's *Gone With The Wind* CD in 2002 was a very impressive debut for the singer, although an encore is way overdue.

"I was raised in New Orleans since I was two, so I have been blessed to have jazz around me all of my life. When I was 12, my front driveway was my stage. At about 7 o'clock, as it was getting dark and almost time to go in and get ready for supper, it was show time for me. I sang to the cars driving down my street. Chaka Khan's 'Feel For You,' Shannon's 'Let The Music Play' and Elton John's 'I Guess That's Why They Call It The Blues' were on my driveway set list."

At American University, she received a degree for a double major in Film Studies and Theater in 1995 and has since worked in commercials, videos, theater and dance. But her main goal has always been to excel as a singer. During the past decade, Machado has freelanced, working with Loren Pickford and occasionally sharing the stage with Jesse Davis, Jason Marsalis and Mark Whitfield. Her performance at the 2002 IAJE Convention with Billy Childs impressed many as has her recording, *Gone With The Wind*.

"I will always love singing jazz. But I also want to widen my musical scope and include singing from other genres that are compatible with jazz. I enjoy writing contemporary songs and I enjoy singing in other languages, namely Spanish at this time. I come from a Cuban family so I love singing the old beautiful songs."

Recommended CDs: *Gone With The Wind* (Summit 1017) is a strong introduction to Christina Machado. Nicholas Payton produced the CD, contributed the arrangements and plays some trumpet solos; another guest is tenor-saxophonist John Ellis. The singer is particularly winning on "Wave," "I'm Old Fashioned" and "What Are You Doing The Rest Of Your Life."

Kevin Mahogany
b. July 30, 1958, Kansas City, MO

Kevin Mahogany's rise to prominence in the early 1990s led to him being considered the first important new male jazz singer in a decade. A superior scat singer, Mahogany mostly performs conventional versions of standards and blues in a warm voice that is slightly reminiscent of Joe Williams.

As a youth, he played piano, clarinet and baritone sax, making his professional debut on the latter with Eddie Baker's "New Breed Orchestra" when he was 12. He began taking singing seriously during his final year of high school. At Baker University, he performed both as an instrumentalist and as a vocalist, forming his own vocal jazz choir. After graduating, he formed two R&Bish groups, Mahogany and The Apollos, that were popular in Kansas City in the 1980s.

However, Kevin Mahogany worked on his jazz singing during that era, and in the early 1990s, he developed a friendship with arranger Frank Montooth that resulted in him being featured on one of Mantooth's CDs. In 1993 Mahogany's debut recording, *Double Rainbow*, was released and he was proclaimed an up-and-coming jazz vocalist. In the years since, he has recorded 10 more CDs (for Enja, Warner Bros, Telarc and his own Mahogany label), including tributes to Motown and Johnny Hartman, toured mostly as a single, and built up an audience for his swinging music.

Recommended CDs: *Double Rainbow* (Enja 7097) made a strong impact when it was released. Each of Kevin Mahogany's recordings, which include *Songs And Moments* (Enja 8072), *You Got What It Takes* (Enja 9039), *Pussy Cat Dues* (Enja 9316), *Kevin Mahogany* (Warner Bros. 46226), *Another Time, Another Place* (Warner Bros 46699), *My Romance* (Warner Bros. 47025), his Motown tribute *Pride And Joy* (Telarc 83542), *Kevin Mahogany Big Band* (Mahogany Jazz), and *To Johnny Hartman* (Mahogany Jazz), have their moments of strong interest, although the Enjas are most highly recommended.

Jenna Mammina
(Jennafer Mammina)
b. October 24, 1964, Benton Harbor, MI

A subtle pop/jazz vocalist whose uncategorizable singing also encompasses folk music, Jenna Mammina always sings with a smile in her voice.

"My family is very musical, so we were either performing or attending concerts at a young age." She sang in church from the age of five, appeared in school musicals, performed with local bands, learned piano and guitar, and often sang with her family from a young age. She attended Central Michigan University, Michigan State University and Laney College in Oakland, settling in the San Francisco Bay area.

Active as a music educator (two of her programs were called "Scat For Cats" and "So You Want To Be A Rock And Roll Star"), Jenna Mammina has led five CDs, starting with 1999's *Under The Influence*. In addition to sharing the stage with the likes of Bobby McFerrin, Bobby Watson, Nancy King, Andy Narell and Steve Coleman, she has had years where she performs with her band 250 times.

"My main musical goal is to wake up each day to music. My parents always taught me to be true to myself; therefore, I perform from my heart."

Recommended CDs: *Under the Influence* has the singer stretching from Elvis Costello to Abbey Lincoln, from "When I Take My Sugar To Tea" to James Taylor with strong contributions made by guitarist Andre Bush. The same can be said in general terms for her other releases: *Just a Little Bit*, *Meant to Be*, *Art of the Duo* (which co-stars Bush) and *Inner Smile*. All of these CDs were released on Jenna Mammina's label Mamma Grace.

Website: www.jennamammina.com

Janis Mann
b. September 5, 1952, Brooklyn, NY

Janis Mann has a very pleasing voice, a witty personality, and the ability to combine together the joy of Ella Fitzgerald with the chance taking of Sarah Vaughan without sounding too close to either. Her range is quite wide, both in notes and in emotions that she expresses while singing.

"I can't ever remember when I was not singing; it was always my favorite thing to do. As a little girl, it was a thrill when I got to stay up late and watch the classic movie musicals with my Mom and Grandma. I remember swinging—yes, literally—on a swing in our backyard in New York and singing for hours. I feel very blessed to have known from an early age what my true passion is."

Mann studied classical piano, and as a teenager, she took up the guitar to accompany herself. She played and sang in the cafes of Paris and Amsterdam in the 1970s, also performing in Israel. After returning to New York and fronting an R&B group, she moved to the Los Angeles area. "Some of the people I met in Los Angeles, where I lived for seventeen years, gave me the support and encouragement to continue to pursue my dreams, especially Linda Hopkins, Ernie Andrews, Andrea Crouch, and Stevie Wonder." In 1993, Janis Mann and her husband relocated to Seattle for a decade. She became friends with Diane Schuur and utilized such players as saxophonist Don Lanphere, pianists Larry Fuller and Randy Halberstadt, and bassist Doug Miller. Among the CDs that she recorded while in Seattle was *So Many Stars—A Tribute To Sarah Vaughan*.

Since returning to Los Angeles, Janis Mann has appeared regularly in local clubs and at jazz parties, recording *A Perfect Time*, which has some particularly inventive frameworks and arrangements by Tamir Hendelman. "I love to sing. I don't think you should ever become complacent in seeking to expand your abilities. As long as I can communicate my passion for music to an audience through recordings and performance, I will feel I am achieving my goals."

Recommended CDs: *A Little Moonlight* (Pancake 101), *Lost In His Arms* (Pancake 201), *So Many Stars* (Pancake 301) and *Let It Happen* (Pancake 401) are all quite rewarding, but *A Perfect Time* (Pancake 501) is the most essential of Janis Mann's five CDs due to the frameworks and her ability to react creatively to every challenge.

Website: www.janismann.com

Renee Manning
b. Brooklyn, NY

Renee Manning is a bluesy and versatile jazz singer based in New York who is greatly underrecorded, only cutting two albums as a leader for the defunct Ken label.

She attended New York's High School of Music and Art and in the 1970s made guest appearances on albums by David "Fathead" Newman and Nat Adderley. Manning was the regular singer with the Mel Lewis Orchestra during 1983–89. She has also sung with a large ensemble co-led by the late Lester Bowie and her husband bass trombonist Earl McIntyre, Chico O'Farrill's Orchestra, Dizzy Gillespie, the Mingus Big Band and the George Gruntz Concert Jazz Band (touring China in 2001). Her diversity is reflected in the fact that she appeared at a Switzerland festival singing in the premiere of *The Magic Of The Flute* (a jazz opera based on Mozart's Magic Flute), and also at two Century of Change concerts that featured music from 1899 to 1919. She currently works as the vocal and choir instructor at the Brooklyn Conservatory.

Despite all of that, Renee Manning has not recorded as a leader since 1991.

Recommended CDs: *As Is* (Ken 013) has the feel of a goodtime blues set, matching Renee Manning with some of the members of the Mel Lewis Orchestra in 1991. *Uhm...Uhm...Uhmmmm* (Ken 022) has music from four different sessions dating from 1986–91. She excels on double-entendre blues and ballads, with assistance from the Mel Lewis Orchestra, Lester Bowie and an octet arranged by Earl McIntyre. But when will Renee Manning record again?

Nancy Marano
b. Hoboken, NJ

A classy singer who has a particularly good feel for swing standards, Nancy Marano has been an important part of the New York jazz scene for 20 years.

She grew up in a very musical family. "My father, Nick Marano, was a professional pianist who was a natural talent in many styles of music, and my mother was a good singer. My grandmother was a mandolin player in Italy, and my aunt and uncle were talented pianists. In addition, my sister June is an opera coach." Marano played piano from the age of five, learned as many songs as possible as a singer, and often accompanied her father to his gigs. "Sarah Vaughan was my idol. But I really began with 'the teacher'—Ella and the songbooks." She attended the Manhattan School Of Music during 1963–67 as a classical pianist but always knew that she was going to be a singer. During that period, she launched her career by singing in jingles and commercials.

After taking time off to raise a family, by 1989 Marano was ready to gain recognition in the jazz world. She formed a duo with jazz accordion player Eddie Monteiro, a collaboration that lasted until 1995 and resulted in three CDs. She joined the faculty of the Manhattan School Of Music, where she taught jazz voice, and eight years later also became an important educator at William Paterson University. In 1996 she was invited to participate in the recording of the *Benny Carter Songbooks* for Music Masters, and that year she also appeared on Dick Hyman's *Swing Is Here* CD for the Reference label.

One of the high points of Nancy Marano's recording career was recording *If You Could See Us Now* in 1999, a project that teamed her with the Metropole Orchestra, singing arrangements by Manny Albam. "That was probably the biggest recording thrill of my life. The musicianship of the orchestra is of such high quality. Working with and becoming close friends with Manny was a lesson in music, integrity, and how to live a proud life in this business."

As a singer, educator and arranger (most of the charts on her *You're Nearer* CD are her own), Nancy Marano has remained a vital force in jazz. "I have been fortunate to have had so much creative freedom on all my projects. As long as

I can pay my bills, and sing the music I love, it is worth it. I hope the day never comes when it is not, because I love this music—planning it, singing it, accompanying myself on it, and arranging it—with my whole being."

Recommended CDs: *The Real Thing* (Perfect Sound 1025), *A Perfect Match* (Denon 9407) and *Double Standards* (Denon 78901) all feature the duo of Marano and Monteiro, a unique and very satisfying group. *If You Could See Me Now* (Koch 6918) is the very special release that has Nancy Marano joined by the Metropole Orchestra. *Sure Thing* (Blueport 7) has the singer swinging with all-star groups from both the East and West Coasts while *You're Nearer* (Munich 427) has her in prime voice while joined by Dutch musicians who perform her arrangements.

Website: nancymarano.com

Kitty Margolis
b. November 7, 1955, San Mateo, CA

An exciting and lively singer who is never shy to stretch herself, Kitty Margolis extends the bebop tradition to Betty Carter and beyond, all with a smile on her face.

"My parents had a lot of jazz recordings, ranging from McKinney's *Cotton Pickers* (a favorite of my West Virginia father) to Lee Wiley (my mother's favorite singer). I'd say we listened to everything up to the bebop era." From the age of 12, she saw live music frequently, often going to the Fillmore West to see everyone from Miles Davis, John McLaughlin and Charles Lloyd to Janis Joplin, Muddy Waters and Frank Zappa. "What those bands all had in common was that they all improvised. That became an important musical value to me from a very young age."

Self-taught on the guitar from age 12, two years later she played guitar and sang harmonies in a group with her friends, emulating such early musical heroes as Joni Mitchell and Bonnie Raitt. At 17, she started to explore the music of such jazz singers as Flora Purim, Eddie Jefferson, King Pleasure and Betty Carter while keeping her mind and music open to world music and pop.

After attending Harvard for two years in the mid-1970s, majoring in visual and environmental studies while singing and playing guitar in a few Western Swing groups, Margolis transferred to San Francisco State to study music and communications. At 21, she stopped playing guitar to concentrate on singing. She sat in with Joe Louis Walker's blues band and at jam sessions hosted by Bobby McFerrin and Pony Poindexter.

Kitty Margolis put together a group that included singer-guitarist Joyce Cooling, trumpeter Eddie Henderson and saxophonist Pee Wee Ellis. A few years later, in 1988, she formed Mad-Kat Records with fellow singer Madeline Eastman and the following year released her first album. She has been a major force on the San Francisco jazz scene ever since, traveling the world, releasing consistently rewarding CDs and teaching at the Jazz School in Berkeley.

"I think that a big part of who I am musically is a direct result of being a kid from San Francisco during a really magical time in history. It left me with the belief that there are no boundaries in music except for the one that people create for themselves and that the industry tries to impose."

Recommended CDs: All of Kitty Margolis' recordings have their memorable moments: *Live At The Jazz Workshop* (Mad-Kat 1001), *Evolution* (Mad-Kat 1004), *Straight Up With A Twist* (Mad-Kat 1006), *Left Coast Life* (Mad-Kat 1008) and *Heart & Soul: Live In San Francisco* (Mad-Kat 53). If only one could be chosen, *Straight Up With A Twist* has some of the more unusual surprises plus guest spots by trumpeter Roy Hargrove and Charles Brown.

Website: www.kittymargolis.com

Tania Maria
(Tania Maria Reis Leite)
b. May 9, 1948, São Luis, Maranhão, Brazil

An exuberant and powerful Brazilian singer-pianist whose performances are full of heat and passion, Tania Maria has been famous in the jazz world ever since she first started recording for Concord.

She was born in the Northern part of Brazil to a family full of amateur musicians.

Tania Maria started studying piano when she was seven and six years later won an important local contest as the leader of a band that her father (who played guitar) had put together for her. She would always be a leader from then on.

Although she studied for a law degree for two years, got married and started a family, she soon decided to switch back to music, making her recording debut when she was 20. She moved to São Paulo, where she sang and played piano in bars and nightclubs. From the start, Tania Maria combined samba and chorinho rhythms with jazz, forging her own style and taking rapid vocals, often scatting in unison with her piano; that became her trademark. She spent time living and performing in Paris, where she recorded several albums. At a concert in Australia, she greatly impressed guitarist Charlie Byrd, who recommended her to Carl Jefferson, the head of the Concord label. After the release of her first Concord album, *Piquant*, Tania Maria became quite famous and, ever since, she has consistently performed at major festivals around the world.

Tania Maria's music, although always including elements from Brazilian music and jazz, has also stretched at times to include pop, fusion and African music, resulting in a largely unclassifiable hybrid that sometimes finds her going over the top with enthusiasm. "I am first a pianist. I also sing, of course, but usually my voice follows the piano. I hope to play music until I die. Music, for me, is the best way to feel alive."

Recommended CDs: *Via Brasil* (Sunnyside 283036) features Tania Maria near the beginning, in 1974–75, playing and singing with a trio in Brazil. Her Concord recordings of 1980–84, *Piquant* (Concord Jazz 4151), *Taurus* (Concord Jazz 4175), *Come With Me* (Concord Jazz 4200), *Love Explosion*

(Concord Jazz 4230) and *Wild* (Concord Jazz 4264), made her reputation and still include some of her finest work. Tania Maria has since returned to Concord for occasional sessions, including the dance-oriented *Outrageous* (Concord Picante 4563), the eclectic *Viva Brazil* (Concord Jazz 4873) and the excellent all-round showcase from 2002, *Live At The Blue Note* (Concord Jazz 2114). Also worth acquiring from other labels are *Bela Vista* (World Pacific 93871), *Europe* (New Note 1003) and *Intimidade* (Blue Note 51935).

Website: www.taniamaria.net

René Marie
b. November 7, 1955, Warrenton, VA

A chance-taking singer who believes in moving audiences through the words she sings, René Marie got a late start in jazz but has been quickly making up for lost time. "As a child, I always felt like I was the person the song was about. It was natural and intuitive for me to insert myself into the song. I was nine the year my mom and dad divorced. I moved with Mom to a city where I didn't know anyone. A neighbor was holding a talent show on his backyard deck for the children. I sang 'A House Is Not A Home,' hoping my Dad would somehow hear it. It was the first time I'd ever sung in front of complete strangers. It was at that moment that I decided that I wanted to move myself and others with music."

A few years later, she led her own R&B band. Self-taught except for two years of piano lessons, she seemed to be on her way to an important career when she married a young pianist. They joined a very strict religious group, and they stopped performing in public. Marie spent the next two decades raising her family, although she continued playing piano, composing and singing at home. Finally, at the age of 41, she was convinced by her oldest son to start singing again. After a family discussion, she began singing one night a week at a local hotel.

Gradually, over a three-and-a-half-year period, René Marie became a full-time singer, was divorced, quit her day job at a bank, and was signed to the MaxJazz label. She has since recorded four albums for MaxJazz and two CDs independently, gaining a strong reputation as a singer who refuses to compromise and only sings music that she believes in.

"I don't think of what I do as a career. Since I've been singing, the high points and turning points were manifest when I stopped doing, saying and singing what was expected of me. I surprised even myself at that boldness. When I said 'No' to predictability, to tradition, to imposed expectation, cleaving to my musical truth like that propelled me forward with much velocity."

Recommended CDs: René Marie first recorded an independent CD, *Renaissance*, as her debut in 1997 under the name of René Croan. Two years later, she cut her initial MaxJazz set. *How Can I Keep From Singing* (MaxJazz 109) is a very impressive program full of surprises such as her scatting on "God Bless The Child," reinvented versions of "Tennessee Waltz" and "Motherless Child," and a passionate "Afro-Blue" plus two of the singer's originals. *Vertigo* (MaxJazz 114) continues in the same vein with a medley of "Dixie" and "Strange Fruit" getting the most notoriety. *Live At Jazz Standard* (MaxJazz 116) has plenty of dramatic moments (including an a cappella version of "How Can I Keep From Singing" and a heartfelt "I Loves You, Porgy"), while *Serene Renagade* (MaxJazz 120) includes nine of her diverse originals. Most recently René Marie recorded *Experiment In Truth* for her own label, mixing together standards that mean a lot to her with topical originals.

Website: www.renemarie.com

Tina Marsh
(Kristin Conway Marsh)
b. January 18, 1954, Annapolis, MD

The vocalist and artistic director of the Creative Opportunity Orchestra, Tina Marsh is an adventurous and versatile singer who is a relatively unheralded force in avant-garde jazz.

She started on piano at age nine, added the flute two years later and first sang in school in the eighth grade. "When I was 19, I left college in Philadelphia to go to New Jersey for a new 'Broadway-bound' musical. It folded and I moved to New York. I always knew that I wanted to reach people through singing. I used to go to hear Joe Beck and David Sanborn play at Mikell's and began to have the music in my imagination. Then, when I moved to Austin in 1977, I dated a percussionist who introduced me to the music of Anthony Braxton, Sam Rivers, Ornette Coleman, late Coltrane, the Art Ensemble of Chicago, Flora Purim, Tomasz Stanko, and others. That was a time of total inspiration. There was a small group of us: saxophone/flute, bass, drums, percussion and me singing. We played constantly, experimented and had a wonderful bohemian existence."

Tina Marsh attended the Creative Music Studio in the summer of 1979, meeting Fred Hess, Roscoe Mitchell, George Lewis and other avant-garde greats. "At the point when the Creative Opportunity Orchestra was started in 1980, or actually just prior to that, I knew that my colleagues and players and other composers would constitute my university." Since that time, she has been busy with the Creative Opportunity Orchestra (CO2), performing with its core group of musicians (which now numbers over 200) plus such guests as Kenny Wheeler, Carla Bley, Steve Swallow, Billy Hart and Roscoe Mitchell. CO2 can be thought of as Austin's equivalent to Chicago's AACM, finding new places and uses for avant-garde jazz although it does differ. Its outreach programs throughout Texas are significant, including Tina Marsh being the artist-in-education for 10 years at South Austin's Becker Elementary School.

Due to her important work, Tina Marsh was inducted into the Texas Music Hall of Fame in 2001. For her own personal future, she simply states, "I want to sing and perform in projects which are truthful and powerful."

Recommended CDs: *The Heaven Line* (CreOp Muse 002) and *Worldwide* (CreOp Muse 005) feature Tina Marsh with 12–13 piece groups. *Out Of Time* (CreOp Muse 007) puts the focus on the singer on standards and originals in

a quartet with pianist Bob Rodriguez, bassist Ken Filiano and drummer Ron Glick. *New Texas Swing* (CreOp Muse 010), which has a quartet that includes saxophonist Alex Coke, is particularly intriguing due partly to a colorful repertoire from such Texas-born performers as Ornette Coleman, Leadbelly, David "Fathead" Newman, Charlie Haden, Coke and Marsh.

Claire Martin
b. September 6, 1967, Wimbledon, London

Arguably the top British jazz singer to emerge during the 1990s (along with Tina May), Claire Martin brings a fresh approach to interpreting vintage standards while including recent pop tunes, done her own way, in her repertoire. "I don't always sing the standards from the Great American Songbook. To enjoy my musical tastes, you must have an understanding and love for contemporary pop music."

She grew up in a house where music was constantly heard. Two of the early turning points that she frequently cites are hearing Ella Fitzgerald's Songbook albums, which inspired her to study singing in London and New York, and seeing Betty Carter at Ronnie Scott's club in 1986, which convinced her to become a jazz singer. "I knew I was a singer when I got my first professional job at age 18 and suddenly realized that I was making my living from singing. Up until then I didn't really have any idea it would happen. I've been very lucky, as I have only had to have one job outside of music." She spent two years singing regularly on the QE2 cruises, gaining valuable experience and building up her repertoire.

Signed to Linn Records in 1991, her debut recording *The Waiting Game* made her famous across England. Soon she was opening for Tony Bennett at the Glasgow International Jazz Festival. The momentum has not slowed down since. By the mid-1990s, she was a regular at the British Jazz Awards, winning the Rising Star in 1994 and the Best Vocalist awards on a regular basis starting in 1995. She has since toured Europe, Australia and the Far East (hers was the first jazz group to perform in Vietnam) and she appeared in New York and Washington, DC. Martin works occasionally with the 92-piece Halle Orchestra in Manchester and is a jazz broadcaster for the BBC on the weekly magazine show *Jazz Line Up*.

Of her cool-toned and open-minded approach to singing jazz, Claire Martin modestly says, "Basically I just make it up as I go along and to me that is very thrilling."

Recommended CDs: Of Claire Martin's 11 CDs for Linn—*The Waiting Game* (Linn 18), *Devil May Care* (Linn 21), *Old Boyfriends* (Linn 28), *Offbeat: Live At Ronnie Scott's Club* (Linn 46), *Make This City Ours* (Linn 66), the pop-oriented *Take My Heart* (Linn 93), *Perfect Alibi* (Linn 122), *Too Darn Hot* (Linn 198), *Secret Love* (Linn 246), *When Lights Are Low* (Linn 260) and *He Never Mentioned Love* (Linn 295)—the ones I would recommend exploring first are *The Waiting Game*, *Offbeat: Live At Ronnie Scott's* and *When Lights Are Low*.

Website: www.clairemartinjazz.com

Sara Martin
(Sarah Dunn)
b. June 18, 1884, Louisville, KY; d. May 25, 1955, Louisville, KY

One of the oldest of the classic blues singers who recorded in the 1920s (being born two years before Ma Rainey), Sara Martin was most comfortable singing popular songs of the era. She started out singing in a church choir and as a teenager was performing in theaters at the turn of the century. She was married for the first time at the age of 16, but became a widow the following year. During a period of time working outside of music in 1908, she married William Martin, keeping his last name. After he passed away in 1916, she returned to music. Already a widow twice, Martin would be married three additional times, with those three marriages all ending in divorce.

Sara Martin worked in Chicago during 1916–22 and, at the urging of Mamie Smith, moved to New York in 1922. Soon she was introduced to pianist Clarence Williams who began recording her. Martin's first record, "Sugar Blues," was a hit. Her deep voice recorded well and she improved as a recording artist throughout the 1920s, although she made most of her records during 1922–25. In 1923 alone, she appeared on 20 record sessions in addition to touring with W.C. Handy's orchestra. Among her best recordings from 1923–25 are "I Got What It Takes," "Nobody In Town Can Bake A Sweet Jelly Roll Like Mine," "New Orleans Hop Scop Blues" and "I'm Gonna Hoodoo You." Vol. 4 in her Document series has many of her most rewarding performances including "Yes Sir, That's My Baby," "That Dance Called Messin' Around," "What's The Matter Now," "How Could I Be Blue," "Cushion Foot Stomp," and three particularly powerful blues during her final session.

Despite her versatility, Sara Martin's recording career came to an end in 1928. She continued performing for a time and appeared in two obscure films: 1927's *Hello Bill* (featuring Bill "Bojangles" Robinson) and *Dark-Town Scandals Revue* (1930). But after temporarily losing her voice in the early 1930s before a stage appearance, she became very religious. From that point on, Sara Martin only worked as a gospel singer. Returning to her hometown of Louisville, she owned and operated a nursing home and worked for her church during her final 20 years.

Recommended CDs: *Vol. 1* (Document 5395), *Vol. 2* (Document 5396), *Vol. 3* (Document 5397) and *Vol. 4* (Document 5398) have all of Sara Martin's recordings as a leader.

Sue Maskaleris
b. December 23, 1957, Montclair, NJ

An excellent pianist and a multi-instrumentalist who is an equally talented vocalist, Sue Maskaleris has thus far only made one CD as a leader, but she is widely respected.

"My father Stephen was a big band bassist (Tommy Tucker, Fran Warren) before becoming a lawyer. He took our family often to hear Duke and Count's bands. Seeing him playing with a Dixieland combo at my grammar school was the 'aha' moment that made me pursue this dream." Maskaleris began piano lessons that year, studying classical music until she was 16 and discovered Chick Corea's "Light As A Feather." She also studied violin from the age of eight, learned to scat with both her violin and piano, plays Brazilian-style guitar, studied harp at the Manhattan School of Music, and took up the five-string bass after winning it as first prize in the Billboard Song

Contest in 1998 in the world music category for her song "No, But I Wish…"

While in high school, Sue Maskaleris directed the girls' vocal group, arranging and writing for them as well as accompanying on piano and guitar. She formed a jazz group with guitarist Ken Sebesky, studying arranging with his father Don Sebesky. "I knew I was going to be a professional singer the minute I sat down at my first piano gig at the bar of East Winds restaurant on Route 22, New Jersey, at age 17, and realized it would double my earning potential." She majored in composition at the Manhattan School of Music. After graduation, she began working regularly on the New York scene, in addition to playing on cruise ships.

Since then, Sue Maskaleris has accompanied Annie Ross, Abbey Lincoln, Cybill Shepherd and Adela Dalto in addition to working with Ralph Lalama, Loren Schoenberg, Jed Levy, Jamie Baum, Romero Lubambo, Michel Urbaniak, Roberta Piket and others. Her composition "Scat" won second place in the 1998 Thelonious Monk Composition Competition, and her compositions have been performed by Danilo Perez, Bob Dorough, Judy Niemack and Roger Kellaway, among others.

The singer-pianist-arranger-composer-producer has thus far just led the lone CD *Unbreakable Heart*. "I would love to perform my own music in concert and at festivals with my groups, where I also perform on my other instruments. I love writing and arranging for jazz choral groups as well as for various instrumentations, and would love to have the opportunity to have these works performed."

Recommended CDs: *Unbreakable Heart* (Orchard 801267) has a dozen of Sue Maskaleris' songs and features her holding her own with a group of all-stars on music that is often Brazilian-oriented.

Website: www.suemask.com

Laurel Massé
b. December 29, 1951, Holland, MI

An original member of the Manhattan Transfer, Laurel Massé suffered from an accident that drastically changed her career, but she has persevered.

The daughter of an opera singer and granddaughter of Leonard Karenendonk, who sang lead baritone with Fred Waring's Pennsylvanians for over 40 years, she had piano lessons in elementary school, played cello as a teenager in Paris, and was self-taught on guitar in the 1960s. She sang in school choruses, church choirs and in high school rock and roll bands.

"I have always sung, and in 1972, people started paying me, so I guess that is when I became a professional." When she was a waitress in Manhattan, she met a cabdriver named Tim Hauser and, together with Hauser, Janis Siegel and Alan Paul, formed Manhattan Transfer in 1972. Performing everything from swing to rock, ballads to pop and bebop, the Manhattan Transfer kept Laurel Massé very busy for the next seven years. The group gradually made it big, constantly touring and recording several impressive albums.

That all came to a halt for Massé in 1979, due to a near-fatal car accident. She was forced to drop out of the group while she spent two years recuperating. She eventually made a full recovery, moved to New York and then Chicago, recorded three excellent albums for the Pausa label starting with 1983's *Alone Together*. In the late 1980s she moved to the Adirondack Mountains in upstate New York, maintaining a low profile.

When she began to re-emerge in the mid-1990s, Laurel Massé often performed a cappella and her repertoire included Celtic songs, classical music and even a Quaker theme, all of it quite spiritual. After recording *Feather And Bone* in 2000, which reflected this "new" music, she returned to jazz. Since then she has hosted a monthly jazz radio show on WAMC, been busy as an educator and still performs occasionally.

"Jazz is a point of view, a joyous exploration of freedom within constraints. I believe that we bring every moment of our lives with us onto the stage. Therefore, it is wise to think, read, observe—really live! I also believe that competition is an artificial construct that can be patted on the head and then ignored, and that all artists have some quality that makes them unique and needed. It is our job, as artists, to continue to explore, expand, and refine forever. Every recording is the best one we could do that day. And then we wake to the next day, able to do more, and better. There is no 'Here I am, I go no farther, I know it all' in music."

Recommended CDs: Laurel Massé's period with the Manhattan Transfer is represented on *Manhattan Transfer* (Atlantic 18133), *Coming Out* (Atlantic 18183), *Pastiche* (Atlantic 19163) and *The Manhattan Transfer Live* (Wounded Bird 540). Of her solo albums, *Again* (Disques Beaupre 820), the spiritual *Feather And Bone* (Premonition 90751) and the privately released *Ballads (Voice Of The Swan)* are available from her website.

LPs to Search For: Laurel Massé's two most bop-oriented releases, *Alone Together* (Pausa 7165) and *Easy Living* (Pausa 7206), unfortunately have not been released on CD yet.

Website: www.laurelmasse.com

Greta Matassa
(Greta Goehle)
b. September 5, 1962, Lockport, NY

One of the best jazz singers located in the Pacific Northwest, Greta Matassa mainly has a local reputation, but deserves to be better known.

"I grew up in a family that loved jazz music and I heard it around the house all the time. I remember listening to Ella, Sarah, Count, Frank, Anita O'Day (who is a huge influence) and Billie. I started singing with them and consider them my teachers and friends. I developed a photographic memory for lyrics and melodies. I formed a jazz group in high school and started playing gigs around the Seattle area when I was 16."

Dropping out of high school as a junior, Matassa worked in Salem, Oregon with pianist-singer Tim Clark, was with heavy metal bands in Seattle, played casuals, worked with guitarist Michael Powers, sang with Jim Rasmussen's Jazz Police (a big band) and became involved in studio work. "I ventured into pop, rock and funk bands, mostly to earn a living. Jazz was always my first love, but I learned a lot about stamina and control from my years in pop bands." She also worked for a decade with the Pacific Northwest Ballet at the Seattle Opera House in a program based on the music of Kurt Weill. A short-lived marriage that resulted in two daughters occupied her part of the 1990s, but she kept on singing. Among her other important musical associations have been those with guitarist Mimi Fox, bassist Barney McClure, pianists Randy Halberstadt and Marc Seales, saxophonist Don Lanphere and drummer Gary Hobbs.

"In the early '90s I began leading my own groups with much success. I found a greater rapport with my audiences because I was seasoned enough to be myself on stage. I never tire of approaching material from the Great American Songbook, old and new, and seeing what might come out this time. I want to do many more recordings and hope to work with some more of the great rhythm sections. And once before I die, I must work with the Basie Band."

Recommended CDs: Although she appeared on small label dates by the Jazz Police, Phil Sheeran and Bert Wilson during 1989–93, Greta Matassa's most significant recordings are more recent: *Two For The Road* (Origin 82411), which she shares with guitarist Mimi Fox, and *All This And Heaven Too* (Origin 82393).

Website: www.gretamatassa.com

Sue Matthews
b. May 17, 1953, Amsterdam, NY

A very good jazz singer whose range spans from swing to performing with symphony orchestras, Sue Matthews is a top-notch improviser with a warm voice.

"I started out listening to Sophie Tucker, which led me to Ms. Holiday, which led me to Fitzgerald, Sinatra, Vaughan and all the rest. I also loved listening to the big bands, especially Duke Ellington." She sang with her church choir at age six and as a teenager sang with folk groups, rock bands, her high school stage band and performed in school musicals. "I recorded my first album with the stage band from my high school on my 16th birthday. It was a great experience." She also studied piano for several years and played the clarinet for a decade.

After graduating from Washington College in 1975 with a degree in Theater Arts, Sue Matthews started working regularly as a jazz singer, often with bassist Keter Betts and pianist Stef Scaggiari, and she sang with the eclectic fusion group Wooden Hands for several years in the 1970s. "I performed at the King of France Tavern of Annapolis' Maryland Inn throughout the 1980s and early '90s, under the watchful eye of owner Paul Pearson. While there I came to know such legends as Charlie Byrd, Ethel Ennis and Monty Alexander."

Sue Matthews, who has thus far recorded three CDs as a leader, has performed at many festivals including regularly at one in County Galway, Ireland, concert halls (she has been the featured artist with the Calgary Philharmonic), clubs and in a show held in Saluzzo, Italy, called *Mozart To Motown*. She has also toured Europe with her group, Guys & Doll, and appears regularly in the Maryland/Washington, DC, area.

"I have been extremely fortunate to spend my life working within a career which I absolutely love."

Recommended CDs: *Love Dances* (Positive 78001) and *When You're Around* (Positive 78011) are from the 1991–93 period while *One At A Time* (Renata 70014) was released in 2002.

Each features Sue Matthews on swing standards, heartfelt ballads and bluesy material.

Website: www.suematthewsmusic.com

Tina May
(Daphne Christina May)
b. Gloucester, England

When it comes to picking the premier female jazz singer from England, some will opt for Cleo Laine while others may go for Claire Martin. I vote for Tina May, a vocalist with a very warm and accurate tone, a strong improvising style, versatility, and a joy in her voice that is a little reminiscent of Ella Fitzgerald.

Both of her parents played piano, and her father was a stride pianist. "We all sang around the piano and harmonized. I played clarinet and my sister played fiddle. We must have been noisy neighbors. I always remember that singing was fun." May played clarinet until she was 17, was self-taught on guitar, and at 16 began studying classical singing, performing in school choirs. While attending University College in Cardiff, she began singing jazz, joining the Welsh Jazz Society. Because she was studying French, she had the opportunity to live in France for a year in 1983, where she met up with the top local jazz musicians, performing at Le Slow Club with the Roger Guerin Big Band and drummer Kenny Clarke. She also worked in theater and comedy revues. "While a student in Paris, I discovered the French vocal group Les Double Six. I felt we were kindred spirits. I had always tried to be an instrument with my voice."

Tina May worked regularly with guitarist Dylan Fowler during the early part of her career and led a nonet called Frevo, which frequently played her originals. Back in England, she acted for a time in a French-speaking theater company called *Bac To Bac*, but late night jam sessions with musical friends convinced her to become a full-time jazz singer. Starting in 1991, she began recording for 33 Records, an association that continues to this day. May performed Duke Ellington's sacred music in concerts with the Stan Tracey Big Band, appeared regularly at festivals, broadcast with the BBC Big Band, first appeared at Ronnie Scott's club in 1993, toured Australia and the Far East, and has rarely slowed down since. Nikki Iles became her regular pianist in 1998.

In addition to her singing, Tina May is a talented composer and lyricist, writing words to bop tunes including a set of Ray Bryant tunes, which she recorded with the pianist as *The Ray Bryant Songbook* in 2002.

"I have always wanted to make good music with good musicians. I am holding on to that goal—as it seems to be working. I always thought that singing is the most wonderful way of speaking."

Recommended CDs: Every Tina May recording is a joy to hear. The ones listed with an asterisk are the ones she thinks are the most representative: *Never Let Me Go* (33 Jazz 005) *Fun* (33 Jazz 013), *It Ain't Necessarily So* (33 Jazz 017), **Time Will Tell* (33 Jazz 029), the set of duets with Nikki Iles called **Change Of Sky* (33 Jazz 039), **Jazz Piquant* (33 Jazz 042), which

features clarinetist-saxophonist Tony Coe, **One Fine Day* (33 Jazz 050), **Live In Paris* (33 Jazz 055), **More Than You Know* (33 Jazz 100) with Tony Coe and Nikki Iles in a trio, *A Wing And A Prayer* (33 Jazz 134), **Sings The Ray Bryant Songbook* (33 Jazz 150) and **I'll Take Romance* (Linn 150), which co-stars tenor-saxophonist Scott Hamilton.

Website: www.tinamay.com

Mary Ann McCall
b. May 4, 1919, Philadelphia, PA;
d. December 14, 1994, Los Angeles, CA

An excellent singer whose music ranged from middle-of-the-road pop to swinging jazz, Mary Ann McCall was most famous for her associations with Charlie Barnet and Woody Herman.

McCall started her career as a singer and dancer with Buddy Morrow's orchestra. After a brief period with Tommy Dorsey in 1938, she joined Woody Herman's band in the spring of 1939. Only four recordings resulted during the stint, including "Big Wig In The Wigwam," which was on the flip side of the original version of "At The Woodchopper's Ball." Later in the year, McCall left Herman to join the Charlie Barnet big band just as Barnet was beginning to make it big. During her seven months with Barnet, she recorded 27 numbers including "Between 18th and 19th On Chestnut Street," "It's A Wonderful World," "Busy As A Bee (I'm Buzz, Buzz, Buzzin')" and "'Deed I Do." None were hits ("Chestnut Street" came the closest) but McCall built up a strong reputation as a pleasing and cheerful singer.

Despite her growing recognition, McCall dropped out of music after leaving Barnet. She resurfaced in December 1947 when she joined Woody Herman's Second Herd, staying until its breakup in late 1949. She added a bit of class to the organization and showed that she had grown as a singer in the interim as can be heard on "P.S. I Love You," "I Got It Bad," "Detour Ahead" and "More Than You Know."

After leaving Herman, Mary Ann McCall had a solo career in the 1950s, impressing musicians but not becoming a major name. McCall cut four obscure titles as a leader for Columbia (1947), six for Discovery (1948) and four for Roost (1950), all of which are long overdue to be coherently reissued. She was married for a time to tenor-saxophonist Al Cohn and worked with Charlie Ventura's band during 1954–55. In addition to recording a few titles with Ventura, McCall led three albums of her own, with one apiece for Regent (reissued on CD by Savoy) in 1956, Jubilee (1958) and Coral (1959), each of which is excellent.

Once again, Mary Ann McCall faded from the scene, singing occasionally in Detroit during 1958–60 before relocating to Los Angeles, where she only performed on a part-time basis. In the 1970s, she returned to records by singing four songs on drummer Jake Hanna's *Kansas City Express* in 1976 and several on Nat Pierce's *5400 North* in 1978, showing that she had not lost her abilities. She also guested at Woody Herman's 40th anniversary Carnegie Hall concert in 1976, singing "Wrap Your Troubles In Dreams." However, that was the final musical act of a strangely truncated career, one that should have gone much further.

Recommended CDs: *Easy Living* (Savoy 93016) features Mary Ann McCall in the 1950s, while Nat Pierce's *5400 North* (Hep 2004) shows that she was still a fine singer later in her life. Otherwise, she can be heard on collections by Woody Herman's Second Herd and Charlie Barnet.

Les McCann
b. September 23, 1935, Lexington, KY

Les McCann gained his original reputation as one of the top funky soul jazz pianists of the early 1960s, leading an instrumental trio in Los Angeles. But once he started singing, it increased his commercial appeal and fame.

Other than four piano lessons from a neighbor, he was self taught. McCann grew up in Kentucky, joined the Navy, and after his discharge in 1956, won a singing contest that resulted in his appearance on the *Ed Sullivan Show*. Despite that, he did not become a singing pianist for several more years. He attended music school, settled in Los Angeles, and formed his trio, Les McCann Ltd., which also included bassist Leroy Vinnegar (succeeded by Herbie Lewis) and drummer Ron Jefferson.

McCann was signed to the Pacific Jazz label in 1960 and was so popular that he led eight albums during 1960–61. Only the fifth record, *Les McCann Sings*, featured his singing. Although he teamed up on records with organist Richard "Groove" Holmes, the Jazz Crusaders, the Gerald Wilson Orchestra, Stanley Turrentine, Ben Webster and Lou Rawls (playing piano on Rawls' classic *Stormy Monday* album), it was not until he signed with Limelight in late 1964 that he was heard again as a singer. From that point on, McCann's vocalizing tended to take precedence over his piano playing.

An expressive singer whose vocals are soulful and as close to R&B and soul as to jazz, McCann had a major hit with "Compared To What," recorded during a legendary and very spontaneous set at the 1969 Montreux Jazz Festival with Eddie Harris. Although he never quite duplicated that success, he came close with his recording of "With These Hands." As a headliner, McCann worked steadily in the 1970s and '80s, often playing electric keyboards with his "Magic Band." In 1994, he had a reunion tour with Eddie Harris. A serious stroke in the mid-1990s knocked him out of action for a time and weakened his keyboard playing for a few years, but his singing was unimpaired and he has remained active up to the present time, never being let offstage until he sings "Compared To What."

Recommended CDs: *Swiss Movement* (Rhino 122 737 572) is a classic even if "Compared To What" was Les McCann's only vocal during the fabled Montreux performance. *Talk To The People* (Atlantic 6028), *Live At Montreux* (Wounded Bird 312), *Listen Up* (Music Masters 65139) and *Pacifique* (Music Masters 65174) all have a generous supply of McCann's gravelly vocals.

LPs to Search For: *Les McCann Sings* (Pacific Jazz 31) and *Live*

At Shelly Manne's Hole (Limelight 82036), which include early McCann vocals, have yet to be reissued.

Susannah McCorkle
b. January 1, 1949, Berkeley, CA; d. May 19, 2001, New York, NY

A decade before the retro-swing movement and years before Linda Ronstadt discovered the Great American Songbook, Susannah McCorkle was one of the first of the singers in the 1970s to begin exploring standards of decades earlier. The fact that she was a world-class singer, very intelligent in her presentations, and had a beautiful voice influenced others to forego R&B, pop and fusion in favor of singing vintage material. She occupies a place similar to tenor-saxophonist Scott Hamilton and cornetist Warren Vache, bringing back superior swing tunes that had been neglected by her generation. She consistently brought out the hidden meanings found in even the most familiar lyrics, even drastically slowing down "There's No Business Like Show Business" to make it into a particularly touching rendition.

Originally, McCorkle planned to become a translator, possibly for the Common Market in Brussels, since she was expert in several languages. While in Italy in the late 1960s, she fell in love with Billie Holiday's music and discovered early jazz, including such singers as Bessie Smith and Ethel Waters. After moving to England in 1971, McCorkle worked with pianist Keith Ingham and had opportunities to perform with trumpeter Dick Sudhalter and cornetist Bobby Hackett. She began to record in 1976, starting with tribute albums of the music of Harry Warren and Johnny Mercer.

McCorkle moved back to the United States in 1980 and was a popular attraction for years, recording regularly for Concord by 1988 and building her repertoire up to 3,000 songs. Over time she gradually modernized her approach from swing to West Coast–style cool jazz of the 1950s, with Allen Farnham being her accompanist and arranger on many projects in later years. She was also an author of both fiction and nonfiction (being particularly proud of her articles on Ethel Waters, Bessie Smith, Irving Berlin and Mae West), a lyricist (writing English versions of songs that were originally in French, Brazilian and Italian) and a teacher/lecturer. In addition to touring with a regular trio, she occasionally performed concerts with orchestras.

Tragically, Susannah McCorkle suffered from severe depression and, as the pressure and disappointments built up in 2001 (being dropped by Concord, not being booked for her yearly engagement at the Algonquin Hotel, growing older, and feeling that life was becoming useless), she chose to commit suicide. She never seemed to realize how much she was loved and admired, and how important she really was.

Recommended CDs: *The Beginning 1975* (Challenge 73233) is an intriguing set of demos, recorded before Susannah McCorkle had made her first record. Her work since that time fulfilled her tremendous potential and she lived up to her billing as a lyricist's dream. All but one of her recordings are available on CD: *The Songs Of Johnny Mercer* (Jazz Alliance 10031),

Over The Rainbow: The Songs Of E.Y. "Yip" Harburg (Jazz Alliance 10033), *The People That You Never Get To Love* (Jazz Alliance 10034), *Thanks For The Memory: The Songs Of Leo Robin* (Jazz Alliance 10035), *How Do You Keep The Music Playing* (Jazz Alliance 10036), *Dreams* (Jazz Alliance 10037), *No More Blues* (Concord Jazz 4370), *Sabia* (Concord Jazz 4418), *I'll Take Romance* (Concord Jazz 4491), *From Bessie To Brazil* (Concord Jazz 4547), *From Broadway To Bebop* (Concord Jazz 4615), *Easy To Love: The Songs Of Cole Porter* (Concord Jazz 4696), *Let's Face The Music: The Songs Of Irving Berlin* (Concord Jazz 4759), *Someone To Watch Over Me: The Songs Of George Gershwin* (Concord Jazz 4798), *From Broken Hearts To Blue Skies* (Concord 4857), and *Hearts And Minds* (Concord 4897).

LPs to Search For: Susannah McCorkle's very first official album, *The Music Of Harry Warren* (Inner City 1141), is the only one that has not yet been reissued on CD.

Bobby McFerrin
b. March 11, 1950, Madeley, United Kingdom

A potentially incredible vocalist, Bobby McFerrin is capable of singing anything. Heard at his best when he is singing a cappella, McFerrin can give the impression of keeping three different voices going at once including falsetto and a deep bass line. By making a sound when he inhales air, McFerrin can put on a display of nonstop creativity. And yet, his career has not been all that it could have been.

Born in England but raised in New York, Bobby McFerrin is the son of the operatic baritone Robert McFerrin. It took McFerrin some time to get his career fully underway, though he picked up important experience performing with a variety of groups, including dance troupes. He became a solo singer in 1977, sang with Astral Projection while living in New Orleans and appeared at the 1980 Playboy Jazz Festival. In 1981, he signed with Elektra and made his recording debut, soon becoming a sensation in the jazz world.

By 1984, Bobby McFerrin was frequently performing concerts that were truly solo, armed with nothing but a microphone and his own creative ideas. He displayed his wit, brilliance and versatility before audiences without any need for other instruments. His recording *The Voice* shows just what he could do. He continued in this fashion for a few years, sometimes teaming up with all-stars. In 1988 he had an unexpected hit with "Don't Worry, Be Happy" (winning a Grammy for the year's best song), which utilized his overdubbed voices in simplistic but catchy fashion.

But then Bobby McFerrin adopted a much lower profile, perhaps a little embarrassed by the hit. Although he formed a 10-piece a cappella group, Voicestra, he drifted toward classical music, becoming a classical conductor, which seemed like a complete waste of his singing talents and of the potential that he had as a temporary "pop star." Although he has done fine work since, including occasionally teaming up with Chick Corea, he has never regained the momentum that he had in the 1980s. While one appreciates his work in music education, conducting classical orchestras (in 1994 he was appointed the creative chair of the Saint Paul Chamber Orchestra) and his appearances on soundtracks, Bobby McFerrin never became the pacesetter among jazz singers that he seemed destined for when he was a bright new star in the 1980s.

Recommended CDs: *Bobby McFerrin* (Elektra 60023) has its great moments (including an unaccompanied version of Bud Powell's "Hallucinations"), but *The Voice* (Elektra 60366) is the classic. Just check out his musical depiction of a washing machine on "Big Top." *Spontaneous Inventions* (Blue Note 46298) is almost as worthy as *The Voice*. *Simple Pleasures* (Capitol 48059), which includes "Don't Worry, Be Happy," is mostly great fun. *Play* (Blue Note 95477) with Chick Corea alternates between having miraculous moments and pure silliness. The more recent recordings, *Medicine Music* (Blue Note 92048), *Bang! Zoom* (Blue Note 31677), *Circlesongs* (Sony 62734) with Voicestra, and *Beyond Words* (Blue Note 34201), all lack the special brilliance that made Bobby McFerrin's 1980s work so special and are a bit disappointing.

Website: www.bobbymcferrin.com

Kate McGarry
(Katherine Genevieve McGarry)
b. January 17, 1963, Pittsfield, MA

A singer whose innocent voice contrasts with her sophisticated music, and one who often falls between creative jazz and folk music, Kate McGarry has long been distinctive and intriguing.

One of 10 children, she sang often with her family while growing up. "My parents always sang to and with us and we would put on talent shows. We would also go camping every year and sing a lot then. It was a means of being close and getting through hard times." She discovered jazz in high school. "My high school music teacher, Richard Berberian, gave me Bill Evans' *Alone Again* and a Billie Holiday record in my sophomore year. I started taking piano lessons in high school from Richard Govoni, who gave me Bill Evans solos to transcribe. Then, the University of Massachusetts sent a trio around to high schools to talk about their program and I found out I could study jazz. Man, was I happy."

After graduating from the University of Massachusetts in Amherst with a degree in Music and Performance in 1985, she joined a local vocal group, One O'Clock Jump. The ensemble had occasional gigs in Monterey and McGarry had the opportunity to appear at the Monterey Jazz Festival as a guest with Clark Terry and Hank Jones. She moved to Los Angeles, where during the first half of the 1990s, she worked regularly in clubs, did some studio work and released her debut recording, *Easy To Love*.

McGarry moved back East in the mid-1990s and spent 1996–99 living at an ashram in the Catskills, meditating and teaching voice and harmonium. "My teacher, Gurumayi, put great emphasis on the study of music and its power to heal and connect a human being with their inner self." In 1999 she was ready to return to the music scene, so she moved to New York City, where she recorded a second CD, *Show Me*, worked with Fred Hersch (participating in his recording inspired by Walt Whitman's *Leaves Of Grass*), and sang in a vocal group called MOSS with Luciana Souza, Theo Bleckmann, Peter Eldridge and Lauren Kinhan. After meeting guitarist Keith Ganz, who she married in 2004, she began working regularly with him in settings ranging from duos to medium-size groups. "He helped me bridge the gap between my folk roots and jazz singing. I'm grateful to him for that."

Since signing with Palmetto, Kate McGarry has had increasing visibility, being discovered by the jazz press, who compares her not only to Betty Carter and Cassandra Wilson but also to Joni Mitchell, Rickie Lee Jones and folk singers. In recent times, she has performed not only with the groups that she leads with Keith Ganz but also with the Maria Schneider Jazz Orchestra, the Jazz Tap Ensemble and MOSS. McGarry recently joined the jazz faculty of the Manhattan School of Music.

"My favorite times in music have been moments where I felt I broke free, and was unlimited by any notions about myself. I'm there singing. I don't even know who I am and it feels so strong and as though everything in me is music."

Recommended CDs: 1992's *Easy To Love* (Vital 015) features Kate McGarry early in her career but already quite recognizable. *Show Me* (Palmetto 2094) and the eclectic *Mercy Streets* (Palmetto 2109) lead directly to Kate McGarry's finest recording thus far, *The Target* (Palmetto 2125), which is full of subtle, sly and surprising versions of mostly unexpected standards (including "Do Something") and originals.

Website: www.katemcgarry.com

Brady McKay
(Wendy Brady)
b. December 13, 1965, Salt Lake City, UT

A fine Dixieland and swing singer who has been branching out more in recent times, Brady McKay is emerging as one of the most potentially significant vocalists on the classic jazz scene.

"My parents were both piano teachers, and my mother wrote children's music and published several albums. I sang on some of them from as early as fifth grade." She studied piano and ballet and started voice lessons when she was 16. After moving to Northern California at 18, McKay performed in regional theater productions, mostly musicals. A turning point for her occurred when she was 23 and a friend gave her a couple of Banu Gibson LPs. Immersing herself in traditional jazz, Brady McKay sang with Stan Mark's River City Stompers during 1988–90 and co-founded the Wooden Nickel Jass Band in 1992. She married one of her main inspirations, trombonist Bob Williams, and also served as band manager for the group.

"After 10 years, I quit Wooden Nickel for various reasons, not least of which was trying to run a band with my husband while raising two children. That was an extremely difficult decision for me. WNJB was an innovative, exciting and dedicated group of musicians to work with." Since that time she has worked with pianist Tom Hook, the Pieter Meijers Quartet, Four Play Jazz, and Hal Smith's Left Coast All-Stars. In addition to appearing as a guest at traditional jazz festivals, Brady McKay has recorded two recent solo CDs. She has also performed duets with guitarist-composer Patrick Grizzell, with whom she looks forward to recording in the future. A high point was getting to sing a duet set with Banu Gibson at the Orange County Classic Jazz Festival in 2006.

"My dedication to jazz has been because of the thrill I get from performing with great players, singing well-crafted songs, and connecting with the audience. A song with good lyrics and lots of room to explore the melody is exciting to me."

Recommended CDs: While her background is in trad settings, *Pieces Of Us* (CT Bop Music 96132), *Moon Swings (Swimming In Lake Me)* and Poplar Jam (CT Bop Music 66940) feature Brady McKay performing swing standards with fine rhythm sections. She is also well showcased on Tom Hook's *Perfect Strangers*, while *Sometimes I'm Happy* teams her with John Sheridan. All of these CDs are excellent, but Brady McKay's definitive recordings are still in the future.

Website: www.bradymckay.com

Robin McKelle
b. January 20, Rochester, NY

Robin McKelle has made a strong impression with her debut CD, showing that she has the ability to make vintage songs sound contemporary and relevant without changing their original meanings or spirit.

"My mother was a liturgical singer, so I was exposed to music from a very young age. I began to study classical piano at the age of five and, after several years of study, I became interested in the sound of jazz harmony. I studied jazz piano and played in the jazz ensemble at school. My piano teacher soon realized that I was a singer as well, so he began to mentor me in the interpretation of singing jazz melodies." She also played French Horn for nine years.

McKelle attended the University of Miami during 1994–96 and Berklee, graduating from the latter in 1999. After a period working in Los Angeles and on tours as a backup singer, she moved back to Boston and started a trio. "I taught voice at Berklee College of Music for three years. Every day, I would tell my students to follow their dreams and never stop. Then one day, it dawned on me that I should take some of my own advice. So I did, and made the decision to leave Berklee." She took third place in the 2004 Thelonious Monk Vocal Jazz Competition and recorded her first CD in 2006.

"I am at a high point right now. I spent most of 2007 performing at many jazz festivals in France and Europe. I am at the beginning of my career, so everything lies ahead."

Recommended CDs: *Introducing Robin McKelle* (Candid 79996) is an impressive start to her career, featuring the singer with a big band comprised of top Los Angeles musicians, making decades-old songs sound like her own.

Website: www.robinmckelle.com

Red McKenzie
(William McKenzie)
b. October 14, 1899, St. Louis, MO;
d. February 7, 1948, New York, NY

A sentimental ballad singer who fit the stereotype of the kind of vocalist who appeals to tough guys crying into their beer, Red McKenzie was a favorite of Eddie Condon. However, his greatest fame was due to his playing of the comb. McKenzie wrapped tissue paper around a comb and turned it into a loud and surprisingly musical kazoo that made his Mound City Blue Blowers a top novelty jazz group in the 1920s.

McKenzie turned to music after he worked as a jockey (an accident that broke both his arms ended that career) and a bellhop. In 1923 McKenzie formed the Mound City Blue Blowers, a group consisting of himself on comb, Dick Slevin on kazoo and banjoist Jack Bland. Their 1924 recording of "Arkansas Blues" sold over a million copies and the group was in great demand for a time. With personnel changes (guitarist Eddie Lang made the band into a quartet by late 1924), McKenzie kept the Blue Blowers together into 1932, recording a dozen titles during 1924–25 and eight other selections for another label as McKenzie's Candy Kids. Its 1929 records featured such major names as Eddie Condon, Jack Teagarden, Coleman Hawkins (in exciting form on "One Hour" and "Hello Lola"), Glenn Miller and Pee Wee Russell. There was also a session in 1931 with Muggsy Spanier, Jimmy Dorsey and Hawkins and a series of dates during 1935–36. By then McKenzie had greatly de-emphasized his comb in favor of singing.

Red McKenzie was quite significant behind the scenes in organizing important record dates including for the New Orleans Rhythm Kings, Bix Beiderbecke, the Spirits of Rhythm and Eddie Condon. He also lent his name to the two classic 1927 sessions by the McKenzie-Condon Chicagoans although he is not actually on those four titles.

In addition, McKenzie led record dates under his own name, and it is on those performances that one can hear him developing as a singer. Although he played comb in addition to singing on the four songs from two dates with his Music Box in 1927–28, his sessions from 1931 on strictly feature him as a singer. While his 1931–32 efforts are with a commercial orchestra, his later recordings have McKenzie backed by jazz combos, often featuring Bunny Berigan or Bobby Hackett. McKenzie, who worked regularly with Paul Whiteman's orchestra during 1932–33, enjoyed singing such sentimental songs as "It's The Talk Of The Town," "Can't We Talk It Over" and "Peg O' My Heart." Although his voice is limited and for acquired tastes, it has a charm of its own.

During 1938–43, McKenzie worked outside of music as a beer salesman for a brewery in St., Louis, an ironic job for an alcoholic. In 1944 he was persuaded by Condon to appear at a few of his Town Hall concerts (by then the comb playing was completely in the past). Red McKenzie made a comeback as a singer during his last few years, led two record dates, and performed at Ryan's in New York before his death from cirrhosis of the liver at age 48.

Recommended CDs: *Volume 1* (Sensation 29) and *Volume 2* (Sensation 30) have all of the early Mound City Blue Blowers recordings. *Red McKenzie* (Timeless 1-019) and *Mound City Blue Blowers: 1935–1936* (Classics 895) contain many good examples of his singing.

Chris McNulty
b. December 23, 1953, Melbourne, Australia

One of the top jazz singers to emerge from Australia, Chris McNulty has been making a strong impression ever since moving to New York in 1988.

She was already quite well known in her native country by then. "I came out of a very traditional working class environment. There were six kids and everyone went to work at 15. Girls were expected to be married and have children by 18–20, so education was thought of as a waste. I was a straight-A student but it didn't much help. It was out to work at 15 and bringing home the board money. I was singing six nights a week by the time I was 16 and also had a steady day gig, which I gave up entirely by the time I reached 18. Then the road literally took me away from family and the safe and simple childhood I'd known, forever."

After singing pop, funk and R&B for years, in 1976 she discovered Billie Holiday, Sarah Vaughan, Carmen McRae and Nancy Wilson. By 1978, when she co-formed a jazz ensemble with the notable Australian pianist Paul Grabowsky, Chris McNulty was a jazz singer. During the next decade she sang in clubs, on television and worked as a studio singer. "Weirdly, by the time I got to NYC in 1985, then permanently in 1988, I was still looked upon as very young and pretty green—little did anyone know." In 1988 she was awarded an International Study Grant from the Australia Council, which made it possible for her to move to New York.

A fearless singer and a fine composer-lyricist, she wrote the official lyrics to Miles Davis' "Blue In Green." She records regularly and travels the world, performing in Europe, Russia and Australia in addition to the East Coast. Along the way, Chris McNulty has worked and held her own with Peter Leitch, Gary Bartz, Paul Bollenback, Gary Thomas, Mulgrew Miller, John Hicks, Frank Wess, Ingrid Jensen, Tom Lellis, Joe Locke, David "Fathead" Newman and many others.

"Being in the presence of such great jazz giants, I sometimes scratch my head, wondering how I got all the way here from West Heidelberg, Melbourne, Australia. I still don't know how I got here really."

Recommended CDs: Chris McNulty's recordings are evidence that she certainly belongs in the major leagues of jazz. *Waltz For Debby* (Discovery 968) was recorded in 1990 and includes her version of "Blue In Green." *A Time For Love* (Amosaya 4545) is a set of standards and matches her with John Hicks, Peter Leitch and Gary Bartz. *I Remember You* (Moptop 4546), *Dance Delicioso* (Elefant Dreams 4547) and *Whispers The Heart* (Elefant Dreams 4549) find her opening up her repertoire to include some pop tunes along with the standards and occasional originals, doing justice to every song with her subtle improvising.

Website: www.chrismcnulty.com

Carmen McRae
b. April 8, 1920, New York, NY;
d. November 10, 1994, Beverly Hills, CA

A very significant singer whose behind-the-beat phrasing, caustic wit and tone are still major influences, Carmen McRae was one of the giants. Her voice may not have been as wondrous as that of Ella Fitzgerald or Sarah Vaughan, but she was a masterful jazz singer.

McRae studied piano from the age of eight and in 1939, her song "Dream Of Life" was recorded by Billie Holiday. Her first major job as a singer was with Benny Carter in 1944, but it would be another decade before she made a strong impression. She worked briefly with the orchestras of Count Basie and Mercer Ellington (with whom she made her recording debut), was an intermission pianist and singer at lesser-known Chicago and New York clubs, and both married and divorced drummer Kenny Clarke.

In 1954 Carmen McRae recorded her first album for Bethlehem. Her Decca recordings of 1955–59 (which deserve to be reissued in a box set) put her near the top of her field. She sang opposite Louis Armstrong in Dave Brubeck's *The Real Ambassadors* in 1961. Her voice was higher than it would be in later years but otherwise she was very recognizable. McRae's recordings of the 1960s and '70s were more erratic due to the often poppish material, much of which she could not save. But her live performances remained a creative joy.

McRae's recordings of 1983–90 feature her at a high level, as she was allowed to record whatever she wanted. Included are sets with George Shearing, Cal Tjader and Betty Carter, and the acclaimed *Carmen Sings Monk*. Her final recording, *Sarah: Dedicated To You*, is a tribute to her idol and friend Sarah Vaughan. Carmen McRae still sounded strong in 1990 but she refused to quit smoking and had to retire in 1991 due to emphysema.

Recommended CDs: *Carmen McRae* (Avenue Jazz/Bethlehem 75990), *I'll Be Seeing You* (GRP/Decca 647), *Here To Stay* (GRP/Decca 610) and *Sings Great American Songwriters* (GRP/Decca 631) feature the bulk of McRae's 1950s recordings. *Sings "Lover Man" And Other Billie Holiday Classics* (Columbia/Legacy 65115) from 1961 was her first recorded tribute to Lady Day, who she considered her main influence. *Alive* (Columbia/Legacy 57887), the Great American Songbook (Atlantic 904), which is highlighted by Jimmie Rowles' "The Ballad Of Thelonious Monk," and *Velvet Soul* (Laserlight 17 111) are among the finest records of her middle period. Pretty much everything that Carmen McRae recorded after 1982 is worthy, particularly, *You're Looking At Me* (Concord Jazz 235), *For Lady Day, Volume 1* (Novus 63163), *For Lady Day, Vol. 2* (Novus 63190), *Any Old Time* (Denon 1216), *The Carmen McRae-Betty Carter Duets* (Verve 314 529 579), *Fine And Mellow—Live At Birdland* (Concord Jazz 342), the classic *Carmen Sings Monk* (Novus 3086), *Dream Of Life* (Qwest/Warner Bros. 46340) and *Dedicated To You* (Novus 3110).

Jay McShann

b. January 12, 1916, Muskogee, OK; d. December 7, 2006, Kansas City, MO

A major Kansas City swing and blues pianist and bandleader, Jay McShann did not start singing until relatively late in his career.

McShann began playing piano when he was 12. He worked as a teenager in Tulsa and Arkansas, attended Winfield College in Kansas, gigged throughout the Southwest, and by the mid-1930s had settled in Kansas City. A pianist with a bluesy sound of his own, McShann was part of the legendary Kansas City jam sessions that included Big Joe Turner, whose blues singing impressed him. He formed his own big band in 1937 and a young Charlie Parker picked up important early experience playing with McShann. One of the last great swing orchestras to emerge from Kansas City, the Jay McShann Big Band, was playing New York by 1940 and recorded for Decca. The label was primarily interested in blues-oriented material and, with Walter Brown singing, McShann had a hit with "Confessin' The Blues."

In 1944 McShann was drafted and his big band broke up. He only served in the military for a few months and spent the second half of the 1940s leading small combos in Los Angeles, often featuring Jimmy Witherspoon. After returning to Kansas City, McShann recorded some selections in 1951, 1955 and 1956 but was otherwise obscure for 15 years.

Because it was often requested that McShann play his band's old hits and he no longer had Walter Brown around, he began to sing himself. A very effective blues and standards vocalist, McShann actually sounded better than Brown. In 1966, for the album *McShann's Piano*, he was heard as a singer on records for the first time, taking three vocals. Throughout the remainder of his career, Jay McShann was known as a pianist-singer, and he sang at least a few numbers on nearly every record date. Having heard Big Joe Turner, Jimmy Witherspoon, Walter Brown and other Kansas City–style singers close up, Jay McShann fit quite naturally into their tradition. He remained a cheerful force and a historic jazz figure up until the time of his death in 2006.

Recommended CDs: Among Jay McShann's numerous excellent post-1968 recordings, all of which feature his fine piano playing, he also takes at least several vocals on *The Man From Muskogee* (Sackville 3005), *After Hours* (Storyville 8279), *The Last Of The Blue Devils* (Collectables 67582), *Just A Lucky So And So* (Sackville 3035), *Hootie's Jumpin' Blues* (Stony Plain 1287), *Havin' Fun* (Sackville 2047) and *Still Jumpin' The Blues* (Stony Plain 1254).

LPs to Search For: *McShann's Piano* (Capitol 2645) from 1966 has not yet been reissued on CD.

Johnny Mercer
(John Herndon Mercer)
b. November 18, 1909, Savannah, GA; d. June 25, 1976, Los Angeles, CA

One of the great lyricists of American popular music, Johnny Mercer wrote the words to over 1,500 songs. His insightful lyrics, which can usually be sung by members of either sex, are consistently optimistic, upbeat and timeless. Unlike most of the other American composers and lyricists, Mercer was also a fine singer and a familiar personality, who frequently performed not only his own music but other pop and jazz songs.

Although he moved to New York in 1927 with hopes of becoming an actor, Mercer was unsuccessful in landing worthwhile parts. However, he discovered that he was very skilled at putting together words, and in 1930 he wrote "Out Of Breath, Scared To Death Of You" for the show *Garrick Gaieties*. In 1932 he won a singing contest, gaining a job as a vocalist with Paul Whiteman's orchestra. Through Whiteman, he met Hoagy Carmichael and had his first real success with "Lazy Bones." Immediately after that hit, Mercer was in demand to write lyrics, moving to Hollywood in 1933 and writing for the movies. During the next 30 years he wrote the words to such songs as "Accentuate The Positive," "And The Angels Sing," "Autumn Leaves," "Blues In The Night," "Bob White," "Charade," "Come Rain Or Come Shine," "Days Of Wine And Roses," "Dream," "Early Autumn," "Fools Rush In," "G.I. Jive," "Goody, Goody," "Hit The Road To Dreamland," "Hooray For Hollywood," "I Remember You," "I Thought About You," "I'm An Old Cowhand," "I'm Old Fashioned," "Jeepers Creepers," "Laura," "Moon River," "My Shining Hour," "On The Atchison, Topeka And The Santa Fe," "One For My Baby," "P.S. I Love You," "Satin Doll," "Skylark," "Something's Gotta Give," "Tangerine," "That Old Black Magic," "The

Days Of Wine And Roses," "Too Marvelous For Words" and "You Must Have Been A Beautiful Baby," among many others.

As a vocalist, Mercer appeared on occasional records in the 1930s. Among his better early recordings are "Dr. Heckle And Mr. Jibe" with the Dorsey Brothers Orchestra in 1933, "Fare-Thee-Well To Harlem" and "Christmas Night In Harlem" from 1934 with Jack Teagarden and the Paul Whiteman Orchestra, "I've Got A Note" with Wingy Manone (1935), a pair of 1938 vocal duets with Bing Crosby ("Small Fry" and "Mr. Crosby And Mr. Mercer"), two guest appearances with Benny Goodman in 1939 ("Cuckoo In The Clock" and "Show Your Linen, Miss Richardson") and "The Old Music Master" in 1942 with Whiteman and Teagarden. In addition to working on the radio with Goodman in 1939, he hosted his own radio show in the early 1940s called *Johnny Mercer's Music Shop*.

In 1942, Mercer founded Capitol Records with Glenn Wallichs and Buddy DeSylva. He was the label's main talent scout, signing Nat King Cole, Stan Kenton and Peggy Lee. He also became a top-notch recording artist for Capitol, having hits as a vocalist with "On The Atchison, Topeka And The Santa Fe," "Accentuate The Positive," "Candy" and "Personality," also recording the delightful "Save The Bones For Henry Jones" with Nat King Cole. His Southern accent was appealing, his choice of notes was flawless and, like Fred Astaire, his subtle phrasing perfectly fit each song even though his improvising was fairly basic.

In 1955, Mercer sold his share of Capitol but remained quite active as a lyricist and occasional vocalist for another decade. In his career, he wrote the scores for seven Broadway musicals, contributed songs to many films, and made quite a few guest appearances on television. After the mid-1960s, the changes in musical taste resulted in him working much less, but Johnny Mercer continued writing and singing until shortly before his death in 1976.

Recommended CDs: The three-CD limited-edition box set *Johnny Mercer* (Mosaic Select 028) has 79 of Mercer's most jazz-oriented recordings of 1942–47 and shows what a fine jazz singer he could be. *Sings Personality* (ASV/Living Era 5430) is a definitive collection of Mercer's 1940s vocal hits and *Sweet Georgia Brown* (Hindsight 152) is a fine set of radio transcriptions from 1944. Finally, *The Huckleberry Verser* (Star Line 9013) finds Mercer in excellent voice in 1972.

Helen Merrill
(Jelena Ann Milcetic)
b. July 21, 1930, New York, NY

Always a very credible and intriguing singer, Helen Merrill puts a lot of thought and planning into her performances and recordings, and has created more than her share of gems through the years.

"I was always interested in all kinds of music including folk, blues, pop, jazz and religious music. I knew that I was going to be a singer, from the age of three." The daughter of Croatian immigrants, she started singing in clubs while a teenager in 1944 as Helen Milcetic, later changing her last name. She was with the Reggie Childs Orchestra

during 1946–47, married clarinetist Aaron Sachs, and had opportunities to sit in with Charlie Parker, Miles Davis and Bud Powell. "My first real professional job was with Earl Hines in 1952. All things stemmed from there. Quincy Jones and trombonist Benny Green were instrumental in getting a contract for me with Bob Shad on Emarcy. The now-historic album with Clifford Brown followed."

Merrill's Emarcy recordings of 1954–58 are consistently rewarding and, in addition to the date with trumpeter Clifford Brown, she used arranger Gil Evans on one of her best recordings a year before he revived his career with Miles Davis on *Miles Ahead*. In 1959 she moved to Italy for four years, touring Europe and Japan. Merrill teamed up with pianist-arranger Dick Katz for a pair of very good Milestone albums during 1967–68 that found her stretching herself while retaining her musical personality. She spent a few years living in Japan, where she has always been very popular, moving back to the U.S. in the mid-1970s.

Since then, Helen Merrill has recorded fairly regularly including a reunion date with Gil Evans and collaborations with Steve Lacy, Roger Kellaway and Torrie Zito. "I was lucky to have lived in NYC, being part of the legendary music with the greatest musicians of the late '40s and '50s. My career has taken me all over the world. I am inspired by creative talent and have taken many chances while never thinking too much about the commercial aspect of my art."

Recommended CDs: Helen Merrill has led over 50 albums in her career. *The Complete Helen Merrill On Mercury (1954–58)* (Mercury 826340) is an exciting four-CD set that covers her first period. For listeners just wanting a sampling of that music, *Helen Merrill With Clifford Brown* (Emarcy 534435) and *Dream Of You* (Emarcy 514074), the latter being her set with Gil Evans, will probably suffice. Other rewarding recordings include *You've Got A Date With The Blues* (Verve 837936), *The Feeling Is Mutual* (Mercury 5588492), *A Shade Of Difference* (Mercury 5588512), which has arrangements by Dick Katz and fine playing by Thad Jones, Jim Hall and Hubert Laws, *No Tears, No Goodbyes* (Sunnyside 3506), which is a set with keyboardist Gordon Beck, *Music Makers* (Sunnyside 3512) with Gordon Beck and either Steve Lacy or Stephane Grappelli, the 1987 reunion with Gil Evans called *Collaboration* (Emarcy 834205), *Duets* (Emarcy 838097) with bassist Ron Carter, *Just Friends* (Emarcy 842007) with Stan Getz, *Clear Out Of This World* (Antilles 314-512654), *Brownie: Homage To Clifford Brown* (Verve 522363), which features trumpeters Tom Harrell, Wallace Roney, Roy Hargrove and Lew Soloff, *You And The Night And The Music* (Verve 537087), the very personal *Jelena Ana Milcetic a.k.a. Helen Merrill* (Verve 543089) and the excellent ballad set *Lilac Wine* (Sunnyside 3020) from 2004.

LPs to Search For: While many of Helen Merrill's recordings from the 1960s have not yet been reissued, *Something Special* (Inner City 1060) is the main one to try to acquire. A very unpredictable and rewarding set from 1967, Merrill is teamed in different combinations with pianist-arranger Dick Katz, Jim Hall, Thad Jones, Ron Carter and drummer Pete LaRoca.

Website: www.helenmerrill.com

Velma Middleton
b. September 1, 1917, St. Louis, MO;
d. February 10, 1961, Freetown, Sierra Leone

Velma Middleton occupies an odd place in jazz history. Due to her excessive weight, she spent most of her career as a comic foil for Louis Armstrong. However, she was an underrated, if limited, singer whose enthusiasm was infectious.

Middleton was originally a comic dancer and she loved to amaze audiences by doing the splits on stage. She visited South America in 1938 with Connie McLean's orchestra and had a solo act before joining Armstrong's big band in 1942. She appears on film in some of Satch's Soundies and already her act was set, with her constant smile, dancing, and humorous interplay with Armstrong. When Louis Armstrong broke up his big band in 1947, it was not long before he had Velma Middleton as a member of his globetrotting All-Stars. Of their duets, "That's My Desire" and "Baby It's Cold Outside" are still funny. Middleton also had occasional chances to sing blues before the comedy took over.

Velma Middleton recorded eight obscure selections as a leader for the Dootone label in 1948 and 1951. She died suddenly in 1961 while on a tour with Armstrong in Africa. She can be heard singing two or three numbers on many Louis Armstrong recordings of the 1950s.

Amos Milburn

b. April 1, 1927, Houston, TX; d. January 3, 1980, Houston, TX

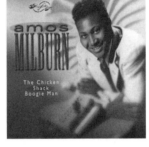

Perhaps it is a bit of a stretch to call Amos Milburn a jazz singer but, like Charles Brown, he crossed over between early rhythm and blues and jazz, both as a singer and as a pianist. But unlike Brown, Milburn never made a comeback after his good luck ran out.

The fourth of a dozen children, Amos Milburn began on piano at the age of five, learning by ear. He was initially inspired by the top boogie-woogie pianists. After lying about his age, he enlisted in the Navy in 1942 at the age of 15, spending a few years overseas. After getting out of the military, he worked in Houston and San Antonio before moving to Los Angeles.

Signing a contract with Aladdin, Milburn had many hits during 1947–53 including "After Midnight," "Hold Me Baby," "Chicken Shack Boogie," "Bad Bad Whiskey," "Thinking And Drinking," "Let Me Go Home Whiskey," "One Scotch, One Bourbon, One Beer" and "Good Good Whiskey." His smooth vocals complemented his barrelhouse piano playing very well, and he was a major name during the era.

As with many of the R&B stars of his generation, the hits stopped in 1954. Milburn, who had many best-selling records about drinking, drank excessively himself. After 1957, he was dropped by Aladdin. He recorded a few numbers for King and Motown during 1961–62 along with a final album in 1976, but his career was largely finished by the mid-1950s. After a long period of increasingly-declining health, Amos Milburn passed away in 1980 when he was just 52.

Recommended CDs: It would be impossible to top the seven-CD box set *The Complete Aladdin Recordings Of Amos Milburn* (Mosaic 7-155) since it includes every Milburn recording prior to 1960, but this is an out-of-print limited-edition series. *The Chicken Shack Boogie Man* (Proper Pairs 102) is a two-CD set from the same period that will suffice for most listeners.

Lizzie Miles

(Elizabeth Mary Pajaund)
b. March 31, 1895, New Orleans, LA;
d. March 17, 1963, New Orleans, LA

A low-down blues singer, Lizzie Miles could also sing Dixieland standards with joy. She made a comeback more than 20 years after her initial success and was at the height of her fame during her renaissance in the 1950s.

Born and raised on New Orleans' Bourbon Street, she left home when she was 14 in 1909 to sing with the Jones Brothers Circus. Miles sang with circuses and minstrel shows for the next eight years and performed in New Orleans with King Oliver, Kid Ory and A.J. Piron before moving to Chicago in 1918. While in the Windy City, she had opportunities to perform with King Oliver, Freddie Keppard and Charlie Elgar's Creole Orchestra. By then she considered Sophie Tucker and her half-sister singer Edna Hicks to be her main influences and she had learned how to sing both blues and early jazz.

In 1921 Lizzie Miles moved to New York. During 1922–30 she recorded 57 songs, mostly with unknown or obscure musicians. The exceptions were two songs apiece with pianist Jelly Roll Morton, a trio with King Oliver, and an all-star group led by drummer Jasper Davis. Among the more memorable selections are "He May Be Your Man But He Comes To See Me Sometimes," "You've Gotta Come And See Mama Every Night," "A Good Man Is Hard To Find," "Georgia Gigolo" and "Don't Tell Me Nothin' 'Bout My Man." Miles did not have any specific hits, but she worked steadily including two years (1924–26) in Europe.

A serious illness kept her out of music during 1931–35. Miles made a comeback, worked with Fats Waller, and recorded eight numbers at a session in 1939 that features her in excellent form. But because her style was considered passé, she was retired from music during 1942–50.

While most of the classic blues singers who made comebacks late in life tended to return in the 1960s with the folk/blues movement, the always-entertaining Lizzie Miles became part of the New Orleans revival jazz scene of the 1950s. She worked steadily in both New Orleans and San Francisco (at the Club Hangover), performed regularly with trumpeter Bob Scobey (1955–57) and was on record dates with Scobey, clarinetist George Lewis, trumpeter Sharkey Bonano and her regular pianist, Bob Camp. She sang vintage standards, vaudeville warhorses, ballads and Dixieland favorites (sometimes in Creole patois) including "Some Of These Days," "Please Don't Talk About Me When I'm Gone," "Careless Love," "Bill Bailey" and "Sister Kate" plus occasional blues, delighting audiences who enjoyed good time jazz.

Lizzie Miles stayed active until after the 1959 Monterey Jazz Festival when she retired to devote herself to religion.

Recommended CDs: *Vol. 1* (Document 5458), *Vol. 2* (Document 5459) and *Vol. 3* (Document 5460) have her early recordings while *Lizzie Miles* (American Music 73) offers a good example of how she sounded in later years.

Big Miller

(Clarence Horatius Miller)
b. December 18, 1922, Sioux City, IA;
d. June 9, 1992, Edmonton, Alberta, Canada

One of the great Kansas City blues shouters, Big Miller is less known than his predecessors and contemporaries because he did not record that frequently and spent his last 25 years living and performing in Canada, but he ranks with the best.

While a teenager, his family moved to Topeka, Kansas, where he studied trombone and bass. After freelancing as a vocalist, he sang with Lionel Hampton in 1949 and then spent the next five years with Jay McShann, a perfect training group for a blues-oriented singer. Miller worked in the mid-1950s with the Fletcher Henderson Reunion Orchestra led by Rex Stewart even though he had never worked with Henderson. Big Miller gained a certain amount of popularity, performing in the main jazz clubs in the U.S. He recorded two numbers for Savoy in 1955, appeared and briefly toured in Jon Hendricks' *Evolution Of The Blues* show, and was signed to Columbia. He also acted now and then, and along the way appeared with Duke Ellington, Count Basie, Dizzy Gillespie and Miles Davis.

Big Miller first sang in Canada in 1962. When he was stranded in Vancouver in 1967 with the breakup of a tour, he began to explore Western Canada and liked what he saw. He moved permanently to Edmonton in 1970 and became a Canadian citizen in 1973. Miller became a very popular figure locally and worked regularly during the remainder of his career including a trip to Japan, visits to Europe, tours with the Nimmons 'N' Nine Plus Six group, and recording with the Tommy Banks Orchestra at the Montreux Jazz Festival. He also had some reunions with Jay McShann including a set with a drummer as a trio at the 1989 Vancouver Jazz Festival.

Big Miller, who could hold his own with Big Joe Turner and Jimmy Rushing, continued performing until he died from a heart attack in 1992.

Recommended CDs: Big Miller's two Columbia albums of 1960–61 are fortunately available as a single CD. *Revelations And The Blues/Big Miller Sings, Twists, Shouts And Preaches* (Collectables 7453) has a full set of his stirring originals and a program of his versions of familiar blues and jazz standards. Miller did not get a chance to record again until 1975 but can be heard later in his career in excellent form on *Last Of The Blues Shouters* (Southland 28), *Big Miller And The Tommy Banks Band And Quartet* (Century II. 10974) and *Live At Athabasca College* (Stony Plain 1151).

LPs to Search For: Big Miller's first album, *Did You Ever Hear the Blues?* (United Artists 6047), has not been reissued on CD yet.

Natasha Miller

b. February 6, 1971, Des Moines, IA

In 2003, singer Natasha Miller met veteran songwriter Bobby Sharp. Their musical partnership has resulted in her CDs having a strong plot and purpose, and Sharp being rediscovered.

"My father is a pianist, and had played standards such as 'Misty' and 'Moonglow' since I was a young child. I began singing with him when I was about two years old." She sang in her church and school choirs and choruses, and is a classically trained violinist. Miller went to the University of Kansas in 1989 for one year on a violin scholarship, and attended Iowa State University and Drake University. Although she made a living as a violinist, including leading the Sapphire String Quartet, she knew that deep down she wanted to be a singer. Miller moved to Northern California in 1995 and gradually became known as a vocalist, accompanying herself on guitar and piano. She performed locally while working days in the advertising industry.

In 2001 Natasha Miller decided that she needed to take the plunge, so she quit her job to work full-time as a singer. During 2002, she recorded two CDs. Then in 2003, while giving an interview on the radio, she was heard by the somewhat forgotten songwriter Bobby Sharp, who was best known for writing "Unchain My Heart." He loved her voice, contacted her, and sent her his songs, many of which had never been recorded or even performed before. Within five months, she presented a concert of his music and two CDs have thus far resulted, helping both of their careers. "This has been the most important and in-depth relationship in music so far for me."

Recommended CDs: *Her Life* (Poignant 001) is a set of Natasha Miller originals, and *Talk To Me Nice* (Poignant 002) has her renditions of standards plus two of her songs. *I Had A Feelin'* (Poignant 003) and *Don't Move* (Poignant 004) are important CDs that feature Miller sounding at her best, interpreting two full sets of Bobby Sharp songs.

Website: natashamillerweb.com

Sophie Milman

b. 1983, Ufa, Russia

A young and beautiful singer with a very attractive voice, Sophie Milman seems to be following in the footsteps of Diana Krall and Jane Monheit, at least in gaining a great deal of publicity early in her career. But she actually has a more flexible voice, does not sound like any of her predecessors, and is at her best when she is able to infuse offbeat material, such as "(It's Not Easy) Bein' Green" and "Matchmaker, Matchmaker," with her own musical personality.

Sophie Milman has already experienced a great deal in life. Born in Russia, her father built up a strong American jazz record collection, not a very easy feat at the time considering that the records had to be bought on the black market. The family was persecuted for being Jewish and moved to Israel when Sophie was seven; fortunately, they were able to take the records with them. Eight years later they moved to Toronto, Canada. By then, Milman was familiar with jazz and the music helped ease the difficulties of learning a new culture and language. She had just appeared at a handful of singing engagements in 2004 when she was signed to a record contract and suddenly found herself becoming a national celebrity.

Sophie Milman has since recorded two CDs, toured around the world and somehow has found the time to work toward a degree in commerce at the University Of Toronto. She is on her way to becoming a major star and her enthusiasm for jazz remains strong.

Recommended CDs: *Sophie Milman* (Linus 29) sold over 100,000 copies, and *Make Someone Happy* (JVC Victor 61446) has done even better. More important, the music is rewarding. The debut CD ranges from "My Baby Just Cares For Me" and "I Can't Give You Anything But Love" to "La Vie En Rose" and "I Feel Pretty." "Bein' Green" is the most touching selection on the equally rewarding *Make Someone Happy*.

Website: www.sophiemilman.com

Phil Minton

b. November 2, 1940, Torquay, England

A remarkable singer whose wide range of sometimes-bizarre sounds has long made him one of the leading vocalists of the avant-garde, Phil Minton's music can be jarring and abrasive but it is never dull.

Minton first heard jazz through Louis Armstrong and sang in church. He took trumpet lessons and played jazz with the Brian Waldron Quintet during 1956–61. Minton moved to London in 1962 and was both a trumpeter and a singer with the Mike Westbrook Orchestra. After living in the Canary Islands for a year and working during 1966-70 in Sweden, he returned to England in 1971. At first, he was back with Mike Westbrook's big band, but soon he was also freelancing and collaborating with many of the top improvisers in Europe, including Peter Brotzmann, Fred Frith, Roger Turner, Derek Bailey and Veryan Weston. He formed the vocal trio Voice with Julie Tippetts and Maggie Nicols, was the lead voice in the revival of Carla Bley's *Escalator Over The Hill* in 1997, and recently has been part of the quartet Roof.

Phil Minton, who has sung in avant-garde operas, engaged in improvisations based on poetry or classical themes, appeared with symphony orchestras, and toured the world in a countless number of settings, has never compromised his musical vision, clicking, quacking, gurgling and making unclassifiable sounds in free improvisations.

Recommended CDs: *Ways* (ITM 163009) is a duet set with pianist Veryan Weston that is relatively accessible due to its crazy wit. *Dada Da* (Leo 192) and *Drainage* (Emanem 4211) are sets of duets with percussionist Roger Turner. Also representative of Phil Minton's music are *Ammo* (Golden Years Of New Jazz 22), *Mouthful Of Ecstasy* (Victo 41), *A Doughnut In One Hand* (FMP 91), and *Slur* (Emanem 4140)

LPs to Search For: *A Doughnut In Both Hands 1975–82* (Emanem 4025) has some of Phil Minton's earlier recordings, which find him moving toward his somewhat revolutionary style.

Website: www.philminton.co.uk

Jane Monheit

b. November 3, 1977, West Islip, NY

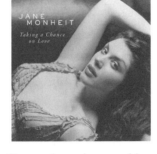

Jane Monheit has such a beautiful voice that one waits with impatience for her to gain more originality and to amass accomplishments. The potential that was displayed when she was 20 is still present 10 years later.

"There was never a time in my life without jazz. I was surrounded by music from birth, and jazz was always a huge part of that. I've been singing since the very beginning, and I have very clear memories of my grandfather recording me when I was very young. Sometimes the tunes were nursery rhymes, but usually it was 'Over The Rainbow.'"

Monheit studied clarinet extensively and learned piano from her grandmother, but singing was always her main focus. She attended the Manhattan School of Music during 1995–99, studying with Peter Eldridge. The most important early highlight was coming in second in the 1998 Thelonious Monk Vocal Competition to Terri Thornton; Tierney Sutton took third place. Monheit gained a great deal of attention from the contest and in 2000 made her recording debut with *Never Never Land*.

Marketed as a young sex symbol with an angelic voice, Jane Monheit competed in publicity with Diana Krall for a time before fading back. She has thus far recorded six CDs and sounds at her best on swing standards (her version of "Over The Rainbow" is famous). Not a major improviser, Monheit has sometimes shown the influence of Broadway show singers and she admires not just Ella Fitzgerald but Judy Garland and Barbara Cook.

"My biggest goal is to be able to do this forever. If I can find a way to always grow as an artist, and stay true to this incredible music, then I know my career will always be meaningful and fulfilling."

We're rooting for you.

Recommended CDs: *Never Never Land* (N-Coded 4207) and *Come Dream With Me* (N-Coded 4219) got Jane Monheit's career off to a fast start during 2000–2001. Her voice sounded great even if her interpretations of standards seemed a bit conservative. *In The Sun* (N-Coded 4234) has her band sounding more modern than her vocals. Her 2003 DVD *Live At The Rainbow Room* is, despite a few good moments, dull due to the overly-arranged material. Nothing looks real on it. In contrast, 2004's *Taking A Chance On Love* (Sony 92495) is her best CD to date, with Monheit sounding comfortable with the vintage material, which includes "Over The Rainbow." *The Season* (Sony 77711) is a forgettable Xmas album and *Surrender* (Concord 30050) is a middle-of-the-road Brazilian-flavored set that is at its best during "So Many Stars."

Website: www.janemonheitonline.com

Antoinette Montague

b. July 21, 1960, Newark, NJ

A fine performer who puts a lot of heart and soul in her singing, Antoinette Montague has been gaining long overdue recognition in recent times.

Her favorite singers to listen to while growing up in Newark were Louis Armstrong and Billie Holiday, and her mother played Ella Fitzgerald records in their house. She started singing when she was five, participated in grammar school talent shows and remembers, "I would sing to the kids in the neighborhood in Newark." While earning an English degree from Seton Hall College, she was in her college gospel choir. "I sang and recorded some contemporary R&B and later with a choir called the Judah Chorale. I was also always sitting in with jazz musicians at the encouragement of friends." She sang with a swing band called "5 Kings and a Queen."

In 1996 she met veteran singer Carrie Smith, and asked her how to sing the blues. Smith became one of her mentors while Montague managed her affairs, negotiating deals for her and eventually becoming her caretaker. She studied with pianist Norman Simmons and was also inspired by knowing and learning from Etta Jones and Della Griffin. Since that time, Antoinette Montague has performed in the New York area with Frank Wess, the Duke Ellington Band and Jack Jeffers in addition to her own groups.

"Music and singing to people have always been in my life in some form.

I found out how I could do it, if I did my lessons correctly, when I watched Carrie Smith, Etta Jones, Shirley Horn, Clark Terry and Lou Donaldson."

Recommended CD: *Pretty Blue* (Consolidated Artists Productions 1003), her only recording thus far, displays Antoinette Montague's powerful voice and ability to make every song sound bluesy.

Website: www.antoinettemontague.com

Barbara Montgomery
b. June 30, 1948, Berkeley, CA

Barbara Montgomery has had many careers besides being a performer. It took some time, but she has carved out a niche for herself as a versatile and continually intriguing jazz singer. "I knew at five that I wanted to be a singer. It just took a while to get there, a few zigs and zags."

After earning a degree at the University of Pennsylvania, she was poised to become a jazz singer in 1970, but soon joined NBC, working behind the scenes for the *Mike Douglas Show*. Since then, Montgomery has worked as a lighting designer, music director (including for Richard Simmons since 1986), producer, publisher, music industry executive and been involved in the production of film and television.

Since returning to performing in 1990, Montgomery has recorded six CDs, including a tribute to Chick Corea (*Dakini Land*), written original music and continued working on major productions. She leads Ladies Night Out, an all-female jazz group, and has primarily performed in the Eastern United States and in Eastern Europe. She has also been a key spokesperson in gun violence prevention.

When asked to name high points from her musical career, Barbara Montgomery says, "Meeting and working (non-musically) with Ella Fitzgerald, Woody Herman, Benny Goodman and Tony Bennett, having the honor of recording the first vocal version of Chick Corea's 'Armando's Rhumba', meeting and performing with Freddie Hubbard, who graciously approved of my lyrics to his 'Little Sunflower', producing (and performing in) a sixty-piece jazz ensemble performance honoring Walter Annenberg and the spirit of giving in 2002, singing in Washington, DC, in 2004 at the Capitol for the Million Mom March in remembrance of the victims of gun violence in America."

Recommended CDs: *Barbara Montgomery* (Mr. Bean & Bumpy 001) was an impressive debut from 1992, featuring the singer on relaxed material plus "Giant Steps." *Ask Me Now* (Orchard 1195) from 1998 shows a lot more seasoning and maturity without any loss of enthusiasm. *Dakini Land* (Orchard 8491) includes her interpretations of six Chick Corea songs. *Little Sunflower* (Mr. Bean & Bumpy 004) is highlighted by her rendering of her lyrics to "Armando's Rhumba," "Little Sunflower" and Duke Pearson's "Idle Moments" and is the CD to get first. While *Noel—One From The Heart* (Two Beans Music 23070) is a fine set of duets with pianist Tom Lawton on Christmas songs, *Trinity* (Mr. Bean And Bumpy 005) focuses on originals and recent material.

Website: www.barbaramontgomery.com

Shawnn Montiero
b. July 9, 1949, Boston, MA

Shawnn Montiero is an exciting singer who considers her main influences to be Carmen McRae and Sarah Vaughan.

The daughter of the late Duke Ellington bassist Jimmy Woode, she heard her parents' records from the time she was three. "During Christian Day Care Summer Camp at about age five or six, I entered the end-of-summer talent show. All the other kids sang songs like 'My Bonnie Lies Over The Ocean,' etc. I sang and scatted 'Lullaby Of Birdland' and won."

Working as a struggling singer in San Jose, California, she was discovered by Mongo Santamaria, who immediately signed her up for his band. She toured with Santamaria for two years, which really got her career going. Since then she has visited Europe frequently, worked with her godfather Clark Terry, and gigged with Kenny Barron, Bobby Durham, Dado Maroni, James Williams and Ed Thigpen. In addition to singing regularly in the Northeast, Shawnn Monteiro teaches Jazz Vocals at Rhode Island College and the Hartt School Of Music.

Recommended CDs: Of her four CDs, *Visit Me* (Monad 134), *Never Let Me Go* (Azzurra 1200326), *I'm Coming Home* (privately issued) and *One Special Night* (Whaling City Sound 22), the latter is something particularly special, teaming her with Clark Terry and her late father in a quintet in 2004.

Website: www.shawnnmonteiro.com

Joe Mooney
b. Mar 14, 1911, Paterson, NJ;
d. May 12, 1975, Fort Lauderdale, FL

Joe Mooney almost became famous a few times during his episodic and unique career, although today he is largely a cult figure. He had a basic but effective voice, a solid sense of swing, and always seemed to be winking at the audience during his interpretations, displaying sly and subtle wit.  Among his admirers were Frank Sinatra and Tony Bennett.

Joe Mooney became permanently blind in the early 1920s. He was already a talented pianist and singer by 1926 (when he was 15), teaming up with his brother Dan on radio. As the Sunshine Boys (they used the Melotone Boys as a pseudonym), Joe and Dan Mooney recorded during 1929–31 and their depictions of pop tunes are cheerful and full of spirit. The Sunshine Boys stayed together through 1936, broadcasting on WLW Radio from Cincinnati.

In 1937, Joe Mooney became the pianist and arranger for Frank Dailey. He joined Buddy Rogers the following year and contributed arrangements for Paul Whiteman, Vincent Lopez, Larry Clinton and Les Brown, plus vocal charts for the Modernaires.

In 1943 he formed the Joe Mooney Quartet, a group that featured him taking vocals and playing accordion (which he had taken up in 1935) while joined by clarinetist Andy

Fitzgerald, guitarist Jack Hotop and bassist Gate Frega. The band was very popular during 1946–49, making recordings that fell between swing and bop. They were featured on a weekly radio show and had a 27-week run on 52nd Street that briefly made them famous. In addition to Mooney's solo vocals, his band featured unusual and advanced group vocals.

After that period ended, Mooney switched to organ, had a minor hit in 1952 with his vocal on "Nina Never Knew" with the Sauter-Finegan Orchestra, recorded an album for Atlantic, and moved to Florida in 1954. Mooney continued performing regularly and he occasionally ventured to New York for television work, gaining a little attention when he recorded two albums for Columbia during 1963–65. However, because he was based in Florida, often running his club The Grate Joy, he had a relatively low visibility. And besides, his music, which always stood apart from what was popular, had little relevance to most of the music audiences of the 1960s and '70s. Joe Mooney died of a stroke in 1975 at the age of 64.

Recommended CDs: *The Sunshine Boys* (Challenge 79039) has all of the recordings by Joe and Dan Mooney during 1929–31, several of which include Tommy Dorsey guesting on trombone. *Do You Long For Oolong?* (Hep 63) has most of the Joe Mooney Quartet's 1946–47 recordings including a radio broadcast. The vocals are hip and sometimes a bit futuristic in a humorous way. The CD concludes with four numbers from 1951 featuring Mooney on organ, leading a group with guitarist Bucky Pizzarelli. *Lush Life* (Koch 8254) is a reissue of Mooney's Atlantic album of 1956, a nice easy-listening set full of charm. *The Happiness Of Joe Mooney/The Greatness Of Joe Mooney* (Koch 7886) on a single disc has Mooney's final two records, his Columbias of 1963–65 which, as with all of his music, fits in its own category.

Monette Moore

b. May 19, 1902, Gainesville, TX;
d. October 21, 1962, Los Angeles, CA

Although she was originally considered a 1920s classic blues singer, Monette Moore (like Ethel Waters) was versatile enough to perform swing, 1930s pop tunes, swinging blues and Dixieland.

Moore grew up in Texas and Kansas City (where she first sang in local venues), moving to New York in the early 1920s. After working as a piano accompanist in silent films, she recorded prolifically as a singer during 1923–25, ironically before her career in vaudeville really caught on. Of her early recordings, the highlights include "Sugar Blues," "Friendless Blues," "I Wanna Jazz Some More," "Nobody Knows The Way I Feel Dis Mornin,'" "Take It Easy" and "Get It Fixed" with some of the sidemen including cornetists Tommy Ladnier, Bubber Miley and Rex Stewart. Moore, who had a sweet and subtle voice that could be powerful, also recorded two songs apiece in 1926 and 1927 plus a medley with pianist Fats Waller in 1932 that was not released for decades. Her theater work apparently kept her too busy to record often.

Moore worked in musical comedies, in Broadway shows, with Charlie Johnson's Paradise Ten at Small's Paradise in 1927–28 (resulting in four excellent recordings including "Don't You Leave Me Here" and "You Ain't The One"), and ran her nightclub (Monette's Club) for a few years in the early-to-mid-1930s. Because of her lack of later recordings (just two titles in 1936, six songs during 1945–47 and an appearance on a George Lewis album in 1953) and her emphasis on stage work, Monette Moore never became famous in jazz despite her abilities. She was Ethel Waters' understudy in shows for

three years, performed in New York, Chicago and Hollywood, worked with Sidney Bechet and Sammy Price, appeared in the 1951 film *Yes Sir, Mr. Bones*, the 1954 version of *A Star Is Born* and had an occasional role on the *Amos 'N' Andy* television show.

Monette Moore's last jobs were working with the Young Men of New Orleans (which was comprised of ancient veterans) in Disneyland during 1961–62 and appearing with Louis Armstrong in the television special *Disneyland After Dark* shortly before her death from a heart attack.

Recommended CDs: *Vol. 1* (Document 5338) and *Vol. 2* (Document 5339) have all of Monette Moore's recordings as a leader during 1923–32.

Barbara Morrison

b. September 10, 1949, Ypsilanti, MI

A soulful singer whose music straddles the boundaries between jazz, blues and R&B (an area also explored by Ernestine Anderson), Barbara Morrison has been a popular attraction in the Los Angeles area since the 1970s. She was originally inspired by her father, who sang doo wop, gospel and jazz.

Morrison first sang in public on the radio in Detroit when she was 10 and has said that she knew she was going to be a singer by the time she was eight. After attending Eastern Michigan University in 1973, she moved to Los Angeles, where she initially sang with the L.A. Smog Control. "It was all jazz and blues when I joined Eddie 'Cleanhead' Vinson's band in 1974. It's been that way ever since."

Since that time, Morrison has worked steadily, both in Los Angeles and on tours of the U.S., Europe, Asia and Australia including a 1986 tour with the Phillip Morris Superband. She has opened for Ray Charles, performed with the big bands of Count Basie, Gerald Wilson, Clayton-Hamilton and Doc Severinsen, and appeared onstage with a long list of notables including Dizzy Gillespie, Johnny Otis, Kenny Burrell, Terrance Blanchard, Monty Alexander, Jimmy Heath, Jimmy Smith, James Moody, Joe Williams, Jon Faddis and the Juggernaut. She is also a professor at UCLA. In 1998, Morrison founded Y.E.S. (Young Educated Singers), an organization that puts on special events and uses the profits to give financial aid and scholarships to young up-and-coming jazz and blues vocalists.

Having appeared on over 20 records, Morrison cites "River's Invitation" from *Visit Me* as her favorite recording. "My goal in life is to leave a legacy to my family and the world, and to set a good example for the future jazz singers."

Recommended CDs: *I'm Gettin' Long All Right* (Chartmaker 14430) is a pretty definitive release, featuring Morrison at her soulful best on such songs as "Confessin' The Blues," "Stormy Monday," "This Bitter Earth" and "Tenderly," making the familiar tunes sound personal. Also well worth picking up are *I Know How To Do It* (Chartmaker 14460), which includes Teddy Edwards' "Don't Touch Me" and "I Ain't Got Nothing But The Blues," *Visit Me* (Chartmaker 15030), *Live Down Under* (Blue Lady/Orchard 1006) and *Live At The 9:20 Special* (Springboard 0012). But perhaps the finest

Barbara Morrison CD is *Live At The Dakota* (Dakota 002), which matches her during a concert with Houston Person and Junior Mance, bringing fresh life to such warhorses as "Please Give Me Someone to Love," "At Last" and "I'd Rather Drink Muddy Water."

Website: www.barbaramorrison.com

Ella Mae Morse
b. September 12, 1924, Mansfield, TX;
d. October 16, 1999, Bullhead City, AZ

Ella Mae Morse was an unusual big band singer because her Texas accent and slight twang showed the influence of hillbilly music, although she was actually a fine jazz vocalist. She was also among the youngest of all singers to be featured with an orchestra during the swing era.

When she was only 14, she called the Jimmy Dorsey Orchestra (which was visiting Texas) in 1938, asking for an audition. Thinking that she was 19, Dorsey hired her. That association did not last long. When the school board sent Dorsey a letter, declaring that he was responsible for her care, he fired her. In 1942, as a 17-year old, Morse joined Freddie Slack's band, immediately having a giant hit with "Cow Cow Boogie." She also scored well with "Mister Five By Five."

In 1943 Morse went out on her own, recording regularly for the Capitol label for the next 14 years. During her solo career, she performed jazz standards, pop novelties, R&B, hillbilly material, country music, bluesy numbers, early rock and roll, duets with Tennessee Ernie Ford, and collaborations with Nelson Riddle's orchestra. Although she did not have any major hits, the versatile singer sounded comfortable in all of the different settings and her recordings of "Buzz Me," "The House Of Blue Lights," and "The Blacksmith Blues" were particularly popular.

Her decision to retire from music in 1957 at the age of 33 was a surprise and she soon entered into a happy 40-year marriage, only performing on a rare basis. Ella Mae Morse, who had such strong musical potential, will always be remembered for her very first recording, "Cow Cow Boogie."

Recommended CDs: *Barrelhouse, Boogie and Blues* (Bear Family 16117) is a five-CD set that has all of Ella Mae Morse's recordings, including her six numbers with Freddie Slack's orchestra from 1942. *The Very Best Of Ella Mae Morse* (Collectables 2732) and *EMI Presents The Magic Of Ella Mae Morse* (EMI 531995) are excellent single-disc samplers of her Capitol recordings.

Lee Morse
(Lena Corinne Taylor)
b. November 30, 1897, Portland, OR;
d. December 16, 1954, Rochester, NY

Although as much of a torch singer as a jazz vocalist, Lee Morse in the 1920s adapted her style to jazz and was backed by top

players. She had an unusually deep voice, a southern accent, a wide three-octave range, and the tendency to punctuate her hotter vocal choruses with some yodeling.

She grew up in Portland, Oregon and Kooskia, Idaho as the ninth of twelve children. Four of her older brothers had a popular vocal quartet (which probably influenced her use of low notes), while her younger brother Glen Taylor would become a senator from Idaho. Married at 18 and a mother at 19, Morse abandoned both her husband and Idaho when she was 21 to sing professionally on the West Coast. She worked regularly in vaudeville during 1920–22, performed on Broadway in several plays, appeared often on the radio, and began recording in 1924.

Morse often accompanied herself on guitar and ukulele and sometimes augmented her vocals with kazoo solos. Her recordings with her "Blue Grass Boys" at various times included such sidemen as Benny Goodman, Red Nichols, Phil Napoleon, Miff Mole, Tommy Dorsey, Jimmy Dorsey and Eddie Lang. Morse, who often wrote her own songs, was at the height of her popularity in the late 1920s, but her excessive drinking and emotional personality caused havoc with her career. She missed some major opportunities, none more important than losing the lead in the Broadway show *Simple Simon* three days before its opening to Ruth Etting, who with Morse's absence was given the chance to debut "Ten Cents A Dance."

Lee Morse's career slowed down drastically in the 1930s. After seven years of regular recordings, she only made a handful of titles during 1932–33. A bad case of strep throat in 1935 knocked her out of action for a time, though she did come back to record four songs in 1938. In 1939 she moved to upstate New York and, although she occasionally performed in local nightclubs, for a time hosted a radio show and recorded four final numbers in 1951, she was forgotten by the jazz and show business worlds. Lee Morse died unexpectedly in 1954 at the age of 57 while visiting a friend.

Recommended CD: *Musical Portrait* (Take Two 420) is a fine overview of Lee Morse's career.

LPs to Search For: *Lee Morse And Her Blue Grass Boys* (Take Two 201) and *Lee Morse Revisited* (Take Two 213) have additional performances from the volatile singer.

Jelly Roll Morton
(Ferdinand Joseph La Menthe)
b. September 20, 1885, Gulfport, LA;
d. July 10, 1941, Los Angeles, CA

As a pioneering jazz pianist, composer, arranger and bandleader, Jelly Roll Morton's accomplishments and innovations (even when he did not exaggerate them) are huge. And although he only recorded one chorus as a singer in the 1920s, his late 1930s recordings often feature him as a touching and wistful singer-pianist looking back nostalgically to early New Orleans.

Because his bragging nature and propensity for tall tales led to him being underrated for decades, Morton's actual musical feats are well worth repeating. As an immediately distinctive pianist, Morton was a very significant figure in the transition between ragtime and classic jazz, improvising and writing with the structures of ragtime as a starting point. As a composer, he penned such future standards as "King Porter Stomp," "Milenburg Joys," "Wolverine Blues," "The Pearls," "Grandpa's Spells," "Mr. Jelly Lord," "Shreveport Stomp," "Black Bottom Stomp," "Winin' Boy Blues," "Don't You Leave Me Here," "Sweet Substitute" and "Wild Man Blues." As an arranger, Morton made superb use of the three-minute limitations of '78' records with a mixture of arranged passages, jammed ensembles and concise solos. As a bandleader he also knew how to bring out the best in his musicians, whether they were virtuosos or primitives. While his often-abrasive personality proved to be his own worst enemy, he was a musical giant.

After brief flings with the guitar and trombone, Morton began specializing on piano when he was 10. The 1900–22 period found Morton (who gave himself the title of Jelly Roll) working at a bewildering assortment of occupations. In addition to playing piano for Storyville's more prestigious bordellos, he was a pool hustler, a boxing promoter, a tailor, a gambling house manager, a comedian in traveling shows, a hotel manager and a pimp. After a formative period in New Orleans, Morton worked throughout the South, visited Chicago as early as 1914, played his brand of jazz in San Francisco the following year, performed music in Alaska, Wyoming, Denver and Tijuana, and called Los Angeles his home base during 1917–22. During the L.A. years, Morton realized that his real calling was being a musician.

For Jelly Roll Morton, the glory years were spent in Chicago (1923–27) and to a lesser extent New York (1928–30). In 1923 he recorded a series of piano solos that feature him in brilliant form. Morton also sounded quite at home on a session with the New Orleans Rhythm Kings that was one of the first integrated jazz record dates. In 1926, he initiated a series of exciting band recordings with his Red Hot Peppers for the Victor label that helped to define classic New Orleans jazz, even as the idiom was beginning to go out of style. And on "Doctor Jazz," Morton took his first vocal.

After moving to New York in February 1928, Morton at first repeated his Chicago successes, but by the following year he was having difficulty hiring musicians who were worthy of his music. Still, despite some undisciplined dates, he recorded occasional classics until his Victor contract ran out in 1930. The onset of the Depression, coupled with the constant evolution of jazz and his personality resulted in Morton going through hard times. He was only on one record date during 1931–37: two songs with trumpeter Wingy Manone's pickup group in 1934. Morton was ripped off by his publishers, rarely receiving royalties even as some of his songs, most notably "King Porter Stomp," were performed nightly on the radio by swing big bands of the mid-1930s. He worked only sparingly, playing anonymously in pit bands for musical revues and in run-down dives. During 1936–38 he played at and managed the seedy Jungle Club in Washington, DC.

In 1938 Morton's fortune seemed to be changing. Alan Lomax of the Library of Congress wanted to interview him about the early days of New Orleans. Morton used the occasion to play and sing music at great length in addition to telling tales. Although he was never paid for all of this work (which totaled eight hours of usable storytelling and music) and the performances were not released to the general public until after his death, Morton created a timeless narrative, punctuated by plenty of proof of his musical greatness. Other than the earlier "Dr. Jazz," it was his first opportunity to be documented singing, and he can be heard on such numbers as "Mr. Jelly Lord," the delightful "Animule Ball," "Pallet

On The Floor," "Honky Tonk Blues," "C.C. Rider," "The Murder Ballad," an uncensored "Winin' Boy Blues" and a few other songs.

In late 1938, Morton decided that it was time for him to make a major impact on the swing world. He returned to New York with some newly written songs and secured some record dates. Unfortunately, none of his new tunes became hits, and such songs as "Good Old New York," "Big Lip Blues," "Get The Bucket" and "My Home Is In A Southern Town" (each of which he sang with a band) never went anywhere. His best later record sessions were made in December 1939, alternating solo piano pieces with numbers on which he accompanied his own heartfelt vocals. Among the latter are "Winin' Boy Blues," "Buddy Bolden's Blues" (also known as "I Thought I Heard Buddy Bolden Say"), "Don't You Leave Me Here" and "Michigan Water Blues."

With his heart failing and his spirit broken for a second time by the indifference of the New York music world, the frustrated Morton moved with his ailing car and all of his belongings to Los Angeles in late 1940, where he hoped to have a fresh start. Although he put together a new band and started to write more music, it was too late. He died in the summer of 1941 at the age of 55, missing the New Orleans jazz revival by just a few years.

Recommended CDs: For Jelly Roll Morton's instrumental music, it is impossible to beat his piano solos on *Ferd "Jelly Roll" Morton* (Retrieval 79002) and the five-CD set *Jelly Roll Morton Centennial: His Complete Victor Recordings* (Bluebird 2361), which has all of his best band recordings. The magnificent eight-CD box *The Complete Library Of Congress Recordings* (Rounder 1888) has everything that Morton recorded for Alan Lomax. The performance sections (including the vocals) of his marathon Library of Congress dates are also available separately on four individual CDs: *Kansas City Stomp* (Rounder 1091), *Animule Dance* (Rounder 1092), *The Pearls* (Rounder 1093) and *Winin' Boy Blues* (Rounder 1094). Probably the best Morton vocal set is the *Last Sessions: Complete General Recordings* (GRP/Commodore 403), which has his 13 solo performances (five with vocals) and a dozen band sides of 1940 (10 of which he sings on), even if most of the band titles (other than "Sweet Substitute") were doomed to obscurity.

Maria Muldaur
(Maria Grace Rose Dominica D'Amato)
b. September 12, 1943, New York, NY

Maria Muldaur deserves an entry in any book on blues singers, jazz vocalists, R&B performers, folk singers and even pop music. Her roots style fits easily into many genres without being confined to any one.

Her tastes in music were eclectic and open-minded from the start. "I had an aunt who loved country music so the first music I remember listening to was Kitty Wells, Hank Williams, Hank Snow and Hank Thompson. In junior high I formed a doo wop girls group called the Cameos and in high school I formed another band, the Cashmeres. I started getting into jazz, blues and folk while hanging out in Greenwich Village, which was my neighborhood. Then in 1962 I was in a bluegrass band with David Grisman called Maria and the Washington Square Ramblers." The following year she joined the Even Dozen Jug Band.

"Victoria Spivey and Sippie Wallace were two genuine blues queens who took me under their wing and taught me about performing, from stage presence to singing techniques. Victoria signed the Even Dozen Jug Band to Spivey Records and turned me on to a lot of early blues. She told me, 'Now Honey, it ain't enough to sound good. You gotta strut your stuff.'"

In 1964, Muldaur joined the Jim Kweskin Jug Band and soon married their guitarist and vocalist Geoff Muldaur. "Geoff was convinced I was the reincarnation of Mildred Bailey." The group lasted for four years and after its breakup, two albums were recorded by Geoff & Maria Muldaur.

In 1974 Muldaur launched her solo career with a self-titled album that had a surprise hit with "Midnight At The Oasis." "I found myself the queen of pop music for a few years there. I never set out to be a pop singer or pop star. I consider much more important high points to be singing a Bob Dylan song, 'Well, Well, Well,' with Mavis Staples, 'It's A Blessing' with Bonnie Raitt, 'Gee Baby Ain't I Good To You' with Charles Brown, 'Louisiana Love Call' with Aaron Neville and "Rockin' Chair' with Hoagy Carmichael."

Maria Muldaur has in the years since explored many types of music that interest her, toured with Dr. John and even recorded a tribute to Peggy Lee (*A Woman Alone With The Blues*). "I made up a character, 'Les Izmore—The Patron Saint Of Music,' and I evoke him every time I sit down with a group of musicians to record or do something creative. In the end, all good music is not about cleverness or virtuosity, but about truth and getting feeling across."

Recommended CDs: Maria Muldaur has recorded quite a few rewarding albums through the years. The single-disc *30 Years Of Maria Muldaur: I'm A Woman* (Shout Factory 30219) is an excellent summation of her career. Among her more jazz-oriented releases are *Sweet And Slow* (Stony Plain 1183), *Louisiana Love Call* (Shout Factory 34343), *Jazzabelle* (Stony Plain 1188), *Meet Me Where They Play The Blues* (Telarc 83460), *Richland Woman Blues* (Stony Plain 1270), *A Woman Alone With The Blues* (Telarc 83568) and *Naughty Bawdy And Blue* (Stony Plain 1319).

Website: www.mariamuldaur.com

Mark Murphy

b. Mar 14, 1932, Syracuse, NY

A brilliant vocal innovator, Mark Murphy can turn a song inside out in his improvisations, jumping between falsetto and low bass notes, or he can treat a ballad with real sensitivity. Based in the bebop tradition, Murphy (like Betty Carter) came up with his own individual way of extending the music. He has also been a highly influential vocal teacher and a lyricist who has written words to the songs of a wide variety of jazz

musicians, from Miles Davis and Charlie Parker to Pat Metheny and Wayne Shorter, not to mention Freddie Hubbard's "Red Clay" and Oliver Nelson's "Stolen Moments."

"I first heard jazz when my Uncle Bill played me Art Tatum's 'Humoresque.' I also soon loved Nat Cole, Miles and Peggy Lee." Mark Murphy sang in his church choir, had piano lessons from the age of seven, and sang with his brother's dance band as a teenager. He studied acting and music at Syracuse University and was encouraged by Sammy Davis Jr., who heard him at a jam session in 1953 and had him join him at his own show that night. Murphy performed with Dee Felice's trio for three years on and off in Cincinnati. He made his recording debut in 1956 when he was 24, cut albums for Decca and Capitol as a typical standards singer, but mastered bop by the time he started recording for Riverside in 1961.

Despite his artistic successes on his Riverside dates, Murphy found work scarce. He spent much of 1963–72 in London, working on radio, television and at European jazz festivals. He collaborated with the Kenny Clarke–Francy Boland Orchestra in 1967 for the Midnight Mood album, but much of his work during those years was as an actor.

It was when Murphy returned to the United States in 1972 that he began to make a very strong impression on the jazz world. His yearly recordings for Muse and High Note put him in the lead among creative jazz singers, only being challenged by Kurt Elling (who in his middle register sounds very close to Murphy) in the past decade. Murphy's body of work, which includes tributes to Jack Kerouac (with the use of some of Kerouac's writing) and Nat King Cole, also includes Brazilian dates for Milestone, a duet album with pianist Benny Green for Milennium, and reissues of his out-of-print Muse sets by 32 Records.

When asked what his future goals were, Mark Murphy simply replied "Go slower and see more."

Recommended CDs: Mark Murphy's recording debut has been reissued as *Crazy Rhythm* (GRP/Decca 670). *The Best Of Mark Murphy* (Capitol 33147) has the high points from his three Capitol records, including a popular version of Steve Allen's "This Could Be The Start Of Something Big." The "real" Mark Murphy emerges on two superior Riverside albums: *Rah* (Original Jazz Classics 141) and *That's How I Love The Blues* (Original Jazz Classics 367). Murphy's European dates for such labels as Fontana, Immediate, Saba and Phoenix are now quite obscure and deserve to be coherently reissued. While the Muse label is defunct, some of the LPs were reissued by Muse before it went out of business, while 32 Jazz has also brought back some of the music. *Stolen…And Other Moments* (32 Jazz 32036) is definitive retrospective of his 1972–91 recordings and *Jazz Standards* (32 Jazz 32063), *Mark Murphy Sings Nat King Cole & More* (32 Jazz 32137) and *Songbook* (32 Jazz 32105) are excellent. Some of the best individual Muse sets are *Mark Murphy Sings* (Muse 5078), *Stolen Moments* (Muse 5102), *Bop For Kerouac* (Muse 5253), *Kerouac: Then And Now* (Muse 5359), *Beauty And The Beast* (Muse 5355), *What A Way To Go* (Muse 5419), *One for Junior* (Muse 5489), which matches Murphy with Sheila Jordan, and *I'll Close My Eyes* (Muse 5436). *Mark Murphy Sings Dorothy Fields and Cy Coleman* (Audiophile 132) is taken from radio programs of the 1970s. Other worthy recordings of the past 20 years include *Night Mood* (Milestone 9145), *September Ballads* (Milestone 9154), *Song For The Geese* (RCA 74321-44865), *Dim The Lights* (Millennium 001), *Some Time Ago* (High Note 7048), *The Latin Porter* (Go Jazz 6051), *Links* (High Note 7077), *Lucky To Be Me* (High Note 7094), *Memories Of You: Remembering Joe Williams* (High Note 7111), *Bop For Miles* (High Note 7126), *Once To Every Heart* (Verve 9872410) and *Love Is What Stays* (Universal 1714489). In 2003, Mark Murphy named as his favorite personal recordings *Rah*, *Bop For Kerouac*, *Brazil Song* and *Song For The Geese*.

Website: www.markmurphy.com

Rose Murphy

b. January 8, 1913, Lima, OH; d. November 16, 1989, Queens, NY

Rose Murphy became known as "The Chee Chee Girl" because she sang "chee chee" in her high-pitched voice somewhere during nearly every number. A fine pianist, Murphy was virtually unknown until the mid-1940s when "I Can't Give You Anything But Love" became her trademark song. Her singing was always bubbly and her style (which included cutesy percussion sounds, giggling and squeals) was considered either infectious or very limited, depending on one's point of view.

Murphy began appearing regularly on the radio around 1945. She made some radio transcriptions in 1947, and recorded for Majestic, Victor and MCA. In addition to "I Can't Give You Anything But Love" (Ella Fitzgerald made an imitation of Murphy's singing a regular part of her routine whenever she performed that song), she recorded such numbers as "When I Grow Too Old To Dream," "Girls Were Made To Take Care Of Boys," "Me And My Shadow," "Busy Line," "A Little Bird Told Me" and "Button Up Your Overcoat."

Other than a Verve album in the mid-1950s (*Chi Chi*), a record for United Artists in 1962 (*Jazz, Joy And Happiness*) and a duet set with bassist Major Holley for Black & Blue in 1980, Murphy made very few appearances on record after 1950. However, Rose Murphy performed often during her last 35 years and was popular in Europe, finding a specialized audience for her eccentric "chee chee" music.

Recommended CDs: *I Wanna Be Loved By You* (Arcade 303835) and *Busy Line* (Body And Soul 2418) have the best of Murphy's 1947–50 recordings. *Rose Murphy* (Audiophile 70) has the 1947 radio transcriptions.

Stephanie Nakasian

(Patricia Stephanie Nakasian)
b. August 29, 1954, Washington, DC

A major bop and swing singer, Stephanie Nakasian is also an important educator. She sang in church and school choirs while growing up, took extensive piano lessons, and studied violin for 10 years. However, she traces her beginnings as a jazz singer to 1980, when she met the great bop pianist Hod O'Brien, who became her husband. By then, Nakasian had a degree in Economics from Northwestern University and an MBA in Finance and International Business. "About eight months after meeting Hod, I realized that I had to decide between singing jazz and trading currency futures on Wall Street, which was my occupation at the time. I made a commitment to try singing for five years without looking back, devoting the time and effort to listening and study. Then after that I would

decide if I 'had the stuff.' The gigs came right away and I've never looked back. I miss the money, though!"

Stephanie Nakasian appeared at the 1982 Kool Jazz Festival, toured with Jon Hendricks and Company during 1983–84, and has since shared the stage with Phil Woods (with whom she recorded her debut), Lou Donaldson, Bud Shank, David "Fathead" Newman, Clark Terry, Scott Hamilton, Harry Allen, Sheila Jordan, Bob Dorough, Dick Hyman and Jim Cullum (on his Riverwalk radio series), not to mention Hod O'Brien. She was the hit of a Stan Kenton Tribute Concert in which she successfully emulated June Christy, and her *Thrush Hour* recording finds her successfully paying tribute individually to 20 top jazz singers, often sounding very close to the original. However, she has long had her own beautiful sound and an extroverted style full of chance taking and exciting moments. In addition, Nakasian teaches jazz voice and vocal jazz improvisation at the College of William and Mary in Williamsburg and has authored *It's Not On The Page! How To Integrate Jazz And Jazz Rhythm Into Choral And Solo Repertoire.*

"I came into jazz because of passion. I saw in this music a youthful, exciting life of ever-changing and ever-experimental adventure, melodies and harmonies; so many possibilities. To sing jazz is to be truly free and to really know who you are and why you're here."

Recommended CDs: *Comin' Alive* (VSOP 73) from 1995 was a notable debut and features some excellent spots for Phil Woods. *French Cookin'* (VSOP 79) has her lyrics to "Nuages," "Isfahan" and "Pent Up House." Her most obscure CD, *Bitter Sweet* (JazzMania 6002), is also excellent. *Invitation To An Escapade* (Chase 8060) has a wide variety of mostly superior material, including quite a few rarities. *Lullaby In Rhythm* (VSOP 110) is her inspired tribute to June Christy, co-featuring tenor-saxophonist Harry Allen. *Thrush Hour* (VSOP 118) has Stephanie Nakasian's tribute to 20 singers, everyone from Ethel Waters to Blossom Dearie. Not to be overlooked is a fine recent CD just released in Japan called *I Love You* (Spice of Life 0004).

Website: www.stephanienakasian.com

Kim Nalley

b. November 14, 1972, New Haven, CT

The owner of the San Francisco club Jazz At Pearl's, Kim Nalley is a bluesy jazz singer who is a little reminiscent of Dinah Washington and Helen Humes in her style and repertoire, although she has her own sound.

Nalley remembers "putting sheets on the clothes lines to make stage curtains with folding chairs in front. My brother and I would try (mostly unsuccessfully) to get the neighborhood kids to pay a nickel for the show. I would sing standards, which didn't fly well with the other project kids, so we would start taking pratfalls to regain their interest. It was ghetto vaudeville."

Taught piano by her great-grandmother, she studied opera and theater at the Educational Center of the Arts during 1986–88, later studying at College of the Holy Cross (1988–89) and history at the University of California, Berkeley (1992–96).

"Singing has always been a way for me to make ends meet. I am a poor little project girl that happened to have a voice and could hear changes. I could work at Kentucky Fried Chicken and make $3.50 an hour, or I could make $40 plus a fancy dinner and free booze in two hours despite being underage. I wanted to be a great lawyer like Thurgood Marshall; singing was just a way to work my way through school."

Moving to San Francisco in the early 1990s, Nalley worked her way through Berkeley by singing each night at little clubs and jam sessions. She was noticed singing at the Alta Plaza without amplification by Michael Tilson Thomas, the director of the San Francisco Symphony. He hired her to perform a set of Gershwin songs with the Symphony, an association that gave her a lot of attention. Since then, she has worked with the Johnny Nocturne Band, Rhoda Scott, David "Fathead" Newman, James Williams and Houston Person, appearing at many festivals including in Europe, Japan, Canada and at Monterey. After living in Switzerland during 2001–2003, she returned to San Francisco where she took over Jazz At Pearl's, which was on the brink of going out of business. In addition, Kim Nalley has acted in several plays including *Lady Day In Love* (playing Billie Holiday), *Spunk* and *Teatro Zinzanni*.

"Jazz is my language and everyone enjoys having a conversation with people in their native tongue."

Recommended CDs: Kim Nalley's debut CD, *Tuesday Live At The Alta Plaza* (MTT), will be difficult to locate. *Million Dollar Secret* (Bullseye Blues 9626) from 1999 features her with the Johnny Nocturne band. Her more recent CDs are *Need My Sugar* (CE Jazz & Blues 111469), a tribute to Nina Simone called *She Put A Spell On Me* (CE Jazz & Blues 211469) and *Ballads For Billie* (CE Jazz & Blues 96754).

Website: www.kimnalley.net

Ray Nance
b. December 10, 1913, Chicago, IL;
d. January 28, 1976, New York, NY

Ray Nance never earned his living exclusively as a singer, but he was arguably the finest male vocalist that Duke Ellington ever had.

Nance took piano lessons when he was six and studied violin for seven years before adding the cornet. As primarily a cornetist but also an occasional violinist, Nance played with the Rhythm Rascals (the band at Land College) and led a sextet in the Chicago area during 1932–36. He was always a very entertaining performer who not only played music and sang but was also a skilled dancer.

Nance was first heard on records during the short period when he was with Earl Hines' big band, taking a vocal on "Jack Climbed A Beanstalk." He was with Horace Henderson's orchestra during 1939–40, recording two sessions and singing "They Jittered All The Time." But all of that was just a warmup prior to his 23 years with Duke Ellington (1940–63).

Nance debuted with Ellington at a concert in Fargo, North Dakota that was recorded, and he found fame due to his much-copied cornet solo on "Take The 'A' Train." He was Cootie Williams' successor as a plunger mute specialist and was Ellington's first and only violin soloist, taking historic solos on the original version of "'C' Jam Blues" and "Black, Brown And Beige." As a vocalist, Nance always sounded hip and swinging, singing such numbers in the 1940s as "Bli Blip," "A Slip Of The Lip Will Sink A Ship," "Just Squeeze Me," "Hey Baby" and his trademark "Tulip Or Turnip." In the 1950s, after Betty Roche (who took a classic vocal on "Take The 'A' Train) departed, Nance took over her spot and adapted it to his own style. Otherwise Nance did not sing that much during the era (Jimmy Grissom and later Ozzie Bailey were the band's regular vocalists), but he could always be relied upon to supply an entertaining encore number when called upon.

When Cootie Williams rejoined the Ellington band after a 22-year "vacation," there was less for Nance to do and he departed in 1963. His post-Ellington years were not that eventful: occasional gigs with small swing groups, unexpected appearances on adventurous records with Chico Hamilton, Jaki Byard and Dizzy Gillespie (the latter with a group also including Chick Corea), a few brief reunions with Ellington and guest spots on an Earl Hines solo set from 1973 that features Nance taking vocals on "Black And Blue" and "I Can't Give You Anything But Love." Although highly thought of as a singer (particularly during his Ellington years), there are no single CDs available that focus on Ray Nance's singing.

Nanette Natal
b. June 10, 1945, Brooklyn, NY

Nanette Natal turned her back on a career in pop and rock music to sing jazz. She deserves to be much more famous, for she is a major jazz singer and a skilled composer.

"I started singing around the house as early as three years old. It was a musical household, with my father playing mandolin and violin with friends and family at parties. I sang songs in Italian. When I was 11, I taught myself the guitar and started writing songs. I attended Queens College in Queens, New York in the mid-sixties, but I was an Art major, having been thrown out of Concert Chorus for improvising on Handel's *Messiah*."

Natal had eclectic taste in music, enjoying everything from jazz, rock and pop music to Handel and Beethoven while growing up. Early on she was a classical singer and a member of the Helen Hayes Young People's Theater Guild, performing in the New York area. She evolved into a rock-blues-folk singer who performed originals, accompanying herself on guitar. She recorded for Vanguard and Evolution in the early 1970s and appeared with Mahalia Jackson, Odetta and Bonnie Raitt. But the record industry found it difficult to classify her.

"It was around 1976 and I was searching for a sound. A producer at Columbia Records was interested in my music if it would go in a pop direction, and he offered me eight hours in the studio to show them what I had to offer. I did my originals, but then I chose 'Sophisticated Lady' as a ballad. I turned a phrase in a way I never had before. When I entered the booth, everyone had a serious expression on their face. The engineer, an old veteran, looked at me and said 'You're a jazz singer.' Suddenly everything started to click; I finally had a category to fit in and it was jazz. It was the turning point in my musical life, my most important day. Needless to say, once I was certain that this was the path I was on, Columbia no longer was interested in signing me and my manager dropped me. But I had found myself musically, which was far more important than a recording contract."

In the late 1970s, producer John Snyder advised her to start her own record label, which became Benyo. Encouraged early on by Cedar Walton and Walter Bishop Jr., she has grown steadily as an improviser, using her technical skills as an asset in her quest to continually be more creative. Since then, Nanette Natal has continued to work in the New York area, has become an important music educator, and has put out eight impressive records on her Benyo label.

"What I love about jazz is the freedom of expression, the opportunity to improvise and to be in the moment. It always pushes me to work harder to find the truth in the work and to keep it real."

Recommended CDs: *My Song Of Something* (Benyo 3333) was the start of Nanette Natal's jazz career, and it is a very impressive beginning. *Stairway To The Stars* (Benyo 3336) has Natal stretching out at great length with her quartet, including a 14-minute version of "You Go To My Head." *Lose Control* (Benyo 3337) is comprised of music from two of her earlier jazz LPs (*Wild In Reverie* and *Hi Fi Baby*). *Is Love Enough* (Benyo 3338) matches the singer with pianist Richard Wyands, while *It's Only A Tune* (Benyo 3339) features her mostly singing original ballads, some of which could become standards if they received enough exposure.

Website: www.benyomusic.com

Shelley Neill
b. January 21, 1951, Newark, NJ

An important singer and educator based in Boston, Shelley Neill is a subtle improviser who is a fine scat-singer. She has a warm voice and a real respect for lyrics.

"I always loved to sing and got praised for doing so when I was a kid. I did all the typical things. I sang in the school chorus in junior high school. I sang in summer camp productions, at school and, like everyone else I knew, I sang along with records. I sang in my high school's annual talent shows. At 14, I sang 'The Nearness Of You' and 'My Funny Valentine' with a trio, and my friend choreographed two dance pieces she performed while I sang with the band."

Among her musical inspirations, Shelley Neill lists Sheila Jordan, Jay Clayton, Sathima Bea Benjamin and Cassandra Wilson, having studied with the former two. Because she has always wanted to retain creative control over her work, each of her five CDs (starting with 1998's *Diaphanous Apertures*) has been released on her own Cobalt Blue label.

When asked about her career, her answer was simple. "I sing. I develop and carry out musical ideas and projects that I am interested in. I turn the work into CDs. I perform, when I can, in venues where people come to listen to music, and avoid singing in places where people come to just eat and socialize."

Recommended CDs: *Diaphanous Apertures* (Cobalt Blue 001) and *Music Sweet Music* (Cobalt Blue 002) mostly feature Shelley Neill's fresh and creative renditions of standards. *The Blues Run Through It* (Cobalt Blue 003) and *Envisioning Blue* (Cobalt Blue 004) "represent my four-year commitment to exploring the impact of blues on jazz from a vocalist's perspective." Her sidemen include pianist Laszlo Gardony and violinist John Blake Jr. *Entrée Blue* (Cobalt Blue 005) has

her returning to standards, although sometimes with bluesy interpretations.

Website: www.cobaltbluemusic.org

Lauren Newton
b. November 16, 1952, Coos Bay, OR

Though she was born in Oregon, Lauren Newton has long been one of the most important singers in the European avant-garde jazz world, constantly expanding her vocal technique to include a wide range of sounds.

"My father played bass and sang in jazz combos. At home we listened mostly to jazz LPs as well as classical music." She had piano lessons and briefly played violin and guitar but her main interest as a teenager was in painting and drawing. Newton attended the University of Oregon and earned a music degree in 1975. "I decided to make singing my profession during my junior year at the University of Oregon, focusing on modern classical music, since jazz was not a part of the curricula at the time. It was in Europe that I began looking for ways of applying my classical training to jazz oriented music and, vice-versa, applying my love of experiment and improvisation to a 'classical' setting."

Newton moved to Europe in 1974, working toward her Master's degree at the Music University in Stuttgart, Germany. After her graduation in 1977, she decided to remain overseas due to the opportunities given her to sing with both contemporary classical and advanced jazz music groups. She became a founding member of the Vienna Art Orchestra, performing at festivals in Europe and touring the United States, Mozambique, India and Thailand through 1989. Newton's voice, whether being used in the ensembles or as a solo instrument, helped give the group a unique and distinctive sound.

Lauren Newton also worked with Bobby McFerrin, Jeanne Lee, Urszula Dudziak and Jay Clayton in Vocal Summit starting in 1982, has been on projects with Anthony Braxton (1998) and Joachim Kuhn, and has frequently performed with bassist Joelle Leandre's quartet since 1995. In addition, there were concerts and three albums with Austrian poet Ernst Jandl, and many performances featuring her singing music written by contemporary classical composers. She has composed music for radio plays (for German, Swiss and Austrian radio) and for film. As an educator, Newton was appointed in 2002 to a professorship for jazz singing and free improvisation at the Musikhochschule Luzern in Lucerne, Switzerland. In the future, she hopes to publish a book on vocal free improvisation.

"I do not perform jazz in the traditional sense but take the freedom of using improvisation and vocalization in the extended sense, that is of being able to develop a personal sound, style and statement either within a certain compositional framework or completely spontaneously. During the '70s, in searching for new ways to use my voice in music, I took the only two paths that were available to me at the time—jazz and contemporary 20th century music. The work-in-progress thereafter brought me together with musicians and music enthusiasts who were just as eager as I to hear the voice in ways beyond the usual singing of melodies with lyrics. In this sense, I have always been singer and composer simultaneously, constantly researching and reveling in the music of the moment."

Recommended CDs: Lauren Newton recorded at least 17 albums with the Vienna Art Orchestra. Of her solo work, 1983's *Timbre*, which was reissued in 1998 as *Filigree* (Hatology 519), was her debut as a leader. In 2004 she named it as among her personal favorites along with *18 Colors* (Leo 245), *Composition 192* (Leo 251) with Anthony Braxton, *The Lightness Of Hearing* (Leo 347), *Timbre Plus* (ARBE 11) and *Artisan Spirits* (Leo 419). *Face It* (Leo 450) is a set of free improvisation duets with Joelle Leandre from 2005 while *Soundsongs* (Leo 473) features Lauren Newton's remarkable unaccompanied improvisations.

Website: www.laurennewton.com

Maggie Nicols
(Maggie Nicholson)
b. February 24, 1948, Edinburgh, Scotland

A major avant-garde vocalist from Scotland, Maggie Nicols often includes aspects of her Scottish musical heritage in her adventurous improvisations.

Born Maggie Nicholson, she used the name Maggie Nichols in 1968 and a few years later shortened it to Maggie Nicols. At 15, she dropped out of school to work as a dancer. The following year she made her debut as a singer, performing in a strip club in Manchester. Around that time, Nicols discovered jazz and began working with pianist Dennis Rose, singing bop, standards and occasional originals. She split 1966 between working as a dancer and hostess in Greece and Iran with the Jon Lei Dancers and performing as a dancer at the Moulin Rouge in Paris.

Her career and life changed permanently in 1968 when she became a member of John Stevens' Spontaneous Music Ensemble. Singing free improvisations with the pioneering band, Nichols performed at Berlin's Total Music Meeting that year with guest guitarist John McLaughlin. From then on, she has been considered one of the leading avant-garde singers.

Maggie Nicols has worked in a large number of settings in the years since. Among her more significant projects have been performing with Keith Tippetts' 50-piece Centipede, being part of the vocal group Voice with Julie Tippetts, Phil Minton and Brian Ely, collaborating with pianist Irene Schweizer and bassist Joelle Leandre as Les Diaboliques, performing with Scottish percussionist Ken Hyder as the Hoots and Roots Duo, in duos with pianist Pete Nu, her daughter, singer Aura Marina and pianist Steve Lodder, and a project with lighting designer Sue Neal called Light And Shade. Other associations have included drummer Baby Sommer, soprano saxophonist Lol Coxhill and Trevor Watts' Moiré Music.

Maggie Nicols, who performs regularly in Europe and Canada, has also been active as an educator (running voice workshops since the 1970s) and as a feminist. She started the Feminist Improvising Group with Lindsay Cooper and organized a women's workshop performance group in 1980 called Contradictions that is still active.

Recommended CDs: Maggie Nicols has recorded a great deal as a sideperson and as a leader. Among her most intriguing releases are *Nichols 'N' Nu* (Leo 127), *The Storming Of The Winter Palace* (Intakt 003), *Transitions* (Emanem 4068) and

a trio of CDs with Les Diaboliques: *Les Diaboliques* (Intakt 033), *Splitting Image* (Intakt 048), and *Live At The Rhinefalls* (Intakt 059).

LPs to Search For: *Voice* (Ikun 110) and *Sweet And S'ours* (FMP 38) are thus far rather scarce.

Website: www.maggienicols.com

Judy Niemack
b. March 11, 1954, Pasadena, CA

An adventurous jazz singer based in Germany who has become a top educator, Judy Niemack always performs intriguing music, pushing forward the bebop tradition.

She sang in her church choir for 10 years and was familiar with the current pop scene but did not hear much jazz until she was 17. "I was introduced to live jazz by a high school friend who was studying saxophone with Warne Marsh, who lived in the neighboring town of Altadena. I often went to concerts of jazz greats at the Lighthouse in Hermosa Beach with a bunch of young musicians who studied with Warne." Niemack studied at Pasadena City College, the New England Conservatory of Music and the Cleveland Institute of Music during 1972–75.

Back in Los Angeles, she took lessons from Warne Marsh, an association that lasted until his death in 1981. He taught her to sing like a horn. After she moved to New York in 1977, Marsh appeared with her for a week at the Village Vanguard. She soon made her recording debut. During the next 15 years she developed into a widely respected singer and lyricist. Niemack has written the words to such pieces as Clifford Brown's "Daahoud," Thelonious Monk's "Misterioso," Bill Evans' "Interplay," Richie Powell's "Time" and works by Don Grolnick, Steve Slagle, Mike Stern, Lee Konitz, Larry Schneider, Richie Beirach and Pat Metheny. In addition, she has had important associations with Toots Thielemans, James Moody, Lee Konitz, Clark Terry, Kenny Barron, Fred Hersch, Kenny Werner and Joe Lovano.

Judy Niemack began teaching in New York in 1980, first sang in Europe in 1982, and in 1993 joined the jazz faculty at the Royal Conservatory of Antwerp, Belgium. In October 1995, she became the first Vocal Jazz Professor in Germany. Niemack also teaches regularly at the Musikene Conservatory in San Sebastian, Spain and each summer is part of the faulty of the Janice Borla Vocal Jazz Camp in Chicago. She married guitarist Jeanfrancois Prins in 1998 and lives in Germany but visits the United States often.

"I enjoy communicating with the listeners, expressing the emotional side of the music through the lyrics, as well as the creative freedom of being part of an ensemble in which each musician spontaneously interacts and improvises within the structure of the song. I love improvising: the risk and joy of creating on the spot is exhilarating."

Recommended CDs: All of Judy Niemack's recordings are at least excellent, for she adds enthusiasm, creativity and lots of surprises to her interpretations of standards, whether singing the lyrics straight, debuting her own words or scatting. One cannot go wrong by acquiring *Blue Bop* (Freelance 009), *Long As You're Living* (Freelance 014), her duets with pianist Kenny Barron on *Heart's Desire* (Stash 548), *Straight Up* (Freelance 18), *Mingus, Monk And Mal* (Freelance 21), which teams her in duets with pianist Mal Waldron, *Night And The Music* (Freelance 26), *About Time* (Sony Jazz 509824), *What's Going On* (Temps 1062) or *Blue Nights* (Blujazz 3353), which has guest appearances from altoist Gary Bartz and trumpeter Don Sickler along with strong contributions from Jeanfrancois Prins.

LPs to Search For: *By Heart* (Sea Breeze 2001) from 1978 was Judy Niemack's recording debut, and she shows a great deal of potential. It is surprising that a decade passed before her next record date as a leader.

Website: www.judyniemack.com

Lisa Nobumoto
b. September 3, 1963, Los Angeles, CA

A versatile singer who has been associated with tenor-saxophonist Teddy Edwards and her late husband pianist George Gaffney, Lisa Nobumoto's music ranges from tributes to Dinah Washington (who she can closely emulate) to R&B and pop.

"My mother played all kinds of music when I was young and she loved such artists as Arthur Prysock, Nancy Wilson, Al Green, and Charlie Pride. I would sing along and really felt emotion from what each of these singers expressed. I became sort of bonded with this music when I was about two or three years old." She sang at family functions and at church, starting with private vocal lessons when she was six.

After attending college, in 1985, she joined and toured with *The Gwen Brisco Show*. "I gained a lot of experience from that organization, touring Australia, Singapore, Indonesia, Germany, Austria, Switzerland, and working a lot in Las Vegas. We worked continuously for two years straight."

Since then, Lisa Nobumoto has worked and recorded with the late Teddy Edwards, led her own combos in Los Angeles, worked extensively in Las Vegas, and performed with Norman Connors, contributing "Adore I Loved" to his upcoming CD. "My musical goals include writing, writing, and more recording of what I have been writing. Jazz is my love, but I also enjoy many kinds of beautiful, great music."

Recommended CDs: *First Time Out* is a privately issued set with the Teddy Edwards Sextet. Lisa Nobumoto also sings on three songs on Edwards' *Blue Saxophone* (Antilles 517527). A CD of her own music is planned in the near future.

Website: www.lisanobumoto.com

Chris Norris
b. ca. 1958; d. 1998, San Diego, CA

Chris Norris was one of the top trad jazz singers of the 1980s and '90s. Classically trained as a vocalist, she was an English Literature PhD and a well-respected professor at the University of California in San Diego.

In 1982 she sat in with the Golden Eagle Jazz Band at their regular gig at the Depot in San Juan Capistrano. Norris' renditions of blues (which she only had started singing the previous years) and 1920s jazz classics so impressed the musicians that she became the band's regular singer. Although inspired by

the recordings of Bessie Smith and Ma Rainey, there was also a little bit of Ruth Etting heard in the cry of her voice as she slid between notes.

A major attraction with the band, Chris Norris would have become better known as a singer if she did not stay based in Southern California. Fortunately she made three albums with the Golden Eagles for the Stomp Off label (plus a few for their own label) and was very well featured, being the band's star attraction. At the Santa Rosa Jazz Festival in 1995, she presented a tribute to Ma Rainey.

Tragically, Chris Norris was struck down by breast cancer, passing away in 1998.

Recommended CDs: *Morocco Blues* (Stomp Off 1192) is the only Chris Norris/Golden Eagles recording thus far put out on CD by Stomp Off.

LPs to Search For: *Oh My Babe* (Stomp Off 1080) and *Young Woman's Blues* (Stomp Off 1100) have plenty of vocals by Chris Norris, who is pictured on the latter's cover.

Helen O'Connell
b. May 23, 1920, Lima, OH; d. September 9, 1993, San Diego, CA

For a time, Helen O'Connell was one of the more popular singers in the swing world. She did not evolve or grow much musically after her period in the spotlight ended, but she will always be remembered for her early 1940s recordings with the Jimmy Dorsey Orchestra, particularly "Green Eyes." She used her limited voice to its advantage and found her place in music history.

After gaining early experience singing locally in Ohio, O'Connell toured for a year and a half with Jimmy Richards' nine-piece band, worked on St. Louis radio, and sang with Larry Funk's band. In 1938, she joined the Dorsey Orchestra. Early on it was decided that she was best on medium-tempo material where her youthful sensuality shone through, so the ballads were left for Bob Eberle. She had minor hits with her versions of "All Of Me," "Embraceable You," "Jim" and "When The Sun Comes Out" (introducing the latter). Her cheerful exuberance helped the Dorsey band, which was struggling during the era.

Things changed when O'Connell and Eberle began to be featured on the same records. Usually Eberle would take a straight vocal chorus and, after a brief instrumental interlude for Dorsey's clarinet or alto, O'Connell was featured swinging on a chorus of her own. In less frequent cases, O'Connell started the piece and Eberle brought it to a conclusion. While the two singers first collaborated on "Do It Again" in late 1939, they hit pay dirt during 1941–42 with "Amapola," "Green Eyes" (O'Connell's squeal on the latter is memorable), "Tangerine," "Brazil" and, in the 1943 Red Skelton movie, *I Dood It*, "Star Eyes." Other O'Connell-Eberle collaborations include "Blue," "Yours," "In The Hush Of The Night," "Time Was," "Jim," "It Happened In Hawaii," "Any Bonds Today," "I Said No," "Not Mine" and "If You Build A Better Mousetrap."

In 1944 Helen O'Connell left Jimmy Dorsey's band to get married. She returned to singing on a part-time basis a few years later (making an appearance in the film *The Fabulous Dorseys*), worked in the 1950s on the *Today* television show, sang whenever she wanted (making occasional recordings), and toured in a nostalgia show in the late 1980s with Kay Starr, Rosemary Clooney and Rose Marie as *Four Girls Four*. But one never got the impression that Helen O'Connell took her singing very seriously or missed it much after leaving Dorsey.

Recommended CDs: Helen O'Connell's hit recordings with Jimmy Dorsey are not available on CD in coherent fashion yet, but *The Best Of Helen O'Connell On Capitol* (Collector's Classics 369) and *Here's Helen/Green Eyes* (Collectables 7300) gives listeners some of her best later records.

LPs to Search For: *The Best Of Jimmy Dorsey* (MCA 2-4073) is a two-LP set that contains O'Connell's most famous performances with Dorsey.

Anita O'Day
(Anita Belle Colton)
b. October 18, 1919, Chicago, IL;
d. November 23, 2006, Los Angeles, CA

Anita O'Day was most unusual among the band singers of the Swing era in that, after the big bands broke up, she never tried to record commercial material and become a pop star. She stuck to jazz and was at her peak during the 1950s. Her career was like a roller coaster and the ride was usually exciting if a bit crazy.

Struggling to make money as a teenager during the Depression, she took the last name of O'Day (which is Pig Latin for "dough") and became a marathon dancer. Although she was never able to hold notes for long, she developed her own distinctive and hip singing style. After working with Max Miller's group in Chicago during 1939–40, O'Day joined Gene Krupa in 1941, just as his band was entering its greatest period. Succeeding Irene Daye, Anita O'Day had hits in "Let Me Off Uptown" (her most famous recording), "Thanks For The Boogie Ride," "Massachusetts" and "Bolero At The Savoy." The former two songs have her engaging Roy Eldridge in spontaneous-sounding dialogue before his solo. Always thinking of herself as one of the musicians, she refused to wear glamorous gowns or to get special treatment.

When the Krupa band broke up in 1943, O'Day was briefly with Woody Herman and spent a year with Stan Kenton (1944–45) where her hit was "And Her Tears Flowed Like Wine." However, she did not care for Kenton's music and was glad to bow out in favor of June Christy, who originally sounded very close to O'Day in her tone and style. Back with Krupa, O'Day helped his new band during 1945–46 by having strong selling records in "Opus No. 1" and "Boogie Blues."

Anita O'Day's solo career began in 1946, and she was immediately open to the influence of bebop, developing her scatting. During 1952–63 she recorded regularly for Verve and was at the top of her game despite having become a heroin addict. The high point of her career, her appearance at the 1958 Newport Jazz Festival, was filmed and is one of the main highlights of the film *Jazz On A Summer's Day*. She is lowdown on "Sweet Georgia Brown" and scats in dazzling fashion on "Tea For Two."

After her Verve period ended, O'Day scuffled and nearly died from heroin. She kicked that habit and in the 1970s wrote her frank autobiography *High Times, Hard Times*. O'Day made a strong comeback for a time, but by the 1980s she was an alcoholic and her voice was going fast. While she continued performing despite her worsening health almost up until the time she died in 2006, her voice was completely gone by the time of 1993's *Rules Of The Road*. *Indestructible* from 2006 is just plain sad and unlistenable. But it had been quite a career with many adventures along the way.

Recommended CDs: *Let Me Off Uptown: The Best Of Anita O'Day* (Columbia/Legacy 65625) has all of her most important recordings with Gene Krupa. *Complete Signature & London Recordings* (Jazz Factory 22824) is a two-CD set that has radio transcriptions from O'Day's periods with Krupa and Kenton plus all of her studio recordings from 1945–50. *The Complete Anita O'Day Verve/Clef Sessions* (Mosaic 9-188) is an out-of-print limited-edition nine-CD box set that features the singer at her peak. Among the individual releases from this box that are available are *The Lady Is A Tramp* (Verve 889 242), *This Is Anita* (Verve 829 261), *Pick Yourself Up With Anita O'Day* (Verve 314 517 329), *Anita Sings The Most* (Verve 829 577), *Anita Sings The Winners* (Verve 837 929), *Swings Cole Porter* (Verve 849 266), *Anita O'Day And Billy May Swing Swing Rodgers And Hart* (Verve 235302), *All The Sad Young Men* (Verve 314 517 065) and *Time For Two* (Verve 559 808). *I Get A Kick Out Of You* (Evidence 22054) and *Mello-Day* (GNP Crescendo 2126) are excellent albums from the 1970s, while *In A Mellow Tone* (DRG 5209) from 1989 is Anita O'Day's last worthwhile recording.

LPs to Search For: *Anita O'Day In Berlin* (MPS 20750) from 1970 was her first recording from her comeback years and finds her back in excellent form.

Sy Oliver
(Melvin James Oliver)
b. December 17, 1910, Battle Creek, MI;
d. May 28, 1988, New York, NY

Best-known as a swing arranger who was a fine trumpeter, Sy Oliver could also be relied upon during his period with Jimmie Lunceford to be a cheerful vocalist, and one of several musicians (along with altoist Willie Smith and tenor-saxophonist Joe Thomas) able to sing as part of Lunceford's glee club.

Oliver grew up in Zanesville, Ohio and began playing trumpet at age 12. While in high school, he worked with Cliff Barnett's Club Royal Serenaders for three years. After graduation, he played with Zach Whyte's Chocolate Beau Brummels and Alphonso Trent, two of the top territory bands. After working in Columbus, Ohio as a teacher and a freelance arranger during 1930–33, Oliver sent some charts to the Jimmie Lunceford Orchestra and was soon asked to join as both a staff arranger and a member of the trumpet section.

Sy Oliver's arrangements helped define the Lunceford sound, his trumpet solos (which were often muted) were attractive, and he took easy-going vocals on such numbers as "Miss Otis Regrets," "Dream Of You," "Four Or Five Times," "The Merry-Go-Round Broke Down" and "Sweet Sue, Just You."

Hot Lips Page

In 1939 Sy Oliver accepted a lucrative offer to join Tommy Dorsey's band, a defection that in time led to Lunceford's decline while giving TD a new musical direction. While with Dorsey, Oliver stuck to arranging except for taking a rare vocal, best of which are "Swingin' On Nothin,'" "Yes Indeed," (the latter two numbers were shared with Jo Stafford), "Chicago" (with the Sentimentalists), "There's Good Blues Tonight" and "Don't Be A Baby, Baby." Oliver served in the military during 1943–45 and continued contributing both charts and occasional vocals to TD through 1950.

Oliver also led short-term big bands of his own starting in 1947, recording for MGM that year and being a musical director for the Decca label for much of the 1950s. Although the emphasis was on his writing, he took fine vocals on "When My Sugar Walks Down The Street" (1949) and some remakes of Lunceford hits in 1950.

Late in his life, Oliver returned to playing and singing, taking vocals on three obscure albums during 1972–76, mostly redoing his earlier Lunceford hits. While singing may have only been the third most important aspect to his musical career, Sy Oliver's accessible and spirited vocals are generally memorable and fit the songs well.

Hot Lips Page
(Oran Page)
b. January 27, 1908, Dallas, TX;
d. November 5, 1954, New York, NY

Oran "Hot Lips" Page was one of the great trumpeters to emerge during the 1930s. He was also a skilled blues singer who was a major part of the Kansas City jazz scene before he moved East.

Page started on the trumpet when he was 12. Living in Dallas, he gained important experience playing in groups behind such blues singers as Ma Rainey, Bessie Smith and Ida Cox. He performed with Troy Floyd in San Antonio and throughout Texas with Sugar Lou and Eddie's Hotel Tyler Band. In 1928, the 20-year-old arrived in Kansas City and soon joined Walter Page's Blue Devils, spending two years with the legendary band, making his recording debut with the unit in 1929. He next joined the Bennie Moten Orchestra. Although he took the trumpet solos on Moten's record dates, the vocals were taken by Jimmy Rushing. After Moten died suddenly in 1935, Page led his own quintet for a few months before joining the Count Basie Orchestra.

If Page had stayed with Basie, he would probably have been one of the stars of the band when the orchestra headed east. But Page signed with Joe Glaser (who was also Louis Armstrong's manager) and went to New York a few months before Basie, forming his own big band. The Hot Lips Page Orchestra lasted on and off through 1938 but never caught on. However, Page was heard as a vocalist for the first time on his 1938–40 record dates, sounding quite effective from the start, particularly on blues.

Page was well featured with Artie Shaw's big band of 1941–42, taking vocals on "Blues In The Night," "Take Your Shoes Off Baby" and a classic two-part "St. James Infirmary." When Shaw broke up the orchestra, Page returned to the small combos and jam sessions in which he excelled. He recorded a hit version of "Baby, It's Cold Outside" with Pearl Bailey in 1949, his "Uncle Sam Blues" was popular during wartime and he easily made the transition from swing to early R&B and back, also being heard in Dixieland settings. He never quite became a big star but he was a beloved figure, passing away in 1954 from a heart attack when he was just 46.

Recommended CDs: *1938–1940* (Classics 561), *1940–1944* (Classics 809) and *1944–1946* (Classics 950) contain all of Hot Lips Page's recordings as a leader during his most important years. *Jump For Joy* (Columbia/Legacy 65631) is an eccentric but mostly rewarding sampler that has his best recordings from 1947–50 plus earlier sideman features.

Joanie Pallatto
b. July 17, 1954, Xenia, OH

A very flexible and open-minded singer, Joanie Pallatto can sing standards quite effectively or go on adventurous flights. As the co-owner of Southport Records (along with her husband pianist/composer Bradley Parker-Sparrow), she has done a major service in documenting the Chicago jazz scene of the past 20 years.

"My mother played guitar while my father played violin and guitar. Each holiday, they would bring out their instruments and play and sing together. I often sang in the kitchen with my mother. She would harmonize, then I would trade off and harmonize to her melody. In ninth grade, I discovered I could really sing, in my correct alto range rather than as a soprano where the teachers had always placed me, and my career path in life was crystal clear."

Pallatto played piano, violin, clarinet, wooden flute and percussion, and attended the University of Cincinnati College Conservatory of Music during 1972–76. She toured with the Glenn Miller Orchestra in 1979 before moving to Chicago, where she met Sparrow in 1980 and sang original music for the first time. She worked in the commercial studios as a voiceover artist and a studio singer for jingles. In 1986, with the start of the Southport label, she recorded her first jazz CD.

Since then, Joanie Pallatto has not only conducted her own solo career, recording regularly and developing her own style, but she has become an expert engineer, and is involved in Southport's recordings, mixing, mastering and general production.

"I feel very fortunate to live a life of music. Expanding my career from performing as an artist to developing as a recording engineer and producer has afforded me the opportunity to be involved in music every day of my life, on many levels. The technical aspects of recording enhance the level of musicality. Using my 'ears' on a daily basis on other musicians' projects helps me to improve my own skills as a musician and engineer."

Recommended CDs: Each Joanie Pallatto recording has its own personality. *Whisper Not* (Southport 0007) from 1986 was her debut as a solo jazz artist. 1994's *Who Wrote This Song* (Southport 21) teams Pallatto with such major Chicago musicians as guitarist Fareed Haque, pianist Willie Pickens and Howard Levy on harmonica plus guest Bob Dorough. She matches creativity with tenor-saxophonist Von Freeman on *Passing Tones* (Southport 0032) and *Fire (With Von Freeman)* (Southport 0035). *Two* (Southport 0046) is a set of intimate duets with pianist Marshall Vente. *Words And Music* (Southport 0067) gives her an opportunity to explore standards, while *The King And I* (Southport 0084) co-stars pianist-composer King Fleming. *We Are Not Machines* (Southport 0093) is an unusual set by Sparrow that has Pallatto improvising on excerpts from a film score. 2003's *Canned Beer* (Southport 0098) is an eclectic project featuring pop, hip-hop, cabaret and world music pieces turned into jazz.

Website: www.chicagosound.com

Tena Palmer
b. Aug, 18, 1962, Halifax, Nova Scotia, Canada

A continually intriguing singer who is very difficult to classify, Tena Palmer gained some fame as a member of the Canadian group Chelsea Bridge, but she has traveled many miles since then.

"In the 1940s, my father was an amateur drummer for dance bands in Halifax. He had a huge record collection and a weekly radio show, featuring music from the 1920s to the '50s. He also ran a deejay service and, as a youth, I worked for him, playing big band jazz and other dance records and tapes for dances. At the same time, I was deeply involved in a highly-developed school band system in Truro, Nova Scotia. I played flute in concert bands, and baritone sax in the jazz ensemble which, in my senior year, won the Canadian Stage Band Festival. We opened for Count Basie at the National Arts Centre, Ottawa; a 'dream come true.'"

Tena Palmer did not sing much as a child, first performing in public as a vocalist during her second year at St. Francis Xavier University. "I was goaded by friends into joining the jazz choir. I got a solo by virtue of the fact that I was the only one who knew 'My One and Only Love.' I picked up lyrics easily and, by the time I began singing in earnest (1983), I had a substantial repertoire. After finishing a two-and-a-half year diploma in jazz performance on saxophone and flute, I was strongly encouraged to complete my music degree as a voice major, which I did." She also privately studied with Janet Lawson and Lee Konitz.

Interested in a wide variety of styles, she also showed interest in Celtic music. "Just when I was reaching be-bop burn-out, I began frequent trips out to the woods to play jigs, reels and the like on tin whistle with fiddlers, mandolin, guitar and banjo players."

After graduating from college in 1984, Palmer moved to Toronto and started working as a singer. She gained fame in Canada for her work with Chelsea Bridge, a group also featuring tenor-saxophonist Rob Frayne, bassist John Geggie and drummer Jean Martin during 1992–96. In 1996 her career and life took an unexpected turn as she moved to Reykjavik, Iceland, where she taught vocal jazz and worked in many different musical areas including electronic music, spoken word, Brazilian music, theater and dance works, Celtic, bluegrass and jazz. During 2001–2002 she worked with the bluegrass septet Gras. In 2003, after a six-month stay in Holland, Palmer moved back to Canada and recorded *North Atlantic Drift*, a set that featured both her ability to write colorful originals and her interest in country music. She currently teaches at Ottawa's Carleton University.

"I plan to continue singing improvised music along with many other styles which inspire my imagination. I am a born improviser and enjoy the freedom to express compositions anew each time; as their meaning changes for me in relation to my personal experience of the moment. Although I sing many other styles of music with great love and commitment, I am at heart a jazz singer and this informs all else that I do."

Recommended CDs: *Blues In A Sharp Sea* (Unity 1065), *Tatamagouche...Next Left* (Unity 144) and *Double Feature* (Unity 150) feature Tena Palmer's voice with Chelsea Bridge, one of the more underrated but worthy groups of the mid-1990s. More recently she has recorded her debut solo CD, *Crucible* (Bad Taste Records), which features experimental music, and the country-oriented *North Atlantic Drift* (TLP/Festival).

Alex Pangman
(Alexandra Ruth Pangman)
b. September 4, 1976, Mississauga, Ontario, Canada

One of the leading swing and classic jazz singers in Canada, Alex Pangman has a real feeling for the vintage music.

"A friend played 'Rosetta' for me on the guitar, I was still a teenager, and this was my initial positive introduction to jazz from the 1930s. I had heard some modern jazz as a child and was not drawn to it. 'Rosetta' was more up my alley, struck a chord with me, and soon after I was heard singing karaoke (of all things) and was asked to join a jazz band." Needing a repertoire, she buried herself in vintage jazz recordings. Among her historic inspirations, she includes Connie Boswell, Mildred Bailey, Louis Armstrong, Maxine Sullivan, Ethel Waters and Annette Hanshaw. "I listened endlessly to 78s and reissued CDs and read a lot of liner notes."

She attended the University of Toronto, studying art, but dropped out when she became ill. "When I returned to health, singing had taken the place of schooling, and had taken up most of my time and desire. The Alleycats were formed and I was officially 'in business.'" Pangman toured Canada with her Alleycats starting in 1998, gaining a great deal of recognition within a brief period of time. She has since worked with such notables as Dick Sudhalter, Jim Galloway, Peter Ecklund, Denzal Sinclaire and trombonist Dan Barrett who dubbed her "Canada's Sweetheart Of Swing."

"This is a people's music and I want lots of people to hear it, dance to it, and sing it in the shower. I also feel it's important to record some of my own jazz compositions, although my main focus will always be on the fabulous inspiring material already in existence."

Recommended CDs: *They Say* (Sensation 18), from 1999, is a debut that shows that Alex Pangman at 22 sounded very much at home with 1920s and '30s standards. *Can't Stop Me From Dreaming* (Sensation 19) features the singer with four different groups, ranging from Bix Beiderbecke-influenced Dixieland to Western Swing. *Live In Montreal* (Real Gone Gal 29) and *Christmas Gift* (Real Gone Gal 30) are her most recent recordings and find no decrease in enthusiasm and joy from the talented young singer.

Website: www.alexpangman.com

Barbara Paris
(Barbara Lynn Perea)
b. October 2, Denver, CO

A fixture in the Boulder, Colorado area, Barbara Paris has grown as a jazz singer through the years, often working with pianist Joe Bonner.

She remembers her father singing jazz to her when she was a child. She performed for years with her church choir, took piano lessons, and started playing the guitar when she was 15. Her debut as a singer was as a teenager at a jazz supper club on Lookout Mountain.

"In 1978 I realized I had to sing to die happy. I had to figure it all out but, once I made up my mind, there has been no stopping." While she often worked outside of music, jazz was always her true love. She was encouraged early on by veteran saxophonist Eddie Shu and altoist Claude Tissendier (best-known for being with Claude Bolling's orchestra); she worked in Europe with Tissendier. Paris had opportunities to sit in with Joe Pass, Freddie Hubbard and the Count Basie Orchestra. She considers her main influences to be Lil Green, Billie Holiday, Etta Jones, Nnenna Freelon and Shirley Horn.

"Meeting Joe Bonner in 1991 was the most important thing that has happened to me as a singer. He took me under his wing and has invented me. In his playing, I heard what was going on inside of me all my life. He encouraged me to record, saying 'You will never again be who you are today, so record it because you can't go back.'"

Recommended CDs: *Where Butterflies Play* (Perea 001), *Happy Talk* (Perea 002), *Day By Day* (Perea 003), which has backing by Nancy Wilson's rhythm section plus Rich Chiaraluce on tenor, and *P.S. I Love You* (Perea 004), a set of duets with Bonner, are all of Barbara Paris' recordings thus far. *Swingballadsblues&bossanovas* (Perea 005) is a fine sampler drawn from these CDs.

Website: www.barbaraparis.com

Jackie Paris
(Carlo Jackie Paris)
b. September 20, 1924, Nutley, NJ;
d. June 17, 2004, New York, NY

Jackie Paris was a pioneering bebop singer whose career was episodic and erratic. He never quite broke through or became well known.

Paris learned guitar early on (an uncle had played guitar with Paul Whiteman) and worked in vaudeville as a child. At 19, he was playing and singing with Nick Jerret's group. Paris spent two years in the Army, and by the time he made his recording debut in 1947, he was quite comfortable with bebop. He became a friend of Charlie Parker, with whom he occasionally worked, became the first singer to record a vocal version of "'Round Midnight," was part of Lionel Hampton's band during 1949–50, and his recording of "Skylark" was popular.

Paris recorded a few albums in the 1950s, guested on a record by the Donald Byrd/Gigi Gryce Jazz Lab, and worked in the 1960s with his wife at the time, singer Anne-Marie Moss. But Paris was off records altogether during 1963–80 other than singing "Duke Ellington's Sound Of Love" with Charles Mingus in 1974, and he worked more as an educator than as a performer. His last recording was in 2001. He remained active up until his death at 79, underrated until the end.

Recommended CDs: Jackie Paris' early recordings, including eight titles during 1947–49 and his first three albums, are all long out of print. *Jackie Paris Sings The Lyrics Of Ira Gershwin* (Japanese King 3011) was originally released by the Time label in 1960. *The Song Is Paris* (Impulse 9065) is considered one of his finest outings though his next recording as a leader did not take place for 19 years. His later recordings include *Jackie Paris* (Audiophile 158), *Nobody Else But Me* (Audiophile 245) and *The Intimate Jackie Paris* (Hudson 1001), the latter featuring Paris as a singer-guitarist (the only time he ever recorded on guitar) while joined in duets by bassist Mike Richmond.

Kim Parker
b. August 22, 1946, New York, NY

The daughter of Chan Parker, Kim Parker's two stepfathers were Charlie Parker and Phil Woods. She made a solid impression as a jazz singer in the 1980s but has been less active musically during the past decade.

"I was introduced to jazz through my family. My grandmother was a Ziegfeld Girl and, after she was widowed at age 33, got a job coat-checking at the Cotton Club. Her house became a frequent after-hours spot for Cab Calloway, Gene Krupa and others. My mother grew up in that environment, and in her late teens convinced my grandmother to take an apartment on 52nd Street. My mother became a fixture on The Street, becoming a club photographer so she could move between clubs and catch all the bands every night. My mother had me, got together with Bird, and there we were—three generations of jazz lovers. My mother, grandmother and I could not have a straight conversation without extensively quoting song lyrics or titles."

Kim Parker won a radio contest when she was five and began performing at summer stock three years later. Just eight when Charlie Parker died, she was 11 when Chan married Phil Woods. "I would sing my little heart out for hours with Phil on piano. He composed many songs for me to sing." She spent a year in Europe when Woods was touring with the Quincy Jones Orchestra. When she sang a program for her high school, her backup band was Phil Woods, Gary Burton, keyboardist Chris Swansen and Steve Swallow.

Parker attended Hofstra University for a year on a drama scholarship and was named "Best Jazz Vocalist" at the Villanova Intercollegiate Jazz Festival. But she decided, at least at that time, not to pursue a career as a singer. Instead she got married in 1967 and became a farmer and a housepainter in Maine. "Because I had grown up with jazz musicians and knew how difficult and spotty that life could be, I shied away from a career until I was 33. I had had my son and he was a great inspiration for me." In 1979, she began to sign in public, soon recording with pianist Larry Gelb. She eventually recorded three albums as a leader (with pianists Kenny Drew, Tommy Flanagan and Mal Waldron), toured Europe regularly, appeared at a variety of festivals, and gained some recognition. But after 1993, she sang less often (though she appeared at four Canadian festivals in 1999 and the Healdsburg Jazz Festival in 2004), owning Designer Crafts in Stroudsburg, Pennsylvania, representing over 300 American craftsmen.

"My goals are to keep discovering tunes which move me, and interpret them in ways that move others. I feel very strongly about the power of a song. To convey a story or emotion in the space of one chorus or one minute is something I will continue to strive for."

Recommended CDs: 1981's *Havin' Myself A Time* (Soul Note 121033), *Good Girl* (Soul Note 121063) and *Sometimes I'm Blue* (Soul Note 121133) are each quite enjoyable, with *Havin' Myself A Time* being a particular delight. Each album finds Kim Parker adding her own personality to the bebop and standards tradition. *A Beautiful Friendship* (Four Leaf Clover 146) from 1996 is more obscure but also quite worthy.

Website: www.kimparker.net

Gretchen Parlato

b. February 11, 1976, Los Angeles, CA

One of the top up-and-coming singers at the moment, Gretchen Parlato has a cool tone, a subtle style, and a real understanding for Brazilian music. She has been praised by the likes of Wayne Shorter, Herbie Hancock and Terence Blanchard, each of whom she has already worked with.

"My father is a jazz bassist, my mother is an artist and web designer, my grandparents were musicians and recording engineers, and my aunts and uncles are singers, dancers and actors. I sang before I could talk. There are some cassette tapes of me at two years old singing in the bathtub, making up my own songs and clapping rhythms while singing. I found a joy for music very early." Parlato attended the L.A. County High School for the Arts during 1991–94 and studied ethnomusicology at UCLA, earning a degree in Jazz Studies in 1998. She started doing studio work while at college and has appeared in several film soundtracks. She was the first vocalist to be accepted into the Thelonious Monk Institute of Jazz Performance, attending during 2001–03, and she also had private lessons with Tierney Sutton. Parlato began to perform regularly at jazz festivals in 2002, a year before she moved to New York.

In 2004, Gretchen Parlato won the Thelonious Monk Vocal Competition and was officially discovered by the East Coast jazz world. That year, when an all-star tribute to Antonio Carlos Jobim was presented at the Hollywood Bowl, she was its youngest performer. In 2005 she recorded her debut CD and she has also recorded as a sideperson with Lionel Loueke, Guilherme Vergueiro (1997–98), Kendrick Scott, Walter Smith III, Terence Blanchard (Flow), Morrie Louden and Sean Jones. In 2007 she performed with Wayne Shorter in Paris.

"I think 'jazz' is such a broad genre nowadays that it allows all of us to bring many other influences into it. There is comfort in its tradition, but jazz should challenge us to move our vision forward. I think it is so important for each of us to have our own unique sound in our art."

Recommended CDs: Gretchen Parlato recorded as early as 1994 but surprisingly only has one CD out as a leader thus far, the privately issued *Gretchen Parlato* from 2005.

Website: www.gretchenparlato.com

Rebecca Parris

b. December 28, 1951, Newton, MA

Rebecca Parris is a powerful singer with a technique comparable to Sarah Vaughan and a bluesy style that hints at the jazz side of Etta James.

She was born into a family of musicians and educators. Parris performed from the age of six, mostly in musical theater. Her parents encouraged her to pursue the study of music. "My mom was a concert pianist and church organist, while my dad (who wore many hats) was also a church organist and choir director. The house was filled with classical and liturgical music. I remember following my mother around the house when I was three, constantly singing my own improvised hymns and etudes. It drove her a little nuts after hearing it for hours. When I ended up a jazz singer she told me she should have seen the 'writing on the wall' then."

Parris began performing early, performing in musical theater from the age of six. In school she had opportunities to play many instruments, including piano, violin and cello, and she taught herself folk guitar in high school. She studied with world-famous vocal coach Blair MacClosky, who was her uncle. Parris started her professional career in music working with various top-40 bands in the Northeast. She attended the Boston Conservatory of Music for 1½ years as a drama major but became bored and returned to full-time performing. After singing rock for a decade, she dedicated herself to jazz in the early 1980s. "I've had such a diverse musical history, but the movement into jazz was inevitable. It was the one arena in which I could finally invest all my study and performance experience and also be as spontaneous as I like."

Rebecca Parris began recording in 1985. Gigging regularly, she has appeared at many major festivals and made guest appearances with Wynton Marsalis, Dizzy Gillespie, Count Basie, Woody Herman, Terry Gibbs and Buddy Rich. She has had friendships with Carmen McRae and Sarah Vaughan, recorded and toured with Gary Burton during 1993–94, and maintained a busy schedule as an educator, clinician and lecturer.

"I have a goal to reinstate music in the public schools that have lost it and to continue that fight until the need for it is totally understood and realized."

Recommended CDs: Rebecca Parris has thus far recorded *A Passionate Fling* (Shira 1001), *Live At Chan's* (Shira 1002), *Double Rainbow* (Shira 1003), *Love Comes And Goes* (Entertainment

Exclusives 1001), *Spring* (Music Masters 65076), *It's Another Day* (GRP 9738), *A Beautiful Friendship* (Altenburgh JGA-0019) with the Kenny Hadley Big Band, a ballad program for *My Foolish Heart* (Koch 7887), *The Secret Of Christmas* 1004) and *You Don't Know Me* (Saying It With Jazz). The last one is a fine straight-ahead set with the singer's trio and guests Gary Burton and tenors Jerry Bergonzi and Houston Person.

Website: www.rebeccaparris.com

Sarah Partridge
b. October 28, 1960, Boston, MA

A singer with a real feeling for lyrics and swing standards, Sarah Partridge has made a strong impression since becoming a jazz singer in 1991. "I love to work around the melody. I love to scat a chorus or trade fours with a musician. You can't do that in any other musical forum. I also love an audience; that's probably the actress in me. I owe them something, not just the music, but a piece of me."

"My parents were huge jazz fans, particularly my father. I began singing along to Chris Connor, June Christy, Dakota Staton, Ella and Sarah at about the age of five. I think the first song I learned the whole way through was 'Lush Life.'" However, her first career was as an actress. Partridge appeared in high school musicals, was a theater major at Northwestern University, and had a role in *Risky Business* opposite Tom Cruise. She appeared in other films, sitcoms, soap operas and commercials in addition to doing voice-overs.

Then in 1991 she was at the Improv in Los Angeles and, at the urging of friends, she participated in a karaoke contest, singing "Summertime." A booking agent was in the audience, assumed she was a professional jazz singer, and got her a gig at a jazz concert. Within a few years Sarah Partridge was singing regularly and had moved to New York.

"The most important association for me was with the late Doc Cheatham. When I moved to New York, he was the first musician to invite me up on a bandstand. Week after week, I would join him for a few numbers at his Sunday Brunch gig at Sweet Basil in the Village. We became friends and started getting gigs together. He was a true inspiration to me, both personally and professionally." She has also worked with a variety of mainstream all-stars including Warren Vache, Harry Allen, Allen Farnham and Keith Ingham, and recorded three CDs as a leader including *You Are There: Songs From My Father*. "The irony of doing what I'm doing now, is that my father was never able to see me do this. He never knew that I recorded anything, or that I actually turned this into something. He was the one who fueled the passion. In many ways, I'm doing this for him."

Recommended CDs: Sarah Partridge's debut CD, *I'll Be Easy To Find* (USA 1055), already finds her sounding distinctive and mature while displaying subtle creativity. *Blame It On My Youth* (Nagel Heyer 92) has guest appearances from Frank Wess, while *You Are There: Songs From My Father* (Nagel Heyer 100) is both a heartfelt and a celebratory tribute to her father.

Ottilie Patterson
(Anna Ottilie Patterson)
b. January 31, 1932, Comber, County Down, Northern Ireland

A colorful and expressive blues singer, Ottilie Patterson gained fame with Chris Barber's trad jazz band in the 1960s.

She first heard Dixieland and swing on the radio during World War II, and had classical piano lessons, teaching herself boogie-woogie. She performed as a singer and pianist on a few occasions as a child. While studying drawing and painting at the Belfast College of Art, she met fellow student Richard Martin who played jazz clarinet and piano. "He introduced me, via 78 rpms, to the music of Jelly Roll Morton, Bunk Johnson, the Louis Armstrong Hot Five and Seven, Kid Ory, and the three great boogie-woogie players: Meade 'Lux' Lewis, Pete Johnson and Albert Ammons. And then Richard introduced me to the singing of Bessie Smith, which really stunned me." Soon she was singing with a local Dixieland group. Since she considered herself a serious blues singer, she left the band when she was asked to sing a novelty pop song. However, two days later she was in Richard Martin's Muskrat Ramblers, performing weekly at the Chalet d'Or in Belfast.

After completing her art studies, Patterson became a teacher but was determined to become a blues singer, preferably in London. "I had in mind the Ken Colyer Traditional New Orleans Jazz Band, which I had heard on record. In 1954 during my summer holiday, I went to London to seek him out. However, the band had broken up and reformed under its trombonist, Chris Barber." She and Barber hit it off very well and she officially joined the group on January 1, 1955, marrying the trombonist in 1959. To Ottilie Patterson's delight, as a member of Barber's band, she had the opportunity to work with some of the artists she most admired, including Big Bill Broonzy, Louis Jordan, Champion Jack Dupree, Muddy Waters, Howlin' Wolf and Sister Rosetta Tharpe. "Singing a duet with Sister Rosetta was one of the greatest experiences of my life. I learned more in three weeks working with Sister than I had in ten years of listening to records." Among the other highlights of her career that she cited was being called up to sit in with Muddy Waters' band in 1959 and being accepted as an authentic blues singer by the musicians.

Ottilie Patterson appeared with the band less often after 1963, retiring in 1973 and divorcing Barber in 1981. She made a comeback in 1983, performing with Chris Barber on an occasional basis for a few years. "I sang my last engagement in the spring of 1991. Although another tour was arranged for later that year, I pulled out since 'one-nighters' and the traveling involved was too exhausting." Erratic health has kept her off the scene since that time, but she is still remembered as one of the best of the blues-oriented singers from England's trad era.

Recommended CDs: Ottilie Patterson recorded regularly with Chris Barber starting in 1955. She is well featured on *Ottilie Patterson With Chris Barber's Jazzband 1955–1958* (Lake 30), *That Patterson Girl* (Lake 244), *40 Years Jubilee* (Timeless CD TTD 586), *Chris Barber's Blues Book Volume One/Good Mornin' Blues* (BGO BGOCD 380) and *Madame Blues & Doctor Jazz* (Black Lion 760506).

Mary Pearson
b. April 30, 1949, Queens, NY

Mary Pearson's recording debut, *You And I*, was such a strong release in 2000 that it alone has put her in this book.

"I've sung all my life, but I did not know I was a jazz singer until 1975 when I heard some guy singing in a club in Chicago and I thought, 'Yeah, that's what I do.' Before, during, and after that, I played folk, sang with a wedding band, performed cabaret, and did some piano bar. Except for Ella's Memorex commercials, my world had been pretty much jazz-free." Her first important jazz gig was at the Surfmaid in New York. "I'd sit in regularly with Claude Garvey and occasionally with Fred Hersch. The owner heard me one night, which landed me my first official jazz singing job. It paid $40 for the duo for a six-hour night. If the place was still there, it would probably still pay 40 bucks a night." The nightly training paid off and she formed her own group in the early 1980s. In 1984 she began to learn to play piano and by 1986 was working as a singer-pianist.

Since then, Mary Pearson has worked regularly in the New York area performing with Dr. Billy Taylor, Harvie Swartz, Lynne Arriale, the DIVA Band, Claire Daly, John Hart and George Gee's Make Believe Ballroom Orchestra. In addition, she whistles on commercials and writes children's musicals.

Recommended CDs: *You And I* (Arkadia 71325) is an unusual and very successful debut. It includes a set of duets in which Mary Pearson interacts on various selections with drummer Steve Nelson, pianists Lynne Arriale and Fred Hersch, guitarist John Hart and bassist Harvie S. A full-length set of voice-bass duets with Harvie S. has yet to be released.

Website: www.marypearsonjazzsinger.com

Denise Perrier
b. November 12, 1939, Baton Rouge, LA

A well respected jazz singer and actress who is an inspiration to younger vocalists, Denise Perrier has been based in the San Francisco Bay area since the 1970s.

Born in Louisiana, she moved with her family to West Oakland when she was five. "I was first introduced to jazz through records and a family 'juke joint.' My family owned a tavern with a jukebox in West Oakland, so I sang along with the records of Billie Holiday, Billy Eckstine, Jo Stafford and other popular singers. I first sang professionally with a San Francisco-based vocal group called the Intervals. Louis Armstrong heard us and took us to Las Vegas to perform in his show in 1963. Then in 1965, an Australian entrepreneur heard me in an Oakland club and hired me to perform in Sydney. The next year I sang with an orchestra on a Singapore radio station, then remained in Hong Kong and sang all around the Pacific Rim for five more years."

Living in New York for the first half of the 1970s, she performed on the cabaret circuit and took vocal lessons from Jack Harold of the New York City Opera. Since settling in San Francisco, Perrier has portrayed Bessie Smith in the play *In The House Of The Blues*, performed in the musical play *One Mo' Time*, sung and produced tribute shows to songwriter Hugh Martin, Duke Ellington and Dinah Washington, and toured Russia 15 times.

"I'd love to record with strings. Also, I'd love to learn Brazilian tunes in Portuguese. Right now I'm singing them in English. I have other projects in mind, but I plan to keep on performing, touring, writing and recording for a long time to come. I love it all. It's my life's work."

Recommended CDs: *I Wanna Be Loved* (Chez Perrier 3331) has Denise Perrier in prime form performing some of her favorite standards, including a few obscurities. *East Meets West* (Chez Perrier 9036) is a little unusual in that it was recorded partly

in San Francisco and partly in St. Petersburg, Russia. *Blue Monday Party: Live At Yoshi's* (Chez Perrier 89093) gives listeners an excellent example of what her live shows are like. All three CDs are rewarding.

Website: www.wireonfire/deniseperrier.com

Billie Pierce
(Wilhelmina Goodson)
b. June 8, 1907, Marianna, FL;
d. September 29, 1974, New Orleans, LA

Singer-pianist Billie Pierce was a blues and New Orleans jazz singer who teamed up in charming fashion with her husband, cornetist-singer De De Pierce.

Born Wilhelmina Goodson and known in her early years as Billie Goodson, she was one of seven sisters who played piano, as did her parents. She worked in the South as a pianist for Bessie Smith, Ma Rainey, Alphonse Picou, Emile Barnes and George Lewis, moving to New Orleans in 1930. In 1935 she married De De Pierce and they performed together during most of the rest of their lives.

The Pierces first recorded in 1953 for the Center label. De De became blind shortly after and retired for a period, but by 1959 he was back playing with his wife. They both became members of the Preservation Hall Jazz Band by 1962, traveling the world representing New Orleans jazz. Billie Pierce's straightforward blues-oriented vocals were always a popular attraction of the group.

Recommended CDs: On January 27, 1961, the Pierces recorded 23 titles in a trio with drummer Albert Jiles. *Blues And Tonks From The Delta* (Original Jazz Classics 1847) and *Blues In The Classic Tradition* (Original Jazz Classics 370) have all of the music.

LPs to Search For: *New Orleans Music* (Arhoolie 2016) is the Pierce's excellent 1959 session for Folk Lyric, featuring Billie singing blues, New Orleans tunes and vintage standards.

John Pizzarelli
b. April 6, 1960, Paterson, NJ

A brilliant guitarist who is a charming and personable singer, John Pizzarelli has been a popular attraction in jazz since at least 1990. His soft and high voice sometimes sings swing standards and at other times is utilized to scat rapid lines in unison with his guitar.

John Pizzarelli
After Hours

The son of guitarist Bucky Pizzarelli, he remembers that, "I grew up listening to and hanging out with Zoot Sims, Joe Venuti, Joe Pass, Slam Stewart and other jazz greats who would come over to our house in Jersey when they were in town. Nat King Cole is the reason I do what I do. I first heard his trio on record when I was 20 and I never looked back. Before that I listened to Michael Franks, Kenny Rankin, James Taylor and Billy Joel." He attended the University of Tampa and William Paterson College during 1978–81 and then worked regularly with his father in the 1980s, performing with Benny Goodman, Zoot Sims, Joe Pass and others at jazz parties.

"I started singing on gigs with my dad in the early 80s. I was singing a song called 'I Like Jersey Best' to a small amount of acclaim in the tri-state area, and Stash Records approached me to make a recording of it and some Nat Cole material in 1983. But it was the *My Blue Heaven* CD on Chesky in 1990 that made me start my own group, sort of break from Bucky, and go on the road with my own trio."

Since then his trio, usually including pianist Ray Kennedy and his younger brother, bassist Martin Pizzarelli, has worked steadily. In recent times the group has expanded to a quartet. Along the way John Pizzarelli opened for Frank Sinatra in a series of concerts in 1993, worked with George Shearing and Rosemary Clooney, and had the lead in the 1997 Broadway production of *Dream*, which was a tribute to Johnny Mercer. Recently he began co-hosting a nationally syndicated radio program, *Radio Deluxe With John Pizzarelli*, with his wife, Broadway and cabaret star Jessica Molaskey.

Recommended CDs: There is no shortage of John Pizzarelli recordings, and all are worth hearing for fans of the singer-guitarist: *I'm Hip—Please Don't Tell My Father* (P-Vine 2332) and *Hit That Jive Jack* (Stash Budget 2508), both from the 1980s, are a bit scarce but excellent early efforts. His other recordings include *My Blue Heaven* (Chesky 38), *All Of Me* (Novus 673129), *Naturally* (Novus 01241), *New Standards* (Novus 63172), *Dear Mr. Cole* (Novus 63182), *After Hours* (Novus 63191), *Let's Share Christmas* (RCA 66986), *Our Love Is Here To Stay* (RCA 67501), *Meets The Beatles* (RCA 61432), *P.S. Mr. Cole* (RCA 63563), *Kisses In The Rain* (Telarc 83491), *Let There Be Love* (Telarc 83518), *The Rare Delight Of You* (Telarc 83546) with George Shearing, the double-CD *Live At Birdland* (Telarc 83577), *Bossa Nova* (Telarc 83591), *Knowing You* (Telarc 83615) and *Dear Mr. Sinatra* (Telarc 83638).

Website: www.johnpizzarelli.com

Karin Plato
b. March 31, 1960, Kindersley, Saskatchewan, Canada

One of Canada's best jazz singers of the past decade, Karin Plato puts her own spin on standards.

Born in a small rural community, "I remember singing as a young child in elementary school as well as singing hymns in the church choir. Later as an older teen, my piano teacher discovered my love of singing and taught me some classical songs as she accompanied me. I studied classical piano and voice at the University of Saskatchewan in the early 1980s, but it was not until 1985 when I moved to Vancouver to attend Capilano College to study arranging and songwriting that I began to get a concentrated exposure to jazz music. While at Capilano College, I was able to study with jazz vocalist Shannon Gunn, who influenced me a great deal and guided me to listen to vocal jazz. I always wanted to be a singer but lacked the confidence to be a lead singer, although I would go to concerts and long

to be making music in that way. After studying in Banff in 1996 and 1998 with Sheila Jordan and Jay Clayton, I knew that I really wanted to pursue studying jazz and become a good jazz singer."

Since that time, Karin Plato has appeared regularly in clubs in the Vancouver area, sang with Linton Garner (Erroll Garner's brother) for several years, appeared at most of the major Canadian jazz festivals and recorded five CDs.

"I have enjoyed sharing the stage with vocalists Denzal Sinclaire and Kate Hammett-Vaughan in different concerts. Denzal brings calm and serenity to a performance and taught me to slow down and become more comfortable with myself on stage. Kate is a fearless improviser and, in sharing the stage with her, I learned to take chances and have fun while doing it."

Recommended CDs: Thus far Karin Plato has recorded her eclectic 1996 debut *Pastiche* (KVP); *There's Beauty In The Rain* (KVP), which has four of her originals along with her subtle transformations of eight standards; duets with bassist Torben Oxbol plus three different guitarists on *Blue Again* (Stikjazz), her Christmas album *Snowflake Season* (Stikjazz); and *The State Of Bliss* (Stikjazz), which has two appearances by Denzal Sinclaire.

Website: www.karinplato.com

Polly Podewell
b. March 31, 1949, Evanston, IL

One of the last singers to have an opportunity to sing with such major swing bandleaders as Benny Goodman, Woody Herman and Buddy Rich, Polly Podewell has a subtle style that is quietly sensuous, particularly on a song such as "It Had To Be You."

She began her singing career performing in a folk group in high school, and as a folk singer-guitarist at a restaurant called The Pig's End while attending college. After earning an M.A. from Erikson Institute in 1973, having studied sociology and psychology ("It helps me deal with musicians"), she studied voice at the American Conservatory of Music in Chicago. "I taught pre-school for a year but I was living above a jazz club called The Bulls in Chicago. I would go down there in the evening and sit with the bands until all hours of the morning, and then get up at 6 a.m. and take a bus to my pre-school teaching job. That could not last forever, so I finally made the decision, not an easy one, to give up my teaching and sing full-time. At the time I had no prospects, but I was young and excited about my future career."

Her big break came during 1979–80 when she sang with the Benny Goodman Sextet. Other notable associations were with Doc Cheatham and Vic Dickenson in 1979, Joe Bushkin, Buddy Rich (on an occasional basis during 1982–87), Woody Herman (his octet in 1984 and in 1986 on tour with his big band) and the Les Brown Orchestra (during 1997–2000).

Since that time, Polly Podewell has mostly appeared at classic jazz festivals and occasionally in the Los Angeles area. "I love to swing. I was so fortunate to have my first big gig with Benny Goodman. I also love to sing the ballads of Gershwin, Rodgers and Hart, Weill, Arlen, etc. There is such beauty in their sadness and how their music and lyrics blend so beautifully together."

Recommended CDs: Polly Podewell has recorded relatively little through the years. *All Of Me* (Audiophile 136) and *I'm Old Fashioned* (Baybridge Records FEX 26B) are pretty scarce. *Don't You Know I Care* (Audiophile 276) with pianist Ross

Tompkins, bassist Dave Carpenter and drummer Jake Hanna is a high-quality set from 1994 that has superior and mostly spontaneous arrangements of standards and vintage obscurities, nearly all of which are first takes.

Lucy Ann Polk

b. May 16, 1928, Sandpoint, ID

A swinging band singer who was also a sensitive interpreter of lyrics, Lucy Ann Polk is best remembered for her association with Les Brown.

She began her career when she was only five, singing with her sister and two brothers as the Four Polks. At nine, she had her own radio show in Spokane. The Four Polks stayed together for quite awhile, having success during the later part of the swing era. A self-sufficient group that included Lucy Ann's vibes plus her two brothers on guitar and bass, they were renamed the Bobbettes when they performed with Bobby Sherwood, and became the Town Criers during their associations with Les Brown (1942–44) and Kay Kyser (1944–46), also performing with Lionel Hampton, Jimmie Lunceford, Bob Crosby and Earl Hines (1946). Tommy Dorsey hired the Town Criers in 1947, using Lucy Ann and her brother Gordon Polk as solo vocalists. When their sister Elva got married in 1948 and retired, the group broke up.

Lucy Ann Polk stayed with Dorsey and had minor hits with "Until" and "Down By The Station" in 1948–49. In 1949 she joined Les Brown's orchestra, staying for five years and winning the Downbeat Readers' Polls of 1951–54 as best female band singer. In 1954 she left Brown to settle in Los Angeles. That year she recorded with the Dave Pell Octet; her second and final album was recorded in 1957.

By the late 1950s she was semi-retired from music, leading a quiet family life with her second husband, baritonist Marty Berman; she had earlier been married to trombonist Dick Noel. Lucy Ann Polk has only emerged on a rare basis since, although she appeared in a few reunion concerts with Les Brown in the late 1990s and gigged as recently as 2005.

Recommended CDs: *Dave Pell Octet Plays Burke And Van Heusen* (Fresh Sound 504) has Lucy Ann Polk's eight numbers from 1954 that formed her own ten-inch LP plus a few instrumentals from 1956. *Lucky Lucy Ann* (V.S.O.P. 6) has her sounding wonderful on standards while joined by a sextet that includes Dick Noel and pianist Marty Paich. She was only 29 at the time, but this recording was essentially the end of her career.

Jim Porcella

b. August 18, 1947, Medford, MA

Originally a drummer, Jim Porcella has developed into a fine singer, whether crooning romantic ballads or engaged in good-natured scatting.

He played in a jazz trio during his high school years and remembers seeing jazz greats at the club Lenny's On The Turnpike. His idols on drums were Art Blakey and Buddy Rich. "My story is somewhat similar to how Nat King Cole began singing. At the age of 19, I was a drummer in a trio working six nights a week in a club owned by, shall we say, a gentleman of influence and power. He thought everyone in the band should sing, so I was given a new job description. My first tune was 'Satin Doll' and fortunately he liked it. I had to add new tunes every night, which became kind of an accelerated learning curve, motivated by fear."

Porcella attended the Berklee School Of Music during 1966–68 and worked with trios led by Mike Sims (1967–77) and James Edward (1978–85), becoming a fixture in the Massachusetts jazz scene. He left jazz for seven years, working as the lead singer of a Top-40 group, but he returned, singing with Dick Johnson's Swing Shift during 1992–94. Since then he has sung with the Artie Shaw Orchestra (under the direction of Dick Johnson), the Louis Prima/Keely Smith tribute show *Prima Vera*, as one of the "3 Swingin' Tenors," and as leader of the swing band Bombay Jim and the Swinging Sapphires.

Recommended CDs: Each of Jim Porcella's solo CDs are enjoyable. These include *Sneak Preview* (Brownstone 921), *You've Got That Look: Live At The El Morocco* (Signature 81847) with the Jeff Holmes Big Band in 1993, *Life Is So Peculiar* (Seaside 137), *Porcella Sings Antonio And Jon* (Seaside 145), which is a set of Antonio Carlos Jobim and Jon Hendricks songs, and *If I Could Dance Like Fred Astaire* (Songkeeper).

Website: www.jimporcella.com

Ginnie Powell

(Virginia Powell)

b. December 24, 1925, Chicago, IL;
d. July 25, 1959, Nassau, Bahamas

Best remembered for her association with bandleader-husband Boyd Raeburn, Ginnie Powell had the ability to stay perfectly in tune no matter what was going on behind her, an important quality when singing George Handy arrangements.

The information below was partly supplied by Bruce Boyd Raeburn, the curator of the Hogan Jazz Archive at Tulane University, and the son of Ginnie Powell and Boyd Raeburn.

Ginnie Powell at 15 was working as a "hostess" at a restaurant, running the jukebox. She met bandleader Bob Strong who asked her to sing instead of just playing records, giving her an impromptu audition. He liked what he heard and soon had her singing on his radio show, *Uncle Walter's Doghouse.* While still in high school, she had stints with the orchestras of Bob Stevens, Cliff Aspergren, Dick Lewis and Norm Faulkner. Within a week of graduating high school in June 1943, she joined Boyd Raeburn's band and went out on the road.

A strep throat temporarily ended that association in October. After her recovery, Powell worked with the big bands of Jerry Wald (recording "Shoo Shoo Baby," "Crazy Blues," "Silver Wings In Moonlight" and "Since You Went Away"), Gene Krupa and Charlie Barnet. She had an audition for 20th Century Fox, but her stammering, which affected her talking but not her singing, ended a possible film career. In July 1945 she returned to the Boyd Raeburn Orchestra, making some impressive recordings and becoming one of the band's main (and most accessible) assets. The music was complex but Powell's singing was warm and melodic, sailing over the futuristic Handy arrangements of "Body And Soul" and "Temptation."

Ruth Price

Whenever the Boyd Raeburn band was struggling or had temporarily broken up, Powell would sing elsewhere and raise money so the band could survive. In 1946 she recorded "Do You Love Me" while with Harry James. She married Raeburn on July 9, 1946 and continued singing with his orchestras even as they failed commercially. In fact, she was practically a co-leader, doing everything she could to keep the band going. But by 1948 it was largely over. She gave birth to two children during the next two years while Boyd Raeburn freelanced in the New York area. She worked as a solo act at country clubs and also appeared on radio and television in the 1950s (including the *Tonight Show*). There were also three dance band albums recorded with Raeburn during 1956—57, including one called *Teen Rock*.

The Raeburns moved to the Bahamas in November 1958, but Ginnie Powell caught meningitis, passing away when she was just 33.

Recommended CDs: Nearly all of Ginnie Powell's recordings were made with the Boyd Raeburn Orchestra. *Jewels* (Savoy 273) has her performing some of her best vocals including "Temptation," "Body And Soul," and "Soft And Warm." *Memphis In June* (Hep 22), which has a memorable Powell vocal on the title cut, and *Jubilee Performances: 1946* (Hep 1) also feature Ginnie Powell with the Boyd Raeburn Orchestra during its prime period.

Ruth Price

b. April 27, 1930, Phoenixville, PA

A straight-ahead jazz and ballad singer with a sweet voice, Ruth Price has during the past decade become famous for running and booking the Jazz Bakery in Culver City, one of the top jazz clubs/concert venues on the West Coast.

She was originally a dancer. "While attending ballet school in NYC, at about age 18, a friend offered me a ride back to Philly for the weekend if I suffered through a Miles Davis performance at Birdland. It turned out I loved it." In 1952 Ruth Price was discovered by Philly Joe Jones and she became a full-time singer, touring with Jones' trio, which at the time included Red Garland and Paul Chambers. She sang with Charlie Ventura in 1954 with whom she appeared on *Bandstand USA* broadcasts, worked with the Billy Taylor Trio, and performed regularly with the Charles Mingus Quartet. Mingus named her as his favorite female singer twice in *Downbeat*. After a period living in New York, in 1957 she moved to Hollywood where she worked with Shelly Manne, recording a notable album with Manne's group. Price also toured with the Harry James Orchestra during 1964–65.

She was married to Dave Grusin for a period in the 1980s during which she retired. After their divorce, Price found herself with a grand piano given to her from a shuttered club. She decided to start one of her own, and the non-profit Jazz Bakery opened its doors in 1991, featuring Walter Norris during its opening night. While she still sings on an occasional basis, Ruth Price's main occupation has been keeping the Jazz Bakery going.

"I'm dyslexic and, I think as a compensation, I am blessed or cursed with remembering almost everything I hear in full, especially songs with their double-memory jog of lyric and music. I am truly in love with songs and worry about the vast repertoire that falls by the wayside for lack of being 'brought alive' by being performed. What isn't heard will be forgotten, and that would be a shame."

Recommended CDs: While her first two albums (from 1956 to 1957) are *My Name Is Ruth Price: I Sing* (Universal 9046) and

Ruth Price Sings With The Johnny Smith Quartet (Fresh Sound 36), her personal favorite is her most famous recording, *Ruth Price With Shelly Manne At The Manne-Hole* (Original Jazz Classics 1770). From 1961, she is in prime voice while assisted by the rhythm section from Manne's trio (including pianist Russ Freeman) on a variety of superior standards.

LPs to Search For: *The Party's Over* (Kapp 1054) is a rarity from 1957, while *Live And Beautiful* (Ava 54) was recorded six years later. *Lucky To Be Me* (ITI 72952) is Ruth Price's only recording under her name since 1963, but this 1983 LP with pianist Tom Garvin and tenor-saxophonist Pete Christlieb is close to definitive.

Louis Prima

b. December 7, 1911, New Orleans, LA;
d. August 24, 1978, New Orleans, LA

Louis Prima had an episodic and rather fascinating career, one that found him becoming a major influence a decade after his death.

Born in New Orleans, Prima first played violin when he was seven, but at 13 he taught himself trumpet. Influenced by Louis Armstrong, both as an instrumentalist and as a vocalist, Prima always had a winning personality, was quick to make fun of his Italian heritage (while simultaneously expressing pride in it), and was a very adaptable performer. He learned his craft while playing nightly in his hometown, leaving in 1932 for New York.

Prima gigged with Red Nichols, freelanced, and in 1934 became a hit for the first time, leading a combo on 52nd Street that fell between New Orleans jazz and swing. He began a series of recordings that found him heading a septet, singing on nearly every song, and sounding happy and humorous throughout. Whether it was a superior swing standard, a Dixieland tune, a jive number or a throwaway, Prima worked his charm and retained his popularity throughout the decade. In 1936 he debuted his song "Sing, Sing, Sing," which was originally a vocal piece two years before Benny Goodman and Gene Krupa performed it at Carnegie Hall as a lengthy instrumental.

In 1939, the Louis Prima Big Band was formed. He had hits with his recordings of "Angelina," "Oh Marie" and "Robin Hood" and worked steadily, but the orchestra never really caught on. He kept the band together most of the time into 1949, although its repertoire near the end leaned pretty heavily on corny Italian novelties.

Louis Prima was at the crossroads of his career in 1952 when he married his young singer, Keely Smith, with whom he had had a hit two years earlier, "Oh Babe." Swing was considered dead and, although Prima was still famous, he was in danger of becoming a dated nostalgia act. But after discovering tenor-saxophonist Sam Butera in New Orleans in 1954, his fortunes changed. Prima put together a wild show that became a sensation in Las Vegas.

Combining his New Orleans jazz trumpet, a repertoire filled with swing standards, Butera's honking R&B-ish tenor, his rollicking group the Witnesses, Keely Smith's ballad vocals,

Prima's Italian humor, a shuffle beat and a rock and roll sensitivity, Louis Prima created music history. He recorded famous versions of "That Old Black Magic" and "Jump, Jive An' Wail," memorable medleys in "Just A Gigolo/I Ain't Got Nobody" and "When You're Smiling/The Sheik Of Araby," and generated a great deal of excitement.

The magic lasted until Prima and Smith divorced in 1961. Prima and Butera continued performing similar shows throughout the decade, although with gradually diminishing success. Prima had one last bit of success. In the animated movie *The Jungle Book*, his voice was used for King Louie and he had a minor hit with "I Wanna Be Like You." After returning to New Orleans, where he and Butera played for tourists, the singer-trumpeter fell into a coma in 1975, passing away three years later. A decade after Louis Prima's passing, he became one of the main influences on the Retro Swing movement, an idiom that used Prima as its inspiration in mixing together a wide variety of styles to create new music.

Recommended CDs: *1934–1935* (Classics 1048), *1935–1936* (Classics 1077), *1937–1939* (Classics 1146), *1940–1944* (Classics 1201), *1944–1945* (Classics 1273) and *1945* (Classics 1374) have all of Louis Prima's recordings during his first dozen years on record. Best are the earlier CDs plus *1940–1944*, which documents his swing era big band. The eight-CD box *The Capitol Recordings* (Bear Family 15776) is not inexpensive, but it has all of the prime Louis Prima/Keely Smith recordings plus two discs apiece of the solo work of Smith and Sam Butera. Listeners who want a sampling are advised to instead pick up *Jump, Jive An' Wail: The Essential* (Capitol 95266), which includes all of the best 1950s/60s recordings.

Flora Purim
b. March 6, 1942, Rio de Janeiro, Brazil

In the early 1970s with the rise of fusion, it looked as if jazz vocalists would have little or no role in the new style. Nearly all of the leading groups (such as Miles Davis, Weather Report, Herbie Hancock's Headhunters and the original Mahavishnu Orchestra) had no real purpose for a jazz singer, and the few contemporary groups that did use singers tended to use ones who were much closer to R&B than jazz. Flora Purim in 1972 became the exception when she sang with the first version of Chick Corea's Return to Forever. Not only was she an innovator in Brazilian jazz, but she also became the leading voice in Brazilian fusion and vocal fusion in general.

Flora Purim remembers, "I was introduced to jazz by my mother who was a classical pianist and used to listen to Errol Garner, Art Tatum and Oscar Peterson. I studied piano from the time I was four until I was 12. Then I switched to acoustic guitar, sang with a vocal jazz group when I was 14, and was 18 when I started singing solo professionally." In 1965 she met her future husband, percussionist-drummer Airto Moreira, and two years later they left Brazil for the Unites States. Purim recorded with Duke Pearson and worked with Stan Getz and Gil Evans. "The turning point of my career was when I helped Chick Corea in 1970 form a group called

Return To Forever along with Joe Farrell, Stanley Clarke and Airto. That gave me the opportunity to create my own style and original music."

After recording two albums with Return to Forever, Purim and Moreira departed as Corea and Clarke went in a more rockish direction. In 1973 she recorded her first American solo album, *Butterfly Dreams*. She became well known for "500 Miles High" and "Light As A Feather" and competed very well in jazz polls in the 1970s. From then on Purim's style was largely set, although she has appeared in many settings including with Carlos Santana, Hermeto Pascoal, McCoy Tyner and Dizzy Gillespie's United Nations Orchestra (early 1990s). Since the mid-1970s, Purim's main musical activities have usually centered around her group that she co-leads with Airto.

"My future musical goal it is to consistently renew myself, and learn from each experience. I want to create new and inspiring sounds for future generations. It is important to follow your dream even if in the beginning people don't necessarily understand or even like what you are doing. Don't get discouraged by bad commentaries and reviews of 'so-called experts,' even teachers that tell you that you have no talent. Always follow your dreams."

Recommended CDs: Flora Purim first recorded in Brazil in 1964. Her two recordings with Chick Corea's Return to Forever are *Light As A Feather* (Universal 9267) and *Return To Forever* (ECM 811978). Purim's most significant solo American recordings were the ones recorded in the 1970s for Milestone: *Butterfly Dreams* (Original Jazz Classics 315), *500 Miles High* (Original Jazz Classics 1018), *Stories To Tell* (Original Jazz Classics 619), *Open Your Eyes You Can Fly* (Original Jazz Classics 1042), *Encounter* (Original Jazz Classics 798) and *That's What She Said* (Original Jazz Classics 1057). More recent recordings include *Humble People* (Concord 43007), *Speed Of Light* (B+W Music 44), *Flora Sings Milton Nascimento* (Narada 12454), *Perpetual Emotion* (Narada 50625), *Speak No Evil* (Narada 43537) and *Flora's Song* (Narada 60321).

Website: www.florapurim.com

Pam Purvis
b. July 1, 1946, Bogalusa, LA

A vocalist who spent her formative years in Louisiana and Texas but is now based in New York, Pam Purvis has not become world-famous, but she has gained universal respect for her singing abilities and her dedication to the music, which she shares with her husband saxophonist Bob Ackerman.

Although she sang as a child and saw some jazz on television, she did not really discover the music until she attended North Texas State as a drama major and heard the NTSU Lab Band. She also attended the American Academy of Dramatic Arts in New York (1967–69). "I had a job while in acting school at a club in the Village called Hillie's where people came in and sang and did comedy. I worked there so that I could get up and sing three songs a night. One night a woman came in who sang some jazz and a beautiful ballad, I think it was 'When Sunny Gets Blue.' I thought then and there that if I could just do that, sit on a stool and sing those wonderful torch songs, that I would be truly happy." After graduating from the Academy, Purvis returned to Dallas, working as a singing waitress until she got hired by a private club and spent a year singing six nights a week with a trio. "After that I realized that I could more easily make a steady living singing in clubs than trying to work in the theater."

In 1974 she began singing at Gulliver's in New Jersey, along the way having opportunities to perform with Chuck Wayne, Joe Puma, Gabor Szabo and Joe Morello. She also met Bob Ackerman who she married in 1975. Since then they have performed together in a countless number of venues, with Pam Purvis often playing keyboards when they perform as a duo. They lived in Dallas during 1978–86 before returning to New York, have performed several times in Europe, Mexico and Brazil. They have thus far recorded nine albums. In addition to performing standards and conventional jazz, Purvis has also performed free improvisations. "In 1993 we started a relationship with Wilber Morris and Denis Charles in the Free Music genre. It was a first time experience for me. We made two CDs together, one of which is completely improvised start to finish and includes the great trumpet player Herb Robertson. The group was called Quartet and the music has opened my ears for singing straight-ahead, adding a real depth to my melodic and rhythmic concepts."

"In the cement on my front porch in front of the door it says 'Music and Love Live Here. Welcome. Pam and Bob.' That pretty much says it all."

Recommended CDs: Pam Purvis' recordings in freer settings are *If I Think Of Something, You'll Let Me Know* (Progressive Winds 1001) and *And Now I Can See Crows Mating In The Mist* (Cadence 1131). Her most recent recordings include *Fools Rush In* (Pam Purvis 35069), *I Had A Ball* (Progressive Winds Music 22956) and *Winter Warm* (Progressive Winds Music 35052).

LPs to Search For: Pam Purvis' debut recording, *Heartsong* (Black Hawk 51201), will be difficult to find.

Website: www.pampurvis.com

Ma Rainey
(Gertrude Malissa Nix Pridgett)
b. April 26, 1886, Columbus, GA;
d. December 22, 1939, Rome, GA

Ma Rainey, "The Mother of the Blues," is considered the first significant blues singer. She is believed to have been performing blues professionally as early as 1902 after having heard a blues sung by a street performer. Born into a family that performed in minstrel shows, Gertrude Pridgett learned about  show business as a child. She appeared in the show *A Bunch Of Blackberries* in Columbus, Georgia in 1898 when she was 12. In 1904 she married song and dance man William "Pa" Rainey and they toured with the Rabbit Foot Minstrels and Tolliver's Circus as "Rainey and Rainey—Assassinators of the Blues."

By 1912, Ma Rainey was a major name in the South, starring with the Moses Stock Co., a revue that also included the young Bessie Smith. Rainey worked constantly during the next 20 years and in December 1923, three years after Mamie Smith and 10 months after Bessie Smith, Rainey finally had an opportunity to record. At 37 she was considered a bit old to be making her recording debut. Rainey unfortunately made all of her records for the Paramount label, which was infamous for using primitive recording equipment and having surface noise that gave its singers a distant presence. One has to listen closely to Rainey's rough and earthy recordings to appreciate her message and her artistry, but it is worth the effort. She recorded 110 performances (counting alternate takes) during 1923–28 including "See See Rider" (which she introduced), "Ma Rainey's Black Bottom," "Blues The World Forgot" and "Titanic Man Blues." On her recordings, Rainey is heard in a variety of settings with groups that include Lovie Austin's Blues Serenaders, all-stars from the Fletcher Henderson orchestra, Louis Armstrong (on the "See See Rider" date) and her Tub Jug Washboard Band (consisting of kazoo, piano, banjo and jug). Like Ida Cox, Rainey stuck to the blues throughout her career, even after it went out of style.

Rainey headed her own tent show in the 1920s and stayed active until 1933. After the death of her mother and sister, she retired to Columbus, Georgia. With her savings, she built and operated two theaters. Ma Rainey died of a heart attack in 1939 when she was 53.

Recommended CDs: Casual collectors will be satisfied with *Ma Rainey* (Milestone 47021), which has her best 23 performances. Completists will opt for *Vol. 1* (Document 5581), *Vol. 2* (Document 5582), *Vol. 3* (Document 5583), *Vol. 4* (Document 5584) and *Vol. 5* (Document 5156).

Ramona
(Estrid Raymona Myers)
b. March 11, 1909, Lockland, OH;
d. December 14, 1972, Sacramento, CA

Ramona gained a certain amount of fame during 1932–37, when she was regularly presented by Paul Whiteman. Both her singing and her sophisticated piano playing bordered on cabaret but crossed over into jazz often enough for her to be included in this book.

Ramona (the name that her mother always called her) grew up in Ashland, Kentucky. She was originally strictly a pianist and was performing each Saturday night at a local hotel by the time she was 12. Ramona worked as staff pianist on the radio in Kansas City for three years and then moved to Pittsburgh where she began to sing on an occasional basis. At 16 she toured with Don Bestor's orchestra, and she also spent a few years having her own stage act on the vaudeville circuit.

While working on Cincinnati radio in 1932, Ramona was discovered by Paul Whiteman, who was greatly impressed by her versatility. Needing a singer to replace Mildred Bailey, he quickly signed her up. "Ramona And Her Grand Piano" appeared regularly on the *Kraft Music Hall* radio series with Whiteman's orchestra, and she was presented at prestigious nightclubs. Ramona also recorded on a regular basis, sometimes as a soloist or with a second pianist (usually Roy Bargy), and on other occasions with a combo taken from the Whiteman big band. Sidemen on her records include trombonist Jack Teagarden, trumpeters Bunny Berigan and Charlie Teagarden and C-melody saxophonist Frank Trumbauer. Among her best records are "Are You Makin' Any Money," "Annie Doesn't Live Here Anymore," "Not For All The Rice In China," "Barrel-House Music," "Raisin' The Rent" and "Anything Goes."

In 1937 Ramona quit the Whiteman organization due to the low pay that she received ($125 a week) for the past five years despite her being a star. She appeared in London quite successfully but, after returning to New York the following year and forming a 12-piece band (Ramona And Her Men Of Music), she found it a struggle and was not able to build upon her earlier fame. Ramona continued working, including on radio, until the birth of her daughter in 1945. She and her fourth husband moved to Cincinnati where she appeared on local radio and briefly had a television show. By 1950 Ramona had retired from show business, content to be a wife and mother.

Recommended CDs: *Ramona And Her Grand Piano* (The Old Masters 116) has many of her best recordings from the Paul Whiteman years.

Sue Raney
(Raelene Claire Claussen)
b. June 18, 1940, McPherson, KS

A classy singer with a beautiful voice, Sue Raney is always in tune and her control over her vibrato is flawless. A superior interpreter of lyrics, she is also a very well-respected vocal teacher in the Los Angeles area.

Her career began very early. When she was four, her mother noticed that she had a potentially great voice. Unable to find a teacher for her young daughter because of her age, Sue Raney's mother took singing lessons herself and then taught them to her child. When she was 12, she had her own radio show in New Mexico, where her family had relocated. Raney's family moved to Los Angeles in 1956 so she could join the Jack Carson radio show when she was just 16, a job that she gained through Frankie Laine, whom she considered her mentor. She performed regularly on Carson's program for ten months. "That was my music school. At 18 I started listening to Ella and Maxine Sullivan and was hooked on how they could swing and deviate from the melody."

She appeared regularly on Ray Anthony's television series and worked as a solo artist from age 18, recording for Phillips and Capitol. Among her fans were Nat King Cole (who wrote liner notes for one of her albums), Joey Bishop (she appeared often on his television show), Don Rickles, Bob Newhart and Frank Sinatra.

In the 1960s, Sue Raney worked with the Four Freshmen in Las Vegas, guested on television variety shows (including Red Skelton, Dean Martin and Danny Kaye) and toured with her own group. In the 1970s she became a studio singer, with her voice appearing on a countless number of commercials. The next decade found her touring with Michel Legrand (singing in front of symphony orchestras) and recording several albums for Discovery. In the early 1980s she taught at the Dick Grove School of Music, and that branched out to become a large private practice. Since then, she has sung with the L.A. Voices and Supersax, the Bill Watrous Orchestra and occasionally with her own trio, which for a time included the late pianist Dick Shreve.

"I love hearing the younger people create. It is so important to keep the music alive so future generations will know and love it as much as I do. That is one of the reasons that I love to teach."

Recommended CDs: *When Your Lover Has Gone/Songs For A Raney Day* (EMI/Capitol 59839) reissues two of Sue Raney's early Capitol albums (from 1958 and 1960), full sets with arrangements by Nelson Riddle and Billy May. *Breathless* (Studio West 107) and *Volume II* (Studio West 108) mostly feature the singer from early 1960s radio and concert performances with jazz groups. *Ridin' High* (Discovery 913), *Flight Of Fancy* (Discovery 931), *Quietly There: The Music Of Johnny Mandel*

(Discovery 939) and *In Good Company* (Discovery 74001) are all from the mid-to-late 1980s and showcase Sue Raney in prime voice while backed by combos headed by pianist-arranger Bob Florence. *Dreamsville* (Discovery 70557) has her singing Henry Mancini songs in 1992, *Autumn In The Air* (Fresh Sound 5017) is a set of ballads from 1997 with pianist Dick Shreve and her recent *Heart's Desire: A Tribute To Doris Day* (Fresh Sound 5045) from 2007 has her paying tribute to one of her idols, sounding quite ageless and as classy as ever.

Kenny Rankin
b. February 10, New York, NY

When sent the questionnaire for this book, Kenny Rankin wrote back, "I am very flattered that you would consider me, but I don't really have a history in jazz, nor do I consider myself a jazz singer. I feel that I am more of a storyteller who takes emotional liberties with the music. I simply sing the story and tell the song."

It is true that there was little in Rankin's earlier work that even hinted at jazz. But in the mid-1990s he began occasionally appearing in jazz clubs, singing vintage standards. While he stuck to the words, he frequently changed the notes during the melody statements, an inventive way of improvising that made songs such as "More Than You Know," "The Way You Look Tonight" and "Love Walked In" sound very different and new.

A recording artist since he was a teenager in the early 1960s, Kenny Rankin played guitar on the 1965 Bob Dylan album *Bringing It All Back Home*, became a regular attraction on the *Tonight Show* (appearing 20 times with Johnny Carson) and wrote such songs as "In The Name Of Love," "Haven't We Met" and "Peaceful." A popular singer/songwriter with a very appealing tenor voice, Rankin has been a household name for decades. His re-emergence on records in 1995 with *Professional Dreamer*, a set of standards, was a surprise and was certainly noticed by jazz singers, who admired his voice and his approach to improvising.

So sorry Mr. Rankin, but you do belong in this book.

Recommended CDs: *Professional Dreamer* (Private Music 82124) will be a revelation for those who would never think that Kenny Rankin and jazz belong in the same sentence. *A Song For You* (Verve 589540) uses the same concept, while *Here In My Heart* (Private 82148) is an equally successful set of Brazilian jazz.

Website: www.kennyrankin.com

Lou Rawls
b. December 1, 1933, Chicago, IL;
d. January 6, 2006, Los Angeles, CA

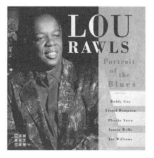

As with Kenny Rankin, much of what Lou Rawls sang during his career would not be considered jazz. Rawls sang R&B, pop, soul and gospel with equal sincerity and skill, but he was also a superior blues and jazz singer, as he showed on an occasional basis. His voice was described by one critic as "sweet as sugar, soft as velvet, strong as steel and smooth as butter."

Rawls started off singing gospel music with his Baptist church choir when he was seven. In high school he sang with local doo wop groups before spending time with the Chosen Gospel Singers and the Pilgrim Travelers. He spent 1955–58 in the Army, rejoined the Travelers and, after a serious car accident put him out of action for a year, he decided to switch to secular music. Rawls was signed to Capitol and his first album, 1962's *I'd Rather Drink Muddy Water* (later renamed *Stormy Monday*), which has him teamed with the Les McCann Trio, remains his definitive jazz/blues record.

Rawls followed that up with at least 20 Capitol albums during the next decade, becoming established in the R&B and pop worlds. He had hits with "Love Is A Hurtin' Thing," "Dead End Street," "Your Good Thing (Is About To End)," and "Natural Man." In 1976 he had his biggest seller with "You'll Never Find (Another Love Like Mine)." A familiar figure on television, voiceovers, in acting roles and musical performances, late in his life he had a reunion tour with Les McCann, which included appearing at the Monterey Jazz Festival. His baritone sounded ageless, largely unchanged from 45 years earlier, making one wish that he had recorded and performed jazz more often during his productive life.

Recommended CDs: *Stormy Monday* (Blue Note 91441) is a classic and shows how powerful a jazz/blues singer Lou Rawls could be, fitting easily into the Big Joe Turner/Jimmy Witherspoon tradition. *Black And Blue/Tobacco Road* (Capitol 54957) combines two other jazz-oriented Rawls sets from the early 1960s. *For You, My Love* (Blue Note 28879) from 1964 and 1968 has both jazz and soul selections while *Live* (Blue Note 4775542) was Rawls' last major jazz date. This 1966 session has the definitive "Tobacco Road," a couple of memorable Rawls monologues, and some of his finest blues singing. Two decades later, *At Last* (Blue Note 91937) from 1989 and *Portrait Of The Blues* (Blue Note 99548) have their moments, ranging from swinging and lowdown blues to Rawls' brand of R&B. But it is a pity that Rawls' reunion tour with Les McCann did not result in any new jazz CDs.

Don Redman

b. July 29, 1900, Piedmont, WV;
d. November 30, 1964, New York, NY

Don Redman had many musical talents. He was one of jazz's first significant arrangers and is given credit for being among the first to divide the ensembles of big bands into trumpet, trombone and reed sections. He was also a fine songwriter who was responsible for "Gee Baby, Ain't I Good To You" and "Cherry," a decent altoist and clarinetist, a bandleader, and an effective vocalist. As a singer, Redman emphasized philosophical lyrics and talked as much as he sang.

Redman started on trumpet when he was three but soon switched to reed instruments. At 12 he could play clarinet, oboe and all of the saxophones. Redman graduated from Storer's College by the time he was 20 and studied music at the Chicago and Boston Conservatories. By 1921 he was in New York, recording on clarinet and alto with Fletcher Henderson's orchestra. After working for a short time with Billy Paige's Broadway Syncopators and making further recordings with Henderson, in 1924 he officially joined Fletcher Henderson (who up to that point had just led a recording band) as both a player and an arranger. While Henderson has often been given credit for his band's early arrangements, nearly all of the charts into 1927 were actually written by Redman.

Don Redman's first recorded vocal, "My Papa Doesn't Two-Time No Time" from April 18, 1924, is one of the earlier scat vocals, predating Louis Armstrong's "Heebies Jeebies" by nearly two years. Redman's arrangements of 1923–24, although advanced and futuristic, were often rhythmically awkward and failed to swing much. That changed after Armstrong joined Henderson's band in the fall of 1924. Armstrong's relaxed legato phrasing, use of space and dramatic way of telling a story was quickly adopted by Redman, whose arrangements (most notably "Sugar Foot Stomp" and "The Stampede") from 1925 on set the standard for big band charts.

Don Redman, who also takes vocals on Henderson's recordings of "Then I'll Be Happy," "Get It Fixed," "I've Found A New Baby," "Tozo" and "The Wang Wang Blues," left the orchestra in mid-1927 when he was given the position of musical director of the new McKinney's Cotton Pickers. He soon made the Cotton Pickers into one of the top big bands, competing favorably with Henderson, and served not only as its main arranger-composer and a soloist but its front man and singer. Of his 11 vocals with the band, the most memorable are on "Save It Pretty Mama," "Will You, Won't You Be My Babe," the initial recording of "Gee Baby, Ain't I Good To You" and "Miss Hannah."

In mid-1931, Redman took the next logical step, leaving the Cotton Pickers to form his own big band. Strangely enough, the Don Redman Orchestra, although working regularly until its breakup in January 1940, never really caught on despite the fact that Redman's arrangements for Henderson and the Cotton Pickers had paved the way for the Swing era. The Redman band did make some fine recordings, particularly during 1931–32 and 1937–40, though it slumped in the middle. Redman's philosophical bent can be heard at its most entertaining during his vocals on "Try Getting A Good Night's Sleep," "It's A Great World After All" and "How Ya Feelin'," and his singing helped to popularize "I Heard" and "How'm I Doin'."

After he gave up his band in 1940, Don Redman primarily worked as a freelance arranger. He put together a special all-star American group to tour Europe right after World War II (1946–47), worked as the musical director for Pearl Bailey in the 1950s, and led a few final instrumental dates during 1957 and 1959.

Recommended CDs: Don Redman's best recordings with his own orchestra, which frequently featured his vocals, are on *1931–1933* (Classics 543) and *1936–1939* (Classics 574). The McKinney's Cotton Pickers CD called *The Band Don Redman Built* (Bluebird 2275) includes their hottest recordings plus Redman's most rewarding vocals with the classic band.

Dianne Reeves

b. October 23, 1956, Detroit, MI

One of the finest singers in jazz today, Dianne Reeves has had a rather eclectic and unpredictable career, sometimes performing R&B and African-based folk music. When she sings jazz there are very few on her level, for she is a superior interpreter of lyrics, a skilled scat singer, and possesses a very warm voice.

Born into a very musical family (keyboardist George Duke is a cousin), she grew up in Denver. Reeves took piano lessons and at 11 realized that she wanted to be a singer. She sang with her high school band (making a recording) and met Clark Terry who became one of her mentors. Reeves studied music at the University of Colorado before moving to Los Angeles in 1976.

Dianne Reeves toured with Caldera, sang with pianist Billy Childs' Night Flight, worked with Sergio Mendes, did studio work, and toured with Harry Belafonte during 1983–86. She made her first record as a leader in 1982 and soon was performing regularly at festivals. She signed with the Blue Note label in 1987, which further increased her visibility and her prominence. It took some time but by 1994 she was committing herself much more to jazz, showing that she is a logical successor to Sarah Vaughan (one of her main inspirations) even though she very much has her own sound. In 2005 she appeared onscreen, singing throughout the George Clooney film *Good Night, And Good Luck*.

Seeing Dianne Reeves live when she performs a jazz set is an exciting experience, and her musical introduction of her band (which contains plenty of ad-libs and scatting) is always a joy. Her very best jazz recordings capture the essence of those performances.

Recommended CDs: Dianne Reeves' best jazz CDs are *I Remember* (Blue Note 90264), *The Grand Encounter* (Blue Note 38268), *The Calling: Celebrating Sarah Vaughan* (Blue Note 27694), *A Little Moonlight* (Blue Note 80252) and *Good Night, And Good Luck* (Concord 2307). *Quiet After The Storm* (Blue Note 29511) and *That Day* (Blue Note 56973) have their strong moments along with other more commercial tracks. Most of Reeves' other recordings are R&B, pop and/or folk-oriented.

Website: www.diannereeves.com

Elis Regina
(Elis Regina Carvalho Costa)
b. March 17, 1945, Porto Alegre, Brazil;
d. January 19, 1982, São Paulo, Brazil

One of Brazil's most beloved singers, Elis Regina was a jazz-inspired vocalist who helped to popularize the tropicalia movement of the 1970s. Due to her moods, insecurities and perfectionism, she was nicknamed "Hurricane" and "Little Pepper." She first sang pro-

fessionally when she was 12 on a local children's television show (*Clube do Guri*), appearing on the show nearly every Sunday for two years. Due to its popularity, in 1960 she made her recording debut as a 15-year-old, cutting three popular records as a teenager and appearing on variety shows. In 1965 when she was 20, her performance of a very emotional "Arrastão" at a major music festival in Rio that was televised made her into a national celebrity. The resulting recording of "Arrastão" was a best-seller, followed by her million-selling LP *Dois Na Bossa*. By then she was the highest-paid singer in Brazil.

In her career, Elis Regina recorded the best works of the top Brazilian composers and her 1974 collaboration with Antonio Carlos Jobim, *Elis And Tom*, is considered a classic. She also recorded an album with Toots Thielemans, although a project with Wayne Shorter fell through. Despite the difficulties of being an entertainer during a period when Brazil was run by a brutal dictatorship that she opposed, her popularity kept her out of jail. Both during and after her career, she sold over 80 million albums.

Elis Regina died in 1982 at the age of 37 from an accidental overdose of cocaine and alcohol.

Recommended CDs: Elis Regina recorded steadily, especially during 1965–80. Among the most interesting releases are *Elis Regina (Orquestra Sob A Direção De Astor)* (Sony 495665), *Samba, Eu Canto Assim!* (Mercury 811218), *Elis Especial* (Polygram Brazil 811220), *Elis Regina In London* (Polygram 558264), *Elis Ao Vivo* (Velas 11140), *Elis And Tom* (Verve 824418), *A Arte De Elis Regina* (Verve 836250), *Nada Sera Como Antes (Elis Interpreta Milton Nascimento)* (Verve 822827), *Millennium: Elis Regina* (Polygram 538200), *Os Sonhos Mais Lindos* (Universal Latino 48217), *Samba, Jazz And Bossa* (Planet Rhythm 780602) and *Definitive Collection* (Wrasse 118).

Irene Reid
b. September 23, 1930, Savannah, GA;
d. January 5, 2008, New York, NY

Irene Reid's career makes one wonder a bit. A talented singer who was influenced in her early days by Dinah Washington and Sarah Vaughan, her ability to straddle the boundary lines between swinging jazz, blues, R&B and gospel was similar to that of Ernestine Anderson. But Reid was mostly obscure despite working steadily.

Born in Georgia, she moved to New York in the late 1940s and in 1948 won the amateur contest at the Apollo Theater for several weeks in a row. Although she worked throughout the 1950s with jazz combos, big bands and organ groups, her only recording was a forgotten single for Savoy in 1955. Reid toured with Count Basie's orchestra during 1961–62, but the association did disappointingly little to help her career. She did finally have an opportunity to make a few recordings, cutting four albums for MGM and Verve during 1963–67 including *Room For One More*, which had her accompanied by a jazz orchestra arranged by Oliver Nelson, but no hits or trademarks songs emerged. She was barely on records during the next 30 years, just popping up on a few pop-oriented dates for tiny labels. Despite that, she kept busy, performing regularly even if the labels did not seem to care.

Finally in 1997, she was signed to the Savant label and during the next few years she recorded six CDs. Fortunately those recordings find her in excellent form late in life, performing the type of accessible soulful jazz that she loved. But why did it take so long for her to be properly documented?

Recommended CDs: Irene Reid's Savant recordings, *Million Dollar Secret* (Savant 2007), *I Ain't Doing Too Bad* (Savant 2012), *The Uptown Lowdown* (Savant 2022), *One Monkey Don't Stop No Show* (Savant 2028), *Movin' Out* (Savant 2032), and *Thanks To You* (Savant 2040), feature her still in her musical prime despite being 67 at the time of the first one, *Million Dollar Secret*.

LPs to Search For: Irene Reid's early recordings, *It's Only The Beginning For Irene Reid* (MGM 4159), *Room For One More* (Verve 8621), *It's Too Late* (Verve 5003) and *Man Only Does* (Verve 5023), have yet to be reissued.

Rita Reys
(Maria Everdina Reys)
b. December 21, 1924, Rotterdam, Netherlands

Known as "Europe's First Lady of Jazz," Rita Reys is a legend overseas, being considered one of the top jazz singers on the Continent since at least the mid-1950s.

After winning several song contests, she sang with the Hawaiian Minstrels in 1941 when she was 16. Two years later she became a member of her father's theater orchestra. Reys also worked and toured with Lex Van Spall, Ted Powder and the Piet Van Dijk Orchestra. In 1945 she married drummer Wessel Ilcken. "He was the most famous Dutch jazz musician in those days, and he introduced me to the jazz scene just after World War II." She worked with his sextet during the next decade. They were based in Stockholm in the early 1950s, recording with baritonist Lars Gullin in 1953. In 1956 she gained a lot of attention when she recorded *The Cool Voice Of Rita Reys With Art Blakey And The Jazz Messengers*.

"During 1956–57 I went to the States for a couple of months. Producer George Avakian had heard me sing in a jazz club in Amsterdam and he invited me. I performed with Jimmy Smith, Art Blakey, Chico Hamilton, Clark Terry, Mat Mathews and others."

A car accident in 1957 resulted in the death of Wessel Ilcken. Reys continued her career and in 1960 married pianist Pim Jacobs. She regularly worked with his trio/quartet up until his death in 1996. Along the way she performed with everyone from Zoot Sims and Oliver Nelson to the Dutch Swing College Band, displaying the influence of her two musical heroes (Ella Fitzgerald and Mel Tormé) but in her own way, caressing ballads and swinging on uptempo tunes. She is most proud of a quartet of songbook records made in the 1970s with a large string orchestra led by Rogier Van Otterloo. During 2004–2005 she celebrated her 80th birthday by coming out with her memoirs (*Rita Reys—Lady Jazz*) and continuing to perform, including television specials, concerts all around the Netherlands, and a special birthday performances in a venue named after her late second husband, the Pim Jacobs Theater.

"What I like the most is singing ballads, like 'The Shadow Of Your Smile' and 'In The Wee Small Hours Of The Morning.' With ballads, a singer is able to really tell his or her story. And for me, that is what singing is about: telling stories, making people laugh, making them smile and sometimes even making them cry."

Recommended CDs: The four-CD box set, *The Rita Reys Story—Songs Of A Lifetime* (Nikkelen Nelis 0500405), does an excellent job of summing up the singer's career during 1953–2000. Other worthy CDs include *The Cool Voice Of Rita Reys* (Columbia 5137), *Marriage In Modern Jazz* (Universal 5497), *Rita Reys Meets Oliver Nelson* (Universal 9143), *Rita Reys Today* (Universal 3066) and 1990's *Swing And Sweet* (Blue Note 7954432) though many are only readily available in Europe or Japan.

LPs to Search For: *Her Name Is Rita* (Epic 3522) is a strong early effort, and Rita Reys thinks highly of *Sings Burt Bacharach* (CBS 53026), *Sings Michel Legrand* (CBS 55037), *Sings George Gershwin* (CBS 80580) and *Sings Antonio Carlos Jobim* (Phillips 6423).

Website: www.ritareys.eu

Ann Richards
b. October 1, 1935, San Diego, CA;
d. April 1, 1982, Hollywood, CA

An excellent singer who looked like a movie star, Ann Richards should have had a major career. Instead her life ended tragically after a long period of obscurity.

She was self-taught on piano and started taking singing lessons when she was 10. Richards began singing professionally in the San Francisco Bay area and had short stints with Charlie Barnet and George Redman. She got what looked like a big break when she joined Stan Kenton's orchestra in 1955. They were married, she became a part-time singer with the band, and she recorded two solo albums plus *Too Much*; the latter with the backing of the full Kenton Orchestra.

But the marriage was a difficult one and ended in 1961, a breakup that she never really recovered from. She posed nude for *Playboy* that year, a daring move that backfired because she was never again taken seriously as a singer. She recorded that year for Atco and made a final album for Vee Jay in 1964, but by then was struggling. Although Richards only turned 29 in 1964, she never recorded again.

Ann Richards' life became aimless and she had long been forgotten by the music world when she committed suicide in 1982 at the age of 46. With better luck, she could have been a contender.

Recommended CDs: All of Ann Richards' albums are worth acquiring. She was better on uptempo material at the time of *I'm Shooting High* (Toshiba 9653) but soon developed into a sensitive interpreter of ballads. *Many Moods Of Ann Richards/ Too Much* (EMI 6672637) combines her second solo recording with her rewarding set with the Stan Kenton Orchestra. *Ann, Man* (Collectables 6321) teams her in a pianoless quartet with guitarist Barney Kessel and trumpeter Jack Sheldon, and is overall her finest recording. Ann Richard's final album, *Live At The Losers*, has been combined with an excellent Mavis Rivers jazz date as *Live At The Losers/We Remember Mildred Bailey* (Vee Jay 18).

June Richmond

b. July 9, 1915, Chicago, IL;
d. August 14, 1962, Gothenburg, Sweden

June Richmond could belt out the blues with the best swing era singers and was also effective on ballads. Despite her talents, she never became a big star.

Richmond worked with Les Hite's band in California and then became one of the very first black singers to be featured regularly with a white band, performing with Jimmy Dorsey's orchestra during much of 1938. None of her seven recordings with Dorsey were hits, although she sounds in particularly fine form on "I Can't Face The Music" and "I Let A Song Go Out Of My Heart." She worked for a short time with Cab Calloway's big band later in the year, recording "Deep In A Dream" and "Angels With Dirty Faces," but was not really needed in an organization dominated by Cab's singing.

Richmond found more of a niche with Andy Kirk's 12 Clouds Of Joy during 1939–42. Her 14 recorded vocals include "Then I'll Be Happy," "Please Don't Talk About Me When I'm Gone," "Wham (Re-Bop-Boom-Bam!)," "Take Those Blues Away," "47th Street Jive" and "Hey Lawdy Mama." Although Kirk's band was starting to decline during this period, Richmond's singing was one of its brightest spots.

After leaving Kirk, Richmond freelanced, appearing in a few black films and Soundies in addition to making guest appearances on the radio. In 1948 she moved to Europe, working in France for a time and eventually settling in Scandinavia. Her obscurity today is partly due to her only leading two record dates in her career: four numbers in 1951 with violinist Svend Rasmussen and four in 1957 with the Quincy Jones Orchestra.

Always overweight, June Richmond died of a heart attack in 1962 when she was just 47.

Recommended CDs: June Richmond's period with Andy Kirk is fully documented on *1939–1940* (Classics 640) and *1940–1942* (Classics 681).

Mavis Rivers

b. May 19, 1929, Upolu, Western Samoa;
d. May 29, 1992, New York, NY

Mavis Rivers had a strong voice, a swinging style, and a feeling for ballads. Although she never quite became world famous, she was one of the first singers chosen by Frank Sinatra to record for his Reprise label.

Born in Western Samoa, she moved to Pago Pago in the American Samoa with her family after Pearl Harbor was bombed in 1941. She debuted singing with her father's band, entertaining American troops. After World War II ended, she moved with her family to New Zealand. Rivers had some local success, particularly on the radio, and made some rare recordings including two titles with cornetist Rex Stewart in 1950. In 1955 she moved to Los Angeles where for a time she worked as a secretary by day and a nightclub singer at night.

Featured at first with a Hawaiian band that had her future husband, bassist David Catingub, she was signed to Capitol in 1959, recording three well received albums. After Frank Sinatra signed her for Reprise, four more albums followed and there was also an all-star jazz date for Vee Jay in 1964 that was a Mildred Bailey tribute album.

Retired from singing to raise a family (she is the mother of saxophonist-arranger-bandleader Matt Catingub), Mavis

Rivers returned to music in the early 1980s. She appeared on some of her son's albums and recorded her own excellent set, *It's A Good Day*, in 1983. She was active on an occasional basis until she suffered a fatal stroke onstage in 1992.

Recommended CDs: Mavis Rivers' Capital and Reprise recordings have yet to be reissued on CD. *We Remember Mildred Bailey* was reissued as both Koch 8551 and in conjunction with an Ann Richards album as *Live At The Losers/We Remember Mildred Bailey* (Vee Jay 18). Her superior 1983 set *It's A Good Day* (Delos 4002) teams her with her son and a quartet with pianist Alan Broadbent, sounding in prime form.

LPs to Search For: Mavis Rivers' Capitol recordings, *Take A Number* (Capitol 1210), *Hooray For Love* (Capitol 1294) and *Sings About The Simple Life* (Capitol 1408), and her Reprise dates, *Mavis* (Reprise 2002), *Sing Along With Mavis* (Reprise 2009) and *Mavis Meets Shorty Rogers* (Reprise 6074), all feature the singer backed by orchestras, coming up with fresh variations of standards.

Judy Roberts

b. October 3, Chicago, IL

An important fixture in the Chicago jazz scene for years, Judy Roberts is equal parts pianist and singer. "Even now, I always perceive myself as a pianist first, vocalist second."

"My dad, Bob Loewy, was a guitarist and arranger in the '30s and '40s. He played with artists like Art Van Damme, Muggsy Spanier, etc., and also did big band arranging for Fletcher Henderson and other groups. He played great albums for me all the time, and we would spend many hours a day listening to and discussing jazz, him at the guitar, and me at the piano." Judy Roberts began playing the piano when she was two but, strangely enough, she never learned to read music. "In grammar school, I was perceived as a kind of 'freak' because I could come up with vocal harmony parts by ear, on the spot, for any songs that were being worked on by the music classes. Consequently, I was dragged around from room to room where I'd sing harmony with the class, and then go on to the next room. Of course I thought it was fun, plus I got to escape from math."

Judy Roberts originally had no intention of becoming a singer. "I was totally into jazz piano. I was a high school senior and had a gig as a pianist with a jazz quintet in the suburbs of Chicago. We were playing a rather rough joint, one of those places where the bandstand is surrounded by the bar. I was playing piano behind the horn players when a tough customer came up to the bar and said to me, 'Sing "Fascination."'' I meekly said (while still playing) 'I'm sorry, Sir, but I don't sing.' So the guy took out a gun, slammed it down on the bar and yelled 'SING "FASCINATION!"' Needless to say, I immediately started singing 'Fascination,' and the next night I was a singing pianist. Since I already knew many hundreds of songs, I was ready."

Although she recorded with bassist Ray Brown when she

was a teenager in the 1960s, Judy Roberts gained her initial fame during 1979–81 when her fusion band recorded three albums for Inner City. When Inner City became defunct, in 1983 Roberts recorded a notable trio album for Pausa with Ray Brown and drummer Jeff Hamilton. After that she seemed to drop off the national radar, but in reality she just concentrated on working in Chicago and has thus far recorded over 20 albums, many for her own private label. Married to tenor-saxophonist Greg Fishman since the 1990s, she has played at many jazz festivals, was on the faculty of Roosevelt University's Chicago College of Performing Arts, written about music for *Chicago Jazz* magazine and teamed up with singer Jackie Allen for duos.

In recent times, Judy Roberts and Greg Fishman have moved to Phoenix. "Sometimes critics don't take me seriously because I am not brooding when I perform. It seems that if an artist is visibly having fun while playing, the music is often perceived as not being 'serious jazz.' Despite this, I will continue to perform, have fun, and share that fun with the other band members and with the audience."

Recommended CDs: *Judy Roberts Band* (Inner City 1078), *The Other World* (Inner City 1088), which includes a popular version of "Senor Blues," and *Nights In Brazil* (Inner City 1138) are recent reissues of Roberts' three Inner City LPs. *My Heart Belongs To Daddy* (Judy Roberts 4742) has Roberts matched with altoist Richie Cole. She teams up with Greg Fishman on *Circle Of Friends* (Judy Roberts 1030), *In The Moment* (Judy Roberts 588740) and the wonderful duet set *Two For The Road* (Judy Roberts 1993).

LPs to Search For: *Trio* (Pausa 7147) with Ray Brown and Jeff Hamilton is one of Judy Roberts' finest straight-ahead albums.

Website: www.judyroberts.com

Sherri Roberts

b. June 28, Greenville, SC

A cheerful singer based in San Francisco, Sherri Roberts puts a lot of heart into her interpretations.

Growing up near Atlanta, she sang regularly in school, performed in musical theater in high school, and sang Renaissance masses and secular chansons while attending Antioch College in Ohio, graduating in 1978 with a theater degree. She learned about jazz from the local public radio station WYSO and the adventurous music department, which booked such artists as Anthony Braxton, Keith Jarrett and Sun Ra. "Finally, when I moved to San Francisco after college and had access to the great jazz station KJAZ and started exploring the repertoire of Billie Holiday and the Great American Songbooks, I was hooked and my fate was sealed."

"I worked in theater in San Francisco for about seven years, both as manager of a professional children's theater and as a freelance performer in (non-musical) shows around town. In 1987 I was burned out on theater management and was ready to try something new. It was then that I started going to open mics and jazz jam sessions. Singing was so important to me, but I had never committed to it as a solo performer, and the time felt right to try. I remember being struck at how rewarding it felt to just stand in front of people, microphone in hand, and communicate through the medium of song. I recognized that exploring the rich emotional life of a character through story could be done far more economically in a four-minute song than a two-hour play; that a well-written song is like a miniature play, distilled down to its musical essence; and that singing, like acting, offers the means to externalize the deeper

internal self. I walked away from the theater and onto the bandstand and never looked back. I hustled up my first gigs around the spring of 1988."

She studied briefly with Jeri Southern and Sheila Jordan and often worked with pianist-singer Flip Nunez during 1990–94. In 1994 she made the first of her three CDs, *Twilight World*. The CDs have traced her growth, and in 2007 Sherri Roberts was singing better than ever.

"I love the happiness I feel when the band and I are swinging. I also love the spontaneity and the fact that there is a common language that allows you to get together with people you have never met before and still make beautiful music."

Recommended CDs: Each of Sherri Roberts' CDs, *Twilight World* (Brownstone 9604), *Dreamsville* (Brownstone 9811), and *The Sky Could Send You* (Pacific Coast Jazz 70001), include joyful and heartfelt moments.

Website: www.sherri-roberts.com

Ikey Robinson

b. July 28, 1904, Dublin, VA; d. October 25, 1990, Chicago, IL

Ikey Robinson should have been a big star. He was an excellent banjoist and guitarist who also occasionally played piano and clarinet, and his singing was versatile enough to cover classic jazz, swing, lowdown blues, hokum and a very credible Cab Calloway imitation. He also lived to be 86 but, due to his decision to spend many decades residing in Chicago, he was out of the limelight and off records during long stretches of his career.

Robinson made his living as a barber during 1918–22 while also having a part-time band. He gave up cutting hair and performed in his native Virginia with the Harry Watkins Orchestra (1922–24) and Bud Jenkins' Virginia Ravens (1924–26). Moving to Chicago in 1926, Robinson worked steadily in town during the next four years. Among his more significant jobs were playing banjo and guitar with the Alabamians, Jelly Roll Morton and Clarence Moore. He recorded with Sammy Stewart's Ten Knights of Syncopation, Clarence Williams and most notably with Jabbo Smith's Rhythm Aces in 1929, although in reality Smith was using Robinson's band. He relocated to New York where he worked during 1930–34, performing with Wilbur Sweatman, Noble Sissle and with his own groups.

All of Ikey Robinson's performances as a leader (except for two songs), which date from 1929–37, are on a single RST CD. In addition to some fine instrumentals, Robinson is heard as a blues singer, scatting and jiving on some hokum numbers, and sounding quite natural as a hot jazz vocalist. In addition to these dates, he recorded as a sideman with Richard M. Jones, the Levee Serenaders (which was led by Jelly Roll Morton), Alex Hill, the Hokum Trio, Clarence Williams (1930 and 1933) and the Fletcher Henderson Orchestra, singing "Take Me Away From The River" with the latter band in 1932. Most intriguing are two numbers recorded as duets with pianist Herman Chittison that have Robinson purposely emulating Cab Calloway in 1933.

Ikey Robinson moved back to Chicago in 1934, where he played with the big bands of Carroll Dickerson and Erskine Tate, appeared on sessions backing blues singers (including many with Georgia White) and gradually slipped away into obscurity. He led local bands for decades but did not record after 1938 until the early 1960s when he played banjo with Junie C. Cobb's group. Robinson worked with Franz Jackson's Original Jazz All Stars later in the decade, guested on sessions led by Little Brother Montgomery and Edith Wilson, toured

Europe and had reunions with Jabbo Smith, staying active until shortly before his death in 1990.

But the multi-talented Ikey Robinson should have done so much more, instead of ending up as a footnote from the 1920s and '30s.

Recommended CD: *Ikey Robinson* (RST 1508) contains all of his recordings as a leader and some of his most important sideman appearances.

Betty Roche
(Mary Elizabeth Roche)
b. January 9, 1918, Wilmington, DE;
d. February 16, 1999, Pleasantville, NJ

Betty Roche was a very talented singer who almost became famous during her two brief associations with Duke Ellington but today is in danger of being forgotten.

After winning an amateur contest at the Apollo Theater, Roche sang with the Savoy Sultans during 1941–42. She had brief stints with Hot Lips Page and Lester Young before joining Duke Ellington in 1943 where she succeeded Ivie Anderson. She was featured at Ellington's first Carnegie Hall Concert singing the "Blues" section of his monumental suite "Black, Brown And Beige." Unfortunately her period with Ellington was during the musicians' union strike and, by the time the strike was settled and Duke was ready to officially record "Black, Brown and Beige," she had already departed.

After leaving Ellington in 1944, Roche worked with Earl Hines, Clark Terry and Charles Brown. In 1952 she was briefly back with Ellington, recording a classic and very hip vocal version of "Take The 'A' Train." But she was soon gone again. She re-emerged during 1956–61 to lead three excellent albums, none of which were big sellers. Betty Roche then slipped away into retirement, spending her last 37 years outside of music.

Recommended CDs: *Take The 'A' Train* (Bethlehem 20-30142), *Singin' And Swingin'* (Original Jazz Classics 1718) and *Lightly And Politely* (Original Jazz Classics 1802) are all excellent, with the edge going to *Lightly And Politely* due to her expert improvising. Her classic recording of "Take The 'A' Train" is included on *Ellington Uptown* (Sony 512917).

Teri Roiger
(Theresa Kathleen Roiger)
b. January 27, 1951, Red Wing, MN

A versatile singer and a skilled improviser, Teri Roiger is also a talented lyricist.

She grew up in Cannon Falls, Minnesota, studied piano from the age of five and spent her teenage years as a church organist. "When I was first living in Minneapolis in the 1970s (attending the University of Minnesota), I met some people who were into jazz, and that was my introduction. I started studying piano with the world-renowned stride pianist and clarinetist Butch Thompson. He discovered my singing talents and I began singing with him. He introduced me to some great artists such as Billie Holiday, Fats Waller, Ella Fitzgerald and Jelly Roll Morton. I was all of a sudden surrounded by people who knew about jazz and was introduced to a whole new world. I fell in love with the music and this changed my life completely."

Her first concert was a duo concert with Butch Thompson. Roiger performed Billie Holiday songs with the Hall Brothers (a top trad band) and toured Europe for three months with Thompson. Returning to Minnesota, she worked with trios and big bands, gradually getting into more modern jazz. She eventually moved to New York where she studied with Jay Clayton, Sheila Jordan, and Jeanne Lee, working with many top musicians including saxophonists David "Fathead" Newman and Dewey Redman, trombonist Roswell Rudd, guitarist Kenny Burrell, pianists Gil Goldstein, Fred Hersch, and Frank Kimbrough, drummers Jack DeJohnette, Al Foster, and Matt Wilson and her husband bassist John Menegon. She also plays occasional solo gigs as a pianist-singer, and teaches jazz at SUNY New Paltz, Williams College and Bard College.

Recommended CDs: Teri Roiger has thus far led two CDs. *Misterioso* (Igmod 49901) has her singing three Thelonious Monk tunes, including her lyrics to the title cut (retitled "Listen To Your Soul") and her words to Kenny Barron's "Sunshower." *Still Life* (Maki 26609) includes her lyrics to two Dewey Redman compositions, the debut of Herbie Nichols' "So It Always Happens," two of her originals and Eddie Jefferson's "I Just Got Back In Town," which has his vocalese lyrics to James Moody's solo on "I Cover The Waterfront."

Website: www.teriroiger.com

Barbara Rosene
b. July 29, 1965, Cleveland, OH

One of the top singers of 1920s and '30s songs, Barbara Rosene was early on influenced by Annette Hanshaw but has since developed her own voice in the vintage music.

"My father was always listening to jazz and big band music and he had a quartet. His father had also been a singer in the '20s and '30s, and had been on the radio in Cleveland." She majored in English at John Carroll University and sang with the choir in addition to performing with a big band and at a small jazz bar. Always interested in early jazz, she says, "Annette Hanshaw, a singer from the '20s and '30s, was singing in a much hipper way than the other white women from that time. I also have listened a lot to Mildred Bailey, who was with Paul Whiteman's Orchestra in the '30s. She has a vulnerable quality that no one else had."

Rosene moved to New York and successfully auditioned over the phone for Vince Giordano, leader of one of the top 1920s-style bands. "In 1987 and '88 I began singing in New York with Vince Giordano's Nighthawks. Vince helped me a great deal, and I stopped doing the 'Sinatra thing' and got really involved with the '20s and '30s music. I took some time off, and when I came back, Vince helped me make my first CD, called *Deep Night*." Since then she has recorded several other albums including one, *All My Life*, that features her performing more "modern" material from the 1930s and '40s, she was featured on the all-star set CD *Celebrating Bix*, she sat in with both Les Paul at the Iridium and the Woody Allen Band ("Getting the 'thumbs up' from Woody was very satisfying"), has performed at top jazz and cabaret clubs in New York and most recently has been touring with the Harry James Big Band led by Fred Radke.

For the future she says, "I want to continue to bring the tunes of the 'Tin Pan Alley' composers to the attention of the public. I think early jazz is sexy and provocative. The lyrics are clever and intelligent, unlike most of the lyrics of today. My music is really American popular music with jazz behind it. I still think the most important thing is the melody; we must hear what the composer wrote."

Recommended CDs: *Deep Night* (Stomp Off 1368) is a tribute to Annette Hanshaw, Ruth Etting and other singers of the late 1920s. *Ev'rything's Made For Love* (Stomp Off 1393), *Moon Song* (Stomp Off 1405), and the recent *It Was Only A Sun Shower* (Stomp Off 1422) continue in that vein, reviving obscurities from the 1920s yet sounding fresh and original in their own way with Barbara Rosene sounding very much like a singer from the era, but not a copy of the past. *Celebrating Bix* (Arbors 19271) has her guesting with all-star classic jazz performers on a few numbers while *All My Life* (Azica 72232) moves her up a decade, singing superior songs from the swing era.

Website: www.barbararosene.com

Annie Ross
(Annabelle Short)
b. July 25, 1930, Surrey, England

One of the hippest female jazz singers of the 1950s, Annie Ross will always be best remembered for her association with Lambert, Hendricks and Ross, although she has had a remarkable career both before and after her time with the premiere vocalese group.

Born to parents who worked in vaudeville, she appeared onstage with them while still a tiny child. She moved to New York and soon Los Angeles at the age of four to live with her aunt, actress-singer Ella Logan. When she was eight, she appeared in an episode of *The Little Rascals*, singing a jazzed-up version of "Loch Lomond." When she was 11, Ross played Judy Garland's younger sister in *Presenting Lily Mars*. At 14, she composed a song ("Let's Fly") for a song contest that had Johnny Mercer and Dinah Shore as the judges. Mercer soon recorded the song with Paul Weston.

At 17, Ross returned to Europe, singing in London and joining composer Hugh Martin and Timothy Gray in a singing trio that performed in Paris. While in Paris, she made her recording debut, "Le Vent Vert," with James Moody. She was involved with Kenny Clarke (Charlie Parker became the godfather to their son), and performed in North Africa with Clarke, Moody and Coleman Hawkins. At 21, she recorded her first session as a leader in New York.

Her vocalese lyrics to "Twisted," based on a solo by tenor-saxophonist Wardell Gray, became a standard and she also had success with her lyrics and recordings to "Farmer's Market" and "Jackie." Ross worked and toured with the Lionel Hampton big band (which included trumpeter Clifford Brown) in 1953, performed in Paris with Blossom Dearie, and starred in London with a revue titled *Cranks* that featured Anthony Newley. When the show moved to New York, she returned to the Big Apple.

In 1957 she was one of a group of singers who attempted to record a recreation of Count Basie's band with Dave Lambert and Jon Hendricks. Lambert and Hendricks were frustrated with the unswinging nature of the singers other than Annie Ross, so they decided to record the project with just their three voices, overdubbing a few times to sound like the Basie orchestra. The resulting *Sing A Song Of Basie* was a sensation and launched Lambert, Hendricks and Ross. Singing with the group would be Annie Ross' main musical activity for the next five years, although she did record three solo albums during that period.

Quitting the group in 1962, supposedly due to her health, she returned to London, resumed her solo career, opened her nightclub, Annie's Room, and then gradually faded out of jazz in favor of acting in films and on stage. While her acting career was quite successful, quite a few years passed before she returned to recording jazz in the 1980s. By then her voice had faded and naturally aged. Utilizing her acting skills, she still performs jazz in New York, often giving dramatic renditions of standards and always answering requests to perform "Twisted."

Recommended CDs: *King Pleasure Sings/Annie Ross Sings* (Original Jazz Classics 217) only has four songs by Ross, but those include the original versions of "Twisted" and "Farmer's Market." *Skylark* (DRG 8470) is a fairly conventional but pleasing album from 1956 featuring Annie Ross singing standards with the backing of a British quartet. *Sings A Song With Mulligan* (EMI-Manhattan 46852) is a gem, matching Ross with baritonist Gerry Mulligan and either Chet Baker or Art Farmer on trumpet. *A Gasser* (Pacific Jazz 46854) is just as rewarding with Ross joined by either Zoot Sims or Bill Perkins on tenor. *Gypsy* (Pacific Jazz 33574) from 1959 is of some interest since Ross is in excellent voice but the material, songs from the play *Gypsy*, are only of occasional interest. The best of her post–Lambert, Hendricks and Ross recordings is 1963–64's *Annie Ross Sings A Handful Of Songs* (Fresh Sound 61), particularly a rather desperate and effective version of "Love For Sale." 1995's *Music Is Forever* (DRG 91446) and 2005's *Let Me Sing* (Consolidated Artists Productions 995) are primarily of historic interest and are only recommended to Annie Ross' most fervent fans.

Dennis Rowland
b. February 3, 1948, Detroit, MI

Dennis Rowland is best known for his period as the singer in the Count Basie Orchestra. The most significant successor to Joe Williams with Basie, Rowland has his own sound within the tradition.

"I was introduced to jazz through my parents' record collection. As a child I would hear strains of Ellington, Basie, Sarah Vaughan, Ella Fitzgerald and Nat King Cole on our brand new 'hi fi.'" He sang in an elementary school glee club and performed throughout his school years in various settings. Rowland took piano lessons from age eight and vocal lessons starting in junior high. He also played flute, including performing in the marching band for three years while attending Kentucky State College (1965–70), bassoon, cello and baritone horn. "I think I always knew that I would sing, act and maybe teach."

Rowland sang and acted in Detroit including a stint with the Jimmy Wilkins Orchestra (1972–77). In 1977 he joined the Count Basie Orchestra, staying until Basie's death in 1984. He was very familiar with Joe Williams, having heard Williams' records with Basie regularly since he was five, but he did his best to infuse the role with his own personality too. After the

Basie period ended, Rowland toured with Grover Washington (1985), Ray Anthony (off and on during 1988–94) and Les Brown (1995). He worked as an actor on stage including *Porgy And Bess*, *Seven Deadly Sins* (with Cleo Laine) and *Chicago* (2003), gigged and recorded with Frank Foster's Loud Minority Big Band, toured Europe, settled in Arizona, appeared in the film *Real Gone Cat*, and recorded three notable CDs for Concord starting in 1995 that display his versatility.

"I sing jazz because, at first, it was an extension of my classic training. Later on as I became more involved and learned more, I realized that jazz touches everyone. The many moods and colors, styles and concepts fit into my life. I only hope I can continue to grow as an artist and as a person so I can give homage to those who have gone before, and hope to those that are coming now."

Recommended CDs: *Rhyme, Rhythm And Reason* (Concord Jazz 4650) is an excellent first effort from Dennis Rowland, who had recently left Count Basie and was showing the influence of that association. *Get Here* (Concord Vista 4693), despite a few commercial selections, finds Rowland stretching out and sounding more original, mixing together some pop and funk with jazz. However, *Now Dig This* (Concord 4751), a tribute to Miles Davis (with the songs dating from 1956–61), is his finest recording so far, finding Rowland coming to terms with the straight-ahead tradition in his own voice.

Website: www.dennisrowland.com

Vanessa Rubin

b. March 14, 1957, Cleveland, OH

A fine singer who emerged in the 1980s and is capable of performing surprising music, Vanessa Rubin has a warm voice and is a warm interpreter of lyrics.

"My introduction to jazz came from listening to the records of my older siblings and parents around the house. Jazz was the predominant music played at home." She sang in school choruses and community talent shows, playing flute and piano in addition to singing. "I knew I was going to pursue singing as my profession when I decided I wanted to be my own boss and make a living out of my passion—singing. I knew it would be jazz after a live performance of 'God Bless The Child' during the talent competition of a beauty pageant of which I was a contestant. I discovered my calling."

After earning a degree in Journalism from Ohio State University, she taught school for several years and sang locally, including recording with the Cleveland All-Stars. In 1982 she took a chance and moved to New York. Rubin studied with Barry Harris, worked with Frank Foster's Loud Minority, and was on her way. When asked to name a few high points that occurred in her career since then, she says, "Working with giants like Pharoah Sanders, Jimmy Heath, Roland Hanna an Billy Taylor, and working with the big bands of Lionel Hampton, Frank Foster and Mercer Ellington. Also singing at the Cairo Opera House with Herbie Hancock, getting an invitation to perform at the White House by special request of the president

of Poland and his wife, and recording with Kenny Burrell, Grover Washington, Etta Jones and Freddy Cole."

Vanessa Rubin, who has recorded five albums for Novus and two for Telarc, has become a household name in the jazz world. "During my years of teaching while pursuing music at night, I was glad to have been able to be a tangible success story, mentor and inspiration to so many of my students, many of whom were not from the US and some of whom were 'at risk.' They were an inspiration to me as well."

Recommended CDs: *Soul Eyes* (Novus 63127), *Pastiche* (Novus 63152), which she names as her personal favorite of her CDs, *I'm Glad There Is You: A Tribute To Carmen McRae* (Novus 63170), *Vanessa Rubin Sings* (Novus 63186), the R&Bish *New Horizons* (Novus 67445), *Language Of Love* (Telarc 83465) and *Girl Talk* (Telarc 83480) are all worthwhile, although the chances are that Vanessa Rubin's definitive recording is still in the future.

Ellyn Rucker

b. August 2, 1937, Des Moines, IA

A sensuous singer with a deep, quiet voice and a superb bop-based pianist inspired by Bill Evans, Ellyn Rucker would be much better known if she did not mostly play in Denver.

She came from a musical family, with a mother who played organ and two other brothers who studied piano. "Our parents took us to see live bands in ballrooms and concerts. I remember seeing Woody Herman and Jazz At The Philharmonic. I sang in the church choir, listened to Lennie Tristano in high school, and loved Bach and movie soundtracks. After school, I put four girls together to sing Four Freshmen–style for assemblies. When I was 16, a club owner sort of demanded that I sing on a gig. I had always liked lyrics and thought singing was another way to express my moods."

Despite her interest in music and her talents, Ellyn Rucker did not become a full-time musician until 1979. Since then she has toured Europe several times, played at the Northsea Jazz Festival three straight years, worked with the late tenor-saxophonist Spike Robinson, and recorded for the Capri label. She is one of Denver's best kept jazz secrets.

Recommended CDs: *Ellyn* (Capri 74007), which features her in a quartet with Pete Christlieb, John Clayton and Jeff Hamilton in 1994, is still one of her finest recordings. Also quite worthy are *This Heart Of Mine* (Capri 74010), *Nice Work* (Capri 74017) with Spike Robinson, *Thoughts Of You* (Capri 74036), *Live In New Orleans* (Leisure 91054) and *Now* (Capri 74058).

Jimmy Rushing

b. August 26, 1903, Oklahoma City, OK;
d. June 8, 1972, New York, NY

Many of the male big band singers of the swing era are barely listenable today, since their overgrown baritone voices were usually showcased on overly sentimental and romantic ballads. Jimmy Rushing was a major exception. One of the great blues and swing singers, Rushing, known as "Mr. Five By Five" due to his portly figure, would have stood out (and not just physically) in any era.

Rushing played violin and piano as a youth, and studied music in high school. By the time he was 18, he was a professional singer. Rushing worked in California during 1923–24, gigged in Oklahoma City, and in 1927 moved to Kansas City where he joined Walter Page's Blue Devils. During his decade in Kansas City, Rushing often participated in the legendary after-hours jam sessions. He recorded his first vocal in 1929 with Page ("Blue Devil Blues") and then, as with most of the Blue Devils, he became a member of Bennie Moten's orchestra, being featured on 10 recordings during 1929–32. Although his voice was higher than it would be during his prime years, Rushing was already a major interpreter of blues.

Rushing stayed with the Moten band until the leader's death in 1935. Shortly after, he joined Count Basie. During his 14 years with Basie, Rushing became nationally famous, as did the band after it relocated to New York in late 1936. Rushing was one of Basie's top attractions, and among his most famous recordings with Count are "Boogie Woogie," "Good Morning Blues," "Sent For You Yesterday And Here You Come Today," "Going To Chicago Blues," "I Want A Little Girl," "Harvard Blues," "Take Me Back Baby," "Your Red Wagon" and "Money Is Honey." While most of his hits were blues, Rushing (like his successor Joe Williams) also loved interpreting standards.

After the Basie Orchestra broke up in 1949, Rushing had a successful solo career. He initially led a septet and then freelanced. Although his style remained unchanged, there were enough fans of mainstream swing to keep him busy during his later years. Producer John Hammond was one of his champions, arranging for him to record for Vanguard (1954–55 and 1957) and Columbia (1956–60). In addition, Rushing recorded as a leader for Excelsior (1946), Gotham (1950), King (1951–52), Parrot (1953), Colpix (1963), Bluesway (1967–68), Master Jazz (1967) and finally RCA (1971). Rushing appeared regularly at the Newport Jazz Festival, toured Europe (including working with Benny Goodman at the 1958 Brussels World's Fair), recorded a set with the Dave Brubeck Quartet, had many reunions with his fellow Basie alumni, was featured prominently in the classic TV special *The Sound Of Jazz* (1957), was part of the Jon Hendricks show *The Evolution Of The Blues*, and had a small role in the 1969 movie *The Learning Tree*.

Jimmy Rushing stayed true to the Kansas City blues, swing tunes and ballads that he loved throughout his career, still sounding in excellent form on 1971's *The You And Me That Used To Be*, recorded a year before his death at age 68. Although a case can be made for Frank Sinatra (who was a very different type of singer), otherwise Rushing was the top male jazz singer to emerge from the swing era big bands. His performances still sound undated, timeless and fun.

Recommended CDs: *1946–1953* (Jazz Classics 5085) has all of Mr. Five By Five's pre-LP dates as a leader. *Oh Love* (Vanguard 79606) and *Every Day* (Vanguard 79607) reshuffle the order of Rushing's three Vanguard albums, but together include all of the music. *Cat Meets Chick/The Jazz Odyssey Of James Rushing* (Collectables 7496) reissues in full two of Rushing's concept albums from his Columbia years, as does *Rushing Lullabies/Jimmy Rushing And The Big Brass* (Columbia 65118). *Five Feet Of Soul* (Roulette 81830) brings back his Colpix session. *Every Day I Have The Blues* (Impulse 547967) reissues on one CD Rushing's two Bluesway dates from 1967 to 1968, which feature him sounding surprisingly comfortable in more modern settings. *The You And Me That Used To Be* (Bluebird

6460) shows that, even at the end of his life, Jimmy Rushing had a commanding presence and a powerful voice.

Jackie Ryan
(Jacqueline Helena Therese Ryan)
b. Greenbrae, CA

An impressive singer with a powerful voice, Jackie Ryan sings quite comfortably in English, Spanish and Portuguese.

"I discovered jazz when I turned on the radio one day when I was a young singer performing rhythm and blues music. Betty Carter was singing 'Spring Can Really Hang You Up The Most.' I heard that, spun around and looked at the radio in awe of this incredible sound; I was smitten on the spot."

Jackie Ryan sang constantly as a child and at 15 began singing professionally. "I joined a band. We wrote and performed our own songs at dances up and down the state. I was belting out gospel and blues (à la Sam Cooke, Mavis Staples and Otis Redding) six to seven nights a week for five hours a night over loud music. After several years, I lost my voice—or let's just say it went from a 3½-octave range to less than one. I started to sound like Miles Davis when I spoke. When I went to the ear, nose and throat doctor, I discovered I had 'bowed vocal cords.' I was told I had to quit singing, talking, laughing or basically making any sounds until I could get my vocal cords to work properly again. It took two years of speech therapy to correct the condition. So I spent my time well. I started to study theory, learned piano, learned to paint, and started listening to the radio a lot. That's when I accidentally discovered jazz."

Since returning to singing, Jackie Ryan has dedicated herself to jazz. She remembers being encouraged by Eddie Jefferson. Among her musical associations are the Rudy Salvini big band, Clark Terry, vibraphonist Terry Gibbs, clarinetist Buddy DeFranco and pianists Larry Vuckovich, Mike Wofford, Jon Mayer, Gareth Williams and Amina Figarova. She is also proud of having Toots Thielemans on one of her records, and most recently saxophonist Red Holloway.

"Sometimes we get bogged down with all the details of trying to get our music heard. It can be a tough life and very challenging in many ways. But, it is nice to stop and think of how very lucky we musicians are to have the opportunity to share our music; with each other and with our audiences. Singing jazz is as free as a human being can get without wings."

Recommended CDs: *For Heaven's Sake* (Blueport 4) from 2000 was recorded live on one night with the Mike Wofford Trio, whom Jackie Ryan had just met. It is an impressive start to her recording career. *Whisper Not* (Jazz House 66) was recorded with British musicians at Ronnie Scott's in London. *Passion Flower* (Open Art 727) has Ryan accompanied by a band with Larry Vuckovich and has both standards (including a Billy Strayhorn medley) and her lyrics to Joe Henderson's "The Kicker" and Barry Harris' "Deep Love." *This Heart Of Mine* (Open Art 728) is a particularly strong all-round set with guest appearances by Toots Thielemans and tenor-saxophonist Ernie Watts while *You And The Night And The Music* (Open Art 729) has Red Holloway on five of the 14 tracks and includes duets with harpist Carol Robbins and guitarist Larry Koonse, plus memorable versions of "Bésame Mucho" and "I Just Found Out About Love."

Website: www.jackieryan.com

Spider Saloff
b. October 14, 1960, Camden, NJ

A classy singer based in Chicago who loves vintage standards, Spider Saloff is also an important radio host.

"When I was 14, I told my parents that I was going to be in the school variety show, to which they responded, 'Doing what?' They were shocked to find out that I really could sing. I had my first professional job in a summer stock theater company shortly after that while still in high school." She studied acting at Glassboro State College and took private voice lessons, but she considers herself largely self-taught as a singer.

"When I was a teenager, I went up to New York City for a weekend. Two of my best friends had run away to NYC to be actors. They took me out to a bar in Greenwich Village and encouraged me to sing. I got up on the stage in my vintage purple silk dress thinking I was Bette Midler, and sang 'Don't Rain On My Parade' to wild applause. Even as a goofy teenager, I could see that this sensation of connecting with an audience would be a part of my life forever."

In 1990, through a friendship with the nephew of George Gershwin, Leopold Godowski III, she had an opportunity to perform for the Gershwin family members. Saloff has since performed many all-Gershwin shows, including in 1998 in St. Petersburg, Russia, at the world's *Gershwin Centennial Celebration*. She also had the honor of performing the American debut of the long-lost Billy Strayhorn ballad "So This Is Love" in 1993.

In 1994, Spider Saloff moved to Chicago and has been part of the local jazz scene after since. She developed, co-created and hosts the syndicated PBS radio series *Words And Music*. "Cranking out an hour-long show every week that examines the works from the Great American Songbook is like recording a new album on a weekly basis." In addition she has recorded several CDs, teaches a group jazz vocal class and performs in the Chicago area.

"Up until about five years ago, my mother would constantly ask me 'So, do you think you'll ever get tired of this show business?' It hasn't happened yet."

Recommended CDs: Of her six recordings, *1938* (Kopaesthetics 101), *Sextet* (Kopaesthetics 103), *Memory Of All That: A Celebration Of Gershwin* (Kopaesthetics 104), *A New Set Of Standards* (Kopaesthetics 106), which has her singing recent songs by Robert Yaseen, *Cool Yule* (Kopaesthetics 107) and *Like Glass* (Kopaesthetics 108), Spider Saloff named *Sextet*,

which features trumpeter Tom Harrell and baritonist Nick Brignola, as her personal favorite so far.

Website: www.spiderjazz.com

Joe Sanders
b. October 15, 1894, Thayer, KS; d. May 15, 1965, Kansas City, MO

Although he outlived his musical partner Carleton Coon by 33 years, Joe Sanders' most significant music was made as co-leader of the Coon-Sanders Nighthawks. Sanders sang with local church choirs and studied piano, choosing music as his career despite being a promising baseball pitcher who earned the nickname of "The Old Left-Hander." During World War I he was a sergeant in the Army, also leading a combo in Texas called the Camp Bowie Jazz Hounds.

In 1918, while on leave in Kansas City, he went to a local music store, picked out a few songs, and started singing one of them. Carleton Coon, who just happened to be in the store, jumped in and harmonized with Sanders, and a friendship was born. After they left the military, they briefly ran a booking agency and then formed the Coon-Sanders Novelty Orchestra. The interplay between the co-leaders along with their individual vocals made the group popular from the start. They recorded one instrumental in 1921 and on December 5, 1922, the band appeared for the first time on the radio, broadcasting from WOAF in Kansas City. Since their radio show did not start until midnight, the group was renamed the Coon-Sanders Nighthawks.

With both Sanders and Coon contributing jazz-oriented vocals (during an era when most male vocalists sounded like either amateurs or frustrated opera singers), the band had a personality of its own. Sanders, in addition to playing piano, contributed to the arrangements, which were both unpredictable and swinging. The Coon-Sanders Nighthawks moved their home base to Chicago and were at their prime when they were based at the Blackhawk Restaurant during 1926–30. They recorded prolifically starting in 1924, and among Sanders' best solo numbers as a vocalist are "Who Wouldn't Love You," "Everything Is Hotsy-Totsy Now," "My Baby Knows How," "I Need Lovin'," "Ready For The River" and especially "Here Comes My Ball And Chain." In addition, his duets with Coon, which include "I'm Gonna Charleston Back To Charleston," "I Ain't Got Nobody" and "Sluefoot," are full of the joyful and carefree spirit of the 1920s.

After spending six months in New York during 1931–32, the Coon-Sanders Nighthawks returned to Chicago. What should have been a successful run at the Hotel Sherman turned into a disaster when Carleton Coon went into surgery for an abscessed tooth that he had neglected. He died on May 4, 1932, from blood poisoning. The Nighthawks were otherwise still intact but the spirit was gone. There were no further recordings, and within a year the group broke up.

Joe Sanders led another big band in the Chicago area for a decade, but it failed to make an impression and never recorded. He later became a studio musician and in the 1950s was a member of the Kansas City Opera Company, passing away in 1965. By then, few realized that, along with Carleton Coon and Cliff Edwards, Sanders had been one of the first male jazz singers to record.

Recommended CDs: *Coon-Sanders Nighthawks, Vols. 1–4* (The Old Masters 111, 112, 113 and 114) has the complete output by the popular and influential orchestra including all of Joe Sanders' recorded vocals.

Jody Sandhaus
b. April 29, Houston, TX

Jody Sandhaus is a fine singer who has a cool tone and delivers her musical message without wasting notes or faking emotions. She considers two of her inspirations to be Irene Kral and Abbey Lincoln.

Sandhaus took classical piano lessons, earned a degree in Liberal Arts at Case Western Reserve University in Cleveland, and studied piano and voice for a semester at the Cleveland Institute of Music. However, it was when she was living in the West Indies that she discovered jazz. "I was living in St. Maarten in a rented home. The owner had left behind 40 or so albums of jazz. There were no phones or TV on the island at the time, so I listened to a lot of music including Benny Goodman, Peggy Lee, Ella Fitzgerald, Maxine Sullivan and others. I recorded the albums on a reel to reel tape and had the music playing constantly in a restaurant I opened. The jazz music became part of the character of the restaurant and changed my life."

Returning to New York, she became part of the local jazz scene. "I was determined to pursue a musical career in the States since I was returning with a blank slate, some money in my pocket, and no pressing responsibilities. I studied at the Herbert Bergoff Studio in Greenwich Village and took a class with the director, Ward Baker, who impressed upon me the importance of singing truthfully. He discouraged the excess hand waving and acting out of a song. This became important to me then and it still is today." In 1992 she met pianist Peter Malinverni, who became her husband, and they have worked together regularly since.

"The fact that one can play jazz with an ensemble of musicians who have never met before, or don't even speak the same language, and make music together with just a song title and key is a beautiful and amazing thing."

Recommended CDs: Each of Jody Sandhaus' recordings, *Winter Moon* (Saranac 1002), *I Think Of You* (Consolidated Artists 954) and *A Fine Spring Morning* (Consolidated Artists 981) feature her subtle improvising, superior storytelling and joy at uncovering obscure gems from the past.

Website: www.jodysandhaus.com

Sandy Sasso
b. May 17, 1949, Rahway, NJ

Sandy Sasso is a veteran jazz singer with a deep and attractive voice who works regularly in the New York area.

Sasso remembers hearing Dave Brubeck's "Take Five" when she was 12. "For me, that was the moment." She studied piano from age six, played flute and violin as a child, studied voice and piano at Westminster Choir College, and graduated from Monmouth University.

Among her many experiences since then have been singing and touring with the Nelson Riddle Orchestra, the Benny Goodman Big Band and the Jimmy Dorsey ghost band, performing with Joe Williams at the Blue Note, and opening for a variety of personalities including Victor Borge, Bobby Short, Bob Newhart, Merv Griffin and Charlie Callas. Sandy Sasso has also led two CDs and appeared at a countless number of clubs and festivals through the years.

"Jazz suffers from botox injections. So much of it is expressionless, so sterile, serious and overly categorized. It has sometimes become exclusionary and elitist. I don't think that this is truly representative of jazz. It is more like everyone is dressed up in 'jazz clothes' and trying to fool people into thinking they look the way jazz should sound while at the same time spouting all this preposterous stuff about respecting the tradition. In jazz, there used to be the expectation (from both musicians and the audience) that we improvise, explore, joke around and experiment. Well the way I look at it is, if you ain't tappin' your foot, I ain't doing my job."

Recommended CDs: *Mixed Grill* (Charlie Boy 1) and *All My Men* (Charlie Boy 2) feature Sandy Sasso mostly performing standards, swinging the songs in her distinctive voice and coming up with fresh variations.

Website: www.sandysasso.com

Cynthia Sayer
b. May 20, 1956, Waltham, MA

Best known as a banjoist (a rarity in jazz today), Cynthia Sayer is also a fine singer who does an excellent job of interpreting early jazz standards.

"As I kid, I enjoyed many kinds of music, including rock, folk, classical, musical theater and jazz. It is only in hindsight that I realize early jazz had some special appeal. I started piano at age six, and piano was my primary instrument through college. Along the way I studied viola for about six years, starting at age nine, and then the drums at age 10. I also messed around on guitar for most of my child and teen years. At age 13 I started banjo lessons only because I wanted a drum set, but my parents got me a banjo instead in the hopes of diverting me from the drums. I realized I'd never get my drums, so I figured I might as well play the banjo. It eventually became my major instrument."

She sang from the time she was a child, learning basic guitar chords originally in order to accompany herself singing. Sayer sang in school shows and in community theater productions. Her first major job was playing in an all-female band at Shea Stadium when she was 17. Sayer graduated from Ithaca College as an English major in 1977. "I never made a conscious decision to be a performer. I just started getting work, and it evolved into my profession. I had intended to have some fun with music temporarily, before attending law school and then going on to do 'real' work, but I never did go back to school. By age 26 I realized that this seemed to be my chosen profession, and I haven't stopped since."

Among Cynthia Sayer's many musical jobs through the years have been playing piano with Woody Allen since 1985, and working with Dick Hyman, Milt Hinton, Buck Pizzarelli, Dick Wellstood and George Segal's band in the 1980s. She has also appeared with the New York Philharmonic (playing *Rhapsody*

In Blue), performed a concert of James Reese Europe's music at Carnegie Hall, been featured on many soundtracks, appeared with fellow banjoist Bela Fleck, and led her own groups in addition to playing with the who's who of trad jazz.

"I should mention that I categorize myself as a professional player who also sings. However, I have worked as a vocalist without playing as well through the years."

Recommended CDs: *Jazz At Home* (Jazzology 270), *String Swing* (Jazzology 370), *Souvenirs* (Plunk Productions) and *Attractions* (Plunk Productions) offer strong examples of Cynthia Sayer's singing and banjo playing.

Website: www.cynthiasayer.com

Diane Schuur
b. December 10, 1953, Tacoma, WA

A popular singer with a beautiful voice, Diane Schuur (widely known as "Deedles") is at her best when she is caressing the melodies of vintage standards.

Blinded at birth due to a hospital accident, she grew up loving music. "At around two years of age, I heard Dinah Washington singing, 'What A Difference A Day Makes' and was thoroughly enthralled by the experience. I remember very clearly sitting in front of a mic singing along with Keddy Lester's 'Love Letters' when I was nine. I listened to Patti Page, Kay Starr and lots of other female vocalists who were popular at the time. Dinah Washington, Nancy Wilson, Ella Fitzgerald and Sarah Vaughan became my main influences. Also, I started playing piano when I was three."

A professional singer from the time she was nine, performing country music, she met George Shearing, who became one of her mentors, when she was 11. Deedles made her debut at the Monterey Jazz Festival in 1975 with drummer Ed Shaughnessy, but it was her appearance in 1979 that was noticed by Stan Getz, who became one of her boosters. Three years later at a televised concert at the White House, Getz featured Deedles, leading to her signing with GRP and quickly becoming a household name in jazz.

Although she had the tendency of screeching in her upper register in the early days, Diane Schuur has greatly moderated that flaw. She often scats in unison with her piano but sounds particularly special when she sings superior melodies. Her career is full of highlights, including appearing with Getz at Carnegie Hall in 1986, recording with the Count Basie Orchestra in 1987 and touring and collaborating with B.B. King, Maynard Ferguson, Ray Charles and Stevie Wonder. She has never lost her popularity and has toured, appeared at clubs and festivals and recorded regularly.

"I love performing jazz because it is never boring and it tests my soul and intellectual skills to the max."

Recommended CDs: Diane Schuur has recorded quite a few CDs. The ones with an asterisk are the ones that I recommend first: **Deedles* (GRP 9510), *Schuur Thing* (Universal/Polygram 9014), **Timeless* (GRP 9540), **Diane Schuur And The Count Basie Orchestra* (Universal 5166), *Talkin' 'Bout You* (GRP 9567), **Pure Schuur* (GRP 9628), *In Tribute* (GRP 2006), **Love Songs* (GRP 9713), *Heart To Heart* (GRP 9767) with B.B. King, *Love Walked In* (GRP 9841), **Blues For Schuur* (GRP 9863), *Music Is My Life* (Atlantic 83150), *Friends For Schuur* (Concord 4898), *Swingin' For Schuur* (Concord 4982) with Maynard Ferguson, *Midnight* (Concord 2209), **Schuur Fire* (Concord 2264) with the Caribbean Jazz Project and *Live In London* (GR2 Classics 0002).

Website: www.dianeschuur.com

Cindy Scott
b. February 3, 1966, Tupelo, MS

Cindy Scott has one impressive CD out and is currently part of the jazz scene in New Orleans.

She sang in her church choir while growing up, taking the part of first soprano. Scott started on flute at the age of 11, attending LSU on a flute scholarship (1984–88), primarily playing classical music. "My junior year, I went to Germany and studied at Tuebingen University. That's where I started singing jazz, in the jazz cellars of the Black Forest. For the next two years, I went to the University of South Carolina and got my Master's in International Business in 1990. While there, I got to sing with the USC Left Bank Big Band and the Progressive Jazz and Fusion Ensemble."

Although she had some gigs after college, Cindy Scott worked in the corporate world for 10 years, living in Houston and only singing occasionally on the side. "In the summer of 2001, I was at a vocal jazz workshop at the University of North Texas, and that whole week I was so anxious and restless and emotional. I felt like I was coming out of my skin. One day, late in the week, it was like I was hit by lightning. I just had to do this. I had to commit myself to being the best musician I could, and that meant figuring out a way to do it full time. I called my husband that very minute, crying, and told him my decision. He said, 'Cindy, I've been trying to tell you that for 10 years.'"

In 2002 Cindy Scott recorded her first CD, *Major To Minor*. In 2003 she and her husband appeared on the reality TV home remodeling show, *House Rules*. "After 100 days of hard labor, Bill and I won the house we remodeled on the show. This allowed me to leave my day job permanently and focus on music." She and her husband moved to South Louisiana so she could accept a full graduate assistantship in Jazz Studies at the University of New Orleans. Although they lost their apartment during Hurricane Katrina, they eventually returned to New Orleans, and Cindy Scott has become an important force in the local scene, both as a teacher and as a singer.

"I love having the freedom to make the music my own. It is not just freedom to personalize this music, it's a requirement. If you don't do that, it's not jazz."

Recommended CD: Cindy Scott's one CD, *Major To Minor* (Catahoula 783 707 626 420), is a strong effort, as she gives standards her own spin and warmth.

Website: www.cindyscott.us

Cynthia Scott
b. July 20, El Dorado, AR

Considering how interesting a life Cynthia Scott has had, it is surprising that she is not better known.

Cynthia Scott was the tenth of 12 children born to a couple who were married for 70 years. She began singing when she was four, starting out with gospel music in her father's church. She sang in high school with an R&B band called "The Funny Company featuring The Sisters Of Soul." "After high school, I moved to Dallas and became an airline stewardess. I didn't like flying, still don't. One day while at a day job, I went through the yellow pages in the phone book and started calling nightclubs to ask if they needed a singer. I posed as my sister and told them that I had a sister that could really sing." After many calls, she landed an audition at the Candlelight Club. "I showed up that Saturday scared to death, but not enough to not go. It went well. The musicians on stage were real jazz musicians and the whole band was great. But I realized that the music I sang in high school from the Motown days was not going to work with these guys."

A little later, Cynthia Scott went on the road as one of Ray Charles' Raelettes, touring and recording with Charles. In more recent times she has performed tributes to Ray Charles at jazz festivals, using some of his alumni. After moving to New York, she performed at the key establishments, and for 10 years was the vocalist at the Supper Club with the 17-piece Supper Club Big Band. Scott was also the featured vocalist with Lionel Hampton, toured with Cab Calloway, performed the music of Duke Ellington with Wynton Marsalis at Lincoln Center, and served as a Jazz Ambassador in 2004, performing in France and five countries in West Africa. She has also sung in Russia and China, and found time to earn a Masters in Music from the Manhattan School of Music.

"I studied acting from a great teacher Uta Hagen, and she taught me that you have to put yourself into your performance. That was a very important lesson for me because I saw it in the church. I can tell when a person is singing outside themselves or a musician is playing in their head instead of their soul or spirit. I appreciate New York for being a great training ground and making me grow up, but my foundation comes from a small town in Arkansas, where I believe the beat of the music was put into my soul. We never needed a metronome."

Recommended CDs: Cynthia Scott has four CDs on her Ttocs label. *I Just Want To Know*, *A La Carte Live* and *Storytelling* are each excellent, but *Live In Japan Boom Boom*, which has her performing eight standards and a blues with the Norman Simmons Trio, is her definitive recording so far.

Website: www.cynthiascott.com

Jimmy Scott
b. July 17, 1925, Cleveland, OH

Jimmy Scott's expertise on ballads, which he often takes at very slow tempos, can result in heartbreaking performances. Aspects of his life were heartbreaking, but he is a survivor who lived long enough to be recognized for his talents and to be thanked by those he influenced, most notably Nancy Wilson.

Afflicted with Kallmann's syndrome, a genetic condition, Scott had his growth stunted at five feet and his voice never changed, staying in the range of a boy soprano. One of 10

children, he sang early on in church choirs. He toured in tent shows and gained some attention for his work with Lionel Hampton (who named him "Little Jimmy Scott") in the late 1940s, having a hit with "Everybody's Somebody's Fool" in 1950. He started his solo career in 1951 and made singles for several labels. Scott signed a contract with Savoy in 1955, which at first seemed like a good move. However, in 1962 when he recorded an album for Ray Charles' Tangerine label, it had to be withdrawn because Savoy claimed he was an exclusive Savoy artist, despite the fact that they refused to record him. Scott struggled for years, having to take a job as a shipping clerk and as an elevator operator in a hotel to make ends meet. Though he recorded an album for Atlantic in 1969, it did not go anywhere or help his situation.

Although he began to perform in clubs again starting in 1985, Jimmy Scott's fortunes did not change until the beginning of the 1990s. He recorded an album for J's Way Records and, when he sang at the funeral of songwriter Doc Pomus, he was signed to Sire Records, beginning a major comeback. Now considered a rediscovered legend, he guested on a Lou Reed album, did some acting, and his 1992 album *All The Way* gained him a great deal of attention. His other recordings for Warner Bros/Sire did even better and he performed and recorded regularly after decades of neglect. Scott recorded four albums of jazz ballads for the Milestone label and led his own group, the Jazz Expressions.

When asked to name some of the high points of his career, Jimmy Scott replied, "Cutting my first record, 'Everybody's Somebody's Fool,' singing 'Why Was I Born' at two presidential inaugurations (Eisenhower's in 1953 and Clinton's 40 years later), singing on movie soundtracks, appearing in a couple of films, being inducted into the Rhythm and Blues Foundation Hall of Fame, and touring Europe, Japan and South America. On the other hand, not being given the opportunity to get the type of recognition I feel I've earned, to play at the type of venues and earn the income of some of my peers, many who claim me as their influence, is a disappointment. It hurts deeply, but I'm still waiting for that opportunity to exploit the abilities and talent I have. I have a saying, 'You may give out a little, but don't give up.'"

Recommended CDs: *Everybody's Somebody's Fool* (GRP 669) has Jimmy Scott's first sides as a leader, performances originally made for Decca. *The Savoy Years And More* (Savoy 17053) is an excellent three-CD overview of Scott's work for Savoy and some later items including nine selections from 1972. Other worthy Savoy sets include *All Or Nothing At All: The Dramatic Jimmy Scott* (Savoy 17567), *All Over Again* (Savoy 263) and *If You Only Knew* (Savoy 17099). *Falling In Love Is Wonderful* (Rhino 3643) finally reissues Scott's lost album for the Tangerine label, while *Lost And Found* (Rhino 71059) reconstructs his Atlantic project. Jimmy Scott made a comeback with *All The Way* (Sire 26955) and since then has recorded *Dream* (Sire 45629), *Heaven* (Warner Bros. 46211), *Mood Indigo* (Milestone 9305), *Over The Rainbow* (Milestone 9314), *But Beautiful* (Milestone 9321) and *Moon Glow* (Milestone 9332).

Website: www.jimmyscottofficialwebsite.org

Annie Sellick
b. February 26, 1975, Nashville, TN

Annie Sellick is a rarity: a resident of Nashville who hates country music. An up-and-coming jazz singer, she performs with enthusiasm and versatility.

Sellick played violin for three years as a child, had 10 weeks of piano, and at 16 taught herself guitar. She earned a degree in gerontology at Middle Tennessee State University. Sitting in with veteran guitarist Roland Gresham's group in a club near the college was the start of her jazz career. Sellick sang regularly with the trio for four years. "I knew when I turned 20 that I had to make a decision that I would stick with my whole life. I didn't want to be flailing around when it came to career decisions. It was going to be either nursing home administration or jazz singing. My dad gave me some timely advice. 'Whatever you do well naturally that most people have to work at, you should do.' I was natural at performing, so that was it."

She moved back to Nashville, attended the Nashville Jazz Workshop (under the direction of pianist Lori Mechem and bassist Roger Spencer), performed weekly with pianist Beegie Adair for three years, and her career was underway. Since then, she has recorded four CDs for her Chalice Music label (including one with organist Joey DeFrancesco), toured as a substitute for Roberta Gambarini with Mark O'Connor's Hot Swing, had a sold-out performance with the Nashville Symphony, and appeared regularly in New York, Atlanta, Montreal and Los Angeles. In recent times Annie Sellick has performed gypsy swing in Europe with her group called Annie and the Hot Club.

Recommended CDs: Annie Sellick's four CDs are *Stardust On My Sleeve* (Chalice 1115029), *No Greater Thrill* (Chalice 1115031), a live date with the Gerald Clayton Trio plus Bruce Forman that is called a *Little Piece Of Heaven* (Chalice 1115030) and *Annie And The Hot Club Play The Songs Of Tom Sturdevant* (Chalice 37101 389426).

Website: www.anniesellick.com

Ingrid Sertso

b. February 26, 1944, Germany

Ingrid Sertso is an important, if sometimes overlooked, contributor to the more advanced styles of jazz as a singer and an educator and behind the scenes. Her adventurous singing has long been open to the influences of music from Europe, Latin America and African.

"My mother was a classical pianist. I studied piano and attended the Conservatory in Heidelberg, Germany. The day my older brother took me to a Count Basie concert is when I knew that I wanted to sing jazz."

Sertso performed in Europe with her own groups and with such notable musicians as Don Cherry, Eric Dolphy, Steve Lacy and vibraphonist Karl Berger. She also taught music. In 1972 she moved to the United States and put out her recording debut, *We Are You* (Calig). Her association with major names continued and she worked with Cherry, Lee Konitz, Sam Rivers, Jimmy Giuffre, Perry Robinson, Leroy Jenkins, Dave Holland, Ed Blackwell and Bob Moses, among many others.

Sertso was on the faculty of the Naropa Institute in Boulder, Colorado (1975–76) and taught at the Banff Centre of Fine Arts in Calgary, Canada. In the late 1970s she became the co-director of the Creative Music Studio in Woodstock, New York with Karl Berger, a position she held for a decade and resulted in her having an impact on the music of many younger musicians.

Sertso toured Europe in 1979, being backed by the Woodstock Workshop Orchestra. She has since performed and taught all over the world including in Europe, West Africa and South America. She had a trio with Karl Berger and guitarist Paul Koji Shigihara that mixed together her poetry with originals and standards. She is currently working with Berger in releasing live CDs from the large archives of the Creative Music Studio on their ACR label.

When asked about future goals, Ingrid Sertso simply answers, "To do more recordings and to be able to help and heal with what I do in music. Music is a healing force of the universe. I hope that I am part of it."

Recommended CDs: Most of Ingrid Sertso's recordings have been for small labels, including Horo, ITM, Trio and India Navigation. *Dance With It* (Enja 8024) from 1994 is one of Ingrid Sertso's best known CDs and serves as a fine introduction to her highly individual singing. *On And On* (Artists-Create-Recordings 001) is a duo album with Karl Berger.

Barbara Sfraga

b. October 28, 1956, Bay Shore, NY

Barbara Sfraga is a very likable singer who sometimes pushes the boundaries of jazz into sound explorations, considering herself a "voicist."

She started playing piano when she was four, switching to organ at 11. "It was all by ear at first because that was so much easier for me, and I was into instant gratification back then." Sfraga was a church organist during her teenage years. She studied classical voice in high school and college, and also played keyboards in rock bands. "While in college, I had the good fortune to take a History of Jazz Piano class with one of the greats, Dr. Billy Taylor. That piqued my interest. Then I discovered Mark Murphy and he blew me away."

Sfraga was a member of guitarist Sal Salvador's quintet, singing reorchestrated big band charts by Salvador, Hank Levy and Teo Macero in a quintet with two guitars. She wrote the lyrics to Chick Corea's "Got A Match," and had a wide variety of other gigs. "I've worked as a singing hostess, played piano and sang for 14 years on a dinner cruise yacht, and played at more than my share of weddings and bar mitzvahs. My turning point came in '97 when I finally decided to musically go for it and take control business-wise as well. By that time, I started to have something to say musically. I wrote out a five-year plan that included a record deal and accomplished everything on that plan within those five years. Growing your art and your business simultaneously is so important. I now give one-on-one consultations to musicians as well as conduct seminars on the biz of music."

Inspired by Mark Murphy who she considers her mentor, Sfraga's first CD *Oh What A Thrill* from 2000 uses her group of the period and has appearances by Murphy and pianist Fred Hersch. Her music has since become freer, and for a time she often led a voice-bass-drums trio.

"The freedom that jazz personifies opens up the music to all that is life. What originally intrigued me was how far one can go out on a limb. No limits, no boundaries. When you move with players who feel that revelation deep inside of the beat, it's a new ride every time. Could be the same ol' chestnuts, but you experience deeper depths and more vibrant colors each time you set sail."

Recommended CDs: *Oh What A Thrill* (Naxos 86047) features Barbara Sfraga turning an eclectic program into creative jazz. *Under The Moon* (A440 Music Group 1025) finds her transforming mostly older standards (along with a Bob Dylan song) into adventurous flights, while *Timelessness Frozen In Time* (SyncTimiCity Productions 2602) emphasizes her diverse originals. All three sets are full of passion and unexpected moments.

Website: www.barbarasfraga.com

Kendra Shank
b. April 23, 1958, Woodland, CA

Kendra Shank is a singer who improvises but always tells stories in her music. Her recent *A Spirit Free: The Abbey Lincoln Songbook* is one of her finest recordings.

She grew up as part of an artistic family (her mother was an actress and her father a playwright), and remembers hearing the album of the Broadway score of *The Threepenny Opera* played on a constant basis when her mother was rehearsing for an important role. Kendra Shank sang in a musical theater production of *Brigadoon* when she was eight. "When I first started learning guitar at age 13, I'd come home from school every day and shut myself in my room and play and sing for hours. I attended open mic sessions in my freshman year of college, playing guitar and singing folk songs. The following summer I busked in the subway and sidewalk cafés in Paris; I was 19." She earned a BA in Art and French from the University of Washington in 1982 and became part of the folk scene for a time. In 1988, while in Paris, Shank became very interested in jazz after hearing a Billie Holiday recording, and she soon became a regular at jazz clubs. "At that time, I was making a living as a solo artist with guitar playing folk, folk/pop, country, and French chansons in bars and coffee houses, but I bought a Real Book and learned a few jazz standards which I played in a sort of folk/jazz hybrid." When she dedicated herself to jazz in 1989, she began studying with Jay Clayton, whom she considers a major inspirational force.

Since then Kendra Shank, who toured the West Coast with Bob Dorough in 1991, has primarily led her own groups and has been performing regularly, often in Europe. In 1992, Shirley Horn recommended her to Mapleshade Records (where she recorded her first CD) and showcased her between her own sets at the Village Vanguard, marking Shank's New York debut. She was based in Seattle until 1997 when she moved to New York. Shank sang wordless horn parts on five songs on guitarist Peter Leitch's *Blues On The Corner* CD for Reservoir. She became good friends with Abbey Lincoln (guesting on her *Over The Years* CD in 2000), was influenced by her, and did a superb job of interpreting her music on *A Spirit Free*. "Abbey, who is a friend, mentor and spiritual guide, has encouraged and inspired me to embrace my folk music roots and all of the music that is in me, and not to be limited by categorization.

She has also encouraged me to play the guitar again, after having neglected it for several years." Kendra Shank has led her quartet (with pianist Frank Kimbrough, bassist Dean Johnson and drummer Tony Moreno) for the past eight years.

Recommended CDs: Each of Kendra Shank's CDs, *After Glow* (Mapleshade 02132), *Wish* (Jazz Focus 028), *Reflections* (Jazz Focus 037), and *A Spirit Free: Abbey Lincoln Songbook* (Challenge 73253), feature her heartfelt and highly original interpretations, with *A Spirit Free* being the true gem of the lot.

Website: www.kendrashank.com

Ian Shaw
b. June 2, 1962, St. Asaph, North Wales

Considered by many to be England's top male jazz singer, Ian Shaw won the "Best Vocalist" award at the 2006 BBC Jazz Awards.

"My father played brass in bands and my mum listened to Radio 2, especially Mel Tormé, Ella and Nancy Wilson. I sang in school choirs and folk groups, and played piano and trumpet from the age of 15."

Shaw studied at the College of Music and attended Trinity College while working in the studios and singing with local rock groups. He recorded an album in 1990 of standards with British blues and rock artist Carol Grimes (*Lady Blue Eyes—Offbeat 93*) but then shifted his focus to singing with his band, Brave New World, and toward more modern jazz. He made his initial reputation by performing regularly at Ronnie Scott's in London and recording standards. Gradually during the 1990s, Shaw became a household name in England, appearing regularly on television. In 1999 he recorded a notable album in the United States, *In A New York Minute*, that matched him with pianist Cedar Walton. He listed the collaboration with Walton as one of the early highlights of his career, along with touring with trumpeter Kenny Wheeler in Europe, and his many projects with Claire Martin.

Since then, Ian Shaw has performed at a countless number of festivals and venues in Europe in many different settings. He has visited the United States a few times, although is still fairly unknown overseas despite recording three albums in the U.S. Most recently, Ian Shaw has recorded a tribute to Joni Mitchell and begun teaming up with trumpeter Guy Barker for a set of duets (with Shaw on piano) of their favorite film music, called *Barker And Shaw Go To The Movies*. "My main goals are to make an album of originals, to record with an orchestra, and to work someday with Joni Mitchell."

Recommended CDs: *Ghostsongs* (Jazzhouse 025), *Taking It To Hart—The Songs Of Rodgers & Hart* (Jazzhouse 036), *The Echo Of A Song* (Jazzhouse 048), *In A New York Minute* (Milestone 1189), *Soho Stories* (Milestone 9316), *A World Still Turning* (441 Records 0020) and *Drawn To All Things: The Songs Of Joni Mitchell* (Linn 276) trace the evolution of Ian Shaw as he explores veterans' standards, originals, pop songs and the music of Joni Mitchell with equal sensitivity.

Website: www.ianshaw.biz

Marlena Shaw
(Marlina Burgess)
b. September 22, 1942, New Rochelle, New York

Because much of her career has found her performing R&B, soul and even disco, it is easy to overlook Marlena Shaw's skills in jazz. She did not seriously explore the music on records until the 1990s, but has recorded a few worthy jazz CDs since then.

Early on, she heard jazz recordings at home. When she was 10 she performed at the Apollo Theater, but her mother refused to give her permission to go on the road at that early an age with her uncle who was a trumpeter. Instead she earned a high school degree and attended the State Teachers' College before dropping out to work as a singer. She gained experience performing at the Catskills, Playboy clubs and other venues.

Signed to Cadet in 1966, Shaw had a hit with "Mercy, Mercy, Mercy." A sassy, extroverted and frequently over-the-top singer, Shaw mostly recorded soul for Cadet, spent four years with Count Basie's orchestra (a period barely documented) and in 1972 signed with Blue Note. By then, the premiere jazz label had gone commercial, and Shaw's output for the label ranged from R&B to disco.

Having established her name and with her hit-making days behind her, Marlena Shaw has since added more jazz to her performances, recording fine sets for Verve, Concord and the 441 label.

Recommended CDs: Marlena Shaw's strongest jazz recordings are 1992's *Is It Love* (Verve 831438), *Dangerous* (Concord 4707), *Elemental Soul* (Concord 4774), *Live In Tokyo* (Sony 18807) and *Lookin' For Love* (441 Records 23).

Website: www.marlenashaw.com

Jack Sheldon
b. November 30, 1931, Jacksonville, FL

Jack Sheldon is a very good bop-based trumpeter, a hilarious if often over-the-line comedian (it is impossible not to laugh at his often spontaneous monologues) and an underrated bandleader. He is also a skilled singer who, as with his trumpet playing, has steadily improved through the years, defying age.

Sheldon began playing trumpet when he was 12 and within a year was playing professionally. "My mother brought home that Clyde McCoy record of 'Sugar Blues.' I was immediately captured, enthralled, enraptured. Then I saw Harry James in the movies and I thought, 'Oh, this is the life for me.' I made myself a trumpet out of tinker toys, and I used to play it outside the YMCA where I'd be swimming in competitions. A little later my mother bought me a trumpet for $100. Soon I was working with Gene Brandt's band at the George Washington Hotel. I was about 13 years old, I had a blue suit and I joined the musicians union. I had to lie about my age. I had a pipe and I painted on a little moustache. Then I worked all over Jacksonville."

Sheldon moved with his family to Los Angeles in 1947 and attended Los Angeles City College before serving in the Air Force, where he played in military bands. After his discharge in 1952, he became an important part of the West Coast jazz scene in Los Angeles, jamming with Charlie Parker and working with Chet Baker (a close friend), Jimmy Giuffre, Wardell Gray, Jack Montrose, Dexter Gordon, Art Pepper, the Dave Pell Octet, Herb Geller and the Curtis Counce Quintet. He toured with Stan Kenton's orchestra in 1958 and Benny Goodman the following year. Sheldon was primarily known as a trumpeter, but always had the desire to sing.

"I started singing when I saw a Gene Autry movie and Vera Lynn sang 'Let's All Sing Like The Birdies Sing'; I just learned it as she sang it. Benny Goodman was the first to let me sing with his band, the one who first gave me the chance. I worked with Stan Kenton before Benny Goodman, but Stan was always afraid that I'd say something outrageous so I never sang with Stan, I just played the trumpet. But he did let me talk. I'd go into big routines. Sometimes I'd be funny, sometimes tragic."

Sheldon was one of the very few jazz musicians to star on his own television series, *Run Buddy Run*, which was on during 1964–65. He was the first musician to record "The Shadow Of Your Smile" (as an instrumental), and he participated with Irene Kral as one of the vocalists on Shelly Manne's *My Fair Lady* LP. As a longtime member of the Merv Griffin Show's orchestra, he made wisecracks and was occasionally featured as both a singer and a musician. He remembers that two singers from the Metropolitan Opera, Jan Pearce and Robert Merrill, both gave him singing lessons backstage. Sheldon continued appearing occasionally with Benny Goodman (including singing "Rocky Raccoon" at Goodman's 40th-anniversary Carnegie Hall concert in 1978) and appeared in the Bette Midler movie *For The Boys*, which led to him forming his own big band.

Today, Jack Sheldon is regularly heard in the Los Angeles area either with his California Cool Quartet (which for a time featured the late pianist Ross Tompkins) or with his orchestra. While leading his big band, Sheldon makes up hilarious monologues, sings swing standards (usually straight but swinging), takes heated and highly personal trumpet solos, and seems to always count off the perfect tempo.

"The more a person studies music, the more appreciative they are of it. Try to sing in tune, with a good sound, that's what I'm trying to do. And I'm so honored to be a part of this, because all my life I dreamed of being a musician. I love the cats."

Recommended CDs: *Hollywood Heroes* (Concord Jazz 4339), *On My Own* (Concord Jazz 4529), *Jack Sheldon Sings* (Butterfly 7701), *Jack Is Back* (Butterfly 7702), *Class Act* (Butterfly 7703) and *J.S.O. Live On The Pacific Ocean* (Butterfly 7704) all feature excellent singing from Sheldon in settings ranging from his big band to duets with Ross Tompkins (on *On My Own*).

LPs to Search For: *Stand By For Jack Sheldon* (Concord Jazz 229) has not reappeared yet.

Website: www.jacksheldon.com

Daryl Sherman
b. June 14, 1949, Woonsocket, RI

A delightful, witty and very talented singer and pianist, Daryl Sherman has a particular feel for swing era standards.

Her father, Sammy Sherman, played trombone and occasional violin with the big bands of Sonny Dunham and Buddy Morrow in addition to his own groups.

"As a first-born toddler, I was awakened when Dad came home from a gig. Sometimes he had other musicians with him, and I got used to singing for company. My first two 'hits' were 'On Top Of Old Moky' (couldn't pronounce 's' then) and 'Goodnight Irene.'"

Daryl Sherman began playing piano when she was six, taught informally by her father and then taking extensive piano lessons that continued through college. As she grew older, she was often allowed to sit in with her father's group, at first as a pianist and then as a singer when she was 12. While in high school she had her first paying musical jobs, and by then Mildred Bailey was becoming a strong influence. She graduated from the University of Rhode Island in 1971 as a Spanish major, although she performed in many ensembles and took a variety of music courses, preparing herself for her career.

Daryl Sherman soon moved to New York. "The following were among those who were kind and generous enough to take me 'under their wing' in New York. I got to either sing/play with them or learn lots just from the privilege of spending time with them: Sylvia Syms, George Duvivier, Milt Hinton, Dick Sudhalter, Red Norvo, and later on, Ruby Braff and Dick Hyman." In 1984 she became the singer with the Artie Shaw Orchestra under the direction of Dick Johnson, picked by Shaw himself. In addition to her own records, which started with *I'm A Dreamer, Aren't We All* in 1983, she has recorded with cornetist Dick Sudhalter, the group Mr. Tram Associates, Dave Frishberg, Barbara Lea, trombonist Dan Barrett, tenor-saxophonist Loren Schoenburg and Bob Dorough. Popular with both prebop jazz and cabaret audiences, she has worked regularly at the Waldorf Astoria, playing Cole Porter's piano, in addition to jazz clubs.

Recommended CDs: All of Daryl Sherman's CDs should interest fans of swing singing: *I'm A Dreamer, Aren't We All* (Baldwin Street Music 204), *I've Got My Fingers Crossed* (Audiophile 264), *Look What I Found* (Arbors 19154), *Celebrating Mildred Bailey And Red Norvo* (Audiophile 295), *A Lady Must Live* (After 9 2019), *Jubilee* (Arbors 19224) with Dave McKenna, *Born To Swing* (Audiophile 316), *A Hundred Million Miracles* (Arbors 19279) and *Guess Who's In Town* (Arbors 19341).

LPs to Search For: *She's A Great Great Girl* (Tono 1001) from 1986 is scheduled to be reissued on CD soon.

Website: www.darylsherman.com

Joya Sherrill
b. August 20, 1927, Bayonne, NJ

One of Duke Ellington's better singers, Joy Sherrill was quite young when she was with Duke and has been associated with him ever since. She was widely praised for her flawless diction.

Sherrill worked with Ellington briefly in 1942 as a young teenager. She wrote the lyrics to "Take The 'A' Train" and in 1944 became a regular member of the group, staying until 1946. She was featured on Duke's hit recording of "I'm Beginning To See The Light" (which was soon dwarfed by Harry James' version) and also starred on such songs as "Everything But You," "I Didn't Know About You" and "The Blues" (from "Black, Brown And Beige").

Sherrill left Ellington when she got married, although she occasionally worked with him through 1950 and guested in 1957 for the television show and album *A Drum Is A Woman*. Otherwise she worked as a solo singer, although without gaining much fame. She acted on an occasional basis and was with Benny Goodman when he toured the Soviet Union in 1962. Joya Sherrill recorded an album of Duke Ellington songs in

1965 and hosted a children's program during 1970–72. She is one of the last surviving members of the Duke Ellington Orchestra of the 1940s along with Herb Jeffries.

Recommended CD: *Joya Sherrill Sings Duke* (Polygram 547266) from 1965 features Sherrill with a combo led by Mercer Ellington that includes such Ellington greats as trumpeter Cootie Williams, Ray Nance on trumpet and violin, altoist Johnny Hodges and pianist Billy Strayhorn. In 1994 she re-emerged at the age of 67 to record *Black Beauty—The Duke In Mind* (Phontastic 8834), another set of Ellington songs. Her voice still sounded strong, making one wonder why she recorded so little through the years.

Ben Sidran
b. August 14, 1943, Chicago, IL

Ben Sidran has had a wide-ranging career as a pianist, keyboardist, lyricist, broadcaster, producer, author and singer.

"I've played piano my whole life, since age five, and I sing like a piano player in the tradition of Mose Allison, Bob Dorough and Fats Waller rather than play piano like a singer. My whole approach to singing is from an instrumentalist's point of view." He was playing jobs as a pianist by 1960 and enrolled in the University of Wisconsin the following year. While there, Sidran was in the Ardells, a blues-oriented band that included Steve Miller and Boz Scaggs. After graduating as an English literature major in 1966, he moved to England to pursue a Master's in American Studies. When the Steve Miller Band was in England in 1967 to record, Sidran was enlisted to join the group. He soon wrote the lyrics to Miller's "Space Cowboy," earning enough royalties to pay for his graduate degrees, which included a PhD in philosophy/musicology. His doctoral thesis was published in 1971 as *Black Talk*. He also did studio work while in England before returning to the U.S.

"Except for fooling around and writing songs in high school, I didn't start singing until my very first recording session as a leader. When I got a record deal with Capitol in 1971, I was informed by the president of the company that I was a singer/songwriter who would be singing on my record. I consider my inspirations as a singer to be Mose Allison, Jon Hendricks, Bill Henderson and Charles Brown."

Since then, Ben Sidran has recorded a series of albums that feature his hipster singing and blues/boogie-woogie oriented piano, organ and keyboards. He has produced recordings for Mose Allison, Diana Ross, Tony Williams, Georgie Fame, Van Morrison and Steve Miller among others. Sidran has also hosted television series, started the Go Jazz label, written his memoirs *A Life In The Music*, created the full-service label Nardis and continued as an active performer.

When asked to name a few high points to his career, Sidran said, "Playing the Carnegie Hall tribute to Eddie Jefferson with Jon Hendricks, Dizzy Gillespie and James Moody gave me a sense of arrival. Touring with Al Jarreau (as his opening act for several months) gave me a sense of proportion as a singer. And touring Europe every year since 1989 has given me a sense of history. But producing Mose Allison's recordings has been a total gas."

Sixty interviews with jazz greats, taken from the five-year period in the 1980s when he hosted *Sidran On Record* on NPR, have recently been made available as a 24-CD box set.

Recommended CDs: Among Ben Sidran's many recordings, a few years ago he named *The Cat In The Hat* (A&M 75021) with tenors Michael Brecker and Joe Henderson, *Bop City* (Go Jazz 6048), which features altoist Phil Woods and *Walk Pretty: The Music Of Alec Wilder* (Go Jazz 6060) as his personal favorites. Other important releases include *Feel Your Groove* (Arcadia 8120), *I Lead A Life* (Universal 6937), *Puttin' In Time On Planet Earth* (Universal 3311), *That's Life I Guess* (Bluebird 6575), *Old Songs For The New Depression* (Antilles 846132), *On The Cool Side* (Go Jazz 6009), *On The Live Sound* (Go Jazz 6008), *Too Hot To Touch* (Go Jazz 6010), *Cool Paradise* (Go Jazz 6001), *Live At Celebrity Lounge* (Go Jazz 6025) and *Nick's Bump* (Go Jazz 6057).

Website: www.bensidran.com

Janis Siegel

b. July 23, 1952, Brooklyn, NY

Of the four members of the Manhattan Transfer, Janis Siegel has had the most extensive solo career. While her work with the Transfer is indispensable, her solo career has also been significant.

"My first public performance was in second grade at a school assembly. My teacher, Mrs. O'Riordan, taught me a song called 'Too-Ra-Loo-Ra (An Irish Lullaby),' which I warbled in front of the whole school. I used to sing with my father in the car. He was a big Bing Crosby fan and I often harmonized on tunes from the '40s. When I was 12, my aunt gave me a guitar and that started me on my way. Along with two close girlfriends, my first singing group, the Young Generation, was born. We were originally called the Marshmellows and then Ethereal. Our repertoire consisted of popular songs of the day like 'Doo-Wah Diddy,' 'Mrs. Brown, You've Got A Lovely Daughter,' and folk songs like 'Lemon Tree' and 'The Cruel War.'" The Young Generation released two singles in 1965 as young teenagers. The trio gradually switched from pop music to acoustic folk, renaming themselves Laurel Canyon. Siegel studied nursing for two years in college but dropped out of school when she decided to become a full-time singer.

In 1972, Janis Siegel met Tim Hauser at a party. He asked her to sing on some demos he was working on and was so impressed that, when he revived his earlier group, called the Manhattan Transfer, she became a permanent member. The Manhattan Transfer made their first recording in 1975 and became very popular almost immediately. In addition to her versatile singing with the group (which ranges from bop to pop, rock and roll to Brazilian), she has also written many vocal arrangements including for the group's hit version of "Birdland."

In addition to her 35 years with the Manhattan Transfer, Siegel has had a steady solo career. Her first solo recording was 1982's *Experiment In White*, and since then she has had seven other recordings, including several with pianist Fred Hersch. She has also appeared on soundtracks, made many guest appearances and been a member of Bobby McFerrin's Voicestra.

For the future, Janis Siegel says that she would like to "continue a path of musical eclecticism, study piano, arranging and orchestration, work with Gal Costa, Bjork, Eddie Palmieri and Joan Osborne, teach and to continue exploring improvisatory singing."

Recommended CDs: All nine Janis Siegel CDs have their great moments. She mentioned four as personal favorites; those are given asterisks. *Experiment In White* (Wounded Bird 8007), **At Home* (Atlantic 81748), *Short Stories* (Atlantic 81989), **Slow Hot Wind* (Varese Sarabande 5552), **The Tender Trap* (Monarch 1021), *I Wish You Love* (Telarc 83551), *Friday Night Special* (Telarc 83566), **Sketches Of Broadway* (Telarc 83597), and *A Thousand Beautiful Things* (Telarc 83630).

Website: www.janissiegel.com

Judi Silvano

(Judith Silverman)
b. May 8, 1951, Philadelphia, PA

An adventurous singer who is never shy to stretch herself and to take chances, Judi Silvano has amassed an impressive body of work while also becoming an influential educator.

"My mother loved both classical music and jazz, so I heard a lot of Ella Fitzgerald and big band music around the house." Silvano studied piano and flute as a child, and studied music and dance at the Temple University College of Music (1969–73). She moved to New York in 1976, performed at loft concerts as a modern dancer, developed her singing, and in 1980 met tenor-saxophonist Joe Lovano, whom she soon married.

Silvano recorded with guitarist Michael Bocian in 1981, improvising freely. In 1987 she co-founded JSL Records with Lovano. She toured Europe with her husband's wind ensemble in 1989 and has often been involved in his projects. By 1990 she was writing vocal arrangements for her own groups, recording her first CD as a leader (*Dancing Voices*) in 1992. During that era, she also became a vocal jazz teacher, teaching voice at Rutgers University's Newark campus, at many summer workshops during the past 15 years, and the Newburgh Performing Arts Academy.

Since then, Judi Silvano has made CDs for Blue Note (1997's *Vocalise*) and Zoho, recorded a duo set (*Riding A Zephyr*) with pianist Mal Waldron, which features her lyrics to some of Waldron's music, presented a long-running vocal series at the Cornelia Street Café in Greenwich Village, and led the ensemble Voices Together (which includes three singers and one dancer). She often collaborates with dancers and poets in multimedia productions and has appeared in a countless number of settings, singing everything from standards to free-form improvisations.

"I want to continue to grow as a musician, develop my compositional skills and deepen my expressive abilities as a vocalist. Bringing music and dance together again has been a truly gratifying way for me to make a contribution to people's experience of their own joy."

Nina Simone

Recommended CDs: *Dancing Voices* (JSL 002), *Vocalise* (Blue Note 52390), *Songs I Wrote Or Wish I Did* (Orchard 6277), *Riding A Zephyr* (Soul Note 121348), *Let Yourself Go* (Zoho 200412) and *Women's Work* (JSL 006) each have their own personalities, ranging from straightforward renditions of standards to sets that emphasize Judi Silvano's wordless singing and more adventurous side.

Website: www.judisilvano.com

Nina Simone
(Eunice Kathleen Waymon)
b. February 21, 1933, Tryon, NC;
d. April 21, 2003, Carry-le-Rouet, France

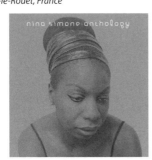

Nina Simone was a completely unique performer. Her music was so wide-ranging throughout her career that it can not be classified as just jazz, folk, R&B, soul, pop or protest music, though it was all of the above plus more.

Born to a poor family as the sixth of seven children, Eunice Waymon started playing piano at the age of four and was considered a child prodigy who was heading toward a career as a classical pianist. She gave a classical piano recital at the age of 10. At 17, she accompanied singers in an attempt to raise money to study at the Juilliard School of Music. She interviewed to study piano at the Curtis Institute but was rejected, and she always believed it was due to racism. Needing to support her family, she started working as a pianist in bars. At a job in the summer of 1954, she was told that she had to sing in order to keep the job. That was the real beginning of her career. Soon she had changed her name to Nina Simone (so her mother would not find out that she was playing popular music), and her focus changed to expressing herself through contemporary music rather than playing classical.

Nina Simone's most jazz-oriented work was in the first part of her career. Her recording debut was a Bethlehem trio album that found her having a hit with her version of "I Loves You Porgy." "My Baby Just Cares For Me" from the album also became a hit when it was re-released in the 1980s. She was next signed to Colpix, where she steadily grew as a singer and pianist while becoming involved in the civil rights movement. In 1964 she moved up to the Philips label and in 1967 switched to RCA Victor. Simone recorded "Mississippi Goddam," which directly addressed the racial situation. Her very emotional "Four Women" talked about life from the viewpoints of four African American women, "To Be Young, Gifted And Black" became famous, and she regularly performed Billie Holiday's "Strange Fruit."

A major name by the mid-1960s, Nina Simone created her own world of music throughout her career, playing at concert halls, festivals and clubs. Never shy to express her displeasure with the establishment (her mood shifts and temper were legendary), she was at her most significant during the 1960s, stretching from protest pieces, current pop/rock tunes that she found relevant, art songs to folk music, a vintage blues and an occasional jazz instrumental. By the early 1970s,

when she left the United States to live overseas, she had made her most important contributions to music, making her final recording in 1993.

Recommended CDs: The two-CD set *Anthology* (RCA 53015) does an excellent job of covering the high points of Nina Simone's career. For those who want to dig into the original albums, the more jazz-oriented collections include *Little Girl Blue* (Bethlehem 3004), *The Amazing Nina Simone/Nina Simone At Town Hall* (Collectables 6206), *Forbidden Fruit/Nina Simone At Newport* (Collectables 6207), *At The Village Gate* (Roulette 95058), *Nina Simone Sings Ellington/At Carnegie Hall* (Collectables 6414), *Nina's Choice* (Collectables 6308), the four-CD set *Four Women: The Nina Simone Phillips Recordings*, which has all seven of her Philips albums from 1964 to 1966 (Verve 065021), and, from the 1980s, *Live At Ronnie Scott's* (DRG 91428).

Frank Sinatra
b. December 12, 1915, Hoboken, NJ;
d. May 14, 1998, Los Angeles, CA

Frank Sinatra was an institution. Considered by many to be the top American singer of the 1940s and '50s (though some hold out for Bing Crosby and many of Sinatra's fans would say "of all time"), his outstanding breath control, phrasing, repertoire, attitude and general style have been extremely influential up to the present day. Many in the jazz world list him as one of their favorites.

But was he a jazz singer? Intelligent and knowledgeable listeners have debated about that for decades. It is true that he often performed with jazz musicians, he always swung, and his renditions of many standards became the definitive way to interpret them. But Sinatra did not change the way he approached a song much after he had it set, his improvising was very minor and, although he greatly appreciated musicians and acknowledged them, he was always the star and the musicians were onstage to accompany him, not to challenge or compete with him. A song such as "Chicago (My Kind Of Town)" and "New York, New York" included no surprises once Sinatra knew how he wanted the arrangement to go, and the same is true of his treatments of hundreds of songs from the Great American Songbook. One could not imagine Sinatra going to a jam session and singing anything that was unexpected. But because he has been so influential on jazz singers, he belongs in this book.

Frank Sinatra first started singing in public in the early 1930s. He dropped out of high school in his senior year and worked at odd jobs until 1935, when he joined a singing group, the Three Flashes, which was soon renamed the Hoboken Four. They appeared on the *Major Bowes Amateur Hour* on radio, won first prize and had opportunities to perform regularly on radio and at shows. After Sinatra left the Hoboken Four later in the year, he worked as a singing waiter at the Rustic Cabin in Englewood, New Jersey. In the spring of 1939, he made his recording debut, cutting "Our Love" with the Frank

Mane band. In June, he joined the new Harry James Orchestra. While James was already a household name due to his earlier association with Benny Goodman, his own big band was two years away from achieving stardom and struggling. Sinatra had opportunities to record with James, and his version of "All Or Nothing At All" would become a hit when it was reissued during World War II. However, when he was offered a much more lucrative contract in November 1939 to join Tommy Dorsey, there was no hesitation on the part of either Sinatra in accepting it or James in letting him go.

Frank Sinatra became famous while with Dorsey during 1939–42. He recorded regularly, whether with the Pied Pipers or as a soloist, was on 16 hit records (most notably "I'll Never Smile Again"), and became extremely popular with teenage girls who were called "bobby soxers" and tended to scream and sigh when he sang. Although their relationship could be rather fiery, Sinatra learned from Dorsey a great deal about breath control and about putting on professional shows.

When he went solo, Sinatra was immediately a big hit, recording regularly for Columbia, singing constantly on the radio and appearing in movies. As the 1940s ended, his popularity began to slip since, at 35, he was no longer a teen idol. His recordings had declined in quality, he was in some lower-level movies, and seemed to be flopping everywhere, including in his marriage to actress Ava Gardner.

But 1953 changed everything. Sinatra won an Academy Award for Best Supporting Actor in *From Here To Eternity*, and he signed with the Capitol label. His recordings for Capitol during 1953–60 found him at his peak. No longer stuck with recording novelties, Sinatra performed the high-quality standards of the previous 25 years while supported by orchestras arranged by Nelson Riddle, Billy May or Gordon Jenkins. Many of his recordings from this era are considered classics, including *In The Wee Small Hours*, *Frank Sinatra Sings For Only The Lonely*, *Swing Easy*, *Songs For Swingin' Lovers* and *Come Fly With Me*. Although not technically jazz records, many are certainly swinging and jazzy, while the ballad dates find Sinatra sounding quite vulnerable as he bared his soul.

As a singer, actor and a personality, Frank Sinatra by the late 1950s symbolized hip and cool to many in the era. His Las Vegas shows with his "Rat Pack" (which also included Dean Martin, Sammy Davis Jr., Joey Bishop and Peter Lawford) became legendary. He started his own label, Reprise, in 1961, and at first his albums continued at the same high quality, including *Ring-A-Ding-Ding* and his collaborations with Count Basie (*Sinatra-Basie*, *It Might As Well Be Spring* and *Sinatra At The Sands*). Also quite noteworthy are *Francis Albert Sinatra And Antonio Carlos Jobim* and an album with Duke Ellington called *Francis A. Sinatra And Edward K. Ellington*. He had pop hits with "Strangers In The Night," "My Way" and "Somethin' Stupid" and, even with the rise of the Beatles and rock, Sinatra prospered. Despite a brief retirement during 1971–73, he remained active to near the end, making his final recordings and concert performances in 1994.

Recommended CDs: Frank Sinatra made an enormous amount of recordings, and his huge studio output is joined by broadcasts, transcriptions and live concerts. A few of the essentials for the serious Sinatra collector include the two-CD set *The V-Discs: Columbia Years: 1943–45* (Columbia/Legacy 66135), the 12-CD *The Columbia Years (1943–1952): The Complete Recordings* (Sony 52877), which has music also available in more piecemeal fashion elsewhere, the four-CD *Complete Capitol Singles Collection* (Capitol 38089), *Songs For Young Lovers/Swing Easy* (Capitol 48470), *In The Wee Small Hours* (Capitol 96826), *Come Fly With Me* (Capitol

96087), *A Swingin' Affair* (Capitol 94518), *Where Are You* (Capitol 33746), *Come Dance With Me* (Capitol 48468), *Only The Lonely* (Capitol 48471), *No One Cares* (Capitol 33741), *Live In Australia, 1959* (Blue Note 37513), *Ring-A-Ding-Ding* (Reprise 27017), *Nice 'N' Easy* (Capitol 33745), *Come Swing With Me* (Capitol 33739), *I Remember Tommy* (Reprise 45267), *Swing Along With Me* (Reprise 1002), *Sinatra And Strings* (Reprise 46970), *Sinatra-Basie* (Reprise 47241), *It Might As Well Be Spring* (Reprise 46972), *September Of My Years* (Reprise 46946), *Sinatra At The Sands* (Reprise 46947), *Francis Albert Sinatra And Antonio Carlos Jobim* (Capitol 46948) and *Francis A. Sinatra And Edward K. Ellington* (Reprise 47243). The true completists will forego the individual Reprise sets and instead acquire the 20-CD *Complete Reprise Studio Recordings* (Warner Bros. 47045).

Denzal Sinclaire
(Densil Pinnock)
b. 1967, Toronto, Ontario, Canada

Denzal Sinclaire's warm voice has a tone similar to that of Nat King Cole and a ballad style not that far from that of Johnny Hartman. However, he also has his own musical personality in the Cole/Hartman tradition, and has emerged as a major crooner from Canada.

Born as Densil Pinnock, he earned a degree in Jazz Performance at McGill University in Montreal. While based in Montreal, he recorded two CDs and appeared as Nat King Cole in the musical *Unforgettable*. After performing at the Vancouver Jazz Festival in 1995, he decided to relocate and, wanting a fresh start, changed his name to Denzal Sinclaire. Fortunately he did not change his voice, and since that time he has continued to evolve and become more individual while holding on to his roots. Sinclaire has won many Juno awards in Canada, toured Canada regularly, performed at jazz festivals and with symphony orchestras, and recorded three albums for Universal, emphasizing ballads. But despite a few visits to the United States, he is at this point best known in his native Canada.

Recommended CDs: As Densil Pinnock, he made a strong impression with *I Waited For You* (Uptown 2737) and a duet outing with pianist Bill Coon, *Mona Lisa* (Universal/Verve 6671). Since his name change, Denzal Sinclaire has recorded three fine sets for Universal: *I Found Love* (Emarcy 1032), *Denzal Sinclaire* (Verve 385782) and *My One And Only Love* (Verve 988422).

Website: www.denzalsinclaire.com

Carol Sloane
(Carol Morvan)
b. March 5, 1937, Providence, RI

A creative jazz singer, Carol Sloane had a fast start in her career and, after some time off the major scene, made a full comeback.

She grew up in Smithfield, Rhode Island, in a musical family in which each member seemed to have a good voice. In 1951 she began singing professionally with a society dance band led by Ed Drew, performing twice a week. "At age 14, I knew without a doubt that I would sing the rest of my life." She performed under the name of Carol Vann and recorded two songs (duets with guitarist George Barnes) in 1953. In 1955 she was married to a local disc jockey, living with him in Colorado and Germany as he served in the Army. They were divorced in 1958 and she returned to full-time music.

She joined Larry Elgart's orchestra, and since he did not like the name Carol Vann, after much discussion she was permanently renamed Carol Sloane. She was on the road with Elgart's band for two years and made a few recordings (mostly wordless vocals) before tiring of the traveling and leaving the group in 1960. While Sloane had a day job as a secretary, she performed at a jazz festival in Pittsburgh where she met Lambert, Hendricks and Ross. Jon Hendricks became a friend and had her learn the book of the group so she could sub for Annie Ross on the rare occasions when Ross was not available. He also successfully talked George Wein into including her at the 1961 Newport Jazz Festival as part of a New Stars program. Her performance received rave reviews, and a few months later she recorded *Out Of The Blue* for Columbia.

However, she never really broke through to become a major name at the time, despite working at many major clubs and appearing regularly on Johnny Carson's *Tonight Show*. After singing at a club in Raleigh, North Carolina, Sloane decided to move there. "From 1969 to 1977, I was living in Raleigh, working as a legal secretary and also singing about every four to six weeks in a jazz club which gained considerable reputation at the time, The Frog And Nightgown. I did record an album during this period, which was subsequently released by the Japanese. Titled *Subway Tokens*, it is a compilation of various live performances in the club. I came back on the scene when Sir Roland Hanna asked me to sing with his group in New York in 1977, and that gig led to my first invitation to tour Japan with the group the New York Jazz Quartet." That year she also recorded her first studio album since 1961.

During the past 30 years, Carol Sloane has been back on the jazz scene. She lived for a time in New York, spent two years back in North Carolina booking a supper club and hosting a radio show, and moved to Boston in the mid-1980s, where she still resides. Sloane has since recorded for Contemporary, High Note and Arbors, performed in Japan several times, and appeared frequently at clubs and festivals as a mature bop-based singer with a sound of her own.

"I am a most straightforward, no-gimmicks kind of singer, steeped in the tradition of Ella Fitzgerald. Although I enjoy many other activities, I am at my best when I am on stage singing."

Recommended CDs: *Early Hours* (CBS/Sony 794) has the music from a demo tape recorded in 1959 with a rhythm section. *Out Of The Blue* (Koch 7810) is her 1961 classic, featuring Sloane with a small group arranged by Bill Finegan. Also worthy but quite rare is *Carol Sloane Live At 30th Street* (CBS/Sony 617) from 1962. Of her later releases (not counting those only available in Japan), *Carol Sings* (Audiophile 211), *But Not For Me* (CBS/Sony 5391), *Love You Madly* (Contemporary 14049), *The Real Thing* (Contemporary 14060), *Heart's Desire* (Concord 4503), *Sweet And Slow* (Concord 4564), *When I Look In Your Eyes* (Concord 4619), *The Songs Carmen Sang* (Concord 4663), *The Songs Sinatra Sang* (Concord 4725), a collaboration with Clark Terry called *The Songs Ella And Louis Sang* (Concord 4787), *Romantic Ellington* (DRG 8480), *I Never Went Away* (High Note 7085), *Whisper Sweet* (High Note 7113) and *Dearest Duke* (Arbors 19350) are all fine efforts.

LPs to Search For: *Carol And Ben* (Honeydew 6608) features Carol Sloane live in 1964 with a quintet that includes the great tenor Ben Webster.

Website: www.carolsloane.com

Bessie Smith

b. April 15, 1894, Chattanooga, TN;
d. September 26, 1937, Clarksdale, MS

She was "The Empress of the Blues," the finest female blues and jazz singer to record in the 1920s. Bessie Smith's singing, even in 1923 when she had to deal with the primitive technical quality of the era's recording equipment and sometimes indifferent accompaniment, was powerful enough to overcome all obstacles. One can only imagine how she would have sounded on record if she had been around in the 1950s. She influenced everyone from Billie Holiday and Mahalia Jackson to Barbara Dane and even Susannah McCorkle, yet no one ever quite sounded like the Empress. Eighty-five years after her first recordings, Bessie Smith still communicates with today's listeners through her passion, intensity, sincerity, musicianship, relevance and sassiness.

She was born to a very poor family and lost both of her parents before she was 10. As a child, Bessie attended public school but sang on the streets as soon as school let out, raising money for her family. In 1912 when she was 18, she became a dancer with the traveling Moses Stock troupe, a company that featured Ma Rainey, the first known blues singer. Bessie learned a bit about show business from Rainey, although she already had a style of her own. Soon she was a major attraction herself, on her way to becoming a headliner. During the next decade she worked with other shows including Fats Chappelle's Rabbit Foot Minstrels and Pete Werley's Florida Blossoms, developing into a charismatic performer whose performances of blues could be hypnotic.

By 1919, Bessie Smith was leading her own *Liberty Belles* show. A major name in the South, Smith was performing in Atlantic City by 1920, the year that Mamie Smith recorded "Crazy Blues." It is surprising that, given the blues craze of 1921–22, it took until 1923 before Smith had her first recording session. She immediately made up for lost time, having a major hit with the very first title she cut, Alberta Hunter's "Downhearted Blues," which sold 800,000 copies. She recorded 28 songs in 1923 alone and 160 during the 1923–33 period for Columbia. Among the other songs that Bessie Smith made famous through her recordings were "'Tain't Nobody's Biz-ness If I Do" (more than a decade before Billie Holiday adopted the song), "You've Been A Good Ole Wagon," "Careless Love," "I Ain't Goin' To Play No Second Fiddle," "Backwater Blues," "Muddy Water," "Trombone Cholly," "Send Me To The 'Lectric Chair," "Mean Old Bed Bug Blues," "Empty Bed Blues" and "Gimme A Pigfoot." Her sidemen greatly improved by 1925 and included Louis Armstrong (who is masterful with Bessie on "Careless Love" and "St. Louis Blues"), cornetist Joe Smith, trombonist Charlie Green, and the brilliant stride pianist James P. Johnson, who was a perfect match with Bessie, particularly on "Back Water Blues."

Although the blues craze had largely died out by 1925–26, Bessie Smith was such a major name that it did not affect her career. She toured in revues (including *Harlem Frolics* during 1925–27 and *Mississippi Days* in 1928) and in 1929 appeared in her only film, a flawed but fascinating 10-minute short, *St.

Louis Blues, that gives today's listeners the only opportunity to see her in action. That year she made her most famous recording, "Nobody Knows You When You're Down And Out." Although the Depression had not hit yet and she was still riding high, that song largely predicted Smith's future.

In the 1920s Bessie Smith was at the height of her fame and she partied constantly, having affairs, drinking excessively and mostly enjoying life. But with the rise of the Depression, hard times began to be felt. Smith was already in the process of gradually reinventing herself from a blues singer to a bluish jazz vocalist. She had shown on such recordings as "Alexander's Ragtime Band," "After You've Gone," "My Sweetie Went Away," "Cake Walkin' Babies From Home," and "There'll Be A Hot Time In The Old Town Tonight" that she did not have to stick exclusively to blues to get her message across. But after recording 14 songs in 1929, she was down to eight in 1930 and just six in 1931 before stopping altogether. After two years off records, the Empress had one last chance to record. Backed by a swing-oriented group organized by producer John Hammond, she put plenty of spirit into "Gimme A Pigfoot" and showed no sign of decline.

In 1934 Smith toured in *Hot From Harlem*, a show that starred Ida Cox, and in 1935 she played at the Apollo Theater a few times to good reviews. She also substituted for Billie Holiday in the show *Stars Over Broadway*. During 1936–37 Smith worked with *The League Of Rhythm* revue and toured with the *Broadway Rastus* show. It seemed as if it was only a matter of time before she would be recording and on her way back to the top again. But on September 26, 1937 Bessie Smith, who was just 43, died in a car accident in which she was a passenger.

Had she lived, she would have been a major part of Hammond's famous From Spirituals To Swing concert at Carnegie Hall in 1938 rather than Trixie Smith. Instead, the concert was posthumously dedicated to her memory.

More than 70 years after her death, Bessie Smith is still the Empress of the Blues.

Recommended CDs: All of Bessie Smith's recordings have been reissued on five two-CD sets accurately titled *The Complete Recordings, Vols. 1–5* (Columbia/Legacy 47091, 47471, 4747, 52838 and 57546). In addition to the 160 recordings, the soundtrack of the film *St. Louis Blues* and the only five alternate takes that exist are included. *Vol. 5* is the least significant of these sets, for its second disc is taken up by a Chris Albertson interview with Smith's niece Ruby Smith, which deals much more with Bessie Smith's personal life than with her music. It is only worth hearing once, but the Empress' recordings are well worth listening to and enjoying scores of times.

Carrie Smith

b. August 25, 1941, Fort Gaines, GA

Carrie Smith became well known for her portrayals of Bessie Smith, although she was versatile enough to sing gospel, classic jazz and swing too.

She suffered through a rough childhood, abandoned by her mother and working odd jobs from the time she was seven. But it was obvious early on that she had a powerful voice, and she appeared at the 1957 Newport Jazz Festival as a member of a New Jersey church choir. Smith eventually switched to secular music and was a relative unknown in 1972 when she caused a stir with her performances with the New York Jazz Repertory Orchestra. She found her greatest fame in the shows *Black And Blue* and *Blues In The Night*. *Black And Blue*, which started in 1985 and reached Broadway in 1989,

teamed her with Ruth Brown and Linda Hopkins, while *Blues In The Night* co-starred Eartha Kitt. She also played Bessie Smith in Dick Hyman's Carnegie Hall production of *Satchmo Remembered*.

Carrie Smith made her first solo recording in 1976 and remained an important figure until her declining health forced her to retire a few years ago.

Recommended CDs: *Confessin' The Blues* (Evidence 26021) brings back Carrie Smith's first album and remains one of her most satisfying recordings. Also quite worthy are *Fine And Mellow* (Audiophile 164), *Nobody Wants You* (Black And Blue 119), *Every Now And Then* (Silver Shadow 203), *June Night* (Black And Blue 197), *When You're Down And Out* (Black And Blue 904) and *I've Got A Right To Sing The Blues* (IPO 1003), a 2002 set with pianist Sir Roland Hanna.

LPs to Search For: *Do Your Duty* (Classic Jazz 139) is one of Carrie Smith's earlier dates and an excellent effort.

Clara Smith

b. 1894, Spartanburg, SC; d. February 2, 1935, Detroit, MI

One of the most popular of the classic blues singers during the 1920s, Clara Smith's recordings have not dated as well as those of Bessie Smith or Ethel Waters, but were fine for the time. Smith picked up early experience working in theaters in the South starting around 1910. She was billed as "Queen of the Moaners" and even "The World's Champion Moaner" due to her bluish singing. Smith, who was not related to the other four blues-singing Smiths (Bessie, Mamie, Trixie and the obscure Laura) or any of the other Smith singers of the 1920s (Clementine, Elizabeth, Hazel, Ivy and Kate), had a sweet voice yet could be powerful under the right settings.

Clara Smith recorded 125 selections during 1923–32, including three duets with Bessie Smith in 1923. Her best numbers are "Every Woman's Blues," "I'm Gonna Tear Your Playhouse Down," "You Don't Know My Mind," "Don't Advertise Your Man," "Nobody Knows The Way I Feel 'Dis Mornin'" (with Louis Armstrong), "Whip It To A Jelly," "Oh, Mister Mitchell" and "I'm Tired Of Fattenin' Frogs For Snakes." Among the musicians who recorded with her were pianist James P. Johnson, tenor-saxophonist Coleman Hawkins, trombonist Charlie Green, cornetist Joe Smith and guitarist-singer Lonnie Johnson. All of her recordings have been reissued on six Document CDs.

Clara Smith ran her own successful Theatrical Club in addition to appearing in Harlem theaters and revues when she was at the height of her fame. Although her last recording was made in 1932, she continued working until a heart attack ended her life in 1935 at the age of 40.

Recommended CDs: *Vols. 1–6* (Document 5364-5369) has all of Clara Smith's recordings. Though she could be weighed down and even defeated by weak accompaniment, when she was teamed with excellent musicians, the "Queen Of The Moaners" consistently showed why she was rated so high at the time.

Jeffery Smith

b. September 14, 1955, Kew Gardens, NY

Jeffery Smith was almost 40 at the time that he recorded his first jazz CD as a leader. A fine ballad-oriented singer with an appealing baritone voice, Smith has been getting attention during the past decade.

"What really got me hooked was receiving Billie Holiday's *Lady In Satin* LP for my 12th birthday. Shortly after, I discovered Shirley Horn and got her *Travelin' Light* album. I played those records till they turned white."

Smith, who played the cello for years, sang in a youth choir from the ages of 12 to 18. When he was 18, he moved to Los Angeles, working as an actor in television and film while occasionally singing in local clubs. In 1985 he moved to New York, acting in plays and again appearing in clubs. He spent 1991–98 living in Paris where he worked with Claude Bolling's orchestra in addition to doing studio work.

After meeting Shirley Horn in 1992, she became Smith's mentor. When he was signed to a three-CD contract in 1995 with Verve, she produced and accompanied him on his first album, *Ramona*, which was dedicated to his mother. Since moving back to New York in 1998, Jeffery Smith has performed at a pair of Louis Armstrong tribute concerts with Wynton Marsalis and the Lincoln Center Jazz Orchestra, co-starred at three sold out concerts with Dee Dee Bridgewater, made guest appearances on recordings, and performed at festivals and New York area clubs.

Recommended CDs: Jeffery Smith's three CDs are *Ramona* (Verve 314 529 468), *A Little Sweet* (Verve 314 537 790) with pianist Kenny Barron, and *Down Here Below* (Verve 314 547 273) with guest appearances by Dianne Reeves and violinist Regina Carter.

Website: www.jefferysmith.com

Lavay Smith

b. November 7, 1969, Lakewood, CA

Many groups emerged, at least briefly, during the Retro Swing movement of the 1990s. Lavay Smith's Red Hot Skillet Lickers has been among the most jazz-oriented and enduring, with its leader-singer becoming a major name. Her vocalizing mixes together aspects of Helen Humes and Dinah Washington, and she sounds like a talent from the mid-to-late 1940s when swing evolved into jump music and R&B.

"I heard the *Johnny Otis Show* while turning the dial on the radio when I lived in Southern California. I loved the music right away and started to listen to his show regularly. After hearing the great music on his show, I started to explore on my own, and started buying a lot of vinyl LPs. I came across an album of Janis Joplin singing old blues, gospel and jazz tunes. I read that she loved Bessie Smith, and paid for Bessie Smith's tombstone, so I bought a Bessie Smith album and it changed my life."

Since her father worked for the U.S. government, Smith spent a few years living in the Philippines, where she made her debut singing in public when she was 15. After a period in Los Angeles, she moved to San Francisco in 1988. The following year she met pianist Chris Siebert. They married and formed the Red Hot Skillet Lickers, a group that has four riffing horns and can often sound like an Illinois Jacquet group from the late 1940s. They have been working steadily ever since, outliving the Retro Swing movement and being a popular attraction for nearly 20 years.

"The highlights have been hearing and meeting great musicians when we do festivals and concerts. I am honored that I met and shared billing with Charles Brown, Ruth Brown, Milt Jackson, B.B. King, Jay McShann, Johnny Otis, Little Jimmy Scott and many others. We've also been on bills with Bobby "Blue" Bland, Ray Charles, Shemekia Copeland, Al Green, Alvin "Youngblood" Hart, Jon Hendricks, Chaka Khan, Wynton Marsalis and many others. What a great way to make a living. I love having four horns playing harmony behind me, and couldn't do it without the support of so many music lovers around the world."

Recommended CDs: Surprisingly, Lavay Smith only has two CDs out thus far, but both are quite enjoyable: *One Hour Mama* (Fat Note 1) and *Everybody's Talkin' 'Bout Miss Thing* (Fat Note 2).

Website: www.lavaysmith.com

Mamie Smith

b. May 26, 1883, Cincinnati, OH;
d. October 30, 1946, New York, NY

Mamie Smith has received something of a raw deal from music historians. Though grudgingly credited with being the first important singer to record a blues ("Crazy Blues") and the one who started the blues craze of the early 1920s, most critics write her off as not being a blues singer on the level of a Bessie Smith or Ma Rainey, and act as if she only had an average talent. Though the former is true, Smith's records show that she was one of the first talented jazz singers to record.

Always a top-notch and versatile performer, Mamie Smith toured in the Midwest during her early years as a dancer and singer. She moved to New York in 1913, performing with the Four Mitchells (a white vaudeville group) and singing in Harlem clubs. She was in the show *The Smart Set* and in 1920 appeared in *Maid Of Harlem*. When Sophie Tucker, the show's star, decided not to make it to a record date, Smith had the opportunity to make her recording debut, singing "That Thing Called Love" and "You Can't Keep A Good Man Now." That day's work made her one of the very first non-gospel black performers captured on record, being preceded only by comedian Bert Williams, James Reese Europe's band and just a few others. Because the record sold well, on August 10 she returned to the studio to record one of the songs from *Maid Of Harlem*, "Crazy Blues," along with "It's Right Here For You." To everyone's surprise, this '78' (due to "Crazy Blues") sold a million copies within six months and started a major blues craze. It also proved that there was a market among black consumers for recordings. Because of "Crazy Blues," during the next four years, scores of singers (mostly black females working in vaudeville) were rushed into the studios, some of whom (such as Bessie Smith and Alberta Hunter) would make music history of their own.

On the 91 selections that Mamie Smith recorded (73 being cut during 1920–23), she went out of her way to use the best musicians available, including trumpeters- cornetists Johnny Dunn, Bubber Miley, Joe Smith and Thomas Morris, trombonist Charlie Irvis, clarinetists Garvin Bushell and Buster Bailey, Coleman Hawkins (a regular member of her Jazz Hounds during 1921–22) on tenor and the great Sidney Bechet on soprano. In addition to the fine musicians, Smith mostly recorded worthwhile material, both blues and vaudevillian-type tunes including "Lovin' Sam From Alabam," "I Want A Jazzy Kiss," "I'm Free, Single, Disengaged, Looking For Someone To Love," "Got To Cool My Doggies Now," "That Da Da Strain," "You've Got To See Mama Every Night Or You Can't See Mama At All," and a classic from 1926, "Goin' Crazy With The Blues." Smith's voice became stronger as the 1920s progressed but unfortunately, after cutting six numbers in 1926, her recording career was finished, other than three unissued songs from 1929 (put out many decades later) and four titles from a 1931 session.

Considered old by then (being 48), she nevertheless had the opportunity to appear in several black films, acting and singing in *Jailhouse Blues* (1929), *Paradise In Harlem* (1939), *Mystery In Swing* (1940), *Sunday Sinners* (1941) and *Murder On Lenox Avenue* (1941); some of the later ones team her with Lucky Millinder's orchestra.

Mamie Smith remained active until 1944, two years before her death at the age of 63. Her pioneering records are still quite listenable today.

Recommended CDs: *Vols. 1–4* (Document 5357-5360) has the complete Mamie Smith. *Vol. 1* and *4* are the best two, though all four CDs will be wanted by 1920s collectors.

Trixie Smith

b. 1895, Atlanta, GA; d. September 21, 1943, New York, NY

One of the most underrated of the classic blues singers of the 1920s, Trixie Smith recorded relatively little in her career (48 selections in all) but ranked high as an expressive vocalist. After attending Selma University, she moved to New York in 1915, where she sang in theaters and revues and was one of the city's first local blues singers. After Mamie Smith's "Crazy Blues" became a best seller, Trixie won a blues contest in 1921 held by the Black Swan label. First prize was a contract with the label.

Trixie Smith recorded 16 titles for Black Swan during 1921—23, including "Trixie's Blues," the initial version of the famous "He May Be Your Man But He Comes To See Me Sometimes" (which with a few changes became a staple for Joe Williams many decades later) and the earliest recording of "My Man Rocks Me With One Steady Roll." Smith's 18 Paramount recordings of 1924–25 include such sidemen as pianist Fletcher Henderson, trombonist Charlie Green, clarinetist Buster Bailey, cornetist Joe Smith and (on four numbers including "The World's Jazz Crazy And So Am I") Louis Armstrong. She also recorded two songs with the Original Memphis Five in 1925 and two versions of "Messin' Around" with cornetist Freddie Keppard and clarinetist Johnny Dodds in 1926.

Other than "Messin' Around," Smith did not record at all

during 1926–37. The decline of interest in classic blues singers led to her being one of the first major vocalists to stop recording, but she was far from inactive. Smith worked frequently in shows and revues during the period, being part of the black show business world in Harlem.

1938 was a comeback year for Trixie Smith. She appeared at John Hammond's Spiritual To Swing concert in a role that would have been filled by Bessie Smith was it not for the latter's death. She also recorded six songs on a session for Decca with soprano-saxophonist Sidney Bechet and trumpeter Charlie Shavers, including spirited remakes of "My Daddy Rocks Me" and "He May Be Your Man." There was one additional title ("No Good Man") cut the following year. Otherwise Trixie Smith continued appearing in shows until ill health forced her retirement in the early 1940s, a couple of years before her death in 1943 at age 48.

Recommended CDs: *Vol. 1* (Document 5332) and *Vol. 2* (Document 5333) contain all of Trixie Smith's recordings.

Valaida Snow

b. June 2, 1900, 1903 or 1905, Chattanooga, TN;
d. May 30, 1956, New York, NY

Valaida Snow was an excellent jazz singer, the finest female trumpeter of the Swing era, a talented arranger and an exciting all-round entertainer. A unique performer for the era, Snow had a relatively enjoyable and eventful life for an African-American woman during the 1920s and '30s, until World War II intervened.

Until recently it was assumed that Valaida Snow was born in 1905, but other years have been offered. Her mother was a music teacher who taught Valaida and her sister Lavaida several instruments, and encouraged them to sing and dance. Valaida became a professional in the early 1920s, playing trumpet and singing in shows. She was featured in the 1924 Noble Sissle/Eubie Blake musical *In Bamville* (later known as *The Chocolate Dandies*), worked in Shanghai, China, with Jack Carter's band in 1928, and that same year headlined at Chicago's Sunset Café next to Louis Armstrong and Earl Hines. In 1929 Snow performed in Europe, the Middle East and the Soviet Union, and in the early 1930s she was back in New York, starring in the Sissle/Blake revue *Rhapsody In Black*. A bona-fide star, Snow never became a household name in the U.S. due to her leaving the country during most of her prime years but she was a major attraction in Europe.

Valaida Snow first recorded with the Washboard Rhythm Kings in 1932, playing trumpet on six numbers and taking the vocals on "I Would Do Anything For You" and "Somebody Stole Gabriel's Horn." She worked in the Grand Terrace revue in Chicago with Earl Hines, appeared in the Blackbirds of 1934, and recorded "Loveless Love" with Noble Sissle. In 1935 she moved to Europe where her series of recordings (31 numbers cut in London during 1935–37 and 10 additional selections made in Stockholm and Copenhagen during 1939–40) are the finest of her career. In addition to taking trumpet solos, Snow sings on most of the titles. She displays a small but flexible voice and a real feel for scatting, influenced by Louis Armstrong in her phrasing, but also displaying her own personality. She also crossed over into cabaret on some of her renditions of ballads.

Unfortunately, she ignored the outbreak of World War II, feeling that her personal popularity would keep her safe while performing in occupied Europe. Until recently it was believed that, after being arrested in Denmark, she spent 1941–43 in a concentration camp before being released in a prisoners' exchange; at least that was the story she told. In any case, she was confined for a few short periods before being sent back to the U.S. in 1943.

Snow was able to resume her career, but she never reached her former level. She recorded 14 songs during 1945–46 and a few additional titles in 1950 and 1953, sticking to vocals, although onstage she occasionally surprised audiences by playing some trumpet. But despite being pretty active during the first half of the 1950s, Valaida Snow was mostly unknown to the general public at the time of her death in 1956 from a cerebral hemorrhage, shortly after ignoring her doctor's advice not to play trumpet on stage.

Recommended CDs: The two-CD set *Queen Of Trumpet And Song* (DRG 8455) has all 41 recordings that Valaida Snow led during 1935–40. Completists may also want to pick up *1940–1953* (Classics 1343) which, after duplicating two numbers, has all of Snow's postwar recordings, which are interesting if somewhat uneventful.

Lisa Sokolov
b. September 24, 1954, Roslyn, New York

A constant improviser who is also an important educator, Lisa Sokolov has always gone her own way musically.

She played piano from a young age and sang throughout her school years in choruses and musical theater shows. "A music teacher in high school turned me on to Coltrane and pointed me in the direction of Bennington College. In my early years, my studies with Jimmy Lyons, Milford Graves and Bill Dixon were pivotal and impressed me greatly. That would be around 1974 at Bennington. After college in the summer of 1976, I went to Paris with a big band. We slowly became a smaller and smaller band, until I was the only one left, so I performed solo. In 1976 I met Jeanne Lee. She became a singing partner, a mentor and a friend. It was through Jeanne that I met William Parker. I began singing with him and his ensemble right away. It was the William Big group, which included myself, Jeanne Lee and Ellen Christie. My association with William continued for decades. I recorded two of his CDs with him, one appearance on a little Huey CD and one Williams Song Cycle CD. He really gave me a spot in the downtown New York world." In addition, she earned a degree in music from Bennington and a master's degree in music therapy from NYU.

Since 1977, Lisa Sokolov has worked with many of the top names in avant-garde jazz, including Cecil Taylor, Rashied Ali, Andrew Cyrille, Mark Dresser, Irene Schweitzer, Butch

Morris and Gerry Hemingway in settings ranging from orchestras to unaccompanied solos, from standards to free improvisations.

Lisa Sokolov has also worked extensively as a music therapist. "I was always interested in the whole human being and in bringing music to people who didn't have access. As an outgrowth of my many years working as a music therapist and teacher, I have developed a method called Embodied Voice Work, which I use in the training of artists, physicians and regular normal neurotic singers and non-singing people who want to learn the language of improvised voice." She taught at NYU in the music therapy department during 1981–91, has taught at the Tisch School of the Arts at NYU since 1985, and has been the director of the Institute for Embodied Voice-Work since 1996, in addition to giving many workshops and seminars.

"My musical goals are to be able to stand in front of a large audience and be able to help move and transform human beings emotionally and spiritually through music."

Recommended CDs: Lisa Sokolov's three CDs as a leader are *Angel Radio* (Laughing Horse 1007), *Lazy Afternoon* (Laughing Horse 1008) and *Presence* (Laughing Horse 1011). *Presence* in particular is quite uninhibited, almost performance art in spots as she acts out the words to a song such as "You Do Something To Me" in a slightly demented and almost startling fashion.

Website: www.lisasokolov.com

Tessa Souter
b. April 3, 1956, London, England

An exotic jazz singer whose music is open to the influence of flamenco, Middle Eastern and Indian music, Tessa Souter is an exciting performer who did not dedicate herself to singing until she was 43.

"My mother got a kick out of her three-year-old singing sophisticated songs and Caribbean lullabies that she had learned from my Trinidadian birth father, who was a singer. We sang in the car, in the house, in the street. Embarrassingly for me (as a child), my mother sometimes used to sing at the top of her voice on the bus. By the time I was six years old, I literally used to wake up singing, which might be why my bedroom was miles away from the rest of the household."

Although it was taken for granted that she would be a singer, Tessa Souter deferred that dream for quite a few years. "I took a major detour by leaving home at 15. I married very young, had my son, and subsequently went to the university to study English literature, becoming a journalist." She wrote for the London *Times*, the *Independent*, *Vogue* and *Elle*, and was a freelance journalist in San Francisco during 1992–96. Eventually she moved to New York and immersed herself in music. Souter won a scholarship to the Manhattan School of Music in 1998 but soon left to study with Mark Murphy. "I was very lucky to be mentored by Mark Murphy for four years, during which time I was his assistant. I learned a lot from him. I also studied with the great Sheila Jordan. I was 42 when I had my first paying gig in February 1999."

Since then Tessa Souter has received consistently favorable reviews, appeared throughout the United States and England, and released her first CD, *Listen Love*.

Recommended CDs: On *Listen Love* (Nara 6277), Tessa Souter gives fresh life to "Caravan" and Pharoah Sanders' "The Creator Has A Master Plan," contributes lyrics to Pat Martino's "Willow" and "Concierto de Aranjuez," and performs songs by Sting, Jon Lucien and Jimmy Rowles ("The Peacocks"). It is a very impressive if long-delayed debut.

Website: www.tessiesouter.com

Jeri Southern
(Genevieve Lilian Haring)
b. August 5, 1926, Royal, NE; d. August 4, 1991, Los Angeles, CA

Jeri Southern's singing fell between jazz and middle-of-the-road pop in the 1950s. She did not have a powerful voice, but she was effective at conveying the feeling of world-weariness, which ironically became reality when she decided to retire prematurely from performing.

Southern started on piano when she was three, with serious lessons beginning three years later. Trained in classical music both in her singing and piano playing, Southern switched to jazz by the time she graduated high school. She attended the University of Nebraska, first performed as a solo pianist in 1944, and moved to Chicago a few years later where she performed in local clubs. Signed to Decca in 1951, she had minor hits in "You Better Go Now" and "Joey," recording most of her best work for the label, which varied from orchestra to combo selections. She also recorded two albums apiece for Roulette and Capitol (including *Jeri Southern Meets Cole Porter*) but chose to retire in 1962 when she was only 36, expressing discouragement at the state of the music business. Jeri Southern became a vocal and piano coach in Los Angeles during her past few decades.

Recommended CDs: *The Very Thought Of You: The Decca Years, 1951–1957* (GRP 671) is a fine single-disc sampler that is drawn from Jeri Southern's six Decca albums. Five twofers that each reissue the contents of two complete albums have been issued. Some will be easier to find than others. Southern's full Decca output is on *You Better Go Now/Your Heart's On Fire* (Jasmine 602), *Southern Hospitality/Jeri Gently Jumps* (Universal 19134) and *Southern Style/Prelude To A Kiss* (MCA 19380). Her two Roulettes have returned as *Southern Breeze/Coffee, Cigarettes And Memories* (EMI 96650), and her Capitol work is on *Meets Cole Porter/At The Crescendo* (Universal 856057).

Luciana Souza
b. July 12, 1966, São Paulo, Brazil

A versatile vocalist who sings in Portuguese and English, and has often set poetry to song, Luciana Souza grew up around music. Her parents, guitarist-singer Walter Santos and Tereza Souza, are successful songwriters who wrote hits for top Brazilian artists including João Gilberto and Elis Regina. Milton Nascimento and Hermeto Pascoal were among their friends. "My parents also wrote jingles for a jingle house, so my first recording was at age three, for a radio commercial. I remember that my father brought home LPs of big bands (Ellington, Stan Kenton and Bill Holman) and singers such as Billie, Frank, Ella,

Sarah and Carmen. My brother introduced me to pianists (he is one), including Bill Evans, Herbie, McCoy and Keith."

There was never any doubt that Luciana Souza would make a career out of music. In addition to singing, she learned piano and guitar and considers her father, Jobim and Pascoal to be her main inspirations. She attended Unicamp University in Brazil for four years and the Berklee College of Music, earning a bachelor's degree in jazz composition in 1988. Souza toured Brazil with Hermeto Pascoal (1991) and the Zimbo Trio (1992), earned a master's degree from the New England Conservatory of Music and relocated to the U.S. Since that time she has worked with Danilo Perez's Motherland Project (2000–2001), Maria Schneider, David Kikoski, Joey Calderazzo, Oscar Castro-Neves, the Paul Winter Consort, Steve Lacy, the Kenny Wheeler Big Band, Donald Brown, John Patitucci, Kenny Werner, Bob Moses and, most recently, guitarist Romero Lubambo in duets. She also taught for four years at Berklee and appeared with symphony orchestras, singing the music of classical composer Osvaldo Golijov.

Luciana Souza's music goes far beyond her roots in samba and bossa nova, for she is a constant improviser who is never afraid to take chances.

Recommended CDs: Luciana Souza's five recordings are 1999's *An Answer To Your Silence* (NYC Records 6030), *The Poems Of Elizabeth Bishop And Other Songs* (Sunnyside 1091), *Brazilian Duos* (Sunnyside 1100), which has a few songs on which her father accompanies her on guitar, *North And South* (Sunnyside 1112) and *Neruda* (Sunnyside 1132). While the latter has music to 10 of Pablo Neruda's poems, *North And South*, which features Brazilian and American standards, is the most accessible of Luciana Souza's recordings to date.

Website: www.lucianasouza.com

Mary Ellen Spann
b. November 26, 1964, Sioux Falls, SD

Mary Ellen Spann is expert at revitalizing vintage ballads and standards, making the results sound fresh, intimate and infectious.

"Music goes way back in our family. My dad played saxophone and had his own big band in high school and college, called the Bud Doyle Music Makers. My mom, one of my biggest musical influences, would sit at the piano and sing 'More Than You Know,' 'Body And Soul,' 'What'll I Do' and 'La Vie En Rose.' My oldest sister, Elizabeth Doyle, is currently a composer, vocalist and jazz pianist in the Chicago area. And my grandfather, George B. German, was a cowboy balladeer, songwriter and radio host of his own program on WNAX in the 1930s and '40s.

"At about the 7th grade I began to realize that my musical tastes were vastly different from all of my peers. At the annual junior high talent show I put together my own medley of 'The Trolley Song,' 'I Got Rhythm' and 'Poor Johnny One Note.' The reality of me being a jazz singer came in high school when my parents introduced me to Skip Hotchkiss, an older jazz piano player who had a swinging bebop Count Basie kind of style that I loved. My parents lined up a recording session at the local studio and we recorded three songs: 'Give My Regards To Broadway,' 'Carolina In The Morning' and 'Before The Parade Passes By.' I still have that recording today."

After high school, Spann studied music and acting at Catholic University of America in Washington, D.C. Moving to New York, she performed a one-woman show, "My Favorite Fellas," in clubs. In 1998 she moved to Dallas, where she

Victoria Spivey

performed with the big band Tuxedo Junction, appearing on two of their CDs (*Live At The Isle Of Capri* and *Up In Harlem On A Saturday Night*). As a leader Mary Ellen Spann has recorded two CDs for her China Alley Records.

Recommended CDs: *Heart Soar* (China Alley 61189) is mostly comprised of Mary Ellen Spann's originals, while *Little Red Robin* (China Alley 47695) puts an emphasis on her interpretations of standards.

Website: www.maryellenspann.com

Victoria Spivey
b. October 15, 1906, Houston, TX; d. October 3, 1976, New York, NY

One of the youngest of all the classic blues singers of the 1920s and among the last ones to be discovered, Victoria Spivey survived long enough to make a strong comeback in the 1960s, and to be an inspiration for later generations.

She began her career playing piano at Dallas' Lincoln Theater in 1919 when she was 12. Spivey, who considered Ida Cox to be her role model, gained years of experience singing and playing music throughout the South, sometimes with Blind Lemon Jefferson. In 1926 she made her recording debut in St. Louis, waxing her trademark song "Black Snake Blues," a record that sold 150,000 copies. She soon moved to New York where she recorded frequently through 1931, often with guitarist Lonnie Johnson who sometimes joined her in vocal duets. Other sidemen include Louis Armstrong (on 1929's "Funny Feathers" and "How Do You Do It That Way"), players from the Luis Russell Orchestra (such as trumpeter Henry "Red" Allen and trombonist J.C. Higginbotham), pianist Clarence Williams and cornetist King Oliver. Some of Spivey's more popular numbers were double-entendre songs, and a half-dozen were extended two-sided records.

Victoria Spivey had a lead role in the 1929 black film *Hallelujah*, although Nina Mae McKinney, who played the "bad girl" who was also a jazz singer, largely stole the picture. Spivey also worked in the *Hellzapoppin' Revue* and toured with Louis Armstrong's big band. In Chicago during 1936–37, she recorded some worthy performances that showed her adapting her blues style well to swing (including recording "Black Snake Swing"). But Spivey, who for a time directed Lloyd Hunter's Serenaders, sang with Jap Allen's band and toured in shows, gave up in 1952, dropping out of music to work as a church administrator, confining her singing to church.

She changed her mind in 1961, recording for Bluesville on part of the sampler album *Blues We Taught Your Mother* and reuniting with Lonnie Johnson for her own *Woman Blues*. The popularity of the folk-blues movement resulted in many veteran blues performers being rediscovered, and she used the opportunity to start her own Spivey label. Her LPs for Spivey tend to look amateurish and low budget in their packaging, but they contain some valuable performances and such sidemen as the young Bob Dylan on harmonica, Eddie Barefield on clarinet and alto, tenor-saxophonist Buddy Tate, Lonnie Johnson, Washboard Sam and pianists Memphis Slim, Little Brother Montgomery, Otis Spann and Roosevelt Sykes.

During the 1960s and early 1970s, Victoria Spivey was treated as a living legend. She starred at folk and blues festivals, appeared at nightclubs as often as she liked, and effectively ran the Spivey label as a serious business, also recording other blues and jazz artists. She stayed busy up until her death in 1976.

Recommended CDs: *Vol. 1* (Document 5316), *Vol. 2* (Document 5317) and *Vol. 3* (Document 5318) have all of the early Victoria Spivey performances. *Woman Blues* (Original Blues Classics 566) was her comeback recording.

LPs to Search For: *Victoria And Her Blues* (Spivey 1002) and *The Queen And Her Knights* (Spivey 1006) are two of her best 1960s recordings for her Spivey label.

Mary Stallings
b. August 16, 1939, San Francisco, CA

A very good singer who makes the conventional seem special (rarely straying from the modern mainstream of jazz), Mary Stallings is most influenced by Carmen McRae and Dinah Washington.

The oldest of 11 children, Stallings sang gospel music early on at her church, but was attracted to jazz. She appeared in jazz clubs as a teenager, sharing the bandstand with the likes of Wes Montgomery, tenors Ben Webster and Teddy Edwards, and pianist Earl Hines. She was a member of Louis Jordan's Tympani Five for a brief time before she was even out of high school, and in 1961 recorded with Cal Tjader. Stallings impressed Dizzy Gillespie, who featured her at the 1965 Monterey Jazz Festival and with his band during 1965–66. She toured the Far East and South America, spent a year in Nevada working with Billy Eckstine and was with the Count Basie Orchestra during 1969–72.

Despite all of that activity, Mary Stalling barely appeared on records before 1990 and was largely unknown. When she had a child in 1972, she went into semi-retirement, not returning to being a full-time singer until the late 1980s. Fortunately she has been better documented since then, recording for Clarity, Concord, Max Jazz and Half Note. While still best known in San Francisco, where she has long been a major part of the local scene, Mary Stallings has traveled more in recent times to appear at festivals and clubs. She is currently still in her musical prime.

Recommended CDs: *Cal Tjader Plays, Mary Stallings Sings* (Original Jazz Classics 284) has the only early example of Stallings' singing. Since 1990, she has been well documented on such fine CDs as *Fine And Mellow* (Clarity 1001), *I Waited For You* (Concord 4620), *Fine And Well* (Clarity 2001), *Spectrum* (Concord 4689), *Manhattan Moods* (Concord 4750), *Trust Your Heart* (Clarity 1018), *Yesterday, Today And Forever* (Concord), *Live At The Village Vanguard* (Max Jazz 112) and *Remember Love* (Half Note 4521).

Kay Starr
(Kathryn Starks)
b. July 21, 1922, Dougherty, OK

Kay Starr, like Dinah Washington, whom her voice resembled, could sing practically anything. Though most famous for her pop hits in the 1950s and her ability to sing country, she was at her best when singing swing standards in a cheerful and sincere style.

Born on an Indian reservation (she is 3/4 American Indian and 1/4 Irish), Starr grew up in Dallas. She began singing very early in life, performing regularly on the radio at the age of seven, singing pop and hillbilly songs. After her family moved to Memphis, she continued on the radio singing Western swing. Around this time she was renamed Kay Starr. When she was 15 in 1937, she joined the Joe Venuti big band. She had brief stints with Glenn Miller (with whom she made her recording debut) and Bob Crosby in 1939, but was mostly with Venuti until 1942. After moving to Los Angeles, Starr worked with Wingy Manone and then gained recognition for her work with Charlie Barnet's orchestra during 1943–45. She also recorded with the Capitol Jazzmen in 1945, cutting "If I Could Be With You."

After signing with Capitol in 1947, Kay Starr became a popular solo artist. During the next 15 years she had such hits as "I'm The Lonesomest Gal In Town," "Angry," "Side By Side," "Bonaparte's Retreat," "Changing Partners," "Someday Sweetheart" and particularly "The Wheel Of Fortune" and "The Rock 'N' Roll Waltz." She became less active in later years but toured in the 1980s with Helen O'Connell, Rosemary Clooney and Margaret Whiting in a group called 4 Girls 4 and continued performing now and then into the late 1990s.

Recommended CDs: *The Complete Lamplighter Recordings 1945–1946* (Baldwin Street Music 305) features Kay Starr on a series of jazz-oriented dates from the mid-1940s with a variety of top swing players, along with earlier appearances with Bob Crosby, Wingy Manone and Charlie Barnet. Her radio transcriptions of 1947 and 1949 are included on *The Uncollected Kay Starr: In The 1940s* (Hindsight 214) and *Kay Starr* (Hindsight 219). *Definitive Kay Starr On Capitol* (Collectors Classics 276) is a two-CD set containing virtually all of Starr's hits plus other very interesting material from her early-to-mid-1950s recordings for Capitol. *The RCA Years* (BMG 12172) has some of Starr's better recordings from 1955 to 1958. Also of strong interest from her post-1960 period are *I Cry By Night/Losers Weepers* (EMI 856 058) *The One, The Only Kay Starr/Blue Starr* (Collectables 2858), *Movin'* (Jasmine 307), *Back To The Roots* (GNP Crescendo 2090) and *Live At Freddy's 1986* (Baldwin Street Music 202). The latter finds a 65-year-old Kay Starr still sounding spirited and joyful.

Dakota Staton

b. June 3, 1930, Pittsburgh, PA; d. April 10, 2007, New York, NY

A powerful and soulful singer who was almost on the level of Sarah Vaughan or her main influence Dinah Washington, Dakota Staton is best remembered for her hit "The Late, Late Show."

Staton attended the Filion School of Music and at 16 starred in the show *Fantastic Rhythm* as a singer and dancer. At 18 she sang with the band of Joe Wespray in Pittsburgh and then spent a few years performing in Midwest night clubs. It was not until 1954, after she had moved to New York, that she began to record, signing with Capitol. Dakota Staton's music straddled the boundaries between jazz, R&B and rock and roll for a time and she looked like a potential

hit maker when "The Late, Late Show" came out in 1957. However, after marrying trumpeter Talib Ahmad Dawud, converting to Islam, and deciding to perform under the name of Aliyah Rabia (she soon changed her mind about that), her commercial potential was greatly lessened.

Staton recorded 10 albums for Capitol plus a memorable collaboration with George Shearing. She switched to United Artists where she recorded three albums but was off records altogether during 1965–71, spending much of the time performing in England. She made a bit of a comeback in the 1990s, recording for Muse and cutting her final project for High Note in 1999 before her health declined and forced her retirement.

Recommended CDs: Six of Dakota Staton's rewarding Capitol recordings have been reissued: *The Late, Late Show* (Collectables 5231), *Dynamic* (Capitol 804), *More Than The Most* (Collectables 5232), *Softly/'Round Midnight* (EMI 533089) and *Dakota At Storyville* (Collectables 5233). *Dakota Staton* (Muse 5401), the erratic *Darling, Please Save Your Love For Me* (Muse 5462), *Isn't This A Lovely Day* (Muse 5502) and *A Packet Of Love Letters* (High Note 7008) are generally worthy recordings from her last period. Her 1957 recording with George Shearing is currently available as *In The Night* (Blue Note 724354231124).

LPs to Search For: Four of Dakota Staton's Capitol albums have not yet been reissued: *Crazy He Calls Me* (Capitol 1170), *Time To Swing* (Capitol 1241), *Ballads And The Blues* (Capitol 1387) and *Dakota* (Capitol 1490); nor have her scarce United Artists records been re-released.

Buddy Stewart

b. September 22, 1922, Derry, NJ;
d. February 1, 1950, New Mexico

Buddy Stewart was an excellent ballad singer who was also a pioneer in singing bebop. He grew up in a show business family and was singing in vaudeville by the time he was eight. Stewart formed a vocal trio when he was 15, moving to New York in 1940. He was a member of the Snowflakes, a vocal group that performed briefly with Glenn Miller and was with the Claude Thornhill Orchestra during 1941–42.

After serving in the military during 1942–44, Stewart teamed up with Dave Lambert to form a pioneering bop singing duo. They recorded "What's This" with Gene Krupa's orchestra in 1945, which is considered the first bop vocal record. They also appeared on some Charlie Parker broadcasts from the Royal Roost in 1948 and recorded "Bebop Spoken Here" with Charlie Barnet's orchestra in 1949.

Otherwise, Stewart worked as a ballad singer with Krupa's band in 1946, he sang wordless lines in ensembles while with Charlie Ventura, and he also performed with Red Rodney, Kai Winding, Al Haig and Charlie Barnet's bebop band in 1949. As a leader, Stewart recorded five selections in 1948, four of which have been reissued on sampler albums by Spotlite.

Buddy Stewart might very well have participated in the vocalese movement of the 1950s, but he died in a car crash in 1950 at the age of 27. A major benefit held at Birdland for his widow and child a few weeks later had performances from some of the who's who of jazz, including a group that featured Charlie Parker, Dizzy Gillespie and the young John Coltrane.

Recommended CDs: Gene Krupa's *1945–1946* (Classics 1231) has eight Buddy Stewart vocals.

Sandy Stewart

b. July 10, 1937, Philadelphia, PA

The mother of pianist Bill Charlap and the wife of the late song-writer Moose Charlap, Sandy Stewart is a fine singer who adds warmth to standards and falls between jazz and cabaret.

She remembers one of her earliest experiences singing was "as a 14-year-old on a local Philadelphia television show. I lied about my age and was the Gretz Beer Golden Girl, working as a singer and moderator. At 16, I was chosen as a jazz singer on NBC radio, performing with pianist Dick Hyman, guitarist Mundell Lowe, bassist Ed Safranski and drummer Don Lamond." That same year she moved to New York, replacing Edie Adams on the Ernie Kovacs television show. During the next 15 years she appeared on television many times including the Johnny Carson and Ed Sullivan shows, acted in the 1959 Alan Freed film *Go, Johnny, Go!* and had opportunities to work with Bing Crosby, Perry Como, Steve Allen, Benny Goodman and various jazz rhythm sections. Her 1962 recording of "My Coloring Book" was a surprise hit, and it gave her visibility for a time.

Sandy Stewart has had a lower profile since then, raising four children, but she occasionally emerges for recordings including an album with her family, a set of Jerome Kern songs (with Dick Hyman) and, most recently, a set for Blue Note in which she is accompanied by her son.

Recommended CDs: *My Coloring Book* (Blue Note 9608) features Sandy Stewart with strings performing folk songs and jazz standards. *Sings Songs Of Jerome Kern* (Audiophile 205) from 1985 is one of her finest jazz recordings. *Sandy Stewart And Family (*Cabaret 5010) is her sentimental favorite, while *Love Is Here To Stay* (Blue Note 60340) is a quiet set of ballads from 2005 performed as duets with her son Bill Charlap.

Maxine Sullivan

(Marietta Lillian Williams)
b. May 13, 1911, Homestead, PA; d. April 7, 1987, New York, NY

Maxine Sullivan had a career similar in its evolution to that of Alberta Hunter and Helen Humes in that she became famous early on, worked for a long time with gradually decreasing visibility, retired from performing altogether, and late in life had a major comeback. Sullivan was one of the first of the "cool jazz" singers (predating the movement by a decade) in that she sang softly, largely stuck to the words and melodies, and always swung lightly. She was an influence on Rebecca Kilgore, Susannah McCorkle and, one would guess, Peggy Lee.

It did not take Maxine Sullivan (who changed her name from Marietta Williams for professional reasons) long to get discovered. She started her career singing on the radio in Pittsburgh with the Red Hot Peppers and, by the time she was 16, she was making her first recordings with Claude Thornhill as her musical director. Her first two numbers ("Stop! You're Breaking My Heart" and "Gone With The Wind") were made

with a band under Thornhill's name on June 14, 1937. Her second effort, which was her debut as a leader on August 6, used an early version of the John Kirby Sextet (with Thornhill on piano) and included two Scottish folk songs: "Loch Lomond" and "Annie Laurie." "Loch Lomond" became a major hit and led to Sullivan recording other lightly swinging versions of folk songs including "Darling Nellie Gray," "Down The Old Ox Road," "I Dream Of Jeannie With The Light Brown Hair," "Drink To Me Only With Thine Eyes," "If I Had A Ribbon Bow" and "Molly Malone."

Although Sullivan soon grew tired of being stereotyped as a jazzy folk singer, "Loch Lomond" did make her famous and kept her working for 20 years. She appeared briefly in the film *Going Places* with Louis Armstrong, was part of the show *Swinging The Dream*, and married John Kirby in 1938, performing with his sextet on and off for several years. They were divorced later in the 1940s.

Sullivan worked with the Benny Carter big band in mid-1941 and then became a successful solo act, mostly performing in New York night clubs. Considered out of the jazz and pop mainstream, she made no records during 1949–54 other than two selections in England in 1953. Sullivan had a burst of activity during 1955–56, including a recorded reunion with the survivors of the John Kirby Sextet and appearing in Leonard Feather's *Seven Ages Of Jazz* show. But after marrying stride pianist Cliff Jackson in 1960, she barely worked in music for quite a few years, instead teaching school and taking nursing classes, though she never did become a nurse like Alberta Hunter. During this period she also took lessons from Vic Dickenson on valve trombone, later switching to flugelhorn.

After singing at a few concerts during 1966–68, in 1969 Maxine Sullivan made a complete comeback and performed regularly during her remaining 18 years. Her style was unchanged from the past and, although her voice gradually aged, it still sounded youthful. She recorded prolifically for such labels as Fat Cat Jazz, Monmouth Evergreen, Riff, Audiophile, Kenneth, Stash, Tono, Concord and Atlantic. Although she grudgingly performed "Loch Lomond" when it was requested (which was at every performance), Maxine Sullivan mostly sang vintage swing standards with the charm and effortless swing that typified her approach.

Recommended CDs: *1937–1938* (Classics 963) and *1938–1941* (Classics 991) have the recordings that made Maxine Sullivan famous. *Loch Lomond* (Circle 47) and *More 1940–1941* (Circle 125) are radio transcriptions of Sullivan with the John Kirby Sextet. She is actually only on 17 of the 44 numbers, but the instrumentals are enjoyable too and show how well her style fit that of Kirby's group. Sullivan's recordings of 1944–48 are on *The Le Ruban Bleu Years* (Baldwin Street Music 303). *The 1950s: Swinging Miss Loch Lomond 1952–1959* (Baldwin Street Music 314) and *A Tribute To Andy Razaf* (DCC Compact Classics 610) cover her work during the next decade. Among her best projects from her comeback years (1969–87) are *Close As Pages In A Book* (Audiophile 203), *We Just Couldn't Say Goodbye* (Audiophile 128), *Uptown* (Concord 4288) and *Swingin' Sweet* (Concord 4351).

Tierney Sutton

b. June 28, 1963, Omaha, NE

One of the most important jazz singers to emerge during the 1990s, Tierney Sutton is an expert scat singer and has such a flexible and well-controlled voice that she can sing anything that pops into her head.

She grew up in Milwaukee. "Although I sang from the

time I was a small child (I sang the lead in Humperdink's children's opera *Hansel And Gretel* when I was five), I knew

nothing about jazz, never heard any, until I was in college. I had a summer job as a singing cocktail waitress at the Heidel House Resort in Green Lake, Wisconsin. Two things happened that summer. One was that I found out that standards like 'My Funny Valentine' and 'Moonlight in Vermont' managed to be great even when sung by the Heidel Honeys with organ and accordion, and two is that I heard a real jazz trio, the Mary Jay Trio, across the street on my night off. It was like taking a musical bath after our tired renditions of stale Donna Summer tunes."

Sutton studied Russian language and literature at Wesleyan University but also spent a lot of time in the music department, which was headed by saxophonist Bill Barron. "When I began singing jazz at Wesleyan, I was lucky because there were tons of instrumentalists who wanted to play, but no other vocalists." She attended the Berklee College of Music for most of two semesters, and studied privately with tenor-saxophonist Jerry Bergonzi.

"It wasn't until 1993 that I decided to do it all the way and ended up moving to Los Angeles. I had planned to move from Boston to New York, but some doors opened in L.A. that led me to the West Coast instead." Since that time she has taught voice at USC, sung with the late trumpeter Buddy Childers and pianist Dave MacKay, been a semi-finalist in the 1998 Thelonious Monk Vocal Competition, performed a series of symphony concerts with pianist-arranger Alan Broadbent in New Zealand, guested with the Les Brown Orchestra, appeared at a countless number of festivals and clubs, and signed with the Telarc label in 2000. Her regular group, with pianist Christian Jacob, Trey Henry or Kevin Axt on bass, and drummer Ray Brinker, has been together for 14 years, while her string of recordings for Telarc (all of which feature her band) has made her nationally famous.

Recommended CDs: *Introducing Tierney Sutton* (Challenge 73111), *Unsung Heroes* (Telarc 83477), *Blue In Green* (Telarc 83522), which is a tribute to Bill Evans, *Something Cool* (Telarc 83548), her Frank Sinatra tribute *Dancing In The Dark* (Telarc 83592), *I'm With The Band* (Telarc 83616) and *On The Other Side* (Telarc 83650) are all excellent and display Sutton's impressive improvising skills. *On The Other Side* is particularly offbeat, featuring slowed-down and often mournful versions of songs that are usually quite happy and joyous.

Website: www.tierneysutton.com

Sylvia Syms
(Sylvia Blagman)
b. December 2, 1917, Brooklyn, NY;
d. May 10, 1992, New York, NY

A superior interpreter of lyrics, Sylvia Syms was called "the world's greatest saloon singer" by Frank Sinatra. Her singing fell between jazz and cabaret, and she made up for

having an average voice by putting a lot of feeling into her interpretations.

After overcoming polio as a child, she became interested in jazz, visiting the clubs on New York's fabled 52nd Street on a regular basis. She befriended Billie Holiday, who gave her some tips, and in 1941 she began singing in clubs, starting with Kelly's Stables. In addition to being a nightclub singer, Syms was an occasional actress. In 1948 she made her acting debut in a revival of *Diamond Lil* after being discovered by Mae West. Syms acted in regional theater throughout her life, including appearing in *South Pacific* and *Hello, Dolly!*

She first recorded six titles for the Deluxe label in 1947, had a surprise million-seller in 1956 with "I Could Have Danced All Night," and made jazz-oriented albums for 20th Century Fox, Prestige and Atlantic. Syms was versatile enough to perform an album with organist Johnny Hammond Smith and revivals of rock and roll songs in jazz settings in addition to the vintage standards. Her 1982 album *Syms By Sinatra* was conducted by her admirer Frank Sinatra. Sylvia Syms died of a heart attack at the Algonquin Hotel while performing a tribute to Sinatra in 1992.

Recommended CDs: *Songs By Sylvia Syms* (Koch 8541) brings back Syms' first album, a 1952–53 project for Atlantic that has her joined by either the Barbara Carroll Trio or a septet led by arranger Johnny Richards. *Torch Song* (Koch 7936) is from the late 1950s with Ralph Burns arranging and directing an orchestra. *Sylvia Is* (Original Jazz Classics 775) from 1965 teams Syms with guitarist Kenny Burrell in a pianoless combo, performing Brazilian songs and standards. *For Once In My Life* (Original Jazz Classics 897) is less interesting due to the weaker material. Of her later recordings, *A Jazz Portrait Of Johnny Mercer* (DRG 91433) and *Then Along Came Bill* (DRG 91402), a 1991 tribute to pianist Bill Evans, are most rewarding.

Grady Tate
b. January 14, 1932, Durham, NC

A world class drummer who has been on an enormous amount of recording dates, Grady Tate is also an occasional ballad singer who, if he were not a drummer, could probably have had a fine career strictly as a vocalist.

Tate actually sang in public before he played drums, starting from the age of four. He performed in church and school until his voice changed when he was 12, but then hardly sang again until he was in his thirties. Self-taught on the drums, he served in the Air Force during 1951–55, studied psychology, literature and theater at North Carolina College, and for a brief period worked as a high school teacher. Tate played drums with organist Wild Bill Davis during 1959–62, moved to New York in 1963, performed with the Quincy Jones Orchestra, and then became a greatly in-demand session drummer. He worked with everyone from Jimmy Smith and Wes Montgomery to Stan Getz, Tony Bennett, Ella Fitzgerald, Benny Goodman and Oscar Peterson, among many others.

Gary McFarland liked Grady Tate's singing voice, and during 1968–69 he contributed arrangements to three albums that Tate led for the Skye label. The music was sometimes a bit commercial, but Tate's expressive baritone voice came across well. Although still primarily a drummer, he has led around a dozen vocal albums in his career (some for Japanese labels), displaying a basic approach and a sound that is influenced by Johnny Hartman. 1992's *TNT* is probably his finest vocal recording and Grady Tate occasionally guests as a singer on the recordings of others.

Recommended CDs: All of Grady Tate's albums as a leader are essentially vocal projects. *TNT* (Milestone 9193), *Body And Soul* (Milestone 9208), *Feeling Free* (Pow Wow 7469), *All Love* (Village 8802) and *From The Heart* (Half Note 4529) all have strong samplings of Tate's warm voice.

Linda Tate

b. July 7, 1951, Chicago, IL

One of the better jazz singers based in Chicago in recent times, Linda Tate is equally skilled at interpreting lyrics and scatting. Her recordings for the Southport label have gained her some deserved attention.

"I have always loved taking bubble baths, and as a child I used to sing songs from movie musicals and Broadway every day in the bathtub. I sang folk songs and accompanied myself on the guitar as a teenager and sang in a choir in college. I wrote original songs and accompanied myself on the piano throughout my teens and twenties. But I didn't really think of myself as a jazz singer until my early thirties (in the 1980s), when I realized that jazz was the music I liked the best and sounded the best singing. Once I discovered the creative possibilities inherent in jazz and my own personal talent to express myself singing jazz, I knew I wanted to do it professionally."

Tate, who received a Bachelor of Music degree when she graduated from Roosevelt University in 1974 (earning a Master's from DePaul University in 1995), became active on the Chicago jazz scene in 1990, the year that she attended Janice Borla's Vocal Jazz Camp. Five years later she made the first of her three CDs for Southport. In addition to performing at local clubs and festivals, she sang in Singapore in 1999 with the Curtis Robinson Quartet, and with the Marek Smaus Quartet in Prague. Her most recent recording, *We Speak Duke*, is a tribute to Duke Ellington that she also performed at the Chicago Cultural Center with seven instrumentalists, three vocalists and a tap dancer.

Recommended CDs: Each of Linda Tate's three recordings, *We Belong Together* (Southport 38), *Time, Seasons And The Moon* (Southport 81) and *We Speak Duke* (Southport 101), are well worth exploring and savoring.

Website: www.lindatate.com

Eva Taylor

(Irene Gibbons)
b. January 22, 1895, St. Louis, MO;
d. October 31, 1977, Mineola, NY

One of the first female jazz vocalists to record who was not a classic blues singer, Eva Taylor was primarily associated with her husband Clarence Williams' pickup recording groups. She had a very likable sound, was in-tune even if her range was small, swung well, and had an easy-to-understand voice. As with Ella Fitzgerald a decade later, Eva Taylor always

sounded happy to be singing.

She began in show business at the age of three, singing with a traveling show and visiting Australia in 1900. Taylor spent much of her childhood performing on stage, visiting Europe (1906), Hawaii and New Zealand in addition to performing throughout the United States. In the early 1920s she moved to New York City, married Clarence Williams, appeared on the radio as early as 1922, and started her recording career. Quite typically, two of the first songs that she cut were a pair of future standards that were not blues: "I Wish I Could Shimmy Like My Sister Kate" and "Baby Won't You Please Come Home."

Throughout the 1920s and early '30s, Taylor recorded constantly, usually in groups led by her husband (those have been reissued along with many instrumentals under Clarence Williams' name by the Classics label) but also 72 selections as a leader during 1922–32 (which fills up three CDs). She was usually backed by all-star jazz players, although occasionally just by her husband's piano. Among the many excellent recordings that Taylor made during this era are "Cake Walking Babies From Home" (with Louis Armstrong and Sidney Bechet), "You Can't Shush Katie (The Gabbiest Girl In Town)," a sweet and definitive version of "When The Red, Red Robin Comes Bob, Bob Bobbin' Along," "Nobody But My Baby Is Getting My Love," "Candy Lips" and the humorous "I've Got The 'Yes We Have No Bananas' Blues."

Taylor also toured with many Broadway productions and revues in addition to appearing regularly on the radio. Things slowed down during the second half of the 1930s and, after recording two final numbers with Williams in 1941, Eva Taylor mostly stopped singing except for rare special occasions. After Clarence Williams died in 1965, Taylor came out of retirement and made a part-time comeback to the delight of vintage jazz fans and musicians. She performed in Europe several times in the late 1960s and early 1970s, recording albums overseas with Dick Sudhalter (1967), the Peruna Jazzmen (1974) and finally trumpeter Bent Persson and Maggie's Blue Five (1976). Although her voice had aged, she still swung and had an infectious smile in her voice.

Recommended CDs: All of Eva Taylor's early recordings under her own name are on *Volume 1* (Document 5408), *Volume 2* (Document 5409) and *Volume 3* (Document 5410). *Edison Laterals 4* (Diamond Cut 303) repeats some of the earlier recordings but also includes some rarities. Most of her other 1920s and '30s performances are on the extensive Clarence Williams series put out by Classics.

LPs to Search For: *The Legendary Eva Taylor With Maggie's Blue Five* (Kenneth 2042) shows that she was still a skilled singer when she was 80.

Jack Teagarden

b. August 29, 1905, Vernon, TX;
d. January 15, 1964, New Orleans, LA

One of the all-time great trombonists, it was often said of Jack Teagarden early in his career that he was virtually the only white male who could effectively sing the blues. Although the truth of that statement (even in the 1920s) is quite debatable, Mr. T. was widely respected throughout jazz by black and white musicians alike. His singing was an integral part of his music.

Teagarden's mother was a ragtime pianist and his younger siblings included trumpeter Charlie, drummer Clois and pianist Norma. Jack started on piano when he was five, switching to baritone horn at seven and trombone at 10. As a teenager he played with his mother for silent movies and with the legendary unrecorded (at least till the 1950s) pianist Peck Kelley as a member of Peck's Bad Boys in Texas. Teagarden also worked with Doc Ross and Johnny Johnson, making his recording debut with the latter in 1927.

When Teagarden joined Ben Pollack's orchestra in June 1928 and came to New York, he made a huge impact. Up to that time, the trombone was considered a harmony instrument behind the trumpet, usually played percussively and with staccato phrasing. While Miff Mole (who played unusual interval jumps) and Jimmy Harrison (with Fletcher Henderson) had helped move the instrument beyond Kid Ory's New Orleans style, Teagarden seemed like a friendly revolutionary. He had no trouble playing the most complex melody lines, always sounded relaxed no matter how difficult the material, and was technically far ahead of his peers while never looking like he worked up a sweat. His singing was in a similar vein, and his numerous recordings of "Basin Street Blues" and "Beale Street Blues" resulted in those songs being closely identified with him along with the touching ballad "100 Years From Today" (which he shared with Ethel Waters and Lee Wiley), "Stars Fell On Alabama" and his theme song "I've Got A Right To Sing The Blues."

Teagarden, who was immediately in demand for record dates, worked with Pollack during 1928–33 and in 1934 signed a five-year contract with Paul Whiteman's orchestra. Although that initially seemed a good move, since it was the height of the Depression and jazz bands were struggling, it was an exercise in bad timing, since Benny Goodman launched the swing era the following year. While his friends formed their own orchestras, Teagarden was stuck playing Whiteman's brand of concert jazz, only being featured on an occasional jazz number. Because of his tie-in with Whiteman, he had to reluctantly turn down an opportunity to lead the nucleus of the Pollack band when the musicians mutinied. The players ended up picking Bob Crosby as their new leader, and Teagarden could only watch the success of the Bob Crosby Orchestra from a distance.

In 1939 when Teagarden was at last free, he finally formed the Jack Teagarden Orchestra, but it was too late. With so many big bands overpopulating the field, it was difficult for Teagarden's ensemble to find its own niche and musical personality beyond the playing and singing of its leader. He kept the band together for seven long years, but at the time that he reluctantly broke it up in 1946 he was so much in debt that he had to declare bankruptcy. Bing Crosby helped Teagarden with his debts, and Mr. T. found life easier when he joined the Louis Armstrong All-Stars in 1947. Both vocally and instrumentally, Teagarden was a perfect match with Armstrong, whether sharing the spotlight on "Rockin' Chair" and "Jack Armstrong Blues" or having a feature on "St. James Infirmary."

In 1951 Jack Teagarden went out on his own, leading a Dixieland sextet. His last 13 years were full of gigs, tours (including Asia during 1958–59) and recordings, with a set of wistful Willard Robison songs from 1962 being particularly rewarding. Although his repertoire did not evolve much, he never lost his joy at playing trombone and singing and he remained one of the greats up until the end.

Recommended CDs: A pair of two-CD sets, *The Indispensable Jack Teagarden* (French RCA 68806) and *King Of The Blues Trombone* (Collector's Choice 279), do a superlative job of summing up Teagarden's early sideman years. *1930–1934* (Classics 698), *1934–1939* (Classics 729), *1939–1940* (Classics 758), *1940–1941* (Classics 839), *1941–1943* (Classics 874) and *1944–1947* (Classics 1032) have all of Teagarden's dates as a leader during 1930–47, including the complete output by his big band. A limited edition four-CD set *The Complete Capitol Fifties Jack Teagarden Sessions* (Mosaic 4-168) reissues six dates from 1955–58. *Think Well Of Me* (Verve 314 557 101) has the memorable 1962 Willard Robison project, and *A Hundred Years From Today* (Grudge Music 4523) reissues a touching reunion by the Teagarden family at the 1963 Monterey Jazz Festival less than four months before Jack Teagarden's death.

Clare Teal
b. May 14, 1973, West Yorkshire, United Kingdom

One of England's up and coming singers, Clare Teal has made a strong impression during the past five years and garnered headlines in the music world when she signed a lucrative contract with Sony.

She grew up in the 1980s loving the singers of the 1930s, '40s and '50s, often listening to her grandmother's 78s which were stored in her parents' attic. "I would imitate all the singers I heard, people like Ella Fitzgerald, Sarah Vaughan, Dinah Washington, Doris Day, Anita O'Day, Peggy Lee, Frank Sinatra and Nat King Cole, as well as all the big band vocalists." She took lessons on piano and clarinet, and studied music at the University of Wolverhampton during 1991–94. Teal gained some experience singing in jazz settings, recorded her debut (the self-produced *Nice Work*), and came in second in a nationwide competition to find the country's best Billie Holiday soundalike.

After spending a few years writing jingles and selling advertising over the phone, when she was 27 she finally decided to do what she really wanted to do: sing jazz. She filled in for Stacey Kent at a jazz festival, and that was the start of her career. Within a year, Clare Teal was recording the first of her three albums for the Candid label. She made such a strong impact that Sony signed and recorded her in 2003, and in 2006 she won the award as BBC Jazz Vocalist of the Year. For the future she hopes "to make the best music I can and bring my blend of jazz and popular music to a much bigger audience."

Recommended CDs: *Nice Work* (self-produced) will be difficult to locate. Of her three excellent Candid recordings, *That's The Way It Is* (Candid 79767), *Orsino's Songs* (Candid 79783) and *The Road Less Travelled* (Candid 79794), Clare Teal names *Orsino's Songs* as her favorite. *Don't Talk* (Sony 5186702) was a big seller, while *Paradisi Carousel* (Sony 708479) finds her stretching beyond standards and vintage material in favor of contributing modern originals.

Website: www.clareteal.co.uk

Clark Terry
b. December 14, 1920, St. Louis, MO

One of the most beloved figures in jazz, Clark Terry's flugelhorn solos are a pure joy. He already had had a full career as a musician before he ever recorded a vocal, but his "Mumbles" character soon became one of his trademarks.

Part of the St. Louis trumpet tradition, C.T. gained experience playing with George Hudson's band in the early 1940s. After serving in the Navy (where he performed with a dance band), he worked with the big bands of Lionel Hampton (1945), Charlie Barnet (1947–48), Count Basie orchestra and septet (1948–51) and Duke Ellington (1951–59). A major soloist with the latter three bands, C.T. became famous in jazz during his long period with Ellington, and he began leading albums of his own in 1955. Beginning in 1957, he started switching his focus to the flugelhorn. Terry worked with the Quincy Jones Orchestra in Europe during 1959–60, the Gerry Mulligan Concert Jazz Band, co-led a quintet with valve trombonist Bob Brookmeyer and became one of the first full-time African American studio players, joining the NBC staff in 1961.

In all of those settings, Clark Terry was strictly an instrumentalist. In 1964, while recording the classic *Oscar Peterson Trio Plus One* album, C.T. made up a pair of satires of early unintelligible blues singers, titled "Mumbles" and "Incoherent Blues." The favorable reaction to his nonsensical vocals led Terry to include similar numbers as a regular part of his performances and occasionally on records.

Despite periods of erratic health, Clark Terry has remained quite active up to the writing of this book, recently celebrating his 87th birthday. He was part of the Tonight Show Band when it was based in New York, occasionally leads a big band (including one fairly regularly in the 1970s), has recorded and toured regularly during the past 45 years, enthusiastically gives a countless number of clinics to young students, and has appeared at virtually every significant jazz club and festival, spreading joy around the world. He has also sung humorous blues, and occasionally a more straightforward number, with Terry's "Mumbles" vocals always being a crowd pleaser.

Recommended CDs: *Oscar Peterson Plus One* (Verve 818 840) introduced "Mumbles." *Clark Terry Mumbles* (Mainstream 56066) from 1968 has five of his vocals, including "The Mumbler Strikes Again," "Grand Dad's Blues" and "Never." *What A Wonderful World* (Red Baron 53750), a tribute album to Duke Ellington and Louis Armstrong, is highlighted by a remarkable version of "Duke's Place" featuring Terry ad-libbing a hilarious monologue. Both Terry and bassist Red Mitchell take some vocals on their duo date from 1986 *To Duke And Basie* (Enja 5011). *Songs Ella And Louis Sang* (Concord 4787) has C.T. and Carol Sloane sharing the singing in joyful fashion without imitating Satch and Ella.

Website: www.clarkterry.com

Sister Rosetta Tharpe
(Rosetta Nubin)
b. March 20, 1915, Cotton Plant, AR;
d. October 9, 1973, Philadelphia, PA

Although she spent much of her career singing gospel music, Sister Rosetta Tharpe had a period in which she sang secular music. Even when involved with religious songs, she was a notable guitar soloist and constantly crossed over into jazz.

Always an exciting performer, Tharpe started her career as a singing evangelist, which was natural for her mother was a gospel performer. By the time she was six, Tharpe was already an impressive acoustic guitarist and, after her family moved to Chicago in the 1920s, she was influenced by blues and early jazz. She gained attention beyond the church world

when she was featured at John Hammond's From Spirituals To Swing concert at Carnegie Hall in Dec 1938. Being the main attraction with Lucky Millinder's orchestra during 1940–43, Tharpe was famed for her versions of "Rock Me," "That's All," "Trouble In Mind," "This Train," "Shout Sister Shout" and "Rock Daniel." Her version of "I Want A Tall, Skinny Papa" must have raised the eyebrows of her followers in the gospel world. Fifteen years before Ray Charles

developed soul music by infusing secular music with the passion and intensity of gospel, Tharpe was already doing the same thing.

In 1943 Sister Rosetta Tharpe became a solo performer and returned to gospel music, where her popularity continued to grow through the years, having a hit in 1944 with "Strange Things Happening Every Day," and a couple years later with "Up Above My Head." She usually played solo but occasionally teamed up with jazz musicians including the Sammy Price Trio, and with Chris Barber's trad band during a 1957 tour of England. Her flirtations with jazz, popular music, the blues and R&B in the 1950s made her controversial to gospel purists, but Tharpe gained a big audience in Europe that allowed her to overcome the conservative backlash. In 1970 she suffered a major stroke but, although it affected her speech, oddly enough she was still able to sing as powerfully as ever. She worked steadily up until the time of her death and is today recognized as gospel music's first national star, and as an underrated jazz singer.

Recommended CDs: *1938–1941* (Document 5334) and *1942–1944* (Document 5335) have all of Tharpe's early recordings, which include her first solo dates, all of her performances with Millinder's band (including radio appearances and V-Discs), "This Train" with Louis Jordan's Tympany Five, and her return to gospel. *Live In 1960* (Southland 1007) and *Live At The Hot Club De France* (Milan 35624) are concert performances from 1960 and 1966 that show just how exciting her singing and guitar playing still were many years after she departed from secular music.

Laura Theodore
b. Cleveland, Ohio

Laura Theodore has extensive experience as an actress in films and television and as a singer in a variety of styles. But it is clear from her series of CDs that jazz is her main love.

"I was a child actor in Ohio at the Children Heights Youth Theater. I performed in over 30 plays (mostly musical comedies) from the age of 11 until I was 17. I also formed my first musical group at 14 (12 kids singing show tunes) and a rock group when I was 17; we liked Grand Funk Railroad and Janis Joplin. But at 19, I bought an Ella Fitzgerald record, played it over and over, and it transformed me. I started singing jazz."

After a bit of travel throughout the U.S. and Canada, and periods living in Denver and Boston (studying jazz composition and music theory at the South Shore Music Conservatory), she moved to New York. Theodore worked as both a stage actor and a singer in jazz and cabaret clubs. She performed at Town Hall with Mercer Ellington's orchestra and at the Cookery for three months, opening for Alberta Hunter. Theodore also became active in appearing on soundtracks, jingles, and in the early 1990s, with a rock group that she co-founded, Q. She played Janis Joplin in the Off-Broadway hit *Beehive* and in a later show titled *Love, Janis*.

Laura Theodore, who recorded her first jazz CD in 1994, has worked with pianist Don Rebic for over 20 years. She has hosted the weekly *All This Jazz* cable show in Manhattan since 1997 and toured the U.S. with her one-woman show *Celebrating The Great Ladies Of American Song*.

Recommended CDs: 1994's *Tonight's the Night* (Bearcat 9481) has appearances by guitarist Joe Beck and trumpeter Randy Brecker. *What Is This Thing Called Jazz?* (Bearcat 9708) is a strong set of standards, *Live At Vartan Jazz* (Vartan Jazz 002) is her only live recording thus far, *We're Only Human* (Etherean Music 7701) is more pop-oriented, while *What the World Needs Now Is Love* (Bearcat 6054) has Laura Theodore returning to jazz quite successfully.

Website: www.lauratheodore.com

Leon Thomas
(Amos Leon Thomas Jr.)
b. October 4, 1937, East St. Louis, MO; d. May 8, 1999, Bronx, NY

Leon Thomas will always be best known for his singing on "The Creator Has A Master Plan" with Pharoah Sanders, and for his tendency to yodel at climactic moments in lengthy improvisations.

Thomas studied music for two years at Tennessee State University. After moving to New York in 1958, he worked with the Count Basie Orchestra during two stints (1961 and 1964–65) but was overshadowed by the accomplishments of his predecessor, Joe Williams. He also performed with Mary Lou Williams, Randy Weston and Rahsaan Roland Kirk. Thomas came into his own working with Pharoah Sanders in the late 1960s, really stretching both his voice and his improvisations, sounding both spiritual and avant-garde while jamming over one and two-chord vamps, not only on "The Creator Has A Master Plan" (originally an instrumental by Sanders that was called "Pisces Moon" before Thomas wrote lyrics) but "Hum-Allah-Hum-Allah-Hum-Allah," and a few similar mystical pieces. Thomas' vocals were popular for a time, proving that even free jazz can catch on commercially under the right circumstances.

Thomas made some albums for the Flying Dutchman label and worked a bit with rock guitarist Santana, but faded from the scene by the late 1970s. He reappeared occasionally, leading a blues-oriented band in 1988, and showing on records that he still had plenty left to say. He was in the midst of a comeback, performing the night before his death, when he passed away from heart failure at the age of 61.

Recommended CDs: Pharoah Sanders' *Karma* (Impulse 153) has a 32-minute version of "The Creator Has A Master Plan."

Blues And The Soulful Truth (RCA 85153) is the only Leon Thomas Flying Dutchman album that has thus far been reissued in full on CD. *Precious Energy* (Mapleshade 5694) is a 1994 collaboration with altoist Gary Bartz.

LPs to Search For: *Spirits Known And Unknown* (Flying Dutchman 115), Leon Thomas' debut as a leader from 1969, has a more concise version of "The Creator Has A Master Plan" plus his interpretation of Horace Silver's "Song For My Father." *The Leon Thomas Album* (Flying Dutchman 10132) displays his versatility including three numbers with "The Super Black Blues Band," while *In Berlin* (Flying Dutchman 10142) is a strong concert performance with altoist Oliver Nelson.

Teri Thornton
(Shirley Enid Avery)
b. September 1, 1934, Detroit, MI;
d. May 2, 2000, Englewood Cliffs, NJ

Teri Thornton made a stir in the early 1960s, was in obscurity for 30 years, and then had a comeback during the last couple of years before her death. Her quotes in this entry are from an interview I conducted with her in 1999.

"I kind of feel like a song belongs to me—just at that moment—and I can do with it what I want, not thinking what someone else has done with it. I feel like it's a brand new song written just for me. Through public performances and recordings, I want to be in contact with as many people as I can. My main goal is that they leave happier after hearing me than when they came in."

Teri Thornton was born and grew up in Detroit. Her mother was a choir director who performed with a local opera company and had her own radio show. Thornton started playing piano when she was three, being mostly self-taught. After winning a couple amateur shows by singing as a teenager, she began to work professionally. In 1956 she worked at Cleveland's Ebony Club. After moving to Chicago, Thornton was introduced to tenor-saxophonist Johnny Griffin. "He took me under his wing. I worked with Johnny for a couple of years and then he preceded me to New York, paving the way for me." After moving to New York in 1960, Thornton was recommended to Orrin Keepnews of the Riverside label by Griffin and Cannonball Adderley (who called her "the greatest voice since Ella Fitzgerald"). She made her recording debut with *Devil May Care* (which has also been issued as *Lullaby Of The Leaves*) during 1960–61. Her powerful voice, a little reminiscent of Sarah Vaughan, made her one of the underrated greats of the period.

In 1962 her second album, *Somewhere In The Night* for the Dauntless label, was very popular, particularly the title cut, which was the theme from the *Naked City* television series. "I knew it was a great song. I only regret that I did not have a high-powered manager who could help me capitalize on its popularity." Booked on Johnny Carson's *Tonight Show*, she forgot the words in the middle of performing "Somewhere In The Night." "The fact that I blew the words on the Carson show, instead of my career being over as I feared, gave me a great deal of impetus. The audience sympathized with me so much that Carson thought it would be a great thing to bring me back on. I was on his show three times in three weeks. That was my claim to fame for many years, forgetting the words."

Thornton was busy during the era, appearing regularly at clubs and having her own television series in England and Australia. She was signed to Columbia and recorded *Open Highway* in 1963, with the title cut being the theme song for *Route 66*. But lightning did not strike twice, the label did not know how to market her (treating her more as a Doris Day–type middle-of-the-road pop singer), and the record did not sell that well. A few years later she largely dropped out of music to raise a family, having three children. She performed now and then in Los Angeles and wrote songs, some of which were recorded by Johnny Griffin, Mel Tormé, Al Hirt, O.C. Smith and Vanessa Rubin. In 1986 she decided to move back to New York and gradually returned to performing regularly.

Sadly, just when her she was gaining recognition in 1998 for her comeback, she collapsed at the Bern Jazz Festival and was diagnosed with cancer. That same year she entered and won the Thelonious Monk Vocal Competition in Washington, D.C. Teri Thornton recorded a fine album for Verve (*I'll Be Easy To Find*) but, after a period of remission, the cancer came back and she died in 2000 at the age of 65.

Recommended CDs: *Devil May Care* (Original Jazz Classics 1017) is one of her finest jazz sets, while *Open Highway* (Koch 8589), despite the inclusion of some commercial string arrangements, is also worth getting, particularly because the CD reissue adds most of another unknown session. Her comeback disc, *I'll Be Easy To Find* (Verve 314 547 755), has a remake of "Somewhere In The Night" and a title cut that was the first song that Thornton ever learned.

LPs to Search For: Ironically, Teri Thornton's best-known recording, *Somewhere In The Night* (Dauntless 4306), is the only one not readily available on CD.

Lisa Thorson

b. September 6, 1957, Midland, TX

A versatile and adventurous jazz singer, Lisa Thorson teaches at Berklee College of Music and is an important vocalist in New England.

Among her earliest musical memories are singing and playing in a ukulele band in Hilo, Hawaii as a child. Along the way she also played guitar, piano and, for seven years, classical cello. Thorson performed in theater from the age of 14. An accident in 1979 resulted in her being permanently confined to a wheelchair, but she has never allowed herself to be confined artistically. "I continued to work in the theater, but sought other musical avenues for expression. I started singing more cabaret style music that turned to jazz with a lot of trial and error, study and exploration. Attending Jazz in July and studying with Sheila Jordan, Max Roach and Billy Taylor changed my life. I was hooked on the soul, integrity, adventure and democracy of the music."

Lisa Thorson spent five years working with the Adaptive Environments Center in putting together programs that make it easier for people with special needs to participate in the arts, and has been active in other organizations that ease the lives of people in wheelchairs. Thorson has recorded several CDs, she led a regular quartet throughout the 1990s comprised of saxophonist Cercie Miller, pianist Tim Ray, bassist David Clark and drummer George Schuller, and she has taught at Berklee since 1996. Thorson is currently involved in *Boswellmania: A Tribute To The Boswell Sisters* and JazzArtSigns, a multi-media production.

"I love the challenge of making jazz new every time with sincerity, not just with flash. I like for the audience to be surprised and laugh with us, cry if warranted, without any gimmicks."

Recommended CDs: Lisa Thorson does her own fresh take on standards during *From This Moment On* (Brownstone 942), *Resonance* (GM Recordings 3039) and *Out to Sea*

(Ellenrobin 593 479), the latter a set of duets with pianist Choo Yoon Seong.

Website: www.lisathorson.com

Martha Tilton

b. November 14, 1915, Corpus Christi, TX;
d. December 8, 2006, Los Angeles, CA

Famous for her association with Benny Goodman and for her hit recording of "And The Angels Sing," Martha Tilton was a cheerful singer who stuck to the melodies and words of the songs she chose to swing.

She was born in Texas, lived in Kansas for three years, and moved with her family to Los Angeles in 1922. Her mother played piano, her father sang at family gatherings, and her younger sister Liz Tilton had a singing career in the 1940s. Martha Tilton gained early experience singing with Sid Lippman's Band at the Coconut Grove and was with Hal Grayson's orchestra during 1933–36. She worked with Three Hits and a Miss in 1936–37, was with Jimmy Dorsey for a few months, and had an uncredited bit (as a singer naturally) in the movie *Topper*. She would appear in nine films in her career (all very small roles) including 1975's *The Queen Of The Stardust Ballroom*.

When Benny Goodman was in Hollywood filming *Hollywood Hotel*, his radio show, the *Camel Caravan*, broadcast from L.A. Tilton appeared on some of the singing commercials and was noticed by the clarinetist, who auditioned her; she was quickly hired. During 1937–39, Tilton was an asset to the band, being an excellent successor to Helen Ward and appearing on over 80 recordings starting with "Bob White" and "I Can't Give You Anything But Love" on September 6, 1937. Other recorded high points include "It's Wonderful," "Please Be Kind," "Feelin' High And Happy," a hit version of Duke Ellington's "I Let A Song Go Out Of My Heart," "This Can't Be Love" and "The Lady's In Love With You." Her version of "Loch Lomond" was popular, and she recorded "Bei Mir Bist Du Schoen" in an unusual version with the Benny Goodman Quartet and trumpeter Ziggy Elman. Tilton repeated the latter two songs at the famous Benny Goodman Carnegie Hall concert of January 12, 1938. But it was 1939's "And The Angels Sing," with lyrics by Johnny Mercer to a Ziggy Elman piece formerly called "Fralich In Swing," that was Tilton's biggest hit.

When Benny Goodman temporarily broke up his orchestra in May 1939, Martha Tilton went out on her own. She appeared on Paul Whiteman's radio shows, dubbed the singing voices for various nonsinging actresses in movies, recorded some radio transcriptions in 1941, recorded "Dreamin' Out Loud" with Artie Shaw, and had her own radio show, being nicknamed "Liltin' Martha Tilton." Although her solo career is today somewhat forgotten, she was the first artist to be signed to the new Capitol label in 1942 and had strong selling records in "I'll Walk Alone," "A Stranger In Town," "A Fine Romance," "Connecticut," and "I'll Remember April." After her period on Capitol ended in 1949, Tilton worked on radio shows and recorded for small labels. She played herself briefly in *The Benny Goodman Story* in 1955, singing "And The Angels Sing."

After the mid-1950s, Martha Tilton gradually became retired, occasionally having reunions with Goodman and appearing on nostalgic big band tours. Her last tour was in the mid-1990s. When she passed away in 2006 at the age of 91, she was the last survivor of the famous Carnegie Hall concert.

Recommended CDs: *And The Angel Sings* (Living Era 5669) is a fine retrospective of Martha Tilton's 1937–55 recordings, including nine numbers with Benny Goodman and a variety of rarities. *The Liltin' Miss Tilton: The Complete Capitol Sessions* (Collector's Choice 142) is a perfectly conceived two-CD set of Martha Tilton's Capitol recordings while *The Complete Standard Transcriptions* (Soundies 4119) is a single disc of her radio transcriptions of 1941–42.

Louise Tobin

b. November 11, 1918, Aubrey, TX

An excellent swing singer, Louise Tobin is one of the last important survivors of the swing era.

"I remember listening to Louis Armstrong on the radio when I was in fifth and sixth grade in school. My older brother played clarinet in high school and he knew how to tune in the jazz station." The tenth of 12 children, Tobin was a natural singer who never had a singing lesson. By the age of 12 she was appearing onstage, and at 14 she won a CBS talent contest. Offered a job with Art Hicks' band, she was able to accept it because her 18-year-old sister went along as a chaperone. In the trumpet section was a young Harry James. Tobin married James in 1935 when she was 16.

She sang with Bobby Hackett in 1939 and ironically became part of the Benny Goodman Orchestra (succeeding Martha Tilton) after James had already left to form his own group. With Goodman, she recorded nine numbers including popular recordings of "There'll Be Some Changes Made," "I Didn't Know What Time It Was," "Scatterbrain" and "What's New." After hearing the unknown Frank Sinatra on the radio, she urged her husband to hire him. She also worked briefly with Will Bradley (recording "'Deed I Do" and "Don't Let It Get You Down" in 1940) and Jack Jenney (with whom she recorded "Got No Time"). In 1943 her marriage to James ended when he became involved with Betty Grable.

After a long period outside of music, Louise Tobin returned to performing in 1961, and she made a strong impression appearing at the 1962 Newport Jazz Festival. In 1966 she started singing with clarinetist Peanuts Hucko, and they were married the following year, a marriage that lasted until his death in 2003. Louise Tobin has been largely retired since the mid-1990s.

Recommended CDs: Other than the titles mentioned above, Louise Tobin recorded relatively little in her career and never led her own album. She can be heard on a few Peanuts Hucko CDs, including *Tribute To Benny Goodman* (Timeless 513) and *Swing That Music* (Star Line 9005), from 1986 and 1990.

Mel Tormé

b. September 13, 1925, Chicago, IL;
d. June 5, 1999, Los Angeles, CA

One of the true giants not only of jazz, but of singing in general, Mel Tormé was one of the great vocalists of all time. His voice, which had a wide range, always seemed to be perfectly

in control even when he was scatting wildly. His breath control bordered on the wondrous (he could hold a note seemingly forever on slow ballads), and he was one of the very few singers to actually improve and get stronger while he was in his sixties. He loved swinging jazz and did his best to perform it throughout his long career.

Tormé's career began virtually at the beginning of his life. He sang a few songs on Monday nights with the Coon-Sanders Nighthawks in 1929 when he was just four. He was a child actor, published his first original song when he was 15, and during 1942–43 was with the Chico Marx Band (which was directed by Ben Pollack) as a singer, drummer and arranger. He co-wrote his most famous tune, "The Christmas Song," in 1944 when he was 19. Nat King Cole's 1946 recording made "The Christmas Song" into a standard. Tormé led the Mel-Tones, a vocal group that teamed up with Artie Shaw in 1945 for a catchy version of "What Is This Thing Called Love." Soon then he began his solo career, recording for Musicraft, and was nicknamed "The Velvet Fog," a title that he hated but somewhat described his voice at the time.

All of that took place before Tormé was 21. He served briefly in the military and did not have much luck in his acting career, but he was a world-class singer. While he did not have major pop hits, Tormé recorded steadily in settings ranging from orchestras to dates with the Page Cavanaugh Trio, sometimes also playing effective piano. While Tormé's recordings of 1947–54 are mostly somewhat obscure now, his series for the Bethlehem label during 1955–57, Tops and Verve, particularly his collaborations with the Marty Paich Dek-tette, contain many classic performances.

Because he made no secret of his love for the music of Count Basie, Duke Ellington and Ella Fitzgerald (a major influence on his scatting style) and his disdain for later pop music, Tormé recorded very little during 1965–73. Attempts at making him into a pop star (which increased after he had an unexpected best seller in 1962 with "Comin' Home Baby") were futile, for Tormé hated it, and the public was unconvinced. He could certainly still sing very well, as he showed on a set with Buddy Rich's big band in 1978 (*Together Again—For The First Time*), but it was not until he signed with Concord in 1983 that the real Mel Tormé was back. In fact, his series of recordings for Concord during the next 13 years rank with the most exciting of his career, and his many CDs with pianist George Shearing are generally classic and quite delightful. He ranked with Joe Williams as the most vital male jazz singer of the 1980s and seemed to enjoy every minute of his rejuvenated career.

A major stroke in 1996 permanently ended Mel Tormé's career, and he passed away three years later. But until then, he was at the peak of his powers.

Recommended CDs: There is no shortage of Mel Tormé recordings. *The Mel Tormé Collection* (Rhino 71589) is a solid four-CD overview of his career although it stops in 1985. *Spotlight On Great Gentlemen Of Song* (Capitol 89941) sums up his 1949–51 recordings well, while *Mel Tormé In Hollywood* (GRP/Decca 617) has an interesting live quartet performance from 1954 that has Tormé both singing and playing piano. The Tormé/Paich magic is heard throughout *Lulu's Back In Town* (Bethlehem 75732), *Sings Fred Astaire* (Bethlehem 30082) and *Swings Schubert Alley* (Verve 821 581). Also quite enjoyable from the mid-to-late 1950s are *It's A Blue World* (Bethlehem 30152) and *Swingin' On The Moon* (Verve 314 511 385). *Two Classic Albums From Mel Tormé* (Rhino 0074) has decent albums from 1962 and 1974, although neither is really classic, and Tormé's meeting with Buddy Rich, *Together Again For The First Time* (Mobile Fidelity 592), is rather scarce. But then there are the Concords. The seven-CD *The Complete Concord Recordings* (Concord 2144) has all six of the Tormé/Shearing albums plus a disc of unreleased material. Other essential Concord releases include *Mel Tormé/Rob McConnell And The Boss Brass* (Concord 4306), *Reunion* (Concord 4360) with Marty Paich, *In Concert Tokyo* (Concord 4382), which is also with Paich, *Nights At The Concord Pavilion* (Concord 4433), *Fujitsu-Concord Jazz Festival In Japan '90* (Concord 4481), *Sing, Sing, Sing* (Concord 4542), *A Tribute to Bing Crosby* (Concord 4614), *Velvet And Brass* (Concord 4667) and *An Evening With Mel Tormé* (Concord 4736). Get one of the Concord CDs and it will become obvious why they are all so highly recommended. The only misfire is a recording with Cleo Laine (*Nothing Without You*) since Laine, despite her beautiful voice, clearly could not keep up with Tormé.

Steve March Tormé

b. January 29, New York, NY

The son of Mel Tormé, Steve March Tormé had a few careers before in recent times concentrating more on singing jazz.

"I first heard jazz by osmosis through the womb. My dad (Mel) was talking music with Nat King Cole, my mom was present and I felt the vibe." His parents, Mel Tormé and former model Candy Tockstein, were divorced when he was 2½, and soon he had a stepfather in Hal March, host of NBC-TV's *The $64,000 Question*. After listening extensively to pop music of the era on the radio, at 12 Tormé knew that he wanted to be a performer. Within a year he had a rock group. After his stepfather died, he started a friendly relationship with his father, learning a great deal from Mel Tormé while still going his own musical way. "I attended Santa Monica College for one semester before signing a record deal and deciding that the road would be a better education."

Steve March Tormé has recorded pop music (starting in the late 1970s), sung on an album with Liza Minnelli, worked as an actor, appeared often on television, hosted music-based TV shows and performed with the vocal group Full Swing. He began to turn toward jazz in the mid-1990s, recording *Swingin' At The Blue Moon Bar And Grille*, which includes a duet with his father on "Straighten Up And Fly Right." Although he occasionally appears at tributes to Mel Tormé, he has a different sound and is developing quickly as a fine jazz improviser.

Recommended CDs: Of Steve March Tormé's three jazz CDs as a leader, *Swingin' At The Blue Moon Bar And Grille* (Frozen Rope 11970), *The Night I Fell For You* (Frozen Rope 30168) and *The Essence of Love* (Rhombus 5006), *The Essence Of Love* shows the most individuality and finds Tormé displaying quite a bit of potential.

Bobby Troup

(Robert W. Troup Jr.)
b. October 18, 1918, Harrisburg, PA;
d. February 7, 1999, Sherman Oaks, CA

Bobby Troup was certainly a multi-talented talent. He played piano well, was a decent actor, wrote quite a few memorable songs and was a solid jazz singer.

Early on, he learned piano, violin, trumpet, saxophone, bass horn and tuba before he settled on the piano. Troup graduated from the University of Pennsylvania's Wharton School of Business with a degree in economics, but his main interest was in music. In 1941 he had his first song hit, "Daddy," and was briefly on the writing staff of Tommy Dorsey. After serving in the Marines during 1942–46, he had a big success with "Route 66," which he wrote while driving West with his

wife of the time, who suggested he write a song about the highway they were on. Troup also had success with other songs including "The Three Bears" (recorded by the Page Cavanaugh Trio), "Lemon Twist," the instrumental "The Meaning Of The Blues," "Baby Baby All The Time" and "You're Looking At Me," the last two made famous by Nat King Cole.

Troup often performed in Los Angeles clubs in a piano-guitar-bass trio that was similar in style to Nat Cole's. He recorded several albums in the 1950s and, although his singing was overly mannered on some of the earlier sessions, he loosened up as time went on. In 1955 he produced Julie London's album *Julie Is Her Name*, which included her big hit "Cry Me A River." They married in 1960 and were always thought of as a team.

Troup was the host of the legendary *Stars Of Jazz* television series in 1958–59, and as an actor he appeared in *The Gene Krupa Story* (playing Tommy Dorsey), the film *MASH* and, along with Julie London, in the 1970s television series *Emergency* before gradually retiring.

Recommended CDs: *The Feeling Of Jazz* (Starline 9009) features Troup in top form in the mid-1950s, singing many of his songs and playing piano. Also quite worthy (all from the 1950s) are *Tell Me You're Home* (Audiophile 98), *Sings Johnny Mercer* (Westside 854) and *Bobby Troup And His Stars Of Jazz* (BMG 35027).

Big Joe Turner

b. May 18, 1911, Kansas City, MO;
d. November 24, 1985, Inglewood, CA

Big Joe Turner had such an accessible blues-oriented style that, no matter how many times the music world changed during his career, from Kansas City blues, boogie-woogie and swing to rhythm and blues, rock and roll and straight-ahead jazz, he always found his own niche without

having to change anything about his singing. So, although he might have sounded inflexible, making every song sound like the blues, he never went out of style.

Turner started off as a singing bartender in Kansas City

clubs, being one of the stars of the many legendary after-hours jam sessions of the 1930s. Boogie-woogie pianist Pete Johnson became his musical partner, and few could outswing them. In 1938, producer John Hammond brought them to New York and presented them with other discoveries at his Spirituals To Swing concert at Carnegie Hall along with pianists Albert Ammons and Meade Lux Lewis. They caused a bit of a sensation and launched a boogie-woogie fad that lasted for a few years. Turner and Johnson appeared at Café Society with the other boogie-woogie pianists and began to record, making "Roll 'Em Pete" and "Cherry Red" into blues standards. Turner was based in Los Angeles for a time, appearing in the Duke Ellington show *Jump for Joy* and recording on different dates with pianists Willie "The Lion" Smith, Sammy Price and Freddie Slack.

Big Joe Turner had no difficulty making the transition from swing to R&B, and in 1954 he helped launch rock and roll with his hit recording of "Shake, Rattle And Roll." He also had strong sellers in "Honey Hush," "Corrine, Corrina" and "Sweet Sixteen." In the 1960s, he remained popular in both jazz and blues settings, and in the 1970s for the Pablo label he recorded with everyone from Count Basie to Dizzy Gillespie, consistently putting on a good show. Big Joe Turner was a powerful musical force up until the time of his death in 1985, always making the blues sound fresh and vital.

Recommended CDs: *Big Bad And Blue: The Big Joe Turner Anthology* (Rhino 71550) is a three-CD set that has many of the high points from Turner's 1938–59 recordings. Other Turner CDs that trace his career in roughly chronological order (with asterisks next to the most important sets) include **I've Been To Kansas City* (MCA/Decca 42351), **Every Day In The Week* (GRP/Decca 621), **Have No Fear, Big Joe Turner Is Here* (Savoy 265), **Tell Me Pretty Baby* (Arhoolie 333), **Big Joe Turner's Greatest Hits* (Atlantic 81752), **Rhythm And Blues Years* (Atlantic 81663), **Boss Of The Blues* (Collectables 6327), **Big Joe Rides Again* (Atlantic 90668), *Singing The Blues* (Mobile Fidelity 780), *Texas Style* (Evidence 26013), *Flip Flop And Fly* (Original Jazz Classics 1053), *Life Ain't Easy* (Original Jazz Classics 809), **The Trumpet Kings Meet Joe Turner* (Original Jazz Classics 497), *Stormy Monday* (Pablo 2310-943), *Everyday I Have The Blues* (Original Jazz Classics 634), **Nobody In Mind* (Original Jazz Classics 729), **In The Evening* (Original Jazz Classics 852), *Things That I Used To Do* (Original Jazz Classics 862), *The Midnight Special* (Original Jazz Classics 1077), *Have No Fear, Joe Turner Is Here* (Original Jazz Classics 905), *Kansas City, Here I Come* (Original Jazz Classics 743) and *Patcha, Patcha, All Night Long* (Original Jazz Classics 887), the last one a set of duets with Jimmy Witherspoon.

Sarah Vaughan

b. March 27, 1924, Newark, NJ; d. April 3, 1990, Los Angeles, CA

Sarah Vaughan had one of the most wondrous voices of the 20th century. She had such control over her wide range that she could effortlessly assay difficult interval jumps, never seemed to miss a note, and could have been an opera singer if her life had been different. She could be out partying all night long, drinking, smoking and getting no sleep, and it would not matter; she still sounded superb the next day from the first note she sang.

Vaughan (who was known to her friends as "Sassy") sang in church as a child and had extensive piano lessons. In 1943 she won an Apollo Theater amateur contest and was hired by Earl Hines as singer and second pianist. She was in the perfect place at the perfect time. Hines' band had taken a major turn to the left as Billy Eckstine persuaded the pianist to hire trumpeter Dizzy Gillespie and Charlie Parker (playing tenor rather than alto, since that was the spot that was open). Although the 1943 Earl Hines Orchestra unfortunately never recorded due to the Musicians Union strike, it was the first bebop orchestra, and Sarah Vaughan constantly soaked up everything she heard. She became arguably the first singer to fully grasp the intricacies of bop, and it would be an influence on her choice of notes throughout her life.

In 1944 Billy Eckstine formed his own bebop orchestra, immediately hiring Vaughan (a lifelong friend), Parker (this time on alto) and Gillespie. Although that band did get to record after Parker had departed, Sassy was only on one so-so title ("I'll Wait And Pray"). However, on December 31, 1944, writer Leonard Feather produced her first record date as a leader. Gillespie was a sideman and his "Night In Tunisia" was sung by Vaughan as "Interlude." Already, she was a major voice. She also recorded "Lover Man" with Parker and Gillespie in 1945.

After spending a few months during 1945–46 with the John Kirby Sextet, Sarah Vaughan launched her solo career, recording steadily during 1946–48 for Musicraft. Among her more memorable recordings are "If You Could See Me Now," "Tenderly" (hers was its first vocal recording), "Everything I Have Is Yours" and "It's Magic." She signed with Columbia in 1949, and during her period with the label she alternated commercial dates with jazz sessions, including one in 1950 that had Miles Davis as her sideman. During much of the 1950s, Vaughan recorded middle-of-the-road pop dates for Mercury and more jazz-oriented outings for Mercury's Emarcy subsidiary, including an immortal set with trumpeter Clifford Brown.

Sarah Vaughan never had an off period, either in the quality of her singing or in her popularity. By the late 1940s she was recognized as one of the most brilliant singers on the scene, and it stayed that way throughout her career. Whether heard with her working trio, with a big band (such as Count Basie's) or with a string orchestra, she soared above her accompaniment and was the star. Musicians loved her, seeing her as one of their own due to her superb singing and the way she treated them as equals. Sometimes she was criticized by some listeners for altering melody lines a bit excessively or going over-the-top with her virtuosity (a criticism also leveled at pianist Art Tatum, trumpeter Arturo Sandoval and other remarkable players) but, when one has the "chops," it makes sense to use them now and then. And a Sarah Vaughan performance was always full of fun, wit and swing.

After recording for Roulette and again for Mercury, Vaughan was off records altogether during 1968–70, not because she was considered out of style but because she could not find the right situation. She came back with albums for Mainstream and some wonderful sets for Norman Granz's Pablo label. Sarah Vaughan did not slow down until the mid-1980s, making her final album in 1987 and succumbing to cancer in 1990 after a lifetime of smoking cigarettes.

When one hears Sarah Vaughan, it is not uncommon to exclaim to oneself, "What a voice!"

Marlene VerPlanck

Recommended CDs: *Young Sassy* (Proper Box 27) is an essential four-CD set that contains all of Sarah Vaughan's 1944–50 recordings, 94 songs in all, including her occasional guest appearances with others, all of her Musicraft recordings and her 1950 set with Miles Davis. She is in wonderful form during a 1947 Town Hall concert issued as *Sarah Vaughan/Lester Young: One Night Stand* (Blue Note 32139). *The Complete Sarah Vaughan On Mercury Vol. 1* (Mercury 826 320), *Vol. 2* (Mercury 826 327) and *Vol. 3* (Mercury 826 333) are two six-CD sets and one that is "just" five CDs (*Vol. 2*), which together contain all of her Mercury and Emarcy recordings of 1954–59. Listeners who wish to be more selective should instead get *Sarah Vaughan With Clifford Brown* (Emarcy 814641), *In The Land Of Hi-Fi* (Emarcy 826 454), *At Mister Kelly's* (Emarcy 832 761) and her collaboration with the 1958 Count Basie Orchestra, *No Count Sarah* (Emarcy 824 057). The limited-edition *Complete Roulette Sarah Vaughan Studio Recordings* (Mosaic 8-214) is an eight-CD set of Sassy's Roulette albums, dating from 1960–63. Some Roulette sets are available individually, most notably *After Hours* (Roulette 55468) and *Sarah Sings Soulfully* (Roulette 98445). *The Complete Sarah Vaughan On Mercury Vol. 4* (Mercury 830 714) features her during 1963–67. *Live In Japan* (Mobile Fidelity 2-844) is a two-CD set that has Vaughan in inspired form at a 1973 concert. Sassy's Pablo years are represented by *I Love Brazil* (Pablo 2312-101), *How Long Has This Been Going On* (Pablo 2310-821), *The Duke Ellington Songbook One* (Pablo 2312-111), *The Duke Ellington Songbook Two* (Pablo 2312-116), *Send In The Clowns* (Pablo 2312-130) and *Crazy And Mixed Up* (Pablo 2312-137). Taken as a whole, this is a good start.

Marlene VerPlanck
b. November 11, 1933, Newark, NJ

Marlene VerPlanck has excelled in three areas: as a studio singer, in cabaret and as a jazz vocalist. Her beautiful voice and her ability to perfectly hit any note she thinks of, along with her respect for lyrics, has made her an important singer for quite some time.

"As a child, I memorized the American Songbook and listened closely to Sinatra, Ella, Peggy Lee, Nat Cole, Dinah Washington and the other greats. I attended Fairleigh Dickinson for a year, majoring in journalism. I dropped out at 19 when I decided that I wanted one day to be in music. I turned to a girlfriend on a bus and said, 'I've decided what I'm going to do: sing.' She looked at me in disbelief and said, 'Oh, that's nice.' From that moment on I found ways to get jobs and never looked back. Fortunately, I met my husband Billy on my first big band, and he guided me into being a good musician. I studied privately with a teacher and I made it a point to study six hours a day, seven days a week, for three years. By then I could read the 'fly specks' off the page."

Marlene met arranger Billy VerPlanck during a stint with the Charlie Spivak Orchestra. They were also part of the last Dorsey Brothers Orchestra. She recorded an album for Savoy in the 1950s before becoming a very busy studio musician for 25 years. Probably her most famous studio gig was singing "Mm-mm good, mm-mm good, that's what Campbell's Soups are, mm-mm good."

After appearing on Alec Wilder's NPR series *American Popular Songs* in the 1970s, she emerged as a jazz vocalist, appearing on many records with arrangements provided by her husband. Marlene VerPlanck continues to record regularly for Audiophile and to tour the United States and Western Europe while being based in New York.

"The thing I love most is singing great songs, working with a great rhythm section, and watching people enjoy themselves. I love introducing folks to obscure material and having them walk away liking it. Some singers dwell on the music. I focus on the words and hope people will understand the story the way the lyricist intended it."

Recommended CDs: *I Think Of You With Every Breath I Take* (Audiophile 62) is a reissue of Marlene VerPlanck's debut recording. *A Breath Of Fresh Air* (Audiophile 109) is from 1968. Since the mid-1970s, she has recorded *You'd Better Love Me* (Audiophile 121), *Marlene VerPlanck Loves Johnny Mercer* (Audiophile 138), *A New York Singer* (Audiophile 160), *A Warmer Place* (Audiophile 169), *I Like To Sing* (Audiophile 186), *Sings Alec Wilder* (Audiophile 218), *Pure And Natural* (Audiophile 235), *A Quiet Storm* (Audiophile 256), *Live In London* (Audiophile 280), *Meets Saxomania In Paris* (Audiophile 288), *You Gotta Have Heart* (Varese Sarabande 5804), *What Are We Going To Do With All This Moonlight* (Audiophile 304), *Speaking Of Love* (Audiophile 320), *It's How You Play The Game* (Audiophile 325), *Now* (Audiophile 330) and *My Impetuous Heart* (Audiophile 334). Each set displays her love for the American popular song.

Website: www.marleneverplanck.com

Claudia Villela
b. August 27, 1961, Rio de Janeiro, Brazil

Claudia Villela, who has a five-octave range, can sing traditional Brazilian music and bossa novas, but is also a fearless improviser who is never shy to push herself and her music.

"My parents gave me a pianola when I turned one and I started writing music soon after. I have pictures of my first gig in my preschool when I was maybe four years old." She heard samba bands throughout her childhood along with her mother singing and her father playing harmonica. As a teenager, Villela performed in clubs in Rio, did studio work and wrote for movie soundtracks. She graduated from the Brazilian Conservatory of Music with a degree in music therapy in 1983. Despite having a great deal of regional success with her band, she moved to Northern California in 1984.

Although she did not speak English at the time, she sang with the Stanford University Chorus and the De Anza College Jazz Singers. Villela won a scholarship to study with Sheila Jordan at New York's Manhattan School of Music. In 1994 she made her debut recording, *Asa Verde*, which featured her original compositions. 1996's *Supernova* teamed her in a group with Michael Brecker and Airto Moreira, while the adventurous *Dream Tales* is a set of free improvisations with pianist Kenny Werner, a practically unprecedented set for a Brazilian singer.

Claudia Villela, who has appeared at many festivals, including quite frequently the Monterey Jazz Festival, has worked regularly with guitarist Ricardo Peixoto since 1994. "Bela Fleck once said of me, 'She is pure music.' I love that though, I'm a mutt."

Recommended CDs: Thus far Claudia Villela has recorded these four rewarding CDs:

Asa Verde (X Dot 25 29), *Supernova* (Jazzheads 9504), *Dream Tales* (Adventure Music 108) and *Inverse Universe* (Adventure Music 102).

Website: www.claudiavillela.com

Eddie "Cleanhead" Vinson

b. December 18, 1917, Houston, TX;
d. July 2, 1988, Los Angeles, CA

Eddie "Cleanhead" Vinson was a cheerful blues singer with a deep voice and an excellent alto-saxophonist who had a tone similar to Charlie Parker. He popularized and frequently performed such classic blues numbers as "Person To Person," "Just A Dream," "Kidney Stew Blues," "Cherry Red," "Somebody's Got To Go," "Old Maid Boogie" and "They Call Me Mr. Cleanhead."

Vinson did not start playing alto until he was 16, but within a year he was sitting next to tenors Illinois Jacquet and Arnett Cobb as a member of the Chester Boone Orchestra. He also worked with the bands of Milt Larkins (1936–40) and Floyd Ray (1940–41). Nicknamed "Cleanhead" after his hair was ruined by a lye-laced straightener, he became well known during his period with the Cootie Williams Orchestra (1942–45), making his recording debut and contributing vocals and occasional solos. After leaving Williams, Cleanhead had his own big band for a year (1946–47) and then led combos during the rest of his life. He wrote two songs that became standards ("Tune Up" and "Four"), though both were copyrighted by Miles Davis. He also had John Coltrane as his sideman in 1952–53.

Although he became a bit obscure during the 1960s, Vinson toured Europe with Jay McShann in 1969 and made a full comeback that lasted until his 1988 death. Eddie "Cleanhead" Vinson was part of both the jazz and blues worlds, welcomed by everyone from Count Basie and Johnny Otis to Oliver Nelson (with whom he stole at the show at the 1971 Montreux Jazz Festival) due to his joyous performances.

Recommended CDs: *1945–1947* (Classics 5017) and *1947–1949* (Classics 5042) have all of Vinson's earliest recordings as a leader. Other later albums that should be picked up are *Back In Town* (Rhino/Bethlehem 76679), *Cleanhead And Cannonball* (Milestone 9324), *Kidney Stew Is Fine* (Delmark 631), *Jamming The Blues* (Black Lion 760188), the out-of-print but exciting *Eddie "Cleanhead" Vinson And Roomful Of Blues* (Muse 5282) and *I Want A Little Girl* (Original Jazz Classics 868).

LPs to Search For: *The Clean Machine* (Muse 5116), *Live At Sandy's* (Muse 5208) and *Hold It Right There* (5243), all from 1978, feature Vinson in excellent form.

Roseanna Vitro

b. February 28, 1951, Hot Springs, AR

A well-rounded singer who can be quite bluesy, Roseanna Vitro sings from the heart and from quite a bit of experience.

"I started singing at four years old and in every possible situation. My family in Arkansas is comprised of gospel/country singers. I sang with my sister Debbie at age 12 on Nashville and Arkansas radio as the Vitro Sisters. I entered talent contests at school, alone with a tambourine, and sang Beatles

songs. In 1971 I moved to Houston. In my early singing days in Houston, while I was a rock and roll and blues singer, I was introduced to Ray Sullenger, a singer for the Paul Whiteman Orchestra. He sang like Mel Tormé and Nat Cole, and played piano, sax and clarinet. When he heard me sing, he said he would coach me for free if I was interested, because he felt I was a great natural singer and a jazz singer. I was 21 years old. That was the first time I'd ever heard of jazz."

While in Texas, Vitro worked with tenor-saxophonist Arnett Cobb, led a popular local group called Roseanna with Strings and Things, and had an opportunity to sit in with Oscar Peterson. After moving to New York, she worked with Kenny Werner, Fred Hersch, Lionel Hampton (going on the road with Hampton for a month in 1981) and Steve Allen. "I sent Benny Goodman a CD when he was looking for a singer. He called me and said he loved my singing and wanted to hire me, but I was already on the road in Texas and couldn't go. Rats!"

In addition to performing and recording regularly, Roseanna Vitro studied Indian classical vocal technique in Bombay in 1998, served as a Jazz Ambassador for the U.S. State Department, and has taught for nearly a decade as the Director of the Jazz Vocal Program at New Jersey City University in addition to conducting other clinics and master classes.

"I want to travel the world, represent jazz music and educate as many ears around the planet about jazz as possible. I am capable of loving and exampling many styles vocally. I am not an easy person to put in a pigeonhole box."

Recommended CDs: *The Time Of My Life* (Sea Breeze 3037) features songs by Steve Allen. *A Quiet Place* (Skyline 1001) and *Reaching For The Moon* (Chase Music Group 8030) are relatively obscure but worthy releases. *Softly* (Concord 4587), *Passion Dance* (Telarc 83385), her Ray Charles tribute *Catchin' Some Rays* (Telarc 83419), *Thoughts Of Bill Evans: Conviction* (Challenge 73208), *Tropical Postcards* (Challenge Records 73244) and *Live At The Kennedy Center* (Challenge 73252) all have their great moments.

LPs to Search For: *Listen Here* (Texas Rose 1001) is Roseanna Vitro's earliest album, recorded in Texas in 1982 and also featuring Arnett Cobb and pianist Kenny Barron.

Website: www.roseannavitro.com

Bea Wain

(Beatrice Weinsier)
b. April 30, 1917, New York, NY

Bea Wain is best known for her big selling records with Larry Clinton's swing orchestra, particularly "My Reverie," "Deep Purple," "Heart And Soul" and "Martha," but that was only a short period in her long life.

"I heard music from practically when I was born. I was singing professionally at four or five on the Children's Hour in New York. My mother took me on the subway, down to the radio station each Saturday. I got $2 a show. I always sang, and when I was in high school, I was on the air every day on my own commercial show."

Born Beatrice Weinsier, her name was changed (without her permission) to Bea Wain on a 1937 recording with Artie Shaw because of lack of space. In addition to her solo work, she led the vocal group Bea and the Bachelors, a vocal quartet that included Al Rinker, formerly of the Rhythm Boys. The group performed on Fred Waring's radio series as part of the larger vocal ensemble V-8, they were part of Kay Thompson's Rhythm Singers, and in 1937 sang on the *Kate Smith Show.* "I had a four- or eight-bar solo on one song and, when I got off the air, I had a telephone call from Larry Clinton who was starting an orchestra and wanted to hire me. He had heard about me and took a chance, having never seen me. We met at the studio during our first record date."

For 1½ years, Wain was Clinton's regular singer, appearing on many hit records. "Most people think I was there much longer. I was married in 1938 and the band spent a lot of time on the road. I quit in 1939 because I had gotten tired of the road and of being away from my husband." Although voted the most popular female band vocalist in a Billboard poll in 1939, ironically she would never be associated with a big band again.

At the height of her fame at the time, she recorded prolifically for RCA during 1939–41. "I chose many wonderful obscure songs but they didn't sell a lot. It might have been a mistake but they sound good today." Wain's basic and straightforward delivery swung lightly and was always quite accessible and sincere. It fit with her girl-next-door image.

She spent most of the war years appearing regularly on *Your Hit Parade,* often opposite Frank Sinatra. Wain had a lower profile by the late 1940s, spending her time raising a family, but she never stopped singing. She was happily married to radio announcer Andre Baruch for 53 years, and for a time they were a team as disc jockeys on WMCA, where they were billed as Mr. and Mrs. Music. The couple also did a regular four-hour talk show for five years in Palm Beach, Florida. Very involved with the Society of Singers (she was one of its founding members), Bea Wain still sings on rare occasions.

"The most important thing is, if you have talent, to be very persevering. Don't let anyone push you around. And when I'm asked what my favorite song is, I always say that it is whatever I'm singing at the moment."

Recommended CDs: *You Can Depend On Me, The Complete Recordings Vol. 1* (Baldwin Street Music 311) and *That's How I Love The Blues, Vol. 2* (Baldwin Street Music 315) contain the bulk of Bea Wain's RCA recordings, although a projected *Vol. 3* has not been released yet. Larry Clinton's *My Reverie* (Living Era 5629) has 14 of Wain's vocals during her period in his band.

Melissa Walker
b. July 4, 1964, Edmonton, Alberta, Canada

A favorite in the New York area, Melissa Walker has long been on the brink of greater stardom in the jazz world.

"My first introduction to a singer unlike any I had heard before was a recording of Lady Day. It was one of the most emotionally beautiful things I had ever heard. After that, I bought the music book called *Lady Sings The Blues* and I learned all of her songs. I was in high school at the time. Then I discovered Dinah Washington, Sarah Vaughan and Carmen McRae."

Melissa Walker attended Brown University in Providence, Rhode Island, during 1982–86 and was set to work toward becoming a lawyer, but she changed her mind. "The one defining moment for me came when I decided not to attend law school despite being accepted. That is when I decided to be a professional singer. I moved to Washington, D.C., where there were so many terrific musicians performing at a high level." She performed locally for a few years and in 1993 produced her first album, *Little Wishes.* After moving to New York and studying with pianist Norman Simmons, in 1997 Walker was signed to Enja. Her three recordings for the label gained her recognition in the jazz world.

Since then, Melissa Walker has appeared with the Lincoln Center Jazz Orchestra and worked with trumpeter Terrell Stafford (her husband), altoist Gary Bartz, pianists Hank Jones, Kenny Barron and Makoto Ozone, vibraphonist Stefon Harris and bassist Christian McBride among others. She was also part of Ray Brown's 75th Birthday Celebration Tour.

"There is nothing like making people's days disappear and transporting them to a new moment through this music. I owe a debt of gratitude to so many superb artists who over the years have taken the time to help nurture my talent and see me through this madness."

Recommended CDs: *May I Feel* (Enja 9335), *Moment Of Truth* (Enja 9365), which is highlighted by a four-song John Coltrane tribute, and *I Saw The Sky* (Enja 9409) each contain strong overviews of Melissa Walker's inventive singing.

Website: www.melissawalker.com

Cathi Walkup
b. February 13, 1948, St. Louis, MO

Cathi Walkup is an important bop-oriented singer influenced by Carmen McRae, and she is also an excellent lyricist.

She first heard music in church and through her mother, who sang around the house. She sang with her school choir in high school. "I did some musical theater for a while, but something was missing. As soon as I started listening to jazz I knew what it was: freedom. In the middle 1970s, I moved to San Francisco and became involved again in musical theater, a Brecht and Weill production in North Beach. I played endless pinball at The Café Babar in the Mission District, where the jukebox was stocked with jazz classics. My friends and I would listen for hours while playing pinball. I remember one time they threatened to toss us out because we kept playing Eddie Jefferson's version of 'Moody's Mood for Love' over and over and over."

She formed a duo with guitarist Don Kurtz, took lessons from Mark Levine and attended workshops run by Kurt Elling and Mark Murphy. Walkup has mentioned pianist Vince DiCiccio, Wesla Whitfield and Madeline Eastman as having helped her at important points in her career. She worked with a group called Mixed Bags in the early 1980s and led Cathi Walkup's Swing Thing a decade later. After issuing a cassette titled *Cathi Walkup Live At The Plush Room,* in 1996 she released her first CD, *Night Owl.* She has since worked primarily in San Francisco and the Pacific Northwest, developing as both a singer and as a lyricist.

"A few singers are starting to record and ask for copies of some of my songs, so of course I want to encourage that. I like for my music to uplift and inform, to be fun, but also make you think. At one concert, I was introduced as 'the thinking person's jazz singer.' I thought that was great."

Recommended CDs: Cathi Walkup's three solo CDs are *Night Owl*, *Living In A Daydream*, which has several of her lyrics, and *Playing Favorites*. In addition, she organized Quint-Essential, which features her and singers Shanna Carlson, Jenna Mammina, Jennifer Lee and Sharman Duran on three songs apiece, and *And A Songbook In A Pear Tree*, which has six different jazz vocalists. All of these CDs have been released on her Flying Weasel label.

Website: www.cwalkup.com

Sippie Wallace
(Beulah Thomas)
b. November 1, 1898, Houston, TX;
d. November 1, 1986, Detroit, MI

Sippie Wallace came from a very musical family. Her two pianist brothers were the boogie-woogie pioneer George W. Thomas, who as Clay Custer recorded "The Rocks" in 1923, and Hersal Thomas, while her niece was singer Hociel Thomas, who recorded 15 blues-oriented selections during 1925–26 (10 with Louis Armstrong as a sideman). Unlike the others, Wallace's career went far beyond the 1920s.

In her native Houston, as a child Beulah Thomas sang and played piano in church, and at night snuck away from her parents' home to see tent and vaudeville shows. Soon she was performing with Hersal Thomas and, as a teenager, she performed in vaudeville shows, moving to New Orleans in 1915. She married Matt Wallace in 1917; their marriage lasted until his death in 1936.

In 1923 Sippie Wallace (who was billed as "The Texas Nightingale"), her husband and her two brothers moved to Chicago. Soon she was discovered and signed by the Okeh label. Her first record date resulted in the popular "Up The Country Blues," and she recorded 43 selections for Okeh through 1927 including her trademark song "I'm A Mighty Tight Woman." Among her sidemen were pianist Clarence Williams, Louis Armstrong, Sidney Bechet, King Oliver and Hersal Thomas. A blues-oriented singer like Ida Cox rather than a more flexible stylist such as Ethel Waters, Wallace recorded less often after the blues craze subsided, just one record date in 1927 and two songs (including a remake of "I'm A Mighty Tight Woman") in 1929.

Hersal Thomas' sudden death in 1926 from food poisoning was a major blow for Wallace, though she continued performing for a time. But after the Depression hit, she moved to Detroit where she stopped performing except in church. Wallace briefly emerged to record two numbers in Chicago with pianist Albert Ammons on one day in 1945 ("Bedroom Blues" and "Buzz Me"), six obscure titles in Detroit in 1958 and a guest appearance on a Victoria Spivey record (a new version of "I'm A Mighty Tight Woman") in 1962, but otherwise stayed in obscurity until 1966.

That year, her old friend Victoria Spivey convinced her to return to music and sing at festivals. Wallace recorded a set of duets with Spivey and also a Storyville album, *Sippie Wallace Sings The Blues*, which finds the 67-year-old performer still in prime form, sounding very expressive on a blues set in which she is accompanied by either Roosevelt Sykes or Little Brother Montgomery on piano. A stroke in 1970 confined her to a wheelchair for a time but, coaxed and championed by Bonnie Raitt, she was back to making occasional appearances by the mid-1970s, recording an album for Atlantic (*Sippie*) in 1982. Her voice was weak but her spirit was still strong.

Sippie Wallace toured with German pianist Axel Zwingenberger during 1983–84 and appeared at her last concert seven months before her death on her 88th birthday in 1986. By then, she was the last of the surviving classic blues singers.

Recommended CDs: *Vol. 1* (Document 5399) and *Vol. 2* (Document 5400) have all of Sippie Wallace's recordings up to 1958.

LPs to Search For: *Sippie Wallace Sings The Blues* (Storyville 4017) is the best of the blues singer's later recordings.

Fats Waller
(Thomas Waller)
b. May 21, 1904, New York, NY;
d. December 15, 1943, Kansas City, MO

Fats Waller was a true phenomenon. He was one of jazz's greatest stride pianists, following in the footsteps and surpassing his inspiration James P. Johnson. He was jazz's first organist, recording unaccompanied solos on the mighty pipe organ as early as 1926. He was a major songwriter, composing such songs as "Honeysuckle Rose," "Ain't Misbehavin'," "Keeping Out Of Mischief Now," "Jitterbug Waltz" and the first anti-racism protest song "Black And Blue" plus dozens of others. And he was a lovable comic personality. In addition, Waller was an excellent jazz singer who often covered up that skill under a riotous wit. Somehow, Waller accomplished all of this while living a nonstop party full of an excess of liquor, women, food and music. Few could keep up with him, either as a partier or as a multifaceted musician. In the 1930s he ranked at the top with Louis Armstrong, Duke Ellington, Cab Calloway and Bill "Bojangles" Robinson as the most famous and beloved black entertainer.

Oddly enough, Waller did not emerge as a vocalist until the early 1930s, when he was already established as a pianist, organist and songwriter. He began playing piano when he was six but ran into problems with his father, a strict Baptist preacher, who only approved of church music. When Waller's mother died when he was 14, he left home and dropped out of school. Through his roommate, pianist Russell Brooks, he met his idol James P. Johnson, who gave him informal lessons and encouragement. Soon Waller was joining Johnson and Willie "The Lion" Smith in playing and battling the competition at rent parties, and at 15 he was the organist at the Lincoln Theater, stomping out tunes while playing for silent movies.

For Waller, the 1920s were a very busy and productive time. He had begun composing in 1918 when he wrote "Squeeze Me" and by the late '20s he was collaborating with lyricist Andy Razaf for the shows *Keep Shufflin'*, *Load Of Coal* and *Hot Chocolates*. He began to record in 1922 when he cut his first piano solos. During the decade Waller was heard as an unaccompanied piano soloist (including on his "Handful Of Keys" and "Ain't Misbehavin'"), as an organist, at the head of hot combos, as an accompanist behind many classic blues singers, on 20 piano rolls, and guesting with the Fletcher Henderson Orchestra, Johnny Dunn, the Louisiana Sugar Babes and McKinney's Cotton Pickers. One wonders how Waller found time for any of this considering his lifestyle.

The one aspect of Waller's talents that was neglected in the 1920s was his singing. Other than a brief vocal on "Red Hot Dan," his voice was not heard on records until 1931. However, that year Waller's witty personality began to emerge on solo piano-vocal versions of "I'm Crazy 'Bout My Baby" and "Draggin' My Heart Around," and on dates with Ted Lewis and Jack Teagarden. Waller worked with the bands of Otto Hardwick and Elmer Snowden during 1931–32 and visited France and England in 1932, but it was upon his return, when he began appearing regularly on the radio show *Fats Waller's Rhythm Club*, that audiences became aware of his wit and comic abilities. Executives from the Victor label were impressed, and in 1934 they signed him up to record an extensive series of recordings with his "Rhythm," a two-horn sextet.

Early on it was discovered that Waller had the ability to turn the worst songs into magic, or at least hilarity, by satirizing, tearing apart or destroying them. Sometimes he would take the most ridiculous lyrics and sing them with sarcasm, while at other times when he found a song that he liked, such as "I'm Gonna Sit Right Down And Write Myself A Letter," he could take a wistful and touching vocal. Sprinkled in every performance was an example of his hot stride piano along with solos from his sidemen, which often included trumpeter Herman Autrey and Gene Sedric on tenor and clarinet.

Not counting piano solo performances, occasional numbers with a big band and alternate takes, Waller recorded 282 selections with his Rhythm for Victor during 1934–42, the great majority of which included his vocals and ad-lib asides. Music publishers were delighted with the results, for many of their turkey tunes would otherwise probably never have been recorded, and fans were entertained by the outrageous nature of some of the recordings.

Waller recorded some gems along the way, including "A Porter's Love Song To a Chambermaid," "How Can You Face Me," "Believe It Beloved," "You've Been Taking Lessons In Love," a very silly version of "Somebody Stole My Gal," "Got A Brand New Suit," "All My Life," "It's A Sin To Tell A Lie," and a pair of hits in "The Joint Is Jumping" and "Your Feet's Too Big." He also did what he could with such duds as "Us On A Bus," "My Window Faces The South," "Why Hawaiians Sing Aloha," "I Love To Whistle," "Little Curly Hair In A High Chair," "You're A Square From Delaware," "Eep, Ipe, Wanna Piece Of Pie," "My Mommie Sent Me To The Store," "I'm Gonna Salt Away Some Sugar" and "Abercrombie Had A Zombie."

Although Waller sometimes became frustrated by the material he was given to record and had occasional dreams of performing more "serious" music, he always sounded as if he were having a great time. His fame grew when he stole the show during his appearances in a pair of otherwise forgettable 1935 movies (*Hooray For Love* and *King Of Burlesque*), his radio programs did well, he visited Europe twice during 1938–39, and his records were solid sellers.

One wonders how long his popularity would have lasted or what he would have done with bebop, R&B and television had he lived longer. Waller kept up his busy pace in 1942–43. He broke up his group Rhythm, continued as a solo act, wrote the score for the musical *Early To Bed*, and made a particularly memorable appearance in the big-budget black film *Stormy Weather*.

Unfortunately his 25 years of hard living and parties caught up with him. On December 15, 1943, while on a train traveling to New York from Hollywood, Fats Waller caught pneumonia and passed away when he was at the height of his fame. He had packed several lifetimes of living, music and fun into his 39 years and still remains a symbol of jazz at its most infectious, swinging and joyous.

Recommended CDs: Virtually every Fats Waller release is full of joy. Concentrating on his post-1930 material when his singing was as important as his piano playing, one can obtain all of his Rhythm studio performances by acquiring *The Early Years Part 1* (Bluebird 66618), *Part 2* (Bluebird 66640) and *Part 3* (Bluebird 66747), *The Middle Years Part 1* (Bluebird 66083), *Part 2* (Bluebird 66552) and *The Last Years* (Bluebird 9883). The three *Early Years* sets are two-CDs apiece, while *The Middle Years* and *The Last Years* are each three-CD sets, so there are 15 CDs in all. *The Complete Associated Transcription Session 1935–1939* (Jazz Unlimited 203 2076), a twofer, features Waller as a solo pianist-vocalist in 1935 and leading his Rhythm four years later on radio transcriptions that give one an idea how he sounded on broadcasts, supplying his own humorous verbal introductions.

J.D. Walter
(John Daniel Walter)
b. July 2, 1967, Abington, PA

Although not yet a household name in jazz, J.D. Walter has greatly impressed virtually everyone who has heard him. He has been compared to Betty Carter and Kurt Elling, but in reality he is an adventurous jazz improviser with his own style and approach.

Growing up in a suburb of Philadelphia, Walter sang with St. Luke's Men and Boys Choir for six years as a youth, spending a year at the American Boychoir School. He attended the University of North Texas during 1985–90 and appeared as a soloist on some of the university's jazz band's recordings. In 1991 Walter studied with Deborah Brown in Amsterdam.

Since then, he has worked with such notables as saxophonists Dave Liebman and Tim Warfield, trumpeters Nicholas Payton and Randy Brecker, pianists Jean-Michel Pilc and Orrin Evans, drummer Art Hoenig and singers Bob Dorough and Mark Murphy.

"A turning point for me was showcasing for many major labels and being turned down, which gave me the opportunity to really find my own direction uninhibited by industry motivations."

Going his own way and developing his own highly individual way of scatting and interpreting lyrics, J.D. Walter has thus far recorded four CDs as a leader or co-leader, become an increasingly influential educator, worked with pianist Orrin Evans' band, and performed frequently in Europe and the Middle East, touring Russia 20 times.

Recommended CDs: *Sirens In The C-House* (Ear 5713), *Clear Day* (Doubletime 187), which is co-led by saxophonist Dave Liebman, *Dedicated to You* with the Steve Rudolph Trio (PACT 1010) and *Two Bass, A Face And A Little Skin* (Dreambox Media 739673107524) all contain examples of J.D. Walter's adventurous and inventive singing.

Website: www.jdwalter.com

Helen Ward

b. September 19, 1916, New York, NY;
d. April 21, 1998, Arlington, VA

In 1936, 19-year-old Helen Ward was at the top of the music world, being the star singer with the Benny Goodman Orchestra and obviously on her way to becoming a household name. Her musical future looked endless, yet she never exceeded or even equaled that height again.

Ward had piano lessons as a youth and as a young teenager began to sing in public. At 16 her accompanist on piano was the future songwriter Burton Lane. After graduating from high school, Ward started singing professionally, including with the sweet bands of Nye Mayhew, Eddy Duchin, Freddie Martin, David Rubinoff and Will Osborne. She also worked on the radio and by late 1933 was a staff singer at NBC. Ward made her first recordings in 1934 with several fairly anonymous studio orchestras.

In the fall of 1934, *Let's Dance* became a regular series on NBC, featuring three bands representing Hot (Benny Goodman), Sweet (Kel Murray) and Latin (Xavier Cugat) music. Since the new Goodman orchestra did not have a singer and Ward was working for NBC, she had an audition and easily passed. Her ability to swing at any tempo, her very accessible voice, and her girl-next-door image were perfect for the band.

Both in the radio series and Goodman's recordings for Columbia and (starting in April 1935) Victor, Helen Ward was one of the main reasons that the band ultimately succeeded, ranking second in importance only to the playing of the clarinetist and the swinging arrangements. Very few band singers of 1935–36 were on Ward's level, particularly at putting warmth and swing into one chorus of a medium-tempo number. Among her best recordings with Goodman are "The Dixieland Band," "You're A Heavenly Thing," "The Devil And The Deep Blue Sea," "It's Been So Long," "All My Life" (with the Benny Goodman Trio), "These Foolish Things," "You Turned The Tables On Me," and her giant hit "Goody-Goody."

But in December 1936 when she was just 20, Ward decided to retire from singing to marry Albert Marx, who in the future would become a major record producer. While other singers were becoming famous due to their associations with major swing bands, Ward was now sitting on the sidelines. On rare occasions she was persuaded to record guest vocals with friends including dates with Teddy Wilson ("There's A Lull In My Life"), Harry James, Bob Crosby, the new Gene Krupa band ("Feelin' High And Happy"), the Joe Sullivan septet and violinist Matty Malneck.

In 1943 Ward and Albert Marx were divorced, and she went back to singing full-time. Unfortunately her timing was bad, for a recording strike kept her off records other than some V-discs with Red Norvo. In fact, few realize that she sang with Harry James as Helen Forrest's replacement during 1943—44, because it was completely undocumented. Ward returned to obscurity for the remainder of the 1940s. In the early 1950s, after the music from Benny Goodman's 1938 Carnegie Hall concert was discovered, released and became a best-seller, Benny Goodman decided that it was time to bring back the swing era by forming a new big band. He hired Ward as his singer; she was still only 37. She recorded five numbers with Goodman's orchestra, including "What A Little Moonlight Can Do" and "I'll Never Say 'Never Again' Again." But a joint tour by the Goodman Orchestra with the Louis Armstrong All-Stars flopped after Goodman, disturbed that Armstrong was the hit of the show, dropped out of his own band, citing health problems. The orchestra, led for the remainder of its commitments by Gene Krupa, soon broke up.

Helen Ward was never again in the spotlight. She made appearances with the Larry Clinton Orchestra and cornetist Wild Bill Davison's Dixieland band in the mid-1950s, recorded an album with the Percy Faith Orchestra that went nowhere commercially, and in 1979 cut an album for her own Lyricon label. She also started writing an autobiography, but it was never completed. Helen Ward passed away in 1998 at the age of 81, 62 years after she had thrown away her chance for fame.

Recommended CDs: *The Complete Helen Ward On Columbia* (Collectors Classics 155) is a two-CD set that includes her earliest Goodman recordings (though not her dates with the King of Swing for Victor), a few freelance sessions and her album with Percy Faith. *The Queen Of Big Band Swing* (ASV/ Living Era 5289) is a fine sampler of her period with Goodman, including her main hits for Victor.

Fran Warren
(Francis Wolfe)
b. March 4, 1926, Bronx, New York

Although much of her later work falls outside of jazz, Fran Warren was a fine band singer during the waning years of the swing era, and her record of "A Sunday Kind Of Love" with Claude Thornhill made that song into a standard.

She started her career working on the chorus line at the Roxy Theater in New York. Francis Wolfe always wanted to sing with big bands, and she just barely caught the end of the swing era. In 1944, at the age of 18, she joined the Art Mooney Orchestra, a short-lived band patterned after Glenn Miller's. She had short stints with the orchestras of Randy Brooks and Billy Eckstine. Eckstine renamed her Fran Warren. She spent 18 months touring with Charlie Barnet. But her greatest fame came while with Claude Thornhill during 1947–48. Her first record with Thornhill was "A Sunday Kind Of Love" and she also recorded other enjoyable selections including "I Get The Blues When It Rains," "Love For Love," "Early Autumn" and "For Heaven's Sake."

Warren's solo career, which started in 1948, included some popular vocal duets with Tony Martin ("I Said My Pajamas And Put On My Prayers" was a big hit) and solo numbers

Dinah Washington

for RCA Victor. She also recorded a few albums in the 1950s and is proud of her version of "Something's Coming." Warren performed in nightclubs, acted in such musical comedies as *The Pajama Game*, *South Pacific* and *Mame*, toured with Harry James for a time in the 1960s and still performs on an infrequent basis.

One often gained the impression that Fran Warren could have cut loose and improvised much more if she had really wanted to. But, at a minimum, her voice always sounded quite warm and expressive on ballads, and she swung on medium-tempo pieces.

Recommended CDs: *The Complete Fran Warren With Claude Thornhill Orchestra* (Collector's Choice 154) includes all 14 of her recordings with Thornhill. *Let's Fall In Love* (Dutton Vocalion 3027) collects together many of her early singles while *Hey There! It's Fran Warren* (Simitar 5631) has the singer joined in 1957 by Marty Paich arrangements. On "Come Rain Or Come Shine" from the latter album, she sounds like Sarah Vaughan in spots but the song ends two choruses too soon. As always, she should have stretched out more.

Dinah Washington
(Ruth Jones)
b. August 29, 1924, Tuscaloosa, AL;
d. December 14, 1963, Detroit, MI

Dinah Washington was an exciting performer, one known as the "Queen of the Blues" although she was proudest of the fact that she could sing anything. Her recordings of 1943–63, particularly those of her first 15 years, are a joy to discover, and she became a major influence on the black female singers who followed her.

Born Ruth Jones, she moved with her family to Chicago when she was three or four. She sang with her church choir, and some of the fervor of the spirituals would always form a part of her style. When she was 15, she was singing both gospel with a professional choir and lowdown blues in nightclubs. She was named "Dinah Washington" by the manager of the Garrick Stage Bar, and in 1943 she was discovered and hired by Lionel Hampton. During her three years with Hampton, Washington recorded surprisingly little with the vibraphonist, but her first session as a leader in late 1943 included her hit version of Leonard Feather's "Evil Gal Blues."

After starting her solo career in 1946, Washington had hit after hit. "Baby Get Lost," "I Wanna Be Loved," "Wheel Of Fortune," "New Blowtop Blues," "T.V. Is The Thing This Year" and "Teach Me Tonight" are only a few of the numbers that made it onto the R&B charts. Like Sarah Vaughan, she recorded in commercial settings for Mercury and jazz dates for its Emarcy subsidiary. Whether it was caustic ballads with string orchestras, belting out a blues with a shouting big band, or jamming in combos (including one remarkable jam session date with trumpeters Clifford Brown, Maynard Ferguson and Clark Terry), Dinah Washington excelled.

Her 1959 recording of "What A Difference A Day Makes" was a major pop hit and changed Washington's career to an extent. Most of her recordings for the next few years were in a similar fashion, being slightly soulful, taken at slow tempos and with string arrangements that would have been better suited for a country singer. "Unforgettable" and "This Bitter Earth" were strong sellers. Her commentary kept nearly all of the performances interesting despite the trappings, her teaming with singer Brooks Benton (particularly on "Baby, You Got What It Takes") was popular, and in concert she was still at the top of her field.

An accidental overdose of diet pills mixed with alcohol ended her life when she was just 39. But no one could accuse Dinah Washington (who had seven husbands) of not living life to the fullest. It would be difficult to imagine what such singers as Nancy Wilson, Aretha Franklin, Diana Ross and Diane Schuur would have sounded like if the Queen had not been on the scene first.

Recommended CDs: Other than Dinah Washington's first four recordings, made for the Keynote label and mostly reissued on samplers, all of her records as a leader are easily available at the moment. *Mellow Mama* (Delmark 451) has Washington's dozen recordings for the Apollo label in 1945. *The Complete Dinah Washington On Mercury Vol. 1: 1946–1949* (Mercury 832 444), *Vol. 2: 1950–1952* (Mercury 832448), *Vol. 3: 1952–1954* (Mercury 832 675), *Vol. 4: 1954–1956* (Mercury 832 683) and *Vol. 5: 1956–1958* (Mercury 832 952) are each three-CD sets that contain all of Washington's studio recordings during a 13-year period, the bulk of her career. Listeners who wish to be more selective should get *The Best In Blues* (Verve 314 537 811) and the encounter with the three legendary trumpeters plus Max Roach on *Dinah Jams* (Emarcy 814 639). Her later commercial years are not without their rewards. *The Complete Dinah Washington On Mercury Vol. 6: 1958–1960* (Mercury 832 956), *Vol. 7: 1961* (Mercury 832 960) and the Mosaic limited-edition five-CD box *Complete Roulette Recordings* (Mosaic 5-227) completely cover the era. In addition, *Live At Birdland 1962* (Baldwin Street Music 301) is an excellent example of Dinah Washington in performance late in life.

Ethel Waters
b. October 31, 1896, Chester, PA;
d. September 1, 1977, Los Angeles, CA

Of all of the female classic blues singers of the 1920s, Ethel Waters was the most successful at evolving into a popular music singer during the '30s. From the start of her career, she showed that she was continually aware of the latest developments in jazz and pop music. Waters was one of the first African Americans to be accompanied regularly by white orchestras and to get decent roles in motion pictures and plays without having to move to Europe.

Ethel Waters, who as a child sang in church choirs, had a

very difficult childhood, working as a maid while just a young teenager. Her singing abilities proved to be her escape route from poverty and hopelessness. She overcame poverty by winning local talent contests, performing early on in Philadelphia and Baltimore, and moving to New York in 1917. Waters was nicknamed "Sweet Mama Stringbean" due to her being tall and thin, an ironic title when one considers that she became heavy during the 1930s.

She differed from most of the other blues-oriented black singers from her era in her flexibility and her very clear enunciation. After Mamie Smith's 1920 recording of "Crazy Blues," Waters recorded two numbers for the tiny Cardinal label in March 1921. She was heard singing and dancing at Harlem's Bucket of Blood club by pianist Fletcher Henderson, who arranged for her to be signed by Black Swan, the first black-owned record label. Her earliest record for the company, "Down Home Blues" (backed by "Oh Daddy"), sold over 100,000 copies and uplifted Black Swan temporarily from its debt. She was Black Swan's top artist for two years until the company was sold to Paramount and during that time, in addition to blues, she also recorded some popular songs including "There'll Be Some Changes Made."

Waters appeared in shows (including *Blackbird* and the *Black Bottom Revue*) and theaters, and by 1925 when she was signed by Columbia, she was considered by many to be second among female blues/jazz singers only to Bessie Smith. On her recording of "Maybe Not At All," Waters pays tribute to both Bessie and Clara Smith by effectively imitating their singing styles and voices.

The 1925–28 period found Waters recording some of her finest performances including "Sweet Georgia Brown," "Go Back Where You Stayed Last Night," "I've Found A New Baby," "Sugar," "Dinah" (the first standard that she introduced) and "Shake That Thing." Her one session with pianist James P. Johnson resulted in four memorable performances including "Guess Who's In Town" and "Do What You Did Last Night."

1929 was a turning point in Ethel Waters' career. She appeared in her first movie, *On With The Show*, in which she introduced "Am I Blue" and "Birmingham Bertha." The film was very unusual for the period (or even 20 years later), because she was treated with the respect due an artist by the white movie characters. Her recordings shifted toward commercial music, with her backing often being by white studio orchestras, although Waters always remained a jazz singer. She introduced Irving Berlin's "Waiting At The End Of The Road" (1929), Eubie Blake's "You're Lucky To Me" (1930), "Stormy Weather" (1933) and the heart-wrenching "Supper Time." While the other classic blues singers mostly faded from the scene, Waters' star continued to rise, and she was one of the most famous black entertainers of the 1930s, influencing Mildred Bailey and Lee Wiley among others.

Waters was the first black woman featured in an all-white Broadway show (*As Thousands Cheer*), starred on a national radio show, and also appeared on Broadway in *Heat Wave* and the 1935 hit *At Home Abroad*. During 1938–39 she toured with a swing octet that was headed by her husband trumpeter Eddie Mallory. In 1939 she starred in the nonmusical drama *Mamba's Daughters*, becoming known as an actress who occasionally sang rather than the other way around. Although unable to completely avoid racial stereotypes, Waters was always dignified in films and shows, even when playing a maid. She starred in the play *Cabin In The Sky* and introduced "Taking A Chance On Love," "Happiness Is A Thing Called Joe" and "Cabin In The Sky." In 1943 she starred in the movie

version and, although Lena Horn often gained the attention, Waters sang all of the hit songs.

After 1940, Ethel Waters rarely recorded, other than 19 numbers during 1946–47 and a retrospective album in the late 1950s. She turned her focus to acting, having small parts in a number of films and more substantial roles in *Pinky* and *The Member Of The Wedding*. In the 1950s Waters was a regular on television in the series *Beulah*. After 1957, she changed course again, dedicating herself to religion after 40 years in show business. From then on her performances (which include two religious albums in 1963) were mostly restricted to church and Billy Graham's crusades.

Recommended CDs: All of Ethel Waters' recordings through 1947 are available on *1921–1923* (Classics 796), *1923–1925* (Classics 775), *1925–1926* (Classics 672), *1926–1929* (Classics 688), *1929–1931* (Classics 721), *1931–1934* (Classics 735), *1935–1940* (Classics 755) and *1946–1947* (Classics 1249). Of those eight CDs, the most essential are *1925–1926*, *1926–1929* and *1929–1931*.

LPs to Search For: *Performing In Person Highlights From Her Illustrious Career* (Monmouth-Evergreen 6812) from 1957 features Ethel Waters (accompanied by her longtime pianist Reggie Beane) for the last time performing many of the hits from her career, still sounding quite viable at the age of 60.

Patty Waters
(Patricia Sue Stonebraker)
b. March 11, 1946, Vicksburg, MS

Patty Waters was an important part of the mid-1960s avant-garde jazz movement, an idiom that, prior to her arrival on the scene, seemed to have no room for vocalists. She made her mark on jazz history, survived the turmoil of the era, and decades later returned as a soft-voiced ballad singer.

She first heard jazz as a child on her family's large radio while sitting at their dairy farm in Iowa. Waters sang at fairs and town functions, had piano lessons from the time she was nine, and in high school won awards in music and drama. She also played organ and tympani. "My parents couldn't afford college for me, so they pushed me to become a band singer. In their eyes, band singers were to be admired. My parents were from the war era and associated the music with romance. I believe my parents had hoped my life could be happy like a Hollywood musical, but I'd say my life has been more like a film noir."

Waters started performing jazz right after high school, working in the Midwest and Pacific Northwest, living in Los Angeles for a little while. In 1964 she moved to New York and, after saxophonist Albert Ayler heard her increasingly adventurous singing at a nightclub, he recommended her to the ESP label. *Patty Waters Sings* starts out with quiet ballads in which her voice is barely louder than a whisper. But on the 13-minute "Black Is The Color Of My True Love's Hair,' she made history with an intense and often shocking improvisation based on the song's words and utilizing screams and shrieks, in a way breaking the sound barrier with her voice. It is still arguably the most significant avant-garde vocal of the 1960s.

Waters also recorded *College Tour* a few months later, an intriguing set that does not quite reach the heights of "Black Is The Color." Unfortunately, other than performing Ornette Coleman's "Lonely Woman" on a Marzette Watts album from 1968, she would be off records for 30 years, dropping out of the scene and moving to Hawaii and later Northern California to raise her son. Patty Waters was a lost legend until she returned to jazz in the late 1990s, performing at the 1999 Monterey Jazz Festival and recording again, although now as a Billie Holiday–inspired ballad singer.

Recommended CDs: *Patty Waters Sings* (ESP 1025) is her CD to get, while *College Tour* (ESP 1055) serves as a strong-follow up. *You Thrill Me: A Musical Odyssey 1962–79* (Water 137) has odds and ends, including commercials and private recordings that add to the singer's small but important discography. *Love Songs* (Jazz Focus 512) is her 1996 comeback album, a set of standards performed with the very sympathetic support of pianist Jessica Williams. *Happiness Is A Thing Called Joe* (DBK Works 523) from 2002 is a brittle and very real tribute to Billie Holiday. Patty Waters sounds both fragile and determined at the same time.

Website: www.pattywaters.com

Leo Watson

b. February 27, 1898, Kansas City, MO;
d. May 2, 1950, Los Angeles, CA

Leo Watson was an eccentric, both as a singer and as a person. An occasional drummer, there was one night when he began a drum solo and refused to stop until the police were called and dragged him away.

As a vocalist, Watson was an innovator in the 1930s, making up words as he went along and becoming a future influence on some of the scat singers of the 1950s, particularly Dave Lambert. Very little is known about his early days. In 1929 he was part of a vocal group that toured with the Whitman Sisters. After the tour, the group became independent and was named the Spirits of Rhythm. The band featured guitarist Teddy Bunn with three of its singers playing a small ukulele called a tiple. Watson worked with the group off and on until 1941.

Otherwise, his associations with bands tended to be brief. Watson recorded with the Washboard Rhythm Kings in 1932 (playing bass and sharing the vocals on two songs), was with an early version of the John Kirby Sextet in 1937, and spent a few months with the big bands of Artie Shaw (recording "Fee Fi Fo Fum," "It's a Strange New Rhythm In My Heart," "Shoot The Likker To Me, John Boy," "Free Wheeling" and "Whistle While You Work" in 1937) and Gene Krupa (recording "Nagasaki," "Jeepers Creepers," "Tutti Frutti" and "Do You Wanna Jump, Children" in 1938). In 1939 Watson led a four-song session of his own that is highlighted by an inventive reworking of "Ja Da." He also appeared on a date led by critic Leonard Feather, taking two vocals.

In the early 1940s Watson moved to Los Angeles, where he became part of the crazy jive vocal movement of 1944–46 that was led by Slim Gaillard (with whom he played drums) and Harry "The Hipster" Gibson. Watson was actually the most creative of the three as he shows on the four remarkable performances that he recorded in 1946 with trombonist Vic Dickenson; his version of "Jingle Bells" is quite nutty.

Unfortunately that was his last recording. After 1946 Leo Watson was completely forgotten and mostly worked at day jobs before his death from pneumonia in 1950.

Recommended CDs: *The Original Scat Man* (Indigo 2098) has 23 of Watson's recordings (nearly his entire discography), including a few selections with the Spirits of Rhythm, his best sides with Shaw and Krupa and all eight of the numbers recorded under his own name.

Frances Wayne
(Chiarina Francesca Bertocci)
b. August 26, 1919, Boston, MA; d. February 6, 1978, Boston, MA

A fine middle-of-the-road swing singer with a straightforward delivery, Frances Wayne had a relatively brief career but was consistent whenever she sang.

Born and raised in Boston, she grew up in an Italian family and spent three years of her childhood in Italy. She started singing professionally when she was 20, initially working in the Boston area, including with her brother Nick Jerrett's swing band. Jerrett's group was forced to break up when most of its members were drafted in 1941. Wayne next sang with Charlie Barnet, recording one selection ("That Old Black Magic") right before the musicians recording strike of mid-1942. After a brief period back in Boston the following year, she was discovered by Woody Herman.

Frances Wayne is best remembered for her work with Herman, which began when the orchestra was in a transition between being "the band that plays the blues" and the First Herd. In addition to appearing on radio broadcasts and cutting V-discs, she recorded 11 selections with Herman, including "I Couldn't Sleep A Wink Last Night," "As Long As I Live," "Saturday Night Is The Loneliest Night In The Week," "Gee It's Good To Hold You" and most notably a hit version of "Happiness Is A Thing Called Joe," a song that had originally been made famous by Ethel Waters. In addition, she had her own obscure six-song session for Musicraft in August 1945 with backing mostly from Herman sidemen.

Wayne married Neal Hefti (who played trumpet and arranged for Herman) in late 1945 and they both left the band by February 1946; her last recording with Herman was fittingly titled "Welcome To My Dream." Wayne and Hefti moved to California where she sang now and then in nightclubs, recorded ten selections for the Exclusive label in 1947, appeared on two songs for a Hefti session and worked briefly with Shorty Sherock's orchestra.

Frances Wayne was in semi-retirement until 1951, when she recorded three songs with her husband. When Hefti formed a big band for a year in 1952, Wayne was his singer and they went on tour together. After that time, she was largely retired except for recording three albums as a leader during 1954–57. Although those records are rewarding, they are rather scarce today. Frances Wayne lived happily in retirement as Neal Hefti's wife until her death in 1978.

Recommended CDs: One of Frances Wayne's three albums has been reissued as half of a CD with an unrelated set by pianist Jack Wilson that is called *The Warm Sound Of Francis Wayne/ The Jack Wilson Quartet* (Collectables 6626).

LPs to Search For: *Frances Wayne* (Brunswick 54022) is mostly a tribute to Ethel Waters, while *Songs For My Man* (Epic 3222) has her interpreting superior standards. In both cases she is accompanied by an orchestra arranged by Neal Hefti.

Ronnie Wells
(Veronica Burke)
b. February 28, 1943, Washington, D.C.;
d. March 7, 2007, Silver Spring, MD

Ronnie Wells was an important force in the Washington, D.C., area as a singer, educator and an organizer of jazz festivals.

Born into a music family, Ronnie Wells remembered spending each Saturday at the Howard Theater from the age of 11, watching many of the giants of jazz who were playing in town. "I sang in the church choir and, at age 13, led my own group, which I directed and accompanied on piano. I attended Howard University from 1960 to 1962, where I majored in liberal arts. I studied music by listening to the jazz greats. In 1962, one of my sisters, Shirley Heard, was performing at a club and invited me to sit in. After singing the first song, that is all it took. I knew then that music had chosen me. I performed for 1½ years during 1960–61 at the Talleyrand and then each weekend for 6½ years at The Top 'O Foolery."

While holding an administrative job, Ronnie Wells became a fixture in the Washington, D.C., jazz scene. She toured Europe and South America and performed regularly with her second husband, pianist Ron Elliston. In addition to recording for her Jazz Karma label, she toured and recorded with the Widespread Depression Orchestra.

Wells was an assistant professor at the University of Maryland's Department of Music during 1983–2002, designing and developing the first Jazz Vocal Techniques Workshop. During her last few years she and her husband ran the Elliston Music Studio for Jazz Studies. In response to public schools cutting back on their music education programs, Wells founded the Fish Middleton Jazz Scholarship Fund and was one of the founders of the East Coast Jazz Festival (which started in 1992). "The music program presents quarterly concerts to feature the greater metropolitan Washington, D.C.'s most talented jazz musicians, and the five-day FMJS East Coast Jazz Festival. The festival's main purpose is to provide a venue for the live scholarship competition. There are 107 events, 86 of which are free and open to the public." Ronnie Wells remained active until shortly before her death from lung cancer.

"When performing a song, the emotion, passion and interpretation are what you are feeling at the time and will never be performed the same way again. Our lives change from second to second. Hence, no matter how many times you perform a song, it is always new, fresh, alive and another journey."

Recommended CDs: Ronnie Wells loved to sing standards, and she particularly excelled on ballads. *After The Lights Go Down Low* (Jazz Karma 906), *Make Me A Present Of You* (Jazz Karma 9009), *After You* (Jazz Karma 9012), *Mostly Ballads* (Jazz Karma 9013), *Here I Am* (Jazz Karma 9016) and *Live At The 10th Annual East Coast Jazz Party* (Jazz Karma 9018) form an excellent cross section of her music.

Carol Welsman
(Mary Carol Welsman)
b. September 29, Toronto, Ontario, Canada

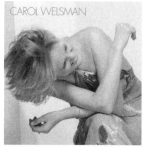

A versatile singer-pianist who is better known in her native Canada than in the U.S. (she currently lives in Southern California), Carol Welsman has been identified with smooth but is capable of performing more creative jazz.

"My father had an eclectic record collection, which included such big bands as Count Basie, Duke Ellington and Woody Herman. I would listen with him often, and, from the age of 12, he'd take me to the concerts. He loves Peggy Lee, Sinatra and Mel Tormé, so I was introduced to the great jazz vocalists at the same time. I started performing at the age of 10 on guitar and singing mostly folk music and bossa novas. It was later in my teens that I developed a jazz repertoire. I am drawn to the minimalist styles of both Peggy Lee and Shirley Horn."

Welsman attended the Berklee College of Music during 1980–81. She also studied voice in France with Christiane Legrand. Back in Toronto, in 1990 she started the Welcar Music label and began to perform locally at first and then throughout Canada. She also became a professor of jazz vocal at the University of Toronto. In 1996 she recorded her debut CD, *Lucky To Be Me*. Welsman's third CD, 1999's *Swing Ladies Swing: A Tribute To Singers Of The Swing Era*, finds her effectively singing swing standards although 2001's *Hold Me* is more in the smooth idiom.

Carol Welsman toured Japan, Italy, Brazil and throughout Canada during 2004–2005 but has yet to catch on in the U.S. She has a pleasing voice and is an effective accompanist on piano to her own vocals.

Recommended CDs: Carol Welsman's seven CDs cover a wide ground: *Lucky To Be Me* (Sea Jam 427 393), *Inclined* (Welcar 363), *Swing Ladies Swing: A Tribute To Singers Of The Swing Era* (Welcar 365), *Hold Me* (Avenue 85659), *The Language Of Love* (Savoy 17196), *What'Cha Got Cookin'* (Columbia 53505) and *Carol Welsman* (Justin Time 220). Try *The Language Of Love* first.

Website: www.carolwelsman.com

Paula West
b. April 5, Camp Pendleton, CA

A subtle singer who adds sensuality and wit to many of her interpretations, Paula West is at times reminiscent of Peggy Lee. Based in San Francisco, her style falls between jazz and cabaret, and she makes swing standards sound fresh and relevant.

West did not hear much jazz until attending San Diego State University, where she discovered Dinah Washington, Billie Holiday and Sarah Vaughan along with the instrumental giants in a jazz appreciation class. After college she moved to San Francisco, sat in at jam sessions, and met pianist Ken Muir, who became her accompanist. She worked as a waitress for

Kate Westbrook

a time until several local musicians, including pianist Larry Vuckovich, hired her and launched her new career. "Singing wasn't something I planned to do. It just ended up this way and I'm glad." She studied with Faith Winthrop and by 1995 was working regularly in both the jazz and cabaret fields. Since then, Paula West has recorded three CDs, toured Europe a few times and performed on the East Coast in addition to singing regularly in the San Francisco Bay area.

"Some high points for me include being on double bills with such greats as Rosemary Clooney, Jimmy Scott and Oscar Brown Jr., working regularly at the Algonquin Hotel, and appearing at jazz festivals and at Jazz at Lincoln Center. I enjoy singing standards because I love lyrics. I love how the songs are open to different interpretations. It is always important to me to try and make a classic sound fresh and make it my own, telling the story and being truthful."

Recommended CDs: Paula West's three CDs, *Temptation* (Original Cast Records 9808), *Restless* (Noir 22) and *Come What May* (Hi Horse 3033), are full of her favorite songs, many of which date from the 1930s through the early '60s.

Website: www.paula-west.com

Kate Westbrook
b. September 18, 1939, Surrey, England

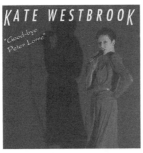

An adventurous singer who also writes lyrics and plays tenor horn and piccolo, Kate Westbrook has been associated with her husband, pianist-bandleader Mike Westbrook, since 1974.

Born in England, she grew up in the U.S. and Canada before returning to England, although she spent a later period in the United States. "At the school I attended in my teens, there were a couple of pupils who were into jazz and they got hold of records from the States. I was intrigued but not yet caught. But driving across America from the East to the West Coast in 1963, I was in Chicago for a while and I heard Charles Mingus' *The Black Saint And The Sinner Lady*, which scared me but made me want to enter that world." She attended college in England. "All of that was in Fine Art and I continue to paint and exhibit in tandem with the music. Musically, I am self-taught, but I have to say that working with fine musicians is a great way to learn."

In 1974 she joined the Mike Westbrook Brass Band on tenor horn and piccolo. "At that time Mike had this small acoustic brass group which played in the streets, a marching band really. On tour, we often played a school in the day and did a concert in the evening. Working in the band with trumpeter and vocalist Phil Minton, I started doing some vocals. In time, this led to writing my own material, generally with Mike, and now I am involved in writing opera, cabaret songs and music theater pieces. In singing, my main interest has been in the lower reaches of my register and in extending my range of vocal colors. I am very fond of consonants and ideas."

Always open to new ideas and sounds, Kate Westbrook has been involved in multi-media productions and creating music that simply cannot be classified. She sings in English, German, French and Italian, both her own lyrics and that of a wide range of composers from several fields. She has recorded more than 20 albums thus far.

"I consider myself very fortunate to have been able to work in music for more than 30 years, and to have earned enough with my writing and performing to be able to carry on until the next project. I do want to continue in this way for many years to come, continuing to reach for new ideas, never resting on old ones or on idioms from the past. Let me die after the second encore."

Recommended CDs: A cross section of Kate Westbrook's talents and eclectic nature can be appreciated after listening to *L'Ascenseur/The Lift* (Jazzprint 130), *Chanson Irresponsable* (Enja 456), *Goodbye, Peter Lorre* (Femme 166442), *Stage Set* (ASC 9), a set of duets with pianist Mike Westbrook called *Love Or Infatuation* (ASC 02028), *Cuff Clout* (Voiceprint 432), which is called a "neoteric music hall," *Art Wolf* (Altrisuoni 186) and *The Nijinska Chamber* (Voiceprint 383).

Website: www.westbrookjazz.co.uk

Carla White
b. September 15, 1951, Oakland, CA;
d. May 9, 2007, New York, NY

Originally a brilliant scat-singer, Carla White developed into a superior interpreter of lyrics while retaining her roots in bebop.

Born in Oakland, she grew up in Bellport, New York. "I grew up in a small town about 60 miles east of NYC out on Long Island. There was no jazz to be heard for a 60-mile radius. However, when I was about 13, I was introduced to this older guy who was a jazz trumpet player who also lived out there. We became friends and he turned me on to Lee Morgan, Miles Davis, Jackie McLean and Coltrane. It was an awakening for me. I fell in love with that music then and there, and I thank God that I'm still in love."

As a teenager, after landing the leading roles in *Babes In Arms* and *Oliver*, she took her first singing lessons. Also after a brief time playing banjo, she switched to the acoustic guitar and studied piano, which she called "a singer's best friend." While her original goal was to be an improvising jazz dancer, she became more involved in singing and acting. White went to a two-year professional training program for actors in London called the Webber-Douglas Academy of Dramatic Art during 1969–71. She also spent a year wandering around Europe and North Africa, singing in the streets. Back in New York, White studied music on and off with Lennie Tristano during 1972–78 and with Warne Marsh for two years.

"The first turning point for me was meeting trumpeter Manny Duran in 1979 while waiting for an elevator. We got to talking about music and soon thereafter we formed a quintet together. It was my first band. We were co-leaders, and Manny was a great mentor to me and gave me the encouragement and confidence I needed to step forward and sing my heart out."

In 1983 the White-Duran band recorded *Andruline* for Stash, her recording debut.

In 1985, she went out on her own. After listening closely to Joe Williams, she became interested in singing lyrics and the change can be heard on her Milestone albums. She toured Europe and Japan, increasing her visibility in the jazz world each year and gaining a strong audience. Although she did not record as often as one would have hoped, each of her albums was something special, showing her continuous growth. She also worked as a voiceover artist, an educator and an occasional actress.

Tragically, Carla White lost her bout with cancer in 2007, passing away when she was 55. She is greatly missed in the jazz world.

"What I love most about jazz is that magical, indescribable feeling of being right in the heart of the moment, the heart of the music, the heart of your heart, the pure and innocent joy of singing, of making beautiful music with your fellow man and sharing it with whoever is listening."

Recommended CDs: *Mood Swings* (Milestone 9158) from 1988, *Listen Here* (Evidence 22109), which was her personal favorite, *Live At Vartan Jazz* (Vartan 016), the obscure *In Mexico* (Jazz Cat 011), *The Sweetest Sounds* (DIW 422) and her final recording, *A Voice In The Night* (Sweet Moon 2357), which was recorded in 2001 but not released until five years later, are all rewarding. Carla White's voice aged from recording to recording, but each CD is an honest and high-quality sampling of how she sounded. She never lost her creativity or love for the music.

LPs to Search For: Carla White's first two albums, her debut, which she co-led with Manny Duran, *Andruline* (Stash 237), and *Orient Express* (Milestone 9147) have yet to be reissued.

Georgia White
(Georgia Lawson)
b. March 9, 1903, Sandersville, GA; d. ca. 1980s?

Although she recorded extensively during 1935–41 when she cut 92 songs, very little is known about the blues-oriented singer-pianist. She moved to Chicago sometime in the mid-1920s and worked at the Apex Club with Jimmie Noone during 1929–30, making her debut by cutting "When You're Smiling" with Noone's Apex Club Orchestra.

Remaining in Chicago, White signed with the Decca label in 1935, who soon promoted her as "The World's Greatest Blues Singer." She often backed herself on piano, but during 1936–37 was accompanied by Richard M. Jones and in 1939 by Sammy Price. Among her other sidemen were guitarists Les Paul, Ikey Robinson, Charlie McCoy, Lonnie Johnson and Teddy Bunn and bassist John Lindsay, with a 1940 session matching her with trumpeter Jonah Jones. White was able to sing lowdown blues, mildly risqué double-entendre tunes and jazz with her barrelhouse-style piano playing fitting her vocals well. Among the high points of her discography are "You Done Lost Your Good Thing Now," "Someday Sweetheart," "Hot Nuts," "I'll Keep Sittin' On It If I Can't Sell It" (which Ruth Brown revived a half-century later), "Little Red Wagon," "You Don't Know My Mind," "Trouble In Mind" (a 1920s classic that she brought back in 1936), "The Blues Ain't Nothin' But…" and "Jazzin' Babies Blues."

Strangely enough, Georgia White did not record again after 1941. She briefly led an all-female band in the late 1940s, worked with Big Bill Broonzy's Laughing Trio in 1949 and

was active in the Chicago area until retiring in 1959. It is not known with any certainty where or when she passed away, but her bluish music is definitely worth discovering.

Recommended CDs: All of Georgia White's recordings are available on *Vols. 1–4* (Document 5301-5304).

Wesla Whitfield
b. September 15, 1947, Santa Maria, CA

A superb interpreter of the Great American Songbook who is both expressive and quite subtle, Wesla Whitfield (whose first name is sometimes listed as Weslia) is at the top of her field in both jazz and cabaret.

"When I was about five, I sang with my two older sisters in a little trio act. I sang harmony because my oldest sister had a strong alto voice, and my middle sister could only sing the melody without getting lost. We performed at various lodge and church functions in Santa Maria."

Whitfield had piano lessons for five years and in college studied violin and guitar. She graduated from Pasadena City College in 1968 and San Francisco State University in 1971. "While singing as a salaried chorister with the San Francisco Opera, and working days running a press in a print shop, my coworkers took me to a Sarah Vaughan concert at the Great American Music Hall. I was knocked out and began listening to every jazz recording and live performance I could find. I never tried to copy anyone though. I've always felt as though I was going in a direction completely different from everyone around me and so was required to be my own inspiration."

In the mid-1970s, Whitfield began to sing full-time, first as a singing waitress and then as a cabaret singer. In 1977 a random street shooting left her paralyzed from the waist down, and she would never walk again. A few years later, she was able to resume singing. She started working with pianist Michael Greensill in 1981; five years later they married. Appearing with Greensill and a bassist, Wesla Whitfield has been quite active during the past 25 years, recording over a dozen CDs and keeping vintage standards alive.

"My whole reason for spending my life as a singer is to interpret the song. I get to tell these stories that can stir the heart and mind and soul of the listener. Since becoming a professional singer in 1972, I've felt as though I'm on a roller coaster with many highs and lows, twists and turns and near misses, requiring an unending process of reinventing myself. Having been classically trained, it is an ongoing task to find my way out of those musical limitations without abandoning my musical principles. In jazz such inventiveness is applauded, and, while I will never feel myself to be an actual jazz singer, I'm thrilled to spend my life moving in that direction. At this point, I hope to keep singing until a few minutes before I die."

Recommended CDs: All of Wesla Whitfield's recordings feature her voice on superior vintage material. There is not a throwaway in the lot, which consists of *Just For A Thrill*

(Myoho), *Until The Real Thing Comes Along* (Myoho), *Lucky To Be Me* (Landmark 1524), *Live In San Francisco* (Landmark 1531), *Nice Work* (Landmark 1544), *Nobody Else But Me* (Landmark 1551), *Beautiful Love* (Cabaret 5007), *Seeker Of Wisdom And Truth* (Cabaret 5012), *Teach Me Tonight* (High Note 7009), *My Shining Hour* (High Note 7012), *High Standards* (High Note 7025), *With A Song In My Heart* (High Note 7040), *Let's Get Lost* (High Note 7062), *Best Thing For You Would Be Me* (High Note 7091), *September Songs* (High Note 7114), *In My Life* (High Note 7132), *Livin' On Love* (High Note 7152) and *Message From The Man In The Moon* (Pismo 102).

Website: www.weslawhitfield.com

Patti Wicks

b. February 24, 1945, Islip, NY

A fine pianist who is also a sensitive ballad singer, Patti Wicks has had a long career and is finally receiving recognition.

She was born two months premature, leaving her visually impaired. At the age of three, she heard her mother play a song on the piano and then, without any encouragement, Patti walked over to the piano and played it back note-for-note. Although she could not see the sheet music put in front of her, she was taught classical music by an innovative teacher, Pat Kleinmeyer. Wicks attended the Crane School of Music at SUNY Postdam, graduating in 1966 with a degree in music education. "I was introduced to jazz as a college freshman by my piano professor. He would play recordings of the jazz greats, from Billie Holiday to Bill Evans, quite frequently before my lessons began each week, as well as at the end of each lesson. I also heard some great playing by fellow music students at a jam session on campus one afternoon, which had quite an impact. I was hooked and wanted to play and sing that incredible music. My first experience singing jazz was with the big band at college for a few concerts. It featured some great young players and excellent arrangements by leader John LaBarbera. I also played and sang in a jazz group on weekends during my junior and senior years at college. Playing and singing have always been of equal importance to me."

"When I came to New York in 1969, I met a bassist, Perry Lind, who helped me to get some gigs and introduced me to other jazz musicians. In 1972 I met Sam Jones and had the honor of having him as my bassist on some gigs. He was very supportive and encouraged me to call the best musicians, whether they were 'names' or not, so I would always be able to grow as a musician by playing with much more experienced players." Other musicians with whom Patti Wicks has worked include bassists Richard Davis, Brian Torff and Mark Dresser, drummers Curtis Boyd, Louis Hayes, Mickey Roker and Alan Dawson, saxophonists Flip Phillips, Frank Morgan and Richie Cole, flugelhornist Clark Terry and singers Anita O'Day, Sheila Jordan, Carol Sloane, Rebecca Parris, Roseanna Vitro and Giacomo Cates.

Patti Wicks moved to South Florida in 1997 but visits New York frequently and has toured Europe several times, particularly Italy. She made her recording debut on 1997's *Root At The Top* and has thus far recorded five CDs that feature both her heartfelt singing and fluent piano.

"Jazz is painting a picture, telling a story using one's personal life experiences to interpret a lyric or play the music with honesty, feeling and with an individual style. There is such a sense of fulfillment and joy in playing and singing jazz that I know I would not have otherwise."

Recommended CDs: *Room At The Top* (Recycled Notes 817) is a very well-rounded debut for Patti Wicks, displaying her small but effective voice along with her sophisticated piano in a trio. *Love Locked Out* (MaxJazz 501) is an all-ballad album that gained her much attention. *Basic Feeling* (Egea 104), *Italian Sessions* (Studiottanta-Fortuna 8021051000216) and *It's A Good Day* (Geco 100001) were recorded for Italian labels and will hopefully be made more widely available domestically.

Website: www.pattiwicks.com

Lee Wiley

b. October 9, 1908, Fort Gibson, OK;
d. December 11, 1975, New York, NY

Lee Wiley did not improvise much, and one could argue that her interpretations fall between jazz and cabaret music, but she had an indescribable charisma and cool sensuality that made her a favorite of many jazz musicians, especially Eddie Condon. Influenced by Ethel Waters and to a lesser extent Mildred Bailey, there was a quiet magic to her best performances.

Wiley ran away from home when she was 19, working on the radio in St. Louis and Chicago. She moved to New York in the late 1920s and made her recording debut with Leo Reisman's orchestra in 1931, having a hit with "Time On My Hands." She soon became associated both musically and personally with composer Victor Young. Under Young's guidance, she had the air of being an upper class cabaret singer whose sophisticated renditions of new material were heard regularly on the radio. With Young she co-composed "Anytime, Anyday, Anywhere" and "Got The South In My Soul." She also recorded a few selections as a leader during 1933–34 (including "I've Got A Right To Sing The Blues"), but a bout with tuberculosis knocked her out of action for a year. After returning to the scene and breaking up with Young, Wiley became involved with the married trumpeter Bunny Berigan and turned her attention toward jazz, appearing on the radio with Eddie Condon and other freewheeling jazz players, and working on the *Saturday Night Swing Club* radio series during 1936–39.

During 1939–43, Wiley made her most important recordings. She was the first singer to devote an entire album (which in those days was a collection of four 78s) to the music of one composer. Her George Gershwin, Cole Porter, Harold Arlen and Rodgers and Hart songbooks came out 15 years under Ella Fitzgerald's and were unprecedented at the time. Porter, Arlen and Rodgers all expressed their approval of her treatments of their songs. Backed by such jazz players as trumpeters Bunny Berigan, Max Kaminsky and Billy Butterfield, cornetist Bobby Hackett, tenor-saxophonist Bud Freeman, clarinetist Pee Wee Russell, Fats Waller on piano and organ, and pianist Joe Bushkin, Wiley recorded definitive versions of "My One And Only," "I've Got A Crush On You," "How Long Has This Been Going On," "Glad To Be Unhappy," "Let's Do It," "Down With Love" and "Let's Fall In Love" among others.

In 1940 Wiley also recorded "Sugar" and "Down To Steamboat Tennessee" while backed by pianist Jess Stacy and cornetist Muggsy Spanier. In 1943 Wiley married Stacy and she urged him to put together a big band. Within five years both the orchestra and their marriage were history. Wiley guested at some of Eddie Condon's Town Hall concerts in 1944–45 and in the early 1950s recorded the well-received *Nights In Manhattan* and a couple lesser-known sets (with backing from a pair of pianists) that were eight-tune songbooks of the music of Irving Berlin and Vincent Youmans.

To Wiley's distress, she was finding it very difficult to compete with younger up-and-coming singers, both stylistically and in her looks (which were very important to her image) as she inevitably aged. Still, she recorded a fine album for Storyville (reissued by Black Lion) in 1954 and appeared at the first Newport Jazz Festival that year. Two records that she cut for Victor during 1956–57 came out well, but their sales were small. Disappointed by the way her career was going, Wiley gradually faded out of music and was largely inactive by the early 1960s.

In 1971, Lee Wiley made a surprise return, recording her final album, *Back Home Again*. She sounded fine on "Indiana" but otherwise was clearly past her prime. The following year George Wein persuaded her to make a surprise appearance at a Carnegie Hall concert that was part of the Newport festival, and she fared pretty well during the emotional comeback, which was released on a CD two decades later. But that was the last time she ever sang in public, closing a 40-year career with a final success.

Recommended CDs: Absolutely essential in one form or another are Lee Wiley's first four songbooks, which are available as *Sings The Songs Of George And Ira Gershwin And Cole Porter* (Audiophile 1) and *Sings The Songs Of Rodgers And Hart And Harold Arlen* (Audiophile 10). Producer Takashi Ono has been putting together a very complete collection of Wiley's recordings, which at this point include the first three songbooks (with many alternate takes) plus her earlier cabaret recordings and radio performances. These are available as *The Completists' Ultimate Collection, Vols. 1–4* (Devil's Music 6001-6004). *Live On Stage* (Audiophile 39) has Wiley's appearances at Eddie Condon's Town Hall Concerts of 1944–45 plus an interesting interview. The two-CD set *Complete Fifties Studio Masters* (Jazz Factory 9811) includes the singer's Columbia and Black Lion records plus a few miscellaneous items. *West Of The Moon* (Mosaic 1008) features Wiley in excellent form in 1956. *As Time Goes By* (Bluebird 3138) duplicates much of that set while containing the majority of the selections from the out-of-print 1957 album *A Touch Of The Blues*. Lee Wiley's final studio album *Back Home Again* (Audiophile 300) has its moments of interest but does not compare historically or emotionally to *The Carnegie Hall Concert* (Audiophile 170), her last performance and a CD that also includes a 1952 rehearsal.

Joe Williams

b. December 12, 1918, Cordele, GA;
d. March 29, 1999, Las Vegas, NV

One of the last and greatest of all big band singers, Joe Williams rose to fame with Count Basie's 1950s orchestra. His post-Basie years with combos were quite busy, and he and Mel Tormé were considered the top male jazz singers of the 1980s and '90s. While a descendant of Jimmy Rushing, Big Joe Turner and the other Kansas City jazz/blues singers, Williams had his own air of sophistication along with a large assortment of double entendre lyrics and phrases. Yet for all his fame with swinging blues, Williams most loved singing ballads.

Joe Williams moved with his family to Chicago when he was three. He learned piano and as a teenager formed a gospel vocal quartet, the Jubilee Boys. Because he did not record under his own name until 1951 when he was already 32, his early career is often overlooked. He was considered an important part of the Chicago jazz scene by the late 1930s. Williams worked with clarinetist Jimmie Noone, the Les Hite Orchestra, Coleman Hawkins, Lionel Hampton and Andy Kirk's Clouds of Joy, making his recording debut with Clouds of Joy in the mid-1940s. He also worked outside of music in slow times, including selling cosmetics door-to-door and being a doorman at theaters.

Things started to improve in 1951 when he started to record as a leader, cutting his first version of "Every Day I Have The Blues" the following year. But Williams was still a complete unknown outside of Chicago when he was hired in December 1954 for the Count Basie Orchestra. Basie had been leading his new band for three years at that point after two years spent heading a combo, and his orchestra's future success was not yet assured. Joe Williams was in the perfect spot at the perfect time. His recording of "Every Day I Have The Blues" on the 1955 album *Count Basie Swings, Joe Williams Sings* was a big hit and became his signature song. He also had success with his rendition of "Goin' To Chicago" (formerly associated with Jimmy Rushing), "Smack Dab In The Middle" and "Alright, Okay, You Win."

Williams was with Basie for six years, going out on his own in January 1961. At first he worked with trumpeter Harry "Sweets" Edison and then generally led quartets for the remainder of his long career. His solo albums were mostly quite rewarding (particularly ones that balanced blues and ballads), he recorded a strong collaboration with the Thad Jones/Mel Lewis Orchestra, and there were occasional reunions with Basie. Even late in life when his voice became a bit raspy, he proved to be a masterful entertainer.

Joe Williams died when, tired of the way that medicine was affecting him during a stay in the hospital, he spontaneously decided to walk a few miles to his home in Las Vegas; the heat got to him.

Recommended CDs: *Joe Williams Sings Everyday* (Savoy 0199) has his pre-Basie recordings of 1951–53. Williams is extensively featured on *Count Basie Swings, Joe Williams Sings* (Verve 314 519 852) and *Everyday I Have The Blues* (Roulette 04826), both of which match him with the Basie band. *A Swingin' Night At Birdland* (Roulette 795335) from 1962 teams him with Harry Edison and tenor-saxophonist Frank Foster on many of his trademark standards and blues. *Jump For Joy* (RCA 52713), *Me And The Blues/The Song Is You* (Collectables 2703), the sampler *The Overwhelming Joe Williams* (Bluebird 6464), the classic *Presenting Joe Williams And Thad Jones/Mel Lewis Orchestra* (Blue Note 30454), *The Heart And Soul Of Joe Williams And George Shearing* (Koch 51002), *Dave Pell's Prez Conference* (GNP Crescendo 2124) and *Joe Williams Live* (Original Jazz Classics 438), which features him with altoist Cannonball Adderley's group, cover his career during 1963–73. Williams' final 15 years are well documented on *Nothing But The Blues* (Delos 4001), *I Just*

Want To Sing (Delos 4004), *Every Night—Live At Vine St.* (Verve 833 236), *Ballads And Blues Master* (Verve 314 511 354), *In Good Company* (Verve 837 932), *Live At Orchestra Hall, Detroit* (Telarc 83329), *Here's To Life* (Telarc 83357) and *Feel The Spirit* (Telarc 83362).

Cassandra Wilson

b. December 4, 1955, Jackson, MS

One of the most important jazz singers of the past two decades, Cassandra Wilson found herself by going back in time musically to country blues, and by opening up her repertoire to include the pop and rock songs of the past 40 years.

Wilson had classical piano lessons for seven years, played clarinet in her junior high school concert and marching bands, and taught herself the guitar. She was a singer-guitarist in a high school folk group, wrote originals, earned a degree in mass communications from Jackson State University, and at the same time sang in local clubs, mostly with R&B, funk and pop cover bands. She learned about jazz from the Black Arts Music Society, spent a year in New Orleans, and in 1982 moved to New York.

Cassandra Wilson studied with trombonist Grachan Moncur III, sat in at jam sessions, and became the vocalist in the M-Base Collective. Inspired by altoist Steve Coleman and the other advanced musicians who developed a new type of avant-funk jazz, she did her best to find a place for her voice in the dense and very crowded ensembles, often singing wordlessly while competing with saxophonists, guitarists, electric bass and drums. She also toured with New Air, a trio headed by saxophonist Henry Threadgill.

After leading two albums that were extensions of the M-Base group, Wilson changed course and recorded *Blue Skies* in 1988, a standards date in which she closely resembled Betty Carter. The next milestone was 1993's *Blue Light 'Til Dawn*, which featured her in an acoustic blues-oriented program. In the years since, she has ventured deeper into country blues, toured as part of Wynton Marsalis' *Blood On The Fields* production, paid tribute to Miles Davis on *Traveling Miles*, and dug up a wide variety of songs from pop, country, soul and rock (including the Monkees' "Last Train To Clarksville"), turning them (with varying results) into modern jazz. Her willingness to tackle post-1965 pop songs has been significant, while her atmospheric versions of bluish originals (sometimes using steel guitar, violin and accordion) have given many of her recordings an eerie atmosphere.

Cassandra Wilson's voice (which often has a bored tone) is an acquired taste but she has been very influential, if not in her sound than in her desire to forego the vintage standards in favor of much more contemporary and unusual material.

Recommended CDs: Cassandra Wilson's M-Base recordings as a leader are *Point Of View* (JMT 834 404), *Days Aweigh* (JMT 834 412), *Jumpworld* (JMT 834 434), *She Who Weeps* (JMT 834 443), *Live* (JMT 849 149) and *After The Beginning Again* (JMT 514 002). *Blue Skies* (JMT 834 419), which was recorded after *Days Aweigh*, is a very different album and it points

toward Wilson's future. *Blue Light 'Til Dawn* (Blue Note 81357) was another important turning point and it ranks with Wilson's best work, as does *New Moon Daughter* (Blue Note 32861), *Rendezvous* (Blue Note 55484), which co-stars pianist Jacky Terrasson, and *Traveling Miles* (Blue Note 54123). *Belly Of The Sun* (Blue Note 35072) ranges from "Wichita Lineman" to Robert Johnson's "Hot Tamales," also including songs by Bob Dylan, James Taylor and Jobim ("Waters Of March"). Much of *Glamoured* (Blue Note 81860) is modern folk music, and the emphasis is on her originals along with some Sting, Dylan, Willie Nelson and Abbey Lincoln ("Throw It Away"), while *Thunderbird* (Blue Note 63398) is electronic and utilizes loops, a new setting for Cassandra Wilson's distinctive voice.

Website: www.cassandrawilson.com

Edith Wilson

(Edith Goodall)

b. September 2, 1896, Louisville, KY;
d. March 30, 1981, Chicago, IL

A star of black vaudeville who could sing blues, Edith Wilson actually made her best recordings late in life. She started performing on stage at Louisville's Park Theater in 1919 when she was 22 (not 12 as is sometimes reported) and caught on as part of an act with her husband pianist Danny Wilson and his sister blues singer Lena Wilson. After playing in Baltimore and on the East Coast, she was discovered by Perry Bradford who had her signed to Columbia in 1921. Her 18 recordings of 1921–22, with backing by Johnny Dunn's Original Jazz Hounds, are quite primitive both in the phrasing and the recording quality, not really doing her justice. She also recorded eight titles during 1924–25 and four during 1929–30, but those are quite obscure.

More important for Wilson was her stage work. She replaced Mamie Smith in the musical revue *Put And Take*, worked in the *Plantation Revue* and was part of the latter show when it was renamed *From Dover Street To Dixie* and moved to London in 1923. In New York she worked in *Dixie To Broadway* and in 1926 toured Europe with the *Chocolate Kiddies* show, which also featured Sam Wooding's Orchestra. She was a world traveler during 1926–29, appearing all over both Western and Eastern Europe (including the Soviet Union) and South America. In New York in 1929, Wilson appeared in *Hot Chocolates*, introducing Fats Waller's early anti-racism song "Black And Blue." That show advertised Wilson, Louis Armstrong and Fats Waller as "The Thousand Pounds of Harmony."

Edith Wilson was a major name in the Harlem show business scene of the 1930s even though there were no recordings, appearing in many shows and with the orchestras of Fess Williams, Cab Calloway, Jimmie Lunceford, Noble Sissle and Lucky Millinder. She had a nonsinging role in the Humphrey Bogart film *To Have And Have Not*, played a regular role on the *Amos N' Andy* radio show and worked in early television. Wilson depicted the character of Aunt Jemima for Quaker Oats in the 1950s, playing the stereotyped part with as much dignity as possible. She retired from show business altogether in 1963 to become an executive secretary for the Negro Actors Guild.

In the early 1970s Edith Wilson made a surprising comeback, sounding in excellent form on recordings and performances with Eubie Blake and Terry Waldo's Gutbucket Syncopators. Her 1973 album *He May Be Your Man (But He Comes To See Me Sometimes)* is a high point; at 76 her voice is surprisingly strong and full of energy. Wilson sounds like an old-time blues and jazz singer rather than a vaudevillian. She also recorded an album in France the following year for the

Wolverine label. Edith Wilson's last appearance was at the 1980 Newport Jazz Festival, nine months before her death at age 84.

Recommended CDs: *He May Be Your Man (But He Comes To See Me Sometimes)* (Delmark 637) is arguably Edith Wilson's finest set of recordings.

Joe Lee Wilson

b. December 22, 1935, Bristow, OK

In the late 1960s/early '70s, Joe Lee Wilson was on the brink of stardom in the jazz world. Like Leon Thomas, he seemed to be pointing the way toward the future of vocal jazz, but unfortunately he soon faded out of the jazz big leagues, moving to Europe in 1977.

Wilson sang in church while growing up. He remembers being impressed by hearing Louis Jordan on the radio and seeing him in movie shorts, but it was seeing Billie Holiday perform in 1951 that made him want to be a jazz singer. "My first gigs were at Santa Monica at Fiddlers Zanzibar around 1953/54. They had jam sessions for four days a week, Thursdays through Sundays. I sang at those jam sessions for two years. They were run by Roscoe Weathers, flute and tenor player, who taught me everything about jazz." Wilson attended the Conservatory of Music in Los Angeles and City College, befriended Eddie Jefferson ("he was my soul mate, father figure and adviser"), gigged in Southern California, and spent some time performing in Mexico before moving to New York in 1962.

Having a deep baritone voice with a three-octave range and an adventurous spirit, Joe Lee Wilson performed with many notable jazz musicians during the 1960s including Sonny Rollins, Lee Morgan, Pharoah Sanders, Jackie McLean and Miles Davis. "Singing with Miles Davis was exciting, and having him come to hear me often. I did not join his band because I did not approve of electronics at that time; of course now I realize he was ahead of his time." In 1968 at an NBC-TV Showcase, Wilson tied for first in the talent contest with Sly and the Family Stone. Since first prize was a record contract with Columbia, the label signed both Sly and Wilson. He recorded three albums for Columbia during 1969–72 but, because his music was so adventurous, all but a few songs were not released.

In the 1970s, Wilson was one of the originators and leaders of the New York Jazz Loft scene, in which musicians ran their own informal clubs and booked modern and avant-garde musicians. He ran his loft (the Ladies' Fort) for six years and organized a loft festival. During that decade he gained some recognition for his singing on Archie Shepp albums (*Things Have Got To Change* and *Attica Blues*) and also worked with Freddie Hubbard.

In 1977, after marrying a British woman, he moved to England and eventually Paris. While his name was largely forgotten in the United States, Joe Lee Wilson has worked frequently in Europe and in recent times recorded for Candid and Philology. He has also been active as an educator.

"Jazz is my religion. When I sing, it is wonderful to see the audience so responsive and happy. This re-endorses my belief that it is a healing music."

Recommended CDs: *What Would I Be Without You* (Knitting Factory 3024) is a reissue of a 1975 album for Rashied Ali's Survival label. A pair of very obscure albums from the 1980s have recently surfaced: *Come And See* (Explore 0024) and *The Shadow* (Explore 0025). Joe Lee Wilson's recent work, *Feelin' Good* (Candid 79210) and *Ballads For Trane* (Philology 707), rank with the finest recordings of his career.

LPs to Search For: Joe Lee Wilson's earliest albums, *Without A Song* (Inner City 1064), *Living High Off Nickels And Dimes* (Oblivion 005) and *Secrets From The Sun* (Inner City 1042), have yet to be reissued on CD. Wilson often sounds like a mixture of Eddie Jefferson and Leon Thomas, but also with his own personality and approach.

Nancy Wilson

b. February 20, 1937, Chillicothe, OH

Nancy Wilson was one of the great jazz singers of the early 1960s, recording a classic set with Cannonball Adderley and other excellent albums. She largely left jazz by the end of the decade but has occasionally returned since, particularly in her later years.

"Listening to Louis Jordan, Billy Eckstein, Jimmy Scott, LaVern Baker, Ruth Brown, Ella Fitzgerald and many others, along with the singing groups of the 1940s and '50s, really inspired my interest in music. I knew early on that I was going to be a singer. The family had gatherings frequently and I always sang. Then later I was in school functions and the choir at church. I really have had no formal training in singing."

She became a professional singer at the age of 15 and appeared on her own local television show, *Skyline Melody*, in addition to singing in clubs. After being in college briefly, in 1956 she dropped out to join a group led by saxophonist Rusty Bryant. Wilson met Cannonball Adderley that same year. In 1959 she moved to New York, worked as a receptionist during the day and quickly caught on in the club scene. Soon she was signed to Capitol, where her first single was her trademark song, "Guess Who I Saw Today."

Nancy Wilson did some of her best work for Capitol during 1960–62 when she recorded five albums including *Nancy Wilson/Cannonball Adderley* and *The Swingin's Mutual With George Shearing*. In 1963 she had a hit with "Tell Me The Truth," which was followed by an important live set the following year. "The live recording from the Coconut Grove was somewhat of a turning point in my career. I think it gave me a greater audience and created a life long association with a huge number of fans."

Nancy Wilson continued recording jazz-inspired dates for a few years, but by the late 1960s she was a national celebrity who had switched to light R&B, pop and cabaret. She worked as an actress, hosted the *Nancy Wilson Show* on television and remained a household name. In 1995 she began narrating National Public Radio's *Jazz Profiles* series. Her most recent recordings for the MCG Jazz have been more jazz-oriented than many of her sets during the previous 35 years, and her voice at 70 is still distinctive and expressive.

"My career has been simple. Tell the story as best you can. You have to like what you're doing. Keep it all simple and to the point."

Recommended CDs: *Something Wonderful* (Capitol 97073), the classic *Nancy Wilson And Cannonball Adderley* (Capitol 48455), which actually only has vocals on half of the selections (but those include "Never Will I Marry," "The Masquerade Is Over" and "Save Your Love For Me"), *The Swingin's Mutual With George Shearing* (Roulette 97935), *My Way* (Capitol 64641), *Yesterday's Love Songs/Today's Blues* (Blue Note 96265) and *Broadway: My Way* (Capitol 64638) show what a fine jazz singer Wilson could be, mixing together the influences of Dinah Washington and Jimmy Scott. *The Nancy Wilson Show* (Capitol 5015712) finds her moving away from jazz in 1964. Jumping ahead 40 years, *R.S.V.P. (Rare Songs, Very Personal)* (Manchester Craftsman Guild 1013) and *Turned To Blue* (MCG Jazz 1022) show that, when Nancy Wilson wants to sing jazz, she always sounds quite credible.

LPs to Search For: *Like In Love* (Capitol 1319) from 1959 is Nancy Wilson's very impressive debut album with Billy May's orchestra. *Hello Young Lovers* (Capitol 1767) from 1962 also deserves to be reissued.

Website: www.missnancywilson.com

Norma Winstone
(Norma Ann Short)
b. September 23, 1941, East London, England

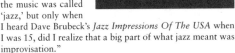

Norma Winstone has long been a very versatile singer. She has been one of the leading avant-garde vocalists in England but can also sing standards and get deep into ballads.

"When I was 12, I heard Ella Fitzgerald and knew that the music was called 'jazz,' but only when I heard Dave Brubeck's *Jazz Impressions Of The USA* when I was 15, did I realize that a big part of what jazz meant was improvisation."

She played piano from the age of seven and attended the Trinity College of Music for three years, starting when she was 11. Winstone started singing professionally at 17. In the 1960s she became involved with the jazz avant-garde, performing with pianists Michael Garrick, Mike Westbrook and John Taylor (whom she married in 1972), trumpeter Kenny Wheeler, saxophonist John Surman and composer Michael Gibbs. She appeared opposite Rahsaan Roland Kirk at Ronnie Scott's in 1966, which gave her a lot of attention. In 1971 she started recording as a leader.

Starting in the mid-1970s, she teamed with John Taylor and Kenny Wheeler as the group Azimuth, recording regularly for ECM. Winstone also developed into a skilled lyricist, with her best known writing being the words for Jimmy Rowles' "The Peacocks" (retitled "A Timeless Place"). She also had the opportunity to record an album with Rowles and collaborated on projects with Tony Coe, Lee Konitz, Fred Hersch and John Abercrombie in addition to singing with the Kenny Wheeler Big Band.

Whether it be recording a CD of Fred Hersch compositions (*Songs And Lullabies*), performing duos with John Taylor (*Like Song, Like Weather*), or leading a group called the "Steve Swallow Project," which features her lyrics to the bassist's originals, Norma Winstone remains both unpredictable and a vital force on the British jazz scene.

Recommended CDs: *Edge Of Time* (Disconforme 1962) was Norma Winstone's impressive debut, *Somewhere Called Home* (ECM 831107) is considered a vocal classic, and *Well Kept Secret* (Koch 7836) is her famous collaboration with Jimmy Rowles on standards. *Manhattan In The Rain* (Pinnacle 1001) also features her expertise with vintage songs. *Like Song, Like Weather* (Koch 7875), *Songs And Lullabies* (Sunnyside 1108), *Chamber Music* (Universal 986 596), *It's Later Than You Think* (Provocateur 2009) and *Amoroso...Only More So* (Trio 576) are five of her most stimulating recent sets. She can also be heard with Azimuth on such CDs as *Azimuth* (ECM 1099), *The Touchstone* (ECM 1130), *Depart* (ECM 1163), *Azimuth '85* (ECM 1298) and *How It Was Then* (ECM 1538).

Website: www.normawinstone.com

Pinky Winters
(Phyllis Wozniak)
b. February 1, 1931, Michigan City, IN

An excellent standards singer who had a long interruption in her career, Pinky Winters is a fixture in the Los Angeles jazz world.

She worked in a dance band while in high school. "I was playing piano with some guys at the local country club, and I got disgusted with my piano solos, which were not that thrilling. I asked if I could take a vocal chorus on 'Guilty.' The leader said 'OK' and the rest is history. It was fun to sing and I felt like I'd been set free. I later played piano with an all-girl band. I started getting little gigs around town (Michigan City, Indiana) on my own, and would learn tunes from the records I was collecting and play them by ear. I didn't go to school to learn technique or tunes. I just practiced on my own, and on my audiences."

After gaining plenty of experience performing in Michigan City, she moved to Denver, where she soon simplified her name to Pinky Winters. Inspired most by Sarah Vaughan, "I lucked out when I met the late Dick Grove, who became my musical mentor. He and I would meet and learn all the tunes in the fake book. I worked in Denver and in Aspen at various clubs, and probably honed my craft for the year and a half I lived there. I moved to Los Angeles in 1953, as did Dick Grove, and I continued to evolve. It never occurred to me to go to school to study singing."

During that early period, she recorded two albums, one apiece for the Vantage and Argo labels. Winters took a long hiatus to raise her two daughters, not singing for 13 years or returning to active performing until the late 1970s. At that time, she taught at the Dick Grove Music Workshops, teaching singers how to improvise. Working mostly in the Los Angeles area, Pinky Winters had Bob Florence as her accompanist during 1978–81 and then Lou Levy for 20 years (1981–2001) until his death. Most recently she has worked with Richard Rodney Bennett. Winters has recorded a few times since her return, displaying a basic and swinging delivery along with a warm voice.

"I hope to continue to work on both coasts, and also in between. My goal is to 'keep the music playing' and strive for excellence."

Recommended CDs: *Pinky* (Norma 5601) was the singer's recording debut. Pinky Winter's 1956 recording *Lonely One* (Universal 9119), featuring pianist Gerald Wiggins, has also been reissued. *The Happy Madness* (Verve 523263) followed 1985's *Let's Be Buddies* by nine years and *Lonely One* by 28. Other worthy CDs from her comeback years include *Shadow Of Your Smile* (3D 307), *Speak Low* (3D 1010), *World On A String* (3D 1503), *As Long As There Is Music* (Koch Jazz 69232) with the Metropole Orchestra, and *Rain Sometimes* (Paradigm 101).

LPs to Search For: *Let's Be Buddies* (Jacqueline 0116), Pinky Winters' "comeback" record from 1985, has not yet appeared on CD.

Website: www.pinkywinters.com

Diane Witherspoon

b. October 26, 1948, Minneapolis, MN

A singer who can really swing hard even at low volumes, Diane Witherspoon is the second cousin of Jimmy Witherspoon and the sister of Shirley Witherspoon, who sang with Duke Ellington in 1969.

"I sang solos and choral arrangements with the Zion Baptist Church choir as a child and performed as a teen with my twin brother Duane." However, it would be some time before she became a professional singer. Witherspoon attended college and worked for the phone company, not deciding to become a vocalist until 1976. Three years later she quit her day job. In 1988 she made her recording debut with Art Maxwell's Tonal Quality on *Latin Up*.

Since then she has led five CDs (including *You May Never Know*, a set of the songs of Cedar Walton with lyrics by John and Paula Hackett) and worked with Walton's trio, Calvin Keys, John Handy, Teddy Edwards, Bobby Hutcherson, Julius Hemphill, Billy Higgins, Eddie "Cleanhead" Vinson, Woody Shaw, Frank Morgan, Red Holloway Ghasem Batamuntu's Nova Ghost Sect-Tet and Rasul Siddik and the Now! Artet.

"My life ain't been no crystal stairs. I've raised three adult children, and overcome drugs and four husbands. My music is a great source of peace, harmony and gift giving, and now I finally get to focus on it full time."

Recommended CDs: Diane Witherspoon's five CDs, all of which are excellent, are *Thanking You* (Tonal Gravity Records 1003), *You May Never Know* (Koch 7879), *The Very Thought Of You* (Miss Soul 1001), *L.A. After Dark* (Summit 381) and *You Called Another's Name* (Docbil).

Website: www.dianewitherspoon.com

Jimmy Witherspoon

b. August 8, 1923, Gurdon, AR;
d. September 18, 1997, Los Angeles, CA

A smooth and sophisticated blues singer who regularly crossed over into jazz and back again, Jimmy Witherspoon was always a joy to hear.

Witherspoon first sang the blues in a rather unusual location, in Calcutta, India. He was stationed overseas during 1941–43 while serving with the Merchant Marines, and performed in India with pianist Teddy Weatherford. In Los Angeles, he sang regularly with Jay McShann during 1944–48, making his recording debut in 1945.

Going solo after 1948, Witherspoon had a big hit recording of "Ain't Nobody's Business If I Do" in 1949. Although Billie Holiday and, before her, Bessie Smith had already made the song famous, it became most closely identified with Witherspoon. He also had success with a string of recordings for Modern and Federal but, despite making a few excellent albums later in the decade, he was overshadowed by the rise of rock and roll, and had been struggling when he was booked at the 1959 Monterey Jazz Festival. However, Witherspoon's five-song set at Monterey, with an all-star band that included trumpeter Roy Eldridge, clarinetist Woody Herman, both Coleman Hawkins and Ben Webster on tenors and pianist Earl Hines, was a sensation and revitalized his career.

In the 1960s Witherspoon worked with Ben Webster, toured Europe with the Buck Clayton All-Stars, visited Japan in 1963 with Count Basie's orchestra, and stayed busy, recording frequently in a variety of settings. While some of his 1970s records tried to establish him in the modern R&B world and were quite commercial, he always remained a blues singer, as he showed on dates in which he utilized guitarist Robben Ford. Witherspoon recorded a particularly excellent set with the Savoy Sultans in 1980. After that time, bouts with throat cancer resulted in his voice being greatly weakened, but he never lost the spirit and continued performing up until near the end of his life.

Recommended CDs: *Urban Blues Singing Legend* (JSP 7778) is a four-CD set that definitively covers Jimmy Witherspoon's 1945–51 recordings, including his performances with Jay McShann. *Spoon So Easy* (Chess 93003) has music from 1954 to 1956 that either did not sell well or was unreleased at the time but does find Witherspoon in fine form. *Goin' To Kansas City Blues* (RCA 51639) reunites the singer with McShann in 1957 and *Singin' The Blues* (Blue Note 94108) has 'Spoon singing the blues in jazz settings during 1958. *The 'Spoon Concerts* (Fantasy 24701) has the legendary 1959 Monterey Jazz Festival set plus ten slightly later songs with Ben Webster and baritonist Gerry Mulligan. Witherspoon's 1963–66 recordings for Prestige include *Baby, Baby, Baby* (Original Blues Classics 527), *Evenin' Blues* (Original Blues Classics 511), *Blues Around The Clock* (Original Blues Classics 576), *Some Of My Best Friends Are The Blues* (Original Blues Classics 575) and *Blues For Easy Livers* (Original Blues Classics 585). *The Blues Is Now* (Verve 367502) teams him with organist Brother Jack McDuff. *Live* (Avenue Jazz 71262) is a good example of his work with Robben Ford in 1976. *With Panama Francis And The Savoy Sultans* (Muse 5288) is a hard-swinging and exciting effort. *Rockin' L.A.* (Fantasy 9660) features Jimmy Witherspoon sounding weaker but still full of spirit in 1988.

Andrea Wolper

b. January 16, Redwood City, CA

Andrea Wolper, who has a very attractive voice, always has a sense of adventure in her singing. "I guess I was just one of those kids who was always singing, making up songs, singing with records, putting on little shows. My mother had been a semi-professional singer as a child and young woman, and she and I sang together; our biggest family hit was 'Sonny Boy.' My parents' record collection exposed me to musicals, classic pop, and a little jazz, so I was absorbing a lot of the repertoire. When I left for college I 'liberated' a few of their records: *Getz/Gilberto*, *Come Fly With Me*, *Ella In Berlin* and Ella's *Cole Porter Songbook*. Somewhere along the way I discovered and fell head over heels with Anita O'Day and Dinah Washington."

She attended the University of California Davis, Berkeley and graduated from SUNY (Empire State College). Wolper worked as an actor, appearing in theater and musicals. But in time she chose singing jazz over acting. "It was like I was home at last, and though it isn't always easy, it's been so right."

In 1994, Andrea Wolper began singing jazz in New York City. She has since performed at most of the key clubs, married bassist Ken Filiano, worked with Art Lillard's Heavenly Big Band, been part of an improvising group with pianist Connie Crothers and Ken Filiano, and recorded two CDs as a leader. She is also a songwriter, lyricist, arranger, educator, writer of fiction and non-fiction, and a political activist.

"Music that involves improvising is a mirror and training ground for life. What's more 'in the moment' than making music? Making it new, present, and alive each time is the ideal, something to reach for."

Recommended CDs: Surprisingly, Andrea Wolper has only recorded two CDs as a leader thus far. Her self-titled debut came out in 1998, while 2005's *The Small Hours* (VarisOne Jazz 3101) features a diverse repertoire, close interplay with Filiano and guitarist Ron Affif, four of the singer's originals, and fresh versions of offbeat standards.

Website: www.andreawolper.com

Lizz Wright
(Elizabeth LaCharla Wright)
b. January 22, 1980, Hahira, GA

Lizz Wright is a young singer with the potential to go in almost any direction, whether it be jazz, gospel, R&B or pop.
"At the age of about six I began singing in church, opening for my dad's sermons. In kindergarten I sang 'Amazing Grace' each morning after the teacher read stories."
Born into a religious family, she remembers, "My first encounter with jazz was Marian McPartland's *Piano Jazz* show on NPR. I was in high school at the time, and I remember thinking that it sounded a lot like church music, except it wasn't about religion." Very active in school choirs, Lizz Wright's voice was noticed early on.

She studied voice at Georgia State and moved to Atlanta. "I left college and began working at Geico as an insurance agent in Macon, Georgia. It was a good job, and a comfortable living, but I was very unhappy. After thinking about nothing but music for those six months, I decided to go back to Atlanta and never stop pursuing music, no matter what happened or didn't happen." Wright joined the vocal quartet In the Spirit, was signed to the Verve label in 2002, and toured with Terence Blanchard's Billie Holiday Tribute.

Strongly influenced initially by Dianne Reeves and inspired by Abbey Lincoln and Nina Simone, Lizz Wright has become increasingly original even as her options include many types of music beyond jazz. She has a great deal of potential and hopefully some of it will be used in the jazz world.

Recommended CDs: *Salt* (Verve 314 589 933) from 2003 is an outstanding debut recording. *Dreaming Wide Awake* (Verve Forecast 314 988 1553) mixes together jazz, pop and gospel.

Website: www.lizzwright.net

Mama Yancey
(Estelle Harris)
b. January 1, 1896, Cairo, IL; d. April 19, 1986, Chicago, IL

The wife of the early boogie-woogie pianist Jimmy Yancey, Estelle "Mama" Yancey had an occasional solo career after his death and proved to be a fine blues singer.

Early in her life, she sang in church choirs and played guitar. She married Jimmy Yancey in 1917 and they lived happily in Chicago. She occasionally sang with her husband in clubs and parties. Mama Yancey made her recording debut with Jimmy Yancey in December 1943, singing "How Long Blues" and "Make Me A Pallet On The Floor." On his session from July 18, 1951, she took vocals on five numbers: "Santa Fe Blues," "Four O'Clock Blues," "Monkey Woman Blues" and remakes of "How Long Blues" and "Make Me A Pallet On The Floor."

Jimmy Yancey died two months later from a stroke. Mama Yancey made occasional appearances during the next two decades and recorded 3½ albums, collaborating with pianists Don Ewell, Little Brother Montgomery, Art Hodes and Erwin Helfer. She remained a symbol of vintage Chicago blues up until the time of her death at the age of 90 in 1986.

Recommended CDs: *Chicago Piano, Vol. 1* (Collectables 7702) has Jimmy Yancey's 1951 session that includes five Mama Yancey vocals. *Maybe I'll Cry* (Steeplechase 9001) features Mama Yancey in 1983 at the age of 87, performing many of the same songs she used to sing with her late husband. She is also featured on five songs on *Chicago: The Living Legends (South Side Blues)* (Original Blues Classics 508) from 1961.

LPs to Search For: *Mama Yancey With Don Ewell* (Winding Ball 102) is an excellent but rare album from 1952. *Mama Yancey Sings, Art Hodes Plays Blues* (Verve/Folkways 9015) from 1965 finds Yancey and Hodes inspiring each other.

Pat Yankee
(Patricia Yankee Rosenaur)
b. July 20, 1930, Lodi, CA

Long associated with Turk Murphy's San Francisco Jazz Band and trad jazz in general, Pat Yankee mixes together the influences of Bessie Smith and Sophie Tucker, both of whom she has portrayed in shows.

Pat Rosenaur (Yankee was her mother's maiden name, which she adopted as her stage name) was originally a tap dancer who at 13 was appearing in shows at the Golden Gate Theater. "I heard jazz for the first time there from Mel Tormé, who was singing with the Chico Marx Orchestra." At 15, she headed for New York, where she worked briefly with Milt Breton's band and then spent a year (1947–48) in Ted Lewis' variety show, singing and dancing. Among the other acts on the vaudeville-type shows were Bill "Bojangles" Robinson and Sophie Tucker. Yankee studied singing with the famous vocal coach Al Siegel. "When vaudeville went out and people were no longer tap dancing, I turned to singing."

Returning to San Francisco, she sang, wrote songs and played piano in nightclubs before spending 1952–56 working at Goman's Gay '90s nightclub as part of a revue. After that period, Yankee formed a singing act and in 1958 joined Turk Murphy's band for the first time, working with the trad group during 1958–62. When she left, she formed Pat Yankee and the Sinners, performing in Las Vegas, Reno and Lake Tahoe. She returned to Murphy for much of 1968–72 before spending nine years living in Madrid, Spain, performing in Europe. When she returned to San Francisco, Yankee rejoined Murphy again, this time staying until the trombonist's death in 1987.

Pat Yankee has had her own band (usually called her Gentlemen of Jazz) during the past 20 years. Her show *To Bessie, With Love* was presented many times during 1994–2002, with narration by Frank E. Reilly. In recent times she has put together a similar tribute to Sophie Tucker in addition to appearing at many classic jazz festivals.

"I've been in this business for 60 years and wouldn't do anything else. I am still going strong."

Recommended CDs: From recent times, *Pat Yankee Sings Saloon Songs* (GHB 470), *Salute To Saloon Songs, Vol. 2* (GHB 570), *Together At Last* (GHB 407), *Remembering Sophie Tucker* (GHB 483) and *Pat Yankee Salutes Louis Armstrong* (GHB 370) give listeners a strong sampling of Pat Yankee's current projects.

Website: www.patyankeejazz.com

Libby York

b. September 15, Chicago, IL

Libby York had several careers before she decided to concentrate on singing jazz. Her two CDs show that, artistically at least, she made a good move.

"My parents both played piano and sang. My dad occasionally sang with the big bands that came to play dances. I heard a lot of Sinatra records around the house and realize that that's where I learned so many tunes." She attended American University in Washington, D.C., earning a Bachelor of Arts in Political Science. York was one of three who founded the Back Porch Café in Rehoboth Beach, Delaware (which is still open after 30 years) and in the 1980s opened a restaurant in Key West, Florida, called the Rose Tattoo. She worked as the stage manager and ran the lights at the Tennessee Williams Fine Arts Center.

"I started singing with a reggae band called the Survivors in Key West, doing three-part harmony with two other singers behind the lead. I also began sitting in with Franklin Micare, a guitarist from New York who was playing at The Pier House. When he invited me to come sing with him on his gig in the Village, I got a sublet and moved to New York."

During her dozen years in New York, Libby York studied with Abbey Lincoln, frequently worked with pianist Renee Rosnes, and was the featured vocalist with Swing Street. "It was not until I really began playing gigs that I understood what being a professional singer means as a lifestyle. All those early years in New York were a wonderful school of hard knocks." Libby York moved back to Chicago in 1994, has sung at many local clubs since then and has recorded three CDs.

"I began singing professionally rather late in my life. I'm so grateful to have the opportunity to do this; it's my therapy. I'm glad to be able to use my voice to hopefully provide a little enjoyment for people in a world where peace seems to be a long sought after and elusive goal."

Recommended CDs: On 1999's *Blue Gardenia* (Southport 64) and *Sunday In New York* (Blujazz 3314), Libby York proves to be a subtle improviser who is respectful of lyrics and particularly sensitive on ballads. *Here With You* (Libby York Music 01374) features the singer with cornetist Warren Vache and guitarist Howard Alden, blending in very well with the swinging musicians and excelling on three vocal-guitar duets with Russell Malone.

Website: www.libbyyork.com

Nora York

b. August 13, 1956, Chicago, IL

An intriguing jazz singer and composer, Nora York has been involved in multi-media presentations and in music that crosses many genres while still retaining her roots in creative jazz.

"I started singing when, as a junior in college, I took a year off for a long trip through Southeast Asia and India and happened upon a job singing in a bar in Bangkok. I liked that pretty well, so upon my return when I moved to New York, I started to study voice. I came to music via the 1980s visual art scene. I began my career on New York City's Lower East Side performance art circuit and moved to jazz performance through the musicians I was working with. I started listening to the horn players, with Ben Webster and John Coltrane being my favorites."

Nora York was always interested in stretching beyond conventional singing and composing. In 1988 she began performing regularly at the Knitting Factory in New York and she started staging compositional theatrical events at Joe's Pub. She collaborated on compositions with Maria Schneider on a regular basis during 1992–94. She teaches "Creative Voice" at NYU, creates performances for visual art spaces, and among her eclectic works are the political *Power/Play* and *I Dreamed I Saw: The Music Of Jimi Hendrix And Stephen Foster*.

Recommended CDs: *To Dream The World* (Evidence 22126) features Nora York as a haunting vocalist on fresh versions of standards and offbeat originals. She collaborated with Maria Schneider for *Alchemy* (Artist Share). *What I Want* (215 Records 2035) is no less intriguing, being very modern folk music that leaves space for improvising.

Website: www.norayork.com

Monica Zetterlund

(Eva Monica Nilsson)
b. September 20, 1937, Hagford, Sweden;
d. May 12, 2005, Stockholm, Sweden

A Swedish actress with a cool-toned, fragile and haunting voice, Monica Zetterlund is most famous in the jazz world for recording with Bill Evans.

She discovered jazz by hearing American jazz singers on the radio, being attracted to the music even though she did not yet know English, and through

Monica Zetterlund

her father who was a musician. She began her career by singing in her father's band and then became quite popular in Sweden due to her voice and her willingness to sing in Swedish in addition to English.

Zetterlund began recording albums in 1958 (there would be over 20 in all), and her tour of the United States in 1960 went well, although her only New York recording with trumpeter Thad Jones and tenor-saxophonist Zoot Sims was not released until 1996. She mostly recorded with Swedish musicians throughout her life, but in 1964 she made the album *Waltz For Debby* with the Bill Evans Trio. She was also proud of recording with the Thad Jones/Mel Lewis Orchestra.

Monica Zetterlund was a fixture in Sweden in films, television series and plays while continuing her career as a singer. She had opportunities to appear on stage with Louis Armstrong, Stan Getz and Quincy Jones, along with the top Swedish players. Her career was cut short in 1999 when she had to retire due to scoliosis, a disease that made it difficult to move. She died in a fire in her apartment in 2005.

Recommended CDs: Virtually all of Monica Zetterlund's recordings are only available as imports, including her Bill Evans set. *The Lost Tapes At Bell Sound Studios NYC* (RCA 63322) is the singer's meeting with Thad Jones and Zoot Sims in 1960. It seems bizarre that 1964's *Waltz For Debby* (Universal 5102682) with the Bill Evans Trio has not been put out in the United States (other than part of an Evans 16-CD set), for Zetterlund's voice fits perfectly with the pianist. *For Lester And Billie*, also known as *Holiday For Monica* (Phontastic 7562), is a 1983 tribute to Billie Holiday and Lester Young.

LPs to Search For: *Spring Is Here* (Dragon 171) features Monica Zetterlund at the beginning of her career on various selections from 1958–60. *It Only Happens Every Time* (Inner City 1082) is Zetterlund's 1977 meeting with the Thad Jones/Mel Lewis Orchestra.

198 OTHER JAZZ SINGERS OF TODAY

Since there have been more than 521 jazz singers in the world and there are quite a few that almost made that list, this section mentions 198 others who are currently active and are worth knowing about, from Helen Abbey to Mr. Z.

British singer **Helen Abbey** started off singing with the Swing Sisters and the Seafood Mamas. She took many years off to raise three children and, after her return to the scene, in 2003 recorded *Simply Me* (Cardinal 514), an effective set on which she covers a variety of familiar standards.

Based in Boston and a fixture on the local scene, veteran **Patricia Adams** traded a long-time career in human resources to work full-time as a singer. She often performs familiar material that is given unpredictable and unusual arrangements. She has recorded several CDs, including the self-produced *Out Of This World*.

From Northern California, **Barbara Adamson** did not decide to start seriously singing jazz until her late 30s, but her debut recording, *Now Is The Time* (Stet 398277) from 1998, is an excellent effort featuring her invigorating a set of standards. It makes one impatient for her long overdue encore.

An avant-garde singer whose free yet often pompous delivery is an acquired taste, the Swiss-born **Irene Aebi** was the wife of the late soprano-saxophonist Steve Lacy. Playing free-form violin and cello in addition to her singing, Aebi primarily recorded on some of Lacy's projects (including some in which she interpreted poetry), although she also had dates with Derek Bailey and other advanced improvisers.

Canada's **John Alcorn** is an actor, a crooner and a jazz-inspired cabaret singer who specializes in the great American songbook. Quite popular in Toronto, his CD *Quiet Night* (JA 002) is a set of Rodgers and Hart songs that includes the rediscovery of the obscure title cut.

A sweet-voiced singer from New York who has the chance-taking spirit of a jazz instrumentalist, **Robin Aleman** has a very impressive self-produced debut recording, *Tonight*. She sings "Tea For Two" in 7/4 time, "Someday My Prince Will Come" in 5/4, revives "Azure" and "Nobody's Heart," and is touching on "In The Wee Small Hours Of The Morning." Aleman has a great future.

Vernelle Anders had spent years performing in nightclubs and supper clubs all throughout the West Coast, Alaska and Hawaii when in 1996 she recorded *At Last* (Music In The Vines 286), a CD not released until 2002. The jazz standards (with a few R&B tunes such as "Respect" included) are all familiar, but Anders' spirited delivery and powerful voice make one wonder why she is a relative unknown in the jazz world.

A veteran singer and educator with an interesting history, **Laurie Antonioli** is from San Francisco. She toured Europe with altoist-singer Pony Poindexter, vocalizing the music of Charlie Parker and Dizzy Gillespie. Antonioli recorded a duet album with George Cables, wrote lyrics to several Joe Henderson songs, worked in the advertising industry in the 1990s, recorded with Richie Beirach, spent 2002 to 2006 as the professor of the vocal jazz department at the University of Music and Dramatic Arts in Graz, Australia, and wrote lyrics to songs by pianist Fritz Pauer, which they performed in concerts. She is currently the Chair of the Vocal Jazz Studies program at the Jazz School in Berkeley. Get her CD with Beirach, *The Duo Session* (Nabel 4705).

Leonisa Ardizzone originally studied opera and learned piano, violin, oboe, clarinet, flute and saxophone. Despite that, her musical career has often taken a backseat to her teaching vocation, which has included being executive director of the Salvadori Center, an organization that teaches architecture, engineering and urban planning. In 2007 she released her debut recording, *Afraid Of The Heights* (Ardijenn 24249), an often dizzying and mostly joyful program of jazz standards with guitarist Chris Jennings in a pianoless quartet. The singer, who has a pleasing voice, definitely sounds as if she is having fun.

Helene Attia is an eclectic singer and songwriter based in Northern California who has a real feeling for French songs and for swinging jazz. She sings in English, French, Italian, Spanish and Portuguese on *The Eyes Of Love* (HA 3731), displaying sensuality, a strong wit and such versatility that she is beyond category, an asset in an over-categorized world.

Margret Avery, who mostly performs in New York, is both emotional and laid-back on *A Place That's Make Believe* (Queenmae). She often emphasizes long notes on her renditions of ballads, contributes five original songs that have insightful lyrics and shows versatility by including a rambunctious "Wild Women Don't Get The Blues."

Born in New Orleans and a lover and interpreter of early jazz, **Vernel Bagneris** wrote, directed and starred in the hit shows *One Mo' Time*, *Further Mo'*, *Staggerlee* and *Jelly Roll*. He is best known in the jazz world as a narrator and singer with Jim Cullum's famed radio series *Riverwalk, Live From The Landing*.

Andrea Baker, a talented bop singer and educator based in Los Angeles, is the wife of tenor-saxophonist Steve Wilkerson. She has recorded several swinging CDs, of which *Table For One* (Dane 0003) is an excellent example of her musical talents.

Although her day job for decades was as a public school teacher, **Margie Baker** is also a popular singer in the San Francisco Bay area, one who always shows her audience a good time. The two-CD live set *Margie Baker And Friends* (CAP 994) features her at the age of 68, still very much in her musical prime.

Amy Banks was born in Minnesota but lives and works in Pennsylvania. While she is an actress and works as a host and commentator on television, she also sings in clubs as often as possible. She has recorded three CDs: a religious set, a Christmas collection and her first jazz recording, *When The Sun Comes Out* (AB 797276), a soulful and pleasing effort that also features pianist Allen Farnham and tenor-saxophonist Tim Warfield.

Lisa Bell, based in Colorado, has worked extensively in the studios, sung background vocals for Bobby McFerrin, worked in musical theater and performed jazz. While her first CD *Dare To Be* (Hapi Skratch 75074) was a typical first start, singing standards, she wrote the majority of the selections on *It's All About Love* (Hapi Skratch 75244). While a bit pop and crossover-oriented in spots, *It's All About Love* displays some promising originality.

A glamorous performer, **Chris Bennett** has been involved in many areas of the music industry during her career, including founding a dance studio while a teenager, performing pop music in shows, songwriting (her originals have been recorded by the Manhattan Transfer and Tina Turner among others), recording a hit disco album in 1978, collaborating as a writer

Steve Blackwood

with Keb' Mo', working in the "smooth jazz" field and, most recently, recording a fine set of show tunes and swing-oriented jazz, *Bennett On Broadway* (Rhombus 7060).

Steve Blackwood, an actor on the soap opera *Days Of Our Lives* since 1997, also enjoys singing in the middle-of-the-road Sinatra/Tony Bennett/Mel Tormé genre. He does a fine job with warhorses on his CDs, which include *Mood Swings* (Rhombus 8008).

A top pop performer in Quebec, **Johanne Blouin** also loves jazz and on a few rare occasions has collaborated with major jazz musicians. *Everything Must Change* (Justin Time 141) finds her holding her own with Bobby Watson, Terrell Stafford and John Hicks, scatting à la Ella and showing that she could be a leading contender in jazz if she had the desire.

Erin Bode has a nice, sweet and clear voice along with an eclectic repertoire that ranges from jazz to contemporary pop, R&B and bluegrass. Her two releases, *Don't Take Your Time* (Max Jazz 118) and particularly *Over And Over* (Max Jazz 121), stretch beyond jazz into other areas that interest her, but she can sing jazz when she wants to.

Melody Breyer-Grell has been singing in New York for quite a few years in addition to being the musical director of the Chez Suzette and, most recently, the Triad. *The Right Time* (Blujazz 3320) shows that, after observing many other singers, she has found her own original conception to performing standards. *Fascinatin' Rhythms* (Rhombus 7074) has her inventive and inspired versions of Gershwin tunes.

Born in Maine and based in the San Francisco Bay area, **Vicki Burns** has a quiet voice and an understated delivery that wins one over. *Siren Song* (Merrymaid 001) has her interpretations of mostly familiar standards plus her title cut and her words to Charlie Haden's "Here's Looking At You."

Terry Cade put out an adventurous and swinging set of standards in 1999, *Sometimes I'm Happy* (Lost Chart 1024). Not much has been heard from her outside of her native Canada in recent times, but she still has strong potential.

Born in Scotland, well versed in several genres of music and a resident of Southern California since the early 1990s, **Roger Cairns** has a charming and versatile style. He is both a crooner and a subtle improviser, which he shows on *A Scot In L.A.* (RC 5858) as he revives one superior obscurity after another.

Brenda Carol sang folk and rock music before settling on jazz. An important figure in Toronto as a singer and educator, she and her husband, pianist Stephen Gardner, co-founded the Darwyn label, resulting in *Brenda Carol* (Darwyn 7208) and *Live At Hot House Café* (Darwyn 10587), both of which feature her adventurous and sensitive singing, coming up with fresh statements on standards.

Amanda Carr has sung with the Artie Shaw, Harry James and Glenn Miller ghost bands, paid tribute to Peggy Lee while with the Everett Longstreth Orchestra, and worked in the studios of Boston. *Soon* (OMS 0920) features her straightforward interpretations of standards, displaying a clear voice and a simple delivery.

Lori Carsillo, who studied in San Francisco with both Kitty Margolis and Madeline Eastman, is in excellent form on *Cole Porter...Old Love, New Love, True Love* (Tru Blu Lu), singing ten Cole Porter songs with the backing of a pianoless trio.

April Caspari, who helps to keep jazz alive in Nashville, singing three nights a week at the Volare Restaurant in the Opryland Hotel, released a fine sampling of her work. *A Snapshot*, which was put out privately, features her displaying sensitivity and subtle swing on nine standards with a local rhythm section.

Based in Atlanta, **Nicole Chillemi** has a sweet-toned voice and a subtle delivery along with a wide-ranging repertoire ranging from swing standards to works by Tom Waits and

Nick Drake. Her second CD, *Mention Of You* (RCAM Records), is filled with expressive and soulful singing that also manages to be haunting.

Born in the Philippines and now based in Los Angeles, **Charmaine Clamor** calls her mixture of jazz and influences from her homeland "jazzipino." Her second CD, *Flippin' Out* (Free Ham 0705), includes both Filipino folk music and jazz standards, sometimes combining the two in the same piece. Her voice sounds lovely in all contexts.

A soulful and powerful singer from New Orleans who excels at blues, gospel and standards, **Thais Clark** sings swing tunes and blues on *Old Feeling* (GHB 441) and holds her own with a top trad band on *With Fessor's Funky New Orleanians* (Music Mecca 2011-2).

Dini Clarke, long a well-respected and influential vocal coach and teacher in the Los Angeles area, is also an entertaining and very musical singer-pianist. Though he has not recorded often enough, *Dini Clarke Sings Duke Ellington* (Dibo Music) offers strong examples of his talents.

A fine singer from Philadelphia who has a husky and expressive voice, **Suzanne Cloud** is also a talented songwriter. *Looking Back* (Dreambox Media 1030) is highlighted by three of her originals and a particularly rewarding version of "Never Never Land."

When **Holly Cole** first emerged, she seemed capable of great things in jazz, performing ironic and inventive versions of standards and offbeat material. However, the Canadian singer has mostly been involved in rock and pop music since the mid-1990s. *The Holly Cole Collection Vol. 1* (Magada 81040) is a good cross section of her career thus far.

Carri Coltrane (who is not related to John Coltrane but adopted his last name due to her admiration for his music) recorded three interesting CDs in the late 1990s. *Flamenco Sketches* (Numoon 3464) features her effectively singing Eugene McDaniels' lyrics to such songs as "Stolen Moments," "Giant Steps," "E.S.P." and the title cut.

Working in voiceover for over two decades apparently helped keep **Lainie Cooke** from being discovered as a talented jazz singer. On *It's Always You* (Harlemwood 0108), only her second jazz CD, she comes up with fresh ideas on standards and obscurities alike while often caressing the lyrics.

Joyce Cooling's roots are in jazz, and she definitely has the talent but has chosen to spend her career in the "smooth" field. *Playing It Cool* (Heads Up 3040) is typical of her pleasing but lightweight easy-listening music.

A fine singer-pianist influenced by Shirley Horn, **Gloria Cooper** mostly performs superior obscurities written by jazz musicians in recent times on *Dedicated To You* (Origin 82450). She teaches at Long Island University in Brooklyn.

Born in Canada and now based in New York, **Sheila Cooper** is a promising young performer, both a warm singer and a skillful alto-saxophonist. *While The World Is In Slumber* (Panorama), her second release, is a good example of where she was in 2003, giving her own spin to standards.

Loretta Cormier from San Antonio switched her career from medical editor at Johns Hopkins to jazz singer. Musically at least, the move makes sense, as can be heard on *Under A Blanket Of Blue* (LC Disc 0202), a collection of standards, some of which are little known.

A veteran singer, **Cynthia Crane** has been an important part of the New York music scene for quite a few years, performing jazz and cabaret in a wide variety of nightclubs. She also co-founded *The Impossible Ragtime Theater*, producing over 100 plays. Of her five recordings, *Smoky Bar Songs For The No-Smoking Section* (Lookout 9302) is a fine sampling of her interpretations of the type of songs that used to be frequently heard by intoxicated and smoking customers.

The daughter of Cleo Laine and saxophonist John Dankworth, **Jacqui Dankworth** has worked as an actress and has sung a variety of music. *Detour Ahead* (Candid 79796) is a solid jazz-oriented set.

Born in Buenos Aires to a French-Romanian Jewish family, **Ondine Darcyl**, who is also a lawyer in New York and a visual artist, primarily sings Brazilian jazz. Her self-titled debut from 2000 on her own Darcyl Records label deserves an encore.

The singer with the Count Basie Orchestra since 2000, veteran **Jamie Davis** has just the right sound for the group. He is featured on his own CD, *It's A Good Thing* (Unity 2517), singing standards, some of which are from the Basie songbook.

After years of singing rock, folk and pop, in the 1990s **E. J. Decker** gradually switched to jazz, where his deep baritone voice (a bit reminiscent of Billy Eckstine and Arthur Prysock) is most at home. He sings melodies fairly straight but with warmth, as displayed on *While The City Sleeps* (Candela 7913).

A promising young singer based in New York, **Sarah DeLeo** sounds like a new singer from the 1950s, being creative within the vintage genre. *The Nearness Of You* (Sweet Sassy Music 1001) is her memorable debut, displaying lots of potential for the future.

Angela DeNiro, who usually sings in groups that include her husband, saxophonist Ron Aprea, is a New York-based bop vocalist who scats well. *My Shining Hour* (CAP 992) features standards plus Aprea originals paying tribute to Phil Woods and Louis Armstrong.

Donna Deussen, who is heard in fine form on 2003's *High Wire* (DD 8212), is most active in Los Angeles and Arizona as both a singer and an educator. Her vocals are cheerful, she has a flexible voice, and she enjoys updating standards with contemporary arrangements while still keeping the flavor of the original song. She is long overdue to record again.

Camille DeVore recorded her debut, *Easy To Love* (Clarion 562), under her maiden name of Camille Schmidt. She has a lovely voice, a real feel for standards, and is one of the top jazz singers based in Omaha, Nebraska.

Darby Dizard has an enthusiastic style, as can be heard on *Down For You* (One Soul 014). Her voice, which used to sing opera, is strong. She has a feeling for jazz, although she sometimes is so full of spirit that she rushes through the lyrics. If she can calm down a bit, she is capable of memorable music.

Sasha Dobson, the daughter of the late pianist Smith Dobson and singer Gail Dobson, is at the crossroads of her career. Her recent release *The Darkling Thrush* (Smalls 0005) is a delightful jazz set that teams her attractive voice with the Chris Byars Octet, but it was actually recorded during 2001–2002. At the 2006 Monterey Jazz Festival, Dobson's performance was less jazz-oriented than Norah Jones' recordings, and her voice sounded run-of-the-mill on consistently dull pop material, so perhaps, at least for now, she is lost to jazz.

A classically trained soprano, a studio singer and an educator, **Julia Dollison** has sung with Maria Schneider's orchestra, no mean feat. Her debut, *Observatory* (JD), which features guitarist Ben Monder in a pianoless trio, is a strong start to her career.

One of France's better jazz singers, **Anne Ducros** has won many prizes in Europe since she began singing jazz in 1986. Out of her five CDs, *Piano Piano* (Dreyfus 36674) is most impressive, featuring her performing standards while accompanied on various selections by pianists Chick Corea, Jacky Terrasson, Enrico Pieranunzi and Rene Urtreger.

Beth Duncan is well known in the Sacramento area for her broadcast journalism work, which includes many years as a news anchor. But earlier in her life she was a singer, and in recent times she has returned to music. Her debut CD, *Orange*

Colored Sky, is filled with powerful singing, inventive arrangements, fresh and often-surprising renditions of high-quality standards and lots of joyful moments.

Bonnie Eisele, the wife of drummer Les DeMerle, is a well-rounded singer who is able to easily handle the demands of DeMerle's fast-moving show, singing ballads, uptempo pieces, Brazilian numbers and vocal duets with her husband. *Cookin' At The Corner Vol. 1* (Origin 82471) and *Vol. 2* (Origin 82491) feature her adding class to the proceedings.

While **Jan Eisen** has often been involved in booking talent and performing in cabaret and non-jazz settings, on *Summer Me, Winter Me* (One Take Productions 74022), she shows that she is a superior jazz singer. The fast-paced program features Ms. Eisen with a pianoless rhythm section as she goes through one song after another, ranging from the obscure "Papa Can You Hear Me" and the Perez Prado hit "Cherry Pink And Apple Blossom White" (when has that ever been sung?) to swing standards that are given Brazilian rhythms.

A singer from Argentina who is now based in Los Angeles, **Taira Elias** has a real feel for both swinging jazz songs and tangos. Her impressive debut, *Living In Dreams* (Winged Being Productions), features her with both the Tom Garvin Trio and a Latin jazz ensemble, excelling in both formats.

Elin (who was born Kathleen Celia Elin Melgerejo) is a Swedish singer who learned Portuguese and sings Brazilian jazz. On *Lazy Afternoon* (Blue Toucan 1805), she proves to be a superior vocalist on bossa novas, a few standards and her own originals. Much more will certainly be heard from her in the near future.

Yve Evans, a Los Angeles-based singer-pianist, is well known for her saucy wit, crazy song medleys and musical talents. She should really be recorded by a larger label, but *4 Jazz C Me* (Noteworthy 30274) gives listeners a solid example of her music and humor.

A highly rated cabaret singer in New York and an actress, **Barbara Fasano** (who regularly teams up with pianist Eric Comstock) can sing jazz when she stretches herself. Her Harold Arlen CD, *Written In The Stars* (Human Child 825), is a strong example of her musical talents.

Normally a trombonist, **Eric Felten** also engages in occasional vocal projects. *Eric Felten Meets The Dek-Tette* (V.S.O.P. 113) pays tribute to the Mel Tormé/Marty Paich recordings of the 1950s, including some alumni (such as Jack Sheldon and altoist Herb Geller) but with new arrangements. Felten does not imitate Tormé and does a fine job.

Rachelle Ferrell, who has a tremendous voice and a huge range, has picked up a large audience through the years. Although she has sometimes sung jazz standards and worked with the likes of Dizzy Gillespie, George Benson, Wayne Shorter and Terence Blanchard, most of her work has been on the pop side of jazz or completely distant in R&B. Her over-the-top vocals tend to lack much subtlety, though her technique is admirable. *Live At Montreux* (Blue Note 38564) features her in jazz-oriented settings.

Ruth Naomi Floyd is unusual in that she is a deeply religious jazz singer who reflects both her faith and her love of advanced jazz in her music, without compromising either. Her voice is superior, she is a strong jazz improviser, and the words she sings deal with her faith but are far from simplistic. *Root To The Fruit* (Contour 40930), her fifth release, is a strong example of her unique music.

One of Colorado's best jazz singers, **Wendy Fopeano** on *Raining On The Roses* (Outside Shore Music 1003) sings her lyrics to several songs (including David Murray's "Morning Song" and her improvised words to Kenny Barron's "Sunshower"). She stretches herself on standards and Brazilian material, making one wonder why she is not nationally famous.

Kimberly Ford

A joyful singer from Santa Barbara who is passionately interested in both jazz and the ocean (she has long been involved in underwater filmmaking), **Kimberly Ford** combines them both quite effectively on her self-produced *Songs In The Key Of Sea*. She performs songs having to do with the sea (such as "How Deep Is The Ocean," "Wave" and "Little Boat") in an attractive voice while joined by a pianoless trio. Her release also includes a short underwater film as a DVD.

Kari Gaffney has a deep sultry voice, swings and is willing to take chances in her improvising. In recent times she has also become quite important in the jazz publicity field. *Satin Doll* (Verbatim 121202), with guitarist-bassist Jeff Williams and Hal Melia on reeds, is an excellent example of her musical talents.

Karen Gallinger works in Orange County as a singer, actress, educator, producer, writer and even a comedian. Most notable are her abilities as a lyricist, having written words to many of Bill Evans' songs, some of which she performs on *Remembering Bill Evans* (Sea Breeze 3041). She is an impressive singer.

Tony Gallo is a fine vocalist from Massachusetts. While his debut CD, *Something To Say* (TG 1297), emphasizes his interpretations of jazz standards, in recent years he has branched out into performing newer material, combining together jazz with R&B, soul, folk and pop, all of it sung with the passion of a blues singer.

Sara Gazarek is a sure bet to have an important career as a singer, for her voice is strong and flexible, and she has a winning style. But whether she will be involved in jazz is more debatable. Her second CD, *Return To You* (Native Language 967), casts her as a slightly jazzy singer/songwriter, singing songs by the likes of Paul McCartney, Leonard Cohen and Billy Joel without much improvising.

Faith Gibson, born in the United States, is making a strong impression on the European jazz scene after a late start. She spent years working in Bonn, Germany, as a freelance translator until she gathered her courage and performed as a singer at her 40th birthday party. After working with a swing vocal trio for a time, she began her solo career, recording *You Don't Know Me* (Juke Joint 016) and displaying versatility, wit and subtle creativity on offbeat standards and her own "Alley Cat Love Song."

One of Cleveland's top jazz singers, **Debbie Gifford** made a strong impression with her self-produced CD, *So Many Songs About Love*, and in her concerts with the Cleveland Jazz Orchestra. In recent years she has been traveling not only in the United States but also in Italy, Spain and France, spreading beyond standards to modern originals that will be featured in her upcoming double-CD, *Open Airs*, recorded in France. She has a straightforward approach to her interpretations that is quite winning.

A powerful bluish singer based in Washington, D.C. who also sings gospel music, **Janine Gilbert-Carter** on *A Song For You* (Jazz Karma 925) puts plenty of feeling into such standards as "There Is No Greater Love," "Please Send Me Someone To Love" and "Someone Else Is Steppin' In."

One of the top jazz singers performing regularly in Chicago (including each Thursday night at the Green Mill with the Swing Shift Orchestra) after a four-year run in New York, **Kimberly Gordon** can be both subtle and sassy. *Melancholy Serenade* (The Sirens 5009) offers an excellent overview of her singing talents.

A superior crooner from Scotland who performs often in England and Europe, **Todd Gordon** considers Frank Sinatra and Ella Fitzgerald to be his main inspirations, although he goes out of his way not merely to imitate the past. *Ballads*

From The Midnight Hotel (TG 10653) features him making vintage standards sound fresh and new.

Kathleen Grace is a promising young singer based in Los Angeles who often teams up with guitarist Perry Smith. On *Songbird* (Monsoon), her eclectic program includes everything from "Red Sails In The Sunset" and "Sunrise Sunset" to her lyrics to Pat Metheny's "I Return To You" and two originals.

It is not every singer who could record a duet album with the remarkable pianist Jessica Williams and not be completely overshadowed. **Carolyn Graye**, a veteran performer from the Pacific Northwest, holds her own on *Songs* (OA2 22006), updating standards while inspired by the pianist's sympathetic accompaniment.

Della Griffin, a professional singer since she turned 20 in 1943, was the leader of the pioneering all-female R&B group the Enchanters (later renamed the Dell-Tones) in the 1950s, took the '60s off due to her marriage and has made a comeback since then. Influenced by Billie Holiday, Etta Jones and Ernestine Anderson, Griffin has recorded three worthy jazz sets for High Note and Savant, including *The Very Thought Of You* (Savant 2001).

A powerful singer with a warm sound on ballads and a very eccentric scatting style, **Miles Griffith** often uses his voice percussively. He has recorded surprisingly little for one who is based in New York. *Spiritual Freedom* (Griffith 1) shows what he can do.

A talented standards singer from Sweden, **Rigmor Gustafsson** made a strong impression while living in New York during 1993–96. Since then she has moved back to Stockholm, recorded several albums for ACT, become particularly popular in Germany and toured much of the world. She has used Randy Brecker and Fred Hersch in her groups, although she usually leads a Swedish combo. *Ballad Collection* (Prophone 080) is an excellent place to start in exploring her recordings.

A veteran singer who has performed jazz, blues, Brazilian music and R&B, **Mercedes Hall** recorded her finest album recently, *Pure Emotion* (West End Jazz 0102). The arrangements are adventurous ("Ghost Of A Chance" alternates between three tempos), and she both displays a warm voice and an inventive improvising style.

A significant songwriter and performer whose career has often stretched far beyond jazz, **Marilyn Harris** is a witty writer and an enjoyable singer-pianist. *Round Trip* (Wrightwood 1569), which matches her with some of the top musicians in Los Angeles, is her most jazz-oriented recording so far.

Jennifer Hart is a versatile singer from Orange County, California, whose music is jazz-based (she scats well too) but includes a wide repertoire that extends to pop and even country. The self-produced *Close To My Heart* is her strongest recording thus far. In recent times she has been teaming up regularly with pianist-arranger Llew Matthews.

A Canadian singer and actress associated with Jeff Healy's Jazz Wizards, **Terra Hazelton** has a growl in her voice and a feeling for 1920s and '30s jazz, as displayed on *Anybody's Baby* (Healeyophonic).

Bruce Henry, who was born in Mississippi and lives in Minnesota, is an eclectic singer whose music on the consistently intriguing *Connections* (Bahlove 1048) ranges from "Equinox" and a vocalized version of Freddie Hubbard's "Red Clay" to "House Of The Rising Sun" and "The Sound Of Music." His deep voice and flexible style make one quickly realize that he can definitely sing.

After success as a writer in Nashville (two of her songs were recorded by Garth Brooks) and as a singer in a wide variety of settings, **Benita Hill** has emerged as one of the country music town's top jazz singers. Her self-produced *I'll See You In My Song* has a few well-known pieces plus some of her originals that sound like vintage swing pieces.

Christine Hitt's *You'd Be So Nice To Come Home To* (Max Jazz 107) from 1999 reminded those in the Midwest who think of her as a pianist and an important educator that she is a fine singer too.

Johnny Holiday showed potential in the 1950s as a ballad and jazz singer, but his career did not go anywhere, and he worked out of music for decades. In 1998 when he was 79, he was given a second chance, and this time he gained some attention. *Johnny Holiday Sings* (Contemporary 14091) has 13 selections from 1998 and 8 from 1954. Despite the passing of 44 years, it is surprising just how good Holiday sounds in both time periods.

A singer with great potential from San Francisco, **Sony Holland** has a voice that seems to always perfectly fit the standards that she interprets. She is able to make familiar tunes sound fresh through her phrasing and feeling. *Out Of This World* (Van Ness 003) was one of the happier jazz vocal releases of 2006. And its follow-up swing, *Bossas, Ballads & Blues* (Van Ness 004) is also filled with exciting singing.

A fine cabaret singer who has been exploring jazz in recent times, **Stevie Holland** on *More Than Words Can Say* (150 Music 07) displays a warm voice and a lyrical style on standards and originals. Joined by a string orchestra, she mostly sticks close to the melodies but will hopefully cut loose in the future.

Ellen Honert may have been born in the Netherlands and be currently based in San Francisco, but her debut CD, *Breath Of The Soul* (Mill Valley), is high-quality Brazilian jazz. She has a real feeling for the music and straddles the boundary line between jazz and middle-of-the-road pop, all with soothing Brazilian rhythms.

The wife of Bob Wilber (an important clarinetist and soprano-saxophonist), **Joanna "Pug" Horton** has occasionally appeared on his records during the past 30 years. *Don't Go Away* (Audiophile 212) is one of the few CDs under her own name. She does not improvise much but swings well.

It is difficult to believe that **Frank Jackson** was 78 when he recorded *New York After Dark* (Kasis 003) in 2003, for his voice could pass for 20 years younger. Based in San Francisco for a half-century, he made it through the lean years by playing piano, but clearly his voice needed to be heard, and he particularly excels on ballads.

A highly expressive and soulful singer based in San Francisco, **Frankye Kelly** spent six months in 2006 performing jazz in Shanghai, China. *Frankye Kelly Sings Songs For My Father*, her third self-produced CD, finds her excelling on a variety of jazz standards that range from "Red Sails In The Sunset" to Abbey Lincoln's "Throw It Away."

The Los Angeles-based **Julie Kelly** gained her initial attention back in 1985 for recording a memorable rendition of "All My Tomorrows" (featuring Bobby Ojeda's brilliant trumpet solo) that helped make the song a standard. Her most recent recording, 2006's *Everything I Love* (Chase Music Group 8075), is her most rewarding set in years.

A hard-swinging veteran jazz singer who puts a lot of personality into her interpretations of standards, **Nancy Kelly** is in top form on the recent *Born To Swing* (Amherst 4422).

A promising swing singer from Toronto, **Maureen Kennedy** on *This Is Always* (Baldwin Street Music 210) delights in reviving such obscurities as "After You," "Humpty Dumpty Heart" and "Winter Of My Discontent."

Based in Philadelphia and blessed with a large voice, **Denise King** mixes together jazz with the power of soul and gospel.

Fever (R.E.D.D. King) features her take on a variety of mostly familiar standards; she mostly finds something fresh to say on each song.

Kathleen Kolman was born in Butte, Montana, and really began exploring jazz after moving to New Hampshire. Her 1999 debut, *The Dreamer* (Walkin' Foot 99001), finds her exploring some lesser-known standards (including an emotional "As Long As He Needs Me" and the swing era tune "You Hit The Spot") along with a few familiar standbys. She has a passionate voice and a versatile style.

While **Kathy Kosins**' background is in R&B from her native Detroit, her solo records have all been strictly jazz. On *Vintage* (Mahogany 54688) she really digs into the past, reviving such unlikely items as King Pleasure's "Tomorrow Is Another Day," Bobby Troup's "Nice Girls Don't Stay For Breakfast," Russ Garcia's "Go Slow" and even "These Boots Are Made For Walkin'." The fresh arrangements and her expressive voice make this CD a keeper.

On *Long As You're Living* (Jizel Music 35611), **Linda Kosut** has succeeded at a difficult task, reviving a full set of Oscar Brown Jr.'s songs and poetry, including the scary "Bid 'Em In," "Hazel's Hips" and Brown's lyrics to "'Round Midnight." Oscar Brown Jr.'s legacy and spirit are felt, even though Linda Kosut is neither African-American nor male.

Lauren Koval is a classy singer who often performs on the Queen Mary in Long Beach. Her self-produced *No Complaints, No Regrets* features her straightforward renditions of a dozen standards with very supportive accompaniment by the Page Cavanaugh Trio.

Celia La combines respect for 20th-century standards and a willingness to stretch herself on *Introducing Celia La* (Lady La Productions 13717), a debut that also features pianist Bill Cunliffe. She displays the influence of Shirley Horn in her use of space and is particularly winning on "Don't Go To Strangers" and "I've Grown Accustomed To Your Face."

A fine singer from Finland who has lived in the United States since 1991, **Sofia Laiti** has retained both her accent and her charm through the years. Her most recent CD is *You Don't Know Me* (Midnight Sun 2709).

Based in Northern California, **Dawn Lambeth** is a superior swing singer who specializes in songs from the 1920s, '30s and '40s. The subtle and basic phrasing of Maxine Sullivan is an influence as Lambeth interacts with some of California's top trad musicians. *Let's Get Lost* (Spanish Shawl Music 002) gives listeners a strong sampling of her talents.

Whether singing solo, teaming up with Reeves Cary as "Girl 'N' Boy Singer" or singing on the Minnesota Zephyr as part of a 1940s-style vocal quartet, **Paula Lammers** is one of the best jazz vocalists performing regularly in Minnesota. Her self-produced *A Blanket Of Blue* features her sounding her best on vintage ballads such as "Isn't It Romantic" and swinging well on "Honeysuckle Rose."

Born and raised in Detroit, **Sheila Landis** sounds quite comfortable whether singing bop or Latin. Often teamed with guitarist Rick Matle, she has regularly put out albums on her Shelan label since 1981. *Riding The Round Pool* (Shelan) is an excellent example of her creativity and interplay with Matle.

A hard-driving singer who puts plenty of enthusiasm and spirit into her performances, **Arlee Leonard** is the daughter of the fine folk roots team David and Roslyn. *Her Wild Honey* (Soulajazz Productions) from 2000 is an excellent debut.

The daughter of bassist-singer Jay Leonhart, **Carolyn Leonhart** has had a diverse career that includes singing with the classical Swiss Percussion Ensemble, touring with Steely Dan and performing with an electronica/lounge group. Her own recordings have tended to be jazz-oriented, with

Kevyn Lettau

If Dreams Come True (Nagel Heyer 2078), which co-stars husband Wayne Escoffery on tenor and soprano saxophones, including several colorful originals.

Best-known for her Brazilian pop/fusion recordings, **Kevyn Lettau** was born in Berlin, moved to the United States at 14, toured with Sergio Mendes for eight years and is actually best known in Japan and the Philippines. *Bye Bye Blackbird* (MCG Jazz 1019) is a bit unusual due to its emphasis on standards, but Lettau's light and accessible style is unchanged from her early days, and the results are easy to enjoy.

Kerry Linder has a real feel for bossa novas and sambas. *Sail Away With Me* (Blue Toucan 892) has her turning such unlikely material as "Song For My Father," "That's All" and "As Time Goes By" into Brazilian jazz songs.

An excellent singer and pianist based in Toronto, **Fern Lindzon** recently released her first jazz recording as a leader, *Moments Like These* (Iatros 01), a set of duets with guitarist Reg Schwager, vibraphonist Don Thompson and bassist George Koller that features her warm singing on nine of the dozen selections, including her lyrics to Wayne Shorter's "Infant Eyes." Lindzon, who also plays modern klezmer music in other settings, is a strong talent.

In the 1980s, **Paula Lockheart** was a link toward much earlier generations of blues and jazz singers, bringing back the styles of the 1920s without overly copying any of her predecessors. *The Incomplete Paula Lockheart* (Flying Fish 70133) is an 18-song sampler drawn from her three Flying Fish albums of 1979 to 1987. It is great fun, though one wishes she would record again.

Although she has had experience in opera, cabaret and particularly in musical plays, **Amy London** is a fine jazz singer based in New York. *When I Look In Your Eyes* (Motema 00011) mostly has her performing offbeat material (some of which comes across as autobiographical) ranging from "Wonderful, Wonderful" and "There's A Boat That's Leavin' Soon" to "Woody 'n You" and "Swingin' The Blues." She is a talent well worth discovering.

A superior storyteller, **Martha Lorin** shows a great deal of versatility on *Come Walk With Me* (Southport 0073). The continually intriguing set of mostly standards arranged by pianist Miles Black matches the singer with some top Chicago musicians, and she handles the unpredictable arrangements quite well.

Elaine Lucia, originally from upstate New York but long based in the Northern California and San Francisco Bay area, has a very attractive voice, hitting high notes with little apparent effort. *On A Sonny Day* (Songflower), her repertoire is intelligent and eclectic, including Chick Corea's "Sea Journey," "I Only Have Eyes For You," her own "I Call You Sonny" and Dave Frishberg's "You Are There." Throughout, her joyful spirit shines through, and she is not shy about taking chances. Hers is a talent just waiting to be discovered.

In her career, **Wendy Luck** has sung and played flute with top avant-garde jazz players, recorded solo meditation sets, performed regularly with a comedy group in New York and gigged all over the world. *See You In Rio* (Wendy Luck 2475) features her sensuous vocals and fluent flute in a Brazilian jazz setting, sounding as if this is what she does full-time.

Pamela Luss is an intriguing singer with a lot of potential. On medium-tempo pieces, she is a superior jazz vocalist, while her renditions of ballads tend to be taken rather straight like a cabaret singer. On *Your Eyes* (Savant 2083), both sides are on evidence, and it will be interesting to see which path she eventually chooses.

Marguerite Mariama keeps busy, being a professor in New York, a dancer, a choreographer and the founder of a performing arts production and consulting firm called From The Inside.

Fortunately she has finally found time to record her debut CD, *Wild Women Never Get The Blues…Well Not Anymore* (Powerlight 12202). Despite the title cut, this is more of a jazz than a blues set, with "Home," "Young And Foolish" and "Love Dance" best displaying her warm voice and spirit.

Lisa Markley mixes together jazz, folk and blues in her music. On *The Sky Is Blue And Sometimes Cries* (Soona Songs 007), she contributes four originals, revives a few forgotten numbers, including "The Dry Cleaner From Des Moines" and debuts songs by some of her sidemen. The music sounds both traditional and brand new, a mixture of usually separate styles that comes across as quite logical and an excellent vehicle for her flexible voice.

One of several fine jazz singers who are based in Nashville, the capital of country music, **Carolyn Martin** has sung a wide variety of music in her career but in recent times has settled on swing standards. *The Very Thought Of You* (Cuppa Joe 101 405) shows the wisdom of that decision for such tunes as "Mean To Me," "Until I Met You" and "Too Marvelous For Words" are a natural fit for her attractive voice and solid sense of swing.

Susan May on her recording debut, *The Rose* (Southport 0102), sounds mature and seems to have a deep understanding for the words of the standards that she sings. That would not be unusual except that she was turning 12 at the time! *Black Coffee* (Southport 0114), recorded in 2005 when she was 13, is slightly better, for she takes a few more chances, and even though most of her repertoire consists of warhorses at this point, her voice is quite attractive, and she is already a fine singer at this very early stage of her career.

Tammy McCann from Chicago has sung opera, R&B, soul (touring as a backup singer for Ray Charles), gospel and jazz, performing in English, Italian, French and German. *Classic* (Katalyst 0015) is her jazz CD, sticking mostly to standards and displaying a warm voice and a swinging style on such tunes as "Happy Talk," "The Nearness Of You" and "The Masquerade Is Over."

Although **Erin McDougald**'s record label is called "Flapper Girl Productions," the music that she performs is mostly from the 1930s through the '50s rather than the 1920s. She loves to caress lyrics and does a fine job with the witty "Nice Weather For Ducks," "I Love Paris," "Where Flamingos Fly" and a three-song "Fall Medley" on her *Auburn Collection* (Flapper Girl 7793).

A throwback to the 1930s in her sound, style and repertoire, **Solitaire Miles** has worked in Chicago with Johnny Frigo and Von Freeman and in New York with Doc Cheatham. Her debut, simply titled *Solitaire Miles* (Seraphic 113743), features Frigo, Freeman, Willie Pickens and other top Chicago musicians joining her warm singing on such numbers as "Comes Love," "I Want A Little Sugar In My Bowl" and "A Kiss To Build A Dream On."

Born in Belgrade, Serbia, **Alma Mimic** came to the United States in 1995 to attend Berklee. Her debut, *Introducing Alma* (CTA 003), is quite impressive, as she comes up with fresh statements on eight standards (including "Infant Eyes," "Corcovado" and "But Beautiful"), her own "That April Day" and the folk song "Sejdefu Majka Budjase." Based on this CD, she clearly has a great future.

Denine Monet is from San Jose, California and frequently performs in the San Francisco Bay area in addition to being a teacher. Her long-overdue debut, *Lady Bird* (Orchard 80 1008), has several songs having to do with birds (sometimes including sound effects) but mostly just gives her a good chance to stretch out. She contributes five inventive originals and also borders on the avant-garde in some of her explorations while staying bop-based.

Singer **Typhanie Monique** and guitarist Neal Alger have performed together regularly in Chicago during the past few years, creating a fresh soulful jazz style even when interpreting well-known standards. The self-produced *In This Room*, which includes a few guests, is an excellent sampling of the type of music they create, ranging from "Caravan" and a pair of spontaneous-sounding pieces to numbers by Annie Lennox and Sting.

From Northern California, **Alexa Weber Morales** on *Vagabundeo/Wanderings* (Patois 3396) gives one the accurate impression that she can sing anything, from jazz to salsa to bossa novas and funk, and in four languages. Her voice is outstanding, she improvises quite a bit, and her music (she contributed five originals) crosses many boundaries while always having the spirit of jazz.

An important singer and educator from Montreal, **Diane Nalini** recently gained attention by adapting the words of William Shakespeare into jazz on *Songs Of Sweet Fire* (EGR 103), although her previous *Tales My Mama Told Me* (EGR 102) is a little more accessible. She has been well praised for her flawless diction and her ability to consistently come up with new ideas.

Bobbe Norris and her husband pianist Larry Dunlap are considered jazz institutions in the San Francisco Bay area, performing bop-oriented tunes and ballads. *Out Of Nowhere* (Four Directions 2004) has Norris in top form in 1999 while joined by Dunlap's trio and two guest horns. On "Invitation," she shares the vocal with Mark Murphy. Bobbe Norris should record much more often.

On *Standard Delivery* (Dead Horse 2731), **Veronica Nunn** performs a set of standards her way, with unexpected twists and turns that keep the music interesting and a little unpredictable. With backing from her husband pianist Travis Shook's trio, she sounds in prime form throughout this program, making many of the warhorses sound like new material. Her years of experience pay off throughout the set, making one look forward to her tackling newer songs in the future.

One of Sweden's top jazz singers of the past decade, **Lina Nyberg** has performed a wide variety of advanced music. *Brasil Big Bom* (Caprice 21785) is a change of pace, for it features her singing Brazilian jazz songs (some of which are her originals) in Swedish with the assistance of Magnus Lindgren on reeds. Even if one cannot understand the words, her placement of notes is impressive, and her feelings shine through.

An important new singer on the Cleveland jazz scene, **Trisha O'Brien** on her 2003 self-titled privately issued debut does a fine job of interpreting standards. She has been traveling more lately and hopefully will be stretching herself musically in the future. She does have a beautiful voice.

At the 2003 Playboy Jazz Festival, the partying crowd was surprised by an appearance from a 13-year-old **Renee Olstead** who sang a powerful version of "At Last." Her first CD from 2004, simply titled *Renee Olstead* (143 Records/ Reprise 48704), has some impressive singing by the youngster, but some of the lyrics on the standards are rather inappropriate for a 14-year-old, particularly in such songs as "Breaking Up Is Hard To Do," "Taking A Chance On Love," "What A Difference A Day Makes," "Midnight At The Oasis" and "A Sunday Kind Of Love." As time passes, hopefully a little more common sense will be used in building up what should be an important musical career.

From California, **Tish Oney** started her recording career in 2001 with the self-produced *Forever Friend*, a fine set of music comprised of six standards and three originals that feature her warm voice. She has since completed her doctoral work in Jazz Studies and has been performing a tribute to Peggy Lee, her singing and her songwriting.

Chrissie Carpenter Oppedisano was born in Los Angeles but has lived and worked steadily in Italy during the past few years. On *Moon Stars And Nights* (Philology 340), she shows a great deal of confidence, swinging hard on "You And The Night And The Music," making "Peel Me A Grape" her own (which is difficult to do) and even finding something fresh to say on the overly familiar "Teach Me Tonight."

Based in the San Francisco Bay area, **Kat Parra** has a beautiful and flexible voice that she uses on her debut CD, *Birds In Flight* (JazzMa), to sing in English, Portuguese and Spanish. A versatile performer, she performs salsa, sambas, Afro-Cuban jazz, Afro-Peruvian music, ballads, a flamenco and music that falls in between those styles, all of it interpreted with enthusiasm, understanding and joy.

Nick Parrott is best known as the regular bassist for Les Paul and for being an increasingly welcome presence on swing and trad sessions. In recent times he has begun to sing, and she has a nice tone and a friendly presence. On a set of duets with pianist Rossano Sportiello, *People Will Say We're In Love* (Arbors 19335), she takes vocals on half of the numbers and fares quite well.

An infectious singer from Brazil, **Rosa Passos** is sometimes compared to Astrud Gilberto, but she has a stronger voice and a more extroverted and openly sensuous style. *Amorosa* (Sony Classical 92068) is a CD that pays tribute on several selections to João Gilberto. This is an exciting release and a perfect introduction to one of today's top Brazilian jazz singers.

A fine ballad singer from Minnesota who only began singing professionally a few years ago, **Tim Patrick** puts a lot of feeling and affection into the songs on his self-produced *The Shadow Of Your Smile*. His interpretations are inviting and accessible, and he does justice to the words he sings.

Annette Peacock has had such a wide-ranging career as an arranger, composer, producer, poet, keyboardist and singer in so many styles of adventurous and avant-garde music that just calling her a jazz singer would not be accurate. By the late 1960s she was an innovator in using her voice through a synthesizer. The year 1972's *I'm The One* (RCA 4578), which has not been reissued on CD yet, is a good example of her unique work.

Though she is originally from Indiana and has performed in the Netherlands and Japan, **Gail Pettis** is today one of Seattle's best jazz singers. On *May I Come In* (OA2 22038), she makes conventional standards and a few offbeat items all sound special with her straightforward and honest interpretations.

Madeleine Peyroux has generated a great deal of attention through the tone of her voice, which can sound very similar to that of Billie Holiday, a quiet charisma and an occasionally mysterious lifestyle. Unfortunately her singing is actually quite limited, even though it definitely has its charm. *Half The Perfect World* (Rounder 11661-3252) has new material, modern folk songs, obscurities and a lone standard in "Smile," all of it interpreted in similar fashion. It is worth checking out but certainly not worth raving about due to the lack of variety and creativity.

One of the better singers based in Denver, **Tina Phillips** performs locally, sometimes with Art Lande or Eric Gunnison on piano. She puts a lot of feeling into her singing, whether scatting or interpreting ballads as she shows on her self-produced *Adventurous Jazz* CD.

The wife of guitarist John Pisano, **Jeanne Pisano** has a very attractive voice, a wide range and the ability to scat the most complex lines. She has worked in the studios, written lyrics and often performed with her husband in the Los Angeles area as the Flying Pisanos. The privately issued *Lazy Afternoon* features Jeanne Pisano accompanied by both John Pisano and Jim Fox on guitars.

Suzanne Pittson

A fine singer formerly in San Francisco who moved to New York to teach at City College, **Suzanne Pittson** is particularly skilled and inventive as a scat singer. *Resolution: A Remembrance Of John Coltrane* (Vineland) has Pittson exploring a variety of songs associated with Coltrane, including two movements from *A Love Supreme*.

John Proulx is a fluent young pianist in the Los Angeles area who also sings in a light voice similar to Chet Baker's. *Moon And Sand* (Max Jazz 503) is an impressive debut featuring both of Proulx's musical talents in a trio.

A spirited singer with a large voice and a happy sound, **Shaynee Rainbolt** made a strong impression with her second CD, *At Home* (33 Jazz 132). Though one could easily imagine her singing on Broadway, she also does a fine job in the jazz world particularly on vintage standards. She is currently recording an album with veteran arranger Russell Garcia.

Maryanne Reall, who performs in Orange County, California, has a sweet voice and puts a lot of heart in her singing. Her debut CD, *In Her Own Voice* (Perfect), is highlighted by "Stars Fell On Alabama," "Romance In The Dark" and a pair of obscurities associated with Billie Holiday ("Mandy Is Two" and "Jim").

One of the most unlikely recording debuts of 2007 was *Ed Reed Sings Love Stories* (ER 001). Not that **Ed Reed**, who has a warm baritone voice and is particularly effective on ballads, was not qualified, but he was 78 at the time. A veteran of the 1950s Los Angeles jazz scene whose heroin addiction made his life difficult for 40 years, Reed emerged in the early 21st century as an ageless singer from the past who still had something important to contribute.

A bit of a cult figure who is considered by some to be a legendary vocal teacher and singer (the hype seems a bit overblown at times), **Rhiannon** has worked with Bobby McFerrin's Voicestra, her own SoVoSo and the earlier group Alive in addition to several a cappella ensembles. The privately issued *In My Prime* shows that she is a superior improviser.

Abigail Riccards, who has lived in Brooklyn since 2003, displays an attractive voice on her recording debut, *When The Night Is New* (Jazz Excursion 116). She takes some chances, including performing "Left Alone" in a trio with trumpeter Ron Horton and bassist Ben Allison, and seems to hit every note she tries for including some wide intervals. There is lots of potential here.

Hanna Richardson's *Something To Remember You By* (La-La 5601) finds the lightly swinging singer paying tribute to Maxine Sullivan with bassist Phil Flanigan's sextet. Richardson has a straightforward style that works well on this set (even if none of Sullivan's folk song hits are included), and there are excellent solos from both Allen Vache and Ken Peplowski on clarinets.

Anita Robles, a potentially explosive talent in Latin music, sings everything from jazz and salsa to pop and funk. *Latina Suave* (AR-2002), which was recorded in her native Argentina, Miami and Los Angeles, is full of variety and has plenty of bright moments from the exciting singer.

Pamela Rose, part of the jazz scene in San Francisco since the late 1970s, loves the Hammond B-3 organ and often utilizes an organist on her records. *Just For A Thrill* (Three Handed 5139) is a soulful jazz set featuring guitarist Danny Caron and either Tony Stead or Wayne De La Cruz on organ on swing standards, soulful numbers and a few surprises. Pamela Rose puts on a joyful and spirited performance.

An actress active in Minneapolis, **Christine Rosholt** took some time before recording her first jazz record, *Detour Ahead* (Idea Dog Productions 13837). While her acting skills add to her appeal, she has an attractive voice, knows how to get the most out of each word, and her phrasing contains plenty of surprises. She is a subtle improviser who clearly loves to sing. Her sensuous version of "Honeysuckle Rose" is a highlight.

When one hears that **Catherine Russell** is the daughter of pianist Luis Russell, who led a notable big band during 1929–34 and played in the Louis Armstrong Orchestra, it would be excusable to assume that she is in her 80s rather than being half as old (Luis Russell lived a long time). After many experiences in the pop music world, she emerged as a fine jazz singer on *Cat* (World Village 468063), performing a few standards, blues and some unusual material, including two Sam Cooke songs and a vocalized version of "Royal Garden Blues" ("Juneteenth Jamboree").

Janelle Sadler, who has sung background vocals for many top acts, finally had a chance to be in the spotlight for her *Don't Make Me Laugh* (Little Precious Records 216) in 2003. She proves to be a skilled and attractive jazz singer with a wide repertoire ranging from "Secret Love" to Jimi Hendrix's "Manic Depression."

Michelle Samuels performs regularly in the New York area. The self-issued *Across A Crowded Room* is rather brief (a few seconds short of a half-hour), but what is included is excellent. Samuels' classical training is evident (her voice has a "legit" quality about it), but she displays warmth throughout the eight lyrical standards that she performs with a rhythm section.

An influential singer, educator, lyricist/songwriter and organizer of events in the Los Angeles area, **Cathy Segal-Garcia** is a strong improviser with a friendly and inviting voice. *Alone Together* (Koyo Sounds 1010), a set of duets with pianist Phillip Strange, is a good place to start in exploring this very talented singer's music.

A very good jazz singer, **Sandi Shoemake** has been the wife of vibraphonist Charlie Shoemake since 1959. She worked in the studios, toured with big bands and been part of the West Coast jazz scene during the past few decades. *Lullaby In Rhythm* (Chase Music Group 8057) is one of her rare solo dates and features her in top form in 1999, swinging standards with fine support from tenor-saxophonist Pete Christlieb, guitarist Bruce Forman and a rhythm section that has her husband on piano.

In 2002 **Rani Singam** switched careers from being a lawyer to becoming a jazz singer. Now a top attraction in her native Singapore, she frequently works with pianist Jeremy Monteiro. Singam's debut, *With A Song In My Heart* (Jazz Note 170702), finds her showing the influence of Sarah Vaughan in spots and sounding quite happy and swinging on standards while joined by a group that includes Monteiro and tenor-saxophonist Greg Fishman.

Keely Smith will always be best known for her association with her husband Louis Prima, but early in her career she was also highly rated for her singing of ballads. Although much of her singing throughout her career was fairly straight, she could sing swinging jazz when it was called upon. During the past decade she has emerged on an occasional basis. 2000's *Swing Swing Swing* (Concord 4882) is an excellent matchup with the Frank Capp Juggernaut. At 68, her voice still sounds quite strong on this fine effort.

The most important new jazz singer to appear during the first half of 2008 was **Esperanza Spalding**. Originally a classical violinist, at 15 she switched to the bass. She attended Berklee (becoming an instructor at 20) and in 2008 the 23-year-old had her debut release, *Esperanza* (Heads Up 3140). Often singing while accompanying herself on bass, she is already a superior scat-singer and a witty and surprisingly mature vocalist.

One of Italy's top jazz singers, **Cinzia Spata** utilizes a mostly American Quartet on *93-03* (Azzurra Music 096). The wide-ranging program includes some of her originals, two tunes by Kenny Wheeler (including "Everybody's Song But My Own") and two jazz standards. Spata, whose background is in swing groups but has evolved into a more adventurous improviser, is a talent worth discovering.

Cynthia Speer, who is based in the Los Angeles area, has a haunting voice that is particularly effective on her heartfelt treatment of ballads, and she always places her notes intelligently. The self-produced *Nature Girl* includes two of her originals, a medley of "I Fall In Love Too Easily" and "It Could Happen To You," and a cooking version of "That Old Devil Called Love."

On *Live At Pearl's* (W. Inc 87768) from 2003, San Francisco–based singer **Wanda Stafford** sometimes recalls prime Anita O'Day in her phrasing and tone. She clearly knows how to bring veteran tunes back to life, she throws in a few unexpected items, and she puts on an entertaining and highly musical performance with her quartet.

Bob Stewart caught the tail end of the big band era, crooning ballads with dance bands before rock and roll ended his career. He captained a fishing party boat for decades but in more recent times has returned to singing the ballads and swing standards that he loves. On *Talk Of The Town* (VWC 4112), his voice sounds fragile and emotional but strong as he really gets into the lyrics, accompanied by a top-notch band that includes trumpeter Glenn Drewes and either Hank Jones or Sir Roland Hanna on piano during most of the songs.

Yevette Stewart has been based in Los Angeles for years, performing regularly in local clubs and abroad. Her soulful renditions of standards are preserved on *The Love Project* (Rhombus 7053), which also includes two Dori Caymmi songs and her own "Loving Me Was The Best Thing That Happened To You."

A middle-of-the-road pop singer whose music sometimes crosses over into jazz, **Curtis Stigers** also plays saxophone and guitar. He started his career playing rock and soul, singing jazz for the fun of it on the side. He eventually switched, sort of, often performing pop and rock songs in jazzy settings with occasional standards. *I Think It's Going To Rain Today* (Concord 2275) is one of his better efforts.

From Toronto, **Melissa Stylianon** modernizes older songs on *Sliding Down* (Sleepin' Bee 1002), contributes five intriguing originals and stretches the mainstream of jazz. She has been one of Canada's more significant singers of the past decade, winning awards and appearing at major festivals.

DJ Sweeney, who is based in Kansas City, adds joy and spirit to each song she interprets. On her self-titled recording debut (which is a bit brief at 36 minutes), she has a lot of fun with swing standards, including "I'm Gonna Lock My Heart And Throw Away The Key." She is joined by some of Kansas City's best players, including guitarist Danny Embrey and pianist Paul Smith, both of whom have worked extensively with Karrin Allyson.

An exuberant and powerful singer who often sounds as if she is throwing a big party, **Sweet Baby J'ai** performs blues and jazz with lots of enthusiasm. Raised in Kansas City and long a fixture in Los Angeles (when she is not touring Asia), J'ai has three CDs out with *The Art Of Blue* (Sunset Music 2245) being a particularly well-rounded set, featuring several of her best originals.

Veronica Swift made her recording debut in 2003, when she was 11. The daughter of Stephanie Nakasian and pianist Hod O'Brien, she has worked with the Young Razzcals Jazz Project. Her privately issued CD, *Veronica's House Of Jazz*, features the great altoist Richie Cole and finds the young singer showing maturity and swing that she obviously inherited from her mother.

Jeannie Tanner sings and plays trumpet and has a repertoire stretching from jazz to pop. Based in Chicago, her voice is

excellent, and on *Tanner Time* (Tanner Time 877319001741) she swings even the non-jazz material along with her originals and such older pieces as "Bernie's Tune" and "I Got Rhythm."

A fine jazz singer from Omaha, Nebraska, **Susie Thorne** has recorded two excellent CDs. *Blue Skies, Clear Day* (Effie 210294) teams her with pianist Christine Hitt, a rhythm section and altoist Jason Swagler on 11 of her favorite standards.

Lee Torchia has in recent years sought to mix together jazz with Indian music, calling it "jazz raga." Years earlier she recorded a fine album, now reissued as the CD *Lover Man* (Jazz Raga 001), with tenor-saxophonist Ricky Ford, pianist Ram Ramirez, bassist Milt Hinton and drummer Mel Lewis. She pays tribute to Billie Holiday through her repertoire rather than trying to copy her, and the results are rewarding.

Dwight Trible has such a powerful baritone voice that he could have been an opera singer. Associated with Pharoah Sanders, the late Horace Tapscott and the advanced elements of the Los Angeles jazz community, Trible certainly believes in the music he performs. *Living Water* (Passin' The Vibe Record) features him performing music by John Coltrane (contributing his own original "John Coltrane"), Abdullah Ibrahim, Wayne Shorter, Andy Bey and Freddie Hubbard.

Donna Tucker, who sings and teaches in Omaha, Nebraska after spending a long spell in Dallas, is impressive on her debut, *Right As The Rain* (Kippie Josh Jazz 50207). She displays a warm and distinctive voice and very good taste in picking out standards to revive.

Steve Tyrell is a crooning pop singer who enjoys singing standards. His voice has been used in many motion pictures, and he formerly worked in A&R, as a producer and as a songwriter. *Standard Time* (Sony 86006) is a good example of his raspy singing (a little reminiscent of Dr. John) and his easy interaction with jazz musicians.

A fine storyteller and a warm interpreter of ballads, the Los Angeles-based **John Vance** is in excellent form on his second CD, *Dreamsville* (Erawan 2007). He is joined by the Jeff Colella Trio, Stacy Rowles on flugelhorn and guitarist Larry Koonse.

Paulien Van Schaik is a fine cool-toned singer from the Netherlands who often teams up with bassist Hein van de Geyn for duets. Their second CD together, *In Summer* (Challenge 70118), has trumpeter Bert Joris making the group a trio for some modern West Coast jazz.

A new talent with an intriguing voice, **Sachal Vasandani** sounds atmospheric on modern ballads but can also dig into vintage swing tunes and blues. On *Eyes Wide Open* (Mack Avenue 1035), there are times when he sounds a little like Michael Franks (in his higher notes) and oddly enough like Art Lund (Benny Goodman's singer in 1946) in his lower register. He shows potential and versatility on this early effort.

Fay Victor, who was raised in New York, has spent much of her career in Europe. She has evolved from a standards singer to an avant-garde explorer but one who has not discarded her roots. *Lucky Old Sun* (Greene Avenue) features both originals and "Laura," ranging from the Doors to Jackie McLean without copying anyone.

Brooke Vigoda, who was associated with pianist Dick Shreve when she lived in Los Angeles, has recently performed in New Jersey with cornetist Warren Vache and bassist Steve LaSpina. A warm singer who loves to unearth obscurities from the 1930s, '40s and '50s, she is planning an upcoming CD.

Singer **Teraesa Vinson** and guitarist Tom Dempsey team up on *Next To You* (Amplified 102) for a set of duets that tone-wise may recall Tuck and Patti. However, their repertoire sticks closer to jazz standards (other than one Dempsey original) while unearthing such gems as Oscar Brown Jr.'s "Opportunity Please Knock" and the lone McCoy Tyner/

Mala Waldron

Sammy Cahn collaboration "You Taught My Heart To Sing." Teraesa Vinson has a pleasing voice and is just at the beginning of what should be a significant career.

Mala Waldron, the daughter of the late great pianist Mal Waldron, has a powerful voice and is also a fine pianist. On *Always There* (Soulful Sound 22241), the music is often R&Bish and is generally lightly grooving but has plenty of improvisation along the way. In her live performances, Waldron is often heard in more avant-garde settings, so her future musical direction is unclear as of this writing.

Anita Wardell, who was born in England, was raised in Australia and moved back to the United Kingdom as an adult in 1989, is a superior bop singer. On *Noted* (Specific Jazz 006), she sings her vocalese to Lee Morgan's solo on "Moanin'" and Cannonball Adderley's "Autumn Leaves" and consistently swings up a storm. She is also a fine improviser, scat singer and interpreter of ballads. Anita Wardell deserves to be famous.

A baritone crooner with a strong and appealing voice, **Lou Watson** is a soulful jazz singer. *Taking A Chance On Love* (Village Notz 92353) has him doing justice to "I Just Found Out About Love," "Just The Two Of Us" and "Fools Rush In."

Joan Watson-Jones is a storyteller who only sings songs with lyrics that she believes in. She performs ten of her favorite standards on *I Thought About You* (Eye Of Samantha 02) and clearly had a great time, particularly on a high-energy version of "It's All Right With Me."

Formerly a pop singer in Singapore, **Anne Weerapass** made the transition to jazz and recorded *Out Of Nowhere* (Jazz Note 170702), her debut jazz CD. It was a good move, for her versions of "The Way You Look Tonight," "So Many Stars" and "So Nice (Summer Samba)" sound different than the typical renditions, displaying plenty of fresh ideas.

Michele Weir is an important jazz educator in the Los Angeles area who is greatly involved in clinics, seminars and teaching at colleges. Her compositions and arrangements have been utilized by symphony orchestras and vocal groups, and she has published vocal arrangements for several publishers. She recently issued a fine set of duets with guitarist Bruce Forman called *The Sound Of Music*, which comprises the title cut plus a variety of standards.

Though a pianist, trumpeter and bassist, **Laura Welland** will probably find her greatest fame as a singer. Based in Seattle, she put together a very intriguing program on *Dissertation On The State Of Bliss* (OA2 22023) that traces the rise, fall and rise again of one's love life through vintage standards.

Her voice fits each of the moods quite well, and the results are superior to most similar attempts by others to portray a love affair in music.

Shea Breaux Wells, who lives in Healdsburg, California, teams up with a quintet of all-stars on the self-produced *A Blind Date* (Ultimate 23647), her definitive jazz set. Her warm and expressive voice is heard at its best on "Baltimore Oriole," "A Night In Tunisia" and a modernized "Blue Skies." She is an up-and-comer.

Judy Wexler has mostly performed in Los Angeles–area clubs. Her debut recording, *Easy On The Heart* (Jazzopolis), is a winner, with the highlights, including Henry Mancini's "Moment To Moment," Oscar Brown Jr.'s "Humdrum Blues," a touching "Tell Him I Said Hello" and "Down Here On The Ground." She interprets the diverse material with sensitivity and understated swing.

Ronny Whyte is a veteran pianist-singer whose tasteful music falls between swing and cabaret. *Walk On The Weill Side* (Audiophile 289) is a particularly rewarding program that features Whyte at his best.

Best known as a lyricist for shows and other singers, **Mark Winkler** also performs on an occasional basis in the Los Angeles area. *Sings Bobby Troup* (Rhombus 7029) is his most successful jazz date, reviving 11 of Troup's best songs (including "Hungry Man," "Lemon Twist," "The Meaning Of The Blues" and of course "Route 66") in addition to introducing Winkler's own "Two Guys From The Coast." Mark Winkler's easy-going style perfectly fits Troup's music.

Deanna Witkowski is an excellent pianist who sometimes uses her voice as a wordless instrument. *Length Of Days* (Artist Share 0010) has her blending in very well vocally with Donny McCaslin's soprano.

The Los Angeles-based **Raya Yarbrough** enjoys switching between pop ballads and jazz scatting while not being shy about utilizing electronics. She excels in all areas, as she shows on her debut *Raya Yarbrough* (Telarc 83658), which includes both standards like "Joy Spring" and "Early Autumn" and originals. Much more will be heard from her.

Mr. Z. (Zaxariades) toured with Jon Hendricks during a six-year period and the influence, along with that of Eddie Jefferson, shows. On *Mr. Z* (Free Ham Records 17769), he revives "Moody's Mood For Love" and some of Jon Hendricks' lyrics in addition to including a few of his own and taking several numbers fairly straight. Mr. Z. has a strong and flexible voice that should not be overlooked.

55 OTHERS WHO HAVE ALSO SUNG JAZZ

Many jazz musicians somewhere along the way have felt compelled to take a few vocals. In some cases it was an obvious mistake, but many have been able to make up for having an average voice by scatting and phrasing like an instrument. Some have developed unusual approaches, while others sing just for the fun of it (their fun, not necessarily the audience's). I will not make an attempt to list or comment on every instrumentalist who has felt like warbling, but the 55 in this section needed to be mentioned.

George Adams (1940–1992) was an emotional tenor-saxophonist who often played in fairly free settings, sounding at his best when he teamed up with pianist Don Pullen. Adams also loved to sing blues in his raspy voice, giving his music a bit of accessibility before he took off on another explosive flight. *America* (Blue Note 93896) has three examples of his singing.

A great New Orleans trumpeter, **Henry "Red" Allen** (1908–1967) loved to count off tempos with a "wamp, wamp" (which sounded particularly funny when he played a ballad). His singing voice was gruff and mildly eccentric, matching his trumpet well. *1935–1936* (Classics 575) has him making "On Treasure Island" and "Take Me To My Boots And Saddle" into hot New Orleans jazz.

Speaking of eccentric, **Ray Anderson** (1952–) is an avant-gardist with a very strong sense of humor. He has greatly extended the range of the trombone (sometimes to hilarious effect), while his occasional singing finds him hitting two notes at once (a minor third apart), which definitely sounds unique. Check him out on *Don't Mow Your Lawn* (Enja 8070).

One of the great songwriters from the golden era of the American popular song, **Harold Arlen** (1905–1986) had one of the closest connections to jazz. However, few probably realize that early in his career Arlen recorded a few vocals with jazz groups, most notably three with Joe Venuti's Blue Four in 1931, sounding quite credible on "Little Girl."

Also surprisingly credible is the lone vocal by **Count Basie** (1904–1984). No, not his stating "One more once" on "April In Paris." On a 1930 recording of "Somebody Stole My Gal" recorded with Bennie Moten's orchestra, Basie sounds quite comfortable scatting for a chorus. Strange that he never did it again on record.

A likable if limited tenor-saxophonist, **Tex Beneke** (1914–2000) became famous with Glenn Miller for singing "Chattanooga Choo Choo" ("Pardon me boy…"), "I've Got A Gal In Kalamazoo" and a few other numbers. Beneke was with Miller's orchestra during 1938–42 and, after Miller's death in 1944, he formed his own orchestra, which, despite his best efforts to forge his own path, ended up sounding like the Glenn Miller Ghost Band. Years passed and Beneke remained frozen in time, still singing "Chattanooga Choo Choo" in 1955, and in 1995. He spent his last 55 years recreating his three main years with Glenn Miller.

One of the greatest trumpeters of the 1930s, **Bunny Berigan** (1908–1942) took reckless chances in his solos (usually succeeding) and his life (dying an alcoholic at 33). He did not have much of a voice and only took a handful of vocals in his career, but one of them was his big hit, "I Can't Get Started."

A solid trombonist, **Richard Boone** (1930–1999) had a bizarre scatting style, a little like Clark Terry's mumbles although even less intelligible. He sang occasionally while with Count Basie (1966–69) and during his later years in Europe. *The Singer* (Storyville 4186) gives listeners an opportunity to see if Boone's singing is inventive or merely annoying.

Henry Butler (1949–) is a dynamic pianist whose music ranges from blues and New Orleans R&B to modern jazz. In addition to his passionate playing, *Blues After Sunset* (Black Top 1144) features some of his most powerful blues-based vocals.

Because he was one of the all-time great alto-saxophonists, a pacesetting arranger, a skilled composer, an important bandleader and an excellent trumpeter and sounded effective on clarinet, tenor, piano and (on one rare occasion) trombone, it was said that **Benny Carter** (1907–2003) could do everything extremely well. But someone making that statement would obviously have never heard Carter sing. He took six vocals on records in the 1930s (including "Synthetic Love" and "Love, You're Not The One For Me") and late in life often liked to sing his "All That Jazz." It is fortunate that Carter could do everything else so well.

Most older trumpeters, particularly those who play swing and Dixieland, eventually succumb to the temptation to sing occasionally so as to rest their chops. **Doc Cheatham** (1905–1997) spent much of his life as a lead trumpeter, not developing into a major soloist until he was already in his 70s and still hitting notes with confidence at 91. He did not sing until late in life, but even there he sounded relatively youthful and confident, interpreting lyrics with charm. *The Eighty-Seven Years Of Doc Cheatham* (Columbia 53215) shows just how much of a wonder he was and how he never really needed to rest his chops, either on trumpet or vocals.

A wisecracking bandleader, a major propagandist for free-wheeling jazz and a decent rhythm guitarist, **Eddie Condon** (1905–1973) also took a few vocals on records in the 1920s, something he would have preferred to forget. A 1929 short film of *Red Nichols And His Five Pennies* has Condon singing several songs. Fortunately he soon decided to use his voice just for talking.

An organist with limitless energy who is largely responsible for his instrument's comeback in the 1980s and '90s, **Joey DeFrancesco** (1971–) loves Frank Sinatra's singing. *Singin' And Swingin'* (Concord 4861) features him singing material associated with Sinatra. Even if it gets close to self-parody in spots, he generally pulls it off by displaying a decent voice and not taking himself too seriously.

Altoist **Lou Donaldson** (1926–) helps keep the bebop tradition alive in his consistent playing. His live performances are not complete without him singing the good-natured blues "Whiskey Drinkin' Woman," a song one could have imagined Eddie "Cleanhead" Vinson performing.

Kenny Dorham (1924–1972) was on many classic sessions during 1946–64, but few of his fans probably know about *This Is The Moment* (Original Jazz Classics 812). While Dorham had sung an occasional blues while with Dizzy Gillespie's band in the 1940s, *This Is The Moment* was his only vocal album and was probably recorded in hopes of it duplicating the sales of Chet Baker. It didn't. Dorham's range (in both notes and emotions) was not much greater than Baker's, and he lacked Chet's charisma.

One of the most competitive of all jazzmen, **Roy Eldridge** (1911–1989) loved to battle other trumpeters. He was also an effective if just occasional singer who could scat well. Fortunately he knew better than to try to trade off with Ella

Fitzgerald. *Happy Time* (Original Jazz Classics 628) from 1975 is full of joy.

Eliane Elias (1960–) is a brilliant pianist who made a strong reputation for herself prior to 1993, the year that she began doubling on vocals. Does the world really need another flat-toned bossa nova singer, particularly when the vocalist is so much better as a pianist? Fortunately Elias has mostly emphasized her piano playing over her so-so singing, which comes across at best as a pleasant distraction.

Don Elliott (1926–1984) was a trumpeter, a fluent soloist on mellophone, a vibraphonist, an arranger and an occasional vocalist. In the late 1940s he was a singer in a group called Hi, Lo, Jack and the Dame. Most of his work in the 1950s was as a versatile instrumentalist. In the late 1950s, he started experimenting with multi-tracking and with changing the speed of taped performances. He overdubbed nine voices on an obscure album, *The Voices Of Don Elliott* (last on LP as ABC-Paramount 190), and he later created the Nutty Squirrels, a sort-of jazz adaptation of Alvin and the Chipmunks. In addition to recording at least three LPs, including *The Nutty Squirrels Go Bird Watching* (Columbia 8389) and *The Nutty Squirrels Sing A Hard Day's Night* (MGM 4272), the Nutty Squirrels appeared in over 100 cartoons, which unfortunately did not catch on commercially.

Bill Evans (1929–1980) was and remains one of the major influences on jazz acoustic pianists. His influence as a singer is a wee bit less, for he only recorded one vocal in his career, and it went unreleased for decades until appearing in the 18-CD set *The Complete Bill Evans On Verve* (Verve 314 527 953). Evans does his best on a humorous "Santa Claus Is Coming To Town."

The short-lived New Orleans trumpeter **George Girard** (1930–1957) was an excellent musician and a fine singer (both with medium-tempo lyrics and scatting) who would have undoubtedly become famous had he not been struck down by cancer.

Nat Gonella (1908–1998) in the 1930s was thought of as England's Louis Armstrong. He always was quick to call Satch his hero, and he emulated both his trumpet playing and his singing (although the latter with a British accent). Gonella had a good-time style and, when he made his final comeback late in life and was no longer able to play trumpet, his singing was still excellent.

Benny Goodman (1909–1986) was one of the greatest clarinetists of all time. But as a singer, he made one wait with impatience for his next clarinet solo. While he did not take it very seriously and of course knew that he was not much of a singer, he still felt compelled to take a vocal every once in awhile despite the lack of demand. Among his attempts at singing are 1938's "Ooo-Oh Boom," some shared vocals with Johnny Mercer on his 1939 series of *Camel Caravan* broadcasts, "Minnie's In The Money" in the 1943 movie *The Gang's All Here*, 1945's "Gotta Be This Or That", which was a minor hit, 1946's "Oh Baby" and "Put That Kiss Back Where You Found It," 1947's "Behave Yourself," "Four Or Five Times" in 1952 and 1955's "It's Bad For Me." The latter pretty well summed up his singing career.

Best known as a guitarist, **Tiny Grimes** (1916–1989) took vocals on "Romance Without Finance (Is A Nuisance)" and "I'll Always Love You Just The Same" that have been played a countless number of times through the years because his sideman on that 1944 session was Charlie Parker.

Pianist **Johnny Guarnieri** (1917–1985) loved to imitate other swing pianists, including Fats Waller, Count Basie and Art Tatum. He took an occasional vocal through the years, including two on the 1978 LP *Stealin' Apples* (Taz-Jaz 1002), on which he sounds like a demented Fats Waller.

Corky Hale does so many things well, including being one of jazz's few harpists, a fine pianist and a flutist in settings ranging from melodic jazz to middle-of-the-road pop and cabaret, that sometimes it is overlooked that she also takes tasteful vocals. She takes two on *Corky* (GNP/Crescendo 2254).

Lionel Hampton (1909–2002) was a brilliant vibraphonist, an exuberant drummer, a hot two-fingered pianist and an exciting entertainer. His vocals were thrown in as a change of pace, starting with Benny Goodman in 1936 and continuing until his final concert. No one really minded them, or remembered them either.

Keyboardist **Herbie Hancock** (1940–) was never a singer, but on many of his records of 1977 to 1988, he seemed to find it difficult to resist the Vocoder, a device that allowed him to "sing" through his synthesizer. Those "vocals" are interesting, the first time around. Joe Zawinul did the same thing 20 years later without any additional success.

Eddie Harris (1934–1996), a very distinctive tenor-saxophonist and an innovator on the electronic sax, was also a funny comedian ("This Is Why You're Overweight" is a classic of its kind) and an occasional singer. He emphasizes the latter on 1972's *Eddie Harris Sings The Blues* (Atlantic 1625).

Milt Hinton (1910–2000) appeared on a zillion dates as a bassist but never sang, except for his funny and insightful "Old Man Time," which he began performing regularly when he was nearing 80.

The great vibraphonist **Milt Jackson** (1923–1999) was a singer before he ever played vibes. From 1978, *Soul Believer* (Original Jazz Classics 686) was one of his few vocal records, and although his voice is pleasant, he proved that he had definitely made the right career move in the 1940s.

Stan Kenton (1911–1979) had a powerful speaking voice but only took one vocal in his entire career, a strictly-for-laughs collaboration with Benny Goodman called "Happy Blues" in which they make fun of each other's music and singing voices.

Actor **Jack Lemmon** (1925–2001) loved to play piano and sing, even though he never did it in his films. In the 1950s he recorded two albums for Epic, and they have been reissued as *A Twist Of Lemmon/Some Like It Hot* (Collector's Choice 205). Though his piano playing is stronger than his singing, he was quite effective at both.

One of the corniest vocalists and clarinetists in jazz history, **Ted Lewis** (1892–1971) became famous for singing "Me And My Shadow" and for his phrase "Is everybody happy?" He can never be totally ignored due to the all-star jazz lineups that he often used in the 1920s and '30s; his overly sentimental cornball singing was in "its own category."

Drummer **Shelly Manne** (1920–1984) only seems to have taken one vocal in his career, but his voice was strong and quite musical. On the hilarious satire of Dixieland and R&B recorded by the Stan Kenton Orchestra that is called "Blues In Burlesque," Manne belted out such lines as "I've got a woman/she's eight feet tall/sleeps in the kitchen/with her feet in the hall."

Influenced by King Oliver and Louis Armstrong in his trumpet playing and by Satch in his singing, **Wingy Manone** (1900–1982) led a series of popular records during 1935–41, also sometimes serving as a sidekick to Bing Crosby. His singing was limited and jivey but effective in small doses, finding its niche somewhere between Louis Prima and Nat Gonella.

Like Shelly Manne, arranger-trumpeter **Billy May** (1916–2004) only took one vocal in his career, and it was on a satirical piece. Unlike Manne, May had a terrible singing voice. On Charlie Barnet's "The Wrong Idea" (the other side of the 78 was called "The Right Idea"), he and the Barnet Orchestra tear apart the corny sweet bands of the 1930s, with May giving the band a new slogan: "Swing and Sweat with Charlie Barnet."

Rosy McHargue (1902–1999), a talented C-melody saxophonist and clarinetist who lived to be 97, loved to sing all of the choruses and verses to completely forgotten vintage tunes of the 1900 to 1930 era. His voice was just okay, but his enthusiasm and knowledge of an endless number of lyrics was always unique.

Glenn Miller (1904–1944) led the most popular swing band of the big band era and had over two dozen major hits. He was wise not to sing on any of them. His only vocal, a single chorus, was with the Dorsey Brothers Orchestra in 1934 on "Annie's Cousin Fanny" and, throughout his life, he preferred not to be reminded of it.

Irving Mills (1894–1985) is best remembered as Duke Ellington's manager and for his ability to get his name listed as co-composer on a remarkable number of songs. He was also a talent scout, a record producer and an occasional singer. Not a great vocalist, he recorded with Ellington on a few rare occasions and with such groups as Irving Mills' Hotsy Totsy Gang, Irving Mills' Modernists and the Whoopee Makers, which were also known as Mills' Musical Clowns.

The lovable tenor-saxophonist **James Moody** (1925–) usually sings a number or two during his shows, invariably "Moody's Mood For Love" and "Bennie's From Heaven." Since "Moody's Mood For Love" is vocalese based on his original alto solo, he is virtually the only singer to improvise on that classic tune, throwing in occasional yodels for punctuation.

The pioneering New Orleans trombonist **Kid Ory** (1886–1973) began to sing on an occasional basis when he made a major comeback in 1944 after more than a decade off the scene. His gruff voice sounded quite at home singing "Do What Ory Said," "Eh, La Bas" and tunes on which he sang in Creole French in the 1950s.

Oscar Peterson (1925–2007) was a truly remarkable pianist, one who was influenced a bit by Nat King Cole. Peterson also sang on a few very rare occasions and, on *With Respect To Nat* (Verve 557 486), he shows why he kept it a secret. During his 11 vocals, Peterson sounds like an exact duplicate of Nat Cole, in his sound and his phrasing. Considering that his speaking voice was different than Cole's, it is somewhat bizarre to hear him sing on this unique set.

Also bizarre, but for a different reason, are the vocals of drummer **Ben Pollack** (1903–1971). An important bandleader who managed to regularly have all of his best players get stolen away from him, Pollack fancied himself a singer by the late 1920s, even hiring drummer Ray Bauduc so he could front his band. Trouble is Pollack had a lousy voice, which he showed on numerous occasions. His trademark closing line, "For your pleasure, Ben Pollack," became a bit of a joke.

In contrast, **Buddy Rich** (1917–1987), who was a song and dance man in vaudeville as a teenager before he became the world's greatest drummer, was a surprisingly good singer. On several occasions in his career, he threatened to give up drumming and make his living as a singer, but that never lasted long, though he did record three vocal albums in the 1950s that are quite worthy.

Jimmy Rowles (1918–1996) was a subtle and consistently creative pianist who seemed to know nearly every song ever written. Starting with a Stan Getz record, *The Peacocks* (Koch 7867), which was a showcase for Rowles in 1975, the pianist regularly recorded vocals during his final 20 years, saying a great deal with his limited and typically subtle voice. His daughter, flugelhornist Stacy Rowles (1955–), has followed in his footsteps, emphasizing ballads and obscurities both in her instrumentals and her vocals, which emulate her dad.

Arturo Sandoval (1949–) is a true powerhouse, being a rather incredible trumpeter, an energetic timbale player, a skilled pianist and a hyper scat singer. When he scats, it as if one is listening to Dizzy Gillespie at three times the speed. He never seems to run out of ideas or breath. Catch him live and be amazed.

Although he rarely took more than an occasional vocal, pianist **George Shearing** (1919–) always loved to sing. An expert accompanist to other singers (including Nancy Wilson, Dakota Staton, Peggy Lee, Nat King Cole and especially Mel Tormé), Shearing in his later years tended to close his shows with a nostalgic ballad.

Actress **Cybill Shepherd** (1950–) enjoys singing standards and has a pleasing if limited voice. In 1976, she persuaded Stan Getz to record with her, and the results have been reissued as *Cybill Getz Better* (Inner City 1037).

Jabbo Smith (1908–1991) had the potential to be one of the greatest trumpeters of all time. In 1929 when he was 20, his recordings with his Rhythm Aces were so exciting that he was rated by many as being second to Louis Armstrong at the time. He was also an excellent singer and a hot scatter. Unfortunately his drinking and unreliability soon resulted in him drifting into obscurity, but in 1929 he had few competitors.

Bassist **Slam Stewart** (1914–1987) became famous for singing along with his bass, humming an octave above his bowed solos. He could be quite witty and speedy in singing the lines, becoming well known first with Slim Gaillard (as Slim and Slam) and then throughout his years with Art Tatum, Benny Goodman and countless others. Major Holley (1924–1990) was one of the few who could do what Stewart did, although he actually hummed in unison with his bass. *Shut Yo' Mouth* (Delos 1024) is a unique CD that features Stewart and Holley playing and humming together.

Frankie Trumbauer (1901–1956) was the master of the C-melody saxophone in the 1920s and '30s, a close associate of cornetist Bix Beiderbecke and one of the greatest of the early saxophonists. While his playing was colorful, his singing on his own records was very limited and often sounded like a monotone, with his vocalizing on "Futuristic Rhythm" being laughable.

An exuberant trombonist with impressive technique and a creative style within the bebop tradition in addition to being a big band leader and an arranger, **Scott Whitfield** (1963–) sang with the Manhattan Vocal Project and in recent times has been teaming up with Ginger Berglund for vocal duets. *Dreamsville* (ArtiosGroup 1200855) is their recent release, an excellent effort.

Clarence Williams (1893–1965), who was a decent pianist, a fine songwriter and a talented organizer of a countless number of record sessions in the 1920s and '30s, was also a cheerful jazz singer who clearly enjoyed being in the recording studio. Among his more memorable vocals are "When I March In April With May," "Farm Hand Papa," "How Could I Be Blue" and "You're Bound To Look Like A Monkey When You Get Old."

Lester Young (1909–1959), one of the greatest tenor-saxophonists of all time, took just one vocal in his career, and it went unreleased until decades after his death. While on a 1952 date with the Oscar Peterson Trio, Young took a good-humored vocal on "It Takes Two To Tango," probably inspired by Louis Armstrong's slightly earlier recording.

Trombonist **Trummy Young** (1912–1984) only sang on an occasional basis, but he did have a hit record of "Margie" while a member of the Jimmie Lunceford Orchestra in the 1930s, a number that he repeated on many occasions throughout his career. He was also an effective foil for Louis Armstrong (both musically and vocally) during his many years with the Armstrong All-Stars.

30 JAZZ VOCAL GROUPS

There have been surprisingly few significant jazz vocal groups throughout the past century. While vocal groups appeared on record as early as the 1890s (mostly spiritual ensembles), and there were occasional hot duos in the 1920s (including the Williams Sisters, who recorded a memorable version of "Sam, The Old Accordion Man"), the Rhythm Boys (which introduced Bing Crosby) can be considered the first important jazz vocal group, starting in 1927. During the swing era, many bands used vocal groups, including the Modernaires, the Pied Pipers and the Merry Macs, but most were closer to pop than jazz. One of the most popular of the vocal ensembles from the time, the Ink Spots, started out as a hot band like the early Mills Brothers before becoming a predictable if charming pop group. Groups of vocalists have been used to sweeten recordings since the 1940s without adding to the jazz content. During the past 30 years there have been a countless number of college vocal ensembles. But if one were to name the truly important jazz vocal groups, a list that included the Rhythm Boys; the Boswell Sisters; the Mills Brothers; Lambert, Hendricks and Ross; the Manhattan Transfer and perhaps Take Six would be considered pretty complete. This section includes those six plus 24 other contenders.

The Andrews Sisters

Although the Andrews Sisters were jazzy at times and performed with jazz backing during their prime years, they were really not an improvising jazz vocal group but a very popular ensemble that swung. Comprised of Patty Andrews (1918–), LaVerne Andrews (1911–1967) and Maxene Andrews (1916–1995), the Andrews Sisters were constantly joyful in their happy music, giving cheer and spirit to listeners during the last years of the Depression and throughout World War II.

Each of the Andrews Sisters was born in Mound, Minnesota. Inspired by the Boswell Sisters, they sang from a young age, appearing onstage locally and on the radio with Patty being the lead singer and soloist. They appeared at the Orpheum Theater in Minneapolis in December 1932, when they ranged in age from 14 to 21. The Andrews Sisters first hit the road in November 1933, becoming part of a vaudeville troupe for six months in the Midwest and then spending several years working with different bands. Their breakthrough year was 1937, when they made their recording debut while being part of Leon Belasco's orchestra; the songs were issued under Belasco's name. In the summer they were signed to Decca, and their second set of tunes as leaders included "Bei Mir Bist Du Schoen," which became a huge hit in early 1938. From then on, the Andrews Sisters were a household name.

The Andrews Sisters were a constant on the best sellers' charts, on radio and in movies. Among their hits (over 110 of their recordings made the charts during 1938–51 and 46 were in the Top 10) were "Hold Tight," "Ferryboat Serenade," "I'll Be With You In Apple Blossom Time," "Boogie Woogie Bugle Boy," "Beer Barrel Polka," "Don't Sit Under The Apple Tree," "Rum And Coca-Cola," "Christmas Island" and, in teamings with Bing Crosby (with whom they had 23 of their hits), "Pistol Packin' Mama," "Jingle Bells," "Don't Fence Me In" and "Ac-cent-tchu-ate The Positive." They sold over 75 million records and appeared in 15 Hollywood B-films during 1940–48.

The Andrews Sisters gradually faded in popularity during 1947–53. Although Patty Andrews tried a solo career during 1953–56, she eventually rejoined the group, which continued until 1966, when LaVerne had to retire after contracting cancer. After a period with Joyce de Young in LaVerne's place, the Andrews Sisters broke up in 1968. Although Patty and Maxene had a reunion for the *Over Here!* show in 1974, they had a permanent falling out the following year and instead continued with their solo careers. The Andrews Sisters will forever be associated with World War II nostalgia.

Recommended CDs: There are many samplers available of the Andrews Sisters. *The Golden Age Of The Andrews Sisters* (Jasmine 74) is an excellent four-CD set that includes virtually all of the high points from their careers up to 1951, while *Greatest Hits: 60th Anniversary Collection* (MCA 11727) is an excellent single disc that covers their musical legacy.

Beachfront Property

Beachfront Property was formed in 1979 to write and record jingles. They first started appearing live as a group in 1988 and made a strong impression during the first half of the 1990s. They had nine singers (Jeff Dolan, Wendy Abeling, Stan Castongia, Renee Kerr, Tom Dustman, Jennifer Dustman, Alyce Ohn, Bill Mumaw and Jill Mumaw) by 1990 so the group was a much larger version of Lambert, Hendricks and Ross or Manhattan Transfer. They recorded fine albums in 1990 and 1993, being down to eight singers at the time of the latter (with Michele Carroll replacing both Wendy Abeling and Renee Kerr). In 1995, they recorded their most recent CD to date, a so-so Christmas album. By then they were at seven singers.

Since that time, Beachfront Property has shrunk down to four singers (with Tom Dustman being the group's artistic director) and expanded their range to include pop and rock and roll in their repertoire, staying active in Southern California but not recording any further CDs during the past 13 years.

Recommended CDs: The year 1990's *Beachfront Property* (Cexton 1848) and especially the boppish *Straight Up* (Cexton 0316) from 1993 are worth searching for. *A Beachfront Property Christmas* (Cexton 2262) is taken a bit too straight, although it is listenable.

The Blue Stars of France

In 1954, Eddie Barclay (head of the Barclay label in France) thought of the idea of recording boppish jazz and pop songs with a vocal octet. Blossom Dearie was in Paris at the time, so he hired her to form a group that became known as the Blue Stars (or Les Blue Stars). Over a two-year period, the Blue Stars recorded three albums. In addition to Blossom Dearie, the original group included singers Christiane Legrand (Michel Legrand's sister), Jeanine DeWaleyne, Nadine Young, "Fats" Sadi, Christian Chevallier, Roger Guérin (normally a trumpeter) and Jean Mercadier. The ensemble, which sang in French, had a surprising hit with their version of "Lullaby Of Birdland."

By the time the Blue Stars recorded their final CD during 1956–57, *Pardon My English*, Blossom Dearie and Fats Sadi had departed, replaced by Ward Swingle (future leader of the Swingle Sisters) and Mimi Perrin. In addition to performing fine music, the Blue Stars are important for leading in future years to the Double Six Of Paris and the Swingle Singers.

Recommended CDs: The Blue Stars' three CDs are *Lullaby Of Birdland* (Five Four 6), which is their definitive set, *Les Blue Stars* (Barclay 760692) and *Pardon My English* (Mercury 111456).

The Boswell Sisters

One of the most exciting jazz vocal groups of all time and easily the best of the "sisters" groups, the Boswell Sisters were in their own category. Unlike other vocal ensembles that simply sang a song straight, the Boswell Sisters utilized key, tempo and mood changes within most of their songs, they alternated lyrics with scatting, and they each had swinging styles and beautiful voices.

Connie (1907–1976), Martha (1908–1958) and Helvetia Boswell (1909–1988) were born and raised in New Orleans. Connie, who was the group's solo singer, contracted polio during infancy and was never able to walk. She always appeared in public in a well-hidden wheelchair, and few knew about her handicap. While each of the sisters played instruments as children, with Connie playing cello, piano, alto sax and trombone, Vet being a violinist and Martha learning piano, only Martha would be a professional musician, accompanying the group on piano. As teenagers in 1925, the Boswell Sisters (who were ages 16 to 18 at the time) made their recording debut with "Nights When I'm Lonely" (sounding like little kids), while Connie had a solo feature on "I'm Gonna Cry."

The Boswells worked locally, and then in the late 1920s they gained attention in Los Angeles, where they appeared on radio five nights a week. In 1930 they began to record regularly. With their adventurous arrangements, which were always full of surprises, their heated singing and their Southern accents (many listeners assumed that they were black), the Boswell Sisters sounded unlike any other vocal group up to that time. By 1931 they were a hit, appearing regularly at New York's Paramount Hotel.

The Boswell Sisters appeared in several films (their best filmed performance is their version of "Crazy People" in *Big Broadcast of 1932*), they visited Europe in 1933 and 1935, and many of their records featured top jazz soloists, including Bunny Berigan, the Dorsey Brothers and Joe Venuti. They held their own with the very best.

Unfortunately when all three sisters got married in 1936, Vet and Martha decided to retire. If the group had stayed together, the great commercial success enjoyed by the Andrews Sisters would have certainly been theirs, for the swing era was just getting going. Surprisingly the Boswell Sisters never had any official musical reunions. Connie Boswell had a reasonably successful solo career during the next 25 years, but the Boswell Sisters were largely forgotten by all but historians and record collectors, only being rediscovered in the 1970s and '80s.

Recommended CDs: All of the Boswell Sisters' regular recordings are on *The Boswell Sisters Collection, Vols. 1–5* (Nostalgia Arts 3007, 3008, 3009, 3022 and 3023). While the first volume is the most essential, each of these CDs has plenty of great moments. Among the high points of the Boswells' discographies are classic versions of "Roll On, Mississippi, Roll On," "Shout, Sister, Shout," "Heebies Jeebies," "Was That The Human Thing To Do," "Put That Sun Back In The Sky," "Everybody Loves My Baby," "There'll Be Some Changes Made," "If It Ain't Love," "We Just Couldn't Say 'Goodbye,'" "Sentimental Gentleman From Georgia" and "Crazy People." Rare material, primarily alternate takes and radio broadcasts, are available on *The Boswell Sisters 1930–1935* (Retrieval 79009) and *Syncopating Harmonists From New Orleans* (Take Two 406).

Bug Alley

It did not last long, but Bug Alley was a most intriguing vocal group. Originally formed in Montreal by singer Karen Young as a folk trio in 1975, it became a jazz group by the following year. Young, Liz Tansey, Steve Cole (also playing guitar) and David Thompson (doubling on bass) formed an intriguing quartet while being accompanied by drummer Andre White and a few guest artists. While Lambert, Hendricks and Ross was a key influence, the band's lone album, *Bug Alley*, also includes a three-song Boswell Sisters medley, "Milestones," their original "Bop Follies" and four features for Karen Young. Bug Alley broke up in 1979, though it had a reunion at the 1981 Monterey Jazz Festival. Karen Young has since had a significant solo career, including duos with bassist Michel Donato.

Recommended CDs: The band's lone album, *Bug Alley*, was originally released as an LP (PM 019) and has been reissued in Japan (Vivid 6174).

The Cats and a Fiddle

The Cats and a Fiddle were similar to the Spirits of Rhythm except that they were a bit more predictable. Founded by guitarist Austin Powell in 1937, the original group also included Jimmy Henderson on tipple, Ernie Price on guitar and tipple and bassist Chuck Barksdale; all four of the musicians also sang. How this group originally gained its name is not known, for they did not have a violin or fiddle in their personnel. After two years of struggling with low-level jobs and gaining brief spots in two Hollywood films, the group was signed to Bluebird in August 1939.

The band had a hit in 1940 with "I Miss You" but suffered a major loss when Jimmy Henderson contracted meningitis and died. Herbie Miles was his first replacement, and he was succeeded during 1941–43 by guitarist Tiny Grimes. Other singers heard through the years with the group were George Steinback, Mifflin "Peewee" Branford, Hank Haslett, Emitt Slay, Shirley Moore and Doris Knighton. The Cats and a Fiddle lasted until 1950, although there were later temporary revivals through the 1950s.

Recommended CDs: Of the group's 32 Bluebird recordings, 27 are on *We Cats Swing For You* (Living Era 3475), their definitive CD.

The Chenille Sisters

The unrelated Chenille Sisters comprised Connie Huber (who also plays guitar, drums and piano), Cheryl Dawdy and Grace Morand. They are an eclectic group that can perform swing à la the Boswell Sisters, original country/folk music or put on shows that are strictly for children. Formed in 1985 in Ann Arbor, Michigan, the Chenille Sisters are based in the Midwest. They have recorded a dozen albums since 1986, appeared on *A Prairie Home Companion*, been featured on PBS and performed at many festivals since then.

Recommended CDs: The most jazz-oriented recordings by the Chenille Sisters are *Mama I Wanna Make Rhythm* (Red House 39) and especially *Whatcha Gonna Swing Tonight* (Red House 50) with James Dapogny's Chicago Jazz Band.

The Cunninghams

Don Cunningham and his wife Alicia have been singing as the Cunninghams since they were married in the early 1970s. Their voices blend together very well, they are both expert scat singers, and although they can perform a wide variety of music, they sound at their best when performing bop-oriented jazz. They made a strong impression in the late 1980s when they were based in Los Angeles and recorded three albums for the Discovery label. In 1996 they moved to Las Vegas, and since then the Cunninghams usually perform close to half the year in Japan, where they are quite popular.

Recommended CDs: Although each of their releases is scarce, the Cunninghams are in excellent form on *Make Me (A Sweet Potato Pie)* (Discovery 70943), *Strings 'N Swing: I Remember Bird* (Discovery 70954) and *Scat Tones M' Bones* (Discovery 70973).

The Delta Rhythm Boys

The Delta Rhythm Boys spanned from swing to R&B and had a surprisingly long run. They were formed in 1934 at Langston University in Oklahoma. The original group had Lee Gaines, Kelsey Pharr, Carl Jones and Traverse Crawford, with pianist Rene DeKnight. The singers transferred to Dillard University in New Orleans in 1936 and two years later started appearing in New York. They appeared in the Broadway shows *Sing Out The News* and *The Hot Mikado* and began making records. Their versions of "Take The 'A' Train" and "Dry Bones" were minor hits, they appeared on sessions with Mildred Bailey, Ella Fitzgerald and Ruth Brown, and were featured on the radio regularly.

Surprisingly the Delta Rhythm Boys were able to continue doing well during the R&B era, appearing in such mid-1950s films as *Rock And Roll Revue* and *Rhythm And Blues Revue*. Because they were so popular overseas while eventually being overshadowed in the United States, the Delta Rhythm Boys moved to Europe in 1956, where they continued working on an occasional basis until Lee Gaines' death in 1987.

Recommended CDs: *Just A-Rockin' And A-Jivin': Anthology Vol. 1, 1941–1946* (Dee-Jay 55108), *Jump And Jive 'Til One O'Clock: Anthology Vol. 2, 1947–1950* (Dee-Jay 55109) and *Radio, Gimme Some Jive: Performances, 1941–1945* (Dee-Jay 55110) do a fine job of summing up the group's history during its prime years. *The Delta Rhythm Boys* (Collectables 6391) finds the ensemble still sounding fine in 1957.

Dick and Kiz Harp

In 1960, the married couple of Dick and Kiz Harp were on the verge of making it big. While Dick played piano and joined in occasionally on vocals, Kiz Harp was the main draw. She had a husky and sensuous yet often playful voice. Based in Dallas during the second half of the 1950s, they played regularly at their 90th Floor club, reminding some of Jackie and Roy, although with their own sound. On *Dick and Kiz Harp At The 90th Floor*, they perform such offbeat material as "You Are Not My First Love," "Too Good For The Average Man" and "Down In The Depths On The 90th Floor" with charm, swing and plenty of unexpected moments. Their fans reportedly included Marlene Dietrich, Tony Bennett, Stan Kenton and Burgess Meredith, and the release of their first album generated a great deal of interest.

But tragically in December of 1960, Kiz Harp suffered a cerebral hemorrhage that caused her death at age 29. A second album, *Again*, was released posthumously. It has additional tunes from the same session that had generated the first date and is of equal interest, but this is all that remains from what could have been.

Recommended CDs: *Dick And Kiz Harp At The 90th Floor* (90th Floor 901) and *Again* (90th Floor 902) are the entire musical legacy of this rewarding if now-forgotten vocal team.

The Double Six of Paris

A descendant of the Blue Stars of France and influenced by Lambert, Hendricks and Ross, the Double Six of Paris was formed in 1959. Led by Mimi Perrin, the group at times during its six years included such singers as Monique Aldebert-Guérin, Louis Aldebert, Christian Legrand, Ward Swingle and Roger Guérin. The Double Six gained its name because it featured six singers who overdubbed their voices, so the recordings had a dozen vocalists. A large portion of their music consisted of vocalese with lyrics in French.

The group broke up in 1965. Mimi Perrin led a similar group with the same name for a year before giving up. Since then, Ward Swingle had great success with the Swingle Singers, and Louis and Monique Aldebert have worked and recorded as the Aldeberts.

Recommended CDs: The Double Six recorded six albums in all. *Les Double Six* (RCA 65659) has all of the music from the group's first two projects, including quite a few songs originally arranged by Quincy Jones and vocalese based on recordings of Woody Herman, John Coltrane, Gerry Mulligan, Charlie Parker, Miles Davis, Stan Kenton and other jazz greats. *Dizzy Gillespie And The Double Six* (Philips 830 224) from 1963 teams Gillespie and pianist Bud Powell with the Double Six on a dozen selections written by or associated with the great trumpeter. *The Double Six Of Paris Sings Ray Charles* (Philips 600-141) was the group's final recording but has not yet reappeared on CD.

The Four Freshmen

Though many have debated over whether the singing of the Four Freshmen would be considered jazz (they are also thought of as easy listening), they have been at least jazz-inspired and their harmonies certainly have been a major influence on other vocal groups, including the Beach Boys.

In 1948, Ross Barbour and Don Barbour formed a barbershop quartet at Butler University in Indiana called Hal's Harmonizers, which also included Hal Kratzsch and Marvin Pruitt. The group became more jazz-oriented later in the year, when Pruitt was succeeded by Bob Flanigan. In September 1948 the unit, which was then called the Four Freshmen, first went on the road. Despite recommendations by Woody Herman and Dizzy Gillespie, the quartet struggled for a time. In 1950 Stan Kenton heard the group performing in Dayton, told his record label, Capitol, to record them, and they were signed. In 1952 they had a hit with "It's A Blue World," and from then on the Four Freshmen were one of the most popular vocal groups of the decade.

Hal Kratzsch was replaced in 1953 by Ken Errair, who left in 1956 and was succeeded by Ken Albers. Don Barbour left in 1960 and was replaced by Bill Comstock. The Four Freshmen, which was always a complete band in itself with its singers also playing instruments (Flanigan played trombone and bass, Don Barbour and Bill Comstock were both guitarists, Ross Barbour played drums, and Hal Kratzsch, Ken Errair and Ken Albers each played trumpet, mellophone and bass), had further hits in "Day By Day" and "Graduation Day." Their string of recordings for Capitol was quite popular, the group appeared regularly on television, they sometimes appeared with Stan Kenton, and their concerts were well attended. Even as the music world went through major changes in the 1960s and '70s, the Four Freshmen continued working. Their personnel changed over time (though the Flanigan-Barbour-Albers-Comstock lineup stayed together during 1960–73), with Bob Flanigan being the final early member before he departed in 1992, but the basic sound has remained the same even as new songs get added to their repertoire. Today, the Four Freshmen are still appearing regularly at concerts and putting on colorful shows, sixty years after the group was born. The current edition comprises Brian Eichenberger (guitar), Curtis Calderon (trumpet), Vince Johnson (bass) and Bob Ferreira (drums), who is the group's veteran as a member since 1992.

Recommended CDs: A limited-edition nine-CD box set, *The Complete Capitol Four Freshmen Fifties Sessions* (Mosaic 9-203), has all of their recordings during 1950–60, including such albums as *Voices In Modern*, *And Five Trombones*, *And Five Trumpets*, *And Five Saxes*, *And Five Guitars*, and *The Freshman Year*. Many of the group's individual sets are available through Collector's Classics. *Live In Holland* (Four Freshmen) from 2006 is a good example of how the Four Freshmen sound today.

Hendricks and Company

When Lambert, Hendricks and Bevan broke up in 1964, Jon Hendricks started a strong solo career, including a four-year stint (1968–72) spent in Europe. After returning to San Francisco, in the early 1980s he put together Hendricks and Company, using his wife Judith, his daughter Michelle and a male singer who at times has been Bobby McFerrin, Kevin Burke or Mr. Z. Sometimes another daughter, Aria Hendricks, gives the group a fifth voice. Hendricks and Company (also known as Hendricks and Family) extends the legacy of Lambert, Hendricks and Ross, not only reviving some of the older charts but giving Jon Hendricks an opportunity to write new vocalese for his vocal ensemble.

Recommended CDs: Jon Hendricks and his family members appear on several cuts on a few of his CDs. *Love* (Muse 5258) and *Boppin' At The Blue Note* (Telarc 83320) have the vocal group's best showcases.

The Hi-Lo's

The Hi-Lo's were considered one of the most innovative jazz vocal groups of the 1950s due to their adventurous harmonies, which decades later would influence Take Six.

The group began in early 1953, when Gene Puerling and Bob Strasen started teaming up with Clark Burroughs and Bob Morse, two singers from Billy May's orchestra. Since two of the singers were tall and two were small, they named their band the Hi-Lo's. They made their recording debut for Trend in April 1953, having a minor hit with their version of "Georgia." Gene Puerling's adventurous arrangements for the group, along with the singers' wide ranges, gave the Hi-Lo's their own musical personality. In 1954 they switched to the Starlite label and continued to stretch themselves. After signing with Columbia in late 1956, they had a strong seller in their LP *Suddenly It's The Hi-Lo's*, and they also recorded *Ring Around Rosie With Rosemary Clooney*. Despite their artistic successes, in general the Hi-Lo's were very much an underground group,

never really breaking through commercially. In 1958 Bob Strasen left the group and was replaced by Don Shelton. After being dropped by Columbia in 1960, the Hi-Lo's made two albums for Reprise that were attempts at capitalizing on the popularity of folk music and bossa nova. Shelton departed in 1964 and was replaced by Frank Howren (briefly) and Milt Chapman before the Hi-Lo's broke up in 1965. In 1977, with the success of Puerling's Singers Unlimited, the MPS label suggested that he put together a Hi-Lo's reunion. The Hi-Lo's with Puerling, Shelton, Morse and Burroughs toured on an occasional basis up to 1994.

Recommended CDs: A strong sampling of the Hi-Lo's recordings can be gained by acquiring *Nice Work If You Can Get It* (Varese Sarabande 5694), *Under Glass/The Hi-Lo's I Presume* (MCA 19393), *Suddenly It's The Hi-Lo's/Harmony In Jazz* (Collectables 6026), *Now Hear This/Broadway Playbill* (Collectables 6465) and *Love Nest/All Over The Place* (Collectables 6694).

Jackie and Roy

Singer Jackie Cain and her husband singer-pianist Roy Kral were a team for 55 years (1947–2002). Roy Kral (whose younger sister was Irene Kral) had his own group as early as 1939, and, after spending four years in the military (mostly playing in Army bands), he made his recording debut in 1947 with Georgie Auld. After Roy and Jackie met, they worked with Charlie Ventura's "Bop For The People" band from 1948 to 1949, often singing unusual material, such as "Euphoria" and "East Of Suez," that featured their flexible voices. Married in 1949, they performed as Jackie and Roy for over a half-century, usually in a quartet with bass and drums. Some of their music was bop-oriented, while some of their projects found them exploring show tunes and more esoteric material. While Jackie Cain performed occasional features and Roy Kral was featured now and then on instrumentals, they became famous for the sound of their two voices together. Jackie and Roy were a constant on the music scene until Roy Kral's death in 2002.

Recommended CDs: Some of Jackie and Roy's most jazz-oriented releases are *Jackie And Roy* (Savoy 92985), *The ABC/Paramount Years* (Koch 7927), *East Of Suez* (Concord 4149), *High Standards* (Concord 4186), *Full Circle* (Fantasy 24768), *Spring Can Really Hang You Up The Most* (Black Lion 760904), *Echoes* (Jazzed Media 1014), *Forever* (Music Masters 65128) and *The Beautiful Sea* (DRG 8474).

Lambert, Hendricks and Ross

Arguably the best jazz vocal group of all time (along with the Boswell Sisters), Lambert, Hendricks and Ross was certainly the definitive vocalese ensemble. In 1957 Dave Lambert and Jon Hendricks worked on a project in which voices would recreate some of Count Basie's classic recordings from the 1930s and '40s. They gathered together a large group of vocalists to sing Hendricks' lyrics to the ensembles and solos of Basie and his band, but discovered that only one of the singers was capable of singing the solos of Lester Young, Buck Clayton, Harry "Sweets" Edison and Count Basie: Annie Ross.

After a great deal of thought, it was decided to overdub their three voices so as to simulate the Basie band. The album, *Sing A Song Of Basie*, was a surprise hit and almost immediately Lambert, Hendricks and Ross became a working band. A popular attraction at clubs and jazz festivals, Lambert,

Hendricks and Ross recorded six albums and featured the three singers individually, scatting together and on complicated vocalese pieces, including singing "Goin' To Chicago" around Joe Williams' voice. There had never been a group like it before, and many vocal ensembles have tried (usually without total success) to bring back the magic of this unique group.

In 1962, Annie Ross dropped out of the band, citing health problems. Her replacement, Yolande Bevan, was an odd choice due to her exotic sound and the fact that she was not a great soloist, although she was fine in ensembles. Lambert, Hendricks and Bevan continued until 1964, when it seemed the right time to break up.

Recommended CDs: All of Lambert, Hendricks and Ross' recordings are available on *Sing A Song Of Basie* (GRP/Impulse 112), *Sing Along With Basie* (Roulette 7953322), which teams the singers with the actual Basie band, *The Swingers* (EMI 46849) and the double-CD *The Hottest New Group In Jazz* (Columbia/Legacy 64933). Among the many high points along the way are their versions of "Little Pony," "Fiesta In Blue," "Jumpin' At The Woodside," "Lil' Darlin'," "Goin' To Chicago," "Four," "Swingin' Till The Girls Come Home," "Cloudburst," "Gimme That Wine," "Summertime" and "Poppity Pop." Lambert, Hendricks and Bevan are not without interest on *Live At Basin Street East* (BMG 25756), *Live At Newport '63* (RCA 68731) and *Havin' A Ball At The Village Gate* (Bluebird 21112).

The Manhattan Transfer

It all started with a cab ride in the early 1970s. Tim Hauser, who had led a short-lived version of the Manhattan Transfer during 1969–71, was working as a cab driver, and one of his fares was Laurel Massé, a waitress who was just starting a singing career. Another day he picked up the conga player for the group Laurel Canyon, who invited him to a party where he met Janis Siegel. After a lot of talking, Hauser, Siegel, Massé and Alan Paul formed the Manhattan Transfer, a group that officially began on October 1, 1972.

Starting as a swing-based band that was open to other styles, the Manhattan Transfer worked locally and then began to catch on in 1975 when they signed with Atlantic. A car accident resulted in Laurel Massé dropping out of the group and Cheryl Bentyne permanently taking her place in 1978. Otherwise, the group's personnel has been unchanged during the past 35 years. Performing swing, bop, vocalese, rock and roll oldies, pop and Brazilian music during their fast moving shows, the Manhattan Transfer has always been both entertaining and very musical. While Cheryl Bentyne and especially Janis Siegel have had strong solo careers, the four singers have remained dedicated to the Manhattan Transfer, which accounts for its longevity and continued relevance and constant success.

Recommended CDs: In the Manhattan Transfer's long discography, its obvious jazz classics are *Vocalese* (Atlantic 81266) from 1985 and 1997's *Swing* (Atlantic 83012). The former has an all-star cast and features the vocalese lyrics of Jon Hendricks, while the latter has the Rosenberg Trio, some Western Swing players and a guest appearance by violinist Stephane Grappelli. But nearly all of the Manhattan Transfer's recordings have at least a few selections of strong interest to jazz listeners, including *Manhattan Transfer* (Atlantic 18133), *Pastiche* (Atlantic 19163), *Extensions* (Atlantic 19258), *Mecca For Moderns* (Atlantic 16036), *Bodies And Souls* (Atlantic 80104), *Live '86* (Atlantic 81723), *Brasil* (Atlantic 81803),

The Spirit Of St. Louis (Atlantic 83394), *Couldn't Be Hotter* (Telarc 83586) and *Vibrate* (Telarc 83603).

The Mel-Tones

In 1943 when Mel Tormé was a drummer, singer and up-and-coming arranger with the Chico Marx Band (directed by Ben Pollack), he met up with five singers who called themselves "The School Kids" since they were all attending Los Angeles City College at the time. One of their key singers, Tom Kenny, who was also their arranger, was heading for the Army, so Tormé took his place. The group, which also included Bernie Parke, Diz Disruhd (soon to be drafted and replaced by Les Baxter), Betty Beveridge and Ginny O'Connor (the future wife of Henry Mancini), had a lot of potential but needed a new leader. Under the name of "The Skylarks," they worked a bit in Los Angeles but without any major success, but in 1944 as "The Mel-Tones," they began to flourish. Tormé's advanced arrangements gave the band its own hip sound and they appeared on radio and even in motion pictures. By year-end they were being billed as Mel Tormé And The Mel-Tones. In 1945 they teamed up with Artie Shaw on a few record dates, with their greatest hit being a particularly catchy version of "What Is This Thing Called Love?"

When Tormé was drafted, the group broke up. However, he was not in the military for long, and in 1946 he brought back the Mel-Tones. But soon Tormé's solo career made the Mel-Tones unnecessary, and they gradually faded away, although they came back (with Louis Jean Norman in place of Betty Beveridge) for the 1949 recording of "California Suite."

Recommended CDs: *A Foggy Day* (Musicraft 70054), *There's No One But You* (Musicraft 70060) and *Velvet Moods* (E 90) have most of the Mel-Tones recordings. The group did not record all that often, but luckily there are a fair number of existing radio broadcasts, including Tormé's *Live With The Mel-Tones Vol. 1* (Mr. Music 7005) and *Live With The Mel-Tones Vol. 2* (Mr. Music 7006).

The Mills Brothers

Today, the Mills Brothers are remembered for being a cheerful middle-of-the-road pop group that sang in conventional fashion in the 1940s and '50s, sort of a male equivalent of the Andrews Sisters. But unlike the Andrews Sisters, the Mills Brothers were an innovative jazz group in their early days, one that has rarely been duplicated.

John Mills Jr. (1911–1936), Herbert Mills (1912–1989), Harry Mills (1913–1982) and Donald Mills (1915–1999) were all born in Piqua, Ohio. They started off singing in church and at their father's barbershop. Harry Mills used to play a kazoo. When the brothers entered a local amateur contest, Harry realized at the last minute that he had lost his kazoo. In desperation, he imitated a trumpet, cupping his hands in front of his mouth. That was so successful that his siblings also worked on developing the ability to imitate instruments. Although John Mills' guitar was the only instrument that they utilized, one would swear that they also had two trumpets, a trombone and a tuba, not only in the ensembles but also during individual solos.

The Mills Brothers at first worked throughout the Midwest in the late 1920s, and they were hired by radio station WLW in Cincinnati. When Duke Ellington heard them, he helped get the group signed to the Okeh label. They moved to New York in late 1930, where they became the first African-

Americans to have a network show on radio. They became a sensation, recorded regularly and appeared in several movies in the 1930s (usually for a song or two); they were a constant on the radio, and they also visited Europe. Billed as "four boys and a guitar," they also collaborated on recordings with Duke Ellington, Louis Armstrong and Bing Crosby and in the movies with Dick Powell. In 1936 tragedy struck when John Mills suddenly passed away from pneumonia. The Mills Brothers' father, John Mills Sr. (1882–1967) took his place as a singer, although a guitarist from outside the family had to be employed from then on.

After the Mills Brothers had a major hit in 1942 with "Paper Doll," which sold six million copies, they stopped imitating instruments and became a much more conventional vocal group, having other hits, including "Opus One," "Glow Worm" and "You're Nobody 'Til Somebody Loves You." Although John Sr. retired in 1957, the Mills Brothers continued working into the 1970s, appearing regularly on television. Donald Mills performed with his son John Mills as late as the mid-1990s as the last remaining Mills Brother.

Recommended CDs: All of the Mills Brothers' recordings of 1931 to 1939, plus some radio appearances and film soundtracks, are available on *Chronological, Vols. 1–6* (JSP 301, 302, 303, 304, 320 and 345). Hearing their versions of such songs as "Tiger Rag," "Nobody's Sweetheart," "Sweet Sue," "Smoke Rings," "Limehouse Blues," "Organ Grinder's Swing," "Caravan," and "Basin Street Blues" should dispel the image of the Mills Brothers as a safe and predictable group. The two-CD set *The Anthology 1931–68* (MCA 11279) sums up the Mills Brothers' entire history quite well. *The Board Of Directors And Annual Report* (MCA 19366) combine together the Mills Brothers two 1960s albums with the Count Basie Orchestra.

New York Voices

In 1986, Darmon Meader, Peter Eldridge, Kim Nazarian and Caprice Fox, all of whom attended Ithaca College in New York, were part of an alumni group formed to tour the European jazz festivals that summer. They enjoyed the experience so much that the following year, with Sara Krieger, they formed New York Voices. Although sometimes overshadowed by the Manhattan Transfer, New York Voices has been one of the top jazz vocal groups of the past 20 years, performing straight-ahead jazz and vocalese plus Brazilian, pop and R&B. In 1989 they signed to GRP and made their first recording. In 1992 Sara Krieger retired and was replaced by Lauren Kinhan. Caprice Fox left the group in early 1994, and New York Voices has since continued with the four voices of Meader, Eldridge, Nazarian and Kinhan. They have recorded seven albums to date under their own name, made guest appearances on a variety of CDs and occasionally performed with the Boston Pops Orchestra.

Recommended CDs: Thus far New York Voices has recorded *New York Voices* (GRP 9589), *Hearts Of Fire* (GRP 9653), *What's Inside* (GRP 9700), *Collection* (GRP 9766), *New York Voices Sing The Songs Of Paul Simon* (RCA 09026-68872), *Sing! Sing! Sing!* (Concord 4961) and *A Day Like This* (MCG Jazz 1031). In addition, they have recorded with the Count Basie Orchestra on *Live At Manchester Craftsmen's Guild* (MCG Jazz 1002), with Don Sebesky for his *I Remember Bill* (RCA 68929), with Jim Hall on *By Arrangements* (Telarc 83436) and with Paquito D'Rivera on *Brazilian Dreams* (MCG Jazz 1010).

The Pfister Sisters

The Pfister Sisters comprises three unrelated singers (Holley Bendtsen, Suzy Malone and Yvette Voelker-Cuccia, with Amasa Miller on piano) who closely emulate the Boswell Sisters. Organized in New Orleans in 1979, the trio has worked together steadily ever since. They mostly stick to vintage swing and pre-swing standards but occasionally perform an original or a later R&B/soul piece. In recent times, Suzy Malone left the group and moved north, but she has been ably replaced by Debbie Davies. Along the way, the Pfister Sisters have appeared with the Neville Brothers, Linda Ronstadt and Maxene Andrews.

Recommended CDs: *New Orleans* (Great Southern 11010) features the Pfister Sisters on diverse material. *All's Well That's Boswell* (Audiophile 309) is a very good tribute to the Boswell Sisters. *Change In The Weather* (Mambo Goddess) is their most recent recording and on the same level as *All's Well*.

Rare Silk

When Rare Silk was formed in 1979, it was a swing-oriented female vocal trio a little reminiscent of the Andrews Sisters and the Pied Pipers with a touch of the Boswell Sisters. The original group consisted of Gaile Gillaspie, Marylynn Gillaspie and Marguerite Juenemann. They appeared with Benny Goodman at the 1980 Playboy Jazz Festival. However, within two years they had greatly modernized their style, with Juenemann departing and Barbara Reeves and Todd Buffa joining up. As a vocal quartet, Rare Silk was exploring music by Freddie Hubbard, Chick Corea and Keith Jarrett among others and seemed to have a great deal of potential. However, after three albums, they broke up in 1988.

Recommended CDs: *New Weave* (Polydor 10028) is a great CD, highlighted by Richie Cole's "New York Afternoon," "Red Clay," "Spain" and "Sugar." *American Eyes* (Palo Alto 8086) is also excellent, while *Black And Blue* (TBA 3976) has not yet been reissued on CD.

The Real Group

One of the finest jazz vocal ensembles around today is an a cappella group from Sweden. Formed in 1984 and initially inspired by Bobby McFerrin, because a lot of their early repertoire came from *The Real Book*, a collection of jazz standards, they jokingly called themselves "The Real Group," a name that stuck. The five-voice group, comprising Katarina Henryson, Anders Edenroth, Peder Karlsson, Anders Jalkeus and Margareta Bengtson (who left in late 2006 and was succeeded by the band's long-time substitute Johanna Nystrom), recorded their first CD in 1987. The singers all attended a post-graduate course at the College of Music in Stockholm, graduating in 1989 and working steadily ever since. During 1992–93 the Real Group was featured regularly in an entertainment show called *Knapp Igen*. It gave them a rare chance to perform with other musicians rather than a cappella. They made several tours of the United States during 1994–98, which gave them an international reputation, but they have mostly worked in Europe. During their 23 years together, the Real Group has performed more than 2,000 times and recorded a dozen CDs. They have evolved from interpreting standards to introducing their own originals, while staying very much a jazz group.

Recommended CDs: The Real Group's most readily available releases are *The Real Group* (Caprice 1), *Nothing But The*

Real Group (Caprice 21376), *Roster* (Caprice 21405), *Unreal* (Town Crier 519), *Live In Stockholm* (Town Crier 522) and *Get Real* (Act 92522).

The Rhythm Boys

Arguably the first important jazz vocal group (if one does not count the team of Carleton Coon and Joe Sanders), the Rhythm Boys were undisciplined but quite inventive. Bing Crosby and Al Rinker were two youths from Washington who in 1926 were working as a duo (with Bing on drums and Rinker on piano) in vaudeville shows. On a whim, they came down to Los Angeles to seek their fortune, staying with Rinker's sister, Mildred Bailey. She gave them their big break by introducing them to Paul Whiteman, who decided to hire them. As a duo, they flopped, but when Whiteman added singer-pianist Harry Barris to the group and they were called the Rhythm Boys, they became a popular attraction. Barris in particular was a colorful performer, using the piano as a prop, scatting wildly, and ending most of the group's performances with a long drawn-out "pahh."

The Rhythm Boys appeared and recorded as a separate unit, as part of Whiteman's big band and sometimes with other Whiteman singers who had a much "sweeter" tone, including Jack Fulton, Austin "Skin" Young and Charles Gaylord. Among their better known recordings were "Mississippi Mud," "I'm Coming Virginia," "Out Of Town Gal," "Changes," "There Ain't No Sweet Man That's Worth The Salt Of My Tears" (the latter two with the "sweet" singers), "That's My Weakness Now," "Because My Baby Don't Mean 'Maybe' Now," "Rhythm King," "So The Bluebirds And The Blackbirds Got Together" and "Happy Feet."

The Rhythm Boys caused Paul Whiteman a lot of grief along the way due to their carousing and unreliability. When Whiteman had to cut back in 1930, they were let go. The Rhythm Boys recorded "Three Little Words" with Duke Ellington and performed with Gus Arnheim's orchestra for a time (recording "Them There Eyes"), but soon Bing Crosby was on his way to the top, and the group broke up. Al Rinker mostly worked behind the scenes during his later years (occasionally taking background vocals), while Harry Barris wrote songs ("I Surrender Dear" and "Wrap Your Troubles In Dreams") and had tantalizingly brief (and usually unbilled) cameos in quite a few films. Were it not for his drinking, Barris had the potential to be a big star. The Rhythm Boys only had one reunion, for a 1943 Paul Whiteman broadcast.

Strangely enough, there is not yet a CD that is dedicated to the recordings of the Rhythm Boys. The best way to get at least a few of their fun performances is to acquire some late-1920s Paul Whiteman sets.

The Ritz

The Ritz (not to be confused with a barbershop quartet having the same name) was formed in the early 1980s as a bop-oriented vocal trio consisting of Daryl Bosteels (who also played piano), Sharon Broadley and Mickey Freeman. During its six recordings, it expanded its repertoire to include some crossover and pop material. By 1991, its personnel had changed and it had four singers: Bosteels, Melissa Hamilton, Val Hawk (also playing guitar) and Christopher Humphrey. The group lasted just a few more years before breaking up, making an impression but not paving any new ground.

Recommended CDs: The Ritz survived long enough to make six albums: *The Ritz* (Denon 1839), *The Spirit Of Christmas* (Denon 72663), *Born To Bop* (Pausa 7190), *Flying* (Denon 3673), *Movin' Up* (Denon 2526) and *Almost Blue* (Denon 7999). Their best recordings were the *Ritz*, *Born To Bop* (which has not yet been reissued on CD) and *Movin' Up*; the latter has guest appearances by Clark Terry.

The Singers Unlimited

The Singers Unlimited were a descendant of the Hi-Lo's. Gene Puerling and Don Shelton were members of the Hi-Lo's, and, after the group broke up, they became active in the jingle field in Chicago, with Puerling becoming a busy arranger. With Len Dresslar and Bonnie Herman, they formed the Singers Unlimited in 1967. Puerling enjoyed using multi-track recording, which made the Singers Unlimited sound like a much bigger group and allowed Puerling to write more complex and dense arrangements than he had for the Hi-Lo's. At first the group worked exclusively in the jingle trade, but pianist Oscar Peterson happened to hear the group and recommended them to MPS. The Singers Unlimited recorded 14 LPs during 1971–81, including sets with the Oscar Peterson Trio (*In Tune*), Roger Kellaway's Cello Quartet, the Art Van Damme Quintet, Rob McConnell's Boss Brass and the orchestras of Robert Farnon and Pat Williams in addition to a cappella projects. Although the Singers Unlimited apparently never performed live and have not recorded since 1981, they are still remembered.

Recommended CDs: *Magic Voices* (Polygram 539130) is a seven-CD set that has the complete Singers Unlimited with the exception of a Christmas album.

The Spirits of Rhythm

A very interesting jive band from the 1930s, the Spirits of Rhythm originally comprised Leo Watson, Wilbur Daniels and Douglas Daniels on vocals and tiples (obscure small guitars), guitarist Teddy Bunn, and drummer-vocalist Virgil Scroggins. Before they settled on the Spirits name, the group was known as the Sepia Nephews, Ben Bernie's Nephews or the Five Cousins. After recording two songs in 1933, they added bassist Wilson Myers to the lineup, recording six other numbers during 1933–34 and four songs with Red McKenzie in 1934. Although the band would seem to have been a natural for the swing era, and it worked on 52nd Street in New York, its only other recordings took place during reunions in 1941: four numbers with singer Ella Logan and just two (one not issued at the time) under its own name. By then, Myers and Scroggins had departed, with Wellman Braud being on bass and Leo Watson switching to drums. The group was best known for its eccentric scatting (Watson in particular) and its goodtime feel.

Recommended CDs: *Spirits Of Rhythm* (Retrieval 79004) is the complete output by the group and includes two earlier numbers by the Washboard Rhythm Kings that have vocals by Leo Watson and Wilbur Daniels, the dates with McKenzie and Logan and four previously unissued performances.

The Swingle Singers

Ward Swingle was a veteran of both the Blue Stars and the Double Six. In the early 1960s he formed the Swingle Singers, which was originally a group of eight freelance session singers based in Paris: Swingle, Christiane Legrand, Jean-Claude Brio-din, Anne Germain, Claude Germaine, Jean Cussac, Claudine Meunier and Jeanette Baucomont. For the fun of it, Swingle had the singers (which included four former members of the Blue Stars) work on singing Bach's *Well-Tempered Clavier*. Backed by a light rhythm, they scatted the notes and found a way to turn Bach into jazz. A record resulted, which was called both *Jazz Sebastian Bach* and *Bach's Greatest Hits*, becoming a hit in the United States.

The Swingle Singers toured the United States and for a time became world-famous, sometimes performing a cappella and sometimes with the quiet backing of bass and drums. During 1963–73 they recorded 12 albums that included pieces by Bach, Handel, Mozart, Beethoven and Chopin, collaborating with the Modern Jazz Quartet on one project. When the group had run its course, in 1973 Ward Swingle moved to England, where he put together a new version of the Swingle Singers that lasted until 1984, not only performing jazz versions of classical pieces but rags, early jazz and big band recreations. By 1984, Ward Swingle had been touring for more than 20 years, written over 200 arrangements and compositions, recorded 24 albums and performed over 2,000 concerts. That year he retired from active performing but remained as musical director of the Swingle Singers. The group has continued touring and recording up to the present time.

Recommended CDs: *Jazz Sebastian Bach* (Verve 824703), *Anyone for Mozart, Bach, Handel, Vivaldi?* (Philips 826 948) and *Place Vendome* (Universal/Philips 9826262) with the Modern Jazz Quartet are three of the Swingle Singers' most important recordings. *The 40th Anniversary Show* (Primarily A Cappella 4530) features the current edition.

Take Six

A remarkable a cappella group, Take Six is both a Christian music ensemble and a group of miraculous singers who perform jazz-inspired music inspired by the harmonies of the Hi-Lo's. In 1980, Claude McKnight formed the Gentlemen's Estate Quartet, an a cappella group at Oakwood College in Alabama. Mark Kibble and Mervyn Warren were also early members of the group, which originally performed as Alliance. They sang in churches and on campus for a few years. By 1985, Alvin Chea, Cedric Dant and David Thomas had joined up. In 1987 the group was renamed Take Six. Their first CD was cut for the tiny Reunion label in 1988 (*Doo Be Doo Wop Bop!*), and they were soon signed to Reprise, gaining a great deal of attention. Take Six has been famous ever since, both in the secular and Christian music worlds. In 1991 Mervyn Warren left the group and was succeeded by Joey Kibble, but otherwise the personnel has remained constant. While Take Six added instruments for a few of their CDs, by 1998's *So Cool* they were back to being a cappella, staying at the top of their field.

Recommended CDs: *Take Six* (Reprise 25670) and *So Much 2 Say* (Warner Alliance 25892) are the group's strongest recordings. *He Is Christmas* (Warner Alliance 26665), *Join The Band* (Warner Alliance 45497), *Brothers* (Warner Alliance 46235), *So Cool* (Warner Bros. 46795), *We Wish You A Merry Christmas* (Warner Bros. 47391), *Tonight: Live* (Warner Bros. 47611), *Beautiful World* (Warner Bros. 48003) and *Feels Good* (Take 6 Records 3018) all have their strong moments, showing how unique Take Six remains.

The Three Peppers

A now-forgotten group, the Three Peppers became prominent shortly before the King Cole Trio, performing in a similar style that pointed toward the direction of Cole's early successes. The Three Peppers consisted of pianist Oliver "Toy" Wilson, guitarist Bob Bell and bassist Walter Williams, all of whom indulged in group vocals. They recorded 24 numbers during 1937–40, including four that added singer Sally Gooding, trumpet, clarinet and drums. Their variety of jive tunes, hot swing numbers and occasional ballads worked quite well. In the 1940s, Wilson departed and was replaced by pianist-singer Roy Branker. Despite making few recordings after 1940 (just an obscure session apiece in 1947 and 1949), the Three Peppers worked regularly and even showed up briefly in the 1943 film *The Lady Takes A Chance*.

Recommended CD: *1937–1940* (Classics 889) has the 24 selections by the Three Peppers from their early days.

THE BEST OF JAZZ SINGERS ON FILM

This is just a sampling of the Hollywood films that have worthwhile appearances by jazz singers, and the DVDs/videotapes that are currently available. There are many more. My previous book *Jazz On Film* (Backbeat Books) has more information about most of these valuable appearances, but these two lists should get collectors started.

41 Hollywood Films

The Best Years Of Our Lives (1946)—Hoagy Carmichael
Beware (1946)—Louis Jordan
Big Broadcast (1932)—Bing Crosby, Boswell Sisters, Mills Brothers, Cab Calloway
The Birth Of The Blues (1941)—Bing Crosby, Harry Barris
Boarding House Blues (1948)—Una Mae Carlisle
Broadway Gondolier (1935)—Mills Brothers
Cabin In The Sky (1942)—Ethel Waters, Lena Horne
A Day At The Races (1937)—Ivie Anderson
The Five Pennies (1959)—Louis Armstrong
Follow The Boys (1944)—Louis Jordan
Get Yourself A College Girl (1964)—Astrud Gilberto
The Girl Can't Help It (1956)—Julie London, Abbey Lincoln
Hey Boy! Hey Girl! (1959)—Louis Prima
Hi-De-Ho (1947)—Cab Calloway
High Society (1956)—Bing Crosby, Louis Armstrong, Frank Sinatra
Hollywood Revue (1929)—Cliff Edwards
Hooray For Love (1935)—Fats Waller
In A Lonely Place (1950)—Hadda Brooks
It's Trad, Dad (1962)—Ottilie Patterson
The Jazz Singer (1953)—Peggy Lee
King Of Burlesque (1935)—Fats Waller
The King Of Jazz (1930)—The Rhythm Boys
The Learning Tree (1969)—Jimmy Rushing
Look-Out Sister (1948)—Louis Jordan
New Orleans (1947)—Louis Armstrong, Billie Holiday
On With The Show (1929)—Ethel Waters
Paradise In Harlem (1940)—Mamie Smith
Pennies From Heaven (1936)—Bing Crosby, Louis Armstrong
Reet, Petite And Gone (1947)—Louis Jordan, June Richmond
Rhythm On The River (1940)—Bing Crosby, Wingy Manone
Ride 'Em Cowboy (1941)—Ella Fitzgerald
Romance On The High Seas (1948)—Page Cavanaugh
St. Louis Blues (1939)—Maxine Sullivan
St. Louis Blues (1958)—Nat King Cole, Cab Calloway, Ella Fitzgerald
Sing As You Swing (1937)—Mills Brothers, Nat Gonella
Stage Door Canteen (1943)—Peggy Lee, Ethel Waters
Stormy Weather (1943)—Fats Waller, Lena Horne, Leo Watson, Cab Calloway
The Strip (1951)—Louis Armstrong, Jack Teagarden
To Have And Have Not (1944)—Hoagy Carmichael
Twist All Night (1961)—Louis Prima
Young Man With A Horn (1950)—Hoagy Carmichael

51 DVDs/Videos

Airto And Flora Purim: The Latin Jazz All-Stars (View Video, 1988)
Alberta Hunter: My Castle's Rockin' (View Video, 1992)
Banu Gibson And New Orleans Hot Jazz (Banjou Productions, 1993)
Birdmen And Birdsongs: Vol. 2 (Storyville, 1998)—Jon Hendricks and Family
The Blues (Storyville, 1991)—Bessie Smith, Ida Cox
Bobby McFerrin: Spontaneous Inventions (A*Vision, 1986)
Boogie In Blues (Rhapsody Films, 1992)—Harry "The Hipster" Gibson
Carmen McRae: Live (Image Entertainment, 1999)
Charles Brown: A Life In The Blues (Rounder, 2003)
Diana Krall: Live In Paris (Eagle Vision, 2002)
Diane Schuur And The Count Basie Orchestra (GRP Video, 1987)
Eddie Jefferson: Live From The Jazz Showcase (Rhapsody Films, 1990)
Ella Fitzgerald: Something To Live For (Winstar Home Entertainment, 2000)
Ellyn Rucker: Live In New Orleans (Leisure Jazz Video, 1992)
An Evening With Nat King Cole (Image Entertainment, 2002)
George Benson: Absolutely Live (Pioneer, 2001)
Harry Connick, Jr: New York Big Band Concert (Sony Video, 1993)
Harry Connick, Jr: Only You (Columbia Music Video, 2004)
Harry Connick, Jr: Singin' And Swingin' (Sony Video, 1990)
Harry Connick, Jr: Swinging Out Live (Sony Video, 1991)
Incomparable Nat King Cole, Volume I (Warner Reprise Video, 1997)
Incomparable Nat King Cole, Volume II (Warner Reprise Video, 1997)
Jazz At The Smithsonian: Alberta Hunter (Kultur Films, 1982)
Jazz At The Smithsonian: Joe Williams (Kultur Films, 1982)
Jazz Band Ball (Shanachie, 1993)—Boswell Sisters, Louis Armstrong, Bessie Smith
Jazz Casual: Carmen McRae (Rhino Home Video, 2001)
Jazz Casual: Jimmy Rushing (Rhino Home Video, 2000)
Jazz Casual: Jimmy Witherspoon and Ben Webster (Rhino Home Video, 2000)
Jazz Casual: Mel Tormé (Rhino Home Video, 2000)
Jazz On A Summer's Day (New Yorker Video, 1987)—Anita O'Day, Louis Armstrong, Jack Teagarden, Dinah Washington
Jazz Voice: The Ladies Sing Jazz, Vol. 1 (Efor, 2005)—Billie Holiday, Nina Simone, Ethel Waters, Anita O'Day, Dinah Washington
Jazz Voice: The Ladies Sing Jazz, Vol. 2 (Efor, 2005)—Ella Fitzgerald, Sarah Vaughan, Carmen McRae, June Christy, Peggy Lee, Lena Horne, Helen Humes
Joe Williams: A Song Is Born (View Video, 1992)

51 DVDs/Videos

John Pizzarelli: Live In Montreal—The Big Band (BMG Video, 1992)

The Ladies Sing The Blues (View Video, 1988)—Bessie Smith, Ethel Waters, Billie Holliday, Ida Cox, Sister Rosetta Tharpe, Connie Boswell, Dinah Washington, Ruth Brown, Lena Horne, Sarah Vaughan, Helen Humes, Peggy Lee

Lady Day: The Many Faces Of Billie Holiday (Kultur Films, 1991)

The Last Of The Blue Devils (Rhapsody Films, 2001)—Big Joe Turner, Jay McShann

Louis Armstrong: Live In '59 (Jazz Icons, 2005)

Louis Armstrong: 100th Anniversary (Passport Entertainment, 2001)

Louis Armstrong And His Friends (Storyville, 2004)

Louis Prima: The Wildest (Image Entertainment, 1999)

The Manhattan Transfer: Vocalese Live (Image Entertainment, 2000)

Maxine Sullivan: Love To Be In Love (Jezebel Productions, 1990)

Nina Simone: Live At Ronnie Scott's (Music Video Distribution, 2003)

The Rosemary Clooney Show: Girl Singer (Concord, 2004)

Sarah Vaughan: Live In '58 And '64 (Jazz Icons, 2007)

Sarah Vaughan And Friends: A Jazz Session (A*Vision, 1986)

Sippie (Rhapsody Films, 1986)—Sippie Wallace

The Snader Telescriptions: The Vocalists (Storyville, 1988)—Peggy Lee, Sarah Vaughan, June Christy, Mel Tormé

The Sound Of Jazz (Music Video Distributors, 2003)—Billie Holiday, Jimmy Rushing

Voices Of Concord Jazz (Concord Video, 2004)—Peter Cincotti, Karrin Allyson, Diane Schuur, Nnenna Freelon, Patti Austin

OTHER BOOKS ON JAZZ SINGERS

Although most of these books were not used in my preparation for *The Jazz Singers*, they are each easily recommended.

Albertson, Chris. *Bessie*. Stein and Day, 1982. (Bessie Smith)

Armstrong, Louis. *My Life In New Orleans*. Da Capo Press, 1954.

Balliett, Whitney. *American Singers*. Oxford University Press, 1988.

Barker, Danny, and Alyn Shipton. *A Life In Jazz*. Oxford University Press, 1986.

Bauer, William R. *Open The Door*. University Of Michigan Press, 2002. (Betty Carter)

Bennett, Betty. *The Ladies Who Sing With The Band*. Scarecrow Press, 2000.

Bergreen, Laurence. *Louis Armstrong: An Extravagant Life*. Broadway Books, 1997.

Calloway, Cab, and Bryant Rollins. *Of Minnie The Moocher And Me*. Thomas Y. Crowell Company, 1976.

Cheatham, Jeannie. *Meet Me With Your Black Drawers On*. University Of Texas Press, 2006.

Chilton, John. *Billie's Blues*. Da Capo Press, 1975. (Billie Holiday)

———. *Let The Good Times Roll: The Story Of Louis Jordan*. University of Michigan Press, 1992.

Clarke, Donald. *Wishing On The Moon*. Viking Press, 1994. (Billie Holiday)

Crowther, Bruce, and Mike Pinfold. *Singing Jazz*. Miller Freeman Books, 1996.

Dickerson, James L. *Just For A Thrill*. Cooper Square Press, 2002. (Lil Armstrong)

Dupuis, Robert. *Bunny Berigan: Elusive Legend Of Jazz*. Louisiana University Press, 1995.

Epstein, Daniel Mark. *Nat King Cole*. Farrar, Straus and Giroux, 1999.

Friedwald, Will. *Jazz Singing*. Charles Scribner & Sons, 1990.

Gavin, James. *Deep In A Dream: The Long Night Of Chet Baker*. Knopf, Borzoi Books, 2002.

Giddins, Gary. *Bing Crosby: A Pocketful Of Dreams 1903–1940*. Little, Brown & Company, 2001.

———. *Satchmo*. Anchor Books, 1988. (Louis Armstrong)

Gourse, Leslie, ed. *The Billie Holiday Companion*. Schirmer Books, 1997.

———. *Every Day: The Story Of Joe Williams*. Da Capo Press, 1985.

———. *Louis' Children*. Morrow, 1984.

———. *Sassy*. Charles Scribner & Sons, 1993. (Sarah Vaughan)

Holiday, Billie, and William Dufty. *Lady Sings The Blues*. Avon Books, 1956.

Jones, Max, and John Chilton. *Louis*. Da Capo Press, 1971.

Kirkeby, Ed, with Duncan P. Schiedt and Sinclair Traill. *Ain't Misbehavin'*. Da Capo Press, 1966. (Fats Waller)

Kravetz, Sallie. *Ethel Ennis: The Reluctant Jazz Star*. Gateway Press, 1984.

Lomax, Alan. *Mister Jelly Roll*. Pantheon Books, 1950.

Miller, Mark. *High Hat, Trumpet And Rhythm*. Mercury Press, 2007. (Valaida Snow)

Nicholson, Stuart. *Ella Fitzgerald*. Da Capo Press, 1993.

O'Day, Anita, and George Ellis. *High Times, Hard Times*. G.E. Putnam & Sons, 1981.

Selk, Len, and Gus Kuhlman. *Lee Wiley: A Bio-Discography*. Self-published, 1997.

Simone, Nina, and Stephen Cleary. *I Put A Spell On You*. Da Capo Press, 1991.

Smith, Jay, and Len Guttridge. *Jack Teagarden*. Da Capo Press, 1960.

Sudhalter, Richard M. *Stardust Melody*. Oxford University Press, 2002. (Hoagy Carmichael)

Taylor, Frank, and Gerald Cook. *Alberta Hunter*. McGraw-Hill, 1987.

Tormé, Mel. *My Singing Teachers*. Oxford University Press, 1994.

Vance, Joel. *Fats Waller: His Life And Times*. Berkley Publishing Co., 1977.

Waters, Ethel, and Charles Samuels. *His Eye Is On The Sparrow*. Da Capo Press, 1950.

Williams, Iain Cameron. *Underneath A Harlem Moon*. Continuum, 2002. (Adelaide Hall)

Yanow, Scott. *Afro-Cuban Jazz*. Miller Freeman Books, 2000.

———. *Bebop*. Miller Freeman Books, 2000.

———. *Classic Jazz*. Backbeat Books, 2001.

———. *Jazz On Film*. Backbeat Books, 2004.

———. *Jazz On Record: The First 60 Years*. Backbeat Books, 2003.

———. *Swing*. Miller Freeman Books, 2000.

———. *Trumpet Kings*. Backbeat Books, 2001.